CE

The London Weavers' Company

The London Weavers' Company 1600-1970

Alfred Plummer

Honorary Librarian
to the Worshipful Company of Weavers

Routledge & Kegan Paul

London and Boston

First published 1972
by Routledge & Kegan Paul Ltd
Broadway House, 68–74 Carter Lane,
London EC4V 5EL and
9 Park Street, Boston, Mass. 02108, U.S.A.
Printed in Great Britain by
Western Printing Services Ltd, Bristol
© Alfred Plummer 1972
No part of this book may be reproduced in
any form without permission from the
publisher, except for the quotation of brief
passages in criticism.

ISBN 0 7100 7272 4

To merry London, my most kindly nurse

Edmund Spenser, *Prothalamion* (1596)

Contents

Contents

Plates

Tables

The history of the London Weavers' Company from the twelfth century to the close of the sixteenth century was written some forty years ago by Dr Frances Consitt. The present work continues the Company's history from 1600 to 1970, or, in other words, from the days of Elizabeth I to those of Elizabeth II. In this volume it has been my aim to present the Weavers' story not in isolation but in its historical setting, and to attempt to bring to life the small but pulsating world in which these London craftsmen lived and worked in good times and bad, through prosperous, cheerful days as well as through great public catastrophes and bitter private suffering. How far I have succeeded, if at all, the reader must judge.

I am grateful to the Worshipful Company of Weavers for the opportunity to undertake the research upon which this book is based, and in particular to Dr Lawrence Tanner, C.V.O., F.S.A., for taking the initiative during his term of office as Upper Bailiff in 1963–4, and thereafter for his unflagging interest in the progress of the work. My thanks are due to successive Upper Bailiffs and especially to the late John Patrick Early who, despite failing health, always gave the project staunch support. At a later stage Dr Tanner, Mr Richard Early and the Clerk of the Company, Mr Romilly Ouvry, read the completed draft and made some valuable constructive suggestions which I now acknowledge with thanks.

Among many other helpful people to whom I am indebted for their perfect courtesy and efficient service I must mention a number of librarians, archivists and keepers of records, such as those at the Guildhall Library, the Shoreditch Central Library, the Bethnal Green Museum and the Greater London Record Office. Also I must thank Miss Rose Dearman for permission to include among the illustrations the portrait of her father, Francis Dearman, who was one of the last of the Spitalfields silk weavers. Finally, I must thank the Company's Beadle, Mr John Jackson, and his wife for their active concern for my comfort and sustenance whenever I was working at Weavers' House, New Wanstead.

Woodford Green
Essex

A.P.

Beaven, *Aldermen*	A. B. Beaven, *Aldermen of the City of London* (1913)
Bell, *Great Fire*	W. G. Bell, *The Great Fire of London* (2nd edn, 1951)
Brett-James, *London*	N. G. Brett-James, *The Growth of Stuart London* (1935)
B.M.Add. MS.	British Museum Additional Manuscript
Cal. S.P.	Calendar of State Papers
Campbell, *English Yeomen*	M. Campbell, *The English Yeomen in the Tudor and Early Stuart Age* (1942; English edn, 1960)
Campbell, *Tradesman*	R. Campbell, *The English Tradesman* (1747)
City of London Records:	
C.C.C. Proceedings	Minutes of the proceedings of the Court of Common Council
Journals	The Journals of the Court of Common Council
Remem.	The Remembrancia of the City of London
Repertories	The Repertories of the Aldermanic Bench
D.N.B.	*Dictionary of National Biography*
George, *London*	M. D. George, *London Life in the Eighteenth Century* (3rd edn, 1951)
Hand-loom Weavers	*Reports on the Condition of the Hand-loom Weavers* (1839–41)
H.O.	Home Office
Lardner, *Silk*	D. Lardner, *A Treatise on the Silk Manufacture* (compiled by G. R. Porter, 1831)
Maitland, *London*	W. Maitland, *The History of London* (1756)
P.C.C.	Prerogative Court of Canterbury
P.R.O.	Public Record Office
Ribbon Weavers	*Select Committee on Ribbon Weavers' Petitions* (1818)
S.P. Dom	State Papers Domestic

Unwin, *Gilds*	G. Unwin, *The Gilds and Companies of London* (4th edn, 1963)
Unwin, *Ind. Org.*	G. Unwin, *Industrial Organization in the Sixteenth and Seventeenth Centuries* (1904)
V.C.H.	*Victoria County History*

Chapter 1

In London under James I

The London weavers in the seventeenth century lived in and around a crowded city, bustling and noisy, lying in a crude crescent along the north bank of the Thames from Wapping to Westminster. Its length was barely six miles and it was some two miles from north to south. Along the south bank of the river, linked to the City by London Bridge—the only bridge—lay Southwark, a pulsating extension of London, in shape like a finger and thumb pointing across marshes and meadows towards Kent and the Continent. The 'Stately Thames enriched with many a flood', gliding on 'with pomp of waters un-withstood', was then the City's main highway; the most safe and speedy of routes, much used by Londoners of all classes upon all occasions, commercial, social and ceremonial; and by visitors from abroad, many of whom came upstream from Gravesend by river ferry-boats.

The tidal estuary of the 'river of Thames', says Stow, is the best way, 'by which all kind of Merchandise be easily conveyed to London, the principal storehouse and staple of all commodities within this realm; so that omitting to speak of great ships and other vessels of burthen, there pertaineth to the cities of London, Westminster and borough of Southwark, above the number, as is supposed, of 2,000 wherries and other small boats, whereby 3,000 poor men, at the least, be set on work and maintained'.[1] All day and every day these small boats—the water-taxis of the seventeenth century—threaded their way between the busy hoys,[2] deep-laden lighters and moored mer-chant vessels, along and across the river, picking up and setting down passengers at the various stairs, piers and landing-stages. There were even ferries with platforms to take a coach and horses.

Elizabethan and Stuart London, though small by modern stan-dards, was to the people of the seventeenth century an enormous city, both absolutely and relatively. By comparison with other cities and towns in the British Isles, London stood forth as fabulously rich and populous. In 1597 a government document estimated that the City of London's rights to 'measurage of commodities' brought into the Port of London was worth as much as all similar rights throughout the whole of the rest of England.[3] Another estimate is that, at the beginning of the seventeenth century, three-quarters of the country's foreign trade paid toll in the London customs house.[4]

At the turn of the century (*c.* 1600) London's population[5]—city, liberties and suburbs—was probably around 225,000 (or a quarter of a million if one includes Westminster, Lambeth and Stepney) distributed as shown in Table 1.1.

Table 1.1 *The population of London c. 1600*

Area		No.
The City within the walls		76,000
The suburbs 'without' the walls:		
(*a*) The Liberties of the City	113,000 ⎫	
(*b*) Out-parishes	36,000 ⎭	149,000
(*c*) Westminster, Lambeth and Stepney		25,000
		250,000

No other city or town had one-tenth of that number of inhabitants. For instance, the City of Norwich with its out-parishes, a leading manufacturing centre in the seventeenth century, had, at most, 17,000 inhabitants,[6] or less than one-fifteenth of the number in London and its environs. Furthermore, London's rate of growth was quite remarkable by comparison with the other cities and towns of the kingdom. Although the birth-rate in London was low and the death-rate appallingly high, because of frequent outbreaks of bubonic plague and other epidemics, the City and suburbs—especially the latter—were continually refilled by immigrants from the provincial towns and the countryside, far and near, and from continental countries, France and Holland in particular. The metropolis was a mighty magnet pulling people, including great numbers of young people,[7] from every direction. It attracted men of status and substance as well as those seeking their fortunes; the affluent, the ambitious, the innocent boy-apprentices and the smart Alecs 'full of cozenage', as Shakespeare (the best eyewitness we could wish for) tells us:

> Disguised cheaters, prating mountebanks,
> And many such like Liberties of sin.

There were, also, refugees from persecution and from justice—'people of desperate fortunes'. 'At length they all to merry London came', pushing and crowding in, 'an immense concourse of men and animals' multiplying the pressing evils of bad housing and primitive sanitation, pestilence, poverty and crime, and creating a perpetual nightmare for the authorities, both central and local. Only by continuous large-scale immigration could London's population have increased at such a rate that the estimated 250,000 of the year 1600 had become an estimated 320,000 by 1625, and 600,000 by the end of the century.[8]

In Elizabethan and early Jacobean times London remained essentially a medieval city in which noblemen, merchants, craftsmen and shopkeepers lived side by side, hard by the haunts of criminals and the hovels of the poor. It was just a jumble of buildings large and small, magnificent and mean; residential, industrial and commercial premises; public buildings; churches set in 'little green churchyard' burial grounds shaded by stately trees; and—to astonish the stranger —many 'fair gardens' like Sir John Hart's, where flowers and fragrant herbs and even fruit could be seen.[9] All this (and much more) was tightly compressed within the ancient defensive wall, with its eight massive gates—Aldgate, Bishopsgate, Moorgate, Cripplegate, Aldersgate, Newgate, Ludgate and Bridge Gate. The monks and friars, it is true, had long disappeared from the streets, their great clusters of monastic buildings having been seized and turned to other uses.

The old walled city had overflowed to form a number of 'liberties'[10] and suburbs which were for the most part nothing better than closely built, noisome slums, huddled immediately 'without' the walls,[11] extending outwards from the edge of the city ditch, which was originally some 200 feet broad and part of the medieval defences, but 'now of later time' (says Stow) '. . . is enclosed and the banks thereof let out for garden-plots, carpenters' yards, bowling allies and divers houses thereon built, thereby the city wall is hidden, the ditch filled up, [only] a small channel left, and that very shallow': in places it had become 'a filthy channel'.[12] The famous Dr William Harvey (1576–1657), discoverer of the circulation of the blood, lived in London during James I's reign and remarked upon 'the filth and offal . . . scattered about' and the 'sulphureous' coal smoke 'whereby the air is at all times rendered heavy, but more so in the autumn'.

Along the few main roads leading outwards from the City gates an unplanned riot of ribbon-development—houses, cottages, sheds and workshops of all sorts and sizes; many constructed of weatherboards— was slowly eating its way towards the nearest villages, such as Bethnal Green and Shoreditch to the north-east, Mile End to the east, and Bermondsey and Lambeth to the south. The result, on both sides of the principal thoroughfares, was a nightmarish maze of ill-paved or unpaved entries, yards, courts, alleys and tortuous, narrow lanes, in which all sorts of activities, legitimate, shady and downright criminal, were carried on. Some of the old mansions and larger houses, abandoned to decay and dilapidation when, for any reason, their original owners moved away, were each divided into as many as twenty or thirty tenements, and soon became part of an unsavoury medley of ruinous rookeries, dirty lodgings, dram shops, inns, taverns and brothels. Coldharbour, the Earl of Shrewsbury's great mansion on the south bank, was demolished in 1600 and 'the site given up to small tenements at large rents'.[13]

In such liberties and suburbs—Cripplegate Without, Bishopsgate Without, Farringdon Without, Southwark—the majority of the respectable 'householders' were master craftsmen: weavers, felt-makers, tanners, wheelwrights, carpenters, coppersmiths, dyers, glovers and the like; each family, with servants and apprentices, all under the same roof, which usually covered their workshop and stores as well. The range and variety of London's crafts were a wonder to behold; and as the decades passed the demand for living and working accommodation was intensified by the incessant immigration of 'foreigners' from the provinces and 'strangers' (aliens) from the Continent.

One of the weavers' chief complaints was that 'most of the poorest sort of strangers are packed and thrust up with their whole families within divers ... tenements ... of very small and narrow compass. ... Insomuch as the City and the Suburbs ... are filled, pestered and much annoyed with many ... troublesome and offensive Inmates.'[14] All this resulted in rising rents which brought forth certain property 'developers'—carpenters, bricklayers, plasterers and chandlers—who saw a chance to make easy money by buying up the leases of premises occupied, often for many years past, by weavers and other craftsmen, and 'dividing of houses, erecting (upon new foundations) Sheds, Hovels and Cottages, putting into every room a family, to the great pestering of the City, Suburbs and places adjoining with Inmates, Aliens and Undersitters'.[15]

Such gross overcrowding in conglomerations of ill-ventilated wood-and-plaster dwellings, separated only by narrow lanes and alleys with kennels full of muck coursing down the middle; with polluted water supplies;[16] with ditches and open sewers running this way and that, and laystalls heaped with rotting refuse in close proximity to the houses; all this was a terrible threat to public health, as the Weavers' Company told the Lord Mayor in 1632, for (they said) it 'brings with it an unavoidable danger to breed contagious and infectious diseases, if God should visit the same with any sickness or mortality'.[17] They had, indeed, good reasons for their fears. The reign of James I was sandwiched between two severe outbreaks of bubonic plague (in 1603 and 1625) and there were a number of comparatively minor visitations in the intervening years. What neither the weavers nor anybody else knew was that the black rats that infested their houses and sheds carried fleas, and these were the deadly distributors of 'the poor's plague', the 'great sickness', which so often struck down with swift 'spotted death' man, woman and child, regardless of rank or calling.

No doubt people's resistance and resilience were buttressed by the widespread interest in 'sports' and contests (accompanied, of course, by gambling), and by the nearness of the countryside. The London populace, high and low, gentry and journeymen, merchants and master craftsmen, loved a fight in any form: cock-fighting, bull- or bear-baiting, fencing with swords 'very little, if at all, blunter on the edge than the common swords are', or a furious fracas between traditional enemies such as men of rival occupations. The Thames watermen, toughened by their ancient trade and masters of the most lurid language, were in every way formidable opponents of those competing upstarts, the coachmen of the 'Hackney hellcarts' or 'four-wheeled tortoises' so detested by John Taylor, the Water Poet;[18] the butchers had a reputation for truculence and a readiness to resort to violence (which is, perhaps, not surprising), and even the weavers occasionally had their militant moments.[19]

It was a community in which men and women alike ate and drank heartily whenever they could, and few were inhibited by prudery or over-conventionality. Laughter and song rose easily to the surface, but so, too, did 'a primitive delight in violence. . . . The physical conditions of life were not easy for anyone. Few anodynes were known and none . . . effective. . . . Familiarity with pain bred, in all classes, a certain stoicism, a deep acceptance of suffering as part of the necessary order of the world and a willingness to inflict it and to see it inflicted.'[20] But although the Cockney craftsmen were often quarrelsome and aggressive, they were not usually murderous either in deed or intent, and they rarely resorted to weapons more deadly than fists and sticks.

This was just as well, for there was everywhere much drinking and drunkenness. There were alehouses and taverns a-plenty, open at all hours. These—especially the taverns—were the pubs and clubs of the period, providing food and drink and a convivial setting for social intercourse, business deals and discussion of the politics of the day. There were noted houses such as the Mermaid, the Mitre, the Gaping Mouth, the Heaven and Hell, the Blew Postes, the Hole in the Wall, and a host of others of all sorts and sizes, fashionable, respectable, obscure, Bohemian, shady; most of them providing lodging chambers, dice-tables, shove-ha'penny boards, and boasting a generous kitchen and a well-stocked wine cellar.[21]

All medieval towns were naturally integrated with local agriculture and the neighbouring rural population. Town traders and craftsmen often hailed from farming families. Many a townsman of today was

but yesterday a boy roaming the fields and woods. The town craftsman knew something about tillage, and the countryman knew something of craftwork. The villages had their craftsmen as well as the
towns. The London Weavers' records show that the sons of yeomen,
husbandmen, market-gardeners and graziers 'of London', or Bermondsey, or Cripplegate, or Shoreditch or St Giles-in-the-Fields were
often apprenticed to weaving. There was continual, day-by-day,
hour-by-hour mingling of townsfolk and country folk, many of
whom were related. Hardly had the nightwatchman, with his dim
horn-lantern, crept wearily homeward, when the early-morning
street traders appeared, crying their wares—eggs, milk, butter and
cream brought in from the nearby farms and fields by countrywomen,
who either went from house to house or settled themselves with their
baskets at every street corner and in any convenient niche. Then
came the higglers bringing fresh vegetables, fruit and poultry.[22]

But for this nearness of the countryside the state of public health
would have been even worse than it was. On Sundays and the occasional holidays such as Whitsuntide, the young men with their
sweethearts, and the older men with their wives and children, believ-
ing, like Thomas Tusser, that 'comfort with labour should sometimes
be had', used to walk by pleasant rural paths to the 'villages out in
the fields' to taste 'rural delights, such as cakes and cream and quarts
of local beer', at 'Bednal Green' or Mile End or Islington; Paddington,
Kennington, Battersea or Camberwell. Writing at the turn of the
century, old John Stow tells us that 'on May day in the morning every
man, except impediment, would walk into the sweet meadows and
green woods, there to rejoice their spirits with the beauty and savour
of sweet flowers and with the harmony of birds'.

In the eastern suburbs, as elsewhere, there were elm, poplar, lime,
and other trees and a variety of wild flowers. The famous botanist
and gardener, John Gerard, found pennyroyal growing wild 'in the
common neare London called Mile Ende[23] about the holes and ponds
thereof in sundry places from whence poore women bring plenty to
sell in London Markets, and it groweth in sundry other commons
neare London'. Other wild flowers were to be seen in and around
Southwark, Bermondsey, Horsleydown[24] and Lambeth. But London
was slowly spreading, and houses were pressing back, now here, now
there, these rural fringes of the suburbs. Stow, writing of Hog Lane,
which ran from 'Algate Without north towards St Mary Spittle without Bishopsgate', says that 'within these forty years[25] [it] had on
both sides fair hedge rows of elm trees, with bridges and easy stiles
to pass over into the pleasant fields, very commodious for citizens . . .
to recreate and refresh their dull spirits in the sweet and wholesome
air'; but it 'is now within a few years made a continual building
throughout, of garden-houses and small cottages; and the fields on

either sides be turned into garden plots, tenter yards, bowling alleys, and such like, from Houndes ditch in the west, as far as White Chappell, and further towards the east'.[26]

The importance of fresh air, and 'free and open walks in the fields about the City', was recognised in Elizabethan times, and in 1593 an Act of Parliament forbade the enclosure (e.g. for building purposes) of any common or waste land within three miles of the City.[27] Moorfields, lying outside Moorgate, was then a swampy, smelly tract of waste ground, partly used as a tenter-ground for the drying of new-woven cloth. But during the decade 1605–15, the City Corporation, encouraged by the King, began to lay out Moorfields with paths and trees as a public open space 'of sweet ayres for Citizens to walk in'.[28]

Against this backcloth and in this setting the London weavers lived and worked and made 'their exits and their entrances'. The Company's records, which give us a large number of weavers' addresses, show that they were congregated mainly in the liberties and suburbs. According to Stow, the weavers had gone from Candlewick Street, where at one time 'both sides the way was nothing but weavers' workshops',[29] their places having been taken by rich drapers and cloth merchants. But in Bishopsgate Without, sometimes referred to as the parish of St Botolph, Bishopsgate, weavers were very thick upon the ground, in alleys, yards and lanes with such picturesque names as Frying Pan Alley, Starlings Rents, Three Tun Alley, Black Bell Alley, Hog Lane,[30] Boar's Head Yard, Half Moon Alley, Woolsack Alley off Gravel Lane, Chequers Alley, Bethlem, Primrose Alley and Petty France—a name which tells its own story.

Northwards, from Norton Folgate to Shoreditch, we find weavers, in gradually increasing numbers, in Coles Alley, Hore Alley and Swan Yard. Outside Aldgate and in Whitechapel weavers were working in Tongs Yard, Castle Street, Sixth Alley and Black Lion Yard. In Cripplegate Without both the 'freedom' part within the City's juris-diction and the 'Lordship' part in the County of Middlesex were closely populated by weavers, who were to be found in such places as Blue Anchor Alley, Bloomer's Rents, Golding Lane, Bell Alley, Goat Alley, Grub Street, Three Leg Court leading off Whitecross Street, Red Cross Street, and spreading slowly along the south side of Old Street in the direction of Hoxton and Shoreditch.[31] Around Moorgate weavers were to be found 'in Moor Lane backside Sugarloaf Court', in Cross Key Court and Little Moorfields.

Over the bridge, Southwark, otherwise known in civic circles as Bridge Ward Without, was administratively part of the City. It was London's popular amusement centre—a district of bear-baiting, fencing contests, inns, taverns and stews—'a naughty neighbourhood'. Here in 1614 arose, Phoenix-like, the new Globe Theatre described by John Chamberlain as 'the fairest that ever was in England'; and here in 1623 (as the same gossip reports):

> The Spanish Ambassador is much delighted in bear baiting; he was last weeke at Paris Gardens, where they shewed him all the pleasure they could both with bull, beare and horse, besides Jackanapes; and then turned a white beare into the Thames, where the dogges baited him swimming, which was the best sport of all.[32]

Southwark, however, played a more useful role, for it was an expanding industrial suburb, to which during many decades, cheap land and low rents had attracted weavers, feltmakers, shipwrights, sawyers, brewers, leather dressers, curriers, glovers and—in nearby Bermondsey—a colony of tanners.[33] Off the main streets were dozens of narrow alleys, some of them nameless; haphazard building had jumbled together tenements, workshops, storehouses, stables and wooden shacks in squalid confusion. Here was a large congregation of master weavers, journeymen and apprentices, natives and aliens, parents and children, some working and sleeping in a single garret or loom-shop.

The official lists of 1618 show fifty-four alien weavers—Dutch, French, German and even two Spaniards—in Southwark,[34] and there were, undoubtedly, much larger numbers of English weavers, both natives of London and its environs and 'foreigners' from the provinces, all engaged in various branches of the weaving trade. They were to be found at such addresses as Crucifix Lane, Barnaby Street, Wild's Rents in Long Lane, St Thomas's Court, Swan Alley, Deadman Place, Five Foot Lane, The Close in Maiden Lane, Horsleydown, and Swan Yard by St George's Church.[35] When, after a sharp internal struggle, the Weavers' Company revived and revised its Yeomanry in the reign of James I, the (reduced number) of sixteen young men 'below the Livery' were organised and allocated in the following districts or 'divisions': for Southwark, four; for Bishopsgate, Cripplegate, Shoreditch and Whitechapel, three each. Later, under the Commonwealth, when 'representatives' of the Commonalty had to be chosen, the numbers attending from Southwark exceeded those from the other divisions.[36] In addition, nearly all the villages adjacent to London had a few weavers: Newington and Walworth, south of the Thames; and Mile End, Poplar, Hackney, Islington and Stepney to the north and east.

These seventeenth-century London weavers, working a twelve- or fourteen-hour day according to the season, manufactured a wide range of goods in wool, linen and silk. It was a time when weaving in the older materials, wool and linen, overlapped with the newer material, silk. The former had not yet 'gone out' of the trade, while silk had certainly 'come in' and was steadily increasing its share of the volume and value of the total output. In the heavy-woollen section there were some rug-makers, fustian weavers and feltmakers among the Company's members, although, strictly speaking, felt is not a woven material. There was always a steady demand for fustian, a cheap, hard-wearing, general-purpose woollen cloth, of which there were 'sundry sorts' (plain, corded, striped, chequered and tufted; some worn 'white' and some dyed), 'a thick, strong sort of goods' very suitable for everyday wear in warehouse or workshop, or by gentlemen who rode a great deal.[37]

It is certain that a significant number of London fustian weavers—masters and journeymen—were at work at least as late as 1675-6.[38] Worsted weavers and weavers of linen—for example, towellings and tickings—are also mentioned in the Weavers' records early in the seventeenth century, and again early in the reign of Charles II, when the Weavers' Court ordered that the business (unspecified) concerning the linen weavers should be considered at the next Full Court. But a steady change-over to silk was probably taking place.[39] In 1611, in connection with the Company's need to raise money in order to subscribe capital for James I's proposed colonisation or 'plantation' of Ulster by non-Irish settlers, the Weavers' Company, by special arrangement with the City Corporation, sought to make free by redemption some thirty English weavers, 'foreign brethren' who (the record states) had served proper apprenticeships and had long 'used the craft' in the City and liberties. The records reveal the branches of the trade to which two-thirds of them belonged (see Table 1.2).[40]

Excluding all the 'unspecified' weavers, and including the taffeta weavers in the silk group, we have: woollen, worsted, and fustian, four (no apprentices); linen, one (no apprentices); silk, fourteen (six apprentices). This serves to indicate, roughly, the trend towards expansion and specialisation in silk at the beginning of the seventeenth century.

Some of the silk weavers specialised in broad weaving, while others made narrow wares such as ribbons, girdles, garterings, braids, and cords or laces, much used as fastenings for both men's and women's garments. Very light delicate fabrics, such as cobweb lawns and tiffanies—i.e. silk gauze—were made by some weavers, while others wove black heavy-dyed silk (commonly called London silk), taffetas and pure silk damasks for people of wealth and fashion—the *beau monde*.[41] But this was not all. Before 1579 the sumptuary laws forbade any man under the degree of a knight's eldest son to wear a velvet jerkin, doublet or hose, or to use satin, damask, taffeta or grosgrain for cloaks, coats, gowns or other 'uppermost garments'. And no woman below the degree of knight's wife could legally wear velvet or silk embroidery or 'netherstocks of silk'. But increasing wealth among the minor gentry and major merchants led to some modification of the laws after 1580, followed by their gradual non-observance in the Stuart period, until, at least in the large towns, every wife felt free, as Thomas Fuller remarked, to set up 'a sail according to the keel of her husband's estate'.[42]

Table 1.2 *The trend towards silk weaving*

Master weavers		Apprentices
Fustian	2	None
Worsted	1	None
Woollen	1	None
Linen	1	None
Silk	9	None
Silk	1	1
Silk	1	2
Silk	1	3
Tuft-taffeta	2*	None
Unspecified	1	2
Unspecified	10	None

* Sometimes written 'Tuftaffety'; a taffeta with a tufted pile.

The humble folk—tradesmen's wives and children, servant maids and the like—were not slow to imitate their 'betters', and the result was a large and expanding aggregate demand, not only for silks, but for various sorts of half-silks and slight-silks in which silk yarn was used, usually as warp, with cotton or worsted or linen as weft. In some of these fabrics the silk yarn was woven so as to create a decorative effect. Such generally useful and comparatively cheap materials —the prices reflecting the qualities and silk content—were much in demand for men's waistcoats, women's 'petty coats', children's clothing, and many sorts of linings and soft furnishings. They 'formed a large part of the London weavers' production and almost the whole of that of Norwich ... even the cheapest (surviving) samples are pleasant to handle and are dyed in good colours'.[43]

The proper manufacturing procedure in silk weaving, according to the customs of the City of London and the Weavers' Company, is described in the Company's records.

A Merchant Silkman may deliver silk [yarn] or other stuff unto any Master Weaver that is a freeman, or other which is admitted a Master by the Bailiffs, Wardens and Assistants of the Weavers' Company. And the silk or other stuff ought to be delivered by weight, and being wrought or fashioned, the owner may receive the same again by weight, and pay the weaver for the workmanship or fashioning thereof, either by the pound or by the dozen, as both parties can agree, allowing sufficient waste upon every pound.

Alternatively, the merchant or silkman might sell the raw material to the weaver at a certain price and buy back the woven fabric at a price high enough to recompense the weaver for his work.[44]

Orris weaving was another important and, for the master weavers, lucrative section of the London weaving trade. This was the manufacture of the gold and silver lace and braid so lavishly used, except in the dullest days of the Commonwealth, to decorate the clothes of persons of rank and fortune—on hats and coats, and even 'shoestrings edged with gold, and spangled garters worth a copyhold'. It was an exceedingly ancient art, as we know from the discovery of a remnant of gold-wire lace, 'black and much decayed, of the old lozenge pattern', found in an Iron Age barrow near Wareham in Dorset.[45] In England gold and silver lacemaking reached such a high point of perfection in the early Stuart period that the customs officers confidently expected the revenue from imports to 'decay'. Indeed, in James I's reign English gold lace was actually exported to India.[46] The Gold and Silver Wire-Drawers' Company received its charter from James I in 1623, and thereafter, in this section of the trade, contacts between the Weavers' and Wire-Drawers' Companies were quite frequent. Finely drawn gold and silver wire spun upon silk, in proportions prescribed by Acts of Parliament, and made up into lace and braid became known as 'statute lace'.[47]

Bone lace, so called either from the bone bobbins used by the lacemakers or because of the bone pins used in pricking out the lace, was a craft in which certain master weavers were interested, chiefly, it seems, as small capitalists supplying materials, employing poor women as lacemakers, and marketing the product. This was, probably, very largely an out-work trade, and those engaged in it were on much the same low income and social level as the multitude of poor people who clung precariously to the fringe of the London weaving trade, including large numbers of young children as well as 'divers ancient people spinners and workers of waste silk . . . a very great number' who had no other means of getting a living.[48]

This, then, was the setting in which the Weavers' Company strove to carry out the functions of a craft gild; searching the craft, enforcing the Ordinances, putting down abuses, and discharging a medley of other duties, ranging from the formulation of high policy to the settlement of trifling disputes.

11

NOTES

1 Stow, *Survey of London* (Everyman edn, 1956), p. 13.
2 The hoy was a small craft, usually sloop-rigged, used to carry passengers and goods—any job, in fact, for which a small coastal vessel was suitable.
3 Quoted W. M. Stern, *The Porters of London* (1960), p. 82.
4 R. H. Tawney, *Business and Politics under James I: Lionel Cranfield as Merchant and Minister* (1958), p. 75: cf. the estimates in P. Deane and W. A. Cole, *British Economic Growth, 1688–1959* (2nd edn, 1967).
5 As there was no census before 1801, exact population figures before that date cannot be obtained. The best estimate, in very 'round figures', is that given above. The problem is fully discussed by N. G. Brett-James in his scholarly book, *The Growth of Stuart London* (1935), Chap. XX; but he reaches no firm conclusions.
6 A. L. Rowse, *The England of Elizabeth* (1950), p. 159.
7 See Chap. 4 on the recruitment of weavers' apprentices.
8 The estimated population of Norwich, the second city of the kingdom, in 1695, was 29,000, and Bristol, the third city, upwards of 20,000.
9 Stow, op. cit., p. 201. A number of the City Companies had gardens adjoining their halls. The Drapers' Company in Throgmorton Street had not only a large garden, but a bowling green as well. Sir John Hart was elected Lord Mayor of London in 1589.
10 The liberties were areas under the City's jurisdiction although not within the walls.
11 London's large-scale extra-mural development had begun in Elizabeth's reign outside Aldgate, Cripplegate and Bishopsgate, and it is noted with some regret by old John Stow, then in his late seventies. Its momentum increased during the seventeenth century.
12 Stow, op. cit., pp. 20, 115–17.
13 A. L. Rowse, op. cit., p. 188, quoting Stow's *Survey* (ed. Kingsford), I, p. 237.
14 MS. 4647, ff.231–2.
15 MS. 4647, ff.360–2.
16 After 1613 piped New River Company's water from Chadwell Spring could be had in London, but the majority of people long continued to use the old sources of supply. For the fortunes of Sir Hugh Myddleton and the New River Company see J. W. Gough, *Sir Hugh Myddleton, Entrepreneur and Engineer* (1964).
17 MS. 4647, ff.231–2.
18 For his biography see W. Notestein, *Four Worthies* (1956), p. 106.
19 Pepys tells us of a battle between the weavers and the butchers in the summer of 1664. 'July 26th Great discourse of the fray yesterday in Moorfields, how the butchers at first did beat the weavers (between whom there hath been ever an old competition for mastery) but at last the weavers rallied and beat them. At first the butchers knocked down all for weavers that had green or blue aprons, till they were fain to pull them off and put them in their breeches. At last the butchers were fain to pull off their sleeves,

that they might not be known, and were soundly beaten out of the field, and some deeply wounded and bruised; till at last the weavers went out tryumphing, calling £100 for a butcher.'

20 C. V. Wedgwood, *The King's Peace, 1637–1641* (1955), pp. 42–3.

21 D. Davies, *A History of Shopping* (1966), pp. 157–8.

22 Fish supplies came through the respectable, and often well-to-do, fishmongers and their traditional enemies, the hawking fishwives, any of whom could set up in trade with 5s., a basket and a piercing voice. They carried their shops on their heads and, although reviled 'for everything from their smell to their morals', they provided a useful service, especially in the poorer districts (D. Davies, op. cit., p. 89). Although the butter was generally of good quality, especially that from Hackney village, much of the milk was contaminated and diluted before it reached the consumers' doorsteps in the milk-maids' pails. See also E. Kerridge, *The Agricultural Revolution* (1967), pp. 177–80.

23 Probably Mile End Waste.

24 Horsleydown was at the end of St Olave's Street, Southwark, on the road from London Bridge to Rotherhithe.

25 1560–1600.

26 Stow, op. cit., p. 116.

27 Brett-James, *London*, p. 73.

28 For a detailed account of the progress and cost of this first of London's public parks, see Brett-James, *London*, pp. 452–9.

29 *England's Advocate, Europe's Monitor* (a pamphlet, 1699).

30 Now Middlesex Street, commonly called Petticoat Lane because of its open-air market in second-hand clothes.

31 *V.C.H., Middlesex* (1911), II, p. 128.

32 R. R. Sharp, *London and the Kingdom*, II, p. 324; W. Notestein, *Four Worthies* (1956), p. 106; E. P. Statham, *A Jacobean Letter-writer* (1920), p. 211.

33 Brett-James, *London*, pp. 405–6, 476; A. L. Rowse, *Shakespeare* (1963), pp. 287–8.

34 *V.C.H., Surrey*, II, pp. 349–50, 359–61. In the Minories, too, Dutch immigrants had increased in numbers, so that there was even a 'churchwarden for the strangers' (E. M. Tomlinson, *A History of the Minories* (1922), pp. 391ff.).

35 In addition to immigrant craftsmen, crowds of destitute persons, beggars, vagrants, vagabonds, and 'other loose persons' congregated in Southwark: indeed, they became so numerous that the City had to appoint a Provost-Marshal to deal with them. Strype says that Southwark had sixteen constables and six scavengers; and we may be sure that they were fully occupied all the time.

36 Southwark 11, Bishopsgate 8, Cripplegate 8, Shoreditch 7, Whitechapel 4 (MS. 4655A/2, ff.6b, 20).

37 The author of *Observations on the Case of the Worsted and Silk Manufacturers and of the Importers of Cotton Wool, and the Manufacturers thereof into Fustian* (c. 1728) complained that a new, inferior, slight stuff of wool mixed with cotton, made chiefly in Manchester, was being called fustian.

38 MS. 4655/8, ff.73b, 79b. In 1673 a Southwark feltmaker was offered the Livery (MS. 4655/7, f.37b).

39 MS. 4655/1, ff.26–8; MS. 4655/3, f.104b; and MS. 4655/4, 27 November 1666: 'Thos. Linsley served a Linen weaver now weaves

ribbon.' MS. 4655/7, ff.70b, 75b reveals linen weavers working in Southwark and 'Bethlem'.

40 MS. 4655/1, ff.8–9, May-July 1611.
41 MS. 4655/1, f.2; MS. 4655/2, f.173; MS. 4655/3, ff.23–4; MS. 4647, ff.169, 175.
42 Campbell, *English Yeoman*, p. 253.
43 Natalie Rothstein, 'The Calico Campaign of 1719–21', in *East London Papers*, vol. 7, no. 1, July 1964.
44 MS. 4647, f.161.
45 F. B. Palliser, *A History of Lace* (3rd edn, 1875), p. 3.
46 Ibid., p. 293.
47 e.g. 9 Wm. III, c. 39 (1698); 15 Geo. II, c. 20 (1742). H. Stewart, *History of the Company of Gold and Silver Wire-Drawers* (1891), pp. 32, 83; cf. M. Postlethwayt, *Universal Dictionary of Trade and Commerce* (2nd edn, 1757), II, art. 'Lace'.
48 MS. 4647, f.478.

Chapter 2

Gild Governance I

Dr Frances Consitt has written the history of the London Weavers' Company from the twelfth century to the close of the sixteenth century. The story begins in the reign of Henry I with a Pipe Roll entry dated 1130, which proves the existence of a gild of weavers in London before that date, and substantiates the Weavers' claim to be the oldest of all the London gilds. The Weavers' status was greatly enhanced in 1155 when the gild received from Henry II the first royal charter ever granted to any London craft.[1] In good times and in bad, despite internal stresses and external struggles (chiefly against the City authorities and alien immigrants), the Weavers not only held their own during medieval and Tudor times but actually made head-way, especially in the 'new era of prosperity' in the sixteenth century, when many London weavers ceased to weave linen and woollen fabrics and turned to silk. By 1603, at the beginning of a new century, a new reign and a new dynasty, the gild of 'Bailiffs, Wardens, Assistants and Commonalty of the Trade, Art and Mystery of Weavers of London' (to give the Worshipful Company its full title), although far from wealthy, appears to have been both vigorous and vigilant. The executive body was, of course, the Court of Assistants, and the control-centre the Weavers' Hall in Basinghall Street.

The Ordinances for the regulation of the Weavers' gild, as ratified in 1577, provided for a body of sixteen men—two Bailiffs, two War-dens (usually referred to as 'the Officers' or 'the Four in Place') and twelve Assistants. The four Officers held office for one year and were seldom re-elected to the same office in the ensuing year. The day of St James the Apostle, 25 July, was (and still is) election day, on which the two present or out-going Bailiffs nominated a person to be the Upper Bailiff, or Master, of the Company for the coming year; and the Wardens and Assistants, usually with some forty or fifty Livery-men assembled in a Common Hall, nominated another person for the chief office. Whichever candidate had the 'most voices' in the assembly

15

was accepted as 'chief and principal Bailiff to rule and govern for one whole year then next ensuing'. The unsuccessful candidate, it seems, with another nominee of the two out-going Bailiffs, was then put before the Common Hall for election to the office of second or Renter Bailiff. Next the two out-going Bailiffs, with the assistance of any 'ancients that were present and which have been Bailiffs',[2] proceeded to choose from among the Liverymen two new Wardens—an Upper and a Renter Warden—to serve for the ensuing year. Usually, but not invariably, the Bailiffs' nominees were elected; but if the Liverymen were displeased with the out-going Bailiffs, or a major issue was causing dissension within the Company, the discontented Liverymen could show their teeth by rejecting the Bailiffs' nominees and voting for other candidates.

The sixteen had self-renewing powers, for they or 'the most parte of them' were enjoined to fill any vacancy among the Officers or Assistants by electing a member of the gild within fourteen days. This Court had to perform a variety of administrative, financial and even judicial functions, some important, some trifling; some calling for technical knowledge, others for wisdom in human relationships. It had to ensure good order and governance within the craft and to check encroachments and illegal practices from without. Its jurisdiction extended two miles from the City gates; an area which included not only Cripplegate, Clerkenwell, Bishopsgate Without, Norton Folgate, Spitalfields, Bethnal Green, Shoreditch and Whitechapel, but also Hoxton, Haggerston, Hackney, Homerton, Old Ford, Stepney, Cambridge Heath, Shadwell, Southwark, Bermondsey, and much of Islington and Canonbury.

The development of silk weaving during the Tudor period gave to the London weaving industry a new impetus, strongly reinforced during the sixteenth and seventeenth centuries by newcomers from overseas, who swelled the numbers of weavers in the liberties and suburbs, and by their artistic talents and special skills in the weaving of figured silks, helped to raise the silk industry to a position of importance in the national economy. But the influx of foreigners and strangers was a never-failing source of new or revived disputes and discontents, with many of which the Weavers' Court of Assistants had to cope.[3]

Over the years the Company had come to accept the impossibility of excluding foreigners and strangers. Some gilds of native craftsmen joined forces in an attempt to keep the strangers out;[4] but the London Weavers, with greater wisdom, evolved several different membership grades or categories to meet the circumstances of various types of craftsmen 'using the art of weaving' (see Table 2.1). The highest grade was, of course, the freeman who had served a full term of legal apprenticeship, or had been admitted by patrimony or redemption.[5]

Such freemen, when they had become also freemen of the City, could use the proud description—'Citizen and Weaver of London'. The lesser grades, usually referred to as 'admissioners' or 'foreign brethren', seem to have been three in number:

1 Foreign Masters,[6] whose qualifications were fully approved by the Company and who were allowed to take apprentices;
2 Foreign weavers allowed to work independently but not to set up as 'householders';
3 Journeymen; weavers who had proved their apprenticeship or capability in the craft, but were not permitted to work except as journeymen.

All such admissioners were sworn to obey the orders of the Company.

A master weaver's status and seniority determined the number of looms, journeymen and apprentices he might legally employ, though the evidence suggests that infringements were neither few nor infrequent, especially in times when trade was good.

Table 2.1 *Grades of gild membership*

	Single looms not exceeding	*Number of:*	
		Journeymen not exceeding	*Apprentices not exceeding*
Denizens or foreigners			
in first year after admission		1	1
in second year after admission	5	2	2
in third and subsequent years		2	3
Strangers (aliens)			
in first year after admission		1	1
in second and subsequent years	4	2	2
Liverymen	6	not stated	4

Bailiffs, Wardens, and past Bailiffs and Wardens were each allowed to have not more than seven single looms[7] and five apprentices. The omission of a limit on the number of journeymen to be employed by Officers past and present and by Liverymen may well indicate the possibility that they could employ an unlimited number of journeymen as out-workers. As the putting-out system became more and more prevalent, so did the employment of unqualified journeymen and apprentices, many of whom worked 'secretly' in obscure holes and corners, difficult for the Company's officers to locate. Many of the admitted journeymen weavers could scarcely rank as skilled craftsmen, for they could not do more than throw a shuttle on plain work. Some hired a loom and 'loom-standing', or helped another journeyman at busy times. Their earnings were, one need hardly say, among the lowest in the trade. At the other extreme were the highly skilled intelligent craftsmen-householders. The weaving of flowered or figured silks, damasks, brocades and velvets called for a high degree of knowledge and skill possessed by comparatively few, whose earnings were consequently high, and could be very high in the busiest times, when the weavers commonly worked a fourteen-hour day.

Amid the ever-increasing mêlée of the metropolis the Company's officers had the task of maintaining its position and status as a craft gild by enforcing its ordinances and trying to preserve high standards of craftsmanship and fair dealing. They had, moreover, to strengthen the Company by securing internal harmony as far as possible, adding competent craftsmen to its membership,[8] and combating the erosive activities of unqualified interlopers and all other types of non-members, English and alien. They had to maintain and, if possible, enhance the Company's prestige, and work in close co-operation with the Lord Mayor and City authorities on a basis of mutual loyalty and support, so that recalcitrant and hostile persons might find themselves confronted not only by the Weavers' Court of Assistants, but ultimately by the more powerful Lord Mayor and Court of Aldermen. The Weavers' Court requested the help of the Lord Mayor when its authority had been challenged or flouted, or when for any other reason it needed to be reinforced by a superior authority.[9]

Members of the Company, on the other hand, could appeal to the Lord Mayor if they felt they had been harshly or unjustly treated by the Weavers' Court. The City of London records contain a statement, written in 1781, of the policy and powers of the City authorities *vis-à-vis* the Livery Companies, conventions which had evolved and gained acceptance through the centuries:

> It appears, that, from early times down to the present century, the Court of Aldermen (which is a court of record) have claimed and exercised a power of superintending and controlling, in many instances, the proceedings of these guilds or companies, which practice the companies appear to have uniformly acknowledged and submitted to. And, by their entries, it appears that the court have created several of the companies . . . livery-companies; have increased and enlarged the livery of others, . . . have translated a member from one company to

another; have claimed and exercised a right of calling before them the masters, bailiffs, wardens, and assistants, to answer complaints of abuse of their trust, oppression of their members, and disobedience and contempt of the precepts and authority of that court (that is the Court of Aldermen); and, for these and such like offences, have imposed pains and penalties, and even committed to prison, . . . and . . . such proceedings of the court of aldermen have been approved and allowed by the judges of the court of King's-Bench.

In respect of the different trades, arts, or mysteries of these companies, or their rules or ordinances for the better regulation thereof, the greater body does not at all interfere, the different companies themselves being the only proper judges in those matters; but in all other cases . . . either respecting the police or government of each company separately, or . . . of the whole body at large, they (the City) have, from the earliest times, from time to time, interposed.[10]

Year in, year out, the Company augmented its ranks by admitting all suitably qualified persons as either freemen or admissioners. In the Weavers' Company, as in the other London Livery Companies, the freedom was usually acquired after serving a formal apprenticeship of not less than seven years, followed by two or three years as a journeyman. This would bring a young man to about the age of twenty-four after which it was open to him to apply to take his freedom, if he had both the inclination and the resources. The son of a freeman, however, had the right to be made free by patrimony, although he might know little or nothing of the art of weaving, and might, indeed, get his living in a totally different trade. Before the middle of the seventeenth century applications for admission by patrimony had to be supported by six citizens (not necessarily weavers) who could testify as to the facts.[11] Later in the seventeenth century only four 'compurgators' were required, and in the eighteenth century two sufficed.[12] Frauds were occasionally detected, such as the one attempted in 1670, when 'Tristram Baker, son of John Baker, weaver, upon report of a merchant taylor and three clothworkers, was made free by patrimony, paid a fee of 3s. 10d. and gave 10s. in lieu of a silver spoon.' But, says a marginal note, 'This was suspected to be a cheat and was therefore put off and not sworn and afterwards the money [was] return'd.'[13] Another cheat was attempted in August 1684, when, according to the minutes, 'Uriah Skipp, son of Thomas Skipp, Weaver, (Hog Lane), upon report of Wm. Daniell, Turner, Randolph Hall, Merchant Taylor, Thos. Horsnaile, Fishmonger, and John Poper, Salter, [was] made free by patrimony. MEMO: A cheat, and to be put out of the Books.' Three months later 'the said Uriah confessed he was not [Thomas Skipp] his son', and that the fraud was contrived at the Bell Inn in St John's Street by one Jones, who had been paid 10*s*., 'and so had three other Reporters—10*s*. a piece'. Just what induced Uriah to confess is obscure, but we do know that a year later all was forgiven and he was made free, this time by redemption by order of the Court of Aldermen. He seems to have had powerful friends.[14]

Redemption, or purchase, was another path to the freedom of the Company. Redemptioners were not, as a rule, qualified weavers, and before the nineteenth century their number was strictly limited, usually by the custom of restricting the right of nomination to a few eminent persons. Thus the Weavers' minutes record that on 20 June 1611.[15]

> . . . upon Certificate made to this Court under the hand of the minister and divers of the parishioners of the Town of Wingham near Sandwich in Kent that Francis Mott the father of John Mott was born in the said town in the year 1551, whereby this Court was satisfied that the said John Mott is the son of an Englishman born and capable of the freedom of this City. It is therefore ordered upon the nomination of the [City] Chamberlain that the said John Mott or Lamott shall be admitted into the freedom of this City by redemption in the Company of Weavers paying to Mr Chamberlain to the City's use the sum of Twenty pounds.

And when John Mott duly received his freedom from the Weavers he presented to the Company a gilt cup with a cover, valued at £5. 10*s*. Five months later John Howe, weaver, was made free by redemption at the request of the City Swordbearer;[16] and in the same year we have the record, already noticed, of no fewer than thirty freedoms by redemption granted by the Weavers' Company as a means of raising the money required to be invested in the Ulster colonisation project.[17] This, of course, was a special case, and the admission of such large numbers of redemptioners is unusual.

There is, however, the admission of William Beckford, a poor weaver, at the request of Sir Henry Yelverton, H.M. Solicitor-General, who asked that Beckford might be 'admitted into the freedom of this City by redemption in the company of Weavers, as one of . . . ten persons to be made free at Michaelmas next'. Sir Lionel Cranfield put forward a similar request in April 1617 on behalf of Richard Hassell, who gave to the Company 'for his admission two silver spoons'.[18] In the following year Richard Child was made free of the City by redemption in the Weavers' Company at the request of the Earl of Pembroke, Lord Chamberlain of H.M. Household, 'the said Richard Child having been apprenticed to William Cooper of

Andover by an indenture dated 27th June 1570'.[19] Also in 1618 the Provost-Marshal of the City presented one William Stevens, 'as the last of two yearly allowed him' by the Weavers' Company to be made free by redemption; and another redemptioner was admitted on a 'report' by the City Chamberlain.

A somewhat surprising entry appears on 16 April 1618, on which day

> six young men in the Lord Mayor's house presented unto the [Weavers'] Court Robert Wright to be made free of this City by Redemption as the last of Three to them granted in the mayoralty of Sir John Loman. . . . Whereupon at the request of the said six young men the said Robert Wright was admitted a freeman of the Company of Weavers *gratis*.[20]

From various redemptioners, who were usually men of substance, the Company received many a silver spoon and piece of plate.[21]

A rather curious situation is recorded in 1655, when

> upon the humble petition of Edward Houghton, who marrying within half a year of the expiration of his apprenticeship is denied his freedom by service, it is ordered by [the Court of Aldermen] in compassion to the petitioner being a poor man and intending no other use of his freedom than to be a Street Porter, that he shall be admitted into the freedom of this City by redemption in the Company of Weavers paying . . . to the use of the City 46s. 8d.

He was 'lovingly received' by the Weavers 'for a fine of 4s.'[22]

It was very unusual, though not entirely unknown, for women to be granted freedom by redemption. During 1668–9 there were, surprisingly, three such admissions. On 23 November 1668 Jane Sutton, Spinster, 'by order of the Court of Aldermen . . . was admitted a freewoman by redemption and paid 16s. 8d.' A week later Mary Rawstone was similarly made free, and in the following April Elinor Stone was admitted; but another entry of this sort does not occur until October 1674, when Mary Skutt 'by order of the Court of Aldermen . . . was admitted a freewoman p.Redemption, & paid 11s. 4d.'[23]

In the 1690s, the Company granted about 150 freedoms a year, of which approximately 86 per cent were taken by servitude, 11½ per cent by patrimony, and slightly over 2 per cent by redemption. During the eighteenth century the total freedoms taken decreased appreciably, while the number and percentages of persons in the three categories show remarkable changes. In the 1790s not more than twelve freedoms were taken each year, on the average. Of these, those taken by servitude represented some 52 per cent, while freedoms taken by patrimony had risen to 17 per cent and by redemption to over 30 per cent. By the end of the eighteenth century the trend was even more markedly in the same direction, less than two-fifths of the freedoms being taken by servitude (see Table 2.2).

Table 2.2 *Methods of qualification, late
eighteenth century*

	Qualified by	%
Freemen admitted {	servitude	39·8
	patrimony	26·5
	redemption	33·7

Thus we see how seriously redemption and patrimony together had eroded the centuries-old craft foundations of the Company.

It is well known that by the so-called 'custom of London', members of a gild could not claim an *exclusive* right to their craft or trade. A London citizen free of a particular company could not, it seems, be prevented from engaging in the craft or trade of any other company. Hence the designation 'mercer', 'fishmonger', 'brewer', 'weaver', after a name, indicates only the company to which the person belonged, not necessarily his actual occupation. From this usage sprang many fantastic incongruities: stationers were freemen of the Fishmongers' Company; men free of the Company of Cooks worked as weavers,[24] and freemen of the Weavers' Company worked as masons, shoe-makers, jewellers and booksellers. There were even paviours in the Goldsmiths' Company. The master carpenter who helped to rebuild Weavers' Hall after the Great Fire was free of the Weavers' Company, and, indeed, served as a Warden in 1668–9. For hundreds of years this illogical but persistent custom was a never-failing source of disputes and discontents among gildsmen, especially the handicraftsmen. Its chief advantage was that it allowed the London citizens freedom of enterprise and mobility of capital. Its main disadvantage was its tendency to weaken gild control over master craftsmen and the quality of their products.[25] The gilds, therefore, strongly advocated some tightening of existing rules and practice. The City Corporation, too, favoured a policy of rationalisation and would bid, order, recommend and exert pressure in particular cases, but they would never attempt any general compulsion, nor would they officially repudiate the custom of London.[26] In 1620, the Weavers having complained that sundry freemen of other companies were using the art of weaving but would not be governed by their orders, the Court of Aldermen ordered that all such persons, 'as well silk-weavers as others, shall be subject to the search, government and correction' of the Weavers' Company, and suggested that officers of the other companies involved should, if they so desired, accompany the Weavers' Officers on their searches. Two years after this the same court expressed the opinion that enforcement of translations of weavers who were free of other companies would result in much bad blood, many lawsuits and set a bad example to all the companies. The Court favoured amicable voluntary arrangements between the companies concerned.[27]

Many translations by mutual consent took place, some without the intervention of the City authorities, others after a hearing before the Lord Mayor and Court of Aldermen. The Weavers seldom raised any serious objections, even when they were losing a member, and men translating to them were often admitted gratis. Thus on 9 October 1610 'William Upton, Citizen and Free of the Carpenters (using the art of weaving) is this day admitted & sworn a brother of this gild, gratis, paying only the Officers' fees.'[28] Two similar translations—one from the Innholders and the other from the Whitebakers—took place in 1618–19.[29] In July 1618 a wax chandler 'using the trade of a weaver' was translated to the Weavers by consent of the two companies,[30] and a little later a cutler, free of the Weavers by patrimony, was translated to the Cutlers' Company. But such translations were not always effected smoothly, as we see from the case of Arthur Pattison, a freeman of the Merchant Taylors who was working as a weaver. Early in 1618 a delegation from the Weavers' Company to the City authorities, 'concerning the translation of such freemen of other Companies using the art of weaving within the liberties of this Gild', complained that Pattison had 'denied and withstood' the Weavers' bailiffs and wardens when they wished to search and had flatly refused to be subject to the Weavers' Company and its rules. During the ensuing inquiry in the Mayor's Court the Weavers produced the inspeximus of 21 Henry VI in support of their case, and the Court decreed that Pattison should be translated to the Weavers' Company immediately, and for the future all craftsmen similarly situated should be translated so as to come under the rules and government of that Company. But the Court hastened to add that this decision must not be taken as a precedent by other companies 'unless they can show forth a grant by authority of Parliament . . . as the Weavers' have done'. Another case at this time was that of John Gadesby, Citizen and Carpenter of London but 'using the trade of a Weaver', who was convicted by the City authorities for keeping more looms and apprentices than the Weavers' ordinances allowed, and promptly thrown into Newgate prison, 'there to remain until he shall conform himself . . . or other order be taken for his enlargement'. Gadesby, it seems, had argued that as he was not a member of the Weavers' Company, their ordinances did not apply to him. The 'other order' referred to was probably his formal translation to the Weavers, for on 28 July 1618 the Carpenters' Company signified their willingness to translate Gadesby to the Weavers 'on Thursday next before the Lord Mayor and Court of Aldermen with six Assistants of the said Company these to be ready to perform the translation and thereupon ... Gadesby to be released out of Newgate'.[31] The Weavers' Company followed up these successes by taking similar action against the Clothworkers and the Wax Chandlers;[32] and when Lawrence Hendricke, a stranger naturalised by royal letters patent, was accused of keeping five apprentices, using seven looms and refusing to pay a fine of £3 'taxed upon him for his offence', the City stood firmly by the Weavers and authorised the taking of proper legal action against Hendricke 'and others in that kynde offending'.[33] But there was apparently little or no improvement in the situation as a whole, for an order in Council, dated 26 June 1622, refers to 'divers obstinate and wilful persons, freemen of other Companies' who utterly refused to conform, thus weakening the position of the Weavers' Company and perpetuating the manufacture and sale of inferior goods. Those who henceforth ignored the Order would do so at their peril—and it seems that many did, for after an interval of sixteen years the Weavers' Company felt impelled to appeal to the highest authority. Towards the end of 1638 a Privy Council presided over by King Charles I heard the Weavers' complaint that the 'Tallow Chandlers, Fishmongers and other Companies delay and refuse to translate weavers free of their Companies contrary to their Charter confirmed by Act of Parliament, His Majesty's proclamation[34] and two several orders of the Court of Aldermen'. The King in Council instructed the City Recorder to see that the ancient Company of Weavers should 'freely enjoy the benefit granted to them', and in their response the Court of Aldermen repeated their view that all weavers of silk, wool, linen, or any other material in London, Southwark, and 'other places pertaining to London', ought to submit to 'the power, jurisdiction, search, supervision and government' of the Weavers' Company, whether they are freemen of the City of London or not, and, notwithstanding that they are free of another company, should be translated to the Weavers.[35] In practice, translations to and from the Weavers' Company continued to be piecemeal and spasmodic. The two years 1662–3 were exceptional, for fifteen men, all 'using weaving', were translated to the Weavers from various other companies, against the loss of only one weaver (translated to the Innholders).[36] In October 1672 Nathaniel Collett, 'an ancient member' of the Weavers' Company but an oarmaker by trade, was translated at his own request to the Shipwrights because they were threatening to sue him;[37] and 'Wm. Bugdon, by Trade a Barber-chirurgeon, lately by order of the Court of Aldermen made a freeman of the [Weavers'] Company', presented his 'humble request to be Translated from this to ye Barber-Chirurgeons' Company inasmuch as the said Compa. do arrest & otherwise molest him for not being a freeman thereof'. The Weavers agreed to release him on payment of £2.[38] An even more handsome 'golden handshake' was received by the Weavers from Nicholas Wye when he paid his 'Livery fine and to be translated to the Brewers' Compa., £10'.[39]

Very few translations, however, were so lucrative for the Company. Some, indeed, were costly, especially when resort was had to legal proceedings. A case in point was that of George Stone, a weaver by trade but free of the Broderer's Company, who was prosecuted in the Court of Exchequer by the Weavers' Company 'in order to force him from the Broderers to the Weavers'. The Broderers' Company appealed to the City, but without success, for the Court of Aldermen ruled that Stone 'ought to be translated to the Weavers, and ... ordered that six [members] of each of the said Companies do attend' before the Court, according to custom, to witness the formal translation. The Weavers usually sent the Four in Place and two Assistants on such occasions, for their attendance signified the Company's consent to the translation. This was usually given, but might be withheld if the candidate was in debt to the Company for unpaid fines, arrears of quarterage and the like.[40] Such attendances usually meant one or more visits to a tavern or coffee house, as we see, for example, from the Renter Bailiff's accounts relating to the translation of Isaac March from the Clothworkers to the Weavers, 'he being a weaver by trade' (Table 2.3).

Table 2.3 *Extract from the Renter Bailiff's accounts*

		£	s.	d.
20 July 1708	Expended attending Court of Aldermen about ye translating Mr. March		16	3
27 July 1708	-ditto-	1	3	0
September 1708	Expended on ye Committee on attending Court of Aldermen on ye translation of Isaac March	1	10	0
	Expended at ye Tavern & Coffee house attending Court of Aldermen		5	6

The attendances and arguments continued so merrily that by the middle of 1709 the case had cost the Weavers' Company over £15 and was still *sub judice*.[41] Even more protracted and expensive was Provey's case in 1781. Samuel Provey, Citizen and Clothworker, was made free of that company by servitude, and in due course became a Liveryman. Some time after this Provey was summoned to take up the freedom of the Weavers' Company, because, they said, he was in business as a weaver. This he consented to do, and was duly sworn in.

When, however, 'after the expiration of several years', the Weavers called upon him to join their Livery and pay the usual fine of £10 'on being clothed', he refused, saying that, as they already knew, he was a Liveryman of the Clothworkers' Company and 'he could not have any additional privilege by becoming a liveryman of the said Company of Weavers'. The latter, having taken the opinion of the Attorney-General, started a test case against Provey, who, advised by the Clothworkers, appealed to the City authorities. In due course the Court of Aldermen decided that the Weavers ought to have applied to the City to have Provey translated (for which there were many precedents), but since this had not been done, Provey was upheld in his refusal to pay a second Livery fine. This case cost the Weavers' Company at least £70.[42]

Simultaneous membership of more than one company, while not at all usual, was certainly not unknown. For example, in 1673 George Harvey, hatmaker, was a member not only of the Weavers' Company but of the Feltmakers' Company in which he 'hath borne all Offices'; and in the following year it is recorded that 'Jasper Curtis, Citizen and Clothworker of London, having also served to ye trade of a Weaver in Wiltshire as per certificate and having married Widow Maynard of this Compa. was admitted a foreign Master and paid 11s. 10d.' A similar case was that of Philip Poles, another citizen and clothworker, who had married the widow of William Wheatley, a linen weaver and 'foreign member' of the Weavers' Company. After he had been arrested as 'an Offender', on the initiative of the Weavers' Company, Poles asked that he might be admitted as a foreign master to exercise the trade of linen weaving, and after careful deliberation his request was granted.[43] Charles Cooling, on the contrary, wished to get away from the Weavers, for, having been twice proposed for the Livery and twice rejected, he took umbrage and asked to be translated 'to any other Company'.[44]

Although Assistants and Liverymen were privileged in respect of the numbers of looms and apprentices they might have, it would be a mistake to suppose that every freeman was anxious to join the Livery or to secure a seat on the Court of Assistants. It is true that some were public-spirited men who had the good of the Company and the trade at heart. Others enjoyed the enhanced status and influence, the prestige and privileges. For an ambitious man, acceptance of the Livery might be an important upward move. As a Liveryman he might get his chance (e.g. by serving on a special committee) to impress the Officers and Assistants, and this could eventually lead to a place on the Court of Assistants and, perhaps, in course of time to the Upper Bailiff's chair. But ambition did not beckon some men in this direction; not everyone was willing to sacrifice time and money by accepting the Livery or serving on the Court of Assistants. Some, indeed, looked upon such calls as nothing but an expensive nuisance, and the records reveal a variety of reasons or excuses for not wishing to serve. In 1663, for instance, two freemen 'warned to be of the Assistants' asked to be excused because they were 'thick of hearing'.[45] (None so deaf . . .!) Ten years later, when the number of Assistants was much depleted by infirmity and death, an attempt was made to fill the vacancies; but there was, apparently, no great keenness to serve, several of those selected urging physical disability, 'distance of habitation', and pressure of business as reasons for their unwillingness to accept nomination.[46] Small wonder that control of the Company's affairs tended to become concentrated in the hands of a few senior members.

In the seventeenth century a conscientious member of the Court of Assistants would attend the monthly and quarterly 'Full Courts' and, in between, the weekly 'Private Courts'. The business of the latter was the binding and turning-over of apprentices and the granting of freedoms. The Full Courts summoned and elected Stewards and Liverymen; elected freemen to fill vacancies on the Court of Assistants; directed the management of the Company's property; appointed the Beadle and Under-Beadle; received the Auditor's reports on the Company's property and charities, and on the annual accounts submitted by the Bailiffs and Wardens. In addition there was the General Court or Common Hall on St James's Day (Election Day), 25 July, attended by the Officers, Assistants and Livery to elect Officers and Auditors for the coming year. Other Common Halls might be summoned to transact special business, such as the consideration and approval of proposed new by-laws and ordinances, or the draft of a petition to Parliament. Usually three or four Officers were present at every meeting, but the Assistants' attendances varied between two and eleven, five or six being a normal number. On Oath Day in August of each year, however, when the new Officers were sworn in, the attendance was usually thirteen or fourteen; and a similar attendance was usual on Audit Days. In and after the last quarter of the eighteenth century regular weekly courts were not held all the year round. From November to March, which was usually the slack period, Private Courts 'for binding and making free' were held fortnightly, weekly Courts being resumed when 'the trade begins to stir again' in April. Quarterly Courts were held on the first Tuesday after each quarter day, except the one in December, which was held on the Tuesday next before Christmas Day.[47]

Candidates for the Livery were chosen by the Bailiffs, Wardens, and Assistants, or 'the most part of them' for the time being, from the body of freemen; and every freeman accepting 'the Clothing' had to pay a 'fine' of £5 to augment the funds of the Company. From 1616 to 1619 twenty-nine new Liverymen were chosen and accepted 'the

Clothing', but others were reluctant, urging various reasons for wishing to be excused.[48] Later, in 1664, four members agreed to 'be of the Clothing' and pay their fines, but twice that number would neither accept nor pay.[49] A Liveryman could be sued by the Company for non-payment of his fine, but this seldom happened: the threat of legal proceedings or some other form of pressure usually sufficed.[50] Acceptance of the Livery was usually marked by a celebration. For example, in February 1690 the Renter Bailiff 'paid for wine 3 worthy persons accepting the Livery, 9s.', and in the summer he 'paid for Canary, Mr. Lamb & Mr. Dent accepting the Livery, 4s.'

Not all Liverymen were prosperous. In 1694 the Court of Assistants resolved that a Liveryman who had 'failed in the World' could have all outstanding fines cancelled and, at his own request, be discharged from the Livery.[51] During the following half-century a number of Liverymen surrendered their Livery gowns and were struck off the Livery, and in cases of need their Livery fines were refunded. In 1752 a Renter Warden-elect pleaded inability to serve and was allowed to resign his gown.[52] Moreover, certain freemen were forced to decline the Livery by reason of their poor circumstances. Thus, when Ivon Le Nain was 'summoned for the Livery' in 1751, he pleaded on behalf of himself and his father, who also had been similarly summoned, that his father 'was quite Superannuated and destitute of all support & provision but what he found for him'; that he could barely pay his way, and therefore he asked that they both might be excused. The Court consented, provided that 'the Representation . . . now given should be found to be true'.[53] The plea of Thomas Handyside, in 1742, was quite different, for he based his refusal to become a Liveryman on the ground that he was not a freeman of the City. The Company, having first taken the Solicitor-General's opinion, sued Handyside in the Court of Common Pleas and won the case.[54]

From 1556 onwards the Bailiffs were empowered to choose two Liverymen 'to be Stewards, which shall provide for the . . . Company's dinner yearly . . . and yearly the said Bailiffs shall appoint such as hath not been in the said Stewardship before time, till it hath gone through the whole Livery, and then to begin again'. In the seventeenth and eighteenth centuries this was the principal burden which a Liveryman might have to bear, and it was usually quite heavy, for, although each Liveryman paid a shilling or two for his dinner ticket, much of the cost of the feast fell upon the Stewards. If a Liveryman chosen in any year 'to serve Steward' wished to be excused, he had to pay a heavy fine—a factor which deterred many a freeman from accepting the Livery. As early as 1610 the records show that Richard Leafield was fined 40s. because he refused to serve as a Steward; and in 1613 John Dorrell was chosen to serve with Gabriel Stone, 'but forasmuch as John Dorrell dwelleth out of the Liberties' viz., at

Loose, near Maidstone in Kent,[55] 'it is ordered . . . that the Beadle shall notify [him] . . . and bring answer to the Court. If a refusal is received, Mark Lyles is appointed in his place and the said Dorrell will be fined according to the Ordinance.' Dorrell paid his fine but asked to be discharged from the Livery.[56] In the second half of the seventeenth century the fines were much heavier, partly because the value of the monetary unit had fallen. Thus in 1669 the Renter Bailiff 'Recd. of Mr. Thomas Bush his fine to be discharged of Steward agst. the Ld. Maiors Day, £12' and 'of Mr. William Winter the like: £12'.[57] In 1704 the Court of Assistants listened sympathetically to Mr Thorp, a freeman, who asked to be excused from 'holding Steward' because 'he had lost £1,000 in nine months last past'; but in the following year the Company brought three rebellious members before the Court of Aldermen for refusing to hold the office of Steward or to pay a fine of £14 a head in lieu. The Court of Aldermen found for the Company and urged the three defendants to do their duty according to the Company's rules.[58] This pattern is repeated throughout the next half-century. Pleas of poverty or serious business losses were usually accepted; but if a man could afford to pay but would not, the Court might take a strong line, as when £20 was 'recovered by Execution on the goods of Jonathan Rigg for his Fine for refusing to serve Steward'.[59]

Inevitably one is brought to the conclusion that, as the decades passed, the Company felt obliged to seek its new Liverymen among the well-to-do: a view supported by the practice, which emerged towards the end of the seventeenth century, of allowing a Liveryman to purchase exemption from the holding of any office in the future by paying a combined fine of £20. Ultimately, in June 1739, the Court of Assistants approved a standing order to this effect.[60] An eminent Liveryman of the Weavers' Company at this period was Thomas Penn, 'Lord Proprietor of Pennsylvania', who was asked 'whether it will be agreeable to him to be Elected a Member of this Court'. He politely declined the invitation but offered to pay a fine of £20 'to be excused from serving all further Offices'.[61] Another eminent freeman (who was free, also, of the Fishmongers' Company) was Alderman John Kirkman, who, having served his apprenticeship to weaving with his father in Coventry, established himself in the London weaving trade about the middle of the eighteenth century. He became a City Alderman in 1768 and a freeman of the Weavers' Company at the end of the following year. Six months later he was 'clothed', paying not only his livery fine but, at his own request, £30 as a composite fine for all other offices. On St James's Day 1770 he was elected to the Court of Assistants in the morning and became Upper Bailiff in the afternoon. He was elected Sheriff of London in 1776, and M.P. for the City in 1780, using Weavers' Hall as his committee rooms. Unfortunately, he died on the last day of the poll, 18 September 1780.[62]

Apart from the occasional Stewardship, the duties of the Livery-men were certainly not onerous. By customs handed down from the Middle Ages and later written into the Ordinances, the Livery were required to assemble to hear a sermon at least once a year, and they were in duty bound to attend the funeral of deceased Liverymen or their wives.[63] They must assemble when summoned by the Court of Assistants, through the Beadle, in Common Hall on the Company's business, or to take part in the election of the Lord Mayor and Sheriffs, Members of Parliament (Burgesses) for the City, or on other important civic occasions. The Renter Bailiff's accounts throw some light upon these functions (see Table 2.4).

The number of the Livery seems to have been about 100 during the greater part of the seventeenth century. Certainly, in 1662, the Court of Assistants 'ordered and agreed' that for the future the upper limit should be 100, and nobody should be admitted to the Livery without the consent of a Full Court.[64] By 1695, however, the number of Liverymen on the books had risen to 149, although the normal attendance at Common Halls was between thirty and fifty. But when some highly important or controversial question was on the agenda the attendance might suddenly swell to a much greater number. In the second half of the eighteenth century the Liverymen's interest in the Company seems to have declined, for despite the raising of the maximum permitted number to 300 in 1724,[65] with actual numbers on the books of 236 in 1730 and 294 in 1740, the attendances seldom exceeded thirty to forty. In addition of course, the Four in Place were present with, perhaps, eight or nine of the Assistants (see Table 2.5).

On the annual Election Days throughout the first half of the seventeenth century the new Bailiffs and Wardens chose four of the Assistants to act as auditors for the ensuing year. During the Commonwealth period, however, the number was raised, by statute, to eight—four Assistants and four from the Livery—to be chosen by the Commonalty. This new arrangement was not, it seems, entirely satisfactory, for in 1655 the Court of Assistants desired 'that it be propounded to the Representatives that when they elect eight Auditors, four of the eight be of them that were chosen the year before, to the end they may be instructed in the manner and way of auditing'.[66] It seems that normally the more literate members were chosen, for the records show that almost every auditor could write, some quite stylishly; whereas many a master weaver could only make a mark. The auditors' duties were not confined to the examination and certification of the Officers' accounts, for they had to check the inventory of property and utensils and see to the replacement of lost or worn items. Old linen was usually given away, but old pewter and

Table 2.4 *Duties of Liverymen as shown in the Renter Bailiff's accounts*

28 March	1615	Three Assistants were fined 12*d*. each (put into the Poor's Box) for failing to attend a sermon at Paul's Cross on 24 March.
2 August	1669	'Paid for supper on Mr. Cade's funeral night, £1. 2*s*. 6*d*.
12 October	1669	'Spent with some of ye Compa. at Mr. Fairvacks funeral, 12*s*. 11*d*.'
18 October	1669	'Recd. of Mr. John Fairvacks, Administrator of Mr. Daniel Fairvacks, a member of this Compa. decd. for the Livery's attendance at ye funeral of the said Mr. D. Fairvacks according to Custom, £5.'
7 February	1676	'Paid for wine for ye Livery attending Mr. Jennings funeral, £1. 12*s*. [and] for tobacco & pipes & coffee, 3*s*. 4*d*.'
17 February	1679	'Spent with Livery electing Parliament men, £2. 10*s*. 2*d*.'
2 September	1680	'Spent with several of the Court visiting Mr. Bearstow, 3*s*. 6*d*.'
13 September	1680	'Spent at ye Funeral of Mr. Bearstow, 10*s*. 8*d*.'
30 September	1689	Expended at a Common Hall electing a Lord Mayor £1. 16*s*. 4*d*.
19 February	1690	Expended at a Common Hall electing 4 Citizens to serve in the ensuing Parliament £3. 13*s*. 2*d*.
29 November	1703	A Common Hall summoned 'about sealing of Black Silk'.
30 June	1704	A Common Hall summoned 'for Election of Sheriffs'.
6 October	1704	'Expended on the Common Hall for the Election of Lord Mayor &c., £2. 11*s*. 7*d*.'
? May	1705	'Expended on the Common Hall & Dinner for Election of Parliament men, £2. 8*s*. 8*d*.' 'Wine for the Common Hall etc., £3. 12*s*. 1*d*.' 'To the Beadle for summoning the Livery, 5*s*.'[67]

silver could be traded in part-exchange for new. For example, in March 1704, 'upon consideration that the Company had two large old Silver Salts that were in a manner useless, it is agreed and ordered that the Renter Bailiff do exchange the same for six lesser Salts'. Also, from time to time, the auditors were asked to report upon the general financial state of the Company.[68]

Needless to say, the auditors had to rely a good deal upon the co-operation of the Clerk to the Company, who was the only permanent official, except the Beadle and the Under-Beadle or Porter. An entry in the Renter Bailiff's accounts under the date 22 July 1686, 'pd. two Porters that carried Gowns, &c. at Mr. Cole's Funeral,

Table 2.5 *Membership of the London Weavers' Company from 1681 to 1820*

Year	Officers and assistants	Livery	Commonalty		Grand total
			Widows	Others	
1681	Not listed Est. 25	105	103	5,170	5,403
1692	25	145	Not listed	6,160	6,330*
1701	24	150	74	5,537	5,785
1710	Not listed Est. 25	183	146	5,495	5,949
1720	25	184	171	4,860	5,240
1730	25	236	217	5,780	6,258*
1740	26	294	123	4,480	4,923
1750	25	218	67	2,303	2,613
1760	25	180	51	1,550	1,806
1770	25	196	27	1,310	1,558
1780	23	170	12	1,172	1,377
1790	24	254	2	924	1,204
1800	25	299	8	651	983
1810	26	281	6	505	818
1820	29	230	6	640	905

* These remarkably high totals have been carefully checked in the Quarterage Book.

2*s.* 6*d.*', brings to mind the Company's Clerk, James Cole, who died in mid-July and was buried a few days before St James's Day. It is not difficult to imagine the sad, kindly thoughts of the senior members of the Court and Livery as they remembered the dedicated services of their late Clerk over an unbroken period of twenty-three years, and especially his almost superhuman efforts during and immediately after the Great Fire in 1666. James Cole's service as Clerk began in 1665, the year of the Great Plague, which meant that he had to cope not only with the aftermath of that dreadful visitation, but with the rescue and safe storage of the Company's charters, records, pictures, plate and other property in the following year, as well as with the preparations, plans and contracts for the rebuilding of Weavers' Hall at a time when the Company, like so many families and corporations, was homeless.

Towards the end of 1683 he was evidently thinking of retiring, for he was training an understudy, one Charles Burroughs, who for eight years past 'had very diligently and soberly demeaned himself in his service'. When the request was put to them, the Court of Assistants, after a long debate, agreed that Burroughs should have the 'reversion' of the Clerkship, provided that Mr Cole would remain in the office 'so long as he should live'.[69]

The Clerk's salary at that time was £4 a year, supplemented by his fees, mainly from apprentice bindings and admissions of freemen. The Company provided him with a rent-free house worth £10 a year, and gave him, fairly frequently, gratuities for special work, such as the drafting and presentation of petitions to Parliament. That there were certain additional perquisites is revealed by such entries in the Renter Bailiff's accounts as 'pd. the Clerk in lieu of 2 Dishes of Meat £1. 1s. 6d.', as part of the Lord Mayor's Day expenses. Moreover, gifts were made to the Clerk's wife and to his maid in recognition of their help on special occasions.[70] In June 1703 the Clerk's basic salary was raised to £10 a year, 'and the said Clerk was thereupon very thankful and returned his hearty thanks'. Three months later he received '£5 as a Common Gratuity for his services the year last past and £5 more for Parliamentary services'.[71] It was important that the Clerk should be, *inter alia*, 'well acquainted with the Searches', and it was a distinct advantage if he could speak French.[72]

The Company seems to have been well and truly served over the years by its Officers and officials. The records reveal very few instances of neglect of duty, incompetence, or suspected or actual dishonesty. The worst case of irregularities in the Company's accounts, coupled with an attempt to 'cook the books', probably to conceal defalcations, occurred in 1649, the first year of the Commonwealth period, when the Bailiffs and Wardens were not elected in the usual way but nominated by Act of Parliament. This episode is vividly described in the Company's minutes:

Whereas William Jackson, John Hooker, John Hewitt and Thomas Hall were chosen Bailiffs and Wardens of the Gild or Company of Weavers upon the first Thursday of March 1649 according to an Act of Parliament then obtained. And for the better obtaining of a stock and Treasure they to discharge the trust reposed in them at the end of their year ought to have [had] their accounts Audited and entered in a Book fairly written, subscribed by the eight Auditors chosen according to the aforesaid Act, and to remain an account of the said Company for ever. All which the said Bailiffs and Wardens did neglect to do, leaving it as an ill precedent and great prejudice to the Gild or Company. But afterwards the said William Jackson with some others did surreptitiously and by fraudulent means, upon the 15th of June 1654, procure the Ledger Book out of the Hall to a scrivener's shop, without the licence, privity, or consent of this Court, and then and there did cause an account to be entered in the name of the Bailiffs and Wardens according to their own directions and contrary to the tenor of the said Act of Parliament and the trust reposed in

them, in consideration whereof We, the present Bailiffs,
Wardens and Assistants . . . do protest and dissent from the
said account and the entry thereof and every thing therein
contained and do declare the same to be null and void. . . .[73]

By 1654 John Hooker, who had been Renter Bailiff in 1649-50, had
prudently removed 'far in the country'. He still owed the Company
over £7, which he showed no intention of paying; but when the
Assistants discovered that he had left £4 in the Beadle's hands and
that the Clerk had possession of Hooker's Livery gown, valued at
30s., they promptly attached both money and gown 'for the use and
benefit of the Company'. Meantime, the Company had been at grips
with John Hewitt, another of the four. Apparently he had engaged
in litigation, allegedly on the Company's behalf, but without its
authority, and had incurred a large debt, amounting to some £200,
which the auditors thought he ought to bear. Hewitt was disqualified
in 1653 from holding any office in the Company in future.[74]

In the 1660s John Biggs, the Company's Beadle, ran into trouble
through overspending (his own money, presumably), and in May
1664 his creditors threw him into prison for non-payment of debts
amounting to £14. Afraid lest he might lose his job and sink even
deeper into debt if he remained in prison, he appealed to the Company, saying that he was 'utterly like to be ruined and undone together with Wife and Children'. The Court of Assistants extended a
helping hand by lending him the £14, 'he being injoyned to give a
bond' to repay the loan by instalments of £4 a year.[75]

Thomas Sharpe, who was Renter Warden in 1684-5, was 'removed
from the place of Warden' because his accounts were in such a complete muddle that a set of supplementary accounts had to be prepared
in order to bring in additional receipts of nearly £75 and unrecorded
expenditure of over £55. But there was no suggestion of dishonest
dealing, and Sharpe was elected Upper Warden in 1687-8.[76]

A much more serious case came to light in May 1694, when the
Court was informed that William Smith, the Renter Bailiff (1693-4),
had made a number of errors in his accounts which, if not set right,
might involve the Company in considerable loss. In spite of pressure
from 'diverse worthy members' Smith had refused to pay certain
debts on the Company's behalf, 'on pretence that he had none of the
Company's money in his hands . . . but that the Company was indebted unto him in several sums'. By way of proof he produced to the
Court 'a figurative account of his receipts and payments'; but the
Court were suspicious and wanted to inspect the Renter Bailiff's
account books. Smith, however, refused this request, and had to be
ordered by the Court to deliver up to the Clerk the account books and
all relevant documents, so that a special committee of auditors might

'inspect, adjust and set right the said Bailiff's account'. But when Bailiff Smith still obstinately refused to divulge certain material information he was strongly suspected of misappropriation of the Company's money. At this point (14 May 1694) a Full Court resolved, *nem. con.*, to dismiss Smith from the office of Renter Bailiff, as being 'a person unmeet to supply that office and place' by 'not keeping a just and true account' and refusing to set it right, which was 'a very notorious fault', and 'for his abusing divers members of this Court with Scurrilous and Gross Language'. One result of this deplorable business was a Court order that in future the Renter Bailiff 'shall lay before the next full Court after every Quarter Day a breviary or summary account of all his receipts and payments in that quarter'.[77]

Later in the same year, 1694, four of the Assistants had their names removed from the list because they had grossly neglected their duties as members of the Court.[78]

NOTES

1 F. Consitt, *The London Weavers' Company from the Twelfth Century to the close of the Sixteenth Century* (Oxford, 1933), pp. 1–4.

2 MS. 4655/3, f.85.

3 Brett-James, *London*, p. 224; Weiss, *French Protestant Refugees* (trans. 1854), p. 253; G. B. Hertz, 'The English Silk Industry in the 18th Century', *English Historical Review*, XXIV (1909), pp. 710–27. During the half-century 1664–1713, according to Hertz, the volume of the English silk trade increased twentyfold.

4 S. Kramer, *The English Craft Gilds* (1927), p. 99.

5 Patrimony: the right or privilege of exercising a craft or trade transmitted from a father to his child by inheritance.

6 The word 'foreign' in this context means a person who had migrated to London from the provinces or from overseas: see MS. 4647, f.365.

7 MS. 4655/1, ff.16–17.

8 Qualified weavers who could 'prove their service' were not excluded because of poverty, age or infirmity; on the contrary, such men were often admitted 'without fees, gratis' (MS. 4655/4, *passim*; MS. 4655/6, f.60b). The misfortunes of John van Merson, a foreign journeyman, led to an unusual payment in kind, for 'having been plundered [in 1674] on his voyage to and from Hamburg, and now presenting to the Company a large brass lanthorn valued at £4, or thereabouts, [he] was admitted a foreign master gratis' (MS. 4655/8, f.11b).

9 e.g., in 1618, 'Giles Boveney, stranger shoemaker, using the art of weaving, never being admitted by this Company, being brought before this Court [of Assistants] by Mr Recorder's warrant, is ordered to pull down his looms forthwith and to leave the trade; otherwise if he be found working again he is to be fined and imprisoned according to the discretion of Mr Recorder' (MS. 4655/1, f.80).

10 City of London Records P.A.R. Book 5, f.44 (2); cf. MS. 4655/1, ff.12, 15.

11 Strictly speaking the father had to be free of the City and his company at the time of his son's birth (P. E. Jones, *The Worshipful Company of Poulterers* (1939), p. 53).

12 MS. 4655/3, ff.2, 6, 10, 17–18.

13 MS. 4655/6, f.21.

14 MS. 4655/9, ff. 38, 71b-72b.

15 MS. 4655/1, f.7.

16 MS. 4655/1, f.13.

17 MS. 4655/1, ff.8–9; see also Chap. 5.

18 MS. 4655/1, ff.44, 54. Lionel Cranfield (1575–1645) is an early example of a business tycoon who turned his talents to government. Having made a fortune as a merchant and speculator, he caught the eye of James I, who appointed him Surveyor-General of the Customs. He became Baron Cranfield in 1621, Earl of Middlesex in 1622, and was Lord High Treasurer of England from 1621 to 1624. During his drive for efficiency and economy in public departments he inevitably made enemies. He was impeached for alleged corruption and imprisoned in 1624; but was soon released and pardoned. From 1625 to 1645 he lived in retirement. See R. H. Tawney, *Business and Politics under James I: Lionel Cranfield as Merchant and Minister* (1958); M. Prestwich, *Cranfield: Politics and Profits under the Early Stuarts* (1966).

19 MS. 4655/1, f.73. Repertories 33, f.270. Wm. Cooper's trade or craft is not specified.

20 MS. 4655/1, ff.72–3, 84.

21 MS. 4655/1, ff.110–12; another redemptioner was recommended by the East India Company in October 1629; MS. 4655/3, f.57b; cf. f.18; see also MS. 4655/15, f.277; MS. 4655/18, f.283; Repertories 127, f.233.

22 MS. 4655/2, f.171.

23 MS. 4655/5, ff.18b, 22b, 53; MS. 4655/8, 5 October 1674.

24 e.g. Mathew Hart of St John Street was 'a weaver but free of the Cooks [and] is Clerk of Bishopsgate Church' (MS. 4658, f.72 (1672)).

25 G. Unwin, *Ind. Org.*, p. 105; F. J. Fisher (ed.), *Essays in the Economic and Social History of Tudor and Stuart England* (1961), pp. 145–6.

26 S. Kramer, *The English Craft Gilds* (1927), pp. 168–72; G. Unwin, *Gilds*, p. 264.

27 Repertories 34, ff.526–526b; W. H. Overall, *Analytical Index of the Remembrancia of the City of London* (1878), p. 103.

28 MS. 4655/1, f.1; see also f.72.

29 MS. 4655/1, ff.82, 103.

30 MS. 4655/1, ff.46, 77; other translations are recorded on ff.64, 84, 86. A member of a declining craft might wish to be translated, e.g. from the Longbow-string Makers to the Weavers (MS. 4655/11, f.159).

31 Repertories 33, f.375; MS. 4655/1, ff.50, 77.

32 Repertories 33, ff.258b, 375; MS. 4655/1, ff.70, 109–10.

33 Repertories 33, ff.297b, 321b.

34 5 September 1619.

35 MS. 4655/1, ff.111–12. The record cites the case of Thomas Scott of Southwark, a weaver not free of the Weavers' Company, who was known to have woven 100 lb. of silk into ribbons.

36 MS. 4647, f.570; MS. 4655/2, *passim*; MS. 4655/3, ff.38b, 48b, 100.
37 MS. 4655/7, f.5.
38 MS. 4655A/3 and MS. 4648/1, 22 January 1672.
39 MS. 4648/1, 18 March 1672.
40 MS. 4655/11, ff.271b, 274, 310b; MS. 4655/12, f.108b.
41 MS. 4648/3, 1708–9, *passim*; MS. 4655/11, f.37b.
42 City of London Records P.A.R. Book 5, f.44; MS. 4655/17, ff.371, 376b–377, 383, 390b, 397–8b, 416, 494. In 1740 Nathaniel Highmore was translated from the Shipwrights to the Weavers, who elected him to their Livery immediately (MS. 4648/5, f.17b; MS. 4655/15, f.60b).
43 MS. 4655/7, ff.43, 87b; MS. 4655/8, ff.93b, 95; MS. 4648/1, 22 May 1676. cf. Kramer, *English Craft Gilds* (1927), p. 169.
44 MS. 4655/15, ff.61–2.
45 MS. 4655/3, f.64.
46 MS. 4655/7, f.35b.
47 MS. 4655/17, f.341; MS. 4655/11, ff.4b, 5, 8b.
48 MS. 4655/1, ff.45–6, 90, 96–7. The Livery fine was increased to £6 in 1680.
49 MS. 4655/3, ff.133b–134; MS. 4655A, 9 October 1649.
50 MS. 4655/5, f.41. A special committee set up in 1740 to bring lawsuits to recover Livery fines and other debts appears to have been very inactive (MS. 4655/15, ff.82b, 83b, 188).
51 MS. 4655/10, f.55b.
52 MS. 4655/16, f.152b.
53 MS. 4655/15, ff.82b, 165b. 167, 201–2, 236, etc., MS. 4655/16, f.18b.
54 MS. 4648/6, 13 July 1742. Maitland, *London*, I, p. 631.
55 Loose was two-and-a-half miles from Maidstone and forty miles from London.
56 MS. 4655/1, ff.1, 23.
57 MS. 4648/1, 18 October 1669.
58 MS. 4655/11, ff.20b, 28.
59 MS. 4655/11, f.131; MS. 4655/15, ff.349, 352; MS. 4655/16, ff.20b, 48b; MS. 4648/6, 29 June 1743.
60 MS. 4655/10, ff.55b, 57; MS. 4655/12, ff.103b, 113, 118b; MS. 4655/15, f.43b.
61 MS. 4655/16, ff.162b, 167. Thomas Penn (1702–75), second son of William Penn, the founder of Pennsylvania, succeeded his father jointly with his two brothers as hereditary proprietors of the province. Thomas Penn returned from Pennsylvania to England *c.* 1747, where he remained, and married in 1751 Lady Juliana Fermor, daughter of the Earl of Pomfret. His name is in the Livery list for 1740.
62 MS. 4655/17, ff.119b, 130–1, 134–5, 138b; A. B. Beaven, *Aldermen*, I, pp. 62, 105, 233, 281; II, pp. 133, 211.
63 In 1613 John Stele paid a fine of 2s. because he was absent from the funeral of a fellow-weaver (MS. 4655/1, f.23).
64 MS. 4655/3, f.44b.
65 MS. 4655/12, f.79b. On St James's Day 1662 'at the choosing of new Bailiffs and Wardens there were present of the Assistants and Livery 41'; a century later, when the Livery numbered 180, the Election Day attendance was barely thirty (MS. 4655/3, f.41; MS. 4655/16, f.266; MS. 4655/17, f.349; MS. 4661, *passim*).
66 MS. 4655/2, ff.167, 174. From July to October 1649 two of the

auditors sat with the Court of Assistants, but this practice was soon discontinued.

67 MS. 4655/1, f.32; MS. 4648/1; MS. 4648/3; MS. 4649B/2. Upper Bailiffs mentioned above: Willian Cade (1653–4); Daniel Fairvacks (1654–5); Edmond Bearstow (1659–60).

68 MS. 4655/11, f.11b.

69 MS. 4655/9, ff.6, 10. Burroughs died in 1694 and was succeeded by Case Shewell, an attorney-at-law; MS. 4655/10, ff.42b, 45, 57.

70 MS. 4648/1, 7 January 1667; MS. 4649B/2.

71 MS. 4655/11, ff.14b, 16b.

72 MS. 4655/11, f.296.

73 MS. 4655/2, f.133; MS. 4646, ff.85b–88; MS. 4655A/2, f.30.

74 MS. 4655/2, ff.11, 18–19, 60, 143.

75 MS. 4655/3, f.128. There were two Compters in the City, one in Wood Street and the other in the Poultry, each under the jurisdiction of a Sheriff. We have the testimony of Ned Ward, who wrote in 1698 that the Poultry Compter stank far worse than a Southwark ditch, a tanner's yard or a tallow-chandler's melting room, and that the prisoners in the hole were 'ill-looking vermin with long rusty beards, swaddled up in rags'. According to Walter Bell, the Compters were places of vile extortion, with large staffs of clerks, sergeants, yeomen, keepers, and turnkeys all demanding their fees from the luckless prisoners from the first moment of their imprisonment. The 'Master's side' was expensive; the 'Knight's side' a little cheaper; but a prisoner placed in 'the hole' could only extricate himself by paying 'garnish' at each door in the ascending scale as he went up higher. Thus a debtor might easily incur even more debts simply by reason of his internment in a Compter. In the first quarter of the eighteenth century prisoners in Ludgate and the two Compters were allowed to take out a box and beg in the neighbouring streets and alleys. But when the City authorities heard of this they thought it 'a Great Dishonour to the Good Government of this City and an obstruction to the passengers in the said Streets on their lawful occasions', and gave orders that the practice must cease at once. At this time, too, Daniel Defoe was moved to make 'A Plea for Poor Debtors', arguing trenchantly that 'Imprisonment for Crimes gets a Gaol Delivery, and Malefactors have their fetters knock'd off, and the Doors set open— either on the left Hand to the Gallows, and the Plantations, or on the right Hand to Liberty—by Court Pardons, Acts of Clemency, and the like; but for Debt, the Gaol is like Hell, from whence there is no Redemption. . . . Kings show Mercy to Traytors, to Murtherers and Thieves . . . but once in Prison for Debt, and we are lost for this World.' Repertories 128, ff.341–2; Bell, *Great Fire*, quoting the *Westminster Gazette*; W. Lee, *Daniel Defoe: His Life and recently discovered Writings* (1869), II, pp. 9–12.

76 MS. 4646, ff.118, 120b, 122.

77 MS. 4655/10, ff.46b–48, 57.

78 MS. 4655/10, f. 56.

Chapter 3

Gild Governance II

The City Fathers, like other municipal authorities, were quite willing to delegate special parts of their duties to the gilds. Cunningham and the Webbs pointed out long ago that with the passage of the centuries the leading gildsmen had become, in effect and up to a point, officers of the municipality charged with the protection of consumers from various forms of fraud such as adulteration of foodstuffs and textile materials, false and shoddy workmanship, and many similar abuses. In addition to these public functions, the gilds took from the shoulders of the civic courts masses of minor cases, such as the hearing and settlement of disputes between masters, journeymen and apprentices plying the same trade or craft. The long-standing rule which prohibited any member of the Weavers' Company from bringing a lawsuit against another member without express permission from the Court of Assistants, was evidently wise, for it ensured that a very large proportion of domestic disputes would be dealt with within the fraternity.[1] This had substantial advantages, especially where a dispute, by its very nature, could not be fairly settled unless the arbitrators or judges possessed expert technical knowledge. 'Let neighbours make an end' was a wise precept, always assuming that any Bailiffs, Wardens and Assistants acting as judges would do so 'in all equity and good conscience'. The following was a typical case involving specialised technical knowledge:

> The difference betn. Mr. Jos. Wright and Will. Burnham his workman touching the returning home of silk short of the quantity delivered being referred to this Court by both their consents, the same was debated and considered, and in as much as the work was all black ... ribbons and some part of it broad ribbon and no waste was returned, it is the opinion of this Court that $\frac{3}{4}$ of an oz. in every pound wt. may well be

allowed by Mr. Wright and more ought not to be demanded by the said Will. Burnham as waste of the said quantity.[2]

Occasionally a special arbitration court was set up *ad hoc*, with instructions to make a full report to the Court of Assistants should a settlement not be reached. Cases involving debts owing from one weaver to another were customarily dealt with by the Court of Assistants, with the willing general assent of the Lord Mayor. Here again, first-hand knowledge of the characters and circumstances of the parties often helped the cause of justice, for in many cases forbearance and a reasonable allowance of time was of the essence of a fair settlement. Payment by easy instalments might be decreed when, for example, it was known that a debtor had a large family of young children, or if he or his journeymen were sick, or if some special misfortune had come upon him.

Disputes about wages and terms and conditions of service are often met with in the Weavers' records. Before the first Spitalfields Act of 1773, weavers' wages in and around London, like those of workmen in other occupations, were regularly assessed and given legal validity by the appropriate magistrates (e.g. in the Cities of London and Westminster, and the Counties of Middlesex, Surrey and Essex) exercising powers conferred in 1563 by the Elizabethan 'Act Touching Divers Orders for Artificers, Labourers, Servants of Husbandry and Apprentices' (5 Eliz., c. 4). This important statute which was based partly on established gild practices and partly on the medieval Statutes of Labourers, sought, in general, to apply a system of wages regulation on a national scale, and so to 'banish idleness, advance husbandry and yield unto the hired person both in time of scarcity and in time of plenty a convenient proportion of wages'.

> And for the declaration what wages servants, labourers and artificers, either by the year or day or otherwise, shall receive . . . the justices of the peace of every shire . . . and every mayor, bailiff or other head officer within any city . . . shall . . . yearly at every general sessions first to be holden after Easter . . . calling unto them such discreet and grave persons of the said county or city as they shall think meet, and conferring together respecting the plenty or scarcity of the time and other circumstances necessary to be considered, have authority within the limits of their several commissions to rate and appoint the wages.[3]

The ideas underlying this Elizabethan legislation were still, in the main, accepted by government and people over a century later. In practice, however, the Tudor statutes were not consistently enforced, and the machinery for the assessment of fair wages does not seem to have been much used beyond the end of the seventeenth century.[4] But there is some evidence that wages in London in the eighteenth century remained 'to some extent customary and traditional, and . . . varied comparatively little till after 1793'.[5]

Among the London weavers, journeymen's wages early in the seventeenth century were usually 2s. 4d. a week, plus food, drink, lodging and washing 'fitting for a journeyman', and the normal hiring period, to which the Weavers' Company gave its approval, was one year, subject to 'three months' warning each to other'. In 1611 the son of a deceased freeman, who was working as a journeyman weaver, was hired for one year at 2s. 4d. weekly, and his master was ordered to pay 20s. to the Company 'for his admission'.[6] There are, however, a few instances of higher or lower rates of wages. In 1617 a journeyman was hired on a two-year contract at 2s. a week; an unusually low rate which is more likely to be due to the long hiring than to length of experience in the trade, because only a month later a newly admitted journeyman was hired for one year at £6, or approximately 2s. 4d. a week. Higher rates of 2s. 6d. and 2s. 8d. are recorded in 1616, 1617 and 1619.[7] The provision by the master of 'reasonable fare . . . sweet and holdsome for man's bodie' as part of a journeyman's wages was normal practice, and the Company would deal promptly with any complaints of non-fulfilment of this part of the employment contract. In other respects, too, the Company would try to secure fair and humane treatment for journeymen. Thus, in 1618, the Company summoned Nicholas Sheming, a master weaver who had neglected for three months to present his journeyman to the Company and had turned him away when he fell sick. The Company fined Sheming 20s., 'which fine is ordered to be [used] towards the relief of the said journeyman in his sickness'.[8]

As to the question of time rates and piece rates of wages, it appears that both methods of payment were actually in use in the seventeenth century and after. In May 1618 the Company fined a weaver 6s. 8d. 'for setting his journeyman at work by the piece and by the pound, contrary to the orders of this Company', and a similar case, involving two journeymen, was dealt with in the following July.[9] Less than a year later, however, John Neave, free of the Drapers but working as a weaver, was admitted to journeyman's status by the Weavers' Company and stated upon oath 'that when he wrought with John van Abyell plain cobweblawn, he was paid 4d. a yard', but later, because his master wished 'to set another in his loom, he would give him but 3d. a yard'. Another entry in the same year shows that a journeyman weaver was weaving silk scarves at 18d. each.[10] Moreover, we find the Weavers' Company placing the seal of its approval upon an agreement to work by weight, made among the gold and silver lace weavers as early as May 1612, when it was

41

ordered and agreed by the Bailiffs, Wardens and Commonalty
of the Gild that no person now using or hereafter using the art
of weaving within the same gild shall work any manner of
plain gold and/or silver lace, or silk and gold lace, or silk and
silver lace, or any lace mixed with gold or silver, for less than
5s. 4d. the pound weight, by avoirdupois commonly called silk
weight.

For gold or silver spangle lace the minimum price was set at 6s. the
pound, and for copper lace or lace mixed with copper, 4s. the pound.
The penalty 'for every ounce worked contrary to this order' was 2s.[11]
The document was signed by the Bailiffs, Wardens and fifty-nine
other members of the Company.

Some nine years later it evidently became necessary to remind
certain members of the terms of this agreement, for on the reverse of
folio 17 is a memorandum stating that 'the persons hereunder named
were summoned to the Hall the 16th of April 1621 . . . and consented
and subscribed to the orders aforewritten concerning Goldweavers';
then follow twenty-eight signatures.

As between masters and journeymen the Company seems to have
striven to be impartial, and while it would not countenance harsh or
unjust treatment of a journeyman, it would not permit a journeyman
wantonly to damage his master's interest. Two cases reported in the
Court minutes in 1654 illustrate this point. In the first case, Mr
William Cade, the Upper Bailiff (1653–4) complained that having
given out work to Anthony Dardley for himself and his father-in-
law's apprentice, Dardley had left his employ 'without giving him
lawful warning', and had taken work from another source. The Court
of Assistants ordered that Dardley must give to Mr Cade a fortnight's
warning for himself and the apprentice and 'receive his work from
Mr Cade as soon as his [other] work is out of the loom, and that he
and the said apprentice do a fortnight's work a piece for his Master
Cade'. In the second case the offending party was a Mrs Carswood
who was ordered by the Court to pay a fine of 13s. 4d. of which 2s. 6d.
was put into the poor's box and 10s. 10d. was given to John Deane,
her journeyman, 'because his mistress had turned him out of work
without warning'.[12]

The Weavers' by-laws and ordinances of 1708 provided that a
journeyman, or a master weaver employed by another master, must
give at least fourteen days' warning of his intention to leave his
employment, 'in case the Loom can be cleared within that time'; but
if this was not possible 'then the journeyman shall clear his Loom
before he departs provided the same can be done within the space of
two weeks longer, before he . . . shall be turned off by, or depart from,
his Master respectively'. It seems, therefore, that a journeyman

could, within limits, delay the date of his discharge by going slow on the piece he had in his loom. On the other hand, the by-law gave an employer some protection against being left with a partly finished piece in a loom while an irate customer clamoured for delivery.

Perhaps it is not too much to say that the most important part of a craft gild's control machinery was the search of the craft. In the London weaving trade the work-places and warehouses to be inspected were even greater in number and variety than the abuses to be detected. Small wonder that the Weavers' Officers, spurred on by the complaints and demands of the Company's rank and file, decided to create a Yeomanry to assist them. In many of the London livery companies the Yeomanry had, by the beginning of the seventeenth century, 'come to be generally identified with the main body of freemen outside the livery', or a substantial proportion thereof. Thus, the Cordwainers' Yeomanry numbered about 150, or one-third of all those who paid quarterage.[13] The London Clothworkers' Yeomanry, too, was a large body with its own wardens and assistants.[14] The Weavers' Yeomanry was quite different. It was a small body of men 'below the livery', usually between sixteen and twenty in number, created to perform a well-defined and responsible task. They were organised in five districts or 'divisions'; they had a foreman instead of wardens, and, apparently, a leader or senior man in each division. The Court minutes dated 5 April 1614 show that since May 1594[15] when the Company agreed that twenty freemen not of the Livery should have leave to assemble once a month, or oftener if necessary, in Weavers' Hall to 'enquire, examine and confer of the offences committed within the gild', as appears by the Indenture of Toleration,[16] this scheme had fallen into abeyance. A petition to the Court asked for its revival so as to create greater unity and concord within the Company, 'much Ease to the Court of Assistants and a general reformation of the abuses'. The Court acceded to this request and a yeomanry of twenty was appointed.

The Weavers' Yeomanry saw themselves, as indeed their comrades of the Commonalty saw them, as the eyes and ears, and sometimes the conscience, of the Court of Assistants. They rubbed shoulders daily with the weavers—masters, journeymen and apprentices—in the Liberties where they lived and worked; they heard the talk in the alleys and workshops; they noticed newcomers; they knew the latest tricks in the trade. They formed, as it were, a bridge between the governing body and the rank and file; between 'the Masters at the Hall' and the weavers in their looms. They were able to make the searches more widespread and thorough, while at the same time they lifted some of the ever-growing burden from the Bailiffs and Wardens. On the other hand, weavers who disliked the search became openly hostile when the searchers who arrived were young, comparatively inexperienced, and below the Livery in status. Many of the elders—some, indeed, on the Court of Assistants—looked askance at the Yeomanry's prying activities, especially if they had something to hide! The more zealously the young men stirred things up, the less popular they became with their seniors who would have preferred to let sleeping dogs lie. Here, undoubtedly, lies the clue to the constant tendency on the part of the Court of Assistants to allow the Yeomanry to fall into abeyance, and even to adopt exclusive or obstructive tactics against that body. The document entitled 'A true Relation of all the proceedings between the Bailiffs, Wardens and Assistants of the Company of Weavers of London and Sixteen men, then of the Yeomanry', which dates from 1625-6, shows clearly that these young men had become a constant thorn in the flesh of the Court of Assistants, and that the latter were resorting to delay, obstruction and petty persecution to resist reforms of the abuses revealed by the Sixteen. On one occasion the Yeomanry were 'shut out of the Parlour and could not be suffered to come and speak for themselves'; pre-arranged meetings were deliberately boycotted by the Bailiffs and Wardens; and promises to admit no more strangers to the freedom of the Company were broken by subterfuges and tricks. On one occasion the Bailiffs and Wardens came to the house of Henry Smith, one of the Sixteen, 'and made search there and demanded a Groat, there being but one penny due for the search by the Orders; and when Smith tendered the penny and would not give him a groat as they demanded, Mr. Wilson took a pewter pint pot for a Distress'. Thereupon Smith complained to the Lord Mayor and Aldermen, who summoned the parties to appear before them; but 'the Masters came not in until they had been three times warned by the Lord Mayor's Officer'. Similar 'searches' resulting in the taking of a piece of pewter by way of distress, were made at the houses of Richard Peircie and William Counley, two of the Sixteen.

As a result of this appeal to the City authorities the Yeomanry evidently retrieved their position, for at the beginning of 1627 they insisted that the Court of Assistants should take notice of various flagrant infringements of the Company's regulations. For example, masters and journeymen were using the weaving trade without having been bound as apprentices, or 'brought up to the trade' by their fathers until the age of twenty-one years; master weavers, members of the Company, were employing unadmitted persons as journeymen; boys bound as apprentices were not being taught the trade but were allowed to 'go at their own will' until the expiration of their indentures, when on the false recommendation of their 'masters' they were made free of the Company; some master weavers had more apprentices bound to them than they were entitled to keep in their households. The Yeomanry conclude by hinting broadly that many abuses which came to the notice of the Clerk and Beadle were never reported to the Court.[17]

Any reforms which may have ensued were evidently short-lived, for early in 1632 'the greatest part of the 16 young men' presented another petition to the Lord Mayor reciting the Indenture of 1594, the order of the Court of Assistants made in 1625 concerning the Yeomanry, that Court's admission that the Yeomanry had done much good by their 'diligent searchings', and its confirmation in 1627 and 1631 of the Yeomanry's full authority 'to search every ones house who used the trade of weaving'. Yet notwithstanding all this, the Bailiffs, Wardens and Assistants had 'utterly dismissed' the Sixteen without just cause, and were still permitting all the old abuses to continue unchecked. For example, they had admitted to the freedom of the Company 'divers Aliens [who] have boys of 16 and 18 years of age to serve for wages as Journeymen and Apprentices to the number of 1,500 and more as by a Catalogue of their names and families may appear'. Moreover, the Sixteen claimed that according to the original agreement with the Court of Assistants, they were entitled to retain the journeymen's quarterages (about £60 per annum) towards their expenses; but 'the Bailiffs will not suffer the Sixteen men to receive the same of the Journeymen, but do gather it themselves and allow the said Sixteen men but £7 a year or thereabouts, among them all, and to discourage them in their duty of search', for without the full proceeds of the journeymen's quarterages, they cannot afford to carry out their weekly searches; nor will it be possible to 'discern' the journeymen 'that have truly served . . . from the Intruders upon the Trade; and if it be not so gathered the greater part thereof will be lost as hitherto hath been'. At this point a group of liverymen joined hands with the Yeomanry by issuing a statement on:

> The true Causes why we of the Livery are unwilling to have any of the Assistants that formerly have been Bailiffs to be chosen Bailiffs or Wardens again:
>> Delivered by divers of the Livery at St. James tide in Anno 1633, when Francis Foster was chosen [Upper] Bailiff.

> It is not that we envy any of your persons, neither is the Cause for that you have been formerly Bailiffs, but that we find by woeful experience that you have been very negligent in punishing of offenders, either found by yourselves in your search or presented by others,[18] which hath been and yet is much prejudicial to the Company generally, and hath encouraged the said offenders to continue in their disorderly practices, and animated others on to Commit the like abuses and disorders. Yea, some of the offenders have said that they have friends in the Parlour who will speak in their behalf, and to our

Knowledge this is true, for many of us hath heard as much from their own mouths, that when the Bailiffs have been ready to give sentence against the offenders, even then one or other of the Assistants hath stept up and pleaded for them, whereby the sentence of Justice hath been stayed, and they emboldened, to continue their disorderly and unlawful Courses . . . you have neglected the punishing of offenders . . . [and] at your Feasts and other meetings have them more frequently in your company than any others of the said Company that demeaneth themselves orderly, whereof we of the Livery have been eye witnesses. . . .[19]

Again, it seems, the authority of the City was exerted on the side of the Yeomanry and the liverymen who supported them, for in 1633, the Court of Assistants, in chastened mood, made an order naming the Sixteen and authorising them to collect the journeymen's quarterages and arrears during their weekly searches or at other times 'to their own use and behoof (and without any Account thereof to be made) for and towards their pains, expenses and loss of time'. Moreover, the Court confirmed the Yeomanry's authority to meet once a month in Weavers' Hall 'in lawful and decent manner . . . to enquire, examine and confer of such disorders and offences' as shall come to their notice, and to summon before them any offenders 'to the end that they may either reform them by entreaty or present them to the Court of Bailiffs, Wardens and Assistants'. If any case had to be taken to the King's Courts the Assistants undertook to accompany and support the Yeomanry, the Company defraying the expenses.[20]

Searches were often resented and occasionally resisted, for they savoured overmuch of prying and snooping, and sometimes smelt strongly of the underhand work of an informer, who might be a rival craftsman or a personal enemy. And when, from time to time, an informer was rewarded by the Company, it must have been extremely galling for his victims. Small wonder, then, that many weavers reviled the searchers; some obstructed them more or less strenuously, while a few resorted to threats and violence. For example, John Jacques, or Davernois, a stranger, was fined £5 in 1616 for refusing to allow the Company's Officers to search his house, and another weaver who obstructed the Bailiffs and Wardens was found to have an excessive number of looms and journeymen. When Samuel Avis called the Bailiff 'a prating fellow' during a search, he was made to apologise and put a shilling in the poor's box. Worse still, a weaver named Love Bramson was ordered to pay a fine of 35s. 4d. for calling one of the Wardens a fool, 'which order he would not submit himself to'; whereupon the Court of Assistants clapped on an extra 30s. for contempt.[21]

The Company's Beadle and the Under-Beadle often stood in some peril from hostile weavers or their watch-dogs. On one occasion the Company decided to pay 20s. to Francis Saville, the Beadle, 'for his pains taken in the Company's business' and by way of compensation because he had been bitten by Mr Halleley's dog. Shortly afterwards, in July 1618, the Company gave Saville licence to 'take his remedie by law against Henry Wheeler for menacing him to take his blood'.[22] A common method of resisting the search was to bolt and bar the way into the premises and to threaten either physical violence or legal action for trespass against any who tried to force an entrance. But the Company's officers were not easily deterred. For example, in 1654 the Company ordered that a writ be taken out against John Allen, a throwster who illegally engaged in weaving, 'for his abusing and opposing the Warden and others with him' when they came to search his house, and authorised the Renter Warden to prosecute in his own name 'at the proper charge of the Company'. The throwster countered by accusing the searchers of causing a riot.[23] On various other occasions the Yeomanry were obstructed, resisted, 'misused' or assaulted.[24] Needless to say, the searchers themselves were not always blameless. When tempers became frayed, hasty and unwise actions might ensue, and the increasing impact of French and Flemish upon English temperaments must have heightened the tension at times. The following Court minute conjures up a picture of a clash between an officious, aggressive Englishman and a typical excitable Frenchman: 'Ordered that Mr. Swinborne be allowed half the charges he paid out of his pocket for the damage he did to the Frenchman in search.'[25] The Renter Bailiffs' accounts abound in entries which record the sums spent in prosecuting refractory members, 'unlawful weavers, Frenchmen, &c.' in various courts, even as far afield as 'Guildford Sizes'. Between July 1679 and August 1680, to take just one year at random, the Company spent nearly £35 upon such prosecutions.[26]

The searchers had a long-standing right to collect from those whose premises they searched a small fee at the rate of one penny per quarter. As not more than one search would normally be made in any year in the seventeenth and early eighteenth centuries, the searchers collected from each household visited a 'search groat' (4d.) as a customary contribution 'towards their travel and charges'. These 'charges' consisted chiefly of the cost of breakfast before the searchers set out and a 'search supper' at the end of the day, with a libation or two at nearby taverns as they made their more-or-less perilous progress through the district or 'division'. For example, in the spring of 1669 the Renter Bailiff 'Paid the Search Breakfast, 4s.' and for the supper, £1. 15s. 6d. This was on 12 March—an unusually early date for the start of the searches. On another occasion they 'expended in search it raining all day, £3. 6s. 6d.' (compared with £2. 13s. 9d. the previous week), which seems to suggest that little serious searching was done that day! After each search small sums ranging in total from 6s. 6d. to 9s. 6d. were paid to the Officers and Yeomanry to cover

Table 3.1 *The cost of searches in the eighteenth century*

Average cost per annum	£	s.	d.
Search expenses	40	10	0
Search groats	31	7	0
Net cost to the Company	9	3	0

personal expenses. A perusal of the accounts from 1670–1 to 1728–9 shows that the search groats collected seldom covered all the expenses of the search, so that the Company usually had to make up the difference; though it must not be forgotten that quarterages due and in arrears were also collected, if possible, by the Officers and Beadles during their searches.[27] During the last quarter of the seventeenth century the search groats collected each year amounted, on the average, to approximately £21. 10s. 0d., while the expenses averaged nearly £24. All the comparable figures for the first quarter of the eighteenth century are much higher (see Table 3.1).

Table 3.2 *Location of weavers in the London liberties and suburbs*

	%
Southwark	30
Cripplegate	20
Bishopsgate	20
Shoreditch	20
Whitechapel	10

During the Civil War and Commonwealth period the commonalties of several of the craft companies, the Pewterers, Saddlers, Clothworkers, Weavers, Founders and Clockmakers, were affected by 'the contagion of the democratic movement', a new, almost incredible phenomenon. The commonalty of the weavers were in the van, demanding a share in the governance of the Weavers' Company and arguing that the jurisdiction over them wielded by that Company must have been founded in the first place upon a 'mutual contract' between equals.[28] 'To such appeals', says Unwin, 'the Long Parliament in its most revolutionary period could not turn a deaf ear.' The Weavers' Company was obliged to arrange for the election by the commonalty of 140 'representatives', as a means of giving effect to the views and wishes of the rank and file.[29] The elections were held in five 'divisions', which reflect, approximately, the distribution of weavers in the liberties and suburbs in the middle of the seventeenth century (see Table 3.2).

Thus, under the Commonwealth, the structure of the Company became:

The Four in Place
The Assistants
The Livery
The Commonalty
  1 The Yeomanry   (16–20)
  2 The Representatives   (140)
  3 The Remainder of the Commonalty

The new machinery was soon set in motion. On 28 May 1649, the Court of Assistants 'ordered for the Dutch and French church[es] to appear at Weavers' Hall at 4 o'clock on Tuesday come sevennight, and the Representatives to appear on the following Thursday at 3 o'clock in the afternoon'.[30] For the next six years, at least, the Court of Assistants worked with the Representatives. For example, the records show that at a General Court or Common Hall of Bailiffs, Wardens and Commonalty held on 6 September 1651, 38 Representatives attended as follows: for Southwark 11, Cripplegate 8, Bishopsgate 8, Shoreditch 7, Whitechapel 4. Six months later, at an Election Day Common Hall, held on 4 March, an unusual date, there were present the Bailiffs and Wardens, eleven Assistants 'and of the Representatives of the Commons about 100'. The meeting elected Officers, eight Auditors, the Clerk (re-elected), a Beadle and a Porter. When, three weeks later, another Common Hall was held to choose a new Assistant, 39 Representatives were present: 14 from Southwark, 12 from Cripplegate, 5 from Bishopsgate, 7 from Whitechapel, but only 1 from Shoreditch.[31] At a similar meeting in 1653 there were two candidates, one nominated by the Court of Assistants and the other by the Representatives, and the Assistants' nominee was elected.[32] In the same year there was talk of proposals for measures likely to benefit both the trade and the Company, and at a Common Hall on 15 August 1653,

Upon reading certain propositions drawn up for the Trade and Company the Court of Assistants and Representatives do

49

agree and order that the Representatives in their several Divisions shall choose persons among themselves to meet with other persons chosen out of the Court and Livery to consider of those propositions and whatsoever else may be thought good and agreed by them for the well governing and benefit of the Trade and Company and to prepare them for an Act of Parliament. And likewise for settling of ordinances with a yeomanry for the finding and reforming of abuses in the Trade. And the Representatives are to give in the names of all those persons which are chosen by them, to the Court of Assistants on the 29th August next, and the persons so chosen are to meet as often as need shall require until the aforesaid business is perfected.

The upshot was that the Court of Assistants chose four of their number, the Livery eight, and the Representatives twelve, and a meeting of this body was convened for the afternoon of 8 September 1653, the Company consenting to pay all expenses and charges incurred by any of those attending the meeting. The actual attendance was eighteen (out of twenty-four). Evidently this was deemed unsatisfactory and the meeting was adjourned for a week, during which the Court let it be known that 'whosoever fails in his appearance (on 15 September) shall forfeit one shilling . . . unless some extraordinary business happen to any of the said persons so failing to appear, which shall be signified by them to Henry Houldrup, Clerk.' Despite this warning only one Assistant, three Liverymen, and five Representatives turned up at the adjourned meeting, and no important business was transacted.[33] Working weavers disliked adjourned meetings for they could ill afford the consequent loss of earnings. But on election days between forty and a hundred representatives would converge on Weavers' Hall, and on at least one occasion, when their nominee had been elected Upper Bailiff, 'they made him a promise that they would stand by and assist him in any business that should be drawn up by him . . . for the good of the trade and Company'.[34]

After the Restoration the election of representatives was quietly dropped. The democratic movement within the craft companies waned, having achieved very little, and the old oligarchic forces 'resumed complete possession of the disputed ground'.[35]

As to the Yeomanry, it is a fairly safe assumption that during the Civil War their functions greatly declined, for many young craftsmen enlisted or were 'pressed', and the 1640s was a decade of general decline in normal activities. A typical case came before the Weavers' Court in October 1648 when Peter Turdevan confessed that he had practised weaving in London and its liberties for over nine years and had been a member of the French Church for ten years (as the minister and elders testified), yet he had never been asked or urged to seek admission to the Company.[36] Evidently the search in that decade was far from thorough. Early in the next decade, however, a marked revival took place. A new Yeomanry was elected and a vigorous search of the craft began to produce results, as the Court records of the investigation and punishment of various offences clearly show.[37] Many weavers, non-members of the Company, had persistently ignored its summonses; lads and maids were being put to work without having been apprenticed; admitted members who were taking too many apprentices and employing 'unlawful workmen' and women were forced into the open. Edmond Gosford, for example, who had three journeymen not free, was ordered 'to bring them to take their freedom betwixt this (March 1655) and Easter'. John Dowse produced to the Court of Assistants a certificate purporting to prove seven years' service in Canterbury, 'but was put by for a report'; and when Henry Degardine 'appeared and produced a certificate of his service beyond sea' the Court was suspicious and 'ordered him to stay at home until he is sent for'. In June 1654, Richard Bowman 'was complained against for keeping one John Pockock who pretended he served at Reading, and the Court ordered him to produce a certificate this day fortnight and the said Bowman to pay the fine of 2s. 2d.'[38] Several immigrants from Canterbury, some of French and some of English descent, were required to produce certificates of service from either the Corporation of Canterbury or the Master and Wardens of the Company of Weavers of that city.[39] Other 'foreigners' were admitted upon the strength of certificates from textile centres such as Norwich and Manchester. David Mitchell, probably an Englishman born, produced an acceptable certificate of his service in Antwerp, and Samuel le Beane produced a deliciously ambiguous affidavit (sworn by a Citizen and Weaver of London) as proof of seven years' apprenticeship under indenture, 'part of which time he served James Bowland of Grub street and part with Sam. Clerke of Norton Folgate, weavers, and the residue thereof he served with Thomas Ewes, which Ewes married the widow of Sam. Clerke without taking any manner of wages upon which certificate the said Sam. le Beane was admitted a foreign brother'.[40]

Whether the high pressure was maintained in the later 1650s is doubtful, but after 1660 the Restoration seems to have revived flagging spirits, at least for a time, and the Weavers shared in the general upsurge of optimism. They even paid their quarterages more willingly. The quarterages collected by the Weavers' Company fell from £136 in 1655–6 to barely £73 in 1659–60; whereas the total for 1660–1 exceeded £221, and for the next three years the annual average was nearly £142.

In 1662 the Company named a Yeomanry of sixteen members

and gave formal authority, in writing, to any two or more of them:

1 to search weekly in any place or places within the Company's jurisdiction all weavers' houses or other places where they 'shall be certified or informed that any weaving is used or to be found';
2 to call upon other persons to assist them, and
3 to examine all such persons 'as they shall suspect not to have served the term of seven years to the trade', and to require the production of relevant certificates of freedom;
4 to report all offenders to the weekly Courts of the Company at the Weavers' Hall;
5 to meet at the Hall as often as need be and to summon before them such persons as are accused or suspected of having 'violated or contemned' the Company's orders and ordinances;
6 to prosecute intruders and offenders at law, provided that the grounds of the proposed action are first approved and allowed by the Bailiffs, Wardens and Assistants; who will then
7 meet the charges from the Company's funds and hold the members of the Yeomanry harmless and indemnified against possible legal consequences of such prosecutions;
8 to receive all journeymen's quarterages and to give an account to the Renter Warden.[41]

A supplementary order issued by the Court of Assistants in August 1662 authorises the Yeomanry to proceed 'by the best and securest way they can find according to Law' against 'all fugitive persons both Aliens and Native that remove from place to place having no certain dwelling and cannot be summoned before the Company'. The Yeomanry were required to give an account of their proceedings to the next Court, and all expenses incurred by them, if approved by the Court, were refunded through their foreman.[42] Occasionally, in the 1660s, three or four of the Yeomanry were allowed to sit with half a dozen of the Officers and Assistants to constitute a 'Bye Court' to deal with matters of which the Yeomanry had special knowledge. It is clear, however, that the Officers and Court of Assistants regarded this special privilege or concession rather jealously and had not the slightest intention of allowing it to go too far. Indeed in 1672, in connection with the handing over of quarterages collected by the Yeomanry the Court stated categorically that 'it is not permitted that ye Yeomanry shall sit in ye Court'.[43]

Armed and encouraged by the Company's confirmation of their status and functions, the Yeomanry went to work with a will, summoning before themselves or 'presenting' to the Court of Assistants a steady stream of offenders or suspects on charges of employing unadmitted journeymen, 'binding apprentices at the Scriveners contrary to the Ordinance', illegally setting up as a master weaver within the Company's jurisdiction, paying wages to an apprentice, producing false and fraudulent work, and so forth. Occasionally, when the young men went too far, the Court had to temper justice with mercy, especially when the accused person was sick or 'very poor and aged'.[44] But the Yeomanry, in no way discouraged, continued to ferret out abuses, issuing 'writs against such persons as have not appeared and are great offenders'. They also helped to collect quarterages.[45] As a mark of the Company's appreciation the Yeomanry were invited to dinner in October 1668;[46] a goodwill gesture which doubtless made for harmonious working in the future. The Court minutes for 2 May 1670 record that 'This day the Bailiffs, Wardens, and some Assistants attended his Majestie & Council about ye French and Dutch Congregations and an order was then made in what manner [their members] should be admitted into this Company', and in the following month the Yeomanry 'are desired to be very active and diligent in discovering' aliens and strangers who work or employ workmen 'contrary to the Rules & Orders agreed and published'.[47] Thus exhorted, they continued the good work with undiminished vigour. Not only the Court minutes but the Renter Bailiff's books and the annual accounts in the 1670s carry entries such as:

'For prosecuting offenders for maken fraudulent Lace' and other 'faulls worke', £5 to three of the Yeomanry, and £4 to John Langley.

Paid Mr. Ranson and other Yeomanry which they expended this year prosecuting Salt and Black, £5. 15s. 0d.

'Paid the Yeomanry their Charge prosecuting refractory persons in Southwark, £32. 5s. 2d.

And again, they paid Lawrence Ranson and Mr Ratcliff for expenses incurred 'in prosecuting refractory Members at Surry Sizes', £8. 14s. 0d.[48]

During the first third of the eighteenth century the Company continued doggedly to search the craft, albeit against ever-increasing opposition from members and non-members alike. Quite early in the century we have the new charter granted by Queen Anne and the accompanying By-laws and Ordinances of 1708[49] which contained the following section:

For deputing a Yeomanry. Item to the end all persons intruding into the said Trade of Weaving may the better be detected and discovered it is ordained that the Court of Assistants . . . shall yearly and every year depute and authorise under the Common Seal . . . twelve or more persons using the said Trade . . . to enter in the daytime into any house, shop, cellar or warehouse where weaving is or shall be used, there to examine whether the Master or Journeymen have duly served the term of seven years to the said Trade . . . or whether he or they be a Member or Members of the said Guild or Company and if upon search made as well by the Bailiffs, Wardens, Assistants and Livery as by the [Yeomanry] so to be deputed any Journeyman shall absent himself from his Loom or work and thereby prevent . . . his examination . . . the Master for whom he works . . . shall tell the name of such person and cause such person to appear at the next Court . . . or otherwise discharge him from his work upon pain of forfeit . . . the sum of ten shillings.

Pressing hard against this attempt to preserve the *status quo* was the growing complexity of the industrial structure and the emergence of increasing numbers of capitalist entrepreneurs, small and large. The Weavers' records throw occasional beams of light upon this process of economic evolution. In 1703, for example, one Burton, a wire-drawer, was accused of

exercising the Weaving Trade not having served any time thereto . . . but it appearing that he did not exercise the Trade with his own hands, and only employed a Free Weaver who employed journeymen and apprentices under him to work upon the materials of the said Burton at a certain rate by the piece, and that the Looms and tackle belonged not to Burton but to the weaver.

The Court decided to seek Counsel's opinion before taking legal action against Burton.[50]

So the struggle continued, many writs being issued and many arrests made. In May 1716 a Full Court of Assistants made a general order 'that the Bailiffs and Wardens have liberty to arrest such persons as . . . break the Charter and Ordinances of this Company', and action was taken in a number of cases.[51] Three years later, in the early stages of the searches for the year 1719, so many persons were refusing to attend the Court when summoned that the Clerk was instructed to enter all such cases in a special book, stating the cause of each summons, and to produce the book at every Court meeting.[52] Meantime, the yearly series of searches continued. In the spring and summer of every year between 1701 and 1725 some twelve searches were made and search groats and quarterages were collected. In April 1726 the Court ordered that 'a Yeomanry be deputed' and that 'the Gentlemen of this Court with such as they think proper go in Search as usual';[53] and this was done, twelve searches being made that year, the search groats amounting to £23. 17s. 0d. But against this the searchers' outlay at the Black Boy in Nicholas Street and the Bull, Cow and Weavers Arms, plus the Search Dinner on 11 August 1726 (an 'Entertainment' which alone cost nearly £26) totalled £44. 15s. 4d., so that the net cost to the Company was about £20—much the same as in the previous year. After the year 1727, in which thirteen searches were made, there appears to have been a gradual decline in this function, probably due to a reluctant recognition of the fact that 'the old order changeth giving place to new' and the game was scarcely worth the candle. Only five searches were made in 1728, none at all in 1729 and only six in 1730. There was a slight increase to eight in 1731, but thereafter the number fell away to four in 1736, the last of the regular periodical searches the Company ever made.[54]

Thereafter only occasional searches were made with special or limited objects. Thus, in June 1740 the journeymen weavers petitioned the Court 'complaining of a great number of persons Exercising the Trade of Weaving without having any Right thereto, to the Ruin and Impoverishment of the Petitioners and their Families', and asking for help 'to prevent the same for the future'. The Court appointed all its members to act as an investigating committee, and the Beadles were instructed to 'make a general search thro' the Streets of Spitalfields and the Places adjacent' and to compile a list of all master weavers there resident. And again, in 1744, the Court of Assistants ordered the Beadles to make a thorough search throughout the whole trade in order to compile a list of apprentices who had not been bound at Weavers' Hall, noting at the same time whether their masters were members of the Company.[55]

Although the weaving of velvet and high-quality figured fabrics, such as silk brocades, demanded many years of training and experience, the weaving of plain materials was much more easily learnt; a fact which attracted all sorts and conditions of men to the weaving trade in and around London. Hence the Company's rules against illegal teaching and the employment of unadmitted journeymen, for such abuses led directly to false and faulty work. Therefore the Company had not only to enforce its regulations limiting the number of apprentices and journeymen a master might properly employ, but it had incessantly to chase a variety of unqualified interlopers—denizens, foreigners and strangers. The cut and thrust of such struggles arising from the Company's exercise of its powers to exclude, compel and punish, inevitably gave rise to personal animosities, rash and offensive remarks, 'evil and reproachful words', and slanderous tales which lost nothing in the retelling.[56] The Weavers' minute books record brief details of a thousand such discordant conflicts—some quickly composed, others bitterly contested—of which only a relatively few examples can be cited here.

There is no evidence that the Company was unreasonably exclusive in its attitude to immigrants to London, whatever may have been the reactions of individuals among the small masters and journeymen. Weavers from established centres of textile manufacture, such as Norwich, Canterbury or the West of England, were admitted without demur if they had proper certificates of service. So were immigrant weavers from the Continent if they could show good credentials as to qualifications and respectability. During the second decade of the seventeenth century the Company made a special effort to bring into membership a number of practising weavers who still remained unadmitted. For example, on 23 February 1613 six such cases were before the Court of Assistants, including that of William Beerstowe who was threatened with arrest at the suit of the Company unless he applied for admission on the next Court day.[57] Three weeks earlier John de Maire[58] had been brought to Weavers' Hall and fined 10*s.* for ignoring no fewer than seven summonses, and 20*s.* more for employing as journeymen three unadmitted strangers. He was ordered to bring to the next Court 'all the indentures of his apprentices and journeymen to be admitted'.[59] A journeyman who came from Barlby in Yorkshire was required to produce a certificate of his apprenticeship to a linen weaver of that town; and a young weaver from Canterbury had to prove not only his formal apprenticeship but 'his honest departure from his former master'. In 1618, Robert Jackson, Citizen and Haberdasher of London, and Robert Clay of York, Saddler, reported to the Weavers' Company that 'William Clay, late apprentice to Symon Pockley of York, Silk Weaver, for eight years from Michaelmas in the fourth year of King James', having duly served his term had 'honestly departed from his country' and was 'of good name and fame and a sufficient workman'. He was admitted and sworn a foreign brother, paying a fee of £3. Another applicant from the provinces, evidently determined to leave nothing to chance, brought with him a certificate 'under the hands of his Master and 3 Justices of the Peace', and on his admission as a foreign brother, 'gave a spoon'.[60]

Strangers (aliens), too, had to show evidence as to character, 'honest departure' from their countries, and sufficient skill as weavers. In such cases the Company welcomed the helpful co-operation of the ministers and elders of the Dutch and French Churches in London, who were usually in a position to say whether an immigrant was sober, honest and a genuine Protestant refugee. Thus Hubert Deleware, a member of the French Church, who declared that he 'was sent hither by his Uncle in anger for yt he would not be a Papist', was required to bring a certificate 'for his good demeanour' from that church within fourteen days.[61] Immigrant weavers who 'intermeddled in the trade' but refused or neglected to seek admission were brought to book by the Company whenever possible, as was Arnold le Mere, stranger, silk box-lace weaver who had been working in Southwark without seeking admission to the Company was ordered to desist or be arrested. 'Maximilian Lombard, stranger, tuftaffatie weaver in Mr. Dunes Alley extra Bishopsgate' was similarly threatened if he failed to apply for admission. Sometimes natives and aliens conspired to evade the by-laws, as when William Walker, a master draper, was found to have four box-lace looms and a stranger journeyman working with him, neither Walker nor the stranger having been apprenticed to weaving or admitted to the Weavers' Company.[62]

The Company's officers had always to be on their guard against deliberate trickery as well as genuine muddles arising, chiefly, from changes or modifications of foreign surnames. For example, Jean de Bois after an interval became 'Boyce' and, later still, 'Wood'; while Jean de Sade became *anglice* as John Sadd. John Marshall claimed that he had been admitted 'by ye name of John Prevoe'; but as this entry could not be traced it was 'ordered that he make it appear better'.[63] The Court became very angry with Thomas Jones, a native of Radnorshire, who said that he had been apprenticed to a London weaver in 1655, and in due course was made free 'upon report of Robert Owen, free of joiners, and John Smith, free Weaver in St. George's parish, Southwark'; but when it was discovered that, in fact, he had never served an apprenticeship, the Yeomanry were authorised 'to sue a disfranchisement against Thomas Jones' and to sue Owen and Smith for giving a false report.[64] Philip Swettman, son of a Dorset husbandman, produced a foreign indenture and nearly secured admission, but the trick was detected in the nick of time and the record expunged.[65] Richard Upchinore gave 8s. in lieu of a spoon at his admission, but was 'afterwards proved a cheat & was not therefore made free'. Two strangers—Isaac Rigoulett and Peter Ruault—produced certificates which were suspect; but fortunately 'better proof' was forthcoming shortly after, and both were admitted as foreign journeymen.[66]

Any master who kept 'servants' and looms in excess of the numbers permitted by the Company's ordinances was liable to heavy penalties. In 1612 the Court of Assistants passed a special resolution that the Ordinances of 1596 concerning the keeping of servants and looms and 'setting up the art of weaving shall forthwith be put in execution' more diligently. During the summer and autumn of that year a number of weavers, including Widow Browne, were ordered to 'reform the number of looms' in their houses. James Cambon was fined 40s. for keeping six looms, and when he refused to 'reform his offence' within fourteen days he was 'comitted to the Compter in Wood street'. Young Edward Daynty, an apprentice in a hurry, had to face the serious charge that he not only 'useth the art of weaving, not yet being admitted', but 'keepeth 3 or 4 looms'. John de Maire, always in rebellion against authority, was fined £5 for keeping no fewer than seven looms in excess of the permitted number and refusing to allow the Bailiffs and Wardens to search his house.[67]

According to Unwin, the searches for false and faulty work brought 'the collective technical conscience of the gild' and the judgment of 'juries of experts' to bear on the methods and products of individual craftsmen.[68] Not only were buyers thereby safeguarded, but honest craftsmen gained some measure of protection against the unfair competition of less scrupulous men. The desperate struggle to secure good standards of craftsmanship and materials of genuine quality was unending; as soon as one piece of dishonesty was scotched another made its furtive appearance.[69] The mixing of good with inferior yarn in the same fabric was an all too common practice, which must have been familiar to Shakespeare who wrote in *All's Well that Ends Well*:

> . . . the web of our life is of a mingled yarn,
> Good and ill together.

John Birckett, a lace-weaver, was caught doing just that in 1617, and was fined 16s. for mixing thread with silk, 'viz., 6s. for his false work and 10s. for abusing the Bailiffs and Wardens in doeing their offices . . . and he is ordered to reform his false work and is sorry for his hasty speeches'. False work was sometimes confiscated, at least for the time being, by the searchers, and some of it was destroyed (though the strict legality of such extreme action is, in some cases, doubtful).[70] Shortly afterwards two weavers who had previously been fined for false work, were each bound by £100 bonds to work honestly in future.[71] The case of Giles Agasse and François Lamblois, two French immigrant weavers, deserves to be noticed. In November 1671 they had attracted attention to themselves by illegally employing one Paulett de Sordez, a Papist, who had neglected to take the oaths of Allegiance and Supremacy.[72] On 22 November 1671 the Renter Bailiff's account records, somewhat ominously, that 3s. 6d. was 'spent with the Informer agst. Agasse, &c.', and five days later—'spent at ye Wt. Hart with several about Agasse's business, 13s. 9d.' Further investigations revealed that the two Frenchmen were 'making false and deceitful wares', and both were heavily fined by the Company, but refused to submit; 'whereupon it is ordered that Mr. Hosea do discourse . . . a Solicitor about ye indicting them for ye fines'. When, in due course, Agasse and Lamblois found themselves before a Justice of the Peace at the Middlesex Sessions they became more submissive, pleading that they 'did not know by putting thread or tape into lace and by covering it over with gold or silver was any fraud . . . but since understanding the Buyer of it from the shop-keeper might be defrauded, and also a damage to those workmen that could not sell the same [genuine] pattern at so cheap a rate', they were resolved never to repeat the offence. By way of deterrent for the future the magistrate imposed upon each defendant a heavy fine of £25 to be paid to the Company, and the money was duly received by the Renter Bailiff in March and May 1672.[73]

Members of the Commonalty who felt incensed by the competition of unadmitted 'intermeddlers' in their craft were the most effective informers. For example, records for 1673 tell us that 'James Smith dwelling in ye Close in Southwark exercises ye trade of weaving of hair plushes, not being bred to ye Trade, but was a Draper at Reading. He was seen working in ye loom by Nich. Gallopine, foreign weaver, who now complains of him and will be ready to attest it.' There is, also, a formal information in writing which runs:

> I, Felix Lee, do declare that John Diamond works with one Denby, a weaver in Thrale Street, and I do conceive he is not capable of using ye Trade; also that John Grant in ye Swan Alley, Minories, keeps 4 apprentices being no Livery man, and also keeps other unlawful workmen.
> This 27 November 1671.
> Ye mark of Felix Lee, George St.
> Witness: J. Cole (Clerk).

Another information is in the form of a memorandum:

> Near Punchinello. Rich. Tucker, waterman at Lambeth Marsh, keeps 5 looms, his wife works, and employs journeymen.
> Will. Matthews ⎱ Weavers, ⎱ Attest.
> Peter Collins ⎰ Lambeth ⎰ this.[74]

Recalcitrant weavers, whether admitted or not, who defied the Company could be sued in the Court of Exchequer. Usually the threat of such proceedings and the imminent risk of arrest and incarceration in one of the Compters was enough to induce a more submissive, less abusive attitude.[75] When Richard Fryer, Weaver, was reported by a married woman to have said 'that he cared not for the Masters of the Company and let them kiss his a . . e' and 'these words he gave in the hearing of Suzan Blackstone in the Blackfriars', the Court of Assistants ordered that 'Fryer shall be committed to the Compter forthwith'.[76] At about the same time (1617–19) several weavers appear to have made a concerted attack upon the good name of Mr Bailiff Rainshall, one putting it about that the Bailiff kept ten looms; another that he had 'three score apprentices'; and yet another, Thomas Browne, said that Mr Rainshall's apprentice, Anthony Wright, 'was unlawfully made free, and that there was a pie or pasty given unto the Master Bailiff which was eaten in Southwark for the making free of his said servant'. The Court fined Browne 33s. 4d., which he at first refused to pay; but one night's sojourn in the Wood Street Compter was more than enough. Next day he paid his fine.[77]

The possibility that such powers were occasionally exercised hastily or unjustly is suggested by the petition of Jo. Wood and Jo. Chambers, Weavers and freemen of London, 'now (October 1645) prisoners in Newgate', to the Lord Mayor, complaining that the 'Masters of the Weavers' Company' had caused them to be committed to prison 'verbally, without any cause declared, where they have lyen prisoners . . . to their extraordinary loss and damage and have not hitherto been so much as called out to any legal trial'. As 'freemen of England' they, quite rightly, demanded speedy release.[78] Usually the Company gave a warning before taking drastic action, as when the Renter Bailiff 'paid & spent' five shillings 'warning 2 refractory Members before the Ld. Mayor';[79] or when three unadmitted weavers, having been summoned, 'carried themselves very stubborn' before the Court of Assistants and were told that if they did not comply with the Company's by-laws and ordinances, there were ways and means 'of enforcing them thereto'.[80]

The sixth item of the Ordinances of 1596 says that 'No person shall teach or instruct in the Arts of weavynge any other person or persons whatsoever not being presented nor admitted into the Guilde', on pain of a penalty of £5. This regulation was, of course, part of the Company's machinery for the control of numbers in the craft, but the fines actually inflicted for this particular offence are relatively few, except in the early decades of the seventeenth century when several cases of illegal instruction are recorded. Between June 1611 and December 1616, John Tice, a weaver, was fined 40s. 'for teaching . . . a Carman the art of weaving, contrary to the laws of the Realm and the orders of this Gilde'; William Seager was summoned and accused of teaching weaving to a chandler and his servant; and Oliver Dunning was in trouble for having taught ribbon weaving to two men— one a victualler who kept the Three Tuns in Bermondsey Street and may have bribed Dunning with beer. Early in 1617, Edward Slipper. an unadmitted 'foreign weaver', was fined the maximum penalty of £5 for daring to teach Richard Evans the art of silk weaving, 'and upon his submission the same fine was remitted to 40s., which he refused to pay and thereupon he was committed to the Compter'. A week later a repentant Slipper was admitted into membership as a foreign brother of the Company; but Evans was ordered to 'leave the art of weaving within one month or else be put in suit'.[81] In 1654 another Evans (Thomas not Richard) when brought before the Court of Assistants said that Nicholas Baker taught him weaving for the sum of 50s., and when Baker was confronted he confessed. Thereupon the Court imposed a fine of 6s. 8d. and ordered him to refund 30s. to Evans, who had to hand over 10s. to the Company and promise 'not to follow the trade of weaving any more'. Another infiltrator, similarly cornered, stated that a stranger named James Provoux had taught him for £3. He was required to relinquish the trade immediately, but whether Provoux was punished does not appear. Thomas Ravenill, however, had to pay a penalty of £5 for illegally teaching two pupils, and when he failed to pay, the Company brought an action for debt against him.[82] It seems, however, that illegal teaching was not stamped out during the seventeenth century for early in the eighteenth century the Livery, in their 'Abstract of the Draught' of a proposed new charter, refer to 'the great Abuses daily practised, in setting to work Boys and Girls and others who serve a year or two, or give 30 or 40 shillings to be taught, and thereby serve no time at all'.

The Company's traditional attitude to the membership and employment of women as weavers is naturally linked with its restrictive regulations on the teaching of the craft, for in the absence of strict control of the latter, women and maids could have been taught, with little difficulty, all but the most skilled branches of weaving. But the male weavers well knew that this would have had the effect of depressing the prices and wages paid for their work; hence the long-standing policy of keeping women and girls out of the looms.[83] For example, in 1649 Richard Simpson was fined 20s. for having six looms 'and two maidens at work in two of the looms'; he was ordered to pull down the looms and not to set any more maidens at work on weaving. Four years later, John Hogg was in trouble for keeping a wench at work for a whole year contrary to the Ordinances, 'for which the Company ordered him to discharge the wench forthwith, and if after she be got work by his means *upon any woven work* then he to pay £5 to the Company'. In 1664 a weaver was fined twenty nobles and ordered to discharge forthwith four wenches who were working in his looms. Attempts were sometimes made to pass off a wench as the master weaver's own daughter, but if the deception was discovered the Company would order 'that the maid be put away'. Even daughters-in-law were not allowed to weave. The Court minutes for May 1667 record that 'Ann White who uses ye trade now appeared, saith her father was a weaver at Manchester & she served him as an apprentice & this attested by John Leach, weaver of London; ordered she procure Certificate thereof out of ye Country within a month'. In the same year a weaver summoned for employing a girl replied that 'she work not in ye loom but was bound to wind silk and [do] other house business'; and another accused of a similar offence pleaded that he had employed her 'out of Charity her husband having beaten her, but she is now returned [to him] who is a freeman; ye Court satisfied'. But the Court was not satisfied with Richard Ainton who, when told to dismiss a woman employee, called them 'a Company of fools'. And even worse was George Chiefe who, having been accused of employing two girls, became 'very refractory and quarrel-some' in the Court Room, and 'being ordered to withdraw he went away and damn'd the Court, and John Chapman and John Daniel heard him'.[84]

Weavers summoned by the Court and sensing trouble ahead, some-times pleaded sickness and sent their wives to face the music or to plead their case, as did a certain Valentine who, having been fined £5 for 'setting up 6 looms contrary to a late order', sent his wife to the Hall with the money. What she said to the Court we shall never know, but the outcome after further questioning was a verdict of 'not proven' provided that Mrs Valentine would agree to put 10s. into the poor's box. Her triumphant return to her husband with £4. 10s. in hand is not difficult to imagine.[85]

So long as they did not invade the looms, women and children were readily accepted as ancillary workers on warping and quilling for the weavers, or by the throwsters on the spinning processes; all at rates of pay far below those of the weavers. This state of things seems to have been quite usual throughout the textile industries of England. The verse describing John Winchcombe's famous early factory refers to,

> . . . one room being large and long
> [where] stood two hundred Looms full strong,
> Two hundred men the truth is so
> Wrought in these looms all in a row.

'Pretty boys' did the quilling, while carding, spinning and such-like tasks were done by

> an hundred women merrily . . .
> And in a chamber close beside,
> Two hundred maidens did abide. . . .

The narrowly restrictive ninth item of the London Weavers' Ordin-ances of 1596 states tersely that 'no woman or mayd shall use or exercise the Arts of weaving . . . except she be the widow of one of the same Guilde'. During the ensuing century, however, some minor modifications were made in practice, if not in strict theory.[86] Girls could be formally apprenticed to weaving and the Company would enrol them and in due course admit them to the freedom as they did Anne Archer, who was apprenticed to Edward Tiplady, Citizen and Weaver, in 1695, and made free of the Company 'upon the report of her Mistress and Edward Barns, Laceman', in 1703; but actual examples are few—probably not much more than 1 per cent of all apprentices bound at the Hall. An even smaller number of daughters of free weavers were admitted by patrimony,[87] like Martha Marriott, daughter of Thomas Marriott, Citizen and Weaver, who was made free of the Weavers' Company in 1712 'upon the report of Samuel Erle, Clothworker' and three other citizens.[88]

Alexander Hosea's legacies account (1686–1766) shows that he employed a number of female lace-makers,[89] and in the eighteenth century there are several records of girls serving their apprenticeships with freewomen of the Weavers' Company who were in business not as weavers but as milliners.[90]

The position early in the eighteenth century is defined in the Weavers' new By-laws and Ordinances of 1708: no weaver 'shall keep, instruct, set to work or bring up in the use, exercise or knowledge of . . . weaving (except to warping) any damsel or woman whatsoever (except the wife, widow or unmarried daughter of a Weaver who shall work for the maintenance of her father or mother)', upon pain of a penalty of £1 a month.

The Weavers, like other craft gilds, regarded a wife as a trade partner having the right to succeed to and carry on the business after her husband's death. Widows, in fact, took over all the rights, privileges and liabilities of their deceased husbands, for example as to the proper number of looms, journeymen and apprentices.[91] Alternatively, a weaver's widow having turned over her apprentices, if any, could go to work for another weaver.[92] If a weaver's widow remarried, unlike a stationer's widow, she could neither retain her rights nor transfer them to her new husband; which meant that if she married another weaver, her rights (looms, journeymen, apprentices, etc.) could not be added to those of her husband. Many such cases appear in the Company's records. For example in 1683 Mrs Fall, a weaver's widow, 'being charged with marrying a cabinet maker, and yet keeping the weaving trade she confessed the same and this Court ordered her to clear her looms and discharge her Apprentices in a fortnight, the which she promised to do'.[93] In 1666 and 1667 two weavers' widows who married seamen were 'ordered to desist' and to leave the trade; and an information was laid against Widow Abel in Coles Alley in Shoreditch 'who had married a Smith [but still] works at ye trade of weaving and employs another woman'.[94] Widow Gosford, having married a dyer, lost her right to keep her apprentices at work in her looms and had to undertake to 'assign them over within a week'.[95] Non-members of the Company who married weavers' widows and then attempted to 'use the trade of weaving' were told 'to desist or be prosecuted'. When Widow Goodale was challenged, in 1667, as to her right to exercise the trade, she declared that her late husband had a good right to his trade, and it was 'ordered she make it appear next Court'. Instead of doing so, however, she 'gave bad words' saying, with more spirit than tact, that 'she will use the trade in spite of ye Company'. The Court promptly reacted by ordering her 'to put away her maid and sister out of ye loom' and to come with her journeymen to the next Court 'to show their right' to use the trade.[96] Mary Cowardine's use of the weaving trade was questioned because, although she was a weaver's daughter, her parents were dead and she was married to a tinman. Her rejoinder was that her husband 'had withdrawn himself and was married to another woman . . . and had not lived with her (Mary) but 10 days in 10 years'. The Court of Assistants insisted that she give up weaving, but allowed her three months' grace. It is a little surprising that in this case the Court did not grant its 'special favour', as it did when Mary Burdge of Petticoat Lane, a glover's widow, was found to be weaving for her father, and on another occasion when a 'foreign journeyman' having married the daughter of Mr Elmer, 'late of the Livery', was admitted a foreign master at the 'earnest suit' of the bride's mother.[97]

The rank and file of the male weavers looked with considerable suspicion and hostility upon any tendency on the part of the Assistants to admit women more willingly than in the past. Their views were expressed in some doggerel verses printed in 1727–8 under the title 'The Weavers' Complaint against the Masters of the Hall':

> . . . now we find the Masters another way has ta'en,
> For to admit the Women to increase their gain,
> For since they hear from Home so many men are gone,
> They think it fit for to admit the Women in their room. . . .
>
> You Widows, Wives and Maidens that hath a mind to be
> Admitted as free Weavers into our Company,
> Three pounds it is the Price, then take my kind advice,
> Your Money tender, they'll a Member make you in a trice.

The Company's quarterage books from 1681 onwards contain nominal rolls of the Officers, Livery and Commonalty, which include the widows remaining in membership and therefore probably still working in the weaving trade. Their numbers rose remarkably in the half-century 1681–1730, from 103 to 217, but decreased sharply during the decade 1731–40 to 123 and continued to fall steadily until, in 1790, only two widows' names appear in the book. Even at their most numerous the widows were never more than a tiny part of the whole membership: slightly less than 2 per cent in 1681 and no more than 3·5 per cent at the peak in 1730.

Another factor, essential to the preservation and progress of any craft, remains to be studied: the recruitment, training and welfare of apprentices. To this we now turn.

NOTES

1 In 1619 a freeman who, without licence of the Court of Assistants, had caused another freeman of the Weavers' Company to be arrested was fined 6*s*. 8*d*., and it was peremptorily ordered that 'the suit between them shall utterly cease' (MS. 4655/1, f.94. See also ff.46 and 101 for similar cases).

2 MS. 4655A/3, *passim*. From various entries it is clear that some journeymen did not work on their master's premises but took materials and wove them in their own home-workshops. The looms they used, however, may well have been the property of the master weaver. Certainly the terms of settlement of another dispute in 1671 includes the phrase 'and the Workman to deliver to his Master his Loom and other things belonging to him'.

3 Bland, Brown, and Tawney, *English Economic History: Select Documents* (1921), pp. 313–16, 325–33.

4 W. S. Holdsworth, *A History of English Law* (1924), IV, pp. 347–8, 382n., 381–2.

5 George, *London*, p. 163; E. W. Gilboy, *Wages in 18th-Century England* (1934), Chap. I.

6 MS. 4655/1, f.12; a similar case is recorded on f.13.

7 MS. 4655/1, ff.25, 44, 49, 51, 58, 67, 91. It seems that long-term hirings were, on the whole, advantageous to the journeymen weavers, for fashions often changed quickly causing fluctuations in demand. Long periods of court mourning caused severe depressions in many sections of the trade, and the weavers often petitioned the King; but not until 1767 did the King (George III) decree shorter periods of court mourning for the future. This evoked a loyal and grateful Address to H.M. from the Weavers' Company (MS. 4655/17, f.71b).

8 MS. 4655/1, f.82.

9 MS. 4655/1, f.73.

10 MS. 4655/1, ff.93, 101.

11 MS. 4655/1, ff.16–17.

12 MS. 4655/2, ff.107–8, 115.

13 Unwin, *Gilds*, pp. 227–8, 250; and see p. 343 on the general position at the end of the seventeenth century.

14 Unwin, *Ind. Org.*, pp. 229–34.

15 MS. 4647, f.215; MS. 4655/1, ff.23, 25, 28; see also W. H. Overall, *Analytical Index of the Remembrancia of the City of London* (1878), pp. 94–5.

16 The Indenture of Toleration, 1594, was made between four of the Assistants and four of the young freemen on behalf of themselves and sundry other young men 'below the Livery'. It is so called because it states that the Assistants 'on behalf of the rest of the Livery . . . thought fit to tolerate the same young men . . . to put in practice their said request and desires', viz. to speed up the discovery and reform of abuses.

17 MS. 4647, ff.179–81, 188–92.

18 Chiefly the Yeomanry.

19 MS. 4647, ff.253–6.

20 MS. 4647, ff.244, 259–63.

21 MS. 4648/1, *passim*; MS. 4655/1, ff.43, 87; MS. 4655/2, f.11; MS.

4655/3, f.145b; MS. 4655/4, ff.84b, 88; MS. 4655/5, f.58. In 1617 the Privy Council and the City Corporation were much concerned about the 'multitude' of 'divers strangers come lately to London with bag and baggage'. The Company made a list 'out of the last search book [now lost] of all such strangers as shall have been found thereby' and sent it to the Lord Mayor (MS. 4655/1, f.52).

22　MS. 4655/1, ff.48, 75.

23　MS. 4655/2, ff.150, 173.

24　MS. 4655/4, f.103b; MS. 4655/6, ff.10–11; MS. 4648/1, 14 August 1675. Many other craft gilds, of course, experienced resistance to their searches; see, e.g., H. Steward, *History of the Company of Gold and Silver Wire-Drawers* (1891), p. 87.

25　MS. 4655/11, f.261. Another intriguing entry reads, 'Allowed Mr. Warden Gwilt for Mistakes on the Search 7*s.* 9*d.*'

26　MS. 4648/1, 1679–80; MS. 4655/12, f.76.

27　MS. 4648/1–3, *passim*; MS. 4646 (Old Ledger Book), *passim*.

28　*The Case of the Commonalty of the Corporation of Weavers of London truly stated* (c. 1649). See also Chap. 9 below.

29　Unwin, *Ind. Org.*, pp. 207–8.

30　MS. 4655A, 28 May 1649.

31　MS. 4655A/2, ff.39, 43b.

32　MS. 4655/2, f.39.

33　MS. 4655/2, ff.43, 46–8.

34　MS. 4655/2, ff.88–9, 93–5, 152.

35　Unwin, *Ind. Org.*, p. 210.

36　MS. 4655A, 30 October 1648.

37　MS. 4655/2, *passim*; MS. 4655A/2, *passim*.

38　MS. 4655/2, ff.23, 113, 173.

39　MS. 4655/2, ff.141, 165, March and October 1654.

40　MS. 4655/2, ff.128, 136.

41　MS. 4655/3, ff.20–1; for examples of action by the Court of Assistants and Yeomanry in 1662 see ff.25, 29b, 30, 33b, 42.

42　MS. 4655/3, ff.44, 44b, 46, 52.

43　MS. 4655/3, ff.128b, 131; MS. 4655/7, ff.2b, 10b.

44　See, e.g., MS. 4655/3, ff.34, 37, 41b, 130b, 151b, 155b.

45　MS. 4655/3, ff.55b, 58; MS. 4655/4, *passim*.

46　MS. 4655/5, 28 September 1668.

47　MS. 4655/6, 2 May and 6 June 1670.

48　MS. 4646, ff.112b, 113; MS. 4649A, 30 July 1672, 3 May 1680. Apart from prosecutions, the out-of-pocket expenses of the Yeomanry, paid through their foremen, averaged about 30*s.* a quarter at this period (MS. 4648/1, *passim*).

49　See Chap. 13 below.

50　MS. 4655/11, f.17.

51　MS. 4655/11, ff.196b, 200–1; MS. 4648/3, *passim*.

52　MS. 4655/11, f.274; MS. 4655/12, *passim*.

53　MS. 4655/12, f.118. The word 'gentlemen' was coming into use in the 1720s in references to the Officers, Assistants and Livery, and the designation 'Esquire' was placed after the names of one or two members of the Court. cf. also MS. 4655/12, f.14b. (1727) in which the phrase 'the Gentlemen of the Trade' is used.

54　MS. 4661, vols 25a, 26b, 28–36a.

55　MS. 4655/15, ff.66b, 67, 188.

56　Ellis Evans, for example, was fined 40*s.* in 1611 for calling the

Weavers' Officers 'beggarly and cut-throat knaves'; he was thrown into the Compter for non-payment, and his appeal to the Lord Mayor failed. See also MS. 4655/1, ff.7, 24, 26, 42–3, 45, 100.

57 MS. 4655/1, ff.14, 21–2, 80, 89, 94, 96–7; cf. the case of Thomas Andrewe (f.36) who was admitted a foreign brother after he had paid 12s. 'for charges of a writ of subpoena and officers' fees for the suit against him in the Exchequer upon St. Andrew's Day'.

58 This man was an unscrupulous troublemaker, who cheated at least one of his journeymen, brought false accusations against others, hurled coarse abuse against the Weavers' Company, became embroiled in lawsuits, and was (1619) imprisoned in Newgate for refusing to pay his fines (MS. 4655/1, ff.46, 100–1, 103).

59 MS. 4655/1, f.24.

60 MS. 4655/1, f.85; MS. 4656/1, f.109.

61 MS. 4655/1, ff.13, 20, 24, 30, 86; MS. 4655/3, ff.58b, 60b, 70b, 89; MS. 4655/4, passim.

62 MS. 4655/1, f.32; MS. 4655A, passim; MS. 4655/3, f.66; MS. 4656/1, passim.

63 Doubtless a corruption of Prévôt. MS. 4655/3, f.68; MS. 4655/4, March 1667.

64 MS. 4655/3, ff.49, 52.

65 MS. 4655/3, f.157.

66 MS. 4655/9, ff.11b, 12b, 34.

67 MS. 4655/1, ff.5–6, 18–19, 22, 30, 33, 42, 47, 53, 66.

68 G. Unwin, Studies in Economic History (1927), p. 96. 'Tho. Crawford . . . presented a piece of 8-penny ribbon' to the Weavers' Court of Assistants, 'which he had given out to one, Thomas Bowman, but the judgement of the Court is that the work was spoiled' (MS. 4655/2, f.124 (1654)).

69 In 1624–5, for example, there were complaints of the illegal use of 'camels hair, barks of trees, and such like . . . base stuffs [which] do fade, molder and wear away before the silk that is therein be half worn out' (MS. 4647, f.169).

70 MS. 4655/1, ff.59, 62, 73, 75, 81. J. R. Kellett, 'The Breakdown of the Gild and Corporation Control over Handicraft and Retail Trade in London' in Economic History Review, 1958.

71 MS. 4655/1, ff.85–6.

72 An extremely unpopular, even dangerous, thing to do in London at that date.

73 MS. 4655A/3; MS. 4648/1.

74 MS. 4655A/3; MS. 4655/7, ff.18b, 93b.

75 MS. 4655/3, ff.21, 33b, 146; MS. 4655/8, f.69.

76 MS. 4655/1, f.104.

77 MS. 4655/1, ff.58, 90, 94. In April 1619, John Kitchen, an awkward, troublesome character, was fined 3s. 4d. for reviling a Liveryman 'calling him knave and drunkard' (MS. 4655/1, f.90), and a case of irresponsible, unseemly gossip and innuendo is recorded on ff.95–6, June–July 1619.

78 MS. 4647, f.338. See also Chap. 9 below.

79 MS. 4648/1, 16 October 1676.

80 MS. 4655A/3, 22 January and 5 August 1672. In 1673, six weavers in Southwark were reported by the Yeomanry as refractory (MS. 4655/7, f.22; cf. also MS. 4655/8, f.90, June 1676). Weavers were not alone in abusing the Company; on one occasion a smith

who had repaired the poor's box was dissatisfied with his pay and called the Company 'beggarly dogs', for which breach of good manners he was made to apologise (MS. 4655/4, 21 January 1667).

81 MS. 4655/1, ff.7, 31, 42, 49–50.

82 MS. 4655/2, f.129; MS. 4655/9, f.20b; MS. 4655/10, f.31.

83 MS. 4655/2, ff.92, 131, 167; MS. 4655/4, *passim*. Among many complaints about the employment of women and girls in looms was one in 1667 against John Mustard, who promised the Company that he would 'dispose of ye girl out of ye loom'; and another against George Clark, who was fined 40*s.* in that year for employing no fewer than five women, contrary to the Ordinances. One weaver was fined 10*s.* for 'countenancing his apprentice to teach a girl the trade of weaving', and in 1674 George Clark was again in trouble for teaching a girl to weave. Despite his admission that this had been going on for ten weeks, he proved defiant and was ordered to be brought before the Lord Mayor (MS. 4655/7, ff.65, 70; MS. 4655/11, f.285b).

84 MS. 4655/2, ff.10, 21, 29, 67; MS. 4655/3, ff.43b, 159b; MS. 4655/4, ff.47, 88b; MS. 4655/11, ff.116, 219b; MS. 4655/13, f.32.

85 MS. 4655A, 11 June 1649.

86 *The Book of Prices* (i.e. piece rates) printed in 1769 is markedly restrictive as to the employment of women and girls, except in wartime.

87 MS. 4656/4, 11 October 1703; MS. 4655/3, f.162b; MS. 4655/4, *passim*; MS. 4648/1, June 1670; MS. 4648/5, ff.7, 8b, 13b, 15b, 22b; MS. 4647, f.553; MS. 4655/15, ff.87, 355. Sarah Brown, executed in 1718 for murder and theft, said she was born in Spitalfields where she learned to weave 'and might by it have got a pretty livelihood'; quoted in George, *London*, p. 181.

88 MS. 4656/5, 8 September 1712.

89 MS. 4653, *passim*.

90 Lace was much in demand for gentlemen's ruffles, ladies' lappets and trimmings of many kinds, and the lace bills of people of fashion were enormous. Thus many thousands of women and girls were employed, but poorly paid. The orris weavers made gold and silver lace and braids. London had two weekly lace markets: at the George Inn, Aldersgate Street, and at the Bull and Mouth by Aldersgate. 'A Lace-Man', said Campbell in 1747, 'must have a well-lined pocket to furnish his shop; but his Garrets may be as meanly equipped as he pleases. His chief Talent ought to lie in a nice Taste in Patterns of Lace, &c. He ought to speak fluently, though not elegantly, to entertain the Ladies; and to be Master of a handsome Bow and Cringe; should be able to hand a Lady to and from her Coach politely, without being seized with the Palpitation of the Heart at the Touch of a delicate Hand, a well-turned and much exposed Limb, a handsome Face. But, above all, he must have Confidence to refuse his Goods in a handsome manner to the extravagant Beau who never pays. . . . ' London was also a great market for the gold and silver buttons worn in large numbers in the world of fashion. The London button-makers worked mainly for lacemen who provided the gold and silver thread and all other materials except the moulds. By the mid-eighteenth century the craft was in the hands of a crowd of women and girls whose numbers reduced average earnings to a low level. The

milliners of the seventeenth and eighteenth centuries did not confine themselves to the making and sale of women's hats; they dealt in a great variety of goods—holland, cambric, ribbons, lawn, lace of all sorts—by the piece or made up into smocks, tippets, neckties, ruffles, handkerchiefs, gloves, caps, hats and hoods; also cloaks and mantuas in plain or figured silk and velvet, trimmed with gold, silver or black lace. Some even sold riding-habits and 'dresses for the Masquerade' (I. Pinchbeck, *Women Workers and the Industrial Revolution* (1930), pp. 203–5, 230–1; A. Clark, *Working Life of Women in the 17th Century* (1919), pp. 141–4; Campbell, *Tradesman*, pp. 147, 207).

91 MS. 4647, ff.506, 537, 545. Ann Pierce, having formerly given a bond with a £60 penalty not to weave unless duly qualified, in fact became qualified by marrying John Munday, who was free of the Weavers' Company, and the bond was then cancelled (MS. 4655/9, f.5b. (1683)).

92 MS. 4655/2, ff.87, 126, 139.

93 MS. 4655/9, f.11. Presumably, 'discharge' in this context means 'turn-over'. The trade rights of a stationer's widow were not lost to her when she re-married, but could be shared by her new husband; this was a valuable asset in the marriage market (E. Arber, *Transcript of Register of Stationers' Company* (1876, V, Intro.).

94 MS. 4655/4, ff.46, 64.

95 MS. 4655/1, f.92; MS. 4655A, *passim*; MS. 4655/2, ff.18, 23, 28.

96 MS. 4655/4, ff.64, 70–70b; MS. 4655/6, f.49b.

97 MS. 4655/2, f.65; MS. 4655/8, f.93b, MS. 4655/11, f.137b. Similar cases in the eighteenth century are recorded in MS. 4655/4, *passim*.

Chapter 4

Freemen of the Future

Industry in the seventeenth century was organised in small local units, of which the most typical was the master craftsman's household, with its living, working and storage accommodation for the family, the apprentices and, perhaps, a young journeyman or two. We have seen that the Weavers' ordinances permitted master weavers to take not more than certain prescribed numbers of apprentices according to their standing as members of the Company, but no limits were placed upon the number of children under fourteen years of age who could be employed on sundry simple but essential tasks. Many master weavers employed young boys 'brought up to the trade' to attend upon them and their journeymen (if any) 'to help him pick his silk clean, to fill his quills, and in a flowered work to draw up the figure.[1] Some of these things these boys are able to do at the age of six or seven, for which they receive 2s., 3s., 4s., or 4s. 6d., a week, which is a great help to their poor fathers and mothers. This they continue till fourteen, at which time they seek for a master and masters also seek for such boys.'[2] The Weavers' records confirm this generalisation. For example, in 1617, Thomas Davie, a master weaver, was eager to employ his boy-servant in the loom, but the Court of Assistants ordered him to keep the boy 'as a winder with him and not to be set to the loom above 14 days before he is bound apprentice to him or some other'.[3] From the eighteenth century comes another example in which a weaver working in Moorfields 'having entertained Jacob Dehorne, a poor lad upwards of 12 years of age who is willing to be bound apprentice but not being of age sufficient, is permitted to keep him until he attains to the age of 14 and then to bring him to be bound'.[4] Such boys, between six and fourteen years of age, with the apprentices and journeymen, all under the direction and supervision of the master weaver, formed the typical industrial unit.

The social importance of apprenticeship was great, for, at best, it provided both technical instruction and moral training throughout late childhood and early adolescence. From the Ancient World to the Augustan Age, as Unwin remarked, the workshop was the only technical school.[5] The importance of the apprentice's inclusion as a member of his master's household, where this was a sober, respectable establishment, can hardly be over-estimated. And when, in the eighteenth century, the taking of 'out-door' apprentices, who were much less under their master's eye, became more and more usual, it was widely deplored as likely to result in 'young lads being left upon the town' and thus subjected to greatly increased temptations to drinking, gambling and disorderly conduct.[6]

By tradition and long usage the craft gilds were regarded as largely responsible for the craftsmanship of their members. This was the ideal, but because of human frailty it was, too often, not achieved. 'It is but too common', wrote Campbell in 1747, 'that they [the master craftsmen] think they have their apprentices for mere slaves, and are under no obligation to spend any of their time in compleating them in their business. . . . Some conceal the secrets of the business designedly, to keep the Apprentice in dependence on them; and others out of mere sullenness and ill-nature.'[7] The Weavers' Company tried to secure adequate instruction and a proper standard of competence in the weaving trade by careful investigation of all complaints of 'insufficient instruction' of apprentices and by insisting upon certificates from the civic authorities when apprenticeship had been served outside its jurisdiction. If an apprentice's father could prove that his son was not being properly treated and taught, the Court of Assistants usually ordered the master 'forthwith to give sufficient surety unto the father . . . for the boy's good usage and his true instruction in his trade', otherwise the apprentice would be transferred to another master.[8] When William Spillmore, apprentice to Richard Sparrey, came to the Court in 1685 and complained of want of sufficient instruction, alleging that he was employed only upon the making of stripe silks, the Court's considered judgment was: (a) 'Richard Sparrey is an ancient and good workman, he having made free [of the Company] 4 apprentices, who were good work-men'; (b) 'the learning to make Stripe Silks is a sufficient instruction [for] most works in the weaving trade, and is always understood as a full discharge of the covenant in the indentures of apprenticeship'; (c) the Complaint is 'vain and frivolous and grounded upon the humour of the apprentice's Mother'.[9]

As a rule an apprentice was bound on the initiative of his father or legal guardian, but a minority were apprenticed by the parishes. The famous Elizabethan Poor Law of 1601 (43 and 44 Eliz. I, c. 2) gave churchwardens and overseers power to bind as apprentices any male children likely to fall into evil ways 'till such man child shall come to the age of 24 years'. This, of course, covered foundlings, who were the responsibility of the parish in which they were found. Some typical examples taken from the Weavers' records for the middle of the seventeenth century are:

> 23rd April 1655. John Clark, son of a tapster of Croydon, apprenticed to a London weaver for ten years by 'Samuel Barnett, Doctor of Divinity, Thos. Morton, Esquire, and others of the Governors of the said parish of Croydon'.
>
> 19th December 1659. Nathan Andrews, 'foundling of ye parish of St Andrew-Undershaft', apprenticed to a weaver for eight years.
>
> 7th March 1659. 'Stephen Brookes of the Parish of St Stephen's, Walbrook, foundling' apprenticed to a weaver for ten years, 'by the Churchwardens of the Parish'.[10]

Very few girls were apprenticed to weaving in London, either by their parents or the parish; but we have a record of Susannah Blackbrow, 'a poor girl of the parish', who was apprenticed to a gold and silver orris weaver in December 1739, and was made a freewoman of the Weavers' Company by servitude in July 1748.[11] Another girl 'was turned by her original master to a weaver who lived with a Billingsgate fishwoman. She sometimes wound quills for the man, but always went to market with the woman, and was also sent out alone to cry periwinkles and crabs, and, at night, radishes.'[12]

In eighteenth-century London the Bridewell apprentices, with their blue coats and white hats, were often to be seen in the streets.[13] Shortly before his untimely death in 1553 the boy king, Edward VI, had given his palace of Bridewell to the Corporation of London to be used partly as a 'house of correction' for ruffians and masterless men and dissolute women found lurking in alehouses, cock-pits, skittle alleys, gambling dens and other 'suspicious houses', and partly as a training school in which boys from Christ's Hospital and former patients of St Thomas's Hospital could be apprenticed and taught certain useful trades. After a long period of delay and experimentation there emerged a training establishment for the children of poor freemen as well as young vagrants. In the seventeenth century there were between seventy and a hundred Bridewell apprentices, and about 140 in the eighteenth century, who served terms of from eight to ten, or even twelve years, in the crafts of shoemaking, gloving, feltmaking, weaving and tailoring. Their instructors, called 'arts-masters', were usually poor freemen of the appropriate gilds or companies, who received from the Bridewell Governors living quarters and workshops, and a capitation grant for each apprentice. But not every arts-master was poor or 'decayed', as appears from the complaint made in 1618 by John Hare, a freeman of the Weavers' Company, that Robert Cotchett, in Bridewell, keeps fourteen looms, 'which he [John Hare] findeth himself agrieved at'.[14] Over a century later the Weavers' records show that Gabriel Bestman, Upper Bailiff in 1727–8, was a Bridewell arts-master, and so was Daniel Nipp, one of the Assistants at that time.[15] A traveller from Germany, Zacharias von Uffenbach, visited Bridewell in 1710 and watched with interest the weaving of plush, plain and flowered velvet, taffeta, damask, woollen curtains and cords, silk girdles, gauze ribbons and silk hand-kerchiefs.[16] Finished goods from the Bridewell workshops were sold to shopkeepers and exporters in the City. The hours of work in Bridewell, as elsewhere, were long, the fare Spartan, and 'correction' frequent and sometimes severe, though the Governors, it seems, discouraged any outright cruelty on the part of the arts-masters. Doubtless many of the boys were 'hard nuts'. Often they absconded; and even those who stayed came to be looked upon as one of the terrors of the London streets, quick to start a disturbance or join a mob on the slightest pretext.[17] Some of them bided their time until the end of their apprenticeship, when they received gifts of new clothes, tools and money, and then immediately decamped, sold the tools, spent the money and sank into some 'mean occupation' such as portering.[18] The steady ones who became freemen were given £10 'to set them up in their trade'.[19] The aims of Bridewell were, indeed, worthy: to pre-vent cime and mendicity by giving poor children a trade and the chance of making an honest living; and success was often achieved, as many entries in the Weavers' records show, e.g.

> 20th November 1648. Thomas Gill, son of a waterman who had died when the boy was very young, was apprenticed to weaving for twelve years and 'was made free upon the report of Mr. Henry Isackson, treasurer of the said hospital' of Bridewell. No admission fees were charged by the Weavers' Company in this case.[20]

> 21st August 1654. An apprentice (apparently an orphan) who came from Oxfordshire, was apprenticed for twelve years and thereafter granted his freedom upon the certificate of the Governors of Bridewell.[21]

> 2nd November 1668. Robert Smith, apprentice, to Edmond Silvester, Weaver, Arts Master of Bridewell, for ten years from Easter 1656 to Easter 1666, 'as was Certified by ye Treasurer of that hospital, made free and paid 3s. 4d.'[22]

> 1st June 1752. 'William Edwards, living in Bride Lane, Weaver, who was bound Apprentice at Bridewell Hospital the 11th April 1745 to James Smith, Citizen and Weaver of London, is made free by Servitude upon Certificate from Robt. Alsop Esqr., Alderman of London, Treasurer of the said Hospital.[23]

The 'Act Touching Divers Orders for Artificers, Labourers, Servants of Husbandry and Apprentices' passed in 1563,[24] and usually called the Statute of Artificers, provided that all apprentices must serve 'seven years at the least'. How far did this minimum period become, in practice, the norm? The Weavers' records for the seventeenth century show that more than one-half of the apprentices bound at the Hall served for seven years; more than one-third served for eight years; while rather less than one-tenth served for nine years or more. The actual percentages are shown in Table 4.1

Table 4.1 *Length of service of apprentices in the seventeenth century*

years	%	years	%
7	55·3	10	1·6
8	35·2	11	0·3
9	7·5	12	0·1

Reductions in the lengths of apprenticeships were sometimes made. For example, John Willey, who had been bound for eight years in 1608, was transferred to another master (reason not stated) and allowed by the Weavers' Company to serve only seven years in all; 'the eighth year is remitted unto him'.[25] In 1619 it was 'ordered and agreed between Robert Lowe and Thomas Hopcroft, his apprentice, that whereas he was bound for ten years and to have at the end of his term double apparel and a cloak and £3. 6s. 8d. in money, the said Robert Lowe is contented and agrees to remit . . . the last year's service . . . in consideration that the money and cloak shall be remitted'.[26] Also, in the same year, an apprentice who had been bound for eleven years was allowed to cancel the last two years.[27]

Apprenticeships for more than seven years seldom occur in the eighteenth century, and terms exceeding eight years are very rare indeed. On the other hand, after 1749 men who had served in the army or navy could obtain special concessions, like Joseph Banks of Bethnal Green, 'who served . . . on board the *Rupert*, Man of War, from 4th September 1740 to 24th November 1748, as by Certificate of Captain Edmund Horn appears', and had been instructed in weaving by James Newman, Weaver, of Virginia Row, Bethnal Green, since leaving the navy (i.e. a little less than two years), and was admitted to the freedom of the Weavers' Company in 1750 under the statute 22 Geo. II which enabled ex-service officers and other ranks discharged after 'the late war' to 'exercise Trades'. Another applicant, Joseph File, had served aboard H.M.S. *Cambridge* and produced the City Chamberlain's certificate to prove it.[28]

No records of apprenticeship premiums appear in the books of the Weavers' Company until 1730, although such payments were customary long before that date. Table 4.2 shows the result of an examination of over 1,500 entries recorded between 1730 and 1795.

Table 4.2 *Apprenticeship premiums*

Sources of premiums		No premiums paid	Total entries examined
Charities and parishes	Private		
241	202	1,080	1,523

The parishes and other charitable trusts usually paid from £2 to £5 for each apprentice. For example, in the middle of the eighteenth century, the parish of St Stephen, Walbrook, paid £2. 10s. to apprentice a boy to weaving, and for another boy All Hallows, Lombard Street, paid five guineas. Christ's Hospital made frequent grants of £5 a head, and Francis Bancroft's and Henry Dixon's charities, administered by the Drapers' Company, made grants of £4 for each apprenticeship. The Weavers' Company administered Richard Jervies's charity which provided that £2 could be spent annually to apprentice the son of a poor weaver of St Leonard's parish, Shoreditch. When this was done the transactions were shown in the Renter Bailiff's accounts, e.g.

> 18th January 1742. Pd. the Churchwardens of Shoreditch for putting out James Alsuxe apprentice to Thos. Ventiman, being the Gift of Richard Jervies, £2.

> 6th July 1747. Paid Jervies's gift for putting out John Vanner apprentice to Wm. Norton. Bound the 4th May last . . . £2.[29]

Various charity schools had funds which they disbursed in a similar way, e.g.

> 1742 The Free School of St Mary, Whitechapel, £3.
> 1747 The Society for Supporting the School in Broad Street, £2.
> 1749 Shoreditch School, £3.
> 1789 Walbrook Charity School, £5. 10s.
> 1791 St Ethelburga's Charity School, £5.
> 1792 Langborn Ward Charity School, £2.
> 1792 The Welch School, £5.
> 1794 Farrington Ward School, £3.

Certain corporations and special groups appear in the records from time to time: e.g., in 1748–50, the Dutch Church in Austin Friars (£10); the French Hospital (£17. 10s.); the French Church in London (£1. 10s.);[30] the Corporation of Clergymen's Sons (£20); and 'The

Cockneys of Shoreditch, charity money from the Cockneys' Feast', two apprenticeship premiums each of £5.

The premiums paid from private sources vary much more widely in amount, for the master weavers seem to have been familiar with the principle of charging what the traffic will bear, which meant that poor men paid no premiums while the well-to-do paid large sums, ranging up to 200 or 300 guineas. The highest premium is recorded in 1783 when Thomas, the son of William Farrow of Monksley in Suffolk, Gentleman, deceased, was apprenticed to Thomas Tatlock, Citizen and Weaver of London, in business as a silk broker in Love Lane, Aldermanbury, for a 'consideration' of £1,000.[31] Other premiums paid by gentlemen ranged from £20 to £400. An 'esquire' living at Chelsea paid 90 guineas; and a Somerset squire paid 350 guineas. A premium of £400 was paid by Robert Le Grand of Canterbury and £380 by Thomas Jones of Hackney, both described as gentlemen. On the other hand, impecunious gentlemen or their executors paid little or nothing; in fact, in the period 1730–95, ten gentlemen's sons were bound without premiums, and the sons of three gentlemen were apprenticed with the aid of three £5 grants from 'charity moneys'.[32] The clergy seem to have been treated in much the same way, but the premiums paid were on a lower scale. In 1753 the Rev. John Hull, a Norfolk parson, paid £150, and in the same year the Rev. Edward Peach, Rector of Titsey in Surrey, paid 100 guineas. On the other hand, in 1755 and 1757, a son of the Vicar of Hendon was apprenticed to weaving without premium, and so was John Castle Dolman, son of the Rev. John Dolman of Brick Lane in the Parish of St Luke, Bethnal Green. Surgeons seem to have been 'assessed' rather highly. In 1758 Stephen Dolignon, son of Peter Dolignon, Surgeon, 'of Cressy-sur-Sarre in Picardy', was bound for seven years to John Hinchcliff, weaver of London, for a premium of 100 guineas; and four years later another surgeon paid a premium of £350. A surgeon practising in Westminster and a barber-surgeon paid £25 and £50 respectively. For the farming fraternity the picture is different. Usually boys from farming families were bound free of premiums, like John Ogilvy, the son of a Scottish husbandman, who came to London in 1753 from Glamis in Angus to be a weaver's apprentice.[33] On one occasion, however, a yeoman paid as much as £100. A Surrey husbandman paid 15 guineas, and a Worcestershire farmer paid £15, but £10 of that sum was 'charity money'. The premiums paid by merchants point to the prosperity of that class in the eighteenth century. One haberdasher paid as much as £300, and another £200; but this is exceptional. A Leeds merchant and a linen draper each paid 100 guineas; and a brandy merchant, a mercer, and a 'Mincing Lane Merchant' each paid £100.

Usually, craftsmen's sons, including sons of weavers, were bound without premiums, for many of them were the sons of neighbours, friends and fellow craftsmen. A pamphlet published in 1719[34] declared that 'where there is one [master weaver] that has money with an apprentice there are fifty that have none at all,[35] and the most they have, when they can get it, is not above £5 or £6 . . .'. Boys brought up in the trade from an early age were preferred, for 'it is much more of advantage to a master to take such a boy without money, than a stranger [to the craft] with money'. Occasionally, however, we come upon exceptions, as when a weaver's executors paid out of his estate, in 1769, a premium of 300 guineas.[36] Again, in 1791, a premium of £300 was paid on behalf of a weaver's son bound to Richard Lea, who was Upper Bailiff of the Weavers' Company in that year. In the following year another master weaver received an exceptionally large premium of £200. Weavers who could command such high premiums must have been in a big way of business.

A fair number of the sons of mariners, porters and labourers of all sorts were apprenticed to weaving, but premiums were seldom demanded except where a grant could be had from a charity. Thus, in 1755, the son of a Clerkenwell labourer was apprenticed to weaving with the aid of '£5 charity money from the Dissenters' School'. A year before, the 'son of Wm. Groocock who died on board H.M.S. the *Woolwich*, Mariner', was bound to a weaver without paying a premium. During the period 1730–95, fifty-six sons of porters, mariners, watermen, chairmen and labourers were apprenticed to weaving without premiums, while premiums were paid—many of them by charities—in respect of thirty-five similar apprenticeships: therefore a ratio of approximately 3 : 2 may be taken as indicating the proportion of non-premiums to premiums paid for lads of this class.

The Weavers' Company did not encourage the binding of girls as weavers' apprentices, and its very small number of freewomen tended to turn towards the millinery business. Probably because they were so few, they could obtain substantial premiums by taking girls as apprentices. Thus, one of the rare records of the apprenticeship of a girl to weaving in London reads:

> 1737. 'Henrietta Griffith, Daughter of David Griffith, Gent., [bound] to Sarah Gabell, Citizen and Weaver, for seven years. £30 consideration; Tuesday 22 November.'

Some three months later we have:

> 6th March 1738. 'Charlotte Quantiteau, daughter of Peter Quantiteau of St. Martin's in the Fields in the County of Middx., Gent., bound apprentice for 7 years to Eliz. Forward of Pater Noster Row, Milliner, Consideration £42.'[37]

In June 1742 Elizabeth Forward, 'Spinster, Weaver of London', took another girl under her wing; the daughter of the Rev. John Milner,

D.D., of Peckham in the County of Surrey, on whose behalf a premium of £60 was paid.[38] A fortnight later 'Christian Clarke, daughter of Charles Clarke, late of Farnham (Surrey), Apothecary, deceased', was apprenticed to Isaac Oake, Citizen and Weaver, for a premium of 30 guineas.[39] In the autumn of 1742 a clergyman's daughter was bound without a premium.[40] Some ten years later another small influx of girl-apprentices is recorded:

1752. Elizabeth, daughter of Geo. Robinson of Sedgefield, Durham, Tailor, bound for 7 years to Sarah Oake[41] Citizen and Weaver of London: Premium £60.

1752. Sarah Hitchin, daughter of a Cheshunt butcher, deceased, bound to Mary Giles, Citizen and Weaver of London: Premium £30.

1753. Sarah Oake took two girls as apprentices; the first for a premium of 20 guineas, and the second—Ann, daughter of John Harper of St. Catherine's Court, Tower Hill, captain of the *King George*, Holland trader—for a premium of 30 guineas.

1758. Susan Walker, daughter of a gunstock maker, 'late of the Minories, deceased, bound for 7 years to John Robinson, Citizen and Weaver of London, husband of Isabella Robinson of Cornhill, Lace Merchant, with whom the said apprentice is to dwell and be instructed in the Lace trade'. Premium 40 guineas.[42]

Mary Gabell appears again in 1769 when Elizabeth Sweet, who had been apprenticed to her eight years before, had set up as a haberdasher and milliner at 34 Fleet Street, and was made free of the Weavers' Company.[43]

Seeing that seventeenth-century communications were slow and all modes of travel hard and hazardous, one might assume that usually a lad would follow his father's trade, or perhaps be bound apprentice to his father; and that he would 'serve his term' of at least seven years in or near his native place. Detailed study of the Weavers' records, however, proves that these assumptions do not hold good for apprentices bound at Weavers' Hall in the seventeenth century. The new apprentices, it seems, formed a not inconsiderable proportion of the great stream of immigrants which flowed incessantly into London from the provinces, from France and from the Low Countries.[44]

Early in the seventeenth century the London Weavers' Company recorded the binding of ten to twelve apprentices weekly, on an average, or some 500–600 per annum. In the middle of the century, the average was about five a week, or approximately 200–250 per annum. After the Restoration the numbers rose sharply, the annual average for the decade 1660–70 being 680, with a high peak of over

750 in the year 1667–8, shortly after the Great Plague and the Fire. During the next twenty years, however, the annual average fell to 430, with a downward trend which became steep over the turn of the century, so that the annual average from 1692 to 1706 was down to 274. This trend continued throughout the first quarter of the eighteenth century, and after 1725–6 the annual total seldom exceeded one hundred. Table 4.3 shows the annual averages for the five decades from 1730 to 1779. By the end of the century the figure was around thirty.

Table 4.3 *The number of apprentices bound, 1730–99*

Years	No.	Years	No.
1730–9	102	1760–9	91
1740–9	88	1770–9	45
1750–9	93	1780–99	30*

* Approximate figure.

In the middle of the seventeenth century only 8 per cent of the weavers' apprentices were sons of weavers and only one lad in fifty was apprenticed to his own father, or, occasionally, to his widowed mother carrying on her deceased husband's trade. All the others had different backgrounds—some markedly different—and a surprisingly high proportion hailed from quite distant counties or provincial towns. The distribution by counties of origin of 1,100 apprentices bound at Weavers' Hall between 1655 and 1664 is set out in Table 4.4. About one-quarter of the lads were Londoners, and another one-sixth came from the Home Counties. The north and south Midlands contributed 309 lads, or about 28 per cent of the total. The West of England sent a hundred, or a little over 9 per cent, and the Eastern Counties eighty-seven, or a little less than 8 per cent. It seems probable that many of the rising generation in those districts were absorbed by the local woollen cloth, worsted and silk manufacturers. The size of the contribution of the north-western counties, sixty-seven apprentices, or over 6 per cent, is somewhat surprising, for there were local textile manufactures in that region; but, perhaps, not sufficient in scale in the seventeenth century to absorb all the young lads coming forward.

Another remarkable aspect of these migrations of the young is the great distances travelled from their homes to London. To make a journey from Cumberland or Cornwall, Durham or Devon, Wales or Ireland, was a prolonged, fatiguing, and often dangerous adventure. Doubtless many of the lads travelled most of the way by sea, in charge of the master of a coasting vessel; but those who journeyed

Table 4.4 *Geographical origins of apprentices, 1655–64*

Apprentices from:	No.
London: i.e. the City, Liberties and suburbs and the City of Westminster	279
Home Counties: Middlesex, Herts., Essex, Surrey, Kent	181
East: Cambridgeshire, Huntingdonshire, Suffolk, Norfolk, Lincolnshire, Rutland, Isle of Ely	87
South Midlands: Berks., Northants., Beds., Worcestershire, Bucks.	169
North Midlands: Warwicks., Derbyshire, Staffs., Notts., Leicestershire	140
West: Wilts., Somerset, Dorset, Gloucestershire, Herefordshire, Devon, Cornwall	100
North-West: Cumberland, Westmorland, Lancs., Shropshire, Cheshire	67
Wales (including Monmouthshire)	23
South: Sussex, Hants, Isle of Wight	19
North-East: Yorkshire, Durham	25
Isle of Man	1
Ireland	8
Jersey, C.I.	1
	1,100

overland had to face extremely bad roads, many little better than the roughest of cart tracks, full of potholes and quagmires. During wet spells floodwater covered low-lying roads and the fords became impassable. Stow, in his *Annales* (1615), speaks of 'long wagons . . . such as now come to London from Canterbury, Norwich, Ipswich, Gloucester, &c. with passengers and commodities'. The poorer sort of people who travelled in these long, canvas-covered wagons at a speed of two to three miles an hour received but scant welcome from the innkeepers, some of whom firmly refused to let them enter their inns; and worse still, as Pastor Moritz noted, anybody travelling a long distance in England on foot was 'sure to be looked upon . . . as either a beggar or a vagabond, or some necessitous wretch'.[45] Wide rivers and estuaries had to be crossed by primitive ferries; and as late as 1724, Daniel Defoe made a ferry-boat passage of four hours in an open boat with fifteen horses, a dozen cows and 'about 17 or 18 passengers, called Christians'.[46] Some of the parents of the new apprentices doubtless contrived to put them in charge of an adult travelling on the same route, for we know that some of the boys were under fourteen years of age. But such adults sometimes proved to be less than trustworthy. For example, in July 1654 John Aubrey complained to the Weavers' Court of Assistants 'that Roger Taylor was sent up to him out of the country to be an apprentice, but he that brought him up put him to Richard Homes contrary to the mind of his friends'. The Court promptly ordered that both parties should send to his friends and 'upon return of their letters the Court will order who shall have him'.[47]

By the second quarter of the eighteenth century the stream of apprentices to weaving flowing into London from the provinces shows a marked change. During the decade 1736–45, 742 new indentures were entered at Weavers' Hall (an average of seventy-four per annum compared with 110 during the decade 1655–64), and of these only seventy came from outside London, Westminster and the Home Counties.[48] From Table 4.5 we see that by the middle of the eighteenth century the flow from the Midlands and the Eastern and Western counties was drying up, and towards the end of the century (1786–95) it had almost ceased, nearly 95 per cent of the lads being drawn from London, Westminster and adjacent counties.

Table 4.5 *Numbers and counties of origin of apprentices whose indentures were entered at Weavers' Hall, London*

	1655–64	1736–45	1786–95
London: i.e. the City, Liberties, suburbs and City of Westminster	279	552	232
Home Counties	181	120	20
East	87	8	—
South Midlands	169	24	4
North Midlands	140	5	—
West	100	12	2
North-West	67	4	1
Wales (including Monmouthshire)	23	2	—
South	19	7	—
North-East	25	2	4
Isle of Man	1	—	—
Ireland	8	2	—
Scotland	—	—	1
Jersey, C.I.	1	—	—
France	—	2	—
Switzerland	—	2	—
	1,100	742	264
Annual average	110	74·2	26·4

The marked slackening of the flow of new apprentices into London during the eighteenth century seems to have been the result of the quickening pace of economic development in the provinces. Modern research in a wide variety of industries other than textiles has led to the conclusion that the progress of technology and the growth of large-scale industry between 1540 and 1740 have been much under-estimated, and that, in fact, 'the introduction of new industries and new machinery, tools, and furnaces in old industries, had brought about technical changes in the methods of mining and manufacturing only less momentous than those associated with the great inventions of the late eighteenth and early nineteenth centuries'.[49] This sort of development can be seen, for example, in Birmingham and the Black Country, from Walsall and Wolverhampton in the extreme north and west, down to Stourbridge and Longbridge in the south-west and south, with Dudley, West Bromwich, Smethwick, Wednesbury, Bilston and Darlaston in the centre and north-west of the region, in which new industries were striking root and existing ones growing lustily, all in considerable variety—swords and guns, glass, leather, saddlery and harness, brass and copper articles such as buckles, buttons and other 'toys'. By the last quarter of the eighteenth century many groups of smiths and miners, scattered, at one time, over a largely agricultural district, had expanded into busy and populous industrial communities. The estimated population of Birmingham town grew from some 5,500 in 1650 to 15,000 in 1700, and over 23,000 in 1731.[50] In Yorkshire and Lancashire also there was marked industrial expansion before the advent of the now-famous inventions in textile machinery. 'By 1700, Yorkshire . . . was fast becoming dominated by the trades and technical arts that supported the woollen industry'; a domination which extended to many of its cities and towns. Bradford, for example, is described in 1800 as 'inhabited by manufacturers, many of them opulent'.[51] In Lancashire, from the last decade of the seventeenth century onwards, the textile industry, centred on Manchester, was pushing ahead persistently and profitably. Bolton and Oldham were already prosperous places. Master manufacturers built new houses with more rooms and decorations (if not, always, more taste) than they or their fathers had been used to. Before 1760, a number of flourishing industries had been developed at Warrington (where Joseph Priestley first made his mark as a teacher at the Warrington Academy): sail cloth, much of it sold to the navy; pins, locks, hinges, foundry work. Throughout the whole region large numbers of apprentices were taken at increasing premiums. 'In the reign of George I even country gentlemen began to bind their sons to the Manchester trade. . . .'[52] Manchester itself 'extended on every side' until by 1800 its population reached 70,000.[53]

The economic and social backgrounds of the weavers' apprentices is, perhaps, an even more interesting study than their places of origin. The Weavers' records of apprentice bindings in the period 1655–64 provide 1,056 cases in which the occupation or status of the apprentices' fathers is clearly stated. The range, both industrially and socially, is remarkable; from gentlemen and yeomen to porters and labourers. The fact that some 400 lads, or 40 per cent, came from an agricultural background is not surprising. Nor is the similar number (382) from the families of craftsmen in textiles, leather, wood, metals and the building industry. But nearly fifty sons of 'gentlemen' seems a surprisingly high number until one remembers that in the seventeenth century the term 'gentleman' had an indefinite and inexact connotation, and that it was not unusual for younger sons of gentlemen to be apprenticed to a trade.[54] R. H. Tawney, writing about 'The Rise of the Gentry, 1558–1640', remarked upon 'the ruthlessness of the English family system, which . . . if it did not drown all the kittens but one, threw all but one into the water'. The poet John Gay, of *Beggar's Opera* fame, was apprenticed to a London silk mercer, while his elder brother served as an officer in Marlborough's army.[55] And again, as Defoe put it, 'our trade being so vastly great . . . no wonder that the gentlemen of the best families marry tradesmen's daughters, and put their younger sons apprentices to tradesmen'.[56] Many shrewd, enterprising and thrifty men in agriculture, trade and industry became prosperous, living comfortably in a 'temperate zone betwixt greatness and want', and were able, in course of time, to raise their status. Thus the line between the prosperous yeomen and many who styled themselves 'gentlemen' became blurred; and a 'crestless yeoman' might well spring from roots older and deeper than those of a new gentleman. 'A Yeoman', wrote Thomas Fuller, 'is a Gentleman in Ore whom the next age may see refined.' When the heralds of Queen Elizabeth I made a 'visitation' in Wiltshire, not a few conceited clothiers who had assumed the status of 'gentlemen' came under inquiry, and either voluntarily 'disclaymed the name of gentleman', or were compulsorily 'disgraded',[57] much to the glee of their neighbours we may be sure. Many a yeoman grew wealthy, like old Woodcock, a man of Kent, 'half farmer and half gentleman', whose horses pulled the plough all week and were 'put into the coach o'Sunday'. In 1664 the son of a well-to-do Lancashire yeoman presented a valuable silver dish to the London Weavers' Company when he was made a freeman.[58]

> Well-to-do yeomen matched their daughters with the sons of
> merchants, clothiers, drapers, or young men of the professions
> . . . and lesser yeomen found their wives among the daughters
> of tailors, weavers, masons, coopers, shoemakers and other
> small craftsmen. Often the way for such marriages was paved
> by members of their own blood-kin who had left the land.[59]

Some prosperous yeomen, it is true, had no desire to climb above their proper place and go about 'ratling in Taffity'.

> Let Gentlemen go gallant, what care I
> I was a yeoman born, and so I'll die.[60]

Such men thought it better to be at the head of the yeomanry than at the tail of the gentry. In general, the yeomen seem to have been farmers of upwards of one hundred acres; they ate 'yeoman bread' made mainly of wheat; and 'they got down to making profits, not just subsistance out of the land'. Some were even better off than the gentry whose land lay alongside theirs.[61] Some supplemented their incomes by engaging, with their families, in spinning and weaving. Therefore, it is not unlikely that certain of the yeomen's sons were sent to London to be well taught the craft, and later returned to their native villages. Among the less prosperous yeomen, as among the husbandmen, the keeping of an alehouse was yet another possible source of supplementary income.

The term 'husbandman' can mean either an occupation or a rank or degree. Thus yeomen and all knights, esquires and gentlemen who engaged in agriculture were husbandmen in the first sense. In the second sense the word denotes a farmer of rank or degree next below the yeoman: usually a small working tenant farmer ranking in both wealth and status between a yeoman and a day-labourer. The latter were landless wage-earners, paid by the piece, day, week or year to work on another man's land. Although they were 'free-born' their rank or degree was low—below the husbandman and well below the yeoman.

The list of professional men whose sons were apprenticed to weaving is not without interest. The 'clerks' in the records were probably for the most part parish parsons, members of the lesser clergy, many of whom came from farming stock. Before the end of the sixteenth century such men commonly had little learning, and many received such poor stipends that they were obliged to engage in some craft, trade or other occupation (e.g. the cure of sick and injured hawks) to supplement their incomes. In Stuart times, however, we begin to hear more and more of their having a study and some books; their social status and incomes were evidently improving, and a growing number had been to a university.[62] Nevertheless, they were, in general, still unable to entertain high ambitions for their sons and daughters. In medicine, too, things were in a transitional state in the seventeenth century and one can discern the trend towards the eighteenth-century position when a Fellow of the Royal College of Physicians was a gentleman, while the barber-surgeons and apothecaries had not yet emerged from the status of 'mere tradesmen'.[63] Musicians likewise were regarded as but small fry in the seventeenth and eighteenth centuries. Campbell, who wrote *The London Tradesman* in 1747, is favourably inclined to music, but contemptuous of musicianship as a 'gainful occupation'.

If a parent finds that his son has got an itch of Music, it is much the best way to allot him entirely to that study. The present general Taste of Music in the Gentry may find him better bread than what perhaps this Art deserves. The Gardens in the summer time employ a great number of Hands; when they are allowed a guinea a week or upwards, according to their merit. The Opera, the Play-Houses, Masquerades, Ridottoes, and the several Music-Clubs employ them during the winter. But I cannot help thinking that any other Mechanic Trade is much more useful to the Society than the whole tribe of Singers and Scrapers.[64]

Analysis of the figures yielded by the Weavers' records in the three decades, 1655–64, 1736–45 and 1786–95 (see Table 4.6), shows that not only were the apprentices drawn mainly from London by the end of the eighteenth century, but before the middle of that century they were drawn, to a substantial and increasing extent, from the families of handicraftsmen, especially weavers and other textile workers. The numbers drawn from farming families—nearly 40 per cent of the total in 1655–64—had become very small (only eighteen apprentices or 7·2 per cent) in the decade 1786–95. The weavers had, so to speak, turned in upon themselves. Weavers' families (chiefly London weavers) provided 272, or 35 per cent of all the apprentices bound at the Hall in the decade 1736–45 (of whom 75 were apprenticed to their own fathers); and 136, or nearly 55 per cent of those bound between 1786 and 1795, of whom no fewer than 59 were apprenticed to their fathers.

The Weavers' apprenticeship records throw a little light upon the question of the incidence of mortality among adult males in the seventeenth and eighteenth centuries. Of all the apprentices bound at Weavers' Hall in the decade 1655–64—a period which follows closely upon the Civil War but does not include the Great Plague of 1665—no fewer than 624 had already lost their fathers by death. The corresponding numbers for 1736–45 and 1786–95 are 252 and 45 respectively. Ratios are shown in the last column of Table 4.7.

These results indicate that in the mid-seventeenth century considerably more than one-half of the nation's children lost their fathers by death before attaining the age of fourteen plus. By the mid-eighteenth century, however, the fraction had fallen to one-third, and fifty years later it was little more than one-sixth.

A father's influence might be removed otherwise than by death from natural causes. Lack of work in London might impel a man to tramp into the provinces, or even to go abroad, for long spells. For example, John Durant was 'abroad in India, Bombardier', when his son was apprenticed to weaving. Unemployment and poverty, or the press-gang, not infrequently forced men to go to sea, and whether they

Table 4.6 *Occupations or status of fathers of London Weavers' apprentices*

	1655–64	1736–45	1786–95
Agriculture:			
Yeomen	185	6	2
Husbandmen	165	10	1
Farmers	—	9	1
Graziers, shepherds, gardeners, cow-keepers, dairymen	13	13	6
Labourers	41	31	8
Handicrafts:			
1 Textile (e.g. weavers, fullers, throwsters, dyers, clothworkers, tailors, etc.)	225	415	150
2 Other materials (e.g. leather, wood, metals, pottery, glass, paper)	157	121	32
Building crafts: (e.g. masons, bricklayers, plasterers, painters, tilers, brick and tile makers)	61	20	4
Food, drink and tobacco trades:	85	54	18
Merchants and general traders: (e.g. haberdashers, tallow-chandlers, higglers, woodmongers)	42	17	6
Transport: (e.g. mariners, porters, carriers, watermen, draymen, coachmen, ostlers)	32	40	8
Personal and professional services			
Clergy and Ministers of Religion	24	7	2
Physicians	3	—	—
Barber-surgeons	3	2	—
Barbers and Peruke-makers	4	7	4
Apothecaries	1	3	—
Musicians	3	—	—
Schoolmasters	1	—	—
Scriveners	1	1	—
Translators	1	—	—
Gentlemen:	49	22	7
	1,096	778	249

Note: Differences between these totals and those on p. 87 arise from occasional omissions, in the Weavers' records, of the place of origin or the father's occupation.

served in the Royal Navy or in merchant ships, the perils were very great, as many contemporary observers and writers realised. Defoe, for instance, writing of seamen in his *Essay upon Projects* (1697) said: 'They are fellows that bid Defiance to Terror, and maintain a constant War with the Elements; who . . . Trade in the very confines of Death, and are always posted within shot, as I may say, of the Grave: . . . always in view of their last moment.' The many memorials to dead mariners in churches like St George's, Ratcliff, serve to remind us that much of the wealth that moved up and down the Thames was purchased, at least in part, at the cost of 'East End courage and East End lives'. Of all the mariners mentioned in the London Weavers' apprenticeship records, four out of every five were dead.[65]

Table 4.7 *Mortality rate among adult males, 1655–1795*

Decade	a Apprentices bound	b Fathers dead	b as % of a
1655–64	1,100	624	57
1736–45	742	252	34
1786–95	264	45	17

Whatever may have been their social status and background, we know that many young recruits to the London weaving industry in the seventeenth century came great distances to learn the craft. Why was this? There is evidence that some had relatives or friends who were members of the London Weavers' Company. There is evidence too, that in many instances a father's sudden or early death made it imperative for the widow to place her older children in apprenticeships or service of some sort. London's size, both absolutely and relatively, and the variety of occupations carried on in the city, liberties and suburbs, meant that the chances of finding places for such lads and lasses were likely to appear better than in the provinces. It also seems probable that although the expansion of provincial industries in the seventeenth century was accelerating, it was insufficient to absorb all the likely lads seeking training and employment. No doubt a powerful attraction was not only London itself—glamorous as it must have seemed to young eyes looking from afar—but the prospects of acquiring the freedom of one of the famous London livery companies with citizenship of London to boot; a glittering prize indeed, for the most ambitious and successful of the young men might, in time, become rich enough to buy land—perhaps in their native counties—and even aspire to the rank and status of 'gentlemen'. But when dreams dissolve, reality remains.

Once the novelty of seeing (and smelling!) the great metropolis had passed, many young lads must have felt desperately homesick and not a little disillusioned with their employment. One apprentice hated it so much that he induced his mother to 'buy him out' of his indentures.[66] On another occasion, when a master weaver complained to the Court of Assistants that his apprentice 'did constantly go away from him to his mother', he was ordered to take the lad back and 'try him out more', and henceforth his mother was not to entertain him without the consent of his master.[67] One apprentice ran away ten times in three months, but eventually he repented, was forgiven and promised 'never to absent himself anymore'. Will Dixon's master complained that Will 'did constantly go from him; and the Court demanding of the apprentice the reason thereof, he said he had no mind to the trade but had a desire to go beyond sea'. When, shortly afterwards, Will Dixon again absconded, the Court gave up and formally discharged the master weaver from his duties under the indentures.[68] Another master whose apprentice had absented himself for seven weeks wished to have no more to do with the lad; but the Court, more lenient, thought that this would be 'extraordinary (i.e. excessive) correction' and ordered the master to take back his apprentice. Even longer absences, such as eighteen or twenty months, were often forgiven provided that in the end the total period of apprenticeship was served.[69] Many of the lads who absconded disappeared completely and their masters never saw or heard of them again; like Thomas Ambros who vanished after serving a year and a half, 'and his master desired he may be crossed out'. Worse still, in the spring of 1667 both of Mr Walker's apprentices went off together. The reason is unknown, and we are left wondering whether their wanderlust had anything to do with young men's springtime fancies, or had they good cause to take a thorough dislike to Weaver Walker and all his works? A month or two later, poor Mistress Jewell, Will Jewell's wife, told the Court of Assistants that 'her son is gone away and [she] thinks he is gone to sea'. This sort of thing was not unusual; many lads ran away to sea, while others went off and enlisted as soldiers.[70]

Eighteenth-century newspapers frequently carried advertisements describing the stature, complexion and dress of runaway apprentices, offering a reward to 'anybody giving intelligence', and adding a warning-cum-inducement such as, 'If any Person entertains the said Apprentice, be it at their Peril; but if he returns he shall be kindly received.' Many of the returned runaways were in a parlous state. Some had sold their clothes to buy food; some were brought in half-starved and in rags; others had consorted with gangs of 'loose, idle and disorderly boys' and had sustained cuts, bruises, and other injuries. Some of the prodigals, having learned a lesson, returned repentant and promised, before the Court of Assistants, to 'become good and faithful servants' to their masters.[71]

It is hardly necessary to point out that absconding was by no means the only way in which an apprentice could plague his master. He could be lazy, slow, and negligent at his work, or wilfully obtuse under instruction. In 1611 there is a record relating to two apprentices who had 'much abused their master' by neglecting their work, 'but had this day humbly submitted themselves unto their master and promised amendment from henceforth of all their former offence'. Another entry shows a master ribbon weaver complaining to the Court of Assistants that his apprentice was lazy and slow, and his output much less than it ought to have been. The Court agreed, but persuaded the master to give his apprentice another chance. The Court minutes sometimes paint a vivid picture in miniature, as when Randall Capper complained

> that his apprentice, Thomas Davies, hath oftentimes abused himself towards his Master, viz., in being drunk on Sunday was sevennight and on Saturday last and hath threatened to spoil both his Master and his fellow servants and refuseth to go to the church on the Sabbath Day and refuseth to serve his Master and to be enrolled according to the custom of London, which he confesseth to be true and hath upon his knees submitted himself to his Master and craved forgiveness for all his faults, which his Master hath freely forgiven.[72]

Weaving is essentially a sedentary occupation and it must have been hard indeed for normal, lively boys to settle down. Many of the tasks, such as quilling and winding, were monotonous, repetitive, devoid of interest, performed in a confined and ill-ventilated space. The working day—6 a.m. to 8 p.m.—was excessively long, even for adults. On the other hand, although Saturday was normally a full working day, it was customary to 'take home' finished work on that day; and many weavers, like other craftsmen, made it a practice to do no work on Mondays, calling the day 'Saint Monday'. As to Sundays, James I's 'Declaration concerning Lawful Sports' (1618) permitted certain 'lawful recreations' such as dancing, vaulting and archery after the end of Divine Service; but during the Commonwealth great austerity gradually descended upon both young and old on Sundays and weekdays alike.[73] In the *Humble Remonstrance of the Apprentices of the City of London* addressed to the Lord Mayor, Aldermen and Common Council in 1647, towards the end of the Civil War, the petitioners ask the City authorities to make a general rule binding upon all. 'Many there are that much wonder we should become such earnest suitors for a little Recreation, or as some please to style it, a Play-day. We answer, 'tis no wonder why they wonder for . . . some [apprentices] are mewed and pend up, and early and late at their labours, whilst othersome enjoy pleasure and great liberty.' Towards the end the document takes on a tone which is anything but 'humble'. After asking for one leisure day a month (excluding Sundays) the apprentices give notice 'that Tuesday, being the 13th of July is our first monthly-day, which (God willing) we are resolved to observe, and whatsoever mischief shall grow or arise from any opposition intended by you, or any, we . . . shall hold ourselves not guilty, but blameless'.

Although the services of apt and conscientious apprentices became progressively more valuable to their masters as the years passed, it was an offence for masters to pay wages to their apprentices at any stage or to allow them to work as journeymen for other masters.[74] In November 1666, shortly after the Great Fire,

> Complaint was . . . made agt. Will. Painter for keeping an appr. of his Brother George Painter 60 miles off not being turn'd [over] and giving him wages (as is affirmed). Ord[ered] that Geo. do take him home or otherwise turn him over, to wch. they agreed and Will. promised for the future to bee more conformable to the rules of this Compa.[75]

In 1692 a weaver was fined 20s. for employing his apprentice as a journeyman and paying him '2s. 6d. or other allowance weekly';[76] and in 1719 we have a complaint that 'the great boys' apprenticed in Canterbury 'were fetched to London before they were out of their time', presumably to be employed as junior journeymen.[77]

The services of senior apprentices or junior journeymen were, it seems, much sought after by master weavers as a form of efficient but cheap labour.[78] Thus, Peter Williams, just out of his apprenticeship, was admitted a journeyman by the Company and promptly hired by a master weaver for three years for 'meat and drink and all other necessaries during that term'.[79] Another lad, John Honey, was apprenticed to Thomas Ashby for the unusually long term of ten years and was assigned to serve with William Piggott for the first eight years. At the end of this period, in August 1618, he returned to Ashby for the final two years, 'in consideration whereof the said Ashby is to give unto his apprentice five pounds a year for his last two years service to be paid weekly, viz., 2s. a week and [he] to be used honestly as a servant should be'.[80] Another apprentice just 'out of his time' was hired for two years at a wage of 1s. 4d. a week, 'and is to have at once, a doublet, a pair of new breeches and a shirt'.[81] Miserly or impecunious or spiteful masters sometimes attempted to keep their apprentices beyond their legal term, as did William Smith who refused to take the necessary steps to make his erstwhile apprentice, John Cozens, free, although he had 'been out of his apprenticeship this four years past'. When the young man secured employment as a journeyman, his new master was fined 3s. 4d. for 'setting him on work, not being free'; but considering the circumstances the Court of Assistants reduced the fine to 1s. 6d. paid into the poor's box.[82]

The sources of cheap labour were not limited to the legally bound apprentices and junior journeymen. The Weavers' records reveal many bitter complaints, emanating usually from the Commonalty, about the admittance of strangers and foreigners (some of whom had never 'served for the Trade'), who 'daily set to work as journeymen, youths of 15, 16 or 18 years of age that come from beyond the Seas,' and also teach 'Boys by the week [so as] to have their work for a time, their Parents or friends finding them diet, apparel and lodging during their learning, which Boys within a year or two become journeymen, working for small wages', whereas members of the Company 'must be 24 years of age before they can be made free of this City to work for wages'. Since the majority of the strangers and foreigners 'dwell in chambers and odd corners, being divers families in one house, having their work wrought by the youths', their expenses are so low that they can easily undersell the legitimate London weavers and 'ingross all the work to themselves and eat the bread out of the mouths of His Majesty's natives', while at the same time they 'fill the City and Kingdom with multitudes of insufficient artificers and handycrafts-[men] . . . who use and exercise a trade before they can master the same'. Moreover, the properly bound and enrolled apprentices, with the natural impatience of youth, resented having to serve seven years or more, became extremely unsettled, and either set up unlawfully to work for themselves in 'private chambers' or else went off to work for 'foreigners' who set up in places remote from London.[83] In 1640 one of the Burgesses of the City was informed by the Weavers that 'there are this day in divers parts of the Realm many persons that have been bound apprentices, who within a short time after have unlawfully departed from their master's service and in remote places set up and used the trade of weaving as masters and journeymen unknown to their said Masters.'[84]

Linked, no doubt, with the prohibition of wage-earning by apprentices was the strict ban on marriage during apprenticeship. Current opinion among sober people on 'over-hasty marriages and over-soon setting up of households by young folk'[85] was voiced by Philip Stubbes in his *Anatomie of Abuses* in 1583, when he deplored the 'marrying of Saucy Boys' under twenty years of age 'without any respect how they may live together with sufficient maintenance for their callings and estate . . .'; often indeed, 'they live as beggars all their life', which 'filleth the land with such store of poor people'.[86] The Weavers' Company shared these views and usually showed little sympathy for weavers' apprentices who rushed into matrimony; but the City authorities seem to have been rather more lenient. When William Kinman, a weaver's apprentice, got married 'a short space' before the end of his time, the Company refused to grant him his freedom. He then appealed to the Lord Mayor and Aldermen who ordered the Weavers to admit him by redemption, on payment to the City of the usual fee of 46s. 8d. The Company accepted this ruling; Kinman was 'lovingly received' and 'he being poor gave 5s.' for his admission. On another occasion 'Rob. Partridge, apprentice to Will. Shippie, did come before the Court to take up his freedom but was put by because he had married in his time'. When Partridge renewed his application a fortnight later, his case was referred to the City Chamberlain who ruled that Partridge should be made free on payment of 46s. 8d. to the City's use; whereupon 'the said Robert Partridge was loving received and made free of this Company. Item: he gave in lieu of a spoon, 6s.'[87] Towards the end of 1666 Lawrence Heath, who had been turned away by his master because he had married after he had served only four-and-a-half years of his apprenticeship, was found to be working (unlawfully) with John Briggs at Swan Yard in Shoreditch.[88] An even more serious infringement came to light three months later when Will Smith, an apprentice who had served only three years, was found to be working with his wife for Thomas Bussett, a member of the Weavers' Company. The Court of Assistants 'ordered that Bussett dispose of him and wife, which he promised', and fined Bussett 16s. 8d. for conniving at the offence.[89]

The Weavers' Company always tried to use its powers to control the number and conduct of weavers' apprentices, to protect them from fraud and ill-usage, and to promote their material, moral and spiritual welfare. Hence its continual insistence that all apprentices to weaving in London ought to be 'presented' and bound at Weavers' Hall,[90] and not at Scriveners' offices nor even before justices of the peace; for such 'irregular' bindings, although quite legal, seriously weakened the Company's grasp upon the whole complicated apprenticeship situation on the London weaving trade. Apprentices who had not been presented and bound at the Hall were not penalised, but masters free of the Company were fined sums ranging from five to twenty shillings because they ought to have known better.[91] In 1632 the Company's Officers complained to the Lord Mayor that 'such as are refused ... at the Hall of the Company do presently fly to other Companies and are received; and to Justices of Peace and Scriveners and before them are bound ... [amounting] to an exceeding great number'.[92] Such practices prevented the emergence of any neat pattern of organisation and administration, and the confusion was increased by the wellnigh unshakeable custom of the City under which 'many freemen carried on a trade which had neither any relation to the craft in which they had served their time nor any connection with the trade of the company of which they were members'.[93] About 1624–5 the Commonalty of the Weavers' Company were alarmed and indignant because three or four men free of other Companies but plying the weaving craft had taken, in less than seven years, no fewer than thirty-seven apprentices; 'and one of their Clerks did say that if one man did bring twenty apprentices on a day to be bound, he would bind them all, by reason that it was for his profit'. No wonder that there was 'a mixture of weavers in most Companies of London'.[94]

The Weavers, like a number of other livery companies, made attempts from time to time to check the steady slide towards a completely chaotic and unmanageable state of affairs. In 1629 they submitted to the Lord Mayor and Aldermen a request to have the apprentices of freemen of other Companies using the art of weaving bound at Weavers' Hall and 'thereby at the end of their said terms may be made free of the Company of Weavers'. The petition was referred to a committee and nothing more seems to have been done.[95] During the Commonwealth the Weavers again raised the matter in a petition to the Committee of Common Council for Trade asking that all persons using the craft of weaving, but free of other Companies, should be required to bind their apprentices to the Company whose trade they use and 'to be regulated in their trade by the ordinances of the said Company according to an Act of Common Council made for the companies of Glasiers and Painter-Stainers *mutatis mutandis*'.[96] At about the same time the Glovers' Company succeeded in obtaining from the City the right to have *all* apprentices to glove-making bound at Glovers' Hall 'upon pain of a fine of £20';[97] and the Carpenters, Joiners, Bricklayers, Feltmakers, and Hatbandmakers joined in asking for a regulation 'enjoyning all persons using their respective trades to present, bind and make free all their apprentices at their respective companies, and to be subject to the search and government of that Company whose trade they use . . .'.[98] So far as the Weavers were concerned, the City attempted to reach a compromise by ordaining in 1658 that everybody using the art and trade of weaving should be subject to the 'search and survey 'of the Weavers' Officers and to the Weavers' ordinances 'touching the exercising of the said trade', and that everybody free of another Company who engaged in weaving must henceforth 'present' every new apprentice to be bound by indenture to one of the Bailiffs, Wardens or Assistants of the Weavers' Company and be immediately turned over to the master presenting him.[99]

Unwin, in his excellent study of industrial organisation in the sixteenth and seventeenth centuries, explained the importance and some of the difficulties of limiting the numbers of apprentices.

The question as to the number of apprentices was always one

of crucial importance in the domestic industries. As a member
of his class the small master was in favour of limitation, and
the interests of the journeyman ran strongly in the same
direction. But there was always a tendency among the more
prosperous and pushing masters, partly arising from a desire to
extend their business and partly from a wish to secure cheap
labour, to keep more than the permitted number of apprentices,
and even to employ boys who had not been bound. When the
small masters of any trade were strongly organised, the
[limitation] rule . . . was usually enforced. But where the final
authority lay in the hands of the trading class, this restriction
. . . was often ignored by the larger employers.[100]

The Weavers' Company did what it could to check abuses connected
with the numbers and enrolment of apprentices, but this was always
an uphill struggle, for the Company had to try to cope not only with
native weavers, i.e. 'denizens', but with 'foreigners' from the provinces and 'strangers' from the Continent. An example of trouble with
a recalcitrant member occurs in August 1612, when Luke Littlewood
was fined 40s. for keeping three apprentices contrary to the Ordinances. When he refused to pay he was committed to the Compter
and ordered to place his third apprentice with another master before
the next Court Day. Two months later he incurred an additional fine
of 10s. for keeping John Littlewood unbound and unpresented contrary to the Ordinances.[101] Another master weaver when cornered
confessed to the Court that he was employing one Griffin, not
admitted, and his boy, and that he had four apprentices himself. He
was fined 20s. A weaver who asked permission to take his own son as
an apprentice additional to his full complement was told to keep his
son at school until one of his apprentices completed his time. The
Court was, however, lenient in certain circumstances. Thus when
Gabriel Stone was fined 20s. for having more looms and apprentices
than the Ordinances allowed, he pleaded in extenuation that 'some of
them came by reason of the marriage of his wife, and that two are
almost out of their time, and some of them sick'. The Court reduced
the fine to seven shillings.[102]

Normally a master was bound not only to teach his apprentice but
to supply him with new clothing and other necessaries during the
course of his period of service and at the end; and there was a clause
in the standard form of indentures which was one of the 'ancient
covenants'. Clerks of London livery companies were expressly forbidden by the City to alter such indentures 'by Razeing out the word
Apparel or any other Covenant therein contained'. In the exceptional
cases where the apprentice's parents or friends undertook to provide
clothing, a separate agreement had to be made between the parties.

No apprentice could be enrolled or turned over by the City Chamberlain unless this rule was observed.[103] The Weavers' Company took very seriously its duty to enforce such clauses. Thus, in June 1617, a master was ordered to make his apprentice free and give him 'a new cloak and a pair of new stockings'; another was ordered to provide his apprentice with a new suit 'within this three weeks', and Widow Holland was peremptorily told to give her apprentice a new suit 'between this day and Sunday next or else the apprentice shall be placed elsewhere'.[104] Three months later, one master was ordered to provide 'some better apparel' for his apprentice, while another, 'having taken one Jenkin Phillips into his service hath sent the boy away and keepeth his clothes, viz., a jerkin, 2 shirts, 2 bandes, one pair of freeze [sic] breeches and 3s. in money', was ordered by the Court of Assistants to hand over the clothes and money to the Company's Beadle. An apprentice whose master had died was turned over to another who was ordered to provide a new suit immediately and, at the end of the apprentice's term, 'double apparel and a new cloak of the value of 20s. or in money 20s.'[105] 'Want of hose and shoes' is a frequent complaint.

The provision of proper bedding was another aspect of welfare upon which the Company kept an eye. For example, when two apprentices complained 'of their bad usages in their lodgings having by their reports lain in one pair of sheets three months or more', the Court of Assistants ordered the master to provide clean sheets every month, otherwise the apprentices would be taken from him.[106] This was substantially in line with the practice at Bridewell, where the apprentices had clean shirts once a week and clean sheets at least once a month.[107] Some complaints, of course, proved frivolous upon investigation, as when Will Dinsdale's apprentice 'did confess before the Court that he wanted for nothing and that his Master did use him as well as any servant in his house'.[108]

The Court of Assistants usually dealt with apprentices' more serious illnesses or injuries by sending them to their homes until they were fit to resume their apprenticeships. Sometimes, however, an apprentice's disability made his training impossible and he was formally discharged from his indentures. In one case, lameness led to a discharge, presumably because the lad could not properly operate the treadles of the loom. Defective sight resulting in the discharge of an apprentice is recorded as follows:

11th June 1694. Prentice discharged. Upon complaint of Ralph Parkinson the apprentice to Thomas Wild, who was bound under 14 years of age and dark sighted and not capable of taking his Trade, being by both sides referred to this Court, it is ordered that each other be discharged from the said Indentures and that the

Master do forthwith return the Boy and his clothes to his father again.[109]

Masters were deemed to be responsible, both as individuals and as members of their gild or company, not only for physical care, but also for the moral and spiritual welfare of their apprentices. By way of aid to both masters and apprentices the Weavers' Company presented to every apprentice bound and enrolled at Weavers' Hall a printed booklet containing 'affectionate advice' on conduct. In Queen Anne's reign, and perhaps earlier, this was called the *Monitor*, and it is on record that in August 1711 the Court of Assistants agreed that 'the Monitor, a paper delivered to the Apprentices, be reprinted at the Company's charge and be delivered to each apprentice'.[110] Early in the nineteenth century it appears that the *Monitor* had, apparently, given place to a small book of 56 pages entitled *Affectionate Advice to Apprentices on their being bound, presented by the Bailiffs, Wardens and Assistants of the Worshipful Company of Weavers.*[111]

The *Advice* begins with an explanation of the necessity for division of labour in human communities and the advantages to boys and youths of taking 'the most proper path' and entering a regular apprenticeship whereby 'the mind becomes fixed to one pursuit' and there is sufficient time to gain a habit of steadiness and a 'full knowledge of the business chosen for him'. The apprentice is enjoined to be modest, civil, cheerful, clean and, above all, obedient to his master 'in all honest things'.[112] When under instruction the apprentice should never appear unthankful or say rudely that he knew it before. He must always be diligent, for he cannot expect kindness from his master unless he is 'constantly employed' in his service. Much emphasis is laid upon strict honesty, truthfulness, frugality and thrift, and a warning is given that neglect to cultivate these virtues coupled with a foolish propensity for idle talk, negligence and inattention will result in loss of good opportunities in the trade, loss of character and friends, and a descent into poverty 'and sometimes into prison'. This frightful fate might overtake an apprentice even more rapidly if he kept bad company whether among his fellow workers or otherwise, for it could—and probably would—lead to gambling and drunkenness. 'Only three-pence a day unnecessarily spent in beer and liquor amounts in the year to £4. 11s. 3d. . . . a sum that would make a working man always respectable in his apparel and independent in his mind.' The apprentice is also warned against play-houses and public gardens: 'theatrical exhibitions have always been considered by the religious part of society as very prejudicial to men's moral habits', while 'public gardens are the constant resort of the profligate of both sexes, and young men of virtue and character should never spend their evenings in them', wasting their time and money, keeping late hours and bad company, and endangering their health and morals—even their souls. On the proper use of leisure time the advice given is frank and full. 'As you will not have much time to call your own, you should put what you have to a good use'; in short, religion and reading. Sunday is for public worship, not for joining parties or 'schemes of pleasure' with the irreligious. On the other six days, the apprentice is told, 'rising early will give you an opportunity to read a few verses or a chapter of your Testament, or of the book of Proverbs, or the Psalms, before you address yourself to God in your morning prayer'.[113] At the other end of the day, 'after your work and before bed-time, if your business allow it, ... read some useful and instructive books ... about serious things'.

When, for any reason, an apprentice had to be 'turned over' to a new master the transaction needed to be approved and recorded by the Court of Assistants. Such a situation could arise when a master retired or died; or when he was found with too many apprentices and was ordered by the Company to reduce the number; or when a master absconded, or went overseas permanently or for an indefinite period; or when both parties to the indenture agreed to the transfer. If the widow of a deceased master decided to exercise her right to continue in the trade, her consent was necessary before her late husband's apprentices could be turned over, for she was entitled to retain them herself if she so wished.[114] In midsummer 1653 the Court was told of a sad case in which a master weaver, Robert Whitney, 'and his wife were both dead, and had left three apprentices masterless'.[115] Occasionally, masters who had immigrated to England from the Continent decided to return to their native lands, and usually their apprentices had to find new masters.[116] Although apprentices normally had only one master during apprenticeship, or two at most, a few had very broken periods of service, like William Richardson, a London weaver's son, who in less than fourteen months was 'apprenticed to Thomas Hall and after his death assigned to Benjamin Proctor and afterwards by him to Will Stone and now [22 July 1650] assigned over to Geo. Fripp, citizen and weaver of London to serve out the remainder of his time from 3rd June 1649'.[117]

The Company had also to cope with various forms of fraud both within its own ranks and outside, as when men falsely holding themselves out as masters free of the Weavers' Company took apprentices and substantial premiums although in fact they had no right to the trade. Forged indentures were sometimes presented in attempts to gain the freedom of the Company and the City.[118] The most persistent and troublesome form of sharp practice, however, was the 'deceitful collusion' between freemen and non-freemen whereby apprentices were formally bound to the former, quickly turned over to the latter, to be employed, as often as not, on all sorts of odd jobs and then fraudulently certified by the freeman, after seven or eight years, as having served a genuine legal apprenticeship. The deceit was aggravated in the eyes of honest men when the so-called apprentices were turned over to foreigners and strangers, the main source of much unfair competition. Early in Charles I's reign, 'The humble Petition of the generality of the Freemen of the Company of Weavers' to the Lord Mayor and Aldermen 'concerning binding and turning over Apprentices to Foreigners and Strangers' states that despite an Order of 3 July 1623 which repealed the 'toleration of turning over apprentices to foreigners', many youths who had not served a proper apprenticeship were still able to become freemen of the City by reason of deceitful collusion between foreigners or strangers and certain freemen, including (it was alleged) some members of the Weavers' Company.[119] Moreover, the parallel practice of turning over apprentices to members of other companies was nearly as objectionable, for 'it is an impossible thing that ever the Masters of the [Weavers'] Company or any of the Sixteen men [i.e. the Yeomanry] . . . should truly know whether any Apprentices so turned over have truly served'. Such practices, it was said, attracted many people, both English and aliens, to London and its Liberties and suburbs, including Southwark, causing increase of 'Inmates' [i.e. lodgers,] the enhancement of the prices of victuals, fuel and other commodities, and a great number of poor in all the parishes adjacent to the City. Moreover, apprentices 'assigned over to foreigners and Strangers' were not kept under proper discipline, 'to the evil example of the Apprentices of Freemen'. Many were allowed 'money or part of their earnings, which no Freeman may do by his oath, and the apprentices of Freemen murmur at their Masters that they have not the like, and repine at their long service, knowing that many of those [other] apprentices . . . have liberty to work as Journeymen or else be at their own pleasures'.[120]

Three years later, in another petition to the Lord Mayor, the Commonalty of the Weavers' Company renewed their complaint against the widespread practice whereby boys and youths were formally apprenticed to freemen and foreigners, 'and afterwards by the freemen reporting to Mr. Chamberlain upon their oaths that these youths (as their own apprentices) have done them good service, when the Reporter lent but his name . . .'. Moreover, this evil example was followed by 'divers Weavers of other Companies and some that are not weavers by trade, as armourers, clothworkers, carmen and others . . . and [this] hath caused a mixture of weavers in most Companies of London'. Thus it had come about that such large numbers of strangers and foreign weavers were living in London and the suburbs, and competition for employment was so intense that many weavers free of the City have become porters, water-bearers, labourers and sellers of fish, fruit, salt, small coals, 'and such servile labour; and others go for soldiers leaving their wives and children in great distress, and divers are enforced through extreme poverty to take relief of the several parishes where they dwell, and others for want of employment take lewd courses, as theft and such like'. The Commonalty asked that the weavers of London may be 'reduced under one government', including all men free of other Companies but using the trade of weaving. 'Divers of the Livery and Yeomanry' of the Weavers' Company supported the Commonalty, citing especially John Renthall, one of the Assistants, as a persistent offender who 'hath these thirty years or thereabout bound divers Boys as to serve with himself and immediately assigns over or sells the terms in the Indentures . . . to Strangers and Foreigners'. The Company's Beadle, also, was accused of having bound twenty apprentices to himself during the past seven years 'and disposed of them in manner aforesaid, not keeping one of them himself'. Many other freemen, it was alleged, were guilty of such abuses, notwithstanding all orders to the contrary.[121] In October 1633 the Lord Mayor set up a committee of Aldermen to investigate and consider the situation, but apparently nothing effective was done, for within four or five years we hear the old familiar complaints against the fraudulent turning over of apprentices by certain freemen for their own 'advantage and lucre'.[122]

There were, of course, good and bad masters, just as there were good and bad apprentices: in fact all shades of conduct are revealed on both sides, from exemplary to utterly base. It was an age of heavy drinking, all day and every day, for the ale-houses and taverns were open at all hours. Nor was it necessary to 'come and get it', for pot-boys kept private houses and workshops continually supplied, so that drinking habits and drunkenness were common features not only of leisure time, but of everyday life and work. Undoubtedly gambling, the club, the tavern and the ale-house were largely responsible for bad masters and bad apprentices.[123] Maitland, writing in the middle of the eighteenth century, wished that a 'good Law' could be passed 'to restrain the destructive Practices of our modern Apprentices', such as 'frequenting of Tavern-Clubs and Playhouses'.[124]

The degrees of ill-treatment of apprentices ranged from verbal abuse and 'nagging'—sometimes by the master's wife—to physical violence which, in certain instances, ended in manslaughter and even murder. Since the apprentice was a member of his master's household he could easily become enmeshed in domestic discords and tensions. The Court of Assistants' order 'that John Shippie . . . do go home with his master and that his mistress shall not abuse him'[125] calls for no comment. The death of a master and the re-marriage of his widow could upset the applecart, as it did when Thomas Hitchman, Master

Weaver, died, and his widow married William Beckford; for Hitchman's apprentice, James Babes, took a strong dislike to Beckford and asked to be turned over. The Court, after inquiry, ordered the apprentice 'to serve the said Mr. Beckford and if that he wanteth either meat and drink or apparel, upon his complaint to the Court they will take care that he shall be provided for'.[126] Various other crises could arise, such as a master's imprisonment, e.g. for debt, or his 'derangement of mind', or his sudden disappearance. In 1693 Daniel Haydon asked to be made free, his application being supported by 'report of John Hall and a Note from his Master now in prison'.[127] When it was reported to the Court that Henry Fisher 'is gone away and hath left [his] apprentice at his own liberty', another master was promptly found for the lad.[128] Another apprentice, Anthony Browne, serving with a master named Cardwell, was turned over to James Mapson, weaver, 'ye said Cardwell being run away'.[129] That the absconding master weavers were not always running away from their wives is proved by such entries as: '28th October 1672. John Tooley, apprenticed to Jacob Pulley, foreign weaver, 8 years from 19th October 1668, ye Mr. and Mrs. going away and leaving the apprentice destitute [he] is turned over to John Twally, foreign weaver.'[130] When in midwinter 1616 Robert Anthonie turned his apprentice out of doors, the Court angrily ordered Anthonie to 'take home his apprentice and use him as an apprentice ought to be used, . . . give him all such necessaries as belongeth unto an Apprentice and . . . pardon him for all his offences heretofore committed against him, without any punishment'.[131]

'Extraordinary' or 'unreasonable' correction of an apprentice usually aroused the Court's wrath and might result in the victim's transfer to another master and the return of the premium, if any. Thus, in 1615, Richard Smith's master was ordered to 'use him well from henceforth or else upon the next misusage he shall be taken from him'. Beating an apprentice 'with a faggot stick' or some similar 'weapon' was held to be 'extraordinary correction' and when the Court was convinced that an apprentice had been 'much abused' in this or other ways, it would order the cancellation of the indenture and the provision of proper apparel for the released apprentice at the master's expense.[132] An accusation of severe maltreatment could bring a master before the magistrates of the City or Middlesex and might result in criminal proceedings. The City of London Repertories and the Middlesex Sessions Records furnish particulars of many cases like that of John Plummer, whose master, John Gilbert, a Stepney framework knitter, had horse-whipped him and severely bruised his arms and shoulders with the butt end of the whip, and had not provided sufficient clothing: 'his shoes have great holes through the soles . . . whereby his health is much endangered'. In the same year

(1736) there was an even more serious case in which James Durant, a ribbon weaver, was tried for the murder of his apprentice, a small boy aged thirteen or fourteen, whom he had brutally beaten with a mop-stick. He was, however, acquitted.[133]

By no means all the lads apprenticed to weaving remained in that occupation: in fact, quite apart from death, disability and absconding, the 'wastage' was considerable. Then, as now, many a youth had to 'taste and see' before he could settle into any particular craft or trade. In 1616 a weaver's apprentice decided that he would rather be a gardener[134] and was released from his original indenture so that he could take service with a gardener at Norton Folgate, who agreed to pay 20s. to the former master. Sometimes the change was in the reverse direction, as when a tallow-chandler's apprentice was transferred to a weaver and was in due course made free of the Weavers' Company.[135] In the *Affectionate Advice* the apprentice is bidden to take comfort from the fact that as every day passes his apprenticeship draws towards its end, 'when he may adopt another trade, or at any rate be his own master'.[136]

Circumstances or happenings which made it necessary to turn over an apprentice to a new master often provided a suitable chance to change his trade. If the new master was in a kindred craft, such as framework (stocking) knitting the break in training was probably not serious, but the same can scarcely be said when the transfer was to a different type of craft, such as one of the wood or metal trades. Yet changes of this sort were often made. Many weavers' apprentices seem to have been attracted by the watchmaking industry in and around Clerkenwell; like Lawrence van der Meulen who was apprenticed to weaving in 1750, turned over after two-and-a-half years to a haberdasher and is described in the records in 1759 as a watchmaker; or Samuel Hodges, turned over after three years from a weaver to a clothworker and entered as a watchmaker when he came to be made free of the Weavers' Company. Another lad went from a weaver to a loriner and eventually became a butcher; while a third left weaving to train as a sword cutler.[137] Thomas Thorogood, who had gone in for carving, was made free of the Weavers' Company by servitude in 1760 despite his master's refusal to appear in his support, 'sending an Excuse that he did not think him worthy of his trouble to attend about'.[138] John Oxley, who was apprenticed to a weaver in 1773, turned over to a leatherseller in 1775 and had become a hatmaker by 1780. Two apprentices to weaving, bound in 1747 and 1749, forsook the craft and, in 1756, one was landlord of the Three Pigeons at Haggerston, and the other was a vintner at the Three Tuns tavern in Spitalfields.[139]

During the eighteenth century there was a distinct tendency for some of the weavers' apprentices to move over to the mercantile side of the textile industry, becoming haberdashers, mercers, silk brokers, lacemen, hosiers and yarn dealers.[140] Thus 'Peter Ponsett living in Widegate Alley, weaver, but going to remove into Elder Street, Norton Folgate, and exercise the Business of a Broker . . . is made free by Servitude'.[141] Two or three enterprising young men went into tea broking between 1774 and 1784, like Charles Triquet junior, who was apprenticed to weaving in 1768, turned over to a grocer four years later, and had become a tea broker before the end of 1775.[142] Several former weavers' apprentices became jewellers and others spectacle-makers. James Nuntley, a weaver's apprentice in 1746, was in business as a barber and peruke-maker fifteen years later, and James Landy, apprenticed to weaving in 1766, had gone into partnership with a 'chymist' before 1773. Nevertheless he was made free of the Weavers' Company without demur. Thomas Jones's son left weaving to take Holy Orders, and another young man, at first apprenticed to his father, a weaver, eventually became a surgeon. James Andrews, who was apprenticed to weaving in 1752, later joined the Royal Navy and was made free of the Weavers' Company in 1760 while serving as a midshipman in H.M.S. *Juno*. Nor must we forget John Hutton, apprenticed to weaving in 1748, who had acquired the status of 'gentleman' twelve years later.[143]

Of course, while some were going up in the world, others were going down, working as watermen, porters, labourers and the like; though probably Will Rogers, who forsook weaving to become a waiter in a coffee-house, did tolerably well out of his tips and perquisites. All in all it appears that between one-third and one-half of those admitted to the Weavers' Company by servitude in the eighteenth century were no longer working as weavers when they took their freedom.

NOTES

1 These were the draw-boys employed by the brocade weavers.
2 *The Just Complaints of the Poor Weavers* (1719), quoted in George, *London*, p. 181. cf. Nicholas Barbon, *Apology for the Builder* (1685), p. 18.
3 MS. 4655/1, f.54.
4 MS. 4655/16, f.100b.
5 G. Unwin, *Studies in Economic History* (1927), p. 96.
6 George, *London*, pp. 275–6.
7 Campbell, *Tradesman*, p. 22.
8 MS. 4655/1 f.93; MS. 4655A, f.38.
9 MS. 4655/9, ff.56b, 72.
10 MS. 4657B. Sometimes the names given to these infants reflected the name of the parish in which they were found; e.g. Lawrence Aldermanbury and Stephen Coleman.
11 MS. 4655/15, f.300.
12 George, *London*, p. 237.

13 According to H. A. Harben's *Dictionary of London* (1918), this distinctive costume was abolished in 1755.

14 MS. 4655/1, f.78; E. Hatton, *A New View of London* (1708), p. 734.

15 MS. 4661/27, opp. f.1. The house-of-correction part of Bridewell, reconstructed after the Great Fire and completed in 1676, included 'a public whipping room, draped in black and having a balustraded public gallery . . . and during the seventeenth and eighteenth centuries the public was admitted to watch the flagellation as one of the more sophisticated London delights' (E. de Maré, *London's Riverside* (1958), pp. 81–2).

16 Quarrell and Maré (eds), *London in 1710* (1934), pp. 54–5.

17 E. G. O'Donoghue, *Bridewell Hospital* (1923), I, Chap. XVIII; II, pp. 69–71, 168.

18 George, *London*, p. 253.

19 Hatton, op. cit., p. 734.

20 MS. 4655A; see also MS. 4655/2, f.51: e.g. thirteen Bridewell apprentices were made free of the Weavers' Company in the three years 1703–6, and a century later the numbers were nearly double; see MS. 4656/4, *passim*; MS. 4655/19, *passim*.

21 MS. 4655/2, f.129.

22 MS. 4655/5, f.10; see also f.41b.

23 MS. 4655/16, f.47; see also f.64b.

24 5 Eliz. c. 4; sometimes referred to as the Statute of Apprentices.

25 MS. 4655/1, f.20.

26 MS. 4655/1, f.88.

27 MS. 4655/1, f.94. 'Double apparel' meant one suit for holy days and one for working days fit for a journeyman weaver.

28 MS. 4655/16, ff.1b, 2, 63.

29 MS. 4648/6 and MS. 4648/6A.

30 In 1742 Philip Jackson, Master Weaver, was summoned for having an apprentice not bound at Weavers' Hall. He said he had lately taken an apprentice 'put out by Charity from the French Church and bound by their Agent', but the boy was only thirteen years nine months of age. As soon as he reached fourteen he would be properly bound at Weavers' Hall; the matter was, therefore, deferred for three months (MS. 4655/15, f.150).

31 MS. 4655/17, f.447.

32 This fits with Defoe's statement that there were 'few families of the lower gentry, that is to say, from six or seven hundred a year downwards, but they are in debt and in necessitous circumstances, and a great many of the greater estates also' (*The Complete English Tradesman* (1725)).

33 MS. 4655/16, f.65.

34 *The Just Complaints of the Poor Weavers* (1719).

35 This is a gross exaggeration: the Weavers' Company records from 1730 to 1795 show a ratio of $1:2\frac{1}{2}$, not $1:50$.

36 MS. 4655/17, f.98.

37 MS. 4655/14, ff.18, 54.

38 MS. 4655/15, f.136.

39 MS. 4655/15, f.137b.

40 Jane, daughter of Rev. John Stuart of Chichester, Sussex.

41 Probably the widow of Isaac Oake.

42 MS. 4655/16, ff.42, 62, 68, 92, 195b.

43 MS. 4655/17, f.105b.

44 'Were above one in ten of the Men now House-keepers in London, born there?' asked John Bellers, the merchant, Quaker, philanthropist and pioneer of social reform, in 1696. See *Proposals for Raising a College of Industry of all Useful Trades and Husbandry*, p. 1.

45 C. P. Moritz, *A Journey to England*, ed. P. E. Matheson (1924); T. S. Willan, *The English Coasting Trade, 1600–1750* (1938), pp. 36, 192. John Taylor's *Carriers Cosmographie* (1637) mentions the points of arrival and departure of ships, barques, hoys and passage boats sailing along the East Coast.

46 Defoe, *A Tour of Gt. Britain* (1724).

47 MS. 4655/2, f.120. Perhaps Richard Homes bribed 'he that brought him [the lad]' to London.

48 The records of Goldsmiths', Grocers' and Fishmongers' Companies show the same trend: see W. F. Kahl's study of apprenticeship in London between 1690 and 1750, in *The Guildhall Miscellany*, no. 7, August 1956.

49 J. U. Nef, article in *Economic History Review*, V, no. 1, p. 22.

50 H. Hamilton, *The English Brass and Copper Industries* (1926), Chap. 5; G. C. Allen, *Industrial Development of Birmingham and the Black Country* (1929), Chap. 2.

51 F. W. Gibbs, *Joseph Priestley* (1965), p. 1; A. Briggs, *Victorian Cities* (1963), p. 139.

52 F. W. Gibbs, op. cit., p. 17; S. J. Chapman, *The Lancashire Cotton Industry* (1904), Chap. 1.

53 A. Briggs, op. cit., p. 85; Deane and Cole, op. cit., p. 111.

54 For example, two sons of a deceased gentleman of Wimbledon in Surrey were apprenticed to weaving on the same day (24 March 1656), one for nine years and the other for seven years (MS. 4657B).

55 P. F. Gaye, *John Gay* (1938), pp. 21–2.

56 *The Complete English Tradesman* (1725).

57 G. D. Ramsay, *Wiltshire Woollen Industry* (1943), p. 46. The Queen forbade the inferior gentry to assume the title 'Esquire'.

58 MS. 4655/3, f.145.

59 Campbell, *English Yeoman*, p. 60.

60 H. Chettle and J. Day, *The Blind Beggar of Bednal Green* (Louvain, 1902), Act II.

61 A. L. Rowse, *The England of Elizabeth* (1951), II, pp. 231, 247; G. E. Fussell (ed.), *Robert Loder's Farm Accounts, 1610–1620* (R. Hist. Soc., Camden Third Ser., LIII, 1936). Campbell, *English Yeoman*, pp. 348, 359–60.

62 A. L. Rowse, *England of Elizabeth*, pp. 427–31, 522; and *Shakespeare* (1963), pp. 11–12.

63 D. Marshall, *English People in the 18th Century* (1956), p. 53.

64 Campbell, *Tradesman*, p. 93. Ridottoes were entertainments consisting of singing and dancing, especially masked balls.

65 MS. 4655/16, ff.1b, 261b. Millicent Rose, *The East End of London* (1951), p. 62.

66 MS. 4655/1, 15 December 1612.

67 MS. 4655/2, f.21, 20 June 1653.

68 MS. 4655/1, f.103; MS. 4655/2, ff.58, 72, 93.

69 MS. 4655/2, ff.20–1, 28; MS. 4655/4, ff.39, 59b, 71b.

70 Repertories 91, f.111.

71 MS. 4655/1, ff.21, 92.

72 MS. 4655/1, ff.12, 65; MS. 4655/4, f.74. Max Beloff has written of two Stationer's apprentices who (c. 1703–5) sometimes went out without their master's permission; who returned at one a.m. after visiting an 'aunt' (!), raided the larder and cellar when the stationer and his wife had retired for the night, and regaled themselves royally on their master's beef-steak and Rhenish wine ('A London Apprentice's Notebook' in *History*, vol. 27 (June 1942), p. 40).

73 On May Day 1654 it was reported that 'much sin (was) committed by wicked meetings with fiddlers, drunkenness, ribaldry, and the like; great resort came to Hyde Park . . . but, most shameful, powdered-hair men, and painted and spotted women' (R. B. Morgan, *Readings in English Social History* (1923), p. 383).

74 MS. 4655/1, f.13; MS. 4655/2, ff.112, 135 (1654).

75 MS. 4655/4, 27 November 1666.

76 MS. 4655/10, f.7b.

77 *Journal of the Commissioners for Trade and Plantations, 1719*, p. 119.

78 MS. 4655/1, ff.24, 94.

79 MS. 4655/1, f.24.

80 MS. 4655/1, f.78.

81 MS. 4655/1, f.71.

82 MS. 4655/1, ff.61, 63.

83 MS. 4647, ff.257–8, 309–12, 322.

84 MS. 4647, ff.585–6.

85 O. J. Dunlop and R. D. Denman, *English Apprenticeship and Child Labour* (N.Y., 1912), pp. 69–70.

86 Quoted in Brett-James, *London*, p. 101.

87 MS. 4655/2, ff.87, 169 (1654–5).

88 MS. 4655/4, 27 November 1666.

89 MS. 4655/4, February 1667.

90 See, e.g., MS. 4655/1, f.14.

91 MSS. 4655/3, f.54b; 4655/4, February 1667; 4655/11, f.217; Repertories 99, f.52.

92 MS. 4647, f.220.

93 W. F. Kahl, 'Apprenticeship and the Freedom of the London Livery Companies, 1690–1750', in *The Guildhall Miscellany*, no. 7 (August 1956).

94 MS. 4647, ff.158–63, 280.

95 Journals 35, ff.63b–64.

96 MS. 4655/2, f.13 (May 1653).

97 MS. 4655/2, f.125 (July 1654).

98 Unwin, *Gilds*, p. 341.

99 Journals 41, ff.178b–179b.

100 Unwin, *Ind. Org.*, p. 117.

101 MS. 4655/1, ff.19–20.

102 MS. 4655/1, ff.19, 53, 78, 80.

103 Repertories 127, ff.468–70 (1723).

104 MS. 4655/1, ff.21, 29, 33, 34, 43, 54, 57.

105 MS. 4655/1, ff.60, 98.

106 MS. 4655/1, f.81.

107 E. G. O'Donoghue, op. cit., II, p. 167. In 'model' workhouses at the end of the eighteenth century clean sheets were provided once a month (E. M. Eden, *The State of the Poor* (1797); see under 'Shrewsbury' and 'Melton').

108 MS. 4655/2, f.16.
109 MS. 4655/1, ff.70–1, 88–9; MS. 4655/10, f.50.
110 MS. 4655/11, f.77.
111 Printed for the Company by W. Holmes, 36 Basinghall Street. Numerous pamphlets and books offering counsel to apprentices and other young people were on sale in the eighteenth century. One of the worst examples is John Ryland's *The Preceptor or Counsellor of Human Life for the Use of British Youth . . . also . . . for the Apprentices of the City of London* (1776); 375 pages of prosy boredom!
112 A footnote adds that 'with a very trifling alteration occasionally, the following hints and advices may become suitable monitors to Errand-boys, Journeymen, and even to young Tradesmen'.
113 Four prayers are printed on pp. 53–6 of the *Affectionate Advice*.
114 MS. 4655/1, ff.19, 71.
115 MS. 4655/2, f.20.
116 MS. 4655/1, ff.44, 51: cf. also f.72, which refers to Philip le Paye, stranger, about to go 'beyond sea'; MS. 4655/9, f.66b.
117 MS. 4655A, 22 July 1650.
118 MS. 4655/3, f.25.
119 In 1612 the Weavers' Company had ruled that 'no person shall bind an apprentice to himself and turn him over to any Alien' (MS. 4655/1, f.14).
120 MS. 4647, ff.193–9.
121 MS. 4647, ff.278–80, 283–5.
122 MS. 4647, f.377.
123 George, *London*, pp. 286, 289.
124 Maitland, *London*, I, p. 267.
125 MS. 4655/2, f.120.
126 MS. 4655/2, f.39.
127 MS. 4655/10, f.27.
128 MS. 4655/1, f.91.
129 MS. 4655/4, f.106b.
130 MS. 4655/7, f.7b.
131 MS. 4655/1, f.47. See MS. 4655/1, f.59, for a similar case in August 1617.
132 MS. 4655/1, ff.35, 66; MS. 4655/3, f.25.
133 *Middlesex Sessions Records*, 1736; quoted in George, *London*, pp. 231, 419.
134 MS. 4655/1, f.46. There were many small-scale kitchen or market gardeners on the fringes of London:'their skill lies in . . . their dexterity in bringing the best and earliest garden products to market. Journeymen have from 9 to 15 shillings a week, according to their skill; and if they are employed as Masters in gentlemen's gardens they have from 10 to 100 pounds a year' (Campbell, *Tradesman*, p. 274).
135 MS. 4655A, 11 June 1649.
136 London Weavers' Company, *Affectionate Advice to Apprentices*, p. 4.
137 MS. 4655/16, ff.176, 181b, 219, 226; MS. 4655/17, f.118.
138 MS.4655/16, f.248b.
139 MS. 4655/16, f.159b.
140 See e.g. MS. 4655/16, ff.176b–177b, 239b; MS. 4655/17, ff.60b, 311.
141 MS. 4655/16, f.214.
142 MS. 4655/17, f.246.
143 MS. 4655/16, ff.152, 248b, 250, 268; MS. 4655/17, ff.44, 202.

Chapter 5

Sources of Income

The Weavers' Company was not, and never had been, wealthy. Its average annual recurrent income during the first quarter of the seventeenth century was approximately £210–£220, derived from three or four principal sources (see Table 5.1).

Table 5.1 *Average annual income of the Weavers' Company*

	Average per annum (1600–1 to 1624–5)		
	£	s.	d.
Master's quarterages (6d. per head per quarter)	60	0	0
Journeymen's quarterages (3d. per head per quarter)	5	7	0
Journeymen's admission fees	2	10	0
Presentation of apprentices, making free, and sundry fines	150	0	0

A weaver's apprentice, bound and presented in the normal way, paid a modest fee of 3s. 4d. on taking his freedom after completing his term of service; but the fees charged to foreign or alien 'admissioners' were much higher: £3 for an Englishman admitted as a 'foreign brother' and £5 for an alien 'stranger' similarly admitted. These were substantial sums for a craftsman to find in those days and it was not unusual for the Company to accept payment by instalments, while in cases of special hardship some reduction of the fee was allowed. Thus, in 1610, Joseph French was admitted a foreign brother for a fee of £3 to be paid by instalments, viz. 10s. on the next quarter day and 5s. on each ensuing quarter day; and a few months later John Trowle, stranger, was ordered to pay 40s., the residue of his admission fee.[1]

At that time the Company owned no real property except its hall in Basinghall Street with an adjoining tenement, and, after 1611, a small share in the Ulster estates acquired by the London Livery Companies in connection with James I's project to 'plant' non-Irish colonists in northern Ireland. This investment, attractive at first glance, yielded nothing to the Weavers and their associated companies for nearly twenty years, but thereafter, throughout a period of 280 years, a substantial income was received on the original capital.

A good deal is already known about the plantation or colonisation of Ulster in the reign of James I, and the contribution made by the Corporation and Livery Companies of London has been dealt with by Professor Theodore Moody in his scholarly study of *The Londonderry Plantation, 1609–1641*, published in 1939. Hitherto, however, there has been no detailed study of the London Weavers' part in the great project. Not that there is any paucity of record material; on the contrary, from the Weavers' minutes and accounts we get a tolerably clear picture of the role of a minor livery company.

Notwithstanding the King's avowed interest in 'plantations, increase of science, and works of industry . . . naturally pleasing to our disposition', Ulster was regarded by many Englishmen as a most wild and perilous province![2] The flight of the two rebellious Irish earls, O'Neill and O'Donnell, in 1607, and the revolt, defeat and death of Sir Cahir O'Doherty in the following year, meant that immense estates escheated to the Crown and seemed to offer a golden opportunity to transform the six confiscated counties into an orderly, prosperous province and at the same time to 'establish the true [i.e. Protestant] religion of Christ among men almost lost in superstition'.[3] So a sort of prospectus was drawn up designed to attract suitable English and Scottish 'planters' or 'undertakers', 'civil men well affected in religion'. For every 1,000 acres allotted to them they were to pay £5. 6s. 8d. to the Crown, but this rent was remitted for the first two years. Every holder of 1,000 acres must build a defensive rampart of lime or stone, called a bawn, and induce their tenants to build their houses near the principal house or castle, and to keep in readiness a store of arms. Nothing could more clearly reveal the unsettled and dangerous situation at that time,[4] and the main reason for the poor response. Another significant sidelight comes from James I's creation of ninety-three baronets, each newly created baronet paying as much as would maintain thirty foot soldiers for three years at 8d. a day 'to assist the King's troops in the reduction of Ulster'.[5]

When one looks at the lions in the path of the Ulster project, the King's decision to try to enlist the help of the City of London and the Livery Companies is not surprising. The proposal was that the City Corporation and Companies should undertake the colonisation of the towns of Derry and Coleraine and large tracts of the hinterland lying around and to the south of the two towns. The Goverment hoped that the City's wealth, reputation and enterprise would be a source of strength to the new venture and an encouragement to other 'undertakers' to come forward. In the spring of 1609, many 'motives and reasons' were put forward to induce the City of London to

> undertake plantation in the north of Ireland, and especially of the late ruined city of Derry. This city, also Coleraine, may with little changes be made impregnable . . . This country . . . supplies such abundance of provision as may not only sustain the plantation but also furnish provisions yearly to the City of London, and especially for their fleets, as beeves, pork, fish, rye, beer, peas, and beans, and in some years will help the dearth of the City. . . . If multitudes of men were set to work proportionately to these commodities, it would ease the City of an insupportable burden of persons who can be spared. . . . Moreover, these colonies may be a means to utter infinite commodities from London to furnish the whole north of Ireland.[6]

At first the Londoners were lukewarm and cautious, but eventually four commissioners, chosen by the City, went to Ulster to make an investigation on the spot. As host and guide the Government cunningly chose Sir Thomas Phillips, privily instructing him to take the party on a conducted tour 'by the best ways . . . to show them the commodities of best advantage, but to keep from them all matters of distaste, as fear of the Irish. . . . They are said to have found all things far better than they expected, yet the Deputy prays God they prove not like their London women, who long today and loathe tomorrow.' It would seem that this prayer was answered. The commissioners' report confirmed 'the King and the City in their resolution to build another London there',[7] and led to an agreement, dated 28 June 1610, between the Government and the Corporation of London by which a new county, to be known as 'Londonderry', comprising Coleraine and adjacent parts of Tyrone, Donegal and Antrim, was created and granted provisionally to the City of London for development by the Corporation and the London Livery Companies. A special 'Society of the Governor and Assistants, London, of the New Plantation of Ulster' was set up and entrusted with the management and administration of the City's estates in Ulster. This 'Irish Society', as it came to be called, was, in effect, a standing committee of the Common Council; 'its governor was always a prominent alderman, and the assistants always included five other aldermen, the recorder, and representatives of the twelve principal companies and of one or two of the inferior companies'.[8] The society's first governor was Alderman Cockaine.

Although the bait was tempting, the Livery Companies showed less enthusiasm than the City Corporation. By the end of February 1611 only the Vintners and seven other principal companies, with ten of the minor companies, including the Weavers, had signified their willingness to accept.[9] The Weavers Court minute book (1610–19) contains the following entry in February 1611:

> It is this day ordered and agreed by the Bailiffs, Wardens, Assistants and Livery of this gild concerning a project to them directed from the Lord Mayor dated the last day of January 1611 for their answer whether they will accept of a proportion of the land in Ulster according to the quantity of this Company's disbursement to be by them undertaken and managed, according to the printed book, for plantation; or that this Company will refer the letting and disposing thereof to the Governor and Committees (as by the same project more at large appeareth). It is now this day with the consent of the Company aforesaid generally agreed that this Company shall make answer to the Governor . . . that they are contented and pleased to accept of a proportion of land to them to be allotted according to their said disbursements.[10]

Strong pressure from the King, exerted through the Lord Mayor, eventually brought in the laggards until, ultimately, fifty-five companies took part. It was now possible to raise capital and allocate the land. The original 'Heads of Agreement' mentioned a sum of £20,000, to be assessed on the companies according to the assessment of the corn rate. By July 1611 this sum was so nearly exhausted that the Common Council decided to call for a further £10,000 from the companies. Eventually, yet another levy of £10,000 was made, so that by the end of 1613 'the whole monies disbursed already in and about the said plantation' and 'the assessment made upon the several Companies towards the plantation in Ireland' was £40,000.[11] These precepts, however, were not accepted submissively by all the companies. The Drapers, for instance, protested that the burden placed upon them was excessive,[12] while others, including the Mercers, Cooks, Brewers, Clothworkers and Salters, were so slow to hand over the 'money rated on them' that their wardens were committed to prison.[13] Meantime, in April 1611, the City Chamberlain was authorised to advance between £300 and £500 'for some few days . . . the same to be repaid with the first monies that he shall receive of the Companies of this City towards the said plantation'.[14] The Weavers, like the Brewers, were at this time facing two large financial liabilities—their contributions towards the City corn stocks or granaries and the plantation of Ulster—for which their funds were totally inadequate. Hence the Weavers' petition to the City for permission to admit as freemen by redemption

> thirty persons Englishmen (born) . . . such as are principal men

now using the Craft of Weaving and have been Apprenticed thereto for the space of seven or eight years, and the reason that chiefly moveth us is for that many of the forren weavers and their families do at this instant and so have time out of mind dwelt and inhabited in this City and liberties thereof.

The City authorities agreed to this money-raising plan on condition that the Company paid 'all such arrearages for the plantation and granaries as are due and owing',[15] and the Weavers promptly appointed a special 'Committee for Redemptioners' consisting of the Officers and four Assistants, to determine how much each redemptioner should pay to the Company for his freedom. The committee fixed a sum of £10 for some of the new freemen and £11. 10s. for the others, and by the beginning of 1612 £172 had been collected from 17 of them, plus £4. 10s. given voluntarily 'towards the charges at the Guildhall'. Shortly afterwards, three of the new freemen were elected to the Livery.[16]

The companies were organised in eleven groups, each headed by one of the 'great' companies, except the wealthy Grocers who preferred to participate singly and not as the head of a group. The Grocers and each of the groups were responsible for raising one-twelfth of the total assessment and for the settlement and improvement of the estates allocated to them. The fifty-five companies subscribed sums ranging from the Merchant Taylors' £4,086 and the Grocers' £3,874 to £20 (Woolmen, Musicians, Bowyers, Fletchers). The Weavers, with the seven other companies named in Table 5.2, were in the group headed by the Vintners.

Table 5.2 *Funds raised for development in Ulster*

Company	£	s.	d.
Vintners	2,080		
Woodmongers	200		
Weavers	100		
Plumbers	80		
Poulterers	80		
Tilers and Bricklayers	80		
Blacksmiths	64		
Fruiterers	64		
Curriers	44		
Overplus from the Grocers	540	13	4
	3,332	13	4

The Vintners appear to have paid the instalments levied by acts of the Common Council by drawing upon their collective funds, recouping

111

later from the minor companies in their group. The Weavers paid in three instalments (£50, £25 and £25) spread over two years, and it seems probable that in addition to the money raised by the redemptioners' fees in 1611–12, they made levies of so much a head upon their members, for in June 1616 Edward Lockwood was 'ordered to pay 10s. at the next Court day towards the plantation of Ireland or else be punished for not doing according to the ordinances of this Company'.[17]

The newly created County of Londonderry lay between Donegal and Antrim; from Lough Foyle and the River Foyle on the west to the River Bann and Lough Neagh on the east, and to the south the boundary ran south-east from the River Foyle some four or five miles above the town of Derry (now Londonderry) to the lower reaches of the Ballinderry river where it flows towards its outlet in Lough Neagh. The chief towns were Derry, Coleraine and Limavady. It was a region in which pockets of fertile land, mainly in the valleys, were interspersed among bogs, barren mountains, and forests from which the settlers drew useful timber for building, barrel staves, fuel, etc. There were good salmon and eel fisheries, the salmon of the River Bann being especially plentiful and a valuable asset. The rural areas were allocated to the twelve companies in 1613 by simply drawing lots; a process which proved too simple, for the extent of each estate was not accurately defined and ambiguities abounded. The aggregate acreage taken over by the London companies seems to have been nearer 400,000 than the 40,000 mentioned in the original grants; a fruitful source of trouble later on. The estates in the Vintners' group lay towards the east and south-east of the county, much of the land bordering the River Bann from Lough Beg northwards;[18] but although the land was in Coleraine, the Vintners had no rights over the town of Coleraine, which the Irish Society retained under its own direct management. Even so, it seems that the Vintners' group received an area measuring nearly 51 square miles, or some 32,600 English acres, out of a total of 290,950 acres allocated to all the City companies. This gives a percentage of 11·2, or rather more than one-ninth of the total acreage; but doubtless this high proportion was counterbalanced, so far as the available data went, by a more than average amount of poor land, bog and mountain. Each of the twelve portions of the county, so allocated, were designated 'manors'. Thus a 'Manor of Vintners' was created and formally conveyed to that Company in the autumn of 1618. 'It is noteworthy', says Professor Moody, 'that in none of the sets of deeds examined is there any mention of the inferior companies that were associated with the principal companies. Their shares in the land dividend were apparently guaranteed only by the act of common council of 27 December 1613, and by a tacit understanding with the principal companies.'[19] This is the basis for the sums received from time to time by the Weavers from the Vintners.

Obviously, land and money would yield nothing unless men could be found to work, manage and improve the estates. Public notices were posted outside the Royal Exchange offering land almost gratis to men willing to settle in Ulster, but there seems to have been little immediate response; Ireland was a long way off and had an unsavoury reputation as a place of chronic insecurity. 'Undertakers' moved in but slowly, and were not always suited to their task.[20] The Lord Deputy reported that

> those sent from England . . . are for the most part plain country gentlemen who promise much but give little assurance of performing. . . . The Scottish come with more port and better assurance, but less money. Some of them . . . bargained with the natives to supply their wants, promising to get them license that the natives may stop upon their lands as tenants which is greatly pleasing to the natives who will strain themselves to stay the uttermost not to be removed from the places of their birth, hoping at some time to find an opportunity to cut their landlords' throats. They hate the Scottish deadly, and out of their malice towards them they even begin to affect the English better than before.[21]

Early in 1616 we find the Irish Society urging each of the companies to send one or two craftsmen to settle in Ulster with their families, taking care to select only 'men that fear God', avoiding drunkards and other disreputable persons. Weavers of common cloth, fustians and new stuffs, feltmakers, hatbandmakers and dyers were urgently needed. The Irish Society sent twelve Christ's Hospital boys to Derry, where ten remained as apprentices while the others were sent on to Coleraine.[22] By 1621–2 the Vintners' Company, it seems, had 'planted' in its manor two British resident freeholders and thirteen British leaseholders or 'reputed leaseholders', the total number of men being given as eighty, of whom sixty-six were armed. This probably represented between twenty-five and thirty families. In addition, 184 native Irishmen were living on the Vintners' estates, probably as labourers or tenants at will. Some six years later another return shows that out of 607 townlands settled by the livery companies, 305 were inhabited by Irish, who continued to maintain eighteen Roman Catholic chapels and twenty-four priests. On the Vintners' lands there were 73 British and 207 Irish 'able men'. The original plan to displace the Irish did not work out, for they were rooted in the soil and their labour was found to be indispensable to the local economy.[23]

Meanwhile capital funds were again running low and precepts to raise a third sum of £20,000 were issued between 1613 and 1616. This meant that the Vintners' group, like each of the others, had to raise an additional sum, to which the Weavers' contribution was another £50 (making a total of £150) payable in four instalments.[24]

What sort of return did the Weavers receive from their Irish investment? The main potential sources of income were (a) the net rents from the tenants on the Vintners' manor, and (b) any dividends paid to the Vintners by the Irish Society from the profits or proceeds of fisheries, ferries, customs dues and rents of houses, gardens, etc. All the returns were intermittent. The first sum shown in the Weavers' accounts as received from 'the Plantation in Ireland' was £11. 1s. 2d. in 1631,[25] nearly twenty years after they had subscribed their first fifty pounds. In the following year £5. 18s. 7d. was received, and in 1634, £5. 9s. 0d. The initial outlays were heavy, certainly well in excess of income in some years; rents fell into arrears, and remote control from London did not make for prompt action or vigorous development. The greatest single obstacle, however, was the growing hostility of the Crown. Charles I, who thought that too much had been given away, tried to take back the Irish estates by accusing the City, the Irish Society, and the Livery Companies of failing to fulfil their obligations. Twice the Irish rents were sequestrated by order of the Privy Council between 1625 and 1628; and in 1631 an information was filed in the Court of Star Chamber against the City and the Irish Society. The proceedings lasted four years and ended disastrously for the defendants. The Court's judgment revoked the original Charter, ordered all the estates to be surrendered to the Crown, and imposed a fine of £70,000. During the next two years the City fought back and ultimately the fine was reduced to £12,000; but Charles, with characteristic obstinacy, flatly refused to relinquish the Irish estates for they were part of his plan so to organise his resources as to become independent of Parliament. It has, however, been doubted whether he was wise 'to alienate the richest and most influencial city in the three Kingdoms for £12,000 and the lands and fisheries of Derry'.[26] Certainly the City's blood was up and, once the Long Parliament was in session, the Corporation petitioned for the restoration of the Irish estates. In August 1641 the House of Commons completely vindicated the City and the Irish Society, and the King was constrained to promise restitution. This, however, was postponed by the Civil War, and it was not until 1657, under Cromwell's Commonwealth, that the *status quo* was at last restored. But there were still dangers ahead, for after the Restoration in 1660 all Cromwellian grants became invalid. In 1662, however, the Irish Society secured from Charles II the restoration of the original grants to the various City companies.[27]

Thereafter, more and larger dividends came in from Ulster. During the fifty years 1664 to 1714 the Weavers' Company received fifteen

payments amounting to over £312.[28] Subsequent payments, from
1715 to 1738, including money received from sales of land, amounted
to £653. 12s. 2d. One of the largest sums was received in October 1729,
when the Vintners wrote to the Weavers requesting the attendance
of their Clerk to receive £150, the Weavers' share of £5,000 'paid in
part of the purchase money of Lands in Ireland by Wm. Conolly,
Esq.' The Weavers responded promptly, and their Clerk, with three
porters to carry and guard the money, was soon at Vintners' Hall
where £150 in gold was handed over. Whereupon the Weavers not
only gave a guinea to the Vintners' Clerk, but a thank-offering of six
shillings to their poor's box.[29]

At a Court of Assistants held on 15 March 1738 the Upper Bailiff
reported that the Vintners' Company was ready to pay to the
Weavers their share, amounting to £392. 12s. 2d. 'of the Purchase
money received . . . on the sale of their Estate in Ireland to Mr.
Conolly'. A résumé and account prepared by the Clerk and entered
in the Court Minute Book stated that the original capital sum paid
by the Vintners' Company was £3,332. 13s. 0d., 'which sum was raised
by several Companies in the proportions following'; then follows a
replica of the list of 1613, showing that the Vintners put up £2,080,
the Woodmongers, £200; the Weavers £100, and so on. The third levy
of £20,000 which raised the Vintners' group's subscriptions to a total
of £5,000 is ignored; which suggests that this portion of the investment had already been paid back, probably around 1655, during the
Commonwealth.[30] The résumé states, further, that in 1673, 'the
Vintners' Company granted a lease of their Manor for the term of 61
years to the Lord Mazareen under a reserved yearly rent of £200'.
In anticipation of the expiry of this lease the Vintners 'contracted
with Mr. Conolly for the absolute Sale of the said Manor for £15,000,
under a reserved Fee Farm Rent of £200 a year, £5,000 of this money
being then paid down by Mr. Conolly, was divided amongst the
Several Companies in the year 1729, and the Weavers' Company
received their proportion of it' (£150). In January 1738 Mr Conolly
paid the remainder of the purchase money and the Vintners drew up
a 'General Account', or final reckoning, which showed that the
Weavers' share amounted to £392. 12s. 2d.[31] According to the Clerk's
statement the Weavers had already received some £366 from the
Vintners since 1679 (see Table 5.3).

These sums, with the £392. 12s. received in 1738, make a total of
£758. 10s.; but the statement is seriously incomplete, since it omits
eight items, amounting in all to £155. 2s. 4d., which are recorded in
the Weavers' accounts between 1701 and 1719. A more complete
account down to 1738 compiled from all the Company's records which
have survived, is given in Table 5.4.[32]

Thus it appears that over the century and a quarter between 1613 and 1738 the Weavers received, intermittently and in unequal amounts, a return of well over £1,000 on their original investment. From the gross total of £1,025 1s. 7¾d., however, certain deductions must be made, viz.:

	£
Refund of the third £50 subscribed by the Weavers between December 1613 and October 1616	50
'Loan' by the Weavers to the Government 'for the service of Ireland' in 1641	40
Gift by the Weavers to the State 'for the service of Ireland'[33]	20
	£110

The net total return is thus reduced to £915. 1s. 7¾d., or an average of approximately £7. 6s. 5d. per annum over 125 years.

Table 5.3 *Receipts from the Vintners*

Year	£	s.	d.	Year	£	s.	d.
1679	101	6	0	1704	13	10	0
1681	11	8	0	1707	7	10	0
1684	9	0	0	1726	60	0	0
1685	13	4	0	1729	150	0	0

Out of the £200 fee farm rent payable by Mr Conolly after 1738 the Weavers could expect to receive in future £6 per annum, as well as 'some small dividend to be made from what the Vintners' Company received from the Irish Society arising from a fishery the Profits of which are divided amongst all the Twelve Companies'.[34] In fact, at the end of June 1741, the Weavers received from the Vintners £21. 17s. 8d. 'for a dividend of 3 years fee farm rent being £200 a year from Mr. Conolly at Christmas last, and for the Dividends from the Irish Society'.[35] At this rate, the original investment of £100 would continue to yield nearly £7. 6s. per cent; a figure identical with the average for the period 1613 to 1738.

From 1740 to the first decade of the twentieth century, the Weavers received, at irregular intervals, over £700 in dividends from the profits of the Irish Society and the fee farm rent from the Irish estates. Finally, between February 1910 and August 1912, the Company received £162, as its share in the capital sum realised by the redemption of the Irish rent charge; a payment which wrote *finis* to a chapter begun exactly three centuries before, early in the reign of the first of the Stuart kings.

Table 5.4 *Income received by the London Weavers' Company (through the Vintners' Company) from Estates in Ulster*[36]

Year	£	s.	d.	Notes
1631	11	1	2	—
1632	5	8	7	—
1634	5	9	0	—
1656	25	1	8	Apparently a refund of money received from the sale of certain pieces of land.
1663	2	2	2	'. . . the Company's proportion for lands in Coleraine in Ireland.'
1664	19	11	11¾	'. . . for the Company's proportion for Coleraine in Ireland.'
1669	12	14	5½	'. . . dividend for rent of land in Ireland.'
1674	15	0	1½	'. . . rent out of Ireland.'
1677	15	0	0	'. . . a dividend out of Ireland.'
1679 (March 17)	15	0	0	'Recd. of the Compa. of Vintners, by them recd. of the Irish Society.'
1679 (June 16)	86	6	0	'. . . for Land at Londonderry.'
1681	11	8	0	'Dividend from Londonderry thro' the Vintners' Company.'
1683–4	9	0	0	'Recd. of the Compa. of Vintners which they rec. of the Irish Society.'
1684–5	13	4	0	
1701–2	40	7	4	'. . . from Ireland.'
1703–4	13	10	0	'Recd. by an Irish Dividend.'
1705–6	15	0	0	'Recd. by an Irish Dividend.'
1707–8	7	10	0	'Recd. from Ireland.'
1712–13	6	15	0	'Irish Dividend.'
1713–14	42	0	0	'Irish Dividend.'
1714–15	15	0	0	'Irish Dividend.'
1716–17	9	0	0	'Irish Dividend.'
1717–18	12	0	0	'Irish Dividend.'
1718–19	15	0	0	'Irish Dividend.'
1727	60	0	0	'Of the Vintners' Company on account of the Horfield Estates, &c. in Ireland.'
1729	150	0	0	'. . . purchase money of Lands in Ireland by Wm. Conolly Esq.'
1738	392	12	2	Balance of purchase money from Mr. Conolly.
	1,025	1	7¾	

Within the Company's membership the natural reluctance to pay dues, and the equally natural propensity to criticise the handling of the Company's money caused a good deal of grumbling, but one seldom finds an outspoken attack on the Court of Assistants like that made by certain Liverymen in 1633 in a document[37] (already referred to in Chapter 3) entitled 'The True Causes why we of the Livery are unwilling to have any of the Assistants that formerly have been Bailiffs to be chosen Bailiffs or Wardens again: Delivered by divers of the Livery at St. James tide in Anno 1633, when Francis Foster was chosen [Upper] Bailiff'. After disclaiming all unworthy motives such as envy, the complainants declared:

> It is not only a grief to us who are of the Livery but to every member that wisheth well to the Company and Trade, that it is evident that you have not been so good husbands for the Company as you might and ought to have been, considering the sums of money you have received for many years past, as may appear by these particulars:
>> By 'Quarterage' and 'search money' considering the multitude that use the trade.
>> By presenting of Apprentices 2s. 6d. a piece, and for turning over many of them to serve Foreigners and Strangers, 2s. 6d. a piece.
>> Also for admitting Journeymen as well Strangers as English.
>> For making men free 3s. 4d. and a Silver Spoon weighing an ounce and a half at least.
>> For admitting English Foreigners £3 a piece.
>> For admitting every Stranger and Alien to use the trade of Weaving, £5, whereof you have admitted many.
>> For every man by you brought in to be of the Livery, £5.
>> Besides such rent as is received for that part of the Hall which is let.
> By which receipt of moneys . . . for many years past, we believe and know that you might now have had a Competent Stock of money in the hall, to have been employed for the good of the generality and relief of the poor of the Company and a good parcel of Land which would have been for the credit of so ancient a Company as ours is. But contrariwise for want of good husbanding and managing . . . moneys in the hall there is little or none, and for Land (the Hall excepted) there is none at all, nor none hereafter like to be, except [we] . . . Choose such men . . . as will take pains for the good reformation of the Trade and Company. For notwithstanding the said Receipts formerly expressed by you received, if any Tax, Tallage or Assessment at any time is to be levied for his Majesty, or for

the service of the City of London, or to buy Corn or otherwise
. . . then such Taxes &c. are gathered of us of the Livery and
Commonalty.

The gist of the Assistants' reply was that the net annual surplus
income available for investment after payment of all expenses and
demands was a great deal less than the disgruntled Liverymen supposed. The Company, they said, has to pay 'many Assessments', such
as subsidies and fifteenths, ship money, corn money, 'the repair of
Paul's, of their own church and of divers other churches in and about
the City, for all manner of duties to the King's Majesty, and [the]
parish where their Hall standeth', as well as the defence of many
suits brought by troublesome and contentious members of their own
and other Companies, whereby they 'are vexed, molested and much
interrupted in their peaceable and quiet government'.[38]

The Weavers, like many other livery companies, expected freemen-
elect to observe the old custom of presenting a silver spoon to the
Company or a cash payment in lieu, when they were made free. The
spoons seem to have differed in size and weight, for we read in
the records of 'a fair spoon' and 'a little spoon', 'a silver spoon of
the value of 21s.', and of two apprentices each of whom gave 'a silver
spoon of the value of 20s.'[39] A more usual value seems to have been
about 8s., while the poorer candidates were often allowed to pay only
3s. or 4s. 'in lieu of a spoon'. During the first decade of the seventeenth
century the Company collected some fifty 'silver and gilt' spoons each
year.[40]

In 1636 the Weavers' Commonalty complained that many young
men were prevented from taking their freedom because of their
inability to pay a fee of 5s. 4d. (i.e. 3s. 4d. to the Company and 2s. to
the Clerk) and to provide a silver spoon weighing at least 1½ oz. This
representation to the Company seems to have received but a cold
reception, for a short time afterwards a petition was presented to the
Lord Mayor on behalf of two named apprentices and 'divers other
poor young men' who had duly completed their terms but could not
afford to give silver spoons. The petition is endorsed: 'Delivered the
27 of July 1637 upon the which the order of 31st of August 1637 was
made for the suppressing of silver spoons taken by the bayliffs.' But
the Weavers' Company refused to be swayed, and in May 1638, a
number of 'poor youngmen weavers' complained bitterly to the Commissioners for Exacted Fees that despite the Lord Mayor's order made
eight months before, the Weavers' Bailiffs were *still* insisting upon the
silver spoons.[41] Even the King himself came in for a share of the
Bailiffs' unpopularity when it became known that in his Letters
Patent, granted to the Weavers' Company on 4 July 1638, he confirmed the custom of 'taking a silver spoon of each person made free'

and stipulated that the proceeds should be used for the relief of poor members of the Company and other charitable and public purposes. Divers young weavers protested that they and some hundreds of others would thereby be kept out of 'the freedom and use' of weaving in London;[42] but this protest fared no better than earlier ones and the old custom continued, modified by exemptions granted to those who could show that they were 'very poor'.[43]

From time to time the spoons were sold and the proceeds credited to income account, as in 1642 when '86 silver spoons white, and 2 gilt spoons, the white spoons weighing 118 oz. ¾ qrs., . . . were sold to Mr. White, Goldsmith, at 5s. 2d. p. oz. which amounts to £30. 13s. 0d. [;] and the gilt spoons, together with 6 other gilt spoons taken out of the Chest with 4 locks, weighing 14 oz. ¾ qrs. were sold to the said Mr. White at 5s. 3d. p. oz. which is £3. 15s. 0d.'[44] In 1637–8 the Company sold 125 spoons for £47. 1s. 10d. in order to pay for repairs to its hearse cloth,[45] and five years later it is recorded that forty-nine spoons brought in £16. 15s. 9d. The price received in 1671, when twenty-one silver spoons weighing 31½ oz. were sold for £8. 5s. 0d., was the same as in 1642.[46]

Two types of 'fine' contributed fairly regularly to the Company's income: (a) fines such as those paid upon admission to the Livery, or on being excused from serving some office such as Steward or Warden, and (b) fines inflicted upon members by the Court of Assistants for breaches of the Ordinances, or other proved abuses. The aggregate amounts from the first of these sources always greatly exceeded those from the second. For example, in January–February 1667, eleven fines for breaches of the Ordinances brought in a total of £4. 6s. 2d., while in August 1669 seven such fines yielded £3. 2s. 0d.[47] These sums together are little more than the admission fine of £6 paid by a new liveryman.

Occasionally, the Company's income was supplemented by voluntary gifts or legacies, such as the sum of £10 bequeathed by John de Freeze in 1618, or the gift in the same year of 'one pair of large Andirons and one pair of little ones all of Brass to be placed in the Parlour chimney'.[48] Sometimes one of the more prosperous members presented a piece of plate.

The actual collection of quarterages was never easy for the Weavers' Officers. The letter of the law was that masters and journeymen must pay their dues quarterly to the Renter Warden at Weavers' Hall on the Mondays next following the usual Quarter Days, but in practice at least two-thirds of the quarterages due, including arrears, were collected by the Beadles during the searches or at other times whenever and wherever they could 'corner' the weavers—in their looms, in a tavern or in the street. Those who neglected to pay and allowed arrears to accumulate rendered themselves liable to imprisonment for debt. For example, the Company fined Isack Blower 6*s*. in 1617 because, despite two summonses, he had not paid his quarterages, and when he persisted in his refusal to pay, he was handed over to the Beadle to be conveyed to the Compter. Blower, however, declined to go, 'whereupon Thomas Harvest, a Sergeant of the Chamber, was sent for, who committed him upon the Lord Mayor's commandment to the Compter, but in going he submitted himself and therefore was pardoned'.[49] On another occasion a weaver who owed 20 quarters was ordered by the Lord Mayor to pay the 10*s*. plus 6*s*. costs, 'and be conformable for the future to the Company and so all differences to be ended between them'; and when James Wilkinson, who owed not less than 49 quarters, was finally brought to book he promised to pay in three quarterly instalments.[50]

The Company was evidently unwilling to hold any large sums of cash in hand, even though the money was locked in the chest fitted with four locks so that the Officers 'in place' could each have a key. Instead, a number of short-term loans were negotiated in order to earn some interest and reduce the risk of loss by fire or stealing. This meant that the Company was occasionally caught short of ready money and was itself obliged to borrow to meet government levies or forced loans, extensive repairs to the Hall, or other abnormal demands. In 1641-2 for example, the Weavers' Company lent £350 to the State, and in the following year a sum of £20 was 'given to the State for the service of Ireland'. It was not unusual for the Company to borrow temporarily from the Officers or Assistants, as we see from the annual accounts for 1650-1 which record the repayment of a loan of £60 to William Cade (who became Upper Bailiff in 1653-4) and another member named Lamott;[51] £20 'Borrowed upon the Company's hearsecloth, and more of small members £12'. At the end of 1651 the Company borrowed £100 from Mr Shippie, an Assistant, 'he to have as security a mortgage on the tenement adjoining the hall, and for interest the rent of £10 p. ann.'; while in 1652-3 loans from 'several persons' amounted in all to £33. 5*s*. 0*d*., and gifts 'for the Company's use, £12. 11. 0'.[52] When, a year later, the Company needed £50 to pay a creditor, the Four in Place lent that sum at interest.[53] The accounts for 1656-7 record a loan of £100 by the Company to John Wells, and at the same time

Debts owing by the Company, vizt., to William Bolnest being money by him lent to pay workmen	£21. 0. 0
To Henry Holdrup (the Clerk) for several disbursements about the Company's business	£14. 18. 5[54]

In 1661 the Company lent, at interest, the unusually large sum of £600 to Arnold Beake, one of its 'ancients', who repaid the money in two instalments during 1662–3;[55] and £400 of this was, it seems, immediately re-lent to a merchant at 6 per cent.[56] Another unusually large loan of £500 was made in 1691 by the Weavers 'to their Majesties [William and Mary] on Security of the Aid Tax', and when it was repaid in the following year with £22 for interest, the loan was immediately renewed.[57]

Towards the end of the seventeenth century the Company began to sell annuities to members or their relatives, e.g.,

1695–6 'Recd. of Mrs. Jane Gressingham £100 for which the Company granted her an annuity of £10';

1698–9 Mrs. Beckett paid £220 for an annuity of £20;

1699–1700 Mr. Saunders paid £200 for 'an annuity of £12 during his life and £8 to Charity for ever after' and Mr. Dixon paid £200 for an annuity of £20 during the life of his wife.[58]

The Renter Bailiff's account for 1730 (see Table 5.5) gives a list of annuities and bonds upon which the Company was then liable.[59] Mrs Gressingham was still alive and drawing her annuity in 1744, by which time she had received from the Company during nearly half a century not less than £480 in return for her original payment of £100.[60]

Table 5.5 *Responsibility of the Company for annuities and bonds*

		£ p. ann.	
Annuities	Mrs. Rebecca Sheldon	20	
	Mrs. Jane Gressingham	10	
	Mr. John Drew	20	
	Mrs. Yates	3	
		53	
Bonds		*Capital*	*Interest*
		£	£
To Mr. Bestman		300	15
Mr. Blowen		200	10
Mrs. Titford		100	5
Mr. Harris		100	5
Mr. Barns		100	5
		800	40

One can detect a moderate degree of correlation between the Company's income and the state of trade and politics. In times of prosperity or when the political outlook appeared promising, the weavers, it seems, felt more optimistic and parted with their money the more readily. On the other hand, in unsettled and critical periods such as the Civil War, the Company's income tended to decrease. The figures, taken from the annual accounts for the years 1641–2 to 1648–9 are given in Table 5.6.[61]

Table 5.6 *Company income and the state of trade and politics, 1641–9*

Year (August to August)	Masters' quarterages collected	Receipts from apprentices' bindings, making free, fines, etc.	Total
	£	£	£
1641–2	109	222	331
1642–3	52	138	190
1643–4	61	115	176
1644–5	74	114	188
1645–6	115	185	300
1646–7	124	277	401
1647–8	91	138	229
1648–9	82	98	180

From August 1642 to the end of 1643 the fortunes of the Civil War were decidedly in the Royalists' favour, especially in the west. Parliament heard the news of Prince Rupert's capture of Bristol on 27 July 1643 'like a sentence of death'. Only Gloucester stood firmly for the Parliamentarians, a bastion between the King's western and northern armies. In 1644, however, the tide began to turn, and Cromwell's success at Marston Moor on 1 July 1644 led on to the decisive defeat of the Royalists at Naseby in June 1645 and the recapture of Bristol in the following September. To contemporaries it must have seemed that the war was over, and this relief appears to be reflected in the Weavers' much increased income in the financial years 1645–6 and 1646–7. But as 1647 passed from spring to summer and summer to autumn, bitter quarrels between Parliament and Army, and the failure to reach agreement with Charles I, culminated in the outbreak of the Second Civil War (in February 1648) and the trial and execution of the King, followed, during 1649–51, by the advent of the Commonwealth. Small wonder that the Weavers were apprehensive and pessimistic in those years and that the Company's income fell heavily from £401 in 1646–7 to £180 in 1648–9.

Throughout the first five years of the Commonwealth the Company's income was low and unresilient, and although it rose sharply in 1654–5 and 1655–6, it fell away again as discontent with the republican regime increased and men began to mutter about bringing the King back. During 1657–60 the Company's income from quarterages, freedoms, apprentice bindings, fines etc., averaged no more than £238, while in 1660–1, the year of the Restoration, the masters' quarterages exceeded £220 (compared with less than £73 in the previous year) and the income from freedoms, bindings, fines etc., rose to £317 from £134 in 1659–60.[62] Undoubtedly this reflects, in tangible form, the general emotional effusion of the time, and, as such, it could not be expected to continue indefinitely at such a high level. The first sharp fall came in 1664–5, when total income fell by some £200 to £380. Then came the impact of those two appalling disasters —the Great Plague in 1665 and the Great Fire in the following year. Needless to say, the Weavers' income fell, but less heavily than one might reasonably expect. The figures, given in Table 5.7, are interesting, for they show the resilience of the Company's members after their misfortunes.[63]

Table 5.7 *Company income and the state of trade and politics, 1664–70*

Year (August to August)	Masters' quarterages collected	Receipts from apprentices' bindings, making free, fines, etc.	Total
	£	£	£
1664–5	117	263	380
1665–6	91	303	394
1666–7	118	375	493
1667–8	129	335	464
1668–9	140	406	546
1669–70	174	495	669

Other fluctuations in the Company's income were caused in 1683–4 and 1684–5 by the unsettled political outlook and especially the Protestants' dread of a Roman Catholic revival if and when James, Duke of York, succeeded his brother, Charles II. The Revolution of 1688 caused another, but less marked, fall in income for a couple of years, until the constitutional and dynastic crisis was resolved.

As a result of the replanning and rebuilding of Weavers' Hall after the Great Fire, the Company was able to increase its income from adjoining tenements by nearly £40 per annum. Before the fire there was only one tenement adjoining the Hall, which was let to a merchant for £10 a year gross. After the rebuilding there were two houses, one on either side of the entry or 'hall gate' in Basinghall Street, each let at £24 a year. One of these, let in the 1670s to Mr Peirson, became known as the Crown Victualling House and later as the Crown House.[64] In 1716 a partial letting of the Hall itself to the Dyers' Company 'for the holding of their Court . . . every month, and for one dinner in each year' brought in £12 a year, £2 of which the Weavers gave to their Clerk, instructing him, at the same time, not to let the Hall in future for balls or burials without leave of the Upper Bailiff. Four years later a similar letting to the Throwsters' Company is recorded, so that in the 1720s Weavers' Hall was being used by three companies.[65]

Early in the eighteenth century the Weavers tried to raise their income above the level of barely £200 a year to which it had sunk towards the end of the previous century. At a full Court in June 1702 the Officers and Auditors were told to 'see . . . what money is due to the Company and to take care the same be got in'; but when three members tried to be helpful by offering to collect the quarterage arrears of persons owing seven years and upwards, for a commission of five shillings in every pound collected, the Court would not agree. The same idea reappeared in a modified form in 1709 when it was resolved that the Beadles should have two shillings in the pound for collecting quarterages 'above 4 years due on the last books'.[66] But the results achieved were negligible, and the Company's income continued to fall until 1731–2 when an *ad hoc* committee of investigation was appointed. The report, presented in May 1732, showed that the Company owed £857, while it was overspending by some £170 per annum. The Court of Assistants, alarmed by the revelation of facts which they ought to have known already, resolved urgently 'to consider of means to pay off the Company's Debt and retrench their future expenses'.[67]

A beginning was made with 'entertainments' at Court meetings, all of which were suspended except those on Oath Day and the four quarterly Courts, and even for these, upper limits were fixed of £4 on each quarter day and £15 on Oath Day. At each private Court total outlay was limited to sixteen shillings. Attention was next directed to the possibility of increasing income, mainly in the form of fines brought in by adding to the numbers elected to the Livery. For example, in 1732 and 1733, thirty-three new liverymen were elected.[68] Not everyone appreciated the honour, and on occasion the Company had to exert pressure.[69] After the decision in the case of *The Company of Weavers* v. *Thos. Handyside* (1742), which confirmed the Solicitor-General's opinion taken by the Company in 1740,[70] a potential liveryman could no longer refuse on the grounds that he was not free of the City.

Two important changes came about in the second quarter of the eighteenth century. Firstly, the searches were discontinued after 10 August 1736, on which date the last search ever made by the Weavers' Company took place. This meant a small saving in expenses since, as we have seen in Chapter 2, the cost of a search usually exceeded the search groats; and an immense saving in irritation and bad feeling towards the Company among those subjected to the search. On the other hand, the Company could not face the loss of income from the quarterages hitherto collected during the searches. Therefore, in September 1736, the Court ordered the two Beadles and the Butler 'to go and Collect the Quarterage of the Liverymen and other members of this Company' living within the Bills of Mortality. For their trouble they were allowed 1s. in the pound on all sums collected from the Livery (raised to 2s. in August 1737) and 2s. in the pound on all money collected from other members; they were directed to pay over the proceeds to the Officers on every Court Day, and 'no money [to] be collected without two of the three of them being present'. Furthermore, the three collectors were required to give security 'to pay treble the Damage for whatever money they shall receive and not give an Account of'. The Clerk was bidden to furnish them with proper authority and 'they shall have Liberty to take the Staff with them whenever they go to Demand any Quarteridge'.[71]

The second and more fundamental change made in the second quarter of the eighteenth century was the Company's abolition of the long-standing distinction between freemen and admissioners, which removed the main barrier to the election of admitted foreign brethren to the Livery. From August 1740 to the end of that year, 59 members were 'called and chosen on the Livery', of whom at least 36 were clearly of French descent.[72] The Company's total membership as recorded in the quarterage books, which had fallen from 5,949 to 5,240 between 1710 and 1720, rose to 6,000 by 1728, and to a peak of 6,330 in 1735–6. The immediate effect upon the Company's income from Livery and Stewards' fines was excellent. No fewer than 64 Livery fines of £10 each were collected in 1740–1, against only 12 in 1738–9. Stewards' fines yielded £90 in 1738–9, £150 in the following year, and £180 in 1740–1. But income from quarterages—never a buoyant source—actually fell from £100 in 1738–9 to less than £70 in 1740–1. The over-all result was an increase in total income from £603 to £1,084 (including a triennial dividend of £21. 17s. 8d. from the Irish Estates), which enabled the Company to clear off £524 of outstanding debts. A typical set of annual accounts from the middle of the century (1750–1) shows total income £575 against total expenditure £452, so that a credit balance of £123 was carried forward. In that financial year the Wardens had collected £20 in quarterages, and the Beadles £46. 13s. 0d.; rents yielded £92, and Livery, Stewards' and Wardens' fines brought in £250.

In the 1630s, as we have seen, and during the Civil War and Commonwealth period, some weavers had criticised the Officers and Court of Assistants because, unlike many other companies, they had failed to acquire property and to provide almshouses for their 'infirme and decayed' members.[73] Where, they asked one another in the loom-shops, alleys and ale-houses, did all the money go? What were 'the Masters at the Hall' doing with it? The Court, well aware of this grumbling, was not unwilling to invest in landed property, if only the Company's finances would permit; but this happy position was not attained until the post-Restoration years, 1660–1 to 1663–4, brought a welcome increase in annual income, fortunately supplemented by a windfall in the form of a legacy of £500 from one John Ash. Evidently this was the opportunity for which the Court had long been waiting, for in November 1662 the Officers were authorised to look at a free-hold farm property at Shenfield in Essex, said to yield a yearly rent of £32. This they did and, in April 1663, agreed with Mr Dax, the owner, a purchase price of £620. The sitting tenant was one William Roman, who rented the farm on a repairing lease, living at that time, it seems, in a cottage on the property, for it was not until 1678 that the Company 'paid for building a farm house at Shenfield, £100'.[74]

After July 1664, when, as the trustees of Rowland and John Morton's Gift, the Company became responsible for another Essex farm, this time at Billericay, some twenty-three miles from London, and four miles from Shenfield, it became necessary—and one may guess, not unpleasant—to pay visits of inspection from time to time to see that the tenants were properly carrying out the terms of their leases. Thus in August 1677 the Officers 'Paid for Coachhire and spent viewing the Land at Shenfield and Billericay with some of ye Compa. £6. 16. 0'. Again, in 1681 the Company 'paid Goodman Bryan at Shenfield in full for making of Hay, £3. 9. 0' and gave him for 'his pains and care' an extra 10s. The Clerk and two Officers spent £2. 15s. 8d. 'going to Shenfield 2 days and for horses', and on another occasion £1. 6s. 0d. was spent 'going to Shenfield to sell the hay' for which they received 'over and above the charges of binding', £22. 16s. 0d. for 24 loads.[75]

Such visits to Shenfield and Billericay, which continued throughout the eighteenth century, were made sometimes by one or two Officers accompanied by the Clerk, and sometimes by a more numerous committee of the Court of Assistants. The larger body usually needed two or three postchaises for two days, which cost between £3 and £4. 10s. In the autumn of 1706, when the tenant of the Shenfield farm was in arrears not only with his rent but with essential repairs to the dwelling house, outhouses and barns, the Court thought it advisable to make an inspection on the spot, taking a carpenter with them. The dilapidations discovered were such that 'the buildings might fall to the ground if not repaired before the winter' if it 'should prove as tempestuous as the last'. Prompt action was taken; the premises were repaired forthwith at the Company's expense.[76] Troubles of one sort or another occurred fairly frequently. One tenant illegally cut and sold a good deal of timber before going bankrupt. Another was threatened with eviction for altering certain fences without the Company's permission. Incompetent farming, lazy tenants and rent arrears were the chief difficulties with which the Officers had to cope. Two entries from the Renter Bailiff's accounts for 1756 must suffice.

23 April.	Paid Postchaise 2 days with Mr. Warden Jennings to Shenfield to sell timber and to Billericay to deliver Ejectments	£1. 12. 0
Ditto	Expenses with Mr. Jno. Richardson who bought the Timber (for £82) and workmen . . . marking the trees to be felled, Turnpikes & Servants	2. 3. 6
7 August.	Paid Expenses to, and at the Assizes at Chelmsford, Witnesses, on the Ejectment of John Cowden, and return to London, 4 days	6. 5. 6.
Ditto	For Postchaise 4 days @ 15s. and Postilion	3. 2. 6.

In addition, the Clerk's bill came to £26. 9s. 4d.[77] Against such expenses we must set the rents received from good tenants and the occasional sales of timber. For example, the Renter Bailiff's accounts show that in 1774 6¾ loads of timber from the Shenfield farm fetched nearly £22, and in 1793 22 mature oaks were felled and sold for £55, young trees being planted in the following year to replace them. Some of the felled timber, of course, was used to repair farm buildings and fences.[78] During the half-century from 1675 to 1725 the Company's average annual gross income from rents (before deductions of land tax) on its properties, whether held in trust or not, increased from £73 to £220.[79]

At the turn of the century there is evidence that some enclosure of waste land had been going on, for in 1805 the Weavers' investigating committee recommended 'that it be one of the conditions of a new lease that the grant of all the waste land already inclosed and proposed to be inclosed shall be made or surrendered to the Company' by the present tenant, the Rev. Mr Salter. But it transpired that the grant had been made by the Lady of the Manor to Mr Salter's son in 1802. He declined to surrender the enclosed land, which measured 1 acre, 2 roods, 20 perches, but offered to sell it for £50; an offer which the Company accepted. In 1807 the Steward of the Manor authorised the Company's tenant 'to lay manure on another piece of waste (some

19 poles in extent) adjoining the Company's land in Priest Lane, so as
to prevent any other person from using the same'. The Court made an
immediate application to the Lady of the Manor for a formal grant
of this second piece of waste, and when this was received, the extra
land was quickly enclosed.[80]

The position in 1819 is revealed in a report of a survey made early
in that year. The farm, 'Situate near the high road from Shenfield to
Billericay', then comprised:

> 9 enclosures of meadow and pasture land; in all—with sites of
> buildings, yards etc.—33a. 2r. 12p.
> The Buildings consist of:
> A small comfortable dwelling house
> A barn
> A butcher's shop
> A stable and other necessary farm erections.

The surveyor's valuation was £98 per annum,

> but considering the convenience of situation near the town of
> Brentwood and close to the junction of two turnpike roads and
> consequently well adapted for the taking in Cattle and the
> dealing therein, for which purposes this Farm is now used, . . .
> it could be let at the clear rent of £105 p. ann. The premises
> have been neglected of late and the tenant who is liable to
> repair buildings and fences, shd. be pressed to do so. There is
> a small quantity of good oak timber as well as a considerable
> number of pollards which it would be advisable to cut. . . .
> All the land being now in grass, a covenant should be inserted
> in any new lease to prevent the breaking up of the same.

After the failure of Thomas Griggs, the tenant, in the summer of 1821,
the Company had some difficulty in reletting the farm and had to
accept a rent of only £65 per annum.[81]

With the rise and development of the stock market in the eighteenth century[82] the Company's sources of income became more
diversified. While it continued to own land and houses both for its
own uses and upon trust for charitable purposes, it began, at least as
early as 1753,[83] to invest trust funds and other surplus money in gilt-
edged securities. This policy was continued over the next forty years,
and towards the end of the eighteenth century the Company's
investments were listed as in Table 5.8.[84]

From 1791 to 1800 the Company's average annual income was
about £800 of which only about £45 came from quarterages, some
£230 from Livery, Stewards', and similar fines, approximately £150
from rents of properties owned by the Company or held in trust for
charitable purposes, and £220 from investments in stocks, over £190
of this sum being earmarked for various charitable uses. During the

Table 5.8 *An account of the estates belonging to the Worshipful Company of Weavers (Renter Bailiff's Account Book 1793–7)*

Company's properties	Date of lease	Rent p. ann. £ s. d.	Terms of years	Rent payable
Farm and buildings at Shenfield, Essex	26 July 1784	31 10 0	21 yrs. expiring Michlmas 1805	Quarterly
Way through farm at Shenfield	23 Dec. 1783	1 0 0	14 yrs. expiring Michlmas 1797	Michlmas
House at Hall Gate in Basinghall Street	20 Dec. 1787	25 0 0	14 yrs. Expiring Michlmas 1801	Quarterly
House at Hall Gate in Basinghall Street	4 Sep. 1788	20 0 0	7 yrs. Expiring Michlmas 1795	Quarterly
Lands in Ulster £100 lent. Quit rent payable Original ground rent £6	—	—	Fee simple	—
Weavers' Hall in Basinghall Street	—	Occasional lettings	Fee simple	
In Trust				
Piece of ground at Shoreditch (Porter's Fields)	24 Mar. 1736	3 0 0	99 yrs. expiring 1835.	Midsummer
Houses in Holborn	20 Dec. 1758	40 0 0	40 yrs. expiring 1799	Quarterly
House in Nicholas Lane	29 Mar. 1775	10 0 0	21 yrs. expiring Xmas 1795	Quarterly
House and land at Billericay, Essex	7 May 1782	14 19 0	21 yrs. expiring Lady Day 1803	Quarterly

Account of stocks

£		
400	5% Bank annuities	Weavers' Company funds
200	4% Bank annuities	Weavers' Company funds
400	3% Consols	Baker's gift
400	East India annuities	Agace's gift
12	Bank Short annuities	Benjn. Mills's gift
800	East India stock	Garrett's charity
216	Bank stock	Carpenter's charity
2,435	5% Bank annuities	Limborough's charity

nineteenth century the Company contrived to bring its expenditure below its income (except on Charities Account) and so was able to invest accumulated surpluses, from time to time, usually in gilt-edged stocks.[85]

NOTES

1 MS. 4655/1, ff.2, 5–6.
2 D. H. Willson, *King James VI and I* (1956), pp. 323–6.
3 T. W. Moody, *The Londonderry Plantation, 1609–1641* (1939), p. 31;
C. Maxwell, 'The Colonisation of Ulster', in *History*, I (1916–17);
Historical Narrative of the Irish Society (1913), pp. 2–4; and G. B.
Harrison, *A Second Jacobean Journal* (1958), pp. 51–5.
4 Maxwell, op. cit., p. 149.
5 Cobbett's *Parliamentary History of England* (1806), I, p. 1508.
6 Harrison, op. cit., pp. 139–40, quoting Cal. S.P., Ireland, III, p. 372.
7 Harrison, op. cit., pp. 153, 157.
8 Moody, op. cit., p. 92.
9 The Ulster project was in competition in the City of London with
the Virginia Company, then making a special effort under its new
charter of 1609, which conferred full governmental powers. No
fewer than fifty-six City companies were providing financial support. Small wonder that Ulster tended to fall into second place.
10 MS. 4655/1, f.5. The 'Orders and Conditions of the Ulster Plantation' were usually referred to as 'the printed Book' (Cal S.P.,
Ireland (1608–10), p. 139).
11 Moody, op. cit., p. 92; *A Brief Historical Narrative of the Origin
and Constitution of the. . . Irish Society, from 1611 to 1898* (?1913),
pp. 4, 13, 16–17; and R. R. Sharpe, *London and the Kingdom*, II,
pp. 28–45.
12 R. H. Tawney, *Business and Politics under James I* (1958), p. 74n.
13 Repertories 29, ff.171, 186, 219b, 235b, 250b, 253b, 254.
14 Repertories 30, f.97.
15 MS. 4655/1, ff.8–9; Repertories 30, ff.78, 110b.
16 MS. 4655/1, ff.10–11, 13. In all, 19 'foreign brethren' are recorded
as made free in this way, but there is nothing to show that the
remainder of the thirty were actually made free of the Weavers'.
17 MS. 4655/1, f.43.
18 Moody, op. cit., Plate I.
19 Ibid., pp. 182–3.
20 E. Hull, *A History of Ireland and her People* (1926), II, pp. 35ff.
21 G. B. Harrison, op. cit., pp. 233–4, quoting Cal. S.P., Ireland, III,
p. 915.
22 *A Brief Historical Narrative of the . . . Irish Society*, pp. 25–6.
23 Maxwell, op. cit., p. 154; Moody, op. cit., pp. 201, 246.
24 This third contribution, or levy, seems to have been repaid during
the Commonwealth, c. 1655.
25 MS. 4646, f.77.
26 C. V. Wedgwood, *The King's Peace, 1637–1641* (1955), p. 165;
Brett-James, *London*, p. 252; R. R. Sharpe, *London and the Kingdom*, II, pp. 111–17.
27 Maitland, *London*, I, pp. 428–9.
28 The Renter Bailiff sometimes recorded losses, ranging from 4*d.* to
1*s.*, on certain clipped coins when he paid out in gold. MS. 4648/1,
passim.
29 MS. 4655/12, f.244; MS. 4648/4, f.222.
30 MS. 4655/2, ff.156–7.

31 MS. 4655/15, f.16
32 No attempt has been made to assess the real value of the sums received at different dates by calculating changes in the value of the pound.
33 MS. 4646, f.83; MS. 4655 (1641), f.6b.
34 MSS. 4655/14, ff.57–9 and 4648/4, f.215.
35 MS. 4648/5, 26 June 1741.
36 MS. 4646 (Old Ledger Book), ff.77–8, 97, 112, 114, 117, 118, 137–155, 163; MS. 4648/4, f.108; MS. 4655/3, ff.106, 142; MS. 4655/5, f.42; MS. 4655/7, f.75b.
37 MS. 4647, ff.253–6.
38 MS. 4647, ff.393–4.
39 MS. 4655/1, ff.5–6.
40 MS. 4646, *passim.* In 1610–11 and 1611–12, seventy-one and eighty-five spoons were collected, and in the following year sixty-six are recorded, with a 'Memo: there is remaining in the house' thirty-eight gilt and silver spoons; which suggests that all the rest had been sold.
41 MS. 4647, ff.423–4, 457–9, 461–3.
42 MS. 4647, f.489.
43 See, e.g., MS. 4655/2, *passim.*
44 MS. 4646, f.82b.
45 MS. 4646, f.92.
46 MS. 4655/3, 10 November 1662; MS. 4646, f.104.
47 MS. 4648/1, *passim.*
48 MS. 4655/1, f.83.
49 MS. 4655/1, f.66.
50 MS. 4655/2, ff.28, 122.
51 Probably John Lamott, Upper Bailiff 1629–30; Alderman 1648; d. 13 July 1655.
52 MS. 4646, ff.83, 88–9b.
53 MS. 4655/2, f.78.
54 MS. 4646, f.91b. William Bolnest was Upper Bailiff in 1656–7.
55 MS. 4646, ff.95, 97.
56 MS. 4655/3, ff.56, 62b.
57 MS. 4646, ff.126–8.
58 MS. 4646, ff.131, 134–5.
59 MS. 4648/4, f.251.
60 MS. 4648/6, August 1744.
61 MS. 4646, *passim.*
62 Also, in 1661–2 the Company received gifts of six cups, two bowls, one salt and one tankard, all of silver (MS. 4646, f.95).
63 MS. 4655/6, f.50b. See also Chap. 10 for details of the rebuilding of Weavers' Hall after the Great Fire.
64 MS. 4655/2, ff.23, 73, 153; MS. 4655/13, ff.89, 148b; MS. 4646, f.254; MS. 4655/16, ff.337, 344b; MS. 4655/17, ff.27, 49, 341, 388. An old cistern, probably lead, taken out of the 'Company's house at the Hall Door' in 1664, which weighed 2 cwt. 3 qrs. 11 lb., was sold at 16s. a cwt., realising £2. 5s. 4d.
65 MS. 4655/11, ff.215b, 241b, 309; MS. 4648/4, f.51.
66 MS. 4655/11, ff.9b, 14b–15, 47b.
67 MS. 4655/13, f.74.
68 MS. 4655/13, ff.78, 80, 99. The Livery fine was £6 at this date, and by paying an extra £14 the liveryman could secure exemption

from serving any and every office such as Renter Warden, Steward, etc., at any future time.

69 MS. 4655/13, f.31b.

70 MS. 4655/15, ff.70, 72b–73.

71 MS. 4655/13, ff.228b, 230, 250.

72 MS. 4655/15, ff.75–7.

73 In April 1649 the Court of Assistants ordered a chest to be provided and all members to raise a 'stock' or fund for the 'good and benefit of the Company, and every member thereof to pay a penny weekly at the least'. But nothing came of this plan (MS. 4655A, 3 April 1649).

74 MS. 4655/3, ff.73, 77, 153b, 157; MS. 4646, ff.96, 112, 251; MS. 4648/1, 24 November 1666.

75 MS. 4648/1, *passim*. In 1684 the Shenfield farm was mortgaged to three creditors to whom the Company owed £312 (MS. 4655/9, ff.22–3).

76 MS. 4655/11, f.31b.

77 MS. 4648/7, April and August 1756; June 1757; MS. 4655/16, ff.153–8, 197b.

78 MS. 4655/17, ff.457, 464, 496.

79 MS. 4646, ff.109–63b.

80 MS. 4655/19, ff.159, 162–8b, 176b, 179b–180, 196.

81 MS. 4655/19, ff.417–18b, 470, 475b, 477, 487b.

82 The first regular list of stock prices, compiled by John Freake, a broker, appeared on 26 March 1714 (E. T. Powell, *The Evolution of the Money Market* (1916), p. 147).

83 In March 1758, after a special sub-committee had reported that immediate liabilities were £220, the Court considered selling £200 3% Bank Annuities bought out of surplus funds in October 1753 (MS. 4655/16, ff.88b, 91).

84 MS. 4648/8, February 1766; MS. 4648/10, *passim*; MS. 4655/17 f.19b.

85 See below, Chap. 18.

Public Service and
Private Interest

It is well known that the gilds were important cogs in the machinery of government from the early Middle Ages down to the eighteenth century. In London the public duties of the gilds and companies included the provision of men for the king's ships and the trained bands; the supply and storage of arms, equipment and gunpowder; and of corn against times of dearth. Moreover, each in its own field was expected to give expert technical advice on the drafting of commercial and industrial regulations, proclamations and Acts of Parliament, and to provide, on request, 'deputations' from among their senior and more respected members to help the customs officers. Since the central government, the municipal authorities and the gilds were, thus, partners in the business of governing the country, governmental regulation and control of industry and trade was not resented as oppressive interference, but accepted as a natural feature of the established order. In an age of high protective tariffs or total prohibitions on textiles and other important classes of imports, the senior members of the Weavers' Company were serving not only themselves, but the Government, when they helped to track down and identify smuggled goods which competed formidably with their own products. Public service and private interest were interwoven. On occasion the London Weavers co-operated with other companies having similar interests, such as the Company of Weavers of Canterbury, or the Gold and Silver Wire-Drawers, when H.M. Customs had seized quantities of prohibited foreign-made lace, fringes, brocades, and embroidery containing gold and silver thread.[1]

Appropriate action sometimes depended upon the initiative of the gilds. In the spring of 1612, for instance, the Weavers' Company appointed four liverymen 'to use their best means to treat with the rest of the Livery to contribute towards the charge of the suit to be prosecuted against such as illegally bring ribands, laces, girdles, corses and corses of tissues or points from beyond the sea' (contrary to the statute 19 Henry VIII, c. 21) and to collect any money freely given by the commonalty and foreign brethren.[2]

Early in the reign of Charles I the Lord Mayor of London set up a committee of aldermen to inquire into 'the great abuse and deceit in making of silk lace uttered and sold within this City', and the committee promptly called to their aid thirteen 'of the most sufficient and best experienced Silkmen and as many Weavers of like skill and experience'. Meeting at Weavers' Hall, they drafted an Act of Parliament 'which should have been put into the Parliament house, but was not done by reason the Parliament broke up so suddenly'.[3] Charles I always evinced interest in English industries, partly—perhaps mainly—because he saw them as promising sources of revenue. Broadly speaking, his policy was traditional and authoritarian, seeking to promote progress by proclamation and development by decree. About the year 1630 one finds the silk weavers complaining bitterly of the 'false and deceitful' dyeing of silk yarn in order to increase weight, thereby damaging the yarn so that it became not only difficult to weave, but produced a fabric poor in colour and much less durable in use. After an inquiry in the Court of Star Chamber, the King issued a proclamation setting up an 'office for surveying and trying of all silk dyed and to be dyed', and strictly commanding 'that no silk dyer do hereafter use any slip, alder-bark, filings of iron, or other deceitful matter, in dyeing silk, either black or coloured; that no silk shall be dyed of any other black but Spanish black, and not of the dye called London black, . . . neither shall they dye any silk before the gum be fair boiled off from the silk, being raw'. The dyers were to receive 16d. per raw pound for all ordinary colours and 18d. for Spanish black. Two surveyors were appointed and the Bailiffs and Wardens of the Weavers' Company were instructed to 'make choice of such able and sufficient men of their Company as shall be needful' to assist the surveyors 'in the searching, discovering and finding out all such falsities and abuses as shall be used and practised in the dyeing of silk'. But thirteen broad weavers, members of the Livery, Yeomanry or Commonalty, were bold enough to protest against these proposals, fearing that the cost and trouble would be likely to 'lie very heavy upon all the Company not only in respect of paying so much upon every pound, but our attendances upon the Office and the difficulty of having our silk out of the same in any convenient [i.e. short] time, to the extreme prejudice of many poor families employed by us and others'. It was hard enough, they said, to compete against 'the multitude of broad silks and stuffs imported from France and Holland'. Therefore they asked that the proposed Bill be dropped and replaced by another whereby (a) the same end as regards the dyeing would be attained with less hindrance and danger to the broad-silk weavers and (b) the importation of broad silks from France and Holland would be prohibited, thus affording greater security to the London Master Weavers 'by whom many thousands of families are employed'.[4] But not until eight years later did Charles I remove, in part, the restrictions imposed by his earlier proclamation so as to permit such silk to be dyed upon the gum (commonly called hard-silk) 'as was proper for making tufted taffetas, figured satins, fine slight ribands, and ferret ribands, both black and coloured; and . . . with a degree of candour not always admitted into the edicts of princes, [said] that he had now become better informed upon the subject'.[5]

Smuggling 'to the great prejudice and damage of ye Nation's commodities' is again mentioned in the Company's records in 1672, when the Commissioners for the Customs asked for help in valuing and selling 'great quantities' of prohibited foreign ribbons and laces, as well as other silks and stuffs on which import duty had not been paid. Without hesitation the Weavers promised to recommend to the Commissioners 'such honest and skilful persons as may make a just appraisement' of the seized goods, and afterwards sell them 'to the best benefit and advantage of his Majesty and ye Seizers and from time to time render a true account thereof, they being only allowed their incident charges therein'. In all, eighteen members of the Company were appointed: two Officers, six Assistants, six Liverymen and four of the Yeomanry.[6] Two years later the Commissioners appointed as searchers and seizers of prohibited and smuggled manufactures two men, a weaver and a mercer, both recommended by the Weavers' Company; and within a few months the Company was asked to recommend yet another person well qualified 'to assist . . . especially in parts remote from London'.[7] There can be no doubt that the Customs authorities needed all the help they could get, for goods such as valuable laces were continually smuggled in in many ingenious ways: inside quartern loaves or ladies' turbans or sewn inside garments such as the back of a gentleman's waistcoat, or hidden in the carcasses of Normandy poultry destined ostensibly for the English market.[8]

During the last third of the seventeenth century the Company was remarkably active in helping to discover and seize prohibited goods; in promoting, supporting or opposing various Parliamentary Bills concerning textiles; and arranging for the submission of evidence (sometimes supported by numerous samples)[9] to Parliamentary Committees: all of which involved the Company in considerable expense. Over £132 was spent in 1671–2 'attending the Parliament' (towards which the Yeomanry voluntarily contributed £10), and, year by year, this item in the accounts increased until, in 1676–7, it reached £233. In the following year, however, the total sum spent attending the Parliament, King and Council and in procuring

Deputations to seize prohibited goods did not exceed £100, of which a sum of nearly £41 was paid to Mr Cole, the Clerk, in July and August 1678, for 'procuring Deputations, Writs of Assistance and Warrants for seizing foreign Ribbons', and 'as a Gratuity for his attendance at Parliament this year'.[10] These payments, which include, of course, the various tips and bribes to persons of high status as well as low, inseparable from such business in the seventeenth century, continued up to and after the turn of the century.[11] In 1689–90, for example, a sum of £235 was spent by the Company, including £30 to the Clerk, 'towards the Charge of Seizing Silks and attending Parliament'; and £5 'paid to Mr. Harrison who seized the 7 horse loads of French goods'. On the other hand, as a partial offset, the Company thankfully received, in 1690–1, 'of the Compa. of Weavers at Canterbury their moiety of disbursements at Parliament, £62. 2s.'

Excessive or misdirected zeal could, on occasion, prove expensive, as was the case when the Company had to pay to Elias Turner the sum of £75 'awarded him for his damages sustained by detaining his Silks', and a further £2. 16s. 6d. to an attorney.[12] At another time certain weavers complained to the Court of Assistants that six pieces of silk made by them had been wrongly seized on behalf of the Royal Lustring Company as being black alamodes and lustrings, which most certainly they were not. The Weavers' Company appointed an *ad hoc* committee to inspect the silks in question and to treat with the Royal Lustring Company and the Commissioners of Customs.[13] The result is not recorded.

The true story of the introduction into England of the manufacture of alamodes and lustrings is to be found in the Weavers' records. It begins with an entry in the Court minutes dated 14 January 1684.[14]

John Larguier and John Quet who lately came from Nimes in Languedoc now appeared and declared that they were lately come from . . . France, that they were fully enabled to weave and perfect Lustrings, Alamodes and other fine Silks as well for service and beauty in all respects as they are perfected in France, and praying to be admitted. The Court considered thereof, and being willing to give all just and reasonable encouragement for the bringing in and completing the carrying on those works here (which have not at any time been used here) for the benefit of the Publique, this Court do . . . consent and permitt that they be allowed six weeks for making an Experiment thereof, and that in the working thereof one or more Members of this Court from time to time supervising the doing thereof that it may be truly understood that they do actually perform the same, then this affair to be considered at a full Court in order to their Admissions.

Not six weeks, but seven months later (on 11 August 1684), John Larguier 'produced a piece of Alamode Silk made in England, the which piece was shot with a piece of coloured silk given him by Mr. Willaw', one of the Assistants. The members of the Court were intensely interested because, as they said, 'the like hath never been made in England, and conceiving that it will be of great benefit to this Nation, do agree that the said John Larguier be admitted a foreign Master *gratis* upon this condition that he employ himself, and others of the English Nation, in making Alamode and Lustring Silks for one year from this day'.[15]

Three years later the Weavers' Company decided to advise the Government not to grant 'a patent for making Alamodes, Lustrings &c.';[16] a position which they maintained during expensive proceedings which dragged on into 1689, as the Company's accounts show (see Table 6.1).

Table 6.1 *Company expenses relating to opposition to a patent*

July 1688, the Renter Bailiff:

paid at the Hall when the Committee and several of the Trade met and went to the King and Council	12*s*. 10*d*.
Spent with the Committee about Lustrings, two meetings and	13*s*. 9*d*.
Spent at Whitehall attending the King and Council and with the Committee and several Members and for Coach hire and boat hire &c.	£2 0*s*. 0*d*.

The Clerk's disbursements in connection with the same business were:

	£	s.	d.
Given my Lord Chancellor's Gent		2	6
Pd. for the Order of Council	3	2	6
Given the door keepers		3	0
To Sir B. Shore	3	4	6
To Mr. Serjeant Trinder	3	4	6
To their Clerks		5	0
For the Order of Council &c., after the hearing	3	2	6
Given the under Clerk		5	0
Coach hire and boat hire		8	2
	13	17	8

Despite considerable expenditure, the Weavers were never able to prevent either the incorporation of the Royal Lustring Company as a joint stock company in 1692, or the grant, in 1698, of a new charter

138

'whereby its powers and privileges were importantly enlarged, and the sole use, exercise and benefit of making, dressing and lustring plain black alamodes, renforces, and lustrings in England and Wales was granted to it for fourteen years'. But this company was stricken down by a deadlier foe than competition, for a change in public taste and feminine fashions largely destroyed the demand for alamodes and lustrings, and the Royal Lustring Company expired at about the same time as its charter.[17]

The pamphlet entitled *Reasons for a Clause to preserve our Manufactures of Silk* (1719 or 1720) makes it clear that the Royal Lustring Company had 'left off the making of Lustrings and Alamodes, . . . [had] divided their Stock, and so in effect are dissolv'd', and that members of the Weavers' Company were already filling the gap. In so doing they observed 'this smuggling trade to increase more and more [and] they have determined to undertake the suppressing of it, if they may have the desired help from Parliament'.

The Weavers' relations with the Throwsters' Company seem to have been less harmonious than with the Royal Lustring Company, for the Throwsters and the Weavers often felt obliged by their respective industrial interests to offer opposing arguments and advice to the government. The Throwsters naturally wished for plentiful and cheap supplies of raw silk, but protection from the competition of foreign-made yarns, while the Weavers were for a free market in both raw silk and yarn, whether produced at home or abroad. Therefore, in the mid-1720s, when the Throwsters drafted a Bill to prohibit the importation of certain thrown silks from Italy, Naples and Sicily, they came up against 'Reasons humbly offered by the Weavers of London' to the Government:

1 that the volume and expansion of the silk manufacture depends upon the weavers' freedom to use every suitable sort of silk yarn, for this has enabled them 'as often as the fashions have altered at home, or new patterns been brought from abroad, immediately to turn their hands to them; and not only to imitate, but to improve them';

2 that Italian thrown silks are essential to the manufacture of various sorts of wrought silks as well as those mixed with worsted;

3 that the restrictions proposed by the Throwsters' Bill would cause loss of trade and serious unemployment among weavers and others who worked for them;

4 that the Weavers, on an average, employ 20 poor persons to every 3 employed by the throwsters;

5 that English thrown yarns are not so good and suitable as the Italian.

In the end, the Weavers' arguments prevailed, to the great relief and satisfaction of many hundreds of journeymen weavers.[18]

In 1739 and 1740, the Weavers' Company was advocating the use of Chinese and Persian supplies,[19] but success was slow in coming. Early in 1750, the Weavers, in co-operation with the Russian merchants, petitioned Parliament to open trade from Persia through Russia so that Persian raw silk would become available to the English silk industry, as it was already to the French and Dutch. After 'constant daily attendance for a considerable time' by a special committee of the Weavers' Company, patience was rewarded and the committee was able to report (June 1750) that, after 'much Labour, Solicitation and Attendance, and at a very considerable expense' of over £400, three Acts of Parliament had actually been procured: (a) an Act to reduce substantially the import duty on Chinese raw silk from 4s. 9½d. to 1s. 11d. per lb.—the same as Italian and other raw silks; (b) an Act to permit the importation of Persian raw silk; and (c) an Act to increase the penalties for seducing artificers away to foreign countries, for buying or receiving purloined or embezzled materials, and for exporting any utensils used in the woollen and silk manufactures.[20]

The emigration—some said 'enticement'—of weavers, woolcombers and other textile workers to continental countries in the eighteenth century was a recrudescence of a movement which had caused alarm in Elizabethan days. It was a drain, actual or threatened, not of scientists, but craftsmen; not of brains, but manual skill. In 1719 representatives of the Weavers' Company gave evidence before the Commissioners for Trade and Plantations on the subject of enticement of artificers into France,[21] and thirty years later we find the Company still grappling with the problem, for in July 1749 information was received that 'Sundry Artificers in the Weaving Manufacture' were preparing to go 'to Spain with divers quantitys of Looms and Utensils for Weaving in order to set up and exercise the said Manufacture in Spain'. This, the Weavers thought, constituted a threat not only to their interests, but to the good of the whole nation. Within a month the would-be emigrants were arrested and 'detained in Custody of his Majesty's Messengers'. On hearing this good news, the Weavers resolved to defray the expenses so far incurred, and to prosecute 'this Affair and the said Artificers . . . to put a stop to the said Destructive Scheme'. By the end of 1749, the Company had paid nearly £7 to witnesses, and the Clerk's bills and other expenses incurred in the 'pursuit of the artificers going to Spain' amounted to more than £54. Nor was this the end, for the Weavers' special committee, having discovered 'the Seducers of the Artificers', had instituted legal proceedings against them at the Company's expense, and had recommended an application to the Government for a more effectual law to prevent such schemes in future (hence the Act of

Parliament mentioned above).[22] Furthermore, in 1751 John Peters, a freeman of the Company, gave an account of his activities and expenses incurred in trying to detect 'divers Foreigners who had been buying up Tools and Utensils for the Weaving Manufacture to send abroad into foreign parts'. He had actually pursued a consignment as far as Gravesend only to find that the ship had sailed. However, when he promised to try to make further discoveries, the Court of Assistants voted five guineas to compensate him for his travelling expenses and loss of time. A few months later, Jacob Sharpe, a Leeds broadcloth weaver recently returned from Spain, told the special committee that 'great numbers of Artificers and Utensils were sent from England and Ireland' to set up a weaving industry there. Whereupon the London Weavers and the Yorkshire Clothiers took joint action to inform the Government.[23]

The sort of activities described above continued more or less intensively in the second half of the eighteenth century. In 1761, for example, customs officers who had seized a quantity of 'foreign wrought silks clandestinely imported', invited the Company to prosecute those found in possession of the goods, which would entitle the Company to a share in any penalties recovered. On another occasion the Weavers and the Wire-Drawers appointed, at the request of the Commissioners of Customs, one member of each Company to attend at the Customs House twice a week to inspect and appraise gold and silver lace and brocades.[24] When, in 1752, a quantity of gold and silver lace, seized at a tailor's shop, was condemned as being of French manufacture, it was publicly burnt and the tailor was fined £100. Thus, in various ways, the Company co-operated with other Companies and bodies of textile manufacturers and merchants, and with the Government, in order to enforce or modify existing laws and to propose and press for new ones.[25] Such co-operation was almost essential in a society steadily growing in size and complexity which found itself with insufficient governmental machinery to handle the increasing volume of public business.[26]

Co-operation with the Commissioners of Customs could, on occasion, yield unusual and unexpected benefits, as it did in the spring of 1764 when word went around among the London master weavers that a customs officer had 'made a very valuable seizure' of a large book and case containing more than a thousand patterns of French silk goods—gold and silver brocades, silver tissues, flowered velvets, lustrings, grograms, sarsenets, satins, etc.—in a remarkable variety of designs and colours. The Weavers, who realised at once the importance of the capture, were delighted and resolved to get possession of the patterns. But the customs officers, well aware of this, cunningly suggested a 'satisfaction' payment of £50 before they would hand over their prize. Whereupon the Company appealed to the

Commissioners of Customs, who agreed to send the precious patterns to Weavers' Hall, where they were deposited in a jealously guarded chest with three locks. Preserved among the Company's papers is an

Acct. of the Number of the French Patterns Delivd. to the Weavers Compa. by the Commrs. of the Customs by Direction of the Lords of the Treasury to be Returned to the said Commrs., taken 19th & 20th July 1764

In the Book	720
In the Case	327
Total	1,047

(Signed) John Hinde
E. Briggs[27]

So great was the interest aroused in the trade that arrangements were made to exhibit the patterns at stated times on certain days. Admission was restricted to 'Silk Manufacturers and Freemen of the Company', and not more than six persons at a time were allowed to inspect the patterns, with at least one Officer or Assistant always present.[28] In the same month of July 1764, the Renter Bailiff 'Paid Messrs. Bland & Trott[29] pursuant to the Order of the Commissioners of Customs for their moiety of the Appraised Value of the Book & Case of French Patterns on their being delivered to the Compa. £26. 5. 0.'

NOTES

1 H. Steward, *History of the Company of Gold and Silver Wire Drawers* (1891), p. 88.
2 MS. 4655/1, ff.15, 18.
3 MS. 4647, ff.166–74. Charles I's second Parliament sat from February to June 1626, and its sudden end boded ill for the future, for Charles clearly stated his fixed opinion that the House of Commons 'was for counsel, not for control'.
4 MS. 4647, ff.614–52; MS. 4655/3, ff.32–3, 44–5.
5 Lardner, *Silk*, p. 58. Apparently this problem cropped up again in 1661 when the Weavers' Company prepared a petition for presentation to the 'Grand Committee of Trade concerning the abuse of heavy dyed silk' (MS. 4655/3, f.16).
6 MS. 4655A/3.
7 MS. 4655/7, f.74.
8 F. B. Palliser, *History of Lace* (3rd edn, 1875), Chap. 27.
9 MS. 4649A, f.28; MS. 4648/1, 13 March 1676.
10 MS. 4646, ff.104, 109–11; MS. 4648/1, July–August 1678.
11 See, e.g., MS. 4646, ff.126–9, 144, 146; MS. 4648/3, *passim*. In August 1708 the Weavers raised £50–£60 'for Parliamentary business' by a special collection, and in the same account ex-

penses of £25 are recorded for 'procuring several Clauses in several Acts of parliament'.

12 MS. 4649B/2, July and August 1690.

13 MS. 4655/11, f.8. An alamode was a thin glossy black silk; a lustring was a glossy silk fabric.

14 MS. 4655/9, f.12. This is *before* the Revocation of the Edict of Nantes in 1685, not after, as has sometimes been supposed.

15 MS. 4655/9, ff.37b–38, 61. In March 1685 Larguier secured the admission of a French journeyman to the Weavers' Company.

16 MS. 4646, f.122.

17 Lardner, *Silk*, pp. 60–1. The Weavers' Company finally withdrew their opposition in October 1692 (MS. 4655/10, f.7). The Royal Lustring Company is mentioned in the Weavers' minutes of 29 February 1712 (MS. 4655/11, f.93b). cf. MS. 4655/11, ff.16b–17b.

18 *The Humble Petition of many Journeymen Weavers* (1728), p. 2. See MS. 4655/12, ff.142b–3, and MS. 4648/4, f.104, which give the cost to the Weavers of opposing the Throwsters' Bill as £16. 10s. 10d.

19 *The Humble Petition of the Silk Weavers, Throwsters and others concerned in the Silk Manufactures* (n.d.); *Votes of the House of Commons* (1739), pp. 141–2; Lardner, *Silk*, p. 66.

20 MS. 4655/15, ff.317b–319, 327b, 344, 349b–350.

21 *Journal of Com. for Trade and Plantations* (1718), p. 441; (1719), p. 122. See also *The Case of the Weavers humbly offer'd to the . . . Parliament of Great Britain* (c. 1719) and *The Case of the Woollen and Silk Manufactures in Great Britain* (c. 1719), which is almost identical in text.

22 MS. 4655/15, ff.327b, 330b, 338b–340; MS. 4648/6A, *passim*.

23 MS. 4655/16, ff.14, 26b.

24 MS. 4655/16, ff.269b–271, 356b.

25 See, e.g., MS. 4655/16, ff.71, 80; MS. 4655/17, f.403b.

26 cf. M. G. Davies, *The Enforcement of English Apprenticeship, 1563–1642* (1956), p. 25.

27 John Hinde was Upper Bailiff in 1765–6; Ebenezer Briggs was the Clerk to the Company.

28 MS. 4655/16, ff.340, 347.

29 Probably the customs officers who made the seizure (MS. 4648/7, 11 July 1764).

Chapter 7

Strangers and Settlers

England has long been an island of refuge for persecuted and oppressed people from the continent of Europe, and the social stresses set up from time to time by the reception and settlement of various streams of 'strangers', as the alien immigrants were called, are part and parcel of our history. Who has not read of the contributions (sometimes much exaggerated) to English industrial development of such people as the Flemish and French weavers? In the second half of the sixteenth century the immigrants came largely (but not entirely) from the Netherlands, flying from 'the Spanish fury', but in the seventeenth century the French Protestants formed the principal immigrant group.[1] Since the refugees were, in the main, either professional people or craftsmen, they tended to settle in urban industrial centres, such as London, Norwich, Colchester, Coventry and Canterbury. In Elizabethan and Stuart London, already overcrowded especially in the liberties and out-parishes, any sizeable influx of population caused considerable concern. A return of aliens in the City of London, Southwark and Westminster in 1563 put the number at 4,534, and twenty years later a total of 5,141 was returned, of whom 1,604 were said to be dwelling and working 'outside the City'. A return made to the Privy Council in 1571 shows that the Netherlanders outnumbered the Frenchmen by approximately 7 or 8 to 1; while in the 1630s the ratio was only 2 to 1.[2] Table 7.1 shows the numbers and distribution of aliens in and around London at that time (c. 1635–9) as given in official returns.

The returns of aliens made by the Lord Mayor of London and the Constables of adjacent parishes[3] show that weavers—mostly silk weavers—and ancillary workers in textiles were concentrated in Bishopsgate, Portsoken and Coleman Street wards, in the four Southwark parishes, and the neighbouring parish of St Mary Magdalen, Bermondsey. No alien weavers are recorded in Cripplegate Within and Without. The statistics are shown in Table 7.2.

144

The total number of strangers returned as dwelling in these wards and parishes was 482, of whom 255, or nearly 53 per cent, were weavers, and another 34 were ancillary textile workers.

Table 7.1 *Numbers and distribution of aliens in and around London, c. 1635–9*

Aliens in	Approx. no.*
City of London	2,550
Liberties (outside the City)	2,000
Southwark	340
Parts of Middlesex adjacent to the City	830
Westminster	840
	6,560

* V. Pearl, *London and the Outbreak of the Puritan Revolution* (1961), quoting from Cal. S.P. Domestic, Charles I.

Table 7.2 *Strangers dwelling in and near London, 1618*

Ward	Total no. of strangers dwelling therein	No. of weavers and other textile workers included in column 2
Bishopsgate	190	138 silk weavers 6 throwsters, threadmakers, and dyers
Portsoken	84	29 weavers 2 silk throwsters 4 silk twisters
Coleman Street	31	10 weavers
Southwark parishes		
St Saviour	13	3 weavers 8 dyers
St Thomas	29	22 weavers
St George	15	3 weavers
St Olave	93	30 silk weavers 3 tape weavers 1 linen weaver 1 orris weaver 3 silk winders 11 dyers
Bermondsey		
St Mary Magdalen	27	14 silk weavers 1 stuff weaver

The Weavers' records of 'admissioners' show that at the beginning of the seventeenth century strangers (aliens) were being admitted at the rate of 9 or 10 per annum, each paying a £5 fee, while 'forren admissioners', chiefly English weavers (who might be descendants of strangers) from the provinces, were joining at the rate of 14 per annum, each paying £3, unless the Company exercised its discretion and reduced the fee, as it did when poverty or other special circumstances were proved.[4] From 1627 to 1630 the comparable rates of admission were: strangers, 7 per annum; foreign brothers, 11 per annum; and from 1637 to 1640 the figures are: strangers, 8 per annum; foreign brothers, 15 per annum.[5]

Since the majority of the Protestant immigrants followed 'manual trades' such as silk weaving and its ancillary crafts, they tended to settle in localities which had a strong Protestant tradition and a population of textile workers.[6] In the vicinity of London such a district lay between St Botolph's without Bishopsgate and the hamlet of Stepney. Stepney had been strongly Protestant 'while Catholicism was still the national religion', and in Elizabethan times Stephen Gosson had been a preacher there and 'had made St. Dunstan's ring with his vituperations against a lax and pleasure-loving age'.[7] Puritans and Dissenters were attracted to the district; indeed, so many refugee strangers settled in Norton Folgate, Shoreditch, Hoxton, Whitechapel and Bethnal Green, that the locality just beyond St Botolph's without Bishopsgate became known as Petty France. Strype, the eighteenth-century editor of Stow's famous *Survey of London*, wrote with approval of the Spitalfields district because it had become

> a great Harbour for poor Protestant Strangers, Walloons and French, who as in former Days, so of later, have been forced to become Exiles from their own Country for their Religion and for the avoiding cruel Persecution. Here they have found quiet and security, and settled themselves in their several Trades and Occupations; Weavers especially. Whereby God's Blessing surely is not only brought upon the Parish, by receiving poor Strangers (*Come ye Blessed of My Father &c. For I was a Stranger and ye took Me in*), but also a great advantage hath accrued to the whole Nation, by the rich Manufactures of Weaving Silks and Stuffs and Camlets: which Art they brought along with them. And this Benefit also to the Neighbourhood, that these Strangers may serve for patterns of Thrift, Honesty, Industry and Sobriety as well.[8]

People began to remark that however poor and hard-worked these strangers might be, they arranged and decorated their homes with a refinement of taste seldom seen in the homes of the English craftsmen.[9]

It was in the eighteenth century that the Methodists and Quakers became influential in Spitalfields and Hackney. George Whitefield, the famous itinerant Methodist preacher, preached to a large congregation in Spitalfields on New Year's Eve 1739, and later on the same day he 'expounded' in Southwark. He returned to Spitalfields in the following months and

> at two in the afternoon read prayers and preached at Christ Church . . . for the Orphan House. The congregation was not so large as might be expected, and that of the poorest sort, so that I began to doubt. But wherefore did I fear? For God enabled me to preach with power, and £25 was collected, to our great surprise. . . .[10]

Although the native London weavers were, on the whole, good-tempered, they could not always bring themselves to take a dispassionate and tolerant view of the strangers' incursions into their preserves. They were, indeed, much torn and divided. Their religious convictions prompted them to be sympathetic and helpful to fellow-Protestants forced by persecution to sacrifice their homes and flee their homeland. Enterprising master weavers were swayed by yet another consideration—the prospect of welcome additions to the supply of labour, especially to the pool of highly skilled craftsmen in the more expensive branches, such as the weaving of figured silk damasks and velvets. The small masters and journeymen, however, held opposite opinions. While they, too, felt sympathy for the parlous plight of the refugees on arrival, they resented any claims to superiority of craftsmanship and feared increasing competition for work and scarce living accommodation from the 'great Troops and infinite numbers of Strangers, Men of Foreign Nations, that daily flock over into this Kingdom and resort to this City', where many of them live and work 'without Order, Check or Controlment'.[11] They were especially hostile to unqualified alien weavers and to those qualified men who sought to evade the by-laws and ordinances of the Weavers' Company. In time of grievous distress and discontent, of slack trade, unemployment and shrinking earnings, the commonalty of native weavers were apt to turn against the strangers with accusations of breaches of regulations, use of the hated engine looms, and other forms of unfair competition, all aggravated by the recollection that when the 'distressed strangers' first came into London they had been 'lovingly received'. During such times of tension it was darkly hinted that some of the strangers were not genuine refugees from religious persecution, but had falsely adopted this role from dishonest or sinister motives.

The London Weavers' Company, as its records show, was careful to inquire whether strangers applying for admission as 'foreign brothers' were respectable and genuine immigrants intending to settle permanently in London, and always refused to countenance unqualified weavers, evasions of its rules, resistance to its searches, and all other irregular and dishonest practices. Thus, when an honest immigrant master weaver assured the Court of Assistants in April 1611 'that his servants, Maximilian Lombard, Stranger, born in Flanders, and Rowland de Chambre, Stranger, born in Turney [Tournai], are men of good name and fame . . . and sufficient workmen in the art of weaving', they were 'thereupon admitted and sworn his journeymen'. During the same month two other respectable alien journeymen, one a member of the French Church in London, were admitted;[12] but in the following spring, James le Calliett was fined 40s. for keeping three alien journeymen unadmitted for three months, and two other strangers were licensed by the Company to work only 'till this day month' and thereafter to be admitted if they could prove their right to exercise the craft, or be discharged if they could not.[13] A little later the Company seems to have relaxed its pressure for a time, but in December 1616 an order was made 'that John Blanchard, stranger silkweaver, and Paul de Rewell in Hedley's Alley shall be arrested at the suit of the Company . . . for using the art of weaving not being admitted'. An even more troublesome case at this period was that of Samuel Witts, who was fined 20s. for keeping too many looms and 13s. 4d. for employing two strangers as journeymen contrary to the Weavers' Ordinances, while his collaborator, Robert Ball, was fined 13s. 4d. for receiving three other alien journeymen ostensibly into his service when, in fact, they were 'neither hired with him nor receive wages nor victuals of him', but were working under cover of his name for the 'use and behoof' of Samuel Witts. Shortly afterwards, Witts incurred a further penalty of £5 for keeping five looms over and above the permitted number, and, with Robert Ball, he was haled before the Lord Mayor because he refused to pay. The 'divers abuses and wrongs by them committed' were recited to the Court which 'straightly charged' the defendants 'to be at all times hereafter obedient to the said Gild', adding for good measure that the City intended to give full support in future to the efforts of the Officers and Assistants of the Weavers' Company to enforce their rules and ordinances. Faced with committal to one of the Compters, Witts capitulated, paid his fines and promised to reform: whereupon the Weavers' Court of Assistants 'gave him back again . . . 20s. . . . which he accepted thankfully'.[14]

During 1618–19, it appears, strangers continued to arrive, some of whom were not acceptable to the Weavers' Company. Some were ordered to 'depart out of this liberty within fourteen days'; others were given leave to work for one month so as to get their bearings and then to depart.[15] But the problem persisted, and in 1622 the central

Government took a hand by setting up a Royal Commission to devise means to protect the interests and livelihood of native craftsmen and so to 'moderate' the strangers 'as may best stand with their conveniency and the present state of the times, and the good and welfare of our own people', not only in London but 'in other cities, towns and places' in England. This 'Commission concerning Strangers', having compiled a list of twenty-four statutes passed between the reigns of Henry IV and Elizabeth I, under which eleven major prohibitions were imposed upon strangers, 'under great penalties', regulating mainly the conditions under which they may dwell and work and sell their wares, remarked that 'the practice of Strangers, as we are credibly informed, is quite contrary to these Inhibitions in every one of these particulars'. Therefore, said the Commissioners, 'the natural subjects suffer much by the neglect of these laws which are so providently made for the wealth of the Kingdom, if all the particulars were examined'.

It is not easy to see what positive results flowed from the Commission's deliberations,[16] except that the London Weavers' commonalty were encouraged to put into writing the 'Grievances which the generality of the Companie of Weavers doe susteine'. They complain, for instance, that a 'great multitude of youths or boys' have 'come lately from beyond the seas, and here are set to work by Strangers, whether they can do the tenth part of their trade, yea or no, without bringing a Certificate of their service for their trade, or of their honest departure from their Countries'. Worse still, many Englishmen and Strangers take such boys 'weekly for small wages . . . to the utter undoing of such as have served seven years for their trade according to the Statute'. Moreover, such 'unlawful' masters continue to flourish 'without government of our Company, for when our Bailiffs and Wardens come to search, they shut their doors against them, and when they are touched with any warrant to come before a Justice, they presently fly to the [French or Dutch] Church for refuge'.[17] Moreover, even if the Company succeeds in bringing them before a justice, 'they use means whereby they are presently released'. And they do not sell their products themselves, 'but they have Wooemen Broakers to sell for them . . .', going daily:

> from shop to shop . . . from one end of the City to the other,
> and all other out places. And they likewise retail at noblemen's
> houses and other places contrary to the Statutes of this
> Kingdom and Custom of this City. . . . By these and such like
> abuses many of our Brethren which have been good house-
> keepers, and have kept many of our own nation at work, are
> constrained to give over housekeeping and become Labourers,
> Porters,[18] Waterbearers, Sellers of Fish and of Fruit. . . .

Others go for Soldiers, leaving their wives and children in most lamentable misery.

But if these abuses were reformed 'the Weavers, which . . . do set on work more poor Children than any three Companies in London, might be able to take a hundred in a year more than now they do from the charge of this City'. The document states in conclusion that 'this writing was drawn . . . by John Counley and William Counley, and by them and others of the Commonalty showed to the Court of Aldermen'.[19]

This statement was in due course referred to a Committee of Aldermen, together with a supplementary petition drawn by the same weavers, in which they asserted that the Weavers' Company already had sufficient powers to put down the abuses complained of, but the Company's Officers were reluctant to take action. 'We are', said the petitioners, 'a great number of poor men which long have groaned under the heavy burthen of want and poverty, not being able by our hard labours and busy industry to maintain our families.' They asked that the established customs of their craft shall be observed and the Weavers' Ordinances properly enforced; that men free of other Companies, but weavers by trade, shall be governed by those Ordinances and shall bind their apprentices at Weavers' Hall; and that all Strangers 'which come from beyond the seas or elsewhere . . . either Master or Journeyman . . . [shall] be governed by the Orders of our Hall'. They asked for strict enforcement of the limitations on the numbers of looms, for many weavers kept more looms than the Ordinances allow, 'yea, some of them twice as many . . . and especially [the] Strangers'. Lastly, they asked for the revival of a Yeomanry composed of 'honest men and sufficient workmen . . . [for] no Company in this City have more need of a Yeomanry than the Weavers'.[20]

Despite this poignant plea so deftly drafted, reinforced by a threat to petition the King if no redress could be otherwise obtained, nothing effective was done and the commonalty's grievances against their Bailiffs, Wardens and Assistants continued to fester for several years, occasionally aggravated almost beyond endurance by cases such as that of the Fleming, James Cassoone, a lawn weaver, who employed two aliens on this work, 'alleging that there is no Englishman can make of the same Stuff, pretending he setteth them to work to teach some of our Native-born in that Art, which he reported the English to be ignorant of'. The infuriated English weavers offered to produce before the Court of Aldermen a number of English lawn weavers who could and did produce work superior to anything made by Cassoone.[21]

At length, some thirty of the commonalty met at the Black Boy tavern in Cornhill on 13 September 1630 and, having discussed their troubles, set up a small committee to draft a petition to the Lord Mayor. They further agreed 'that every man shall assess himself according to his own willing mind freely and willingly towards so honest a business' by giving weekly contributions to be continued 'until the said Suite be ended'. Then follows a list of thirty names headed by William Counley, of whom thirteen each gave or promised 12*d*., but nothing is recorded against the other names.[22] When the petition was ready, William Counley, Samuel Seaton, Robert Warde and one other presented it to the Lord Mayor. In essence, it was an indictment of the Officers and Assistants of the Weavers' Company, declaring that the petitioners, 'with the rest of the Company [were] much oppressed and kept in extreme poverty and want by reason that the Statute against Intruders upon our Trade who never served for the same is not duly executed', despite the orders for its 'well government' made by the Lord Mayor and Aldermen, which have been ignored 'by the Masters of the Company', so that just 'as many offenders [are] suffered and permitted to continue as heretofore they have done'. The Yeomanry, too, were apparently not receiving proper support from the Officers and Assistants, for the petitioners ask that 'ye said 16 men may be enjoined to continue a weekly search . . . and also that such abuses as they shall find and present unto the Masters may be forthwith reformed'.[23]

This attack was too much for 'the Masters at the Hall', who promptly countered by branding Counley and his companions as conspirators harbouring sinister intentions not disclosed in their petition. The four men were therefore summoned to appear at the next Court of Aldermen, where, notwithstanding the peril in which they now stood, Counley, Seaton and Warde (the other man had faded away!) stoutly maintained that those who met at the Black Boy did not, as the 'Masters' alleged,

> sociate themselves together for some evil purpose, [but] to make known the great negligence of the said Bailiffs, Wardens and Assistants . . . and it is well known to us all that by reason of the Bailiffs &c. taking sums of money and valuable gifts of intruders to allow them to use the Trade of Weaving, there are many now where, if the Orders were put in execution, there would not be any.

Furthermore, the Bailiffs and others associated with them, 'knowing themselves to be faulty' and wishing to 'continue in their bad dealing without being discovered', were trying to hinder the commonalty 'in their honest proceeding . . . although many hundred households be undone thereby'. Doubtless the Company's Officers and Assistants were somewhat shaken by this exposure, but nothing more positive seems to have resulted. It may be that the City Fathers, whatever their private thoughts and sympathies, were reluctant to become involved in the Company's internal dissensions.[24] However, some two years later they did call to the attention of the King in Council the 'extraordinary enlargement of the suburbs, where great numbers of traders do enjoy, without charge (i.e. taxation), equal benefit with the freemen and citizens of London'; a statement which is echoed in a Royal Proclamation of 1637 deploring the intrusion, into places within three miles of the City, of aliens and non-apprenticed folk, and the resultant 'false wares' and overcrowded 'noysome and contagious' suburbs.[25] Meantime, the Weavers' commonalty had attempted to petition the King in June 1635, and later had put forward the additional accusation that many alien immigrants were fugitive criminals or deserters from foreign armies.[26]

The Weavers' pressure was maintained up to the beginning of the Civil War. Indeed, in February 1641 the draft of a Bill 'for the preventing of divers abuses in the Trade of Weaving' was thoroughly considered and, eventually, approved by the Weavers' Court of Assistants and thirty-one Liverymen. The document referred to 'the multitude of aliens and strangers born' who had flooded into various parts of the kingdom, especially into or near the cities of London, Canterbury, Norwich, and Westminster, where they had set up in trade, engaging servants and journeymen, mostly aliens.[27] Evidently the intention was to force the strangers to conform to the Company's ordinances on membership, apprentices, false fabrics, etc., and to suppress the activities of illegal alien brokers and hawkers.[28]

During the Civil War the agitation against aliens was thrust aside by more fundamental issues; but in 1653 the tough old problem reappeared. Thus, in March–April 1653 the Weavers' Company summoned a journeyman, 'Abr. Rinnelbrooke, not admitted', and his master, 'a Frenchman in Peticote Lane', to prove their right to the trade and their willingness to take up membership, or else . . .; and another Frenchman in the same street was sued because he had 'put an Englishman out of work' and had refused to obey the Company's summons.[29] Less than four months later, the Weavers' Company, evidently much concerned, issued a solemn declaration of policy.[30]

Whereas divers persons born in foreign nations do dwell and reside in this Commonwealth setting up and exercising as masters the trade of weaving contrary to several statutes in that case provided, some whereof were constrained to come out of their own countries for conscience sake and others have here inhabited many years and married English wives, and in the late war have manifested much affection to the Commonwealth by adventuring themselves in the public service and contributed their estates likewise, and others of them have lately come over into England and are not members of the Church and yet do use and exercise the trade of weaving to the great damage and dishonour of the Commonwealth and prejudice of this Corporation. It is therefore fit and so ordered by this Court that such of the said aliens as lived any considerable time and declared their affection to the Commonwealth and prove their service to the trade of weaving as aforesaid shall be admitted as members of this Company and so become subject to the government thereof. And that such others of the aliens as are lately come over shall not be permitted to exercise the said trade of weaving any longer, but be proceeded against according to the law and statutes of this nation.

The Company appealed to the Elders of the Dutch and French Churches for their co-operation in carrying this policy into effect; but the Elders were on the horns of a dilemma, for they could hardly go all the way with the Weavers' Company without abandoning their Christian duty to succour recently arrived refugee members of their congregations. They did, however, try to influence those members of their congregations who had exercised the weaving trade for many years without joining the Weavers' Company, to apply for membership, and in a limited number of instances they were successful, especially in the 1660s after the Restoration. Some of these 'admissioners' had been living and weaving in England for twenty to twenty-five and even thirty years.[31] Yet, despite their long period of settlement many were obviously still very poor. A few examples must suffice.

John Doozen, a Stranger, and a very poor man with a wife and 'a great charge of Children', was admitted a foreign journeyman gratis.

Peter Clement, a Frenchman, was ordered to give up weaving in London because he had been in England only two years; and Nicholas Rufine was fined 13s. for 'employing 2 Frenchmen who have been in England but 6 months . . . and was to turn them away presently, which he promised'.[32]

Jeremiah Terry 'brought Martin Grere who came from Cambrai about 1½ years since, his parents being Papists and he a Protestant; [the Court] ordered that he procure an attestation of his service within a month and this Court will further consider'.

Two Frenchmen, 'lately come from Cambridge for Religion, one of them being there formerly imprisoned upon that account and ye other having renounced Papacy openly in the French Congregation', were regarded as exceptional cases and therefore admitted.

Paul Turpine, a Walloon, who had 'used the trade for 40 years', was admitted a foreign master; and 'Henry Messelles, a High German, having been here 8 years, and his service of 7 years at Hamburgh attested now . . . and inasmuch as he hath married ye Widow of John

Green, Weaver, deceased, and especially for ye last consideration he is admitted a foreign Master for £4; now paid in part 40s.'[33]

Towards the end of 1668 'Some of ye Gentm. of ye French and Dutch Congregations appeared at this Court declaring that by reason of a Persecution in France [they] prayed ye Kindness of this Compa. as heretofore to admit such as shall come.' At the next Court they had their answer: that in the past the Company had always tried to preserve good relations with the French and Dutch Churches; but they

> have now very great grounds to believe that ye foreign members have and do invite more Strangers over (and they come) under pretence of a Persecution. But if that calamity shall really happen and this Court sensible thereof being satisfied that [the immigrants] were brought up and have right to this trade, this Court will as heretofore continue their favour and kindness to them and as they doubt not will be satisfactory to both Churches.[34]

We are now approaching the decade preceding the Revocation of the famous Edict of Nantes, which had been promulgated in 1598 by Henry IV of France in an attempt to propitiate his Protestant subjects after his own decision to embrace Catholicism. 'This edict', says Victor Duruy, the French historian, 'proclaimed the modern principle of toleration in matters of religion, and the corollary that the state should hold aloof from religious disputes in order to impose on all respect for the public peace.' The repeal of 'what remained of the Edict' nearly ninety years later[35] by that all-powerful autocrat, Louis XIV, was not an isolated event; it was the last staggering stroke in a prolonged persecution which destroyed all promise of continuing toleration and was at certain times and in certain places savage and merciless.

> Huguenot emigration overseas . . . had continued steadily during the first half of the seventeenth century. At times, when government policy at home was tolerant, it was a mere trickle, at other times, under the spur of renewed mistreatment, it was a stream. When the first measures of Louis XIV convinced all who did not deliberately shut their eyes to it that it was wiser to prepare for worse days than to hope for better ones, the exodus became a river; and after 1685, when the Edict of Nantes was repealed and Protestantism in France finally, officially wiped out, it rose to a torrent.[36]

What Louis XIV had in mind was the 'winning back' to Mother Church of the French Protestants in the sacred cause of religion and national unity, so that eventually he might be able to 'offer to God a wholly Catholic France'. But the path was dangerously steep, and conversion by persuasion soon slid into coercion by legal sanctions, followed in time, by a further slide into forcible extirpation of heresy. 'If God preserve the King,' wrote Madame de Maintenon in 1680, 'there will not be one Huguenot left twenty years hence.'[37] All sorts of pressure were used, some ingenious, some tempting—'consciences were bought for money'—some openly brutal like the 'Dragonnades' which began in Poitou in March 1681. Dragoons, who were deliberately billeted in Protestant households as 'booted missionaries' to bring about the conversion of their hosts and their families to Roman Catholicism, 'were allowed every license, except murder and rape'.[38] In June 1681 Louis XIV issued an edict lowering from twelve to seven years the age at which 'conversion' of children of Protestant parents would be accepted as valid. Some five weeks later, Charles II declared publicly that he felt bound by honour and conscience to assist Protestants persecuted for their faith.[39]

Repercussions of this bitter conflict of faith and conscience can be traced in the London Weavers' records over many years. The Company was in consultation with the French and Dutch Churches in London in 1669, and in December of that year had business before the King and Council 'touching aliens and foreigners'. Again, on 4 May 1670 'the Bailiffs, Wardens and some Assistants attended his Majesty and Council about the French and Dutch Congregations' and the admission of their members to the Weavers' Company: proceedings which cost the Company nearly £30.[40] In June 1670 the Elders of the two Congregations 'came [to Weavers' Hall] and returned their thanks to this Court for their civility to many of their members shewn, desiring a continuation of the same'. The admission books are, unfortunately, missing between 1646 and 1695, but the Court minutes indicate that an abnormal number of 'strangers' were admitted after 1670 on giving satisfactory proofs of training and experience in weaving in cities and towns such as Paris, Rouen, Tours, Tournai and Lille.[41] The fact that, in September 1672, the Company took the further step of having its admission oath for masters and journeymen translated into French[42] suggests that large numbers of French weavers were still flowing into London and that the migration was expected to continue. This was fully thirteen years before the Revocation of the Edict of Nantes.

One of the chief points of the settlement between the Weavers' Company, the Dutch and French Congregations, and the Government was that henceforth master weavers were to employ at least as many English journeymen as strangers. But within five or six years, it seems, the agreement was being evaded and many aliens or strangers were working as master weavers, taking apprentices and employing journeymen, although such so-called 'masters' were not regarded as sufficiently qualified to be admitted to membership of the Weavers' Company. In 1676–7, although the King in Council had asked the Company to adopt a lenient and liberal attitude, the Court of Assistants 'ordered that henceforth no Alien or Stranger born shall be admitted Master except it be debated and agreed by a full Court, and in that case also to be very sparing in admitting any Master but upon some weighty grounds or reasons'.[43] Mounting complaints of the employment of excessive numbers of strangers are to be heard again in the early 1680s, as the flood-waters of immigration from France began to rise to new and alarming levels. For example, in March 1685, when several freemen complained that 'many foreign members now employ more French than English', the Weavers' Court promptly asked for names, and the very next day had ten accused members before them at Weavers' Hall. Some confessed and were fined, including one who pleaded that he did not understand English. Another stated that usually he employed seven men, four of them English; but recently 'two of the English went away of their own accord'. The rest denied the allegations and the Yeomanry were ordered to search during the ensuing week to discover the true facts if possible.[44]

Meanwhile a public policy of sympathetic welcome to the French refugees was being pursued. When, in August and September 1681, more than 600 'distressed poor Protestants', mainly weavers, clothiers and fisherfolk, arrived in the Thames in a number of small vessels, Charles II, wryly remembering that he had himself been a refugee for many years, announced that he felt bound 'to comfort and support all such afflicted Protestants who . . . shall desire to shelter themselves' under his protection. He promised to grant free letters of denization and liberty to ply legitimate trades and handicrafts. The King's subjects followed his lead by collecting £14,000 in 1681 for the relief of distressed immigrants.[45]

The final blow fell on 22 October 1685 when the Instrument of Revocation ended the legal existence of what its enemies called 'la réligion prétendue réformée'. Many French Protestants who had so far managed to hold on, now found their situation intolerable and the prospects of relentless persecution horrifying. The refugee river became a torrent indeed. It is estimated that between 200,000 and 250,000 Frenchmen, mainly town-dwellers, emigrated. Reims, Tours, Nîmes, Rouen, lost over half their workers—clothworkers, clockmakers, jewellers, shipwrights; some of France's best artist-craftsmen, such as the glassmakers and the weavers of gorgeous figured-silk fabrics, fled; 9,000 out of 12,000 silk workers left Lyons; many teachers, doctors, lawyers, merchants and bankers also left; a migration well described as 'a serious haemorrhage of industry, of skill and capital'.[46] Within a year of the Revocation 15,500 French Protestant refugees had been helped by generous public and private subscriptions to settle in England; all but 2,000 of them in and around London. By 1688 some 800 of London's houses, newly built after the Great Fire, were filled by them.[47]

Generous subscriptions from King Charles and his subjects created a fund of no less than £200,000, and a committee chosen from the chief immigrants was charged with the distribution of £16,000 a year among poor refugees and their descendants. The first annual report presented by this committee in 1687 stated that help had been given to 140 persons of quality and their families; 143 ministers of religion; 144 lawyers, physicians, burghers and traders; and to upwards of 15,000 artisans and workmen. 'Weekly assistance was granted to the sick, and to those whom great age prevented from earning their own living by labour'—in all about 300 persons; and 600 French artisans and workmen were enabled to migrate to America.[48] Precise figures do not exist, but Weiss estimated that between 1681 and 1690 some 80,000 French refugees came to England, of whom at least one-third settled in London—mainly in Spitalfields, Bishopsgate, Shoreditch, Southwark, Cripplegate, Soho and Seven Dials.[49]

The high proportion of silk weavers among the French refugees[50] intensified the London Weavers' problems of membership and control. Although the Company was always ready to admit as a 'foreign brother' any weaver who could produce reliable evidence of his training and experience in weaving,[51] there were always many weavers who exercised the craft within the area of the Company's jurisdiction but remained outside the fold. Thus in 1750 James Massu, who had been 'bred a weaver in France' and had plied his craft in England for ten years, agreed to take up membership. In the following year Peter Desert, applying for membership, was able to prove to the Court of Assistants that he had served an apprenticeship with his father in Normandy and had settled in Spitalfields about the year 1730. The case of John-Baptist Caron, also a native of Normandy, was somewhat similar, and he was admitted after producing a certificate from his former master in France, supported by the testimony of certain French weavers then resident in London, who had known him as a boy. Abraham Levesque who had served his time with his father, a worsted weaver in Havre de Grace, and had been in the weaving trade in England since 1724 (nearly thirty years), was made free by servitude.[52] But the English-born journeymen still complained that many 'unlawful workers and Foreigners' were employed by the French masters, who encouraged such men to the great detriment of weavers who had served a proper apprenticeship. Worse still, the unlawful workers were teaching others. The journeymen asked the Company to compel such men to take up membership if they were adequately qualified, or to expel them if they were not. Pressed in this way the Company took action from time to time, but the task was enormous and far beyond the Company's resources.[53]

For more than half a century after the Revocation in 1685 the Company, although willing—nay, anxious—to admit qualified strangers to its membership, was not disposed to admit them to the Court of Assistants or even to the Livery. For the year 1738 we have a list of the names of those who attended a Common Hall, comprising the Four in Place, 14 Assistants and 75 Liverymen—over ninety in all—but there are very few foreign names: Deheulle, Grelier, Duthoit and possibly three others which seem to be foreign surnames anglicised.[54] But in the 1730s a change took place. The distinction between freemen and admissioners was abolished, and admissions of 'foreigners' and 'strangers' were no longer separately recorded. Furthermore, a common admission fee of only 3s. 4d. was charged. By the end of the decade some early effects of these changes can be detected. For example, a list of ten new Liverymen made in December 1740 contains no fewer than seven French names.[55] In addition, James Ouvry was offered the Livery, but preferred to pay a fine of £10 to be excused.[56] Another name of considerable interest is that of Peter Ogier of Norton Folgate who came from Poitou and 'having duly served an apprenticeship and exercised the trade of a [silk] Weaver for many years', paid a fee of £5 and was made free of the London Weavers on 2 October 1738. It was through this man (who became Upper Bailiff of the Company in 1760–1) that the now-famous Courtauld family made contact with the silk industry, for in 1749 or 1750 Samuel Courtauld (1720–65), Goldsmith of Cornhill, married Peter Ogier's daughter, Louisa.[57] One of the children of this marriage was George Courtauld, born in Cornhill in September 1761 and apprenticed fourteen years later to Peter Merzeau, a silk throwster in Spitalfields. In 1782 George Courtauld, having completed his apprenticeship, set up for himself in the same craft, but his business never flourished and three years later he emigrated to America, just two years after the American colonies had won their independence. It was his son, Samuel, born in Albany on 1 June 1793, who later came to England and founded in Essex the great industrial enterprise which is today world-famous and world-wide in its business connections.[58]

Very soon after the disappearance of the distinction between freemen and admissioners a public emergency provided the 'strangers' and their immediate descendants with an opportunity to stand up in defence of their own fundamental interests and, at the same time, to prove that they were second to none in their loyalty to King George II, the British Constitution and the cause of Protestantism. This emergency was the Jacobite rising in 1745. After the defeat of Sir John Cope by the Young Pretender at Gladsmuir, better known as Prestonpans, in the early autumn, and the subsequent southward penetration of the invading Highlanders, a state of alarm gripped the citizens of London, who over-estimated the strength and determination of the invaders and evinced little confidence in the officers commanding the numerically superior English forces. At this juncture —26 September 1745—

> the colony of silk manufacturers at Spitalfields waited personally upon their King, and assured him of their unswerving loyalty and readiness to take up arms for his cause against the Popish Pretender if need required. The English manufacturers joined in the deputation, which comprised representatives of 133 firms. Each firm had endeavoured to induce their workpeople to give a like promise and the total number of men which Spitalfields thus offered to furnish was 2,919.

Of this total, 2,056 men (i.e. workmen, servants and dependants) were employed by 96 master weavers or firms of Huguenot origin; while the remaining 863 men were employees of 37 'English' manufacturers. The largest numbers of volunteers were entered against the names of Captain James Dalbiac (80), Peter Campart (74), Daniel Gobbee (70), Lewis Chauvet (65), Godin and Ogier (60), Abraham Jeudiome (60), John Rondeau (57). Among those offering smaller numbers were Obadiah Agace and Sons (41), John Ouvry (33), Daniel Cabbinell (30), Ogier and Sons (28), James Ouvry (19), and Peter Lekeux (18).[59]

Fortunately, the services of the men of Spitalfields were never called upon. On 6 December 1745 the Jacobites, having advanced as far as Derby, decided to retreat towards the Border, for it was deemed too hazardous to go further. Although pursued by superior Hanoverian forces, the Jacobites succeeded in reaching Scotland, where they turned and defeated a considerable force of their pursuers at Falkirk on 17 January 1746. This, however, was 'their last gleam of success'. Weakened by disputes among their leaders and desertions from their ranks, they were overwhelmed at Culloden on 16 April 1746—a defeat which crushed for ever the Stuart cause.[60]

NOTES

1 Hudson and Tingey (eds), *Records of the City of Norwich, passim*; Brett-James, *London*, pp. 18, 141, 228. The French Protestant Church in Threadneedle Street in the City of London was founded in 1550.

2 R. E. G. and E. F. Kirk, *Returns of Aliens . . . in London*, Part I (Huguenot Soc., 1907), p. xiv.

3 Cal. S.P. Dom., James I, 1618; printed in R. E. G. and E. F. Kirk, op. cit., Part III, 1598–1625, pp. 180–230.

4 MS. 4656/1, ff.18, 20, 105, 108, 122; e.g. 'Gedeon Le Scalliat, Inglishman, borne at Canterbury, was the 30 April 1627 admitted a brother . . . for £3', payable by instalments, 'for all wch. payments his father, Peter Le Scalliat hath given his word'.

5 For examples see MS. 4656/1, ff.137, 140.

6 Remem., VII, f.151.

7 M. Rose, *The East End of London* (1951), pp. 10, 79.

8 Strype, *Stow's Survey* (1720), IV, p. 48.

9 Justin McCarthy, *The Reign of Queen Anne* (1905), p. 415.

10 *Whitefield's Journals* (1960 edn), pp. 195, 202. On the project to build an Orphan House near Savannah in Georgia see pp. 395–6. For an appraisal of Whitefield's character and influence as a preacher see Lecky, *History of England in the eighteenth century* (1901), III, pp. 50–67.

11 MS. 4647, ff.228–9.

12 MS. 4655/1, f.5.

13 MS. 4655/1, ff.14–15.

14 MS. 4655/1, ff.48–50.

15 MS. 4655/1, ff.71, 90–1.

16 W. Cunningham, *Alien Immigrants to England* (1897), p. 176.

17 MS. 4647, ff.296–8.

18 On porterage as the last resort of those 'washed up by the tides of political and social change', see W. M. Stern, *The Porters of London* (1960).

19 MS. 4647, Ordinance and Record Book, ff.157–8, 162–3, 320–1, 324–9.

20 MS. 4647, ff.162–5, 214.

21 MS. 4647, ff.206–8.

22 MS. 4647, ff. 200–2.

23 MS. 4647, f.215.

24 MS. 4647, ff. 203–5, 215–17; Repertories 41, f.148. Twenty years later, under the Commonwealth, Wm. Counley appears as one of the eight 'representatives' for Cripplegate, and was actually elected an Assistant in June 1651, but refused to take the oath. On 27 October 1651 he is listed as an Assistant, so evidently the oath difficulty had been surmounted (MS. 4655A/2, June and October 1651, ff.9b, 20).

25 Brett-James, *London*, pp. 226, 231–2; MS. 4647, ff.334–7.

26 MS. 4647, ff.257–8, 300–3, 309–12, 672–3.

27 cf. S. Smiles, *The Huguenots in England and Ireland* (1867), p. 338.

28 MS. 4655/1, ff.105–8. The draft Bill was sent to the Speaker of the House of Commons in March 1641.

29 MS. 4655/2, 28 March, 4 April 1653.

30 MS. 4655/2, f.24.

31 MS. 4655/3, f.31b. Not a few of these immigrants settled first in the provinces (e.g. at Canterbury) and later—in certain cases many years later—moved to London. This could mean that some were referred to in the Company's records as 'foreign' brethren, not as 'strangers'.

32 MS. 4655/3, ff.37b–38, 39b, 43b. A minimum of three years' residence was usually required at this period. See, e.g., MS. 4655/5, ff.20–1b.

33 MS. 4655/4, f.46; MS. 4655/5, ff.16, 34b, 36b–37b, 55.
34 MS. 4655/5, ff.22, 25.
35 At Fontainebleau on 22 October 1685 (W. S. Browning, *A History of the Huguenots* (1845 edn), p. 380).
36 Otto Zoff, *The Huguenots* (1943), pp. 323–8.
37 Vincent Cronin, *Louis XIV* (1964), pp. 265–71.
38 Such methods were used over a large part of France (C. Weiss, *History of the French Protestant Refugees from the Revocation of the Edict of Nantes* (1854), pp. 62–70).
39 Weiss, op. cit., p. 211; Browning, op. cit., pp. 365–9 and Chap. LX.
40 MS. 4655/6, f.27; MS. 4648/1, 22 August 1670.
41 MS. 4655/6, ff.35–8, 44.
42 MS. 4655/7, f.1.
43 MS. 4655/8, ff.81, 112b–113.
44 MS. 4655/9, ff.3, 29b, 61–2.
45 Brett-James, *London*, Chap. XIX.
46 G. R. R. Treasure, *Seventeenth-Century France* (1966), Chaps 7 and 24; Brett-James, *London*, pp. 488–90; Cronin, op. cit., pp. 265–71.
47 C. H. Ward-Jackson, *A History of Courtaulds* (1941), pp. 4–5.
48 Weiss, op. cit., pp. 223–4. As late as 1838 William Bresson of Spitalfields stated that 'there are some who still receive pensions from this fund' (*Hand-loom Weavers*, Appendix, p. 76).
49 Weiss, op. cit., pp. 214–15.
50 W. Minet and W. C. Waller (eds), *Register of the Church known as La Patente in Spitalfields from 1689 to 1785* (1898), Introduction.
51 MS. 4655/11, f.159. On 25 October 1714 five French journeymen were admitted, and in the next month three more 'Upon the report of Gabriel Grellier and Jean Rayman . . . of their services in Poictou in France according to the custom there.'
52 MS. 4655/16, ff.2, 32b, 34, 60b–61, 72.
53 MS. 4655/16, ff.74, 80b, 119b.
54 MS. 4655/15, f.11.
55 Chevalier, Gourges, Guenin, Desormeaux, Pillon, Auber and Bourdon.
56 MS. 4648/5, f.8, 1 December 1740.
57 MS. 4655/15, f. 31; C. H. Ward-Jackson, op. cit., p. 6.
58 Ward-Jackson, op. cit., especially Chap. 2. It was in 1793 that George Courtauld ended one of his letters from America with the words: 'May God bless old England. In a political sense she is corrupt and abominable, but I love her private character, and her manners are congenial to my own.' He returned to England in 1794 and did not go back to the U.S.A. until 1818–19. He died there in August 1823. cf. D. C. Coleman, *Courtaulds: An Economic and Social History* (1969), I, *passim*.
59 The weavers' deputation was led by Sir William Baker, Alderman, Bassishaw Ward, 1739–70; Upper Bailiff, Weavers' Company, 1739–40; Colonel of the Orange Regiment, 1745–62; *Proceedings of the Huguenot Society of London*, II (1887–8); Beaven, *Aldermen*, II, p. 128; P. W. Kingsford, in *History Today*, May 1971.
60 The last battle of the '45 was the hard-fought, small-scale naval action in Loch nan Uamh on 3 May 1746, but, unlike Culloden, this was not a decisive battle (J. S. Gibson, *Ships of the '45* (1967), Chap. 2).

Chapter 8

Two Early Inventions

On 9 August 1675 ominous tidings reached Weavers' Hall that a number of persons 'many of them weavers by trade, are now got together in a large Body in and about Spitalfields, and the Court [of Assistants] being altogether ignorant of their intentions', after disowning and protesting against the assembly as a potential danger to the public peace, sent a deputation to the Lord Mayor 'to desire his Lordship to use his authority for the suppression thereof'.[1] The cause of the trouble was quickly discovered. The weavers were out in violent protest against the use of 'engine looms', which were manually operated multi-shuttle 'great looms' for the weaving of narrow or 'small wares' such as ribbons, garterings, tapes and laces: all greatly in demand in the seventeenth century. For three days (9–11 August) mobs of weavers, variously estimated at from 30 to 200 strong, anticipated the Luddites by rampaging through Shoreditch, Hoxton, Whitechapel, Stepney and Clerkenwell, breaking into houses, tearing out the wooden looms and burning them in the streets.[2] This the rioters did because, they said, one man with these engine looms could do as much as twenty men on single looms, and although the quality was less good, they feared the loss of their employment and the consequent starvation of their families. These fears drove the disturbances like a tidal wave eastwards to Stratford-by-Bow and into Essex, and southwards over the river into Southwark and adjacent parts of Kent.[3] In London itself, the Privy Council, hurriedly summoned, issued a proclamation; regular soldiers were called out; while the trained bands were mustered and ordered to march about to make a show of force. A number of the rioters were arrested, and for a time, stood in peril of charges of treason; but times were hard and a good deal of sympathy was felt for the poorer weavers. In the end the culprits were punished by three days in the pillory, plus imprisonment until heavy fines (e.g. 500 marks) were paid.[4]

The earliest known example of an engine loom seems to have been a four- or six-ribbon loom invented in Danzig between 1579 and 1586. The city authorities, however, feared that the general use of the new loom might reduce a great many weavers to beggary, so 'they suppressed it and caused the inventor to be privately strangled or drowned'.[5] At Leyden in 1604 there appeared a ribbon loom said to have been able to weave twelve pieces simultaneously. Despite strong opposition this loom was quickly adopted, and a few years later it was brought into England (where it was often referred to as the Dutch engine loom), much to the consternation of the native single-loom weavers.[6]

This invention enabled the weavers of narrow wares to weave a large number of pieces—say 12 or 16 or 24—side by side, by the simultaneous actuation of that number of shuttles. In the machine's earliest forms the shuttles carrying the weft were made to pass through the warp by the action of cog-wheels working on the teethed upper edges of the shuttles. When the cog-wheels were reversed by the weaver, the shuttles passed back. Later the loom was much improved by the introduction of the fly-shuttle principle, all the shuttles being propelled simultaneously by 'the ladder', an oblong frame in which the cross-pieces acted as the hammers or 'hands' by which the shuttles were kept in motion. The 'ladder' slid horizontally in a groove made in the batten, and was put in motion by a handle operated by the weaver, so that each crossbar of the ladder was made to strike or drive, alternately to right and left, upon one of the two shuttles between which it was placed.[7]

Although the engine looms were not power-driven in the seventeenth century, their effects were so greatly feared that 'the authorities' on the Continent—the weavers' gilds and even some governments, central and local—sought to prohibit their use. Nevertheless, by about 1720 the battle for restriction was clearly lost, and thereafter the open use of engine looms increased rapidly, encouraged, often, by certain princes who licensed their use as a welcome means of raising extra revenue. In time, the application of water-power (and, eventually, steam-power) to drive the looms followed, despite early technical difficulties arising from the delicate nature of silk yarn.[8]

In England, no sooner were the new-fangled machines brought into the country than the battle commenced. Official documents dating from 1616 refer to alien weavers 'bold of late to devise engines for working of tape, laces, ribbon and such, wherein one man doth more among them than seven English men can do, so as their cheap sale of these commodities beggareth all our English artificers of that trade'. Then followed repeated denunciations of 'that develishe invention of looms brought in by strangers . . . with looms of 12 to 24 shuttles, worked by one man's hands, which takes away the work of a dozen men' and causes 'the destruction of many poor'.[9] On this subject the voices of the London weavers were heard loud and often down the earlier decades of the seventeenth century. In 1624–5, for example, the 'generality' of the Weavers' Company complained of the use of 'an Engine or loom brought into England from Holland in recent times, and now being set up in and about London and its suburbs'. The number was put at about forty-four, some having 10, 16, 20 and even 24 shuttles to each 'engine'; and 'when set on work' it was estimated that they could 'take away the living' of some 486 poor but industrious persons. The use of the engine loom, said the London weavers, was already prohibited in Holland 'because it took away the living of a great number of poor' who had always worked upon single looms, on which the work was 'very sufficiently wrought, and many children set on work by the same'. In this way the men had kept themselves and their families from idleness and begging. An interesting feature of this document is a supplementary petition added at the end, in which the weavers themselves seem to have sensed vaguely the futility of attempting to hold back the march of technical progress:

> But if your Worships do conceive the said Engine to be
> beneficial for the Common Wealth because one man may do as
> much work as ten can upon single looms, then we humbly
> entreat [you] to . . . order that none may use the said Engine
> but only such as are Weavers by trade; for they which now use
> them are [mostly] . . . Merchants and other Tradesmen, but
> not Weavers by trade.[10]

Apparently no effective action followed this plea, for within seven or eight years we find the Weavers' commonalty making a formal protest to the Elders of the Dutch and French Congregations in London, because certain aliens 'have brought into this Kingdom an Engine very hurtful to our Trade'. Between 1635 and 1637, the native weavers complained that many such engines 'have been set up by Alien Merchants and others in London and the suburbs' (although they would not be permitted to use them in their own countries), and asked the Government to suppress all 'the new invented late used Engines',[11] because their introduction had taken away the work 'whereby two thousand of the native-born subjects' children of 7, 8, 9, 10 and 12 years of age were employed till they were fit to perform other work'. Also many old men who used to weave tapes, ribbons and laces on single looms had lost their only means of subsistence, while the children formerly employed 'now lie idle in the streets ready to perish'.[12] At this point Charles I intervened by including in his letters patent, granted to the Weavers' Company in 1638, an express prohibition of the use of engine or great looms, 'whereby much deceit is practised', after 4 July 1638.[13]

The reference to merchants as the owners of many of the newly installed engine looms is interesting and significant, for it throws a ray of light upon early industrial capitalism. These looms were among the first of the machines which have led by degrees to the capitalistic organisation of industry, and, through their grouping together, to the factory system. They were comparatively complicated pieces of mechanism and could be successfully constructed only by the best loom-makers. The cost of each loom was between £6 and £12, and the London riots of 1675 revealed small groups of from five to ten looms concentrated in one place and operated, presumably, by hired journeymen working, under supervision, for the loom-master or owner. The minimum capital investment, therefore, might be between £50 and £120. By 1750, in Lancashire, where the adoption and use of the engine loom was unhampered, at least 1,500 'Dutch' smallware looms were in use in the parish of Manchester alone, grouped in the workshops of a superior class of master weavers or 'undertakers' whose employees were not small masters but wage-earning 'hands', and likely to remain so.[14] Many of these masters had acquired, through the engine looms, 'such large and opulent fortunes as hath enabled them to vie with some of the best gentlemen of the country'.[15] The engine loom's superior productivity lowered costs and prices, and so led to expansion of the market. We can see quite clearly the makings of a bitter struggle between the single-loom narrow weavers and the thrustful men aiming to exploit the much greater potentialities of the multi-shuttle looms.

In London this struggle was a long one, for although opposition and prohibitions could retard in some degree the adoption of the engine looms, their alluring advantages perpetually beckoned the more enterprising weavers and merchants. Little is heard of the matter during the Civil War and Commonwealth, although an entry in the Weavers' Court minutes on 5 May 1651 suggests that the controversy was not completely dormant: 'Mr. Jo. Jones did declare in the hearing of Mr. Richard Collard that Mr. Thos. Westwood[16] did keep a great loom with many shuttles.' Whether this was true or not, the information suggests that official policy was still against the use of the engine looms.

After the Restoration and the return of high fashion the demand for silk ribbons and other narrow wares showed a marked expansion, and so did the use of engine looms. This inevitably evoked renewed opposition which is reflected in the Weavers' records. For example, in 1666–7 the use of engine looms was complained of in Southwark, Spitalfields and Low Leyton, and the Court of Assistants resolved that 'when ye Yeomanry upon their Search [in 1667] bring a return of what Number there are', a course of action will be decided upon.[17] Towards the end of 1667 a meeting of Officers and Assistants, with seven Liverymen and ten of the Yeomanry, agreed that 'divers Engine Looms of late months set up ... will be destructive of ye trade', and the Yeomanry were 'desired with all speed to enquire into the number that are used, what quantity of ribbons are supposed to be made therein, and touching the deceitfullness thereof'. On 12 December 1667 the Yeomanry were able to present to a 'full Court' of Assistants, Livery and Yeomanry the names 'of divers persons who keep engine looms';[18] they also reported 'that by discourse with ye Shopkeepers they find them disliking to ye use of these looms and [they] offer their assistance to this Compa. in that affair'. The commonalty presented a paper giving their views and a promise to help, if need be. The meeting appointed a committee, including two of the Yeomanry, 'to consider and endeavour ye suppression of ye said Engine Looms',[19] and shortly afterwards the Weavers' Company asked for the help of the City Corporation in procuring parliamentary authority for the same purpose. This petition was referred to the Common Council,[20] but nothing further is recorded, and the agitation seems to have died down until October 1670, when the Weavers' Court of Assistants,

> upon the motion of the Yeomanry and serious consideration ... of the great evils to the trade of weaving by (i) the frequent importation of foreign-wrought silks and stuffs, broad and narrow, and (ii) by the use of the broad or tape loom, it was agreed that a Bill be presented to Parliament for the remedy thereof.[21]

But apparently no remedy was found, for in August 1675, as we have seen, the weavers' rank and file poured into the streets and began to show what *they* meant by 'suppression' of the hated looms.

This rioting and destruction shocked the Weavers' Company into activity once again. Another inquiry was instituted, and in October 1675 'several of the Yeomanry, especially those in Southwark', complained bitterly that they and 'the whole trade of weaving do exceedingly suffer by the use of the Engine Looms' to weave silk ribbons. The Company decided to petition Parliament,[22] and the account books show that the fees and other expenses incurred in so doing during 1675–6 exceeded £23. Retaining fees were paid to Sir William Jones, to the Attorney-General, and to a certain Captain Cressett 'for soliciting during the Sitting of Parliament & at ye King and Council'. The Common Sergeant and Sir John King were also retained. After the hearing everybody went to dinner—'above 40 present'—which cost the Weavers' Company £4. 8s. Finally, in April 1676, Mr Taylor, a solicitor, received £2. 10s. for services rendered 'about the dispute of the Tape or Engine looms depending before the King and Council'.[23]

After a careful inquiry the Government came to the conclusion that, in fact, the engine looms did quite good work, and 'if these Looms be encouraged it will prevent the great Importation that is now dayly of Dutch and French ribbon', so that 'more poor Men, Women and Children will be employed by them than the Single Looms do or can employ'. Moreover, if engine looms

> be suppressed here . . . the Dutch and French using them will much undersell us and serve our Markets at home and abroad, so the suppressing them here will only enrich the Dutch and French and ruin ourselves and Trade. . . . That by the same reason the Single Loom weavers complain of the Engine Looms, many [other] . . . envious people will complain of the Engines for Water Mills, Saw Mills, and Engines for splitting of iron, and Ploughs, and printing presses, and Cranes for Wharfs, and many other Ingenious, useful and profitable inventions now in England, but we doubt not but Ingenuity will find encouragement in England.[24]

Thus was the door opened wide to the engine-loom weavers, whether they worked independently or in the employ of capitalist entrepreneurs. That the opportunities were not neglected we see clearly from the Weavers' records for the first half of the eighteenth century, which show engine weavers springing up in all the industrial or textile districts in and around London, e.g., Upper and Little Moorfields, Hoxton, Shoreditch, Saffron Hill, Cripplegate, Smithfield, Aldersgate, Holborn, Bishopsgate Within, Blackfriars, Whitefriars, Newington Butts, and Twister's Alley, Bunhill Row. Apprentices were openly bound to engine weavers at Weavers' Hall, and some of the boys of Bridewell were trained on engine looms and eventually became free of the Weavers' Company.[25] Among the engine weavers admitted to the freedom in the eighteenth century we notice Peter Swinton an 'engine or tape weaver' working in Southwark in 1757, who had migrated from Middlewich in Cheshire where he served his apprenticeship from 1728 to 1735. Samuel Johnson, an engine weaver living at Kensington in 1769, had served his time in Manchester. Another engine weaver, Andrew Fleming, living and working in Charterhouse Lane near Smithfield, had been apprenticed in early childhood to his father, a Dublin weaver, and had been a competent weaver since the age of twelve. He was made free of the London Weavers' Company in June 1751.[26]

Despite the comparatively high productivity of the engine looms, the earnings of the journeymen working in them seem to have been rather low, and even lower were the earnings of the remaining single-loom weavers who were trying to compete with the growing numbers of engine-loom weavers. Campbell, writing in 1747, says: 'The whole tribe of narrow-weavers make but poor bread, and less in proportion to the coarseness of the materials they use. The common run of them may earn about 9s. a week.' He adds that in London and its suburbs 'the livery-lace and ribbon weavers are most generally found'. No doubt the earnings of 'the common run' remained low because 'the plainer goods' (e.g. tapes) were being 'made more cheaply in the country'.[27]

This trend continued, especially when power looms were introduced in the provinces, but not in London. Early in the nineteenth century the weaving of tapes, ribbons and similar narrow wares on power looms was introduced and perfected in towns like Congleton, Leek, Derby and, of course, Coventry, which became 'the great city for the manufacture of ribbons in England', employing 6,000–7,000 operatives in the city itself in 1838, and 10,000–11,000 more in the surrounding countryside, though not all were working power looms at that date.[28] In London the use of the old-fashioned hand-operated engine looms continued well into the nineteenth century. According to Richard Cray's eyewitness description of 'the Condition of the Silk Weaving Trade', written between 1836 and 1838,[29] there had been about 600 engine looms at work in the Spitalfields district in 1824, but in 1838 there were only 100, mostly 16-shuttle and 20-shuttle looms; 'the rest all gone to the power looms' in Coventry, Exeter, and other places away from London.

Another early invention which, like the engine loom, points forward to the revolution in our textile industries in the eighteenth and nineteenth centuries, is the 'stocking engine' or knitting frame. This was nearly contemporaneous with the engine loom, for it was invented about the year 1589 by William Lee, a native of Calverton, near Nottingham, where he is said to have inherited 'a pretty freehold'. It seems probable that Lee was born in 1564, for he matriculated as a sizar at Christ's College, Cambridge in May 1579. Later he transferred to St John's College, and proceeded B.A. in 1582. He took Holy Orders and we know that in 1589, the year in which he is generally supposed to have completed his famous invention, he was parish priest of Calverton. During the next two years he worked with his brother, James, practising with, and improving his machine, after which he moved to Bunhill Fields in London where he set up a stocking frame or frames, doubtless hoping to find a good market among the London merchants and people of quality.

On Lee's stocking frame in its improved form the knitting was done by about 100 needles:

> set in an engine or frame composed of about 2,000 pieces of smith, joiners, and turners work after so . . . exact a manner that . . . it far excels in the ingenuity, curiosity and subtility

of the invention and contexture, all other frames or instruments of manufacture in use in any known part of the world. The machine had a series of rigid hooks with a second series of moving hooks at right-angles to them. The stitches were cast on the series of rigid hooks and then the movable hooks, manipulated by a simple mechanical action, were inserted on the rigid hooks. The yarn was then laid horizontally under the rigid hooks and the stitches were drawn over it by the movable hooks.

Lee's invention was, for those times, a remarkably advanced and complex mechanism. Operated by a treadle, it was capable of making 'in a moment almost, two hundred meshes of loops, without requiring much skill or labour in the workman' or knitter,[30] and it proved to be 'the basis of all subsequent inventions in the field of knitting and lace-making machinery'.[31]

It is not surprising that the ingenious inventor of this machine expected to receive the grant of a patent from Queen Elizabeth I, and the story goes that between 1596 and 1598, after many failures, Lee succeeded in knitting a pair of silk stockings—a rare luxury at that time—perfect enough to be presented to Her Majesty. Nevertheless, neither Elizabeth I nor James I ever granted a patent to the inventor, despite an apparent absence of opposition from vested interests, which contrasts sharply with the determined resistance put up, as we have seen, against the engine looms. It is scarcely surprising, therefore, that Lee, bitterly disappointed in his own country, accepted an invitation from Henry IV of France, through his famous minister, Sully, to migrate to France and work under the powerful patronage of the French King. Taking with him three stocking frames and nine weavers Lee began to manufacture stockings in Rouen early in the seventeenth century. From this point the accepted story has been that Lee and his men worked happily under royal patronage until the assassination of Henry IV on 14 May 1610, after which Lee's enterprise ceased to prosper, and within a short time the inventor, impoverished, died in Paris. There is, however, in the London Weavers' register of admissions of 'strangers and foreigners' between 1600 and 1646 an entry which seems to throw a somewhat different light upon the matter. On folio 48, under the heading 'Admissions in the yeare 1608', we read:

William Lee weaver of Silk stockings by Ingyn was the Seaventh day of March 1608[32] admitted a forren brother for Three Pounds whereof he payd Fortie shillings in hand and the rest he is to pay whensoever he shall sett up anie Loome or Sapyn to use the Art of weaving and is sworne I say for 03.00.00

—and on folio 47:

> William Lee. Rec. of him when he was admitted in pte. of
> payment the sume of 02.00.00.[33]

There can be little doubt that this refers to William Lee, the inventor
of the stocking frame. Since he was not a native of London, he would
have to join the London Weavers' Company as a 'forreign brother',
and the entry quoted above suggests that Lee was preparing the way
for a return to England at least fourteen months *before* the assassination of his patron, Henry IV of France. No further mention of William
Lee has been found in the Weavers' records nor any note of the payment of the outstanding balance of his admission fee, which suggests
that although William Lee may have planned to do so, in fact he
never did set up a loom or sapin within the Company's jurisdiction.
The story hitherto accepted that he died in Paris at some time after
the middle of 1610 may well be true.

Whatever the truth may be as to Lee's fortunes in France, it seems
certain that the use of his invention in England spread rapidly during
the seventeenth century, after James Lee, assisted by Aston, a
former apprentice of William Lee, and six or seven journeymen, all
recently returned from France, set up frames in Old Street Square.
Although the initial cost of each stocking frame was as high as £80–
£90 in the first half of the seventeenth century, the productive
capacity, also, was high. Even the earliest stocking frames could
work ten to fifteen times as fast as a hand-knitter, and could be
manipulated by a child of twelve. Later, operatives using an improved form of the machine could make shaped stockings by throwing
some of the hooks out of action at certain stages.[34] Doubtless many
of the recruits to this new manufacture came from the ranks of the
skilled silk weavers of Spitalfields, Cripplegate, Norton Folgate,
Shoreditch and Whitechapel. Direct figures are not available,
but there are a few fragments of indirect evidence. The burials
register of St Giles without Cripplegate indicates that in that
parish one 'weaver' in seven was a stocking weaver or framework knitter.[35] The Weavers' Company records of apprentice
bindings in the eighteenth century which show the fathers' occupations, point to a certain concentration of stocking makers in Spitalfields, Whitechapel, Shoreditch and Moorfields, but not in very large
numbers.

During the first half of the seventeenth century, the master
stocking makers had no separate gild or company, so they were 'dispersed among divers Companies of London and elsewhere', including,
of course, the London Weavers' Company, to which, as we have seen,
William Lee himself had applied to be admitted. Not until 1657 did
the framework knitters achieve incorporation as a City livery com-

pany;[36] and it was at the Frameworker Knitters' Hall in 1710 that the German traveller, Zacharias Conrad von Uffenbach, saw a portrait (since lost) of William Lee.[37]

The stockings produced by the English framework knitters were, on the whole, so well made that they were highly valued on the Continent in the seventeenth and eighteenth centuries. According to Lardner, England exported 'vast quantities of silk hose', even to Italy, and the quality was so superior that 'Keyslar, in his Travels through Europe, as late as the year 1730, remarks that at Naples, when a tradesman would highly recommend his silk stockings, he protests they are right English'.[38] Woollen stockings, also, were made on stocking frames by the London framework knitters.[39] According to Campbell's *London Tradesman* (1747), the stocking loom 'has received several improvements ... till it has arrived at the Perfection of a compleat Engine, whereon stockings of all sorts can be wrought with great Art and Expedition'. The stocking weaver, he said, needs ingenuity and a fair amount of strength, but it is by no means impossible for an apprentice of average intelligence to acquire a tolerably good grasp of the craft in three years. 'With the closest application' journeymen can earn 9s. to 10s. a week: they are paid so much for each pair of stockings, 'and if they have not a loom of their own, [they] allow the Master 2s. a week for the use of his'.[40]

NOTES

1 MS. 4655/8, f.55b.
2 *V.C.H.*, *Middlesex* (1911), II, p. 97. The engine looms were valued at £6 to £7. 10s.
3 George, *London*, p. 187; M. Beloff, *Public Order and Popular Disturbances, 1660–1714* (1938), p. 82.
4 J. C. Jeaffreson (ed.), *Middlesex County Records* (1892), IV, pp. 60–5.
5 J. Beckmann, *A History of Inventions, Discoveries and Origins* (4th edn, 1846), II, pp. 528–9, quoting a work by Lancellotti published in Venice in 1636.
6 MS. 4647, f.312, where 1610 is suggested as the most probable date.
7 In Lardner's *Treatise on ... the Silk Manufacture*, compiled by G. R. Porter and published in 1831, it is stated that 'with one of these looms a diligent workman may weave one yard in an hour of as many narrow ribands as the loom is qualified to produce at the same time ... being seldom under eight or beyond twenty-eight' (pp. 226–7). Thus the output from a 20-shuttle loom would be 20 yards per hour. For a drawing of an engine loom see Lardner, *Silk*, pp. 228–9.
8 Beckmann, op. cit., II, pp. 527–33.
9 Cal. S.P. Dom., James I, 1619–23, LXX and VIII, pp. 112, 271, quoted in Lipson, *Economic History of England* (1956), III, pp. 52–3.
10 MS. 4647, Ordinance and Record Book, 1577–1641, f.157.
11 MS. 4647, ff.297, 302, 345–7, 672.
12 MS. 4647, ff. 358–60.

13 MS. 4636, cf. MS. 4655/1, f.106; Cal. S.P. Dom., Charles I, 25 May 1638.

14 A. P. Wadsworth and J. de L. Mann, *The Cotton Trade and Industrial Lancashire, 1600–1780* (1931), pp. 104–5, 285; James Ogden, *A Description of Manchester* . . . (1783), p. 82.

15 S. J. Chapman, *The Lancashire Cotton Industry* (1904), p. 20.

16 Upper Bailiff, 1657–8.

17 MS. 4655/4, ff.9b, 51b. A memorandum, probably dating from *c.* 1675, records that Thomas Avering, an apprentice, had committed a double offence, for he had run away from his master and 'now works at an Engine with Fra. Browne, Long Alley' (MS. 4655/8, f.146).

18 Unfortunately, the names and numbers were not entered in the minutes.

19 MS. 4655/4, ff.92–3, 95b.

20 Repertories 73, f.67.

21 MS. 4655/6, ff.64, 72b, 77b, 79. The Yeomanry volunteered to subscribe £10 towards the cost of printing and promoting the Bill, and early in 1671 the Company borrowed £100 at 6 per cent for this purpose and to pay workmen.

22 MS. 4655/8, f.66b.

23 MS. 4655/8, ff.72, 81b; MS. 4648/1, 1675–6, *passim*.

24 Quoted by Wadsworth and Mann, op. cit., pp. 102–3.

25 MS. 4655/15, ff.302, 331b, 332b; MS. 4655/18, f.224; Quarrell and Maré (eds), *London in 1710* (1934), p. 54.

26 MS. 4655/16, ff.19b, 21b, 173; MS. 4655/17, f.104.

27 Campbell, *Tradesman*, p. 259. cf. *Ribbon Weavers*, evidence.

28 Ribbon-making was introduced in Coventry at the beginning of the eighteenth century by a Mr Bird, 'who is supposed to have been assisted in its first establishment by some of the French refugees' (*Handloom Weavers*, vol. 24, p. 3).

29 Written at the request of the London Working Men's Association. Cray had been a silk weaver in Spitalfields for many years and was familiar with the industry and district from the inside. See B. Mus. Add. MS. 34,245B, ff.3–17.

30 J. Beckmann, op. cit., pp. 361–8.

31 A. Wolf, *A History of Science, Technology and Philosophy in the 16th and 17th Centuries* (1950), p. 465; C. Singer and others, *A History of Technology* (1957), III, p. 185.

32 i.e. $160\frac{8}{9}$.

33 MS. 4645/1, ff.47, 48.

34 A. Wolf, op. cit., pp. 465–6.

35 MS. 6419/7, *passim*. Gravenor Henson's guess that London had 400–500 knitting frames in 1664 is probably too high.

36 F. A. Wells, *The British Hosiery Trade* (1935), pp. 23–8, 35. See also an article by J. D. Chambers in *Economica*, November 1929.

37 Z. C. von Uffenbach, *Merkwürdige Reisen durch Niedersacksen, Holland und England* (1753), II, p. 571. An engraving of this picture is in the Museum of the Commissioners of Patents.

38 Lardner, *Silk*, p. 26; J. S. Burn, *The History of French, Walloon* . . . *and other Foreign Protestant Refugees settled in England* (1846), p. 256.

39 *Journal of Commissioners for Trade and Plantations*, 1718, p. 441.

40 Campbell, *Tradesman*, pp. 214–15. A new frame at that date might cost between £7 and £8.

A Time of Conflict and Calamity

During the quarter-century from 1641 to 1666 the London Weavers, like thousands of other people, passed through three major calamities —civil war, plague and fire. One cannot say 'lived through' for many did not survive the Civil War, which took its toll mainly of the younger men, while the Great Plague of 1665 ravaged all regardless of age or sex. Fortunately, few people lost their lives in London's Great Fire in 1666, but the destruction of property within the City— buildings, stores, furniture, tools and equipment, records and all sorts of personal belongings—was enormous. Few Londoners in those disastrous days escaped without damage 'in mind, body or estate'.

It is well known that one of the most decisive factors in the Civil War situation was the attitude of London, with its great concentration of wealth and population and its nine regiments of trained bands which were beyond doubt the most efficient in the kingdom at that time.[1] The great importance of London was fully appreciated by both sides. Whoever had the capital firmly in his grasp held the ace of trumps. In 1641–2, the sympathies of many leading City men, especially the members of the chartered trading companies and the great livery companies, lay with the Crown. The City Fathers turned only very gradually—many of them with extreme reluctance—against the King. Some, indeed, never did turn. At the beginning of 1642 the sympathies of the Lord Mayor, the Recorder and the majority of the Aldermen were still with the King; but they were finding it increasingly difficult to ignore the rising anti-royalist temper of the mass of ordinary Londoners.[2] Unfortunately for his cause, Charles I utterly failed to consolidate these potentially favourable forces; on the contrary, he not only did much to antagonise them, but seems to have been completely blind to the dangers of so doing. He regarded London's wealth as an inexhaustible reservoir from which great loans could be drawn and, later, shabbily repudiated at his royal will. His high-handed attempt to deprive the City and the livery companies of their Irish estates, the many accusations brought against them and the heavy fine imposed, were not easily forgotten. Nor was Strafford's contemptuous threat to have 'some of the Aldermen hanged up'. Charles's rigid attitude weakened the position of moderate men and opened the path to power to the parliamentary puritans, who were a well-organised radical minority party receiving strong popular support from the crowds of weavers, pewterers, saddlers, clothworkers and other craftsmen in the industrial liberties and adjacent suburbs.[3] On the whole, the members of Parliament for London, Westminster and Southwark, and the City's Common Council members were for the Parliament, and although there was a far from negligible Royalist faction in the City which the King tried to stir up into a sort of 'fifth column', its strength steadily diminished as its partisans slipped away to join the King's forces in the field.[4]

The Weavers' Company had begun to feel the financial pressure of the Government's demands in the late 1630s, and its records show that between 1638 and 1642 several unusually large sums, ranging from £175 to over £300, had to be borrowed, presumably to meet the precepts issued through the Lord Mayor. The actual outbreak of hostilities certainly did not relieve the financial pressure; it merely meant that the demands came from Parliament instead of the King. By 1642 the Weavers' Company was over £800 in debt,[5] and on 10 October 1642 the Court of Assistants 'with consent of the Livery' ordered that sixty-nine pieces of plate weighing over 800 oz., which were kept 'lock'd upp by the Bailiffs and wardens in the chest with 4 locks', should be 'sold to paie Assessments and other monies taken up at Interest for the use of the State, City and Company'. An inventory dated 2 September 1641 lists this plate as follows:

5 Broade gilt bowls	1 Parcel gilt bowl
10 Standing gilt cups with covers	8 Beer bowls, white
3 Double salts, gilt with covers	25 Wine cups, white
5 Gilt cups with covers	1 Silver salt
2 Single salts with covers	3 Beakers, white
1 Gilt 'Tanker' [? tankard]	1 large Beer bowl, white
3 Parcel gilt bowls	1 'Chalfendish', white[6]

The white plate fetched 4s. 10d. an ounce and the gilt 5s. 3d.; so that the sale realised some £200. In addition, 26 silver spoons, weighing 37¾ oz., were sold for £9. 5s. 7d.[7]

The financial demands arising from the Civil War and its aftermath kept the Weavers' Company in a state of insolvency, with expenditure running always ahead of income. Towards the end of 1648 the Company had to convene a special court to consider a warrant from the Committee of Arrears demanding payment of £33, being arrears of a levy for the Army covering a period of nineteen months. But only the Renter Bailiff and four Assistants attended and 'nothing was resolved upon'. By the spring of 1652 the Court of Assistants was so hard pressed that it 'ordered and agreed . . . that every one that is able and willing to lend 20s. a man for a year for and towards the payment of the Compa. debt . . . shall have it repaid again out of the Incomes of the Compa. as the same do come in'.[8] Meantime the arrears of £33 owing to the Government had been paid by the Renter Bailiff, William Cade, out of his own pocket, as we learn from the following Court minute:[9]

2nd March 1654

Whereas Mr. Will. Cade now Upper Bailiff and master of this Company declared to this Court of Assistants and Representatives that in the year 1648 he being then Renter Bailiff of the Company, at which time there was due from the Company in taxes for the Army the sum of £33, and the Company being not able to pay the same, he, Mr. Cade, at the request of the Court of Assistants did lend to the Company the aforesaid sum which was paid to the several Collectors for the Army, and had the Hall mortgaged for his security; and upon the change of government, Mr. Hewitt being chosen master of the Company, he the said Mr. Cade made a demand of his money which Mr. Hewitt denied to satisfy, but put him to suit for the same, in which suit he expended the sum of £22. 16. 11, as did appear by his account produced. Now forasmuch as Mr. Cade has observed the estate of the Company to be but mean and at present not able to satisfy the said debt, and for that he was willing to unite the Company and for the good of the same did fully and freely forgive the Company the aforesaid debt of £22. 16. 11; and for which love and kindness of his the Court of Assistants and Representatives did return him thanks.

Money, however, was only the means to an effective amalgam of men and weapons. To this, too, the livery companies were in a position to make a very substantial contribution, by encouraging their young freemen and journeymen and the senior apprentices to volunteer, and by bringing forth the weapons already in their keeping, for they had a statutory duty to 'find and keep' weapons and make them available to the proper authorities when required. In the Weavers' records, under date 2 September 1642, there is a list of the arms 'Lent unto the Parliament for the expidition of the Earle of Essex and was by the direction of Parliament':[10]

	Valued at
2 new corselets with headpieces and pikes	35s. each
1 old corselet and headpiece with a new pike	?
3 new muskets	2s. 8d. each

3 rests for muskets	5s.
6 swords	6s. each
6 belts	14s. each

These arms and items of equipment were formally handed over to Captain Langham and two other officers, the warrant authorising the loan being deposited with 'Mr. North, one of the Constables of this parish of Bassishaw'.[11] In 'A list of the Names of the Several Colonels, and their Colours, with the Lieutenant-Colonels . . . appointed by the Committee, for the ordering of the Militia of this Honourable City of London', dating from 1642, Captain Langham is named as Lieutenant-Colonel of the White Regiment, then serving under its Colonel, Alderman Penington, a leading puritan radical, who was very shortly to become Lord Mayor (1642-3).[12]

A week after Captain Langham's visit to Weavers' Hall the troops under the Earl of Essex left London and marched to Northampton where they joined forces with troops from the Midlands. Essex's orders were 'to rescue His Majesty's person, and the persons of the Prince and the Duke of York out of the hands of those desperate persons then about them, and to bring the sovereign home again to his loving Parliament'. The opposing armies moved very slowly and it was not until 22 October that Essex intercepted the Royalists just south of Warwick. This attempt to hold up their advance towards London[13] failed, and after the indecisive battle of Edgehill, near Kineton, on 23 October 1642, the Royalist army continued its slow but menacing march towards London, which the Parliamentarians felt forced to defend with all the means they could muster. Even before the fight at Edgehill, according to Whitelocke, 'the Parliament having notice' of the King's intention to capture London, ordered the trained bands to be made ready and the immediate 'passages' into the City to be fortified. In October 1642 the Committee of Militia increased the pressure to put the City in a strong 'posture of defence'. Trenches were dug and ramparts thrown up to cover the main roads into London; craftsmen and shopkeepers were ordered to 'forebeare their trades' and help with the digging and carrying of earth; great numbers, including many women

> From ladies down to oyster wenches
> Labour'd like pioneers in trenches,[14]

and amazed the Venetian Ambassador by working even on Sundays.[15]

Meantime the Royalist threat to London was creeping perilously close. Early in November 1642, after the King's forces had captured Brentford, 'the Alarm came to London, with the same terror as if the Army were enter'd their Gates'. On 8 November Lord Brooke and Sir Henry Vane went to the Guildhall to appeal for a greater effort: let every available man follow the drums and fight courageously 'and this shall be the day of your deliverance'. Parliament proclaimed an indemnity to all apprentices who enlisted without the consent of their masters. Soon 9,000 men had mustered on the artillery ground by Finsbury Fields.[16] On 10 November the new defences were manned, and on 12–13 November a defensive force of some 24,000 men— largely citizen-soldiers newly enlisted as 'auxiliaries'—was drawn up at Turnham Green across the Royalists' line of advance. Here a fierce pitched battle, with London as the prize, seemed imminent. The Londoners' morale was high, for they felt that they were defending their hearths and homes, and they were greatly heartened by the cartloads of food and drink sent to the 'brave Boys' at Turnham Green by busy wives and sweethearts in London. Moreover, the confrontation, lasting many hours, revealed the relative smallness of the King's army, which was outnumbered by approximately two to one.[17] Eventually the Royalists withdrew through plundered Brentford towards Reading, leaving the Londoners to celebrate an important, if bloodless, victory.

But they did not relax their efforts. Spurred on, perhaps, by the rumour that Prince Rupert had sworn to take *and sack* the City, Parliament decided, in February 1643, to expand the existing small-scale and rather hasty fortifications into a comprehensive scheme designed to protect the City (not forgetting Southwark), the liberties and some of the out-parishes. All through the spring of 1643 this work went on apace. Once again everybody joined in: the men of the trained bands with their colours; many hundreds of porters in their 'white frocks'; and a host of substantial citizens with their wives and families, including 'the whole company of gentlemen Vintners . . . with their wives, servants, and wine porters'.[18] Doubtless, the weavers, too, were glad to join in (although many of the masters and journeymen were not physically fit for hard manual labour), for business in the luxury trades was almost at a standstill. A number of strong-points were constructed in the Spitalfields area, e.g. at Shore-ditch, Hoxton, Brick Lane, Hackney Road and Mile End Green, all near the Weavers' homes and workplaces.[19] William Lithgow, an energetic Scot who walked round the whole perimeter of London at this time, saw 'a trench dyke . . . running through Wapping fields to the further end of White-chappell, a great way without Aldgate', where a large fort was under construction. He also saw some 4,000 weavers and great companies of tailors, clothiers and feltmakers marching to and from the fortifications, carrying shovels, mattocks and flags. Southwark, too, where many weavers, feltmakers, and other industrial workers lived, is mentioned as in process of being fortified. Already these defences were manned by 'foot centinals', supplemented by 'fourteen horse troupes that scoute the high-wayes both day and night', making two circuits every night.[20] A Royalist commentator in *Mercurius Aulicus*, the Cavaliers' penny weekly news-sheet, also remarked upon the digging of deep trenches

> to be filled with water from the New River and the River of Lee which runnes by Bow, wherein the new Elect rebaptize themselves, and call it by the name of Jordan . . . [and] they goe from house to house to list and persuade all Apprentices, and others of able bodies, to man these workes . . . every householder being commanded to send both men-servants and maid-servants, with their spades and baskets. . . . And . . . on Wednesday night, the women-labourers . . . had drawne themselves into a Regiment of their owne, and came marching homewards through the streets with their Spades and Pick-axes, with so much confidence and impudence as might make it manifest that when the men thinke fit to cast off their loyalty, the women are not bound to retaine their modesty.[21]

In all, twenty-four forts were constructed, linked by some eighteen miles of trenches, and when the men of the London trained bands were called upon for service in the field, the forts were manned 'with volunteers and those who were too old or too busy to be full-time soldiers'.[22]

London's defences were never, after all, tested in battle. The fighting flared up in the North, the West Country and the Midlands, and in it the London infantry stubbornly stood their ground in more than one desperate battle.[23] Even Prince Rupert's cavalry 'could make no impression upon their stand of Pikes'. But London itself, although sometimes alarmed, was never besieged, nor even seriously threatened as it was in 1642; which was fortunate for the Parliamentarians, since London was the control-centre of their organisation and the main source of their strength.

When the Parliamentarians realised that a long war was probably unavoidable, they set up such governmental machinery as seemed essential, using the halls of certain of the livery companies, including Weavers' Hall, as government offices. In November 1642, when a government ordinance imposed a regular weekly tax to be levied in London and Westminster, a committee, based at Haberdashers' Hall, was set up to work out appropriate assessments, while a parallel committee, sitting at Weavers' Hall, had the task of collecting the taxes so assessed. This committee had power to appoint collectors for each parish, to levy distress and, as a last resort, to call upon the trained bands to help it to deal with recalcitrants; a necessary provision, for large numbers of influential citizens 'denied to contribute money to public safety' and had to be coerced.[24] In 1645, a busy Committee of Arrears sat at Weavers' Hall, and later the hall was used as one of the public treasuries. Here it was that General Lord

Fairfax, desperate for money to pay his troops, seized upwards of £27,000 in December 1648 on account of the £40,000 which, it was alleged, the City owed the Government at that time. 'That the extreme necessity of the Forces before Pontefract may be supplied', wrote Fairfax in his order to Colonel Dean,

> you . . . are hereby required, with the assistance of such forces as may be needful, to march into the City of London, and there to seize upon all such sums of Money as you shall find in the publique Treasury at Goldsmiths Hall, Haberdashers Hall, and Weavers Hall, or in any of them, giving to the Keepers of the said Treasuries respectively, Receipts . . . for the Sums, or number and proportions of Bags so seized; all which Sums . . . are . . . to be conveyed into Blackfryers, there to be disposed of for the end aforesaid.[25]

During the early years of the Commonwealth 'Weavers' Hall might properly be denominated their Exchequer . . . [for] from this place Parliament was accustomed to issue bills, . . . in the nature of our exchequer bills, and which were commonly known under the name of "Weavers' Hall Bills".'[26]

The stresses and strains of such 'distracted times' weakened traditional disciplines and provided opportunities for the airing of long-standing grievances as well as new-fangled notions. In earlier centuries the common man had tried, spasmodically and with little success, to make himself heard; but now the Civil War gave him 'a chance, briefly, to taste the possibility of power and to speak his mind'. John Taylor's pamphlet entitled *A Swarme of Sectaries and Schismatiques*, published in 1641, refers slightingly to 'the strange preaching (or prating) of . . . Cobblers, Tinkers, Pedlers, Weavers, Sowgelders, and Chymney-Sweepers'.[27] In London, the voice of the 'commonalty' was raised in criticism of the City's government, as well as that of many of the livery companies. At least twelve companies, including the Weavers, were affected; and Unwin thought it 'highly probable that few of the companies containing a rank and file of craftsmen escaped the contagion of the democratic movement',[28] which manifested itself in startling demands that the companies' oligarchic constitutions should be reformed on democratic lines. For example, in 1644 the commonalty of the Stationers' Company claimed the right to be present at elections of officers, and in the following year a young man of their commonalty dared to accuse the Master and Wardens of sundry misdemeanours.[29] The Weavers' Company had somewhat similar trouble in 1643, when two disgruntled members of their commonalty, John Wood and John Chambers, made a disturbance at the election of the Bailiffs and Wardens. The Company invoked the City's aid, and after considerable delay, the

Court of Aldermen sent Wood and Chambers to Newgate gaol where they were held without trial for no less than twelve weeks. The prisoners sued out a writ of Habeas Corpus and the Officers of the Weavers' Company 'by their own confession' spent £150 in defending the case.[30] They accused certain 'ill-affected' members of making a combination and plotting to overthrow the 'ancient and approved government' of their Company, and voted a levy of 10s. a head to meet the expenses of defending the Company's 'rights and immunities'.[31] The Court minutes reveal that the customary dinner on Lord Mayor's Day was in jeopardy. Three Stewards had agreed to serve, but because of 'great divisions at present in this Company which threateneth the ruin thereof', no dinner was held in 1648 and the money already advanced by the Stewards was returned to them.[32]

The case for preserving the *status quo* was set forth in *A Breviate of the Weavers' Business before the Honble. Committee of the House of Commons in Star Chamber* in 1648, in which 'this manner of electing the officers of corporations by a certain select number of rank and degree (as is practised in London and other popular Cities)' is justified as being 'good and agreeable with the Law for the avoiding of popular disorder and confusion'; a view upheld long ago 'in a case of Law by all the Judges'. The commonalty's counter-blast and proposals for reforms were embodied in a document entitled *The Case of the Commonalty of the Corporation of the Weavers of London truly stated* (c. 1649), and 'humbly presented to the consideration of the honourable House of Commons'.[33] It opens with an impressive argument, based upon a simple form of the theory of the social contract:

> All legal jurisdiction over a number of people or society of men must either be primitive or derivative. Now primitive jurisdiction is undoubtedly in the whole body and not in one or more members, all men being by nature equall to other and all jurisdictive power over them, being founded by a compact and agreement with them, is invested in one or more persons who represent the whole and by the consent of the whole are impowered to govern by such rules of equality towards all as that both governors and governed may know certainly what the one may command and what the other must obey, without the performance of which mutual contract all obligations are cancelled and the jurisdictive power returns unto its first spring—the people from whom it was conveighed. And doubtless whatever power our governors of the Corporation of Weavers may pretend and plead for, if they have any rationally, they had it at first from the whole body.

As to the rights and privileges granted by royal charter, the commonalty argued that:

there is not any one liberty that is granted to them (the governors) but what is also granted to the meanest member of the said Company . . . not to so many particular men but to the whole society and what power soever any person or persons were afterwards invested withall must of necessity be by the consent, election and approbation of the whole body . . . our Egyptian Taskmasters . . . plead custom and Presidents [precedents] both which they will find but . . . rotten props to support their worm-eaten Soveraignty.

In 1650 the Weavers' commonalty published a short pamphlet addressed to 'the High Court of Parliament' and entitled *The humble Representation of the Commonalty of the Weavers Company . . . together with the Charge against the Mr. Bayliffes and Governors. . . .*[34] In this document, which contains no reference to the social contract and is more factual than philosophical, the 'distressed Commonalty' state that 'many thousands of the poorer sort of us . . . are like to perish' because 'thousands of intruders are suffered into our trade, . . . aliens eate the bread out of our mouths [and] our inheritance is possest by strangers', who enjoy as much privilege as 'we that have served for it'. The Officers and Assistants are accused of admitting

aliens to be members for sums of money . . . [having] brought in by their own confession 312 strangers to be masters . . . and taken for their admittance £5 a man, which amounted to £1,560. . . . They object that the strangers admitted are broad weavers and deal not in the commodities that we trade in, viz., ribbon, lace, etc. The objection is false; for most of us can, and many of us have wrought, as good broad stuffs as are nowadays made, and would do still, were it not for the vast number of strangers. . . . And if it be demanded how . . . they got the trade into their hands, we answer that at the beginning of the war many of us and our servants engaged for the Parliament, and in our absence, they, being generally malignant, staying at home, and keeping servants all of their own country, never employing any English . . . by degree got all the trading, so that now the war is ended, and we returned to follow our callings, we can get no employment. By which means many hundreds have been forced to leave the trade, as to be porters, labourers, water-bearers, etc., and many forced to take relief from the several parishes wherein they dwell.

Furthermore, it was alleged that the Officers and Assistants had continually procrastinated and had arbitrarily dismissed the Yeomanry; the case of Wood and Chambers was raked up and the charge of wasting 'the stock and treasure of the companie' was repeated. By way of remedy for all this, the commonalty claimed the right to take part *directly* in the election of the Bailiffs, and not indirectly through the Livery, who were not elected by the commonalty and were in no sense their representatives. The outcome was that Parliament empowered the Weavers' commonalty to elect 140 representatives to act for them, with results which have already been outlined in Chapter 2.

Any dangerous ideas of a democratic colour which the common man may have entertained during the Civil War and the Commonwealth period, faded fast when the Restoration brought back his customary sports and pastimes. The old traditional forces resumed possession of the disputed ground, and oligarchy retained its powerful (and often corrupt) hold for a further 200 years.

It is unfortunate that the Weavers' Court minute books covering the early 1640s are missing, so that we get no glimpses of the enlistment of the young men in the six 'auxiliary' regiments, some 18,000 strong, raised by Parliament in London during the early days of the Civil War to augment the existing trained bands. The details of the sale of the Company's plate in 1641 and the collection of arms and equipment from Weavers' Hall in 1642 are recorded as separate memoranda on spare folios in an earlier minute book. Not until the survivors return and apply to be made free of the Company do we find references to their military service. The earliest record occurs on 21 May 1649 when Robert Newton, son of Giles Newton, carpenter, who had been apprenticed to a London weaver for seven years from 1 March 1640, 'and was employed in the States service' from the beginning of 1642 until July 1646, was made free, his four-and-a-half years of military service being counted as part of his term of apprenticeship.[35] Such exemptions seem to have been common practice, whatever the length of war service, as we see from many examples in the Weavers' records.[36] In the summer of 1649,

> Noah Sterling, son of William Sterling of Godmanchester, in the County of Huntingdon, Tanner, apprenticed to John Leyland, citizen and weaver of London, for 8 years from 9 May 1642, was made free by report of John Hoare, citizen and weaver of London, for his service, and also produced a certificate that Noah Sterling served as a private soldier in Capt. William Parker's troop, my Lord Fairfax his regiment, from 20th June 1648 until the 26th March 1649, and also an affidavit underneath the said certificate of the truth thereof.

Thomas Richardson, the son of a Lancashire chapman, who had been apprenticed to a London weaver, was made free, he having been in 'the States service when ye fight was at Brainford' (Brentford); and William Wilson, the son of a Wiltshire labourer, who had been similarly apprenticed in April 1641, was made free after serving for over two years in the army. All through the second half of 1649 and the following spring we see the discharged warriors returning to civilian life. Thus, in July 1649, Thomas Bon, son of a joiner who lived in Keswick, and William Pym, son of a Buckinghamshire labourer, were both made free on production of recent certificates of their military service. And Thomas Jackson, whose father lived in Burton-upon-Trent, was made free by virtue of five-and-a-half years' service with his master, a London weaver, 'and also by report of Colonel Pride,[37] present in Court, and by certificate under the hand of Richard Kemp, Captn, doth appear for his service to the State the remainder of his Time', viz., two-and-a-half years. At the same meeting of the Court of Assistants, Robert Smith handed in a certificate signed by Captain Peter Crispe 'for part of his time in the State's service' and Thomas Daniel's military service was vouched for by Captain Nathaniel Kirke. Richard Haselwood was able to prove that he had served under Captain Langham; and between August 1649 and April 1650, eight other apprentice-soldiers proved various periods of war service ranging from one to four years.[38] During 1651 the pattern is very similar. For example, John Gissopp, son of a Derby weaver, served three years of his apprenticeship term with a London weaver 'and 4 years he served the Parliament as it appears by an order of the Committee of Indemnity bearing date 13th May 1651 directed to the Master and Wardens requiring them to make him free, and [he] was sworne and paid 3s. 4d.'[39] Thomas Ellis, who came from a Yorkshire family, had served under the Earl of Warwick on the Parliaments' side for no less than seven years; and John Cooke, son of a Cumberland yeoman, had served for five years.

One of the most interesting entries made at this period tells us that in February 1651 the Court of Aldermen had before it the petition of Henry Houldrup to be admitted into the freedom of the City on the grounds 'that he hath served to the trade of weaving five years with a freeman and having out of his good affection to the Parliament adventured himself with his five apprentices in their service, wherein four of them lost their lives, hath put themselves out of that good way of livelihood wherein he was settled'. This petition was powerfully recommended by none other than 'the Lord General Fairfax and Major General Harrison in his behalf' and the Court ordered that Houldrup should be admitted to the freedom of the City by redemption in the Company of Weavers, 'paying to the Master Chamberlain to the City's use the sum of 46s. 8d.' Accordingly, he was 'lovingly received' by the Weavers; so lovingly, indeed, that he became Clerk of the Company (c. 1652).[40]

In November 1651, Colonel Pride gave a certificate of war service to Ephraim Marshall, son of a Berkshire labourer, who had been in the Parliament's army for seven years. Shortly afterwards, Robert

Kember, a Southwark lad, was made free on the certificate of John
Addis, cornet of a troop of horse in Captain Charles Bowles's company. John Hill, who had been apprenticed to weaving for ten years,
proved by 'a certificate signed by Captain Clarke' that he had spent
eight of them in the army.[41] John Hutchens declared that after
serving four years as a weaver's apprentice, he was pressed into the
King's service; and Francis Papworth, when challenged to prove his
'full term', was able to show that he had spent two years with his
master, two years in the army, and although he had been away a
further three years in Barbados, he 'had given his Master content'.[42]
Altogether some forty men are named in the Weavers' records of
admissions to the freedom of the Company, including Henry Houldrup and his apprentices, as having served in the Civil War, nearly
all of them on the side of Parliament.

Another London weaver whose name has come down to us, written
into the chequered history of England, is Richard Blomfield, who was
serving in the Parliamentary army under the Earl of Essex when it
was forced to surrender to the Royalists at Lostwithiel in Cornwall in
1644. Blomfield was one of some thirty witnesses who gave written
evidence against Charles I during his trial in January 1649. The
report runs thus:

> Richard Blomfield, Citizen and Weaver of London, aged 35
> years, or thereabouts . . . saith that at the defeat of the Earl
> of Essex's Army in Cornwall he . . . was there, . . . At which
> time he saw the King at the Head of his Army, near Foy
> (Fowey), on Horseback; and further saith that he did then see
> divers of the Lord of Essex's souldiers plundered, contrary to
> the Articles then lately made, near the person of the King.[43]

Apparently, Blomfield was not asked to explain what he meant by the
word 'plunder' in this context; but the probable meaning may be
gathered from the evidence of another witness, Humphrey Browne,
a Rutland husbandman, aged twenty-two, who said that when
Newark Fort in Leicester was surrendered to the King's forces 'upon
Composition that neither Cloaths nor Money should be taken away
from any of the Soldiers of that Fort which had so surrendered nor
any violence offered to them'; as soon as the Fort was surrendered 'the
King's soldiers, contrary to the Articles, fell upon the Soldiers of the
Fort, stript, cut and wounded many of them'; and the King, who was
present 'on Horseback, in bright Armour' refused to put a stop to
these abuses.[44]

The accusation of 'plunder', but not the King's acquiescence, is
partially confirmed by the Royalist soldier, Richard Symonds, who
tells in his *Diary* what he saw on 2 September 1644, when the Parliament's army surrendered.

> These regiments I took note of after three or four had passt
> . . . Colonel Davies, white colours, Citty London . . . Colonel
> Whichcote, greene, Citty London . . . The King himselfe ridd
> about the field and gave strict command . . . that none of the
> enemys were plundered . . . Yet, notwithstanding our officers
> with their swords drawne did perpetually beate off our foot,
> many of them (the Parliament's soldiers) lost their hatts, &c . . .
> Our foot would flowt at them . . . and then would pull their
> swords, &c away, for all our officers still slasht at them.[45]

Several entries in the Weavers' books after 1660 show that not all
weavers were on the side of Parliament. For example, the father of
one weaver's apprentice alleged that he had been 'forced to go beyond
the sea because he would not take up Arms against the King', and
for this reason his son was born in Holland. William Short, son of a
glover living in Southwark, was made free of the Weavers' Company
after serving only five-and-a-half years of his eight-year term of
apprenticeship because 'he did produce a certificate that he had
served his Majesty at his happy Restoration'. In 1664 another
apprentice who proved that 'he was a soldier at the restoration of the
King' was made free forthwith; and Edward Edwards was granted
exemption from a major portion of his apprenticeship when he produced a certificate showing that he 'went into His Majesty's wars and
was a soldier at H.M. Restoration'.[46]

In midwinter 1664–5, 'a time of great Extremity', the Lord Mayor
wrote to the London Livery Companies reminding them of the
'pressing great necessities of the multitude of poor within the City
and Liberties, much aggravated by the hard season and dearness of
seacoals and the smallness of the collection yet appearing from the
several wards'. To this appeal the Weavers' Company responded by
sending 40 shillings. Shortly afterwards the Company was called
upon to provide 35 quarters of wheat as its contribution towards a
total stock of 10,000 quarters to be provided by the livery companies
as a whole;[47] a reserve designed to guard against famine and famine
prices for breadstuffs in the City. But far worse tribulations were in
store, for in the second half of 1665 London's population was deci-
mated by the worst outbreak of bubonic plague in the city's long
history. The inhabitants of many large cities in Britain and abroad
had come to expect these periodical visitations of pestilence, which
the majority looked upon as the 'sad and sore judgements' of God
upon a sinful people. London had suffered many of these 'judgements', such as the outbreak of 1603 which killed between 30,000 and
31,000 people and prevented James I, newly arrived from Scotland
after the death of Elizabeth I, from entering the capital of his
southern kingdom. In 1625 another severe outbreak, which carried

off more than 35,000 Londoners, coincided (not inappropriately) with the beginning of the disastrous reign of Charles I. Eleven years later plague caused the deaths of yet another 10,000 to 11,000 of London's population. The climax of calamity, however, was reached in and around London in the summer of 1665, when at least 70,000 people— probably many more—met their deaths by bubonic plague[48] which crept up insidiously upon individuals, families, households, neigh- bourhoods and eventually whole parishes, striking again and again, regardless of age or sex, rank or occupation. This was the worst and, mercifully, the last of these terrible scourges to fall upon London, subjecting the populace to a slow torture, unrelenting and lethal, devilishly drawn out through a dry, sweltering summer and well into the late autumn.

The general 'pattern' in 1665 was similar to that of the severe visitations of 1603 and 1625, with the highest incidence of plague deaths in the overcrowded, insanitary industrial liberties and out- parishes, such as St Giles, Cripplegate, St Mary, Whitechapel, St Leonard, Shoreditch, St Olaves and St Saviour, Southwark and St Botolph, Aldgate. 'Death hath pitcht his tents,' wrote Dekker, '. . . in the sinfully-polluted Suburbs . . . the skirts of London.' According to John Gaunt's estimates, first published in 1662, the most rapid growth in London's population in the earlier half of the seventeenth century took place in ten of the parishes immediately 'without' the walls, and of these Cripplegate, Whitechapel and the Southwark parishes—all teeming with weavers and other industrial workers—had become terrible slums, even worse, far worse, than those which disgraced the Victorian era.

The incidence of the plague in 1665 was exceedingly severe in the parish of St Giles without Cripplegate, which was the largest city parish and included the whole Ward of Cripplegate Without, a densely populated district outside the City wall, characterised by narrow streets and alleys, foul open ditches, heaped garbage and refuse of every description. This district, extending from the wall to Old Street and from Aldersgate Street to Moorfields, was originally a fen consisting mainly of malodorous stagnant pools, which had gradually been filled up with the City's rubbish and debris to form foundations for buildings. When the earlier, well-to-do residents moved away, their places were quickly filled, indeed over-filled, by an industrial population of weavers, glovers, tailors, cordwainers, carpenters, wire- drawers, pinmakers, coopers and other craftsmen, together with large numbers of victuallers, carmen, porters and labourers. Cripplegate, long known as generally unhealthy and a bad place for fever, was severely hit by plague in 1603, 1625, 1636 and 1641; and here, in 1665, with everything in its favour, the plague struck more savagely than ever before.[49] From 29 recorded plague deaths in June 1665 the num-

ber soared to over 700 in July and 4,600 in August, when a high peak
of horror was reached. In September the total, at 1,340, was still
grim, but less than one-third of that of the previous month. One
contemporary observer, John Tillison, a minor official of St Paul's
Cathedral, thought that 'the miserable condition of St. Giles, Cripplegate . . . is more to be pitied than any parish in or about London'.[50]

The first plague death in Cripplegate, it seems, occurred during the
last week in May 1665, and on 2 June we have a record of the death
from plague of 'John Barker, weaver in Old Street'. Thereafter, for
nearly four weeks, no weavers nor any members of weavers' households in Cripplegate died of the plague. But on 29 June the fortunate
spell came to an end with the deaths from plague of George Smith,
weaver, and Alexander Watkins, 'weaver in Barbican'. In July the
deadly attack began in earnest and by the end of the month, according to the burials record kept by Nicholas Pyne the devoted and
heroic parish clerk of Cripplegate, the plague had wiped out 28
weavers, 13 weavers' wives, 41 sons and daughters, 16 male 'servants'
(mostly journeymen weavers, no doubt) and 3 female servants; a total
of 101 persons. In August the figures rose to a ghastly crescendo:
83 weavers, 160 of their wives and children, and 31 'servants'—in all,
274. For September the total was much lower at 126, though still a
good deal higher than the July total. The plague deaths among
weavers, their families and 'servants' in Cripplegate during the seven
months June–December 1665, during which time 162 weavers and
365 members of their households died, are summarised in Table 9.1.[51]

Table 9.1 *Plague deaths among weavers, their families, journeymen
and other servants in the parish of St Giles without
Cripplegate, from 2 June 1665 to 31 December 1665*

1665	Weavers	Weavers' families			Weavers' 'servants'		Total
		Wives	Sons	Daughters	Male	Female	
June	3	—	—	—	—	—	3
July	28	13	20	21	16	3	101
August	83	37	59	64	23	8	274
September	40	13	28	22	21	2	126
October	4	3	3	3	5	—	18
November	4	—	—	—	—	—	4
December*	—	—	1	—	—	—	1
	162	66	111	110	65	13	527

* No weavers or members of their households died of plague in Cripplegate after
10 December 1665.

These figures cloak a multitude of domestic tragedies and a black
hell of human misery. A few examples of deaths by plague among
weavers' households must suffice. At the beginning of August 1665,
Richard Poole lost two sons and a daughter in two days. John New

saw his son and daughter die on 6 August, and followed them himself three days later. Thomas Leeke was buried on 13 August, and his two sons on the next day. During the four days 14–17 August, Thomas Crawley, his wife, son, two daughters and a journeyman—a household of six persons—were wiped out. Between 18 and 23 August Sebastian Bugg, his wife, his daughter and his servant, Mary Seamans, were all carried off. A similar tragedy opens on 19 August with the burial of Dorothy, daughter of Nicholas Holmes, and concludes with the burial of his son and two other daughters on 24–25 August: four children gone in six days. Again, between 23 August and 5 September, William Fell lost his journeyman, his wife and three daughters. And as late as 4 October Felix Bragg was buried and on the same day his wife and son, 'both in a coffin'.

Analysis of the recorded deaths from plague among people in other occupations in Cripplegate indicates that the weavers considerably outnumbered members of other large crafts, such as the cordwainers, tailors and glovers (see Table 9.2).

It was not only working-class folk who died in the pestilence, for the plague was no respecter of persons, and actually carried off such eminent officials as the City Coroner and the Remembrancer (both in

Table 9.2 *Recorded plague deaths among craftsmen and other workers in the parish of St Giles without Cripplegate, June–December 1665*[52]

Craft or trade	No.	Craft or trade	No.
Weavers (including 23 stocking weavers)	162	Bricklayers	10
Cordwainers	73	Printers	9
Tailors	67	Tobacco-pipe makers	9
Carpenters and joiners	47	Barbers	8
Glovers	47	Buttonmakers	8
Smiths 18 Blacksmiths 6 Coppersmiths 3	27	Curriers	8
		Dyers	8
		Sawyers	7
		Turners	7
Wire-drawers	27	Pewterers	6
Coopers	18		
Pinmakers	12		
Needlemakers	10		
Victuallers	36	Labourers	53
Butchers	13	Porters	44
Vintners	9	Coachmen & Carmen	13
'Servants' including journeymen, household and brewers' servants			252
Total			990

September 1665). But it is true that the City within the walls suffered less than the liberties and out-parishes.[53] Moreover, many well-to-do people could, and did, leave London to seek safety in the country (as Pepys notes in his *Diary* on 21 June). A number of the clergy fled; but others remained and died with their parishioners, while some who stayed survived. The vicar of St Leonard's, Shoreditch, died at his post; so did the curates of St Giles's and St Saviour's in Southwark. In the parish of the Weavers' Company, St Michael's, Bassishaw, the temporary incumbent, his wife and three children all died of plague early in September. The vicar of Stepney stayed with his sorely stricken flock and, as by a miracle, survived. The burial register of St Giles, Cripplegate, shows that five 'ministers' died of plague in that parish; also five chirurgeons and an apothecary, four scriveners, four 'pedagogues' and two solicitors.[54] The same parish lost three churchwardens and its efficient and devoted parish clerk who, steadfast in the face of death, kept such excellent records. Dr Parker, who had medical charge of the stricken ward of Cripplegate Without and the parish of St Stephen, Coleman Street, died on duty.[55] Doubtless a few of the more prosperous master weavers with their families left London. Some of these, indeed, already resided in satellite villages such as Hackney, where they may have felt safe; but, as it proved, no place was entirely safe, though some were safer than others. As a contemporary observer remarked of those who went away for a time but came back too soon, 'Divers persons and familyes at the return home to the City have mett with what they fled from . . .'[56]

Over the river, in Southwark, there lived a large colony of weavers, probably half as many again as in Cripplegate, as well as many feltmakers, shipwrights and other craftsmen, watermen, porters and labourers—a dense industrial population in whose ranks the plague tore great gaps. It was from Southwark—'a sad place through the plague', as Pepys remarked—that John Allin wrote his vivid eyewitness accounts of the plague's ravages, in letters which the addressees were reluctant to receive for fear of infection. 'Mr. Symond Porter, Mr. Miller's brother-in-law, dyed last Tuesday (of the plague)', he wrote on 18 August; 'I am afrayd to write to Mr. Miller of it, least hee should bee afrayd of my letter; but pray let him know. . . .' Allin was a priest who had given up his living at Rye in Sussex for conscience's sake in 1662. He was also a dabbler in alchemy and astrology, an amateur student of medicine, and an intelligent on-the-spot observer. In 1665 he was living in the parish of St Olave, Southwark, and there he remained unscathed while 'spotted death ran arm'd through every street', destroying at least 2,785 lives in that parish alone. The dreadful sickness is, he says, 'very mortal where it comes; many whole familyes . . . totally swept away'. Allin tells of his 'brother [-in-law], Peter Smith, who was abroad on Lord's day last, in the morning; towards evening a little ill, then tooke something to sweate, which that night brought forth a stiffness under his eare, where he had a swelling that could not be brought to rise and breake, but choacked him; he dyed Thursday night last . . . it is a great mercy now counted to dye of another disease'.[57] And again, on 24 August, 'I am, through mercy, yet well in the middest of death . . . and the plague pitt open daily within view of my chamber window.'

In London's East End—the liberties and out-parishes spreading northwards and north-eastwards from Bishopsgate and Aldgate—the aggregate industrial population was larger than in Southwark and at least twice as large as in the Cripplegate district. As living conditions were not markedly better,[58] doubtless the incidence of deaths among the closely packed weavers in this district was much the same as in Southwark and Cripplegate: probably upwards of 1,000 deaths among weavers and their households. The parish of St Botolph, Bishopsgate, suffered some 2,500 deaths by plague. In the neighbouring parish of St Botolph, Aldgate, there was a great plague pit into which, according to Defoe, 1,114 corpses from Aldgate and Whitechapel were thrown in a single fatal fortnight.[59] St Leonard's, Shoreditch, too, was heavily hit. In mid-July it was reported that the plague 'is much at Hogsden' (Hoxton), and in August–September the plague deaths in the parish were not greatly below those in Bishopsgate parish. Doubtless it might have been written of many a luckless weaver, as it was of Daniel Saul—'Here lies the body of [a] Spittlefields weaver, and that's all.' Nor did the industrial workers, including some weavers, living in the squalid slums of Clerkenwell escape the plague, which made its appearance early and stayed long. At its worst in the month of August it killed nearly 600 people.[60]

Further afield, the extensive semi-rural parish of Stepney, comprising eight hamlets, at first seemed immune from the plague; but in August and September the number of plague deaths soared to the appalling total of 3,247 in the five weeks ending 3 October. According to Walter Bell, the aggregate of recorded plague deaths in Stepney parish in 1665 was 6,583, which may be compared with the figure of 7,150 in Cripplegate and 9,887 for all the parishes inside the City wall.

Obviously, such an onslaught of pestilence would tend to dislocate or halt all normal activities; and this indeed happened to a certain extent. Commercial intercourse between Scotland and south-east England, and between France and England, ceased in July 1665, while people of rank and fortune hastily left London. Trade withered, causing high unemployment and 'great wants and extremities' among craftsmen, shopkeepers and the poor. On 28 July the Lord Mayor called upon the City Companies to devote to the relief of their poor members one-third of the money saved by the cancellation of their customary feasts and festivities. The evidence to be found in the

Weavers' records suggests only a shrinkage or reduction of the
Company's normal activities, not a complete breakdown. By the end
of June 1665 about three-quarters of the normal annual searches of
the craft had been made and much of the search groats and quarterages collected (see Table 9.3). Nevertheless, as we saw in Chapter 5,
the Company's accounts showed an appreciable fall in income in the
financial years 1664–5 and 1665–6.

Table 9.3 *Effect of the plague on Company income*

Year	Bailiff's receipts from presentments, free-doms, fines, etc. £	Masters' quarterages collected £
1663–4	466	149
1664–5	263	121
1665–6	303	91
1666–7	375	118

The credit balance 'due to the house' (i.e. to the Company's funds) in
1664–5 was only £20. 18*s*., whereas in the previous year it had been
£289. 16*s*. 5*d*.[61] The periodical payments to the Company's pensioners
were maintained, though the amount paid out fell from £42. 5*s*. in
1663–4 to £31. 17*s*. 6*d*. in 1665–6, which suggests abnormal mortality
among the pensioners and that the vacancies had not been filled
promptly. During the plague period the Company's usual dinners
were not held, so that expenditure decreased as well as income.

The Weavers' records covering the years 1666–7 show an abnor-
mally large number of turn-overs of apprentices whose masters had
died in the plague. The turn-over rate averaged seven or eight a month,
and in February 1667 the Court of Assistants decided that 'no fee be
demanded for permitting turn-overs', except one shilling for the
Clerk. For several years after 1665 echoes from the dreadful days of
'the great sickness' can be heard in the Weavers' minute books. For
example, in March 1667 Oliver Pecarr 'saith all ye Neighbourhood
are dead, and [he] cannot prove his service'. But, after further
inquiry, proof was forthcoming and he was admitted a foreign
brother. Three years later 'John Lingar appr. to Peter Sergeant,
Weaver, decd., 7 years from 16th July 1660, upon report of his
Service till ye Sickness time at wch. time his Mr. & Mrs. dyed, & by
Certificate [that he had continued in weaving] he was made free and
paid 3*s*. 4*d*., gave a small spoon and in money 1*s*. 8*d*.'[62]

Hard on the heels of the Great Plague came the Great Fire; both
appalling disasters, but very different in their incidence and effects.

The plague was most deadly in the extra-mural parishes, while nearly all the fire damage occurred within the walls of the old city. The tale of the outbreak of fire in the small hours of 2 September 1666 near the northern end of London Bridge during an exceptionally hot dry summer has often been told: its three days of havoc among the old wooden houses overhanging the narrow streets and alleys; the strong steady wind fanning the flames and driving them irresistibly from Thameside up to the very heart of the city; the acute shortage of water; the citizens' early reluctance to pull down buildings in the path of the fire; and the struggling streams of panic-stricken people of all classes flying from the frightful furnace, as from Hell itself, 'in a great *sauve qui peut*'. In all, St Paul's Cathedral and more than 80 other churches, upwards of 13,000 houses, large and small, and the halls of 44 of the 51 livery companies were burnt down.[63]

Earlier in the seventeenth century some such disaster had been dimly foreseen. Both James I and Charles I were much concerned about the fire-risk represented by so many timber-framed buildings, tar-coated wooden sheds, and stocks of inflammable goods tightly packed into such a small area. John Evelyn's *Diary* mentions the warning he had given to the King and his advisers in 1661 in his little book, *Fumifugium*, on the grave dangers of storing wood, coal and similar materials in 'wharfes and magazines' within the City.[64] Their removal 'would be a means to prevent the danger of fireing, those sad Calamities' which all too often begin in such places. Although 'certain engines for the quenching of fire within this City in time of danger' had been provided by the City Corporation in 1627 at a cost of £250, apparently no fully comprehensive plans to deal with a major fire were ever made.[65]

Certain it is that on 2 and 3 September 1666 the fire raging in the City and hourly increasing its hold met with no effective opposition, so that Tuesday, 4 September, the day on which Weavers' Hall was destroyed, was the most dreadful of all. On that day the fire destroyed the church of St Lawrence Jewry, the famous Blackwell Hall cloth market, the Triple Tun Tavern and, sweeping through the Guildhall, put an end to the famous twin giants, Gog and Magog. From narrow Coleman Street and its still narrower alleys the flames spread swiftly to Basinghall Street, destroying the merchants' houses, the parish church of St Michael, Bassishaw and the neighbouring halls of the Weavers', Masons', Coopers' and Girdlers' Companies.[66] In addition the Weavers lost the tenement adjoining their hall, which had been let to a merchant for £10 per annum, and a house in Bread Street which they had bought in 1661 for £200.[67] This, like the hall, soon became nothing but an ash-strewn site.[68] On this same day the Grocers' Company lost their hall, but their muniments were saved and, later, they recovered from the debris 200 lb. of fused silver, the remains of their plate. Goldsmiths' Hall suffered the same fate, but here both plate and records were saved. Old St Paul's, also, was destroyed that day, and the unquenched fire, roaring onwards before the wind, burst through the city wall into the liberties beyond Ludgate. The entry in John Evelyn's *Diary* for 4 September shows us the fire raging through Fleet Street, the Old Bailey, Newgate and Paul's Chain to the cathedral. 'Paul's is burned, and all Cheapside' is Pepys's six-word summary in his *Diary* under the same date; and when he wrote to his father that evening, 'the post-house being burned, the letter could not go'. In the opposite direction, however, the fire did not quite reach Bishopsgate, leaving a part of Bishopsgate Within, including Sir Thomas Gresham's great house and the Leathersellers' Hall, unburnt,[69] so that the weavers and other craftsmen living in the courts and alleys near the gate had a wellnigh miraculous escape.

It was fortunate, indeed, for the Weavers' Company that their hall was in Basinghall Street and not in Thames Street,[70] so that the fire did not reach them until the third day, by which time their energetic, dauntless and devoted Clerk, James Cole, helped by the Beadle and Porter, had managed to remove to safety nearly all the pictures, the great chests containing the Company's precious ancient charters, and most of their records and plate. Exactly how he accomplished this most successful salvage operation we do not know, but it cannot have been easy. The conveyance of heavy and bulky objects through narrow streets cluttered and obstructed by the belongings of other people all trying to do the same thing must have been almost impossible. Porters, now in tremendous demand, were able to exact from desperate citizens rates of hire which became hourly more and more extortionate; while other men ostensibly porters, turned out to be thieves, 'wicked wretches that make their gain by the common calamity'.

Among the most vulnerable of all the valuables saved from Weavers' Hall were two bags each containing £200 in gold. The story is that in November 1664, the City Corporation, having promised Charles II a loan of £100,000 'for his present great affairs',[71] was trying to raise some of the money from the livery companies. The weavers were asked to provide £800 and to be 'sure and expeditious' about it. After anxious deliberation their response was an offer of £500, which the City flatly rejected. Apparently there was nothing for it but to submit and run more heavily into debt. This the Company did, obtaining £200 from Mistress Sarah Tutchin, a wealthy widow,[72] and another £200 from Samuel Hewson, gentleman, giving as security bonds under the Company's seal. By the beginning of September 1666 the Company was in a position to repay these loans and the money—gold coin in bags—lay at the Hall ready to be handed over to the lenders. At this very moment the Great Fire swept through the city, and the two creditors must have despaired of ever seeing their money.

However, all was not lost, as we discover from two entries in the Renter Bailiff's account book:[73]

Oct. 11, 1666	Paid Mr. Sam. Hewson due p. Bond £211. 10. 0	
	Expended with the said Mr. Hewson (he abating the Compa. about £5 & above 4 mo. Int. for preserving his Money at the time of ye Fire, it lying ready)	0. 16. 10
Dec. 13, 1666	Recd. of Sarah Tutchin (for preserving her money at ye Fire . . .)	0. 15. 0

Fortunately a great many of the Company's record books were rescued, but the Court minute books covering the years 1620 to 1650 (inclusive) have been lost, as have the Renter Bailiff's account books before 1666.[74] The Freedom Admission books for 1647 to 1694 are missing, and it is possible that the one in use in 1666, running from 1647 onwards, was destroyed in the Fire. For more than a year it was thought that the Ordinance and Record Book,[75] dating back to 1577 and containing copies of the Company's Ordinances and various petitions setting forth the weavers' grievances, had also been destroyed in the fire, but in December 1667 a Court minute tells us that

> Whereas a large Book wherein was a Copy of the Company's Ordinances and other concerns . . . was lately found by one Taylor and presented back to ye Compa. by Peter Welch, a Member thereof; it was thought fit and ordered that Mr. Bail. Heginbotham do give unto ye said Mr. Welch 20s. and that his quarterage be remitted.[76]

A grateful Company did not fail to reward its Clerk and his helpers for their prodigious and largely successful efforts. On 22 October 1666 it voted to 'Mr. Cole, the Clerk, for his Charges by him expended in removal & securing the Company's Money, Plate, Charters, Household stuff, etc. from the late dreadful fire, and for his pains and care therein; £50'; and gave to the Beadle and the Porter gratuities of £5 and £4 respectively. Early in the following December the Court of Assistants ordered 'that the Clerk's Bill of Expenses . . . now examined and approved, being £37. 17. 0. . . . be allowed him and £12. 3. 0 more for saving the Company's monies, plate and goods in ye dreadful fire . . . as ye free gift of this Court, and £5 to his wife as a loving remembrance'.[77]

NOTES

1 Maitland, *London*, I, pp. 373–4, 377; Sir Charles Firth, *Cromwell's Army* (1942), pp. 11, 17.
2 V. Pearl, *London and the Outbreak of the Puritan Revolution* (1961), pp. 104, 225.
3 V. Pearl, op. cit., pp. 31–7, 100, 116, 256–7.
4 Sir Charles Firth, 'London during the Civil War', in *History*, II (1926–7), pp. 25–9.
5 MS. 4655/1, ff.115–16; MS. 4646, ff.82b, 84.
6 MS. 4655/1, f.113.
7 MS. 4646, f.83.
8 MS. 4655A/2, 25 March 1652, f.43b.
9 MS. 4655/2, f.90; MS. 4655A/2, ff.13–14b, 29b–30.
10 MS. 4655/1, f.116.
11 Here again a great difference in degree is seen between the duties of major and minor livery companies. For example in 1642 the Merchant Taylors had 153 swords, 70 pikes, 32 halberds and black-bills, 52 muskets, 40 musket rests, 50 corselets, 300 cwt. of musket bullets, 300 cwt. of match and 40 barrels of gunpowder (Herbert, *Livery Companies*, I, p. 127). During the Civil War the Weavers' Company kept 3 barrels of gunpowder in a garret at their hall, where it seems to have deteriorated, for in 1648 'three barrels of decayed powder' were sold for £7 (MS. 4655A, 4 September 1648; MS. 4646, f.85b). The infantry weapons at this date were the pike and the musket; the proportion of pikemen to musketeers being about 1:2. The physique of the pikemen was usually superior to that of the musketeer, his armour was heavier and in close fighting the issue was often decided by 'push of pike'. The musketeer had little armour; his main defence against cavalry were hedges, dykes, and five-foot stakes called 'Swedish feathers', which he could stick in the ground in front of his position. His musket fired a bullet weighing about one ounce, and he carried his powder in a bandolier worn over the left shoulder. All his equipment was heavy and cumbersome—musket, coils of match, musket rest, bandolier and stake. The 'supporters' of the arms of the Honourable Artillery Company were a pikeman and a musketeer. The musket was effective up to 400 yards, but marksmanship was often poor. Indeed, it has been said that the smooth-bore musket was actually inferior to the long bow in range, accuracy, penetration and rate of fire (Firth, *Cromwell's Army* (1902), *passim*; John Buchan, *Oliver Cromwell* (1941), pp. 109–10; C. H. Roads, *The British Soldier's Firearm* (1966), Foreword by Lord Cottesloe; G. A. Raikes, *History of the H.A.C.* (1878–9), plate facing p. 68).
12 Isaac Penington was a substantial merchant, especially in textiles, and had interests in breweries. He was elected Sheriff in 1638; Alderman in 1639; Prime Warden of the Fishmongers' Company, 1640–2; one of the City's M.P.s in the Short and Long Parliaments. An uncompromising Parliamentarian, he helped to raise money for the cause and energetically forced on the fortification of London. He was a member of the Court which tried and condemned Charles I, but he did not sign the execution warrant. See *D.N.B.*; V. Pearl, *London and the Outbreak of the Puritan Revolution* (1961), pp. 176–

184, 198–206; John Nalson, *True Copy of the Journal of the High Court of Justice for the Tryal of King Charles I* (1684), Appendix; Clarendon, *History of the Rebellion and Civil War* (1704 edn), II, p. 76.

13 C. V. Wedgwood, *The Great Rebellion: The King's War, 1641–1647* (1958), p. 120.
14 Samuel Butler, *Hudibras*.
15 Whitelocke, *Memorials of the English Affair* (1682), p. 60, quoted in Brett-James, *London*, pp. 269–72; Cal. S.P., Venetian, 1642–3, pp. 191, 256.
16 Clarendon, *History of the Rebellion and Civil War in England* (Oxford, 1704 edn), II, p. 57; C. Hibbert, *Charles I* (1968), pp. 190–1.
17 C. V. Wedgwood, op. cit., p. 143.
18 Brett-James, *London*, Chap. XI.
19 Ibid., pp. 279–80. 'Weaving . . . was an unhealthy occupation . . . done in small, crowded rooms in horribly insanitary dwellings, and the air was carefully excluded by paper pasted over the cracks of the windows, to prevent the silk from losing weight and so making the weaver liable to deductions from his earnings. . . . It is no wonder that the weavers were a diminutive race' (George, *London*, p. 194).
20 W. Lithgow, *The Present Surveigh of London . . . with the several Fortifications thereof* (1643), in *Somers Tracts* (1810), IV, pp. 534–45.
21 Quoted by Firth, *History*, II (1926–7), p. 29; cf. Wedgwood, op. cit., pp. 163–4.
22 Brett-James, *London*, pp. 283, 288.
23 C. Firth and G. Davies, *Regimental History of Cromwell's Army* (1940), I, p. xvii and II, p. 424; Maitland, *London*, I, pp. 373–7.
24 In December 1642 Parliament authorised the extension of this tax to the whole kingdom (V. Pearl, op. cit., pp. 253–5, 266).
25 R. R. Sharpe, *London and the Kingdom* (1894), II, pp. 216, 295; *A Letter of H. E. Thomas Lord Fairfax to the Lord Mayor of London . . .*, 9 December 1648.
26 Herbert, op. cit., I, p. 182.
27 C. V. Wedgwood, *The Common Man in the Civil War* (1957), pp. 4, 6, 22. cf. Unwin, *Gilds*, p. 336.
28 V. Pearl, op. cit., Chap. IV; Unwin, *Ind. Org.*, p. 207; C. Hill, *The Century of Revolution* (1961), p. 154.
29 Blagden, *The Stationers' Company: A History, 1403–1959* (1960), p. 134. cf. C. Welch, *History of the Company of Pewterers* (1902), II, p. 105; Unwin, *Gilds*, p. 339.
30 Repertories 57, Part II, f.255; City Records MS. 22.43; *The Humble Representation of the Commonalty of the Weavers Company* (1650), p. 5.
31 MS. 4655A, 3 October 1648.
32 Ibid., 19 February and 18 June 1649.
33 Printed at length in Bland, Brown and Tawney, *English Economic History: Select Documents* (1921), pp. 307–12.
34 Guildhall Library Pam. 2037.
35 MS. 4655A.
36 Cromwell's Ordinance of 2 September 1654 decreed that any soldier who had served in the armies of the Parliament or Commonwealth between 1642 and 3 September 1651 for not less than four

years should be free to practise his trade or occupation, all legal restrictions notwithstanding. This was confirmed by Parliament in 1656 and re-enacted in slightly different form by Charles II, after his restoration, for the benefit of the men of Monk's army (C. Firth, *Cromwell's Army* (1902), pp. 275–6).

37 Thomas Pride (birth-date unknown); died 1658; a fanatical Anabaptist, rose from obscure origins to the rank of colonel. As Lieut.-Colonel he commanded Edward Harley's regiment of foot at Naseby, at the storming of Bristol, and the capture of Dartmouth, rendering much distinguished service. He served under Cromwell at the battles of Preston, Dunbar and Worcester. He is famous for 'Pride's purge' on 6 December 1648, when on orders from Fairfax he excluded Presbyterian M.P.s from the House, thus leaving only a 'Rump' of some fifty members. He was a member of the Court which tried Charles I, attending all sittings except one, and signing the King's death warrant (*D.N.B.*; and Nalson, *Tryal*, Appendix. cf. C. V. Wedgwood, *The Trial of Charles I* (1964), pp. 41–2).

38 MS. 4655A, *passim*.

39 MS. 4655A/2, ff.7, 19.

40 See MS. 4655(2), f.47, and MS. 4646, Old Ledger Book, f.92.

41 MS. 4655/2, f.127. For similar entries see ff.41, 49, 66, 121.

42 MS. 4655/2, f.109.

43 Nalson, *Tryal*, pp. 61, 71–2; C. V. Wedgwood, *The Trial of Charles I* (1964), pp. 148–9; A. Woolrych, *Battles of the English Civil War* (1961), p. 82.

44 Nalson, *Tryal*, p. 72; C. Hibbert, *Charles I* (1968), pp. 225–6 gives a comparable report of the plunder of Leicester after the siege and surrender, the King being present and making no effort to check the sack of the city. On the other hand, the Roundheads sometimes plundered the Royalists; e.g. after the fall of Reading (C. V. Wedgwood, *King's War* (1958), p. 205).

45 Richard Symonds, *Diary of the Marches of the Royal Army* (1859), pp. 66–7.

46 MS. 4655/3, ff.78b, 86b, 129.

47 MS. 4655/3, ff.168b–169. In famine years approximately one-seventh of the City's grain consumption was supplied by this method (N. S. B. Gras, *The Evolution of the English Corn Market* (1951), p. 450).

48 F. P. Wilson, *The Plague in Shakespeare's London* (1927), *passim*; W. G. Bell, *The Great Plague in London in 1665* (1924), *passim*.

49 W. Denton, *Records of Cripplegate Without* (1883), pp. 10, 142–3; J. J. Baddeley, *An Account of the Church and Parish of St. Giles without Cripplegate* (1888), p. 20; Bell, op. cit., pp. 144, 182; and *The Great Plague* (a pamphlet, 1958), p. 2. The statistics of the incidence of the plague must not be taken as accurate. Without doubt the numbers of plague deaths are understated. The sources of information were the 'searchers of the dead', who were usually poor old women glad to earn a few pence for this unpleasant and risky service. They had no medical knowledge and were open to bribery. Although they soon learnt to recognise the signs of death by plague, they might be induced by relatives to report the cause of death not as 'plague' but as fever or spotted fever. Since the deaths increased rapidly, as they did from July to September, many dead were carried direct to the plague pits or to burial in

the fields, so bypassing the parish church and clerk. Moreover, a number of the searchers, sextons and parish clerks were themselves struck down by plague, which further hindered the keeping of exact records.

50 Quoted by Bell, *The Great Plague*, p. 177.

51 St Giles without Cripplegate Register, 1663–7, *passim*. In the pre-plague decade, 1655–64, the yearly burials averaged 1,124 (Denton, op. cit., p. 201).

52 MS. 6497/7, St Giles without Cripplegate Register, 1663–7, *passim*.

53 Less than one-sixth of all the plague deaths recorded in London occurred in the parishes within the walls.

54 MS. 6497/7, St Giles Register, 1663–7. The five ministers all died of plague between 6 and 30 September 1665.

55 Jeaffreson, *Middlesex County Records* (1892), III, pp. 377, 379.

56 In July 1665 plague passes were introduced, with the intention of checking the spread of the disease by preventing plague 'contacts' from leaving London. Thus the plague pass (now preserved in the Guildhall Library, London) issued to Mary Walker, a servant, was signed by two churchwardens of the parish of St Andrew Under-shaft and certified that she and her master's whole family and all the neighbouring inhabitants 'are and by God's blessing have been free from being visited with the infectious disease of the Plague or pestilence'. Mary Walker, it seems, found employment at the Cross Keys Inn in Evesham, where her pass was discovered in the wood-work during rebuilding in 1939. But the device was in general evidently not effective, for we know that the plague spread dis-astrously into many ports and provincial towns, some as far away as Derbyshire, Cheshire and Tyneside.

57 B.Mus. MS. 4182, f.31; Bell, *Great Fire*, Chap. XI.

58 Ibid., pp. 259, 269.

59 Ibid., pp. 151–3. See MSS. 4515/4 and 9222/2 for the greatly in-creased numbers of burials in St Botolph's without Bishopsgate and St Botolph's, Aldgate.

60 Bell, *Great Fire*, p. 272.

61 Of which £113. 19s. was reported as 'lost by error', leaving an actual credit balance of £175. 17s. 5d. to be carried forward.

62 MS. 4655/4, ff.36, 49b; MS. 4655/6, 20 June 1670.

63 Southwark, protected by the river, was unscathed in the fire of 1666, but just ten years later it had its own great fire, in which 600 houses were burned down or blown up to check the spread of the flames. See Brett-James, *London*, p. 407.

64 Evelyn, *Fumifugium* (1661, reprinted 1961); *Diary*, 5 and 13 September 1666.

65 Brett-James, *London*, Chaps I–IV; Repertories 41, ff.214, 217b.

66 John Bedford, *London's Burning* (1966), *passim*.

67 MS. 4655/3, ff.14, 33b; MS. 4646, f.94.

68 Later sold to a scrivener for £140; see below, p. 201.

69 Bell, *Great Fire*, p. 211.

70 Fishmongers' Hall was the first of the livery companies' halls to be destroyed, and with it the Fishmongers, like the Watermen, lost nearly all their possessions. 'The Watermen, busiest of all people in saving the property of others, seem to have shown no practical concern in saving their own. The Fire was the wherrymen's harvest time. Their boats were at every man's disposal, at rates rising

to ruinous sums as the fire progressed' (Bell, *Great Fire*, pp. 28, 39).

71 This astonished Pepys: see his *Diary*, 10, 19 and 21 June 1666.

72 Her husband William Tutchin lent £100 to the Company in 1663, and he was alive when this money was repaid in 1664; but by 1666 he was dead and his executors were dealing with his estate. Therefore it is not unlikely that he died of plague in 1665 (MS. 4646, f.96; MS. 4648/1, 23 August 1666).

73 MS. 4648/1, and MS. 4655/3, f.160.

74 The Renter Bailiff's account book (MS. 4648/1) begins on 8 September 1666, four days after the burning of Weavers' Hall; and a new Court Minute Book (MS. 4655/4) was opened on 22 October 1666, when the Court of Assistants held their meeting at Carpenters' Hall.

75 MS. 4647.

76 MS. 4655/4, f.95.

77 MS. 4648/1, 22 October 1666; MS. 4646, f.100; MS. 4655/4, 22 October and 3 December 1666.

Chapter 10

Building Anew

The Weavers, gazing at the smouldering ruins of their Hall, must have felt almost overwhelmed by the tremendous physical and financial problems confronting them. They had to pull down the ruined shell and clear from the site mountains of masonry and charred timbers when everybody else all over the City, immersed in similar work, would be competing for labour and transport. Then they had to find men, materials and money to build anew. They could look for no help from insurance, for fire insurance was not 'invented' and developed in London until more than a decade after the Great Fire; so how could they raise the money, and how much would they need? No grants from public funds were to be had. All donations coming in from other parts of the country were, quite properly, designated for the relief of London's poor, whose plight in the long, hard winter of 1666–7 was pitiful in the extreme.[1] Apart from these funds, self-help was the order of the day. All in all, it was a situation in which initial hesitation is excusable and some delay not surprising, especially after the awful ravages of the plague only a year before. Even the rents from the house in Bread Street and the tenement adjoining Weavers' Hall would cease, for these premises, too, had been gutted.

An immediate practical problem facing the Court of Assistants was to find a meeting place where the present emergency could be discussed and ordinary business transacted. The choice lay between hiring accommodation at a tavern from time to time or securing partial use of one of the few companies' halls that had escaped destruction. They first tried the taverns which, although not over-expensive, were likely to prove distracting, at least for some. Three weeks after the Great Fire, 8s. 6d. was 'spent at ye Pope's Head with most of ye Assistants' and on 6 October 1666 a full Court dinner was eaten at the Angel in Moorfields,[2] at a cost of £1. 11s. 2d. Meantime the Weavers approached the Armourers, Loriners, Carpenters and Leather Sellers. The negotiations with the Armourers and Loriners came to nought, although the Weavers spent over £2 'with the Loriners when the Compa. were agreeing for the use of their Hall'. A temporary arrangement was come to with the Carpenters—the Court met at their Hall on 17 and 22 October 1666—and a somewhat more permanent one with the Leather Sellers, whose hall had originally been the refectory of the Benedictine nuns of St Helen's Priory, Bishopsgate. The Leather Sellers had bought it after the Dissolution and had added panelling and a rich plaster ceiling.[3] Here, on 5 November 1666, the Weavers held a Court meeting, having agreed to pay a rent of £4 a quarter, and 1s. 6d. for every fire during the winter months.[4] At Christmas 1666 or shortly after, the Clerk of the Leather Sellers' Company was given 'a piece of gold for his kindness' to the Weavers, while the Leather Sellers' Beadle received 5s.

At a Court held a fortnight later, at which the Bailiffs, Wardens and four Assistants were present, Bailiff Heginbotham reported that 'he had employed persons to cleanse the ground at the Hall', and his action was approved.[5] Little more could be done in the depth of winter, but early in the spring of 1667 the sap began to rise again not only in the trees but in the citizens also. In mid-March, Mr Fluellin, the tenant of the house adjoining 'ye late Hall', was pressing for something to be settled, and so was Mr Mason, the tenant of the Company's house in Bread Street. After somewhat protracted negotiations, Fluellin agreed to accept £200 'in consideration of his surrender of his interest in the ground on the front of the Hall; that he leave the rubbish and material belonging to the ground, and pay the rent to the time of the fire'.[6] Although the terms of the settlement with Mason have not come to light, we know that the site in Bread Street was sold to Thomas Bostock, a scrivener, for £140 (and £2 to the poor of the Company)[7] in order to augment the new Hall building fund. The Renter Bailiff supervised the 'measuring the Hall', with some workmen and Jonah Lewis who, although he was by trade a master carpenter, was a freeman of the Weavers' Company and became one of the Weavers' wardens in 1668–9 during the rebuilding of the Hall.[8] In April 1667, the Company agreed certain rates of remuneration with Lewis, who promised 'that the whole should be ready for tiling by Michaelmas next', while the master bricklayer, Thomas Seagood,

having brought up ye Foundation of ye Common Hall with the Company's materials be day work, now agreed to provide all materials of Bricklayers' work with workmanship for the Superstructure and to accept . . . seven pounds p. rod being reduced to a brick and a half being allowed running measure; and to perform the tiling workmanlike, he finding good and sound tiles, etc. . . . . and to have after the rate of 28s. p. square.[9]

A month or so later a paling fence was erected around the site of the old Hall and tenements, the Merchant Taylors were approached 'touching a parcel of ground near ye Hall', and a payment of £25 was made for preliminary work. The site measured 91 feet from east (back) to west (front) on the north side, and 87 feet 10 inches on the south side. The frontage facing west towards Basinghall Street was 36 feet, and the back boundary measured 28 feet 9 inches.[10]

At this point (June 1667) we meet the 'surveyor' (i.e. architect), Edward Jerman, when the Weavers invited him to view 'the Hall and ground' and present a 'draught' (i.e. a plan or set of plans) to the next Full Court.[11] Jerman was one of the special commissioners appointed to survey London after the Fire and to guide the work of reconstruction. The King appointed Christopher Wren, Hugh May, formerly King's Paymaster of the Works, and Roger Pratt who had been surveyor of St Paul's. To these the City added the three City Surveyors, Robert Hooke, Edward Jerman and Peter Mills. In the spring of 1667 Jerman had been unanimously chosen by a joint building committee of the City Corporation and the Mercers' Company, as 'the most able known artist (besides Mr. Mills)' that the City then had, to rebuild the Royal Exchange upon the old foundations and to design 'the pillars, arches, and roof according to the rules of art for the best advantage of the whole structure'. In due course the Lord Mayor and Edward Jerman, with a deputation, laid the plan and elevation before Charles II, who gave his approval.[12] Jerman also designed new halls for the Drapers, Vintners and Mercers, and is known to have been consulted by the Apothecaries. The Fishmongers' and Haberdashers' Halls are also attributed to him, but this awaits confirmation by documentary evidence.[13]

July 1667 was a time of intense activity for the Weavers' Company. On 8 July the Court resolved unanimously that two houses 'be forthwith built on ye front of ye Hall' and three days later, at a Common Hall attended by 'part' of the Assistants and about thirty of the Livery, 'it was fully agreed that the Hall and appurtenances adjoining be forthwith rebuilded'; and the master bricklayer was instructed 'to get Labourers to cleanse the cellars there and to lay in lime'. It was further decided to elect on Election day '6 or 8 persons of ye Livery to join with ye Bailiffs, Wardens and Assistants in this affair'.[14]

We have a fairly full report of the Election day proceedings on St James's Day, Thursday, 25 July 1667, when the Bailiffs, Wardens, Assistants and about thirty-six of the Livery

> Being met at Leather Sellers hall according to Summons they
> put on their Gowns and Hoods and from there walked to St.
> B[otolph], Bpsgt. Church where was a sermon preached by

Mr. Hall late Preacher of St. Mich: Bassishaw. Sermon being ended, the Company returned back to ye Hall, [where] the Bailiffs, Wardens and Assistants sat in Court by themselves, [and] after some consideration ye Bailiffs nominated . . . Mr. Abra. Broadway (being in course) to go in Election for Principal or chief Bailiff for the year ensuing, and Mr. Rich. Bailey . . . for Second or Renter Bailiff . . . and presented the same to the Livery, whereupon the Bailiffs, Wardens, Assistants and Livery being sat together for nomination of others to go in Election with those above-named, a Petition was sent into the Court . . . in the name of, and subscribed by the whole Yeomanry and divers of the Commonalty, setting forth their great satisfaction in the Government of this Company by the very great endeavours of the Bailiffs and Wardens, by ye help of ye Assistants, the year last past, and making it their earnest request that the said Bailiffs and Wardens might be chosen and prevailed with to hold again for the year now next ensuing; which petition was read and well considered . . . ,

with the desired result: Mr Benjamin Ducane and Mr George Heginbotham were re-elected Upper Bailiff and Renter Bailiff respectively.

Afterwards such as have been Bailiffs (according to the Ordinances) went to Election and there upon chose Mr. Richard Bailey and Mr. Mathew Porter to be Wardens for the year ensuing. Which being declared, they all made their earnest suit and request to be excused from that Service, but the Court likewise desiring them to hold and execute the same . . . they all declared their willingness to hold . . . for which this Court returned their thanks. Afterwards the Livery chose and elected

Mr. Will James	Mr. Thurman
Mr. Alex. Hosea	Mr. Russell
Mr. J. Upcher	Mr. G. Savile
Mr. W. Jenings	Mr. Soames

to be a Committee to join with the Bailiffs, Wardens and Assistants touching the rebuilding of the Hall.[15]

We have the minutes of the first meeting of this Special Committee, held at the Sun tavern in Bishopsgate on 26 August 1667, at which the master mason, Thomas Cartwright, and the master carpenter, Jonah Lewis, were present. Edward Jerman, also, seems to have been there, for the minute runs:

Agreed by the Committee that the Doorcase to the Hall, piers and other ornaments drawn for the 2 houses at ye front of ye

Hall and Gateway to the hall shall be with stone as is demonstrated in the Draught now presented by Mr. Jerman.

Mr. Cartwright, the Mason, now demanded £185 for the work in the front [and] promised that it should not exceed that price, and would use his endeavours to bring it to a less charge which he therefore hints, in hopes Stone may be procured at a cheaper rate than now it is.

Agreed that Mr. Lewis immediately proceed to the getting up the first storey. . . .

Mr. Deputy Cade and Mr. Adams are desired to buy 10,000 Bricks to rub for ye front.

Agreed that ye whole Committee be from time to time summoned, and any 5 [members] meeting, to act.[16]

On 23 September 1667 the Committee for Building met again (this time at the Angel in Moorfields) and agreed 'that there be no Belconies to the houses building at the Hall'. Advances of £60 each were voted to the master carpenter and master bricklayer, and the latter was authorised to try to buy 20,000 bricks at 20s. per 1,000[17] and 10,000 tiles at around 25s. per 1,000.

A continual careful watch had to be kept, of course, upon the financial position. Although a two-years' accumulation of silver spoons was sold in September 1667, the Company had to borrow £200 at the end of the year 'to pay workmen'.[18] Rigid economy was the order of the day. By the beginning of January 1668, when one of the houses was nearing completion, and the Court agreed 'that ye Compa. sit in their own Building by ye next Court', and that 'Mr. Cole, ye Clerk, do let the house he now live's in . . . and that as soon as one of the Compa. houses be fitted, the Clerk do live there and ye Compa. use the same until the Hall be rebuilt and accommodation can there be had'. So, on 27 January 1668, a full Court and dinner, 'being ye first at the Compa. new Buildings', was held in one of the new houses beside the Hall gateway.[19]

The Court now concentrated its attention upon the Hall itself, and resolved that 'when the Hall is rebuilt Mr. Lewis do see Mr. Jerman's directions performed by all the workmen concerned'.[20] Throughout 1668 the work went forward briskly. The Committee for Building met at least seven times, and the Bailiffs and Clerk had many a meeting (usually in a tavern) with the master bricklayer and master carpenter. Towards the end of 1668, the removal of 449 loads of rubbish from the site indicated the beginning of the final phase; a further fifty loads were carted away in January 1669, and the cellar was pumped dry. Three labourers 'that dug a vault in the kitchen' were paid 4s. 6d., and 9s. 10d. more 'for carrying out ye rubbish'; while others were hired to 'clean the street by the hall'. But much interior work remained to be done by the joiners, plasterers, plumbers, painters and carvers. In the middle of April the Company paid 16s. to a labourer 'that helped the Mason ten days in the great Kitchen', and to some of the carpenters 'breakfast money about the Turret, 2s. 4d.', because the turret, which had weather-board cladding,[21] was not finished and some extra effort was called for.

In less than two years a new brick building faced with stone had been constructed from cellar to turret. Looking directly on to Basinghall Street were two houses which provided a façade, and between them there was an entry from the street to a small courtyard around which were built the main Hall, the Court Room (or parlour), two kitchens and the office. The principal rooms—the Hall and Court Room—were approached by a handsome staircase at the top of which were a pair of equally imposing carved oak doors.[22] The joiners had to wainscot the walls of the Hall 'one foot above ye Seats or Benches' and to construct a screen of wainscot.[23] The Hall floor had to be laid, and tables and forms had to be made so that the Hall could be used not only for formal business but for dining. The joiners had also to make the main gates on Basinghall Street, which were 'of two leaves and a hatch of two leaves'. Below stairs, when ovens were 'set up . . . for the Company's service', the cook's advice was asked. Also a water-course was constructed from the Hall to the street, and a 'house of easement' was located in a convenient part of the cellar.[24]

Nearly all the materials were supplied and the labour engaged and paid by the master craftsmen, of whom thirteen were employed by the Company during the rebuilding operations; a bricklayer, a carpenter, a mason, a plumber, three plasterers, a painter, two smiths, a glazier, a joiner and a carver. As the work progressed the Company reimbursed these master craftsmen by instalments ranging from £20 to £100, paid usually every five or six weeks. From the Renter Bailiffs' accounts a summary of these payments can be made (see Table 10.1). It will be noted that all the glazier's work and nearly half the mason's was charged to the two houses—mainly for work on the Basinghall Street façade, no doubt. The Company paid £80 'for six fother and three hundred wt. of lead at £13 p. fother, used in and about ye Hall',[25] and £49. 18s. for 36 spruce deals (34 feet long) 'for the Hall floors and tables'. The water-carriage of this timber, wharfage, cartage and porterage cost £1. 15s.[26]

Not only the prices of materials, but craftsmen's and labourer's wages may be noticed in passing. Thomas Manley, writing in 1669, says that 'within these 25 years the wages of joiners, carpenters and bricklayers in London and within a 40 miles' radius have risen from 1s. 6d.–1s. 8d. a day in 1644 to 2s. 6d.–3s. a day in 1669, and this not since the dreadful fire of London only, but some time before'.[27]

Walter Bell found carpenters' wages a little higher: 2s. 6d.–3s. 6d. a day, according to the type of work; and unskilled labourers' wages 1s. 6d. for a ten-hour day. The Weavers were paying slightly more in 1669, 1s. 7d.–1s. 8d. a day (though on one occasion they paid only 1s. 9d. for one-and-a-half days). Journeymen masons received 2s. 6d. a day, earning 15s. a week when fully employed. But the building industry was notoriously seasonal. During the winter months earnings fell because of frosty weather and the shorter days, and there was much unemployment, which could assume serious proportions in a long, hard winter.[28]

Table 10.1 *Rebuilding the Weavers' Hall and two houses, 1667–9*

Summary of payments to master craftsmen and merchants								
Kind of work or materials	*The Hall, Court Room, etc.*			*The two houses*			*Total*		
	£	s.	d.	£	s.	d.	£	s.	d.
Bricklayer's	435	1	2	206	3	10	641	5	0
Carpenter's	825	0	0	361	1	11	1,186	1	11
Mason's	93	13	2	88	2	4	181	15	6
Plumber's	200	0	0	66	0	0	266	0	0
Plasterer's	90	0	0	59	2	0	149	2	0
Painter's	62	0	0	13	10	0	75	10	0
Glazier's	—			13	7	0	13	7	0
Smith's	50	0	0	21	2	6	71	2	6
Joiner's	170	0	0	—			170	0	0
Carver's	30	0	0	13	10	0	43	10	0
Lead	80	0	0	—			80	0	0
Timber	51	13	0	—			51	13	0
	2,087	7	4	841	19	7	2,929	6	11

The rebuilding of Weavers' Hall had cost, as we see, over £2,900 exclusive of much extra expenditure on new furnishings and equipment. This, in the 1660s, was a great deal of money, perhaps equal to about £100,000 at 1970 values. How did the Weavers raise such a large sum? Three ways were open and all were tried; (a) a thorough, strict marshalling of the Company's normal sources of income, such as quarterages, fees and fines; (b) an appeal for voluntary subscriptions; (c) borrowing.

In spite of the great ordeal by plague in 1665, the Company's financial position in 1667–8 was not at all bad. The credit balance on the Bailiffs' and Wardens' accounts in August 1667 was nearly £273. Shortly afterwards a Mr Portman, goldsmith, repaid to the Company a debt of £100 with interest; thirty-nine new Liverymen were admitted each paying a fee of £5; and the site of the burnt-out house in Bread Street was sold, as we have seen, for £140. Thus they had over £700 to begin with. Then, in October 1667, the Court resolved 'that our Master do meet once a week with some few of ye Compa. . . . to inquire of ye dwellings of persons in arrears for quarterage', the better to collect every available shilling 'for carrying on ye Rebuilding of ye Hall'. These regular weekly meetings for 'reading out ye Quarter Books' produced good results, for the Masters' quarterages collected in 1668–9 amounted to £140. 7s. against £129. 3s. for the previous year, and in 1669–70 a record total of £174. 3s. 4d. was brought in. Moreover, during the same three years (1667–70) the Company's revenues from presentments of apprentices, making free, and other fees and fines, rose from £335. 11s. to £495. 3s. 1d.;[29] an increase of nearly 48 per cent.

The first voluntary subscription towards the rebuilding fund was 5s. given spontaneously by one William Mitchiner early in August 1667.[30] Shortly afterwards the Company ordered a book or books of printed 'forms of promise of Subscriptions towards the cost of rebuilding the Company's Hall', each completed form being a solemn promise, over the subscriber's signature or mark, to pay a specified sum.[31] Some members paid their money forthwith, but others did not, or could not, and from the addresses roughly noted on the forms it seems certain that the officers had to 'chase' many of them. Indeed, the accounts show that on 22 August 1670, £15. 16s. 3d. was paid to the Clerk 'for collecting £126. 10. 0 subscribed towards building the hall at 2s. 6d. p. £'.[32] In a list, dated August 1668, of 'Voluntary Contributions towards rebuilding ye Hall', the largest sums are £25 given by Mr William Cade, one of the Company's staunchest and most generous 'ancients', £20 given by 'Mr. Benjamin Ducane, Master', and a similar sum from the philanthropic Mr Alexander Hosea. The Upper Warden gave £7 and the Renter Bailiff and Renter Warden each contributed £5. Other gifts ranged from £15 to 2s. 6d. including 5s. each from three weavers' widows. Altogether 113 names appear in this list and the total subscribed was £285. 12s. A year later (August 1669) a second list showed 167 names and a total of £108. 4s. 4d.

Meanwhile an approach to the French and Dutch Congregations brought in £49. 10s. during 1667–8. The gifts from the French Protestants, though small, are especially praiseworthy, for their church had been totally destroyed in the Great Fire and they were so impoverished that they could no longer afford to pay their aged pastor the small allowance on which he and his family had been subsisting.[33]

Collections continued during the year 1669–70, in which 209 subscriptions yielded a total, from all sources, of £165. 12s. 6d. By this time, however, the Hall was built and enthusiasm had cooled: in 1670–1 the number of subscriptions fell to 66 and only £82. 8s. 2d. was collected.[34] Clearly, the effort on this front had been justified, for about £700 of new money had been brought in, which meant that the amount of the Company's original funds had been nearly doubled.

But there was still a wide gap between the Company's normal income plus voluntary gifts and its total outlay, which had to be bridged by borrowing; and this was done, very wisely, by raising a number of relatively small loans ranging from £50 to £400 among its wealthier members and their friends. Between September 1667 and September 1669 the Clerk lent £400, some of it free of interest; Edmond Smith lent £100, Will. Raven £200, and Thomas Marriott £300, while Mr Cade's legacy brought in a timely £50. In November 1669 the Company 'received of John Wilcox in gold which was borrowed at 6 p.c. int. under the Common Seal of ye Company, £400'.[35] These loans were usually for short terms only and were repaid or renewed at the lender's option: at first glance a hand-to-mouth method, but certainly the best available to the Company at the time. Moreover, it was cheaper than borrowing in 'the market', which in those days usually meant the goldsmiths. Walter Bell says that interest rates were high in the reign of Charles II, '8 and 9 per cent being common'; and again, writing of the building of the City churches, 'money had to be borrowed at high rates of interest on the security of the Coal Dues'.[36] Yet the Weavers' Company was able to borrow privately on security less good than a statutory tax, at much lower rates—5, $5\frac{1}{2}$ or, at most, 6 per cent. The accounts show that the Company borrowed £1,850 in the two years 1670–1 and 1671–2;[37] much of this, however, was not new debt, but to repay short-term loans falling due.[38]

In 1668 the Company decided 'not this year to attend ye Lord Mayor by water by reason of their great charge in building'. It was also decided to let on lease the two houses in front of the Hall as soon as possible; but 'none of ye houses to be let to any that sell Drink'. A fine of £120 and a rent of £20 per annum for a term of twenty-one years was proposed, unless the prospective tenant was in victualling or certain 'other noisome trades' likely to be destructive to the buildings or inconvenient to users of the Hall, when a rental of £40 was to be demanded. Eventually the house north of the gateway was leased, in March 1669, to John White, Gentleman, for £20 per annum and a fine of £110.[39]

Meanwhile the buildings were rising steadily and the workmen had to be paid. In the autumn of 1668 the Clerk was told that he must 'vigorously betake himself to ye Collecting of ye Subscription Money', and in January 1669 £300 was borrowed at 6 per cent. Less than three months later, the 'Bricklayer's work of ye Common Hall' was 'admeasured in presence of ye [master] Bricklayer', who would naturally expect payment shortly afterwards. In the middle of May Mr Reynolds the joiner received £20 'on account for ye screen'; the carver and master mason also received payments on account. And so it continued: as the money came in it was immediately spent, and whenever the funds gave out, the Clerk or one or other of the Officers or Assistants came to the rescue with a loan.[40]

Midsummer 1669: St James's Day approaching, and with it the prospect of a jolly housewarming on the occasion of the Election Day feast. We can see the preparations going forward. On 12 July, the Officers went by water to buy two dressers; one for the great kitchen, at a cost of £7. 16s. 1d., and a much smaller one for the 'upper kitchen' (probably a sort of servery) for which they paid only 19s. 6d. Then a load of faggots and billets was delivered 'to neale the ovens'. A week later 'divers labourers' were paid £1. 16s. 10d. 'for removal of Stones and Cleansing the hall of Stuff and Rubbish agt. the Election day'. Brooms, baskets, mops, a pail and a bowl were bought, and the workmen were given 'tips' to ensure that all outstanding jobs were finished in time. Five shillings went to the carpenters 'for striking Scaffolds'; the plasterers and their labourers (eight in all) shared 13s. 6d. when the Hall ceiling was finished; the glaziers and masons received 4s. The courtyard was raised and levelled. All the new spruce-wood floors were cleaned, and 13s. 6d. was spent on fragrant 'nose-gaies and strewings';[41] the Court carpet was scoured, the pewter was cleaned with oil and whiting, tables and stools were borrowed, the table-linen laundered, glasses and candles bought. New gowns for the Officers and a new chest to keep them in had already been ordered. On the walls hung the portraits—astonishingly rescued from the Fire —of Queen Elizabeth and the early Stuarts. The eight pieces of tapestry recently bought from Mr Gerrard Vanheytheyson (merchant and member of the Dutch Congregation) for £102[42] also adorned the walls, and two men were paid 6s. for 'watching ye hangings in ye hall 3 nights'. Some of 'the Marshall's men' were hired to stand at the Hall gate; no 'spoiling the ship' on this very special occasion! We can be certain that ample supplies of beer, wine (they liked their claret) and victuals were laid in: the pasties alone cost £6. 18s. A typical menu would include pullets and bacon, venison, roast turkey, roast beef, pies, tarts, custard and fresh fruit. Although the total cost of the Election Day feast in 1669 cannot be given because separate figures are not available for that year, an estimate of £70 to £80 is probably not very wide of the mark. This, too, was an occasion calling for a display of the Company's plate, which, at this date, included four silver salts, six silver cups, a silver bowl and trencher plate, two 'great standing bowls', or loving cups, with covers, and a handsome silver tankard.[43] The Election Day service was held at St Giles's, Cripple-gate.[44]

So, after nearly three years of struggle and stress, the Weavers were again under their own roof. Never a wealthy Company, their rapid recovery was both remarkable and praiseworthy. Only five other London livery companies—the Butchers, Cutlers, Innholders, Pewterers and Painter-Stainers—completed the rebuilding of their halls before 1670. Five other halls were finished in 1670; four in 1671, and three in 1672. Walter Bell paid a well-deserved tribute to the livery companies' part in the City's recovery from the great disaster when he wrote:

> In private enterprise the Livery Companies led the way in the rebuilding of the City. This stands to their lasting credit. Never in all their long history has their public spirit been displayed so decisively as after the Fire of London. The disaster fell upon the Companies with crushing severity . . . yet . . . the first practical thought of the liverymen was the immediate restoration of their Halls . . . and the boldness of their example gave the utmost encouragement to the citizens, then sadly needing encouragement in their unparalleled distress.[45]

As for other public buildings, it was four years before the rebuilding of any of the City churches began, and eight years elapsed before the foundations of the new St Paul's were excavated. The Weavers' parish church of St Michael, Bassishaw, was rebuilt by Wren between 1672 and 1682, and the rebuilding of the Guildhall with its adjacent civic offices (all enlarged) went on until the close of 1675. On the other hand, Edward Jerman's Royal Exchange was finished and publicly opened in September 1669, and Blackwell Hall, the famous cloth market by the Guildhall, was rebuilt and open for trade by 1671.

It would be a mistake to suppose that all work in and about the Weavers' Hall ceased in 1670, for a number of extra amenities and improvements, including the Hall garden, were added during the following decade. Englishmen had long been interested in gardens, and more than one City company—the Grocers, Drapers, Pewterers and Leather Sellers, for example—could look with pride upon a pleasant, well-kept garden adjacent to its Common Hall; 'a refreshing sight in the heart of the City'. After the Fire, the Weavers leased from the Merchant Taylors for £8 a year some extra ground which they laid out as a garden to their new Hall. But first, in January 1671, the Company decided to enlarge its 'parlour and gallery adjoining'[46] by building out at first-floor level on pillars or columns over part of the garden ground, so that beneath the extension at ground level a paved walk or 'pallasadoe', sometimes referred to as the 'piazza', was created, to which there was access from the main gate and courtyard by way of stone steps 'put between the Bosses (underneath the Parlour and Gallery) and Pillars in the front yard, for more ornamentation thereof'.[47] According to the draft of an inscription which has survived,

This Court Parlour was wainscotted and painted
at the charge of the 16 Yeomanry men of this Company,
Mr. Robert Partridge being Foreman,
Ano. 1671[48]

The story, continued in the Renter Bailiff's account book, reads: 'Paid Thomas Prater back his subscription (£1) he having contributed with the Yeomanry towards beautifying the Parlor. . . . Paid back to Mr. Benson wch. he formerly paid as Subscription towards building the hall he now presenting a watch for ye Court: 10s.' and 'Paid for a case of Walnut tree for the watch presented by Mr. Benson £3. 10. 0.'[49] Between December 1671 and February 1672 the Company bought twelve 'rushy chairs', a 'Clerk's table' and 'a shovel, fork, tongs and chimney irons' for the Court parlour. The chairs cost 7s. 4d. each; the table, 12s. and the set of fire irons, 6s.[50]

Other parts of the building, too, were improved or embellished. In 1671 the Company paid £3. 10s. for 'a Copper fixed in the great Kitchen', and the walls of the hall, behind the tapestry hangings, were lined with deals or battens to preserve the tapestry from damage by damp.[51] In the same year a sum of £12. 10s. was paid to William Newman, a carver, for work done in the Parlour and the 'leopards' heads and other images upon the Hall Stairs'. These were, apparently, carvings of leopards' heads alternating with wivern on the newels of the balustrading posts. There must have been at least eight of these carvings, inspired, no doubt, by the Company's arms and supporters. Unfortunately, they were liable to get damaged—especially on Lord Mayor's Day, St James's Day and similar festive occasions; indeed, in 1672 the carver received 13s. for replacing one Libbitts Head (carried off, perhaps, as a trophy) 'and mending ye things on ye stairs'.[52]

All this extra work and furnishing brought on another shortage of funds, and although the Beadles sallied forth and collected £21. 18s. 4d. of new money for the building fund in the first half of 1672 (receiving a gratuity of £3 for their pains), the Court expressed its concern that 'the Company may not run further into debt'.[53]

In the spring of 1672 the Company began to cultivate its garden. Abraham Jourdan, gardener, a member of the Weavers' Company, was appointed 'to set and plant ye ground with flowers and herbs for which he is to be discharged his arrears of quarterage being 15s.' His regular pay was 10s. a quarter and free breakfasts. The garden certainly had gravel paths and probably a lawn, but we do not know what sort of plants Abraham Jourdan tried to grow in it in 1672-3. We *do* know, however, that £4 was paid in August 1672 for 'a Screen of Prospective painting now standing in the Garden'.[54] The account books show that the Company continued to cultivate and improve its garden for a great many years. In 1726, for example, the gardener, Skipworth, was paid £4. 2s. 9d. 'for Gravelling and fitting up the Garden'; and in 1740 the Company paid £1. 16s. 'for four loads of gravel and planting new fig trees in the room of those killed by frost'. The Clerk received an annual allowance of £3. 3s. 'for taking care of the Garden . . . planting new Trees, etc.', and the gardener's retaining fee was £2. 2s. a year.[55] By this time the rent of the garden had risen from £8 to £15 per annum.

When John Adlam, Clerk to the Weavers' Company, died in 1737, Henry Smart was appointed his successor. Although the new Clerk held office for only three years, he made a number of improvements in his apartments and in the Hall garden, which were listed and appraised after his death in March 1741 (see Table 10.2).

Table 10.2 *Improvements to the Clerk's apartments and the Hall garden, c. 1737–41*

Item	£	s.	d.
A Chimney piece with marble slabs, tiles and urn over the chimney in the Little Parlour	6	6	0
A Marble and Wooden Chimney Piece fixed, a Marble Slab fender, tiles and urn in the Study	8	0	0
Two Leaden Garden Pots	1	16	0
A Settee in the Garden		7	0
A Stone Pedestal with Hercules of Lead	9	9	0
Two Stone Figures, a small Hercules and a piece of Painting	5	5	0
A Stone Basin and Rock Work	2	10	0
Two Bells with five Pulleys	1	5	0
	34	18	0

This sum was paid over by the Company to Henry Smart's widow in March 1745.[56]

But meantime, in November 1743,

> Complaint being made of Damage being done last Lord Mayors day to the Statues in this Company's Garden, and other Disorders committed, and that the Sons of George Smith the Beadle were suspected of doing the same, Or that they could Discover [i.e. reveal] who did the same, *Ordered* that George Smith do give Notice to his Sons that they Appear at the next Court to answer the said Complaint.

What transpired we do not know, for the records tell us nothing except that in August 1744 the Company paid a guinea to have the statues mended.[57] Over forty years later, Hercules was still in the Weavers' Hall garden, with two companions or attendants, Venus and Faunus. But in June 1778, the Court of Assistants resolved unanimously,

> that the statue of Hercules in the garden and the two statues
> of Venus and Faunus ... which was removed previous to the
> late improvements at the Hall, be presented to John Baker,
> Esqr., a worthy member of this Court and the most ancient
> Member of this Company as a Testimony of the respectful sense
> this Court entertain of his Services and Attachment to the
> Rights and Interests of this Company and the Trade in General;
> and that the same (statues) be conveyed to Mr. Baker's house
> at this Company's expense.[58]

Trouble more persistent and potentially destructive than frost in the garden, or occasional damage to the statues, arose from water and rising damp in the Hall basement and ground floor. In May 1740 and again in February 1741 water from the well 'overflowed the Kitchen';[59] and during 1756–7 the Company put in hand 'lathing and plastering the kitchen under the Hall in such manner as shall be needful to prevent the Damage ... by the Damps rising from the Well made in the kitchen to carry off the waste water'. Two years later, Mrs Skinner, the tenant of the house on the south side of the Hall gate, then known as the Crown alehouse (but formerly known as the Surgeons' Arms and later as the Queen's Head tavern, 'complained of receiving great damage by some defect in the water course leading from the forecourt to the Hall gate, the water running into her cellar upon her butt heads and spoiling the beer'. Repairs were put in hand, on the advice of a surveyor, in 1760, and it is significant that in December of that year the Company paid 12s. 6d. for '5 sacks of charcoal used to dry the Hall, Court room, etc.'[60] In 1781 'repairs of the House late the Crown [alehouse]' cost the Company £125, and in 1785, in addition to interior whitewashing and repairs to the Hall roof and chimneys, the paved floors of the cellar and kitchen were raised fifteen inches and a drain was laid from the well in the cellar to the sewer in the street.[61] Rising repair bills were causing so much concern at that time that in 1787 the Court of Assistants called for an account of the sums spent upon the Hall during the last seven years. The building was, after all, about 120 years old, and it had been erected at a time of extraordinary pressure upon building labour and materials. In 1792, when the Company decided to have 'the brickwork round the Court Yard in front of the hall stuccoed', the plasterer thought that the new work 'would soon decay from the age of the walls', which, he recommended, should first be repaired and painted 'as the best method to preserve them'. The plasterer's, bricklayer's and painter's estimates for this work exceeded £64.[62]

Five years later, after St James's Day, 1797, the Livery expressed a wish for better accommodation at their public dinners, and raised the double question 'whether it is practicable or advisable to rebuild or enlarge the Hall; and . . . what funds can be appropriated for those purposes'? A surveyor estimated the cost of enlarging the Hall so as to provide additional room for fifty persons, with ancillary alterations and a general repair of the whole premises, at about £1,800; but he felt bound to add that he 'could not advise so large a sum to be laid out upon a building which is so ill-constructed and very old', especially as part of the new work would have to be done on the garden, which was leasehold ground. As to the proposal to build a new Hall, the surveyor reported that 'there is not space sufficient for it and other necessary appartments without taking down the two front houses'. This scheme might well cost some £4,800, in addition to the loss of the rents from the two houses. Faced with these figures, the special committee advised the Court that *all the property* of the Company is not only inadequate to such expenses . . . but that the annual income is little more than sufficient to defray the annual taxes and unavoidable necessary repairs of their Hall and premises'. The Officers and Assistants liked the idea of a new Hall, because it would enhance both 'the respectability and convenience' of the Company. But did the Livery think that £4,800 could be raised 'by subscription or otherwise'? If not, then (the Court asked) would it be 'proper, expedient, or agreeable, to have the entertainment on St. James's and Lord Mayor's Days provided at some tavern, where there are good rooms large enough for all the company who usually meet together on those days'? An alternative course was suggested early in the new year (1798) when a builder named Benson came forward with an offer 'for enlarging and altering the Hall at an expense not exceeding £35'. This amount seemed so reasonable, so much more in keeping with the Company's resources, that the offer was promptly accepted, the old seventeenth-century Hall was reprieved and remained in use for another half-century.[63]

NOTES

1 Pepys, *Diary*, 28 December 1666 and 2 January 1667; Evelyn, *Diary*, 6 March and 4 April 1667. Fire insurance seems to have been first proposed in Oldenburg *c.* 1609, but rejected for the curious reason that 'Providence might be tempted'. In London immediately after the Fire the main emphasis was upon fire-fighting. In 1667

the Common Council divided the City into four quarters, each to be equipped, parish by parish, with leather buckets, ladders, and brass hand-squirts. All the City Companies were required to provide buckets, 'engines', and other appliances 'proportionable to their abilities'. Nicholas Barbon is said to have been instrumental in opening the first fire-insurance office 'at the backside of the Royal Exchange' in May 1680. These early fire offices used the popular coffee houses to advertise their schemes. The first premiums quoted were 8 per cent for timber houses and 4 per cent for brick-built structures (B. Lillywhite, *London Coffee Houses* (1963), p. 21; J. Beckmann, *A History of Inventions, Discoveries and Origins* (4th edn, 1846), I, pp. 241–2); Thomas De Laune, *Angliæ Metropolis; or the Present State of London* (1690 edn), pp. 351–3.

2 MS. 4648/1. The Pope's Head, in Pope's Head Alley, Cornhill, kept by John Sawyer, a vintner, was burnt down in the Fire, and during its rebuilding, John Sawyer is known to have opened a temporary tavern in the parish of St Helen's, Bishopsgate, a neighbourhood which narrowly escaped the Fire (B. Lillywhite, op. cit., p. 724. cf. Pepys, *Diary*, 14 November 1666).

3 A. L. Rowse, *The England of Elizabeth*, p. 196, quoting J. E. Cox, *Annals of St Helen's, Bishopsgate*. cf. W. H. Black, *History and Antiquities of the Company of Leathersellers* (1871), pp. 49, 74.

4 MSS. 4646, ff.99–100; 4648/1 and 4655/4, f.10.

5 MSS. 4655/4 and 4648/1. George Heginbotham was an Auditor in 1653; elected an Assistant in 1663.

6 MS. 4655/4, ff.35, 57b, 58, 83. The sum of £4. 3s. 4d. was paid in October 1667.

7 MS. 4655/4, f.96b. Thomas Bostock claimed £347, after the Fire, in respect of four messuages in Candlewick St and Bush Lane; he was doubtless in urgent need of a site for other premises in 1667 (B.M. Add. MS. 5099, ff.35–55). After the fire 28 Livery Companies were involved in litigation before the 'Fire Judges', but the Weavers, fortunately, were not (B.M. Add. MS. 14,331; *Analysis of Decisions of the Commissioners for settling the City Estates*).

8 MS. 4646, Old Ledger Book, f.102. Lewis was elected an Assistant in March 1665.

9 MS. 4655/4, ff.116, 116b.

10 MSS. 4648/1 and 4650. Peter Mills and John Oliver, *The Survey of Building Sites in the City of London after the Great Fire of 1666* (1962), IV, f.42b.

11 MS. 4655/4, f.59b.

12 E. W. Brayley, *Londiniana* (1829), III, 82–7, gives a view of the South front of the new Royal Exchange. A. Pugin and J. Britton, *Illustrations of the Public Buildings of London* (1838), II, 42–5; opposite p. 42 is a drawing of the south elevation of the Royal Exchange by 'Edw. Jerman, Arch. 1667'. Jerman's date of birth is unknown; he died in October or November 1668, at the height of his powers and in the midst of a great mass of rebuilding work on the Royal Exchange and at least four (perhaps six) companies' halls. Jerman's Royal Exchange, which was burnt down on the night of 10 January 1838, had a wooden clock tower, an inner cloister, and a 'pawn' or upper floor for the sale of ribbons, gloves, etc. There was a statue of Charles II by Grinling Gibbons, and one of Sir Thomas Gresham by Edward Pierce (C. Welch, *Modern*

History of the City of London (1896), pp. 178–9. See also Robert
  Hooke, *Diary 1672–1680* (1935)).
13 Colvin (ed.), *Dictionary of Architecture.*
14 MS. 4655/4, ff.61–61b, 63b.
15 MS. 4655/4, f.66.
16 MS. 4655/3, ff.72b, 74b. Thomas Cartwright, one of the best and
  busiest mason contractors in London, was Edward Jerman's head
  mason and supervised the completion of the masonry of the Royal
  Exchange from the architect's drawings after Jerman's death.
  Immediately after the Great Fire, Cartwright worked on the Compter in the Poultry, Holborn Bridge, Bridewell, Moorgate, Ludgate
  and the Fleet Ditch, and between 1670 and 1691 he was employed
  on three of the City churches—St Mary-le-Bow, St Bennet Fink
  and St Antholin's. He was also chief mason at London Bridge in
  1672–3, but seems to have resigned because of pressure of other
  work. D. Knoop and G. P. Jones, *The London Mason in the Seventeenth Century* (1935), pp. 38, 38n., 41, 87. The other master craftsmen
  employed by the Weavers' Company (1667–9) were Thomas
  Seagood, bricklayer; Thomas Griffith, William Hollingshead, Henry
  Hodson, plasterers; Samuel Ems, plumber; John Oliver, glazier;
  Thomas Reeve, painter; Mr Reynolds, joiner; John Roberts,
  William Newman (after 1670), carvers; Solomon Hinchman, Walter
  Drew, smiths. Merchants: Richard Bailey, timber; John Moore,
  lead.
17 MS. 4655/4, f.80. This price was probably for bricks of good quality;
  lower qualities could be had at about 14*s.* per 1,000, according to
  Bell, *Great Fire*, p. 282.
18 MS. 4655/4, f.77b.
19 MS. 4655/4, ff.97b, 98. The dinner cost £2. 2*s.* 10*d.*
20 MS. 4655/4, f.99.
21 MS. 4655/15, f.304.
22 These cost £27 (MS. 4648/1, July 1672).
23 Later described in Maitland, *London*, II, p. 790, as 'a Screen of the
  Ionick Order'.
24 MS. 4655/5, ff.45b, 55b.
25 A fother of lead is 19½ cwt. Stow speaks of 'fodders' of lead.
26 MS. 4648/1, November 1668 and August 1669; and MS. 4650.
27 *Usury at Six Per Cent. Examined* (1669), quoted by Webb, *History
  of Trade Unionism*, p. 20n.
28 Knoop and Jones, op. cit., p. 63. For a study of real and money
  wages in the building industry see E. H. Phelps Brown and S. H.
  Hopkins, 'Seven Centuries of Building Wages', in *Economica*, N.S.
  XXII and XXIII (1955–6).
29 MS. 4655/4, f.82; MS. 4646, Old Ledger Book, ff.101–2; and MS.
  4648/1.
30 MS. 4655/4, f.70, and MS. 4648/1.
31 Weavers' signatures and marks occur in various places in the
  records, reminding us of Shakespeare's joke '. . . dost thou use to
  write the name, or hast thou a mark to thyself like an honest plain-
  dealing man?' The Weavers' Subscription Book (1669–75) gives 50
  marks and 118 signatures—some well-written but many labori-
  ously penned, suggesting that the signatory could just about write
  his name and no more. The percentage of signatures is 70·2. Professor Campbell found that the signatures on over 2,500 wills,

leases, and bonds indicated that between 60 and 70 per cent of English Yeomen could write their names in the early seventeenth century; but it is impossible to say what proportion could do more than this (Campbell, *English Yeoman*, pp. 263, 274). For the middle of the nineteenth century, Mayhew's *London and the London Poor* gives the numbers of signatures or marks in marriage registers.

32 MS. 4648/1.
33 MS. 4655/4, ff.106b, 107. Bell, *Great Fire*, p. 309, quoting Cal. S.P. Dom. 1666–7, pp. 385, 461.
34 MS. 4646, Old Ledger Book, ff.103–4.
35 MS. 4646, ff.102–3; MS. 4648/1, 1 November 1669.
36 Bell, *Great Fire*, pp. 283, 311.
37 MS. 4646, ff.104–6.
38 See, e.g., MS. 4655/5, f.72 and MS. 4655/6, ff.1b, 5b. The Pewterers paid 6 per cent until 1676–7, and thereafter, 5 per cent. See Welch, *History of the Pewterers' Company*, II, p. 153.
39 MS. 4655/4, ff.43b, 45b–46, 92b, 119b.
40 MS. 4655/5, ff.5b, 31b, 41, 42b, 55b, 58, 64b, 65, 71.
41 In 1678 the 'strewings, etc.' were provided by the Company's almspeople, who received 2s.
42 MSS. 4655/3, f.63b, and 4650, 29 July 1669.
43 MSS. 4646, ff.89b, 94–6; 4655/3, f.31b. See also Appendix 1.
44 MS. 4648/1. The preacher received a fee of £1 for his sermon; the clerk and the sexton had 6s. each and the bell-ringers shared 5s. between them.
45 Bell, *Great Fire*, pp. 272–3.
46 Probably a music gallery.
47 Thomas Cartwright, the master mason, did this work for £50. MS. 4655A/3.
48 MS. 4655A/3; MS. 4655/6, ff.41b, 57b, 65b, 74, 78b; MS. 4655/9, ff.24, 26; MS. 4655/12, f.116; MS. 4649A, ff.1b, 18b.
49 MS. 4648/1, 14 November 1671; MS. 4649A, f.8.
50 MS. 4648/1.
51 MS. 4655/6, f.42; MS. 4655A/3, 18 September 1671.
52 MS. 4649A, September 1671 and February 1672. cf. J. G. Milne (ed.), *Catalogue of Oxfordshire 17th-Century Tokens* (1938), p. 19.
53 MS. 4655/7, ff.17b, 18, 37, 56b.
54 MS. 4655A/3; MS. 4649A, ff.14, 14b, 16; MS. 4648/2.
55 MS. 4648/4, f.88; MS. 4648/5, ff.3–4.
56 MS. 4655/15, ff.13–14, 96, 97b, 220b. Henry Smart's successor as Clerk was Ebenezer Briggs.
57 MS. 4655/15, f.183; MS. 4648/6, 20 August 1744.
58 MS. 4655/17, f.298b; John Baker's letter of thanks is entered at f.307, and a minute (f.441b) records his death in 1783. During spring and summer 1778, John Bassington, the gardener, planted in the Hall garden 3 spruce firs, '16 dozen of daisies, 4½ dozen of flower roots, one mint, one sage, 2 coxcombs, 2 Frickloes, 2 globe ameranthus', and 1s. 6d. worth of grass seed.
59 MS. 4648/5, ff.21, 27.
60 MS. 4655/16, f.226b; MS. 4655/17, f.83; MS. 4648/7, 1 December 1760. The Clerk's Report on the Charities, 1742, f.9. During 1761–2, 43 new Liverymen were 'called', so that their fines would help to provide money to pay the workmen's bills (MS. 4655/16, ff.280b, 295b).

61 MS. 4648/10, 6 July 1781; MS. 4655/17, ff.505–6. The Hall and two
    adjoining houses were insured in 1778 for £2,400.
62 MS. 4655/18, ff.223–4b.
63 MS. 4655/18, ff.339b–340b, 342b. In 1781 the Weavers had renewed
    their lease of the garden ground from the Merchant Taylors for
    fifty years at an increased rent of £20 per annum (MS. 4655/17,
    f.289b). In May 1793 Mr Benson was paid nearly £60 for extensive
    repairs to the Hall.

Chapter 11

Pageantry and Good Cheer

The visible symbols of the many strong links between a city and its gilds lay largely in the ceremonial and pageantry of important public occasions, when lavish processions and 'tryumphs' created impressive spectacles. The organisation of civic processions or 'ridings' as they were commonly called,[1] necessarily raised the question of the order of precedence. In London, down to the end of the fifteenth century, the final decision in cases of doubt or dispute was made by the Lord Mayor. But as the livery companies grew more influential and proud of their standing and functions in the City and, indeed, in the State itself in certain respects, so they waxed more jealous of each other and more pernickety about their privileges. Consequently, inter-company disputes about precedence became not only more frequent, but more intricate and difficult to settle.[2] By the beginning of the sixteenth century the problem had become so tiresome that there emerged a general wish to reach, once and for all, a lasting settlement. Thus, in 1515–16 a specially convened Court of Aldermen worked out an order of precedence using as their principal guide the order followed in the mayoralty of Sir Edmund Shaa in 1482–3; and the order of precedence promulgated in 1516 is the one used today as regards the Companies incorporated before that date.[3] This is:

1 Mercers	11 Vintners	21 Tallow Chandlers
2 Grocers	12 Clothworkers	22 Armourers
3 Drapers	13 Dyers	23 Girdlers
4 Fishmongers	14 Brewers	24 Butchers
5 Goldsmiths	15 Leather Sellers	25 Saddlers
6 Merchant Taylors	16 Pewterers	26 Carpenters
7 Skinners	17 Barbers	27 Cordwainers
8 Haberdashers	18 Cutlers	28 Painter-Stainers
9 Salters	19 Bakers	29 Curriers
10 Ironmongers	20 Wax Chandlers	30 Masons

31 Plumbers	37 Tilers and	43 Woolmen
32 Innholders	Bricklayers	44 Scriveners
33 Founders	38 Bowyers	45 Fruiterers
34 Poulterers	39 Fletchers	46 Plasterers
35 Cooks	40 Blacksmiths	47 Stationers
36 Coopers	41 Joiners	48 Broderers
	42 Weavers	

The principle or principles, if any, on which the order was worked out has never been stated and is still something of a mystery. Certainly the antiquity of a company did not come into it, otherwise the Weavers would rank first and not forty-second. Nor does membership seem to count: a 'great' company did not necessarily mean one having a great number of freemen. We are left, then, with wealth or 'estate', and here light begins to break through. Although no attempt seems to have been made in 1516, or earlier, actually to value the estates owned by the various companies and the charitable trusts administered by them, yet each of the first twelve companies in the order of precedence did own 'great' or 'very considerable' estates and their annual payments to charitable uses were substantial, especially when we reflect upon the high commodity value of the unit of money in the Middle Ages.

There is little room for doubt that *indirectly* a Company's wealth tended strongly to carry it upwards towards the 'top twelve'. The Lord Mayor and Aldermen needed, from time to time, to be able to call upon a number of the companies to provide a goodly concourse of horsemen, impressively clothed and caparisoned, to support them and to enhance the dignity of the City on ceremonial occasions, such as royal marriages, coronations, the return of the monarch from a victorious war, the arrival of a new ambassador, and so forth. For example, in the first year of Richard III's reign the Common Council directed a certain number of men from each livery company (406 in all) to ride 'in murrey-coloured[4] coats . . . to meet the king on his entering the City'. The thirteen companies named at the head of this list are: Mercers, Drapers, Grocers, Fishmongers, Merchant Taylors (30 men each), followed by the Haberdashers (28 men), Goldsmiths and Skinners (24 men each), Ironmongers, Salters and Dyers (10 each), Vintners (8), Scriveners (4). A very similar (though not exactly the same) order was arranged when Richard's conqueror, Henry VII, entered the City in 1487; and again, in 1509, when Henry VIII and Queen Catherine were crowned, the 'order of crafts how they shall stand' was much the same.[5]

When war or invasion threatened, the companies were expected to supply and equip contingents of able-bodied men; and, broadly speaking, the wealthier the company, the larger its armoury and the size of its contingent. When the Spanish Armada menaced this island in 1588 the livery companies made their contributions to the force of 10,000 men required from the City. The Grocers sent 500 men and 'the other Companies according to their rank'. From Bassishaw, a small ward, a quota of 177 men was required and presumably the Weavers' contingent was included in this number. In other emergencies or crises, too, when the King asked the City for loans, the City, in turn, asked the livery companies to help according to their resources.

Moreover, not only military but economic threats had to be met and warded off. Every company was responsible for the purchase and storage of a stock of corn (and, later, of sea-coals also) which could be sold at reasonable prices to the poorer citizens in time of dearth. Clearly, only the wealthy companies could finance such transactions on any adequate scale. A few examples of corn quotas and the monetary assessments based upon them in 1603–4 are set out in Table 11.1.[6]

Table 11.1 *Corn quotas and monetary assessments*

	Quarters of corn	Assessment to raise an aggregate of £400		
		£	s.	d.
Great companies				
Merchant Taylors	936	37	8	9
Grocers	874	34	19	2
Mercers	820	32	16	0
Vintners	520	20	16	0
Minor companies				
Weavers	25	1	0	0
Masons	25	1	0	0
Woodmongers	20		16	0
Turners	17		15	7
Glaziers	8		5	4

It is significant that the list agreed in 1516 is headed by twelve companies of whom ten are companies of merchants. Only two—the Goldsmiths and the Clothworkers—have a craft basis, and even they were mixing merchant functions with craftsmanship by the beginning of the sixteenth century. Some of the Goldsmiths, indeed, were about to develop into financiers as well. This preponderance of wealthy companies of merchants is not surprising, for it was much easier to make and accumulate money by trading than by plying a handicraft such as weaving or carpentry. In the eyes and estimation of successive generations of the City Fathers those companies stood highest who were willing *and able* to give the greatest amount of aid and support, especially on important ceremonial occasions or in times of crisis.

Not only did the livery companies make their contributions to civic processions, but on all solemn occasions, such as funerals, marriages, coronations, royal visits and the like, the Liverymen in their uniforms took up their appointed places in the streets. Great companies, such as the Mercers, Grocers and Drapers, occupied about five times as much length of 'standing' as the lesser companies, like the Poulterers and Weavers. Platforms or scaffolds two feet high with rails in front of them were erected to give the onlookers a better view as well as protection from the horses.[7] The celebration of Marlborough's victory at Blenheim was such an occasion. On 4 September 1704, at a Full Court, the Weavers' Company

> Ordered that the Carpenter provide stands for the Company to stand at the reception of her Majesty on the thanksgiving day for the late most glorious victory obtained by the Arms of her Majesty and her Allies upon the Rhine under the command of his Grace the Duke of Marlborough over the united forces of France and Bavaria at Blenheim. And that a Dinner, music and other necessaries be provided for that solemnity.[8]

When George I, at his accession, planned a state entry to London on 20 January 1715, the Weavers began to make preparations in the previous September. Four members undertook to act as Stewards and to 'make as good an Entertainment for the Company as of Lord Mayor's Day and defray all the charges, except the carpenter's bill for erecting the stands'. The committee decided that 100 feet of stands should be constructed and covered with 'blew bays'. Next they engaged five trumpeters, four swordsmen and seven banner-carriers, all of whom were to have new clothes. Ten gallons of white and red wine and a supply of bread were provided at the stand; but 'no liveryman to bring a son or other person but shall be dismissed', and there was to be 'no dinner at the charge of the Company'.[9]

Apart from such occasional special 'solemnities' there were two outstanding days in the Weavers' year. The first was Lord Mayor's Day when the Company took part with the other livery companies in the Lord Mayor's procession and rounded off the day with a dinner for the Livery at Weavers' Hall; and the second was the Company's Election Day (St James's Day, 25 July), when the election of officers for the ensuing year in a Common Hall was followed by a dinner. In order to carry through such important functions in a style befitting the dignity and prestige of a City Company it was necessary to have a hall, a ceremonial barge, and all the ancillary trappings and 'furnishings', such as gowns and liveries, plate, pewter, napery, banners, streamers and ribbons. There must be a church service with a sermon on St James's Day, and to enliven the evening's entertainment a 'consort' of musicians, who were usually 'not so much praised for their long, as their well Playing'.[10]

The Lord Mayor's procession, which has arisen from the custom of swearing-in the new Lord Mayor at Westminster Hall, seems to date from the early part of the thirteenth century. But not until the fifteenth century did some of the chief citizens go from the City to Westminster on the River Thames, which was for centuries 'High Street, London', the City's principal thoroughfare. One authority[11] says that when William Warderne was chosen Lord Mayor in 1422 the Brewers' Company 'ordered that the Aldermen and Craft should go to Westminster with him, to take his charge in barges without minstrels'. But according to Humpherus, historian of the Watermen's Company, the first Lord Mayor to go by water was Sir John Norman (Draper) 'who having at his own expense built a noble barge, had it decorated with flags and streamers, in which he was this year [1453] rowed by watermen with silver oars, attended by such of the city companies as possessed barges, in a manner so splendid that "his barge seemed to burn on the water" '.[12]

At first this river pageant was not an annual event, but in course of time it became so, except in periods of great calamity such as the Civil War and its aftermath, or the Plague of 1665 and the Fire of 1666.[13] John Evelyn tells us that the Lord Mayor's Show in 1661, provided by the Grocers' Company and held on the river, was 'the first solemnity of this nature after twenty years'.[14] In the following year, on 23 August 1662, both he and Pepys saw the magnificent river procession when a great fleet of barges, including, of course, those of the London companies, rowed upstream with the morning tide to Chelsea to meet and welcome to London, Catherine of Braganza,[15] Charles II's Queen, as the royal couple came down-river from Hampton Court after their honeymoon. Pepys, with a friend, had walked that morning all along Thames Street, but could not get a boat. 'I offered', he says, 'eight shillings for a boat to attend me this afternoon, and they would not, it being the day of the Queen's coming to town from Hampton Court.' But he was not the man to miss such a splendid spectacle, so he walked to White Hall,

and up to the top of the new Banqueting House there, over the Thames, which was a most pleasant place . . . and all the show consisted chiefly in the number of boats and barges; and two pageants, one of a King, and another of a Queen, with her Maydes of Honour sitting at her feet very prettily; . . .
Anon come the King and Queen in a barge under a canopy

with 1,000 barges, I know, for we could see no water for them,
nor discern the King nor Queen. And so they landed at White
Hall Bridge [i.e. jetty], and the great guns on the other side
went off.

Evelyn had a very different viewpoint, for he was afloat in a

new-built vessell, sailing amongst them . . . the most magnificent
triumph that ever floated on the Thames . . . innumerable
boates and vessells, dress'd and adorn'd with all imaginable
pomp, but above all the thrones, arches, pageants and other
representations, stately barges of the Lord Maior and
Companies, with . . . musiq and peales of ordnance both from
the vessels and the shore. . . . His Majestie and the Queene
came in an antiqu-shap'd open vessell, covered with a state or
canopy of cloth of gold, made in form of a cupola, supported
with high Corinthian pillars, wreath'd with flowers, festoons,
and garlands.

Evelyn thought that 'it far exceeded the Venetian Bucentoras, etc.
on the Ascension, when they go to espouse the Adriatic'.[16] Two years
later he saw a 'most magnificent triumph by water and land of the
Lord Mayor' (Sir John Lawrence), and afterwards dined at the Guildhall.[17] Thousands of humbler Londoners gathered 'Along the shore
of silver-streaming Thames' took delight in these displays, with their
gleaming squadrons of bedizened barges gliding majestically in gilded
procession, their oars flashing, their gay banners and streamers
'gloriously displayed' as the breeze wafted the sound of music across
the water.[18] Strictly speaking, a 'pageant' was either a portable
image, such as a giant, mounted on a barge or a trolley, or a stationary
tableau vivant, such as a group of maidens posing as mermaids. Two
notable early-seventeenth-century aquatic processions were 'London's Love to the Royal Prince Henry', on 31 May 1610; and 'An
Entertainment by Water at Chelsey & Whitehall' when Prince
Charles was created Prince of Wales in 1616.[19] Another grand river
procession enriched the wedding festivities of Princess Elizabeth,
daughter of James I, and Prince Frederick, the Elector Palatine.[20]
In the sixteenth and earlier centuries the City companies used to
hire barges when they were needed, but in the seventeenth century
a few of the wealthier companies deemed it more dignified to appear
in 'faire Barges' of their own, which were the Rolls-Royces of their
time, symbols of status and prestige. The Goldsmiths' first ceremonial
barge was specially built in 1616, and forty years later they built a
new one at a cost of £100.[21] In 1640 the Merchant Taylors built their
first barge at a total cost of £120.[22] The much less wealthy Weavers'
Company always hired a barge at that period. For example, on

13 October 1612, John Johnson, waterman, who had been appointed bargeman to the Company in 1611 *vice* John Sprincklett, bargeman, 'lately deceased', was 'hired to provide a barge for the Company on the Lord Mayor's feast day next for the sum of 40*s*. whereof he hath received in part 10*s*. and the Court have given him 12*d*. more in earnest'. In addition, four whifflers were chosen, and two men to serve 'as drum and fife' were paid 5*s*. each for the day.[23] In October 1618 two watermen were engaged 'to serve the Company for fifty shillings with a convenient barge for the Livery on the Lord Mayor's Day next ensuing',[24] and in the following year Richard Jones, a freeman of the Weavers' Company but evidently working as a waterman, was appointed 'to provide a sufficient barge for the Livery of this Company on the [next] Lord Mayor's Feast Day . . . according to the custom hitherto used and so from year to year henceforth so long as the Company shall be well served by him and his assigns and not otherwise'.[25]

On the morning of the Lord Mayor's Day the Weavers' Company assembled in their hall, whence they went in procession to embark in their barge, proceeding as follows:

First Division (*leading*)
    The Pensioners with half the drums and fifes

Second Division
    The Yeomanry
    The Ensign
    Seven Trumpeters, wearing gay cloaks, 'to sound through the streets'[26]
    Drums and fifes

Third Division
    The Company's standard and banners carried by men wearing scarves or sashes of taffeta in the Company's colours of blue and yellow
    The Liverymen in their liveries

Fourth Division
    The Gentlemen Ushers carrying white staves
    The Beadle, with the Leading Staff or Mace ⎫
    The Under-Beadle ⎪
    The Clerk ⎬ wearing their
    The Upper Bailiff ⎪ gowns
    The Renter Bailiff ⎪
    The two Wardens ⎪
    The Assistants ⎭

At the river stairs the Officers, Assistants and Livery embarked. 'And [John Tatham tells us] the Lord Mayor, Aldermen and their

Attendants take to their Barges, and the several Companies . . . to the like, adorned with streamers and Banners', the chief ones being the Royal Standard, the Union Jack, and the banner of the City of London. At the stern were the Company's arms carved, painted and gilded, with the Company's banner flying above. It was customary to have at the prow a carved group of mythical figures, such as Neptune with tritons and sea-horses, or other gods and goddesses.[27] The Weavers may have had a leopard with a shuttle in his mouth. The rudder, too, was usually gaily decorated with conventional designs, paintings of dolphins, and so forth. To the music of 'Hoe-boys, Cornets, Drumms and Trumpets'[28] the gay argosy rowed up-stream towards Westminster, saluted on the way by 'several peals of Ordnance, in token of Love. Being landed there, they make a lane or guard from the bridge [i.e. landing stage or jetty] to Westminster Hall.' And again, on the return voyage,

> they are entertained by several pieces of Ordnance as
> acclamations of joy: the Body (or Lord Mayor's party) making
> . . . for Baynard Castle, but the several Companies to Pauls
> Wharf and other places in order to making a guard or lane
> from Pauls Wharf all along Thames street and up Dowgate hill
> and so through Walbrook unto the Stocks, where the Scenes or
> representative Tryumphs appear, along Cheapside into Pauls
> Churchyard round by Pauls Chain . . .

so the Lord Mayor and his whole procession, riding 'in great pomp', came at last to the Guildhall, where a splendid dinner awaited them.[29]

The land part of the procession also was colourful, splendid and sometimes unusually exciting. From year to year the companies vied with each other in the invention of magnificent and novel devices. The Grocers on one occasion spent nearly £900—a great sum in the seventeenth century; and at another time the Fishmongers con-structed:

> a large stack of fabric, at the one end whereof a ship, floating,
> rigg'd and man'd; at the other end a rock with various figures;
> one representing Oceanus, who is said to be God of Seas and
> the Father of Rivers. . . . To show his majesty, he walks or
> treads upon his watery regiment, several fishes are discovered
> to play at his feet, and Trytons sporting themselves; four
> virgins cloathed in white loose garments, and their brows
> circled with sage, representing the nymphs that frequent rivers.

The Skinners, in 1671, 'added to their traditional wilderness a wild beast, a group of satyrs dancing to the music of Orpheus, and a bear performing on a rope; whilst in 1689 they introduced a number of live dogs, cats, foxes and rabbits, which being tossed hither and thither amongst the crowd afforded great diversion':[30] except, perhaps, to those onlookers who were bitten or clawed by the terrified, infuriated animals.

Nobody familiar with seventeenth-century social habits will be surprised to learn that the feasting began on the river voyage. The walk down to the river created a thirst and the river air made the voyagers hungry. On the Weavers' barge it was customary to provide canary wine and cakes at the expense of the Stewards acting for that day. In the 1670s, however, a group of members pointed out that the increase in the number of Liverymen 'for some years past' had made more onerous the financial burden on the two Stewards 'making the feast on the Lord Mayor's day'. Consequently the Stewards:

> have omitted to send any greater quantity of Canary and Cakes to ye Livery going in ye Barge than the usual allowance of Six Gallons of Canary and twenty dozen of Cakes, which hath been so small and hath given great discontent to the Liverymen. And this Court taking into consideration as well the said great number of Liverymen as the . . . dearness of provisions at that time of year when all the Companies of London do feast, and being unwilling to oppress any of their Members with too great charge, but rather to do some act as may lessen the charge and encourage the Stewards cheerfully to undertake and perform that office . . . it was unanimously agreed by the Court that instead of two there shall be three Stewards . . . for the future, upon these terms and conditions, that the Stewards do pay ye Trumpets and other Musick used on that day not exceeding the charge of £4, and do send to the Livery in the Barge Ten Gallons of good Canary and forty dozen of Cakes, all which . . . is computed to ye charge of six pounds, or thereabouts, and [the Stewards] do also perform ye customary part of ye Stewards in returning ye Linen, Pewter and Hall clean in like manner as the same shall be made ready for the service of that day.[31]

These victuals were as nought compared with the feast after the Show, when the generous menu included venison, sirloins of beef, roast turkeys and ducks, boiled fowls, geese pasties, mutton pasties, veal fillets, pork and bacon, rabbits, calves' heads, tongues and udders. The choice of fish was limited usually to oysters and cod; but vegetables were served in great variety, from asparagus and 'spinnage' to 'colly flowers' and sprouts, with cabbage, carrots, turnips, beans, peas and onions also in the list of 'possibles'. We also encounter such items as suet, raisin and currant pudding, large apple pies costing four shillings each, and marrow puddings at five shillings each. The Weavers' accounts show that their feast on Lord Mayor's Day, 1675,

including many incidental items, cost £44. 16s. 6d., and in the following
year, £45. 10s. In 1677, however, the amount 'paid and laid out for
the service of the Company on the Lord Mayor's Day' was £74. 16s. 7d.;
a sum which includes items connected with the barge and the procession as well as the feast. A typical folio from the Renter Bailiff's
account book is set out in Table 11.2. The total expenses for Lord
Mayor's Day 1689 were very similar, namely £77. 8s. 6d.

Table 11.2 *Typical expenses for Lord Mayor's Day*

31st October 1687. Paid on the day following the Lord Mayor's Day	£	s.	d.
pd. 5 Porters		12	6
pd. 6 Fencers and for their Dinners	1	1	0
Given the Watermen that carried the Colours		3	0
pd. for Cords, packthread and match		1	8
pd. for 2 dozen of wooden dishes		5	0
Given the Almspeople		6	0
pd. the Trumpeters	3	15	0
pd. 2 Drummers and one fife		15	0
pd. for fruit		8	4
pd. Mr. Rhodes's bill [the Barge Master]	9	4	0
pd. for Oysters	2	1	0
pd. Mrs. Burroughs's bill for washing linen [scouring] pewter &c.	2	5	0
pd. the Poulterer's bill	6	8	0
pd. Mr. Pierson for beer and ale	1	18	0
pd. Mr. Hollis for wine	10	16	0
pd. Mr. Rymill the cook	13	0	0
pd. Mr. Sumers the butcher	7	0	0
pd. Mr. Snow the butler	1	15	0
pd. the Beadles for summoning the Livery, and attendance		10	0
Given the Clerk as customary	1	1	6
pd. Mr. Soames for Ribbons on the Lord Mayor's day	9	1	6
pd. Mrs. Jones for looking after the Buttery		2	6
pd. for Cakes	1	0	0
pd. the Shipwright's bill	4	10	0
pd. the Oarmaker's bill	1	9	0
pd. for Gent. Usher's staves		2	8
	79	11	8

These outlays show a slight upward trend between 1677 and 1697:
the average annual expenditure during the decade 1677–86 was
approximately £72, while in the following decade it was nearly £86.
In 1694, when there was anxiety about the Company's solvency, it
was said that the two yearly feasts had recently 'run the Company

mightily behind hand and in debt'.[32] Therefore, by the turn of the century the Company had adopted a more economical policy, reducing its Lord Mayor's Day expenditure to £60 or £65; a policy adhered to, by and large, for many years. Indeed, in October 1738, the Court of Assistants,

> taking notice of the approaching solemnity of the Lord Mayor's day and seriously considering the low circumstances of this Company and the heavy Debt with which it is at present Incumbred and being sensible that it will not be in the power of this Company to attend with that decent appearance which their inclination as well as duty requires, without plunging this Company into further and almost inextricable difficulties, *Resolved:* That this Company cannot appear in Publick to pay their duty to the New Lord Mayor on Lord Mayor's day next.

In 1743 a dinner was provided, but the cost was kept down to £50.

No small part of the Company's financial difficulties in this period can be traced to its barge, which, with all its grace and grandeur when afloat on festive occasions, was an expensive luxury. It was built for the Company in 1673 by John Graves, shipwright, for £115, including eighteen oars but not the painting and gilding. The dimensions were; length 72 feet; breadth 11 feet; the 'house' to be 34 feet long. Mr Reeve, a painter-stainer, undertook to 'paint the Barge according to models now presented as to figures' and to gild the mouldings of capitals, washboards, carved work, arms and supporters,[33] leopards' heads, 'and other fit and convenient parts'. He agreed also to plain-grain the interior and paint all benches, forms and oars 'in a blue colour'. The banner and pendant staves too were to be painted, but the colour is not specified. All this work to be done 'within the rate of £55'.[34] The silk banners, streamers and pendants, painted by one Edmond Pickering, cost £75, including the silk. The shipwright received £5 more than the sum first agreed upon. The inventory of 1677 and the total cost are shown in Table 11.3.

When the barge was finished in October 1673, a barge master, a steersman and a crew of eighteen oarsmen had to be engaged and properly clothed. Recruitment was easy, for the 'office of Barge Master and the position of watermen regularly employed by the Lord Mayor of London and the Livery Companies were eagerly sought after by the watermen of the River Thames for the reason that they were generally exempted by the Admiralty from impressment to serve in the Navy. The appointments were formally registered by the Watermen's Company.'[35] As to clothing, two long coats in blue satin (for the barge master and steersman), twenty caps and eighteen white linen waistcoats, embellished with the Weavers' arms on tin badges were bought for £11.[36]

Table 11.3 *The Company's barge*

		£
Inventory	One long and large Streamer	
	One King's Arms	
	One City Banner	
	One Ensign of the Company	
	One Company's Banner	
	Two large Pendants	
	Thirty small Pendants, &c.*	
	[Seven green cushions were added later.]	
Cost	Building the Barge	120
	[The cost of the carving is not separately stated]	
	Painting, staining and gilding	55
	Banners, streamers and pendants	75
	Total	250

* MS. 4649A, ff.17b–20; MS. 4646, f.203.

A special fund was opened to raise the money to pay for all this, and in less than nine months a total of £207. 10s. was collected from eighty-five voluntary subscribers, mainly members of the Court and Livery. To this must be added 'Justice Ricrofts money upon the Masters forgetfulness, £2'.[37] This left a deficiency of over £50 on the barge account, to say nothing of the expenses of storing and maintaining the new vessel in the future. A bargehouse was essential, for without it the barge would deteriorate rapidly and the cost of repairs and repainting would become very high. Eventually, the Weavers agreed to pay £9 to the Tallow Chandlers' Company for building a bargehouse at Chelsea, and a yearly rental of £1. 10s.[38] The barge master received £2 a year, and the watermen shared £5 between them. In addition the barge master and steersman each received new coats every year to the value of £1. By the eighteenth century these costs had risen and, instead of a cap, the barge master wore a hat trimmed with gold lace. Table 11.4 shows items in the accounts for 1725.[39]

Table 11.4 *Barge uniform expenses in 1725*

Items	£	s.	d.
Lace for a Waterman's hat		5	6
4½ yards blue cloth @ 8/–	1	16	0
7 yards yellow Shalloon @ 1/6		10	6
3 yards white fustian		11	0
	3	3	0

There were, moreover, a number of incidental expenses, such as 'dressing' the barge, £5; breakfast for the watermen, 12s.; 'paid the Shipwright for trimming the Barge, £3. 14. 0'; launching the barge, £1. 2s. 6d.; 'given Mrs. Powneys men upon taking water, 2s. 6d.'[40] A typical list of expenses incurred 'by the Company's going out in thier Barge' to attend the new Lord Mayor is given in Table 11.5.

Table 11.5 *Expenses in using the Company barge*

October 1728	£	s.	d.
for 4 yds. of Cloth and 5 yds. of Shalloon as per bill for			
Barge Master	1	19	6
Gold lace for his hat		7	6
For Gentlemen Ushers		5	0
Ribbons to Mr. Daintry (for cockades for the Livery)	12	2	0
A Bottle of Wine on making 'em up		2	0
Cakes for the Barge	1	8	0
Cups for the Barge and Staves for Gentlemen Ushers	1	2	0
Ale for the Barge		18	0
For Gilding the Barge Master's Badge & Buttons		13	6
Wine for the Barge	4	10	0
Musick for do.	3	10	0
The Barge Master's Bill	11	7	6
Repairing the Barge for one year to Bernard (the shipwright)	6	0	0
Rent for the Bargehouse*	6	0	0
	50	5	0

* At Chelsea; rented at this date from the Apothecaries' Company.

An additional payment of £18. 17s. 6d. 'for Wine in the Barge, Lord M. Day' brought the total to £69. 2s. 6d.[41]

The loan of the Company's barge to others was seldom permitted. In October 1710, however, the barge was allowed to go to Brentford 'to carry friends to vote for Esquire Barker and Mr. Austin [parliamentary candidates], they being at the charge thereof and making good any damage she may sustain thereby, and any Member of the Company may go therein being of the Livery and a Freeholder'. On a different occasion, the Upper Bailiff, Mr Edmunds, 'in consideration of the great services' rendered by him 'during the service of his several offices', was given leave to use the barge, with certain members of the Court and Livery, 'for the accommodation of themselves and wives', and the Company paid £5 to the watermen for the day; but added that this was 'not at any time hereafter to be drawn into precedent or example'.[42] In 1716 the barge was lent to a group of dyers for a summer's day on condition that they employed the Weavers' barge master and promised to make good any damage to the barge or tackle; but in 1721 a request from the Dyers' Company for the use of the barge 'on the next swan hopping' (? upping) was refused. On another occasion leave was given to the 'Four in Place', 'at their time and convenience to take out and use the Company's Barge at their own expense and upon the condition of insuring it and the Company from any accidents'.[43]

By the early 1720s, it seems the barge was becoming rather a burden. In October 1721 £20 had to be borrowed from the Clerk because the Renter Bailiff had 'not money enough to proceed to the payment of the Poor', and, at the same Court, it was resolved 'that this Compa. do not attend my Lord Mayor on the next solemnity with their Barge'. They did not, however, cancel the Company's dinner, nor did they contemplate giving up their barge permanently. On the contrary, they decided that the barge should go out on Lord Mayor's Day 1723.[44] Seven years later such grave doubts arose as to the vessel's seaworthiness that the Court resolved not to risk a voyage on Lord Mayor's Day 1730, and appointed a committee to 'wait on the Lord Mayor elect' to explain and apologise for 'the Barge not attending him for this time'.[45] The barge builder received £10 in all for 'things done to the Barge',[46] but these repairs were only a stop-gap, and although the barge made the voyage to Westminster and back in 1731 without sinking, the Court was soon forced to admit, most reluctantly, that 'the Company's present Barge is not fit and safe for their attendance on the Lord Mayor's Solemnity any farther'. The tenancy of the bargehouse was given up in 1732, the barge cloth, banners and streamers were put into store, and the old barge was broken up in 1733.[47] For a time they hoped to build a new barge in the near future; but financial stringency prevented this. So much money was absorbed by the official proceedings leading up to the approval of the new By-laws in 1737 that the Weavers could not even provide a stand on Lord Mayor's Day.[48] It was the same in 1738 when the Court 'resolved unanimously That this Company cannot appear in Publick to pay their Duty to the New Lord Mayor on Lord Mayor's Day next'. Unfortunately they forgot to explain and apologise in advance to the Lord Mayor elect and, early in December, were summoned to show cause why the Company did not march in the procession. No voyage by barge is mentioned. Again, in 1741, the Company wished to be 'excused from marching in the procession', and there is no mention of the barge.[49]

In the Weavers' eyes the annual feast on Election Day ranked equal in importance with that on Lord Mayor's Day, and during the last quarter of the seventeenth century the Company spent on average approximately £66 on each of its Election Day 'entertainments'. Indeed, during the period 1675 to 1695 the annual average was £71. Since there was no grand procession and water pageant on

Election Day, it follows that the feast on that day must have been the more sumptuous. We must not forget, however, that:

> Whereas it was formerly a custom to invite the wives of the Liverymen . . . upon the Lord Mayor's Day to dine at the Hall, this Court finding it very inconvenient in many respects have therefore ordered that from [25 June 1663] henceforth they shall be invited to dine at the Hall on St. James's Day annually; and it is also further ordered . . . that there shall be three persons of the Livery yearly elected Stewards to perform the said office and charge, on the said day, and that there shall be a sermon preached before the Company.[50]

After 1662 the numbers dining in Weavers' Hall on Election Days made it necessary to use the Court Room as well as the Hall.[51]

We can picture the setting: the Court Room furnished with nine Spanish tables, eighteen leather chairs, a velvet chair, a small table, two wainscot forms and two joint stools; a 'cloth carpet' on the floor, and on the walls the King's arms and the Company's arms framed, and half-a-dozen pictures. In the Hall itself there were three Spanish tables (which, of course, had to be supplemented by tables temporarily set up for the feast days), and, adorning the walls, 'eight pieces of Tapestry Hangings', oil paintings of Queen Elizabeth, King James I, King Charles I, King Charles II, and James, Duke of York, 'The King's, the City's and the Company's Arms carved', five pictures of benefactors and a list 'wherein are written the Benefactors towards the Building the Common Hall'. On the floor was a 'Turkey-work Carpet'.[52] Flowers and herbs were 'strewed' and nosegays provided by a number of poor women who usually received sixpence each, but sometimes more. The two or three porters at the gate were small master weavers or journeymen hired for the day and glad to earn a little extra money, like 'John Wood, living in Mile End New Town, Weaver, who works to Mr. [Benjamin] Champion, [who] was appointed one of the Porters . . . in the room of Old Dukes who is incapable'.[53] The victuals, cooked in the Hall kitchen, were served by beribboned waiters, while a band of music played in the musicians' gallery.[54] For this the group of musicians received £2. 10s. in the seventeenth century and £3. 10s. in the eighteenth century, plus 2s. 6d. 'for playing when paid their Money, according to Custom'.[55] On the tables stood a number of silver and silver gilt tankards, salts, bowls and cups, glistening bravely in the candle-light; for every livery company is proud of its plate, displays it on all important occasions, and regards it, also, as a valuable asset easy to realise should the need arise. The Weavers' Company marked the dawn of the seventeenth century by making a substantial purchase of plate from a goldsmith dwelling at the sign of the Bottle in Westcheap. Table 11.6 shows the items bought.[56]

Table 11.6 *A purchase of plate by the Company*

Items	£	s.	d.
3 Beakers parcel gilt, weighing (together) 40 oz. @ 6s.	12	0	0
2 Bowls, all gilt, weighing 28½ oz.	8	11	9
1 Salt } 1 Standing Cup } gilt, weighing 58 oz.	19	10	10
3 Bowls, all gilt, weighing upwards of 50 oz. @ 6s. 4d. p. oz.	15	18	1
9 Bowls, white, weighing over 70 oz. @ 5s. 5d. p. oz.	19	2	6
3 Beakers, white, weighing nearly 25 oz. @ 5s. 5d.*	6	15	2
	81	18	4

* 'Memo: that the above mentioned was bought with [the proceeds of] 19 dozen and five silver spoons' which realised £74. 8s. 6d.; and the balance of £7. 10s. was paid in cash.

The Weavers' plate was, from time to time, augmented by gifts and purchases, and diminished by sales. For example, in 1618, Thomas Rainshall[57] presented a silver cup when he was made free, and a silver bowl was given by William Stevens of Redriffe who became Renter Bailiff in 1619–20 and Upper Bailiff in the following year.[58] During the Civil War, as we have seen, the Company sold much of its plate and had to acquire a new collection when better times returned. In the 1660s several additions and one sale were made. A silver salt engraved with the Weavers' arms and his name was presented in 1663 by William James, a Liveryman, who became Upper Bailiff in 1674. During the summer of 1663 the Court resolved that 'two fair silver salts be bought against St. James's Day and so many spoons be forthwith sold as will pay for the same'. Actually two cups as well as 64 spoons, weighing together over 107 ounces, were sold at 5s. 1½d. an ounce, realising £27. 10s. 3d.[59] Four years later, the two sons of Arnold Beake, on taking their freedom, gave in lieu of the customary spoons, a silver cup and a silver trencher plate.[60] In 1677 the Company's stock of plate amounted to close upon 500 oz.[61] By 1685 a large silver tankard weighing 40 oz., two cups 'with Ears' and a chased cup had been acquired, but a sugar dish and five small cups had been disposed of; which resulted in a net addition to the plate of some 51 oz.,[62] making a grand total of 550 oz.

For many years the Company kept its plate in a large chest in the Clerk's office, but in May 1690 a carpenter was paid 5s. 'for joists used in the place where the Plate was hid';[63] an entry which brings to mind the troublous, unsettled time of the English Revolution, when

Dutch William was brought in to displace the discredited second James. Fortunately the Weavers' Company sustained no losses during this 'Convulsion of State',[64] with its anti-Catholic riots, but evidently they had taken precautions. Some years later, around the turn of the century, the Weavers sold a number of their pieces of plate and bought others (notably six silver salts), thus decreasing, on balance, the total quantity. In 1756, after the imposition of the plate tax, the Company was assessed on 300 ounces.[65]

We can see, then, the setting when the Livery dined. The actual menu for the dinner on Election Day 1672 has survived:

Pullets and Bacon
2 Venison p. Upper Table
1 Venison p. each of other Tables
Roast Turkey
Umble Pye
Roast Beef, a piece to each Table
Roast Capons
Custard
Tart
Fruit, 2 dishes to each Mess[66]

The cook's bill usually came to about £45; the butler received £2. 10s., and the consort of musicians a similar sum. The wine bill was always substantial, for although wine was cheap by modern standards, great quantities were consumed, and usually, for the Lord Mayor's and Election days together, the cost was between £20 and £30. In 1727 £11. 8s. was paid 'for Wine on Lord Mayor's day, vizt. twelve gallons of Old Canary & 20 of Old Port'.[67]

Smoking became an established social habit in the seventeenth century in defiance of King James I's grave warning against it in his *Counterblaste to Tobacco* (1604) as a danger to the lungs and a cause of soot deposits 'in the inward parts of men'.[68] At all public dinners tobacco and clay pipes were provided as part of the 'entertainment'. In 1668–9 the Company bought '10 lbs. of Tobacco for the whole year' at 2s. 6d. a pound and two gross of clay tobacco pipes at an average price of 2s. 5d. a gross. For Lord Mayor's Day, 1687, two lb. of tobacco were bought at 2s. a pound, and in the following year the Company 'paid the pipe maker for pipes for a year, 14s. 6d.'

Usually the Election Day sermon was preached by the Rector of St Michael's, Bassishaw, the Company's parish church, which was nearly as old as the Weavers' Gild, for the first church was founded in 1140.[69] Occasionally, however, a special preacher was invited. Thus, in 1681 at the height of the intense public excitement which centred on Titus Oates and the alleged 'Popish Plot', 'it was by several of the [Weavers'] Livery desired' that the Reverend Dr Titus

Oates should be invited to preach before the Company on St James's Day; 'which Proposal was ... maturely debated and ... upon an Argument ... that the Doctor's Father was a Weaver, it was resolved that some Members of the Court should wait upon the Doctor'. On 26 July 1681 the *Loyal Protestant and True Domestick Intelligence* reported: 'Yesterday Dr. Oates (according to promise) preached before the Master, Wardens, and the whole Society of the Company of Weavers. ... There was a very great Auditory; after which the Doctor was invited to a noble Dinner in Weavers Hall.'[70]

Titus Oates (1649–1705) was the son of Samuel Oates, a Norwich weaver, who turned to preaching for the Anabaptists and became Brother Oates of Lamb's Church in Bell Alley, Coleman Street (only a stone's throw from Weavers' Hall) and, later, chaplain to the regiment of Colonel Pride, a fanatical Anabaptist who (it was said) had been a brewer's drayman before he joined the Parliamentary army. After the Restoration Samuel Oates switched to the Church of England and was given the living of All Saints, Hastings. His son, Titus, a consummate confidence trickster, was 'hosanna'd' for more than two years (1679–81) as 'the Saviour of the Nation' from a Popish plot to destroy King Charles II and the Protestant religion in England— a 'plot' which had, in fact, been fabricated in 1678 by Titus Oates himself and Israel Tonge, rector of St Mary Staining. For many feverish months the voluble, inventive, audacious Oates had a credulous Protestant London at his feet.

> Prodigious actions may as well be done
> By weaver's issue, as by prince's son

was Dryden's satirical comment. Although the King remained sceptical, a great wave of anti-Catholic hysteria swept through the nation; 'fear, hatred and credulity were the ruling passions of the hour, and held sway over the Lords of the Privy Council as over the meanest beggar in the streets'.[71] The London Weavers' Company was no exception: hence their Election Day invitation to Oates, and the 'noble Dinner' after his sermon.[72]

The approach of Election Day was a perennial reminder that the Hall with its furnishings and equipment needed (like the barge) to be 'repaired and beautified' from time to time. A fresh coat of whitewash for the walls of the Hall and the Court Room cost about £10, and 'refreshing' the tapestry hangings (purchased when the Hall was rebuilt after the Fire) cost £4 in 1680.[73] Windows, too, were cleaned and mended 'against St. James's Day'. In 1707, £10. 19s. 8d. was paid for a new chair 'embellished with gold lace' for the Upper Bailiff, and early in 1709 six Russian leather chairs were bought for £2. 8s. the set.[74] Two dozen new 'Princes Metal' candlesticks were bought for the Hall on one occasion,[75] and at other times quantities of pewter dishes and similar utensils. Such a soft metal as pewter very quickly became damaged or worn out in general use, or melted in the oven, and had to be replaced.[76] Moreover, some of it was stolen every year, especially during the two feasts.[77] A few losses, usually of trencher plates and napkins, seem to have been regarded as normal, but in 1715–16 the losses assumed alarming proportions; e.g. 'All the table cloths and all the napkins but three, lost or worn out. Two dozen and eight trencher plates lost at Feasts. Two pie plates and one flagon lost or worn out.'[78] Even a long spit—one of six—disappeared from the kitchen![79] Apparently it proved impossible to solve the mystery of the disappearing dishes, for in 1738 the Court, disturbed yet again by a report on the pewter, ordered that the butler 'do take all the Company's Pewter under his Care and that after every Entertainment he report the State thereof to this Court'.[80] In 1768 the Weavers again substantially renewed their pewter, as we see from the

Acct. of New Pewter Bot. for the Compa. of Thomas
Swanson, 25th July 1768, in Exchange for the Compas.
Old Pewter, wt. 6 cwt. 0 qr. 6 lb. at 8d. (per lb.)
52 dishes in three different sizes
24 flat dishes
16 soup dishes
24 Pie Plates

	£	s.	d.
All the best fine Pewter,			
4 cwt. 3 qr. 7 lb. at 14d.	31	8	10
2 7-inch best Stands		9	0
More Pewter Bot. 7th Nov. 1768 for Pastys—⎫			
4 Oval Soup Dishes, 7 lbs. @ 18½d. ⎭	2	2	10
	34	0	8
Recd. by Old Pewter above	22	12	0
Ballance	11	8	8

In addition, ten flagons and one chamber pot were bought, but the prices are not stated.

Without doubt many interlopers, mingling with the throng, managed to get into and out of the Hall on Feast Days and some of them, as well as the members' servants, carried away not only pewter and linen but victuals also—a malpractice which certainly continued for at least a century. In 1674 the Court issued the following statement:

For as much as at some former feasts at the Hall some persons' attendants on those days, and others, have used to carry out victuals from the Hall to Taverns & Victualling houses near thereabouts, which hath been taken notice of by some

Members to their great dislike, as if the credit and honour of the Company were thereby (as indeed it is) greatly prejudiced, and by means thereof oft times pewter and linen is carried out with the same, to the loss thereof. It is therefore ordered that the Officers attending at the Gate on those days do not permit any persons whatsoever to carry any victuals out of the Hall, but that the 4 in place do dispose of the broken victuals to the poor of the Company.[81]

Such measures may have had a temporary effect, but there seems to have been no permanent improvement, for as late as 1769 the Court decreed:[82] 'that no Sons or children of the Liverymen or other Persons not of the Livery . . . be admitted into this Company's Hall on next St. James's Day, except the Stewards' Friends, who are not to introduce more than two each, who are to be presented to Mr. Upper Bailiff and approved by him . . . this resolution [to] be printed at the bottom of the Summons given to the Livery.' The Court also ordered that 'strict Charge be given to the Porters at the Hall Gate, that on no pretence they leave the Gate both at the same time, and that they take care to Admit none but the Livery without the special leave of the Upper Bailiff'; and, as a further check, that a 'Third Person be appointed to stand at the Hatch', and the Hall gates should be kept shut 'during the Entertainment and the Company's continuance in the Hall'.[83]

Richard Sturley, an old pensioner living in one of the Company's almshouses in Porters Fields, was an interloper of a different kind. On St James's Day 1746 he caused a commotion by deciding to dine with the Livery in Hall, 'where, by his Behaviour, he gave great offence to divers of the Liverymen'. The result was a prompt and peremptory order 'that for the future no Pensioner of this Company shall upon any account be admitted to Dine at any of the Publick Entertainments . . . either on St. James's Day or Lord Mayor's Day'. The Beadles were told to exercise strict vigilance and 'if any . . . Pensioners shall hereafter appear at any of the said Entertainments' they must 'remove them accordingly'.[84]

Such incidents serve to remind us that behaviour at public dinners in the eighteenth century was often much less decorous and dignified than is customary today, and, incredible though it may appear, even the Lord Mayor's Banquet was no exception. In 1780, for example, the year of the Gordon Riots, William Hickey, who was for many years in the East India Company's service, was invited by his friend, Alderman Woolridge, to be his guest at the banquet to mark the beginning of Sir Watkin Lewis's mayoralty. So, on 9 November 1780, we see William Hickey, dressed in a 'full suit of velvet', driving with the alderman to the Guildhall at about 4.30 p.m., an hour before the arrival of the Lord Mayor and his procession. Here is Hickey's astonishing eyewitness account of what followed:

> At six we sat down to a profusion of turtle and venison, followed by all the etceteras of French cookery, with splendid dessert of pines, grapes, and other fruits. . . . The heat from the crowd assembled and the immense number of lights was disagreeable to all [although] the Lord Mayor's table was . . . considerably elevated above the rest. The wines were excellent and . . . served too [at the high table] with as much regularity and decorum as if . . . in a private house; but . . . in the body of the hall . . . in five minutes after the guests took their stations at the tables the dishes were entirely cleared of their contents, twenty hands seizing the same joint or bird and literally tearing it to pieces. A more determined scramble could not be, the roaring and noise was deafening and hideous, which increased as the liquor operated, bottles and glasses flying across from side to side without intermission. Such a bear garden . . . I never beheld. . . . This abominable and disgusting scene continued till near ten o'clock, when the Lord Mayor, sheriffs, nobility, &c., adjourned to the ball and card rooms and the dancing commenced. Here the heat was no way inferior to that of the hall and the crowd so great there was scarce a possibility of moving.[85]

By this time William Hickey had had enough and went home to bed 'completely exhausted'.

The expenses of each of the Weavers' annual feasts were customarily defrayed by two (later, three) Liverymen chosen to be Stewards for the occasion. Some of the wealthier or more generous members accepted this rather onerous office without demur, but among the majority there was usually so much reluctance that the Company often had to bear some part of the expense, by allowing the payment of a fixed 'fine'. Thus in 1648 a payment of £10 would secure exemption from the duty of 'holding Steward'. In 1660 and 1661, immediately after the Restoration, the Stewards were allowed, out of the Company's funds, one-fifth of the cost of the dinner on Lord Mayor's Day; and in 1669 the two Stewards chosen 'against my Lord May's day' were granted 'Twenty Nobles towards their charge on that day . . . in respect the Company have received fines of two Stewards, [who were discharged on payment of £12 each] and the Livery being greatly increased'.[86] Some Liverymen were unwilling to pay anything at all and offered excuses, more or less genuine, such as urgent journeys out of town, business losses, advanced age, and 'infirmity of the body'. Very occasionally, the Company met with a blunt refusal 'couched in very disrespectful language'. Others were unwilling to 'hold Steward' because of all the personal frictions that could arise in the kitchen and catering departments. For example, in October 1664 the two Stewards charged with the dinner preparations on Lord Mayor's Day asked the Court's permission to engage another cook, for when they thought that all the arrangements were well in hand, Mr Adams, a deputy cook, 'did fly off'. When the Court asked questions, the head cook said 'that the Stewards had drove of the time [delayed] so long that they [the cooks] could not provide themselves of men to help them'. As a matter of urgency the Court gave the Stewards 'leave to make choice of a cook for this present time'.[87]

Members' reluctance to hold the office of Steward increased roughly in direct ratio to the rising cost of providing the dinners. Matters came to a head in 1674, when the Court of Assistants, 'designing (if possible) that the feasts should be managed to general satisfaction', proposed in future to shift the entire cost of the feasts from the Stewards to the Company, on condition that 'the first seven in course of Stewards' should each 'pay down £14; the next succeeding fourteen, £12 a piece, and all the rest of the Livery . . . £10 a piece'. Moreover, every person accepting the Livery in future should pay £16 'in lieu of the ancient fine for the Livery [£5], the Rent of the Bargehouse [£1], and to be discharged forever from the place, office or charge of Steward [£10]'. These recommendations were debated and agreed at a Common Hall which also decided that all present or future Liverymen refusing to comply with the new order 'shall be liable to be elected . . . Stewards for the said feasts . . . as hath been heretofore used and accustomed'; the fine for refusal to serve as Steward if so elected was fixed at £14. Among the next group of liverymen to be summoned was a Quaker, 'Mr Selwood, [who] offered to hold and perform his part of the charge provided it be with moderation and there be no excess, which the Company could not well understand, and so he departed.'[88] During the first quarter of the eighteenth century each of three Stewards was required 'to undertake to find and provide one third part of an Entertainment' or to pay £15 in lieu, and usually it was less expensive 'to fine' because one-third of the actual expenses might amount to £18 or £20 at the least.[89]

The Weavers' Lord Mayor's Day dinners were discontinued for a period in the mid-eighteenth century, probably because of the cost and the difficulty of obtaining willing Stewards. In October 1765, however, a 'considerable number' of the Livery asked the Court to 'have an Entertainment provided as formerly on Lord Mayor's day, and that the same might be continued in future, as the discontinuing of it for some years had given great Disgust and Dissatisfaction to the Livery in General'. Certain Liverymen expressed their readiness to serve as Stewards or to 'pay their Fines whenever it came their Turns'. Thus encouraged, the Court, 'being desirous to show a proper attention to the Livery', resolved to hold an entertainment on the next Lord Mayor's Day; whereupon the Livery 'went away well satisfied'.[90]

At the dawn of the nineteenth century, when the country was at war with France, the problem of public dinners arose once again. In 1800 the usual dinners on Election Day and Lord Mayor's Day were not held because of the scarcity and high prices of provisions, the unsafe state of the Hall premises and the heavy expense of repairing them. Two years later, in an attempt to economise, it was decided that 'the Entertainment for the Court and Livery on next St. James's Day be provided at the "Mermaid" in Hackney'. In 1804 there was a proposal to discontinue for a time one of the two public dinners, because the Livery had increased so much that every dinner was costing about £150; 'and as the Entertainments in the country [e.g. at Hackney or Greenwich] on St. James's days seem to give general satisfaction to the Livery, the Court wished to suspend the dinner at the Hall on the Lord Mayor's Day.' Although twenty-three Liverymen were against this proposal, it was ultimately resolved (in June 1805) to discontinue the Lord Mayor's Day dinners 'for some years to come'.[91]

There is reason to suppose that the Election Day dinners also were suspended for a time, because in May 1825 the Court of Assistants asked the Officers to look into the Company's ability to provide a dinner for the Livery on St James's Day that year (see Table 11.7). Having looked at these figures, the Court resolved (though not unanimously) that a Livery dinner should be provided on St James's Day 1825, and that the July Court dinner, which usually cost upwards of £25, should not be held.[92]

Among the minor convivial occasions there was Oath Day in August, when the Officers elect were sworn in; and Audit Day in December, usually about a week before Christmas, when the four Auditors (all members of the Company) having completed their labours, were entertained to dinner as a token of the Company's appreciation of their voluntary vigilance. The expense of the Oath Day dinners seems to have been shared between the Officers and the Company. Thus in 1666 the record runs: 'Allowed to the 4 in place towards their Charge in the Oath Day Dinner, the Yeomanry being invited thereto, p. Order, £3.' In 1689 a 'third part of the Oath Day Dinner' paid by the Company, came to £6; and nearly twenty years later (1708) the Company's share was £17. 10s. 6d.[93] The Audit dinner in 1666 cost £2. 15s. 6d., and in 1689 the Company paid £2. 13s. 2d. for 'Dinner, Wine and Oysters, being Audit Day'. Sometimes these dinners were served in Weavers' Hall, but at other times the assembled company adjourned to a tavern, such as the King's Arms in Cateaton Street, or the Angel in Moorfields. During the eighteenth century many Audit Day dinners were held at the London Tavern as a sort of pre-Christmas celebration.[94]

After the Court of Assistants had completed their business the members usually went to dinner, sending the bill to the Company.[95] From time to time, the Court issued 'orders' enjoining strict economy and setting upper limits upon spending; e.g. £1. 5s. for a 'private' (monthly) Court dinner and £3. 10s. for a quarterly Full Court dinner.[96] During a financial famine in 1738 a memorandum was added to the Court minutes:

> 6th February 1738.
> After the Business of the Company was over [i.e. a committee for binding and making free] the four Officers and the three gentlemen of the Court of Assistants had a Dinner which came to fifteen shillings and sixpence and was paid for by themselves and not at the Expense of the Company. This is Entered as an Example proper to be followed by the other Gentlemen of the Court.[97]

Table 11.7 *Estimate of numbers attending and cost of a Livery dinner, 1825*

Court of Assistants	24	
Livery appearing by the Books as living	247	
	—	271
Not to be found, residence unknown	67	
Out of the Kingdom	9	
Insane or superannuated	3	
Residing 10 miles (or more) from London	13	
Not paid Stewards Fines	20	
	—	112
		159
On an estimate that one-fourth of this number may not attend, deduct		39
Probable number to attend a Livery Dinner		120

To provide a dinner for 120 persons and guests, say 130 in all:

	£	s.	d.
Dinner at 5s. per head	32	10	0
Dessert at 1s. 6d. per head	9	15	0
Wine, $1\frac{1}{2}$ bottles per head, at 5s. p. bottle	48	15	0
Tea and Coffee at 1s. per head	6	10	0
Waiters and extras at 1s. per head	6	10	0
	104	0	0

I.e., 16s. each.

A few items from the accounts help us to visualise the sort of meals enjoyed by the Officers and Assistants when they dined together (see Table 11.8). The entry 'Paid Mr. Ham for Beef & Lamb' seems to have a rather jolly lilt, doubtless well suited to the occasion.

Table 11.8 *Dining expenses of Officers and Assistants*

Date	Item	£	s.	d.
1672 November	2 Calfs heads for Court Day Dinner		5	7
December	2 Legs of Mutton for Court Day Dinner		6	8
1673 January	4 pullets		7	0
	A lamb pasty		12	6
	Oysters		4	4
	Wine (3½ quarts Canary)		7	0
February	Sirloin of beef		8	6
1687 August	'Fish & Hartichokes'		6	6
October	2 Pigeon Pies @ 8s. 6d.		17	0
	Wine		13	0
	Tobacco		2	0
1725 February	'Dressing ye Dinner, Wine &c. being 15 in Compa. and 3 came upon ye Clothing [Livery]: all as by bill on ye Fyle'	2	4	2
October	'For beef & Greens on Michaelmas Day	1	18	6
	For Beer, Ale, Pipes and toBaco same day'	1	12	0
1726 September	4 tongues & 2 udders		15	0

The wives of Officers, Assistants and Liverymen seldom appear in the records, but certain items in the accounts for 1725 are not without interest (see Table 11.9).

Table 11.9 *Entertainment expenses*

Date	Item	£	s.	d.
21st June 1725:	for 12 quarts fine old Port wch. was dranck at ye Dinner for ye Court & There wife	1	0	0
	Paid Adlam's bill at ye Ladys Entertainment		16	6
	4 Large Buttocks & 2 Large Sourloynes beef, cabbidge & carrots	2	8	8
	Pd. Cook's bill for Dinner for Assistants & their Wives, 2nd June last	23	10	0
	Pd. Wido. Heron's[98] bill for Wine from 10th Feby. to this day, including wine for the above mentioned Dinner	11	9	0

After one of the Court dinners, the Upper Bailiff, 'being lately married ... now presented to every Bailiff, Warden and Assistant (and intends also to them that are absent) a pair of Gloves, as hath been heretofore accustomed'.[99]

Sundry events or particular duties which cropped up from time to time were deemed to justify a little dinner or at least a 'drinking'. The Officers, for instance, occasionally spent 18s. or 19s. on a dinner, which might include victuals such as 'a quarter of lamb and a barrel of oysters', after paying out pension money to the poor, who were 'treated' to beer, ale and bread at a cost of 6s. 4d. Less frequently, £3 or £4 was spent on a journey into Essex to view the Company's land near Billericay; or some 13s. when 'looking over the Plate & Goods of the Compa.' On one of their visits to Billingsgate 'to taste Oysters as Customary' the Upper Bailiff and Wardens managed to spend nearly £1.[100] 'A Treat for the Canterbury Masters', when they came to London in the spring of 1690, was hospitably provided by the Weavers' Company.[101] In 1770 the Weavers' delight in having Alderman John Kirkman as their Upper Bailiff was expressed in the form of a dinner given at the White Hart tavern for the Officers and Assistants on the occasion of 'Aldn. Kirkman's first taking the Chair'.[102] When the Company received on behalf of its poor members a legacy of £30 under the will of Solomon Hesse who died in 1796, a pre-Christmas dinner was held in December 'for the Court and Mr. Hesse's Executors', which cost nearly £11.[103] Even the lectures or sermons delivered under the Limborough Bequest resulted in 'the Court, Church Wardens of Spitalfields, Rev. Mr Foster (the Lecturer) &c.' dining together. Gildsmen through the centuries have remained faithful to the tradition that no opportunity for conviviality should ever be neglected.

NOTES

1 Chaucer's *Cook's Tale* tells of a pleasure-loving victualler's apprentice who, '. . . whan ther any ridyng was in Chepe, Out of the shoppe thider wolde he lepe—'
2 As a result of a compromise decision given by the Lord Mayor in 1483 on an obstinate dispute between the Skinners and the Merchant Taylors, these companies rank sixth and seventh in alternate years.
3 Repertories 3, f.66v.
4 i.e. mulberry-coloured.
5 W. Herbert, *History of the Twelve Great Livery Companies* (1837), I, pp. 102n., 124.
6 John Nicholls, *Progresses of King James I* (1828), pp. 400–1. In the seventeenth century the Grocers were required to buy and store 675 chaldrons of sea-coal; the Mercers, 488; the Vintners,

375; but the Weavers' quota was only 27 chaldrons (Maitland, *London*, I, pp. 273, 431–2).

7 P. E. Jones, *The Worshipful Company of Poulterers of the City of London* (1939), pp. 141–2.

8 MS. 4655/11, f.20.

9 MS. 4655/11, ff.154b–156, 165.

10 John Tatham, *London Tryumph* (1658).

11 H. G. Carr, 'Barge Flags of the City Livery Companies of London', reprinted from *The Mariner's Mirror*, July 1942, pp. 222–30.

12 H. Humpherus, *History of the Company of Watermen* (1874), I, pp. 8–9, 50. This work contains a number of references to the Lord Mayors' processions on the Thames.

13 It was discontinued after 1856.

14 Evelyn, *Diary*, 29 October 1661.

15 Catherine brought from Portugal an unprecedentedly large dowry: half a million of money, Tangier, the Island of Bombay, and free trading rights to Brazil and the East Indies—'a key for English merchants to the treasure trove of the world' (A. Bryant, *King Charles II* (1931), p. 135).

16 Pepys, *Diary*, 23 August 1662; Evelyn, *Diary*, same date.

17 Evelyn, *Diary*, 29 October 1664.

18 Anne Petrides, *State Barges on the Thames* (1959).

19 J. G. Nichols, *London Pageants* (1831), pp. 5–6n.

20 E. de Maré, *London's Riverside*, p. 255.

21 Unwin, *Gilds*, p. 274; Herbert, op. cit., I, p. 100 and note.

22 R. T. D. Sale, *The Barges of the Merchant Taylors' Company* (1933), p. 9.

23 MS. 4655/1, f.20. Originally, a 'whiffler' was a sort of jester or clown chosen from among the freemen; he wore a vizard, carried a whip, and was supposed to clear a way for his Company.

24 MS. 4655/1, f.82. No doubt the two watermen were to act as barge master and steersman.

25 MS. 4655/1, f.102.

26 In 1675 John Browne in Blue Maid Alley, Southwark, trumpeter, engaged to bring not less than 6 or more than 8 trumpeters on Lord Mayor's Day, for 10*s.* a head, to sound through the streets (MS. 4655/8, f.146).

27 Sale, op. cit., p. 24.

28 In 1671 and 1672 the Weavers hired two barges, one to carry the musicians, and paid a hiring charge of £6 for the two (MS. 4648/1; MS. 4648/2).

29 John Tatham, op. cit.; N. Luttrell, *A Brief Historical Relation of State Affairs from 1678 to 1714*, I, p. 25.

30 Unwin, *Gilds*, pp. 290–1; E. de Maré, op. cit., p. 126.

31 MS. 4655/7, ff.48–9, 29 September 1673.

32 MS. 4655/10, f.50b.

33 The supporters to the Weavers' arms were granted on 10 August 1616 and are 'Two Wyvers ermine on their Wings displayed garnished gold two Roses gules, langued and membred of the same.' The choice of the 'wyver', an heraldic two-legged dragon, was probably suggested by the phonetic similarity of the words 'wyvers' and 'weavers'. Heraldic supporters are usually human, beast, bird or fish forms, which appear to support or uphold the shield; they should not 'lounge upon it', nor squat or lie down comfortably, nor

should they seem to emerge from behind the shield, thereby creating a pleasant but unheraldic Alice-in-Wonderland impression. Certainly the Weavers' supporters cannot be so criticised, for they appear to be a formidable pair, whose attitudes suggest unwinking vigilance and strength bordering upon ferocity (A. C. Fox-Davies, *A Complete Guide to Heraldry* (1925), Chap. 26; J. Bromley and H. Child, *Armorial Bearings of the Guilds of London* (1960), pp. 263–5; W. Gardner, *The Calligrapher's Handbook* (ed. C. M. Lamb, 1956), p. 174).

34 MS. 4655/7, ff.10, 29, 47b.

35 Sale, op. cit., p. 57.

36 MS. 4649A, f.20b; MS. 4646, f.203.

37 The list of subscribers appears at the back of MS. 4648/2.

38 MS. 4649A, f.35; MS. 4655/8, ff.17b, 18b, 23b. Annual repairs to the bargehouse ranged from 13*s.* in a fortunate year to over £18 in a year such as 1704, when a great storm caused considerable damage (MS. 4648/3, 17 January 1704).

39 MS. 4655/8, f.64; MS.4648/1, 13 October 1679; MS. 4648/4, ff.18, 88, 132, 181.

40 Probably for sweeping the lane leading to the waterside: cf. MS. 4648/3, 13 November 1704.

41 MS. 4648/4, ff.214, 236.

42 MS. 4655/11, ff.59b, 65b, 165b, 202b.

43 MS. 4655/12, ff.3, 226.

44 MS. 4655/12, ff.7b, 32b.

45 MS. 4655/13, ff.16, 20.

46 MS. 4648/4, ff.264–6; MS. 4655/13, ff.41, 54.

47 MS. 4655/13, ff.13, 74b, 99, 120.

48 MS. 4655/14, ff.12–13.

49 MS. 4655/15, ff.33, 116b; MS. 4648/5, f.9.

50 MS. 4655/3, f.82.

51 MS. 4655/16, f.148.

52 MS. 4646, ff.203, 249, 289b–296.

53 MS. 4655/16, f.51.

54 MS. 4648/10; MS. 4648/4, f.244.

55 MS. 4648/4, ff.133, 225.

56 MS. 4646, f.306.

57 Probably a son of John Rainshall, who was Renter Bailiff in 1617–1618.

58 MS. 4646, ff.70b, 71.

59 MS. 4655/3, ff.31b, 84b, 88.

60 MS. 4655/4, f.86.

61 MS. 4646, f.203. For the Inventory of October 1677 see Appendix 1.

62 MS. 4646, f.249.

63 MS. 4649B/2, 19 May 1690.

64 MS. 4646, f.293.

65 MS. 4646, f.288; MS. 4648/3, 27 March 1704; MS. 4648/7, 23 July 1756.

66 MS. 4655A/3.

67 MS. 4648/4, ff.89, 137. In August 1669, 4*s.* 4*d.* was paid to a cooper for bottling a hogshead of claret. 20 dozen glass bottles @ 4*s.* a doz. and 2 gross of corks cost £4. 5*s.* Canary wine cost 6*s.* 8*d.* a gallon and claret 2*s.* 8*d.* in 1669.

68 Smoke, wrote King James, 'makes a kitchen . . . in the inward

parts of men, soiling and infecting them with an unctuous and oily kind of soot, as hath been found in some great tobacco takers that after their death were opened. . . . This filthy novelty [is] loathsome to the eye, hateful to the nose, harmful to the brain, dangerous to the lungs . . . resembling the horrible Stygian smoke of the pit that is bottomless.'

69 It was rebuilt in 1460, and after its destruction in the Great Fire it was rebuilt from designs by Sir Christopher Wren and completed in 1679.

70 The *Loyal Protestant and True Domestick Intelligence*, 16 and 26 July 1681; N. Luttrell, *A Brief Historical Relation of the State of Affairs*, I, pp. 112, 125–6. The Weavers' Court minute book covering the year 1681 is lost.

71 Jane Lane, *Titus Oates* (1949), pp. 142–3.

72 On 31 August 1681 (little more than a month after Oates preached to the Weavers) Charles II expelled Titus from his privileged lodging in Whitehall, and his decline began. He badly overplayed his hand by attacking James, Duke of York, who had Oates tried on a charge of *Scandalum magnatum*. The result was the award of overwhelming damages against Oates of £100,000. At a second trial, in 1685, Oates was convicted of perjury: 'perjury which had been the direct means of sending at least eleven innocent men to die by the most horrible form of execution ever invented. . . . there was no precedent for so complex and heinous a crime' (ibid., pp. 275–6, 299–300, 317–18).

73 MS. 4649A, 26 July 1680.

74 MS. 4648/3, August 1707 and March 1709. This Upper Bailiff's chair is still in the Company's possession. See Plate 10.

75 MS. 4655/18, f.128. Princes metal was an alloy of copper and zinc.

76 MS. 4646, ff.93, 109; MS. 4648/1, August 1676.

77 MS. 4649A, 21 August 1682. In 1659–60 the Company bought nearly seven hundredweights of new pewter; and the accounts for 1675–6 show that the Renter Bailiff 'paid for some new pewter & exchanging of old, £19. 14. 0.'. For '12 pewter flagons and engraving the same' the Company paid £5. 12s. in 1682. The inventory taken on 2 October 1702 shows that a quantity of old pewter had been sold, including eight flagons with covers, one ten-pound dish, and six dozen plates, and by way of replenishment a dozen new pewter dishes, ranging from 7 lb. down to 2½ lb. and fourteen dozen trencher plates had been bought.

78 MS. 4646, f.290b; cf. also MS. 4655/11, f.299b.

79 MS. 4646, f.285; memo to inventory, 18 October 1716.

80 MS. 4655/14, f.70.

81 MS. 4655/8, ff.9b, 12b.

82 See e.g. MS. 4655/15, f.201.

83 MS. 4655/17, ff.108b, 115b.

84 MS. 4655/15, f.254.

85 A. Spencer (ed.), *Memoirs of William Hickey* (1918), II, pp. 297–8.

86 MS. 4655A. 16 October 1648; MS. 4655/2, ff.55–6; MS. 4655/3, f.14; MS. 4655/6, f.8b. One noble=6s. 8d.

87 MS. 4655/3, f.157b.

88 MS. 4655/8, ff.3, 5b, 6, 7b, 47. Liverymen who were slow to pay their Livery dues might suddenly receive a visit from the Clerk or a summons to 'hold Steward' for one of the feasts (MS. 4655/10, f.56).

89 MS. 4655/11, f.280; MS. 4655/12, f.54b.
90 MS. 4655/17, f.11b.
91 MS. 4655/19, ff.58b, 61b, 93, 102b, 143, 148, 156b.
92 MS. 4655/20, f.3.
93 MS. 4648/3, August 1708.
94 MS. 4648/1, 6 October 1666; MS. 4655/12, f.124b; MS. 4648/8, 19 December 1770.
95 Thus on 11 December 1666 a Court dinner at 'ye *White Hart*' cost the Company £1. 1s. 9d. In 1668 £2. 7s. 3d. was spent on 'a Fish Dinner for the Court', and £5. 4s. 4d. was paid 'for a full Court Dinner all ye Yeomanry invited'.
96 MS. 4655/8, f.79b; MS. 4655/12, f.226, 240–1.
97 MS. 4655/15, f.10.
98 MS. 4648/4, ff.31, 36. Martha Heron was hostess of the Three Tuns in Bishopsgate Street,
99 MS. 4655/7, f.70.
100 MS. 4648/4, f.8.
101 MSS. 4649B/1 and 2, 3 October 1687; 27 March 1688; 22 April 1690.
102 MS. 4648/8, 3 October 1770.
103 MS. 4648/11, 23 November and 20 December 1796.

Chapter 12

Worthy Benefactors and Charitable Gifts

The concept of brotherhood within the craft which lay at the root of the gild system implied a duty to be 'loving, gentle and friendlie one to another' and to help brother-craftsmen who, although honest, sober men and competent at their trade, had become Misfortune's unwilling guests or were aged, infirm and 'much decayed'. Within the scope of this duty the dependants—wives and children, widows and orphans 'in low circumstances'—were included; so, also, was the provision of seemly burial for deceased members if the expenses could not be otherwise met.[1] Before the seventeenth century the charity dispensed by the Weavers' Company seems to have taken the form of occasional gifts or doles to relieve particular cases as they came to the notice of the Court of Assistants. The money for this came mainly from the 'poor's box' which was placed on the table at every Court meeting ready to receive the voluntary bounty of the benevolent as well as the not-so-voluntary gifts of those whose excusable offences the Court was willing to overlook on condition that the offender agreed to put a specified sum in the box. We know that in 1600–1, the total so collected was £1. 6s., but for many years after that date there is little precise information: only the Commonalty's vague grumblings, in 1636, that 'more might have been distributed ... and more Charitably employed' to relieve the necessities of the Company's poor.[2] The yearly average of the poor's box collections for the last quarter of the seventeenth century was £26; and for the first quarter of the eighteenth century between £68 and £69. In 1662 the Court ordered that the poor's box money 'shall be given to the poor quarterly',[3] and five years later it was resolved 'that particular care be taken that none be relieved out of ye Box but such as truly belong to ye Compa.'[4]

In the seventeenth century, especially in the second half, the old forms of charity, considerably increased in total amount, were supplemented by new, more systematic charitable gifts, such as regular pensions in money or kind, and the provision of almshouses for aged poor weavers or their widows. The increasing prosperity of certain master weavers resulted, from time to time, in generous legacies or gifts *inter vivos* of money or property. Among the earliest of these was Ralph Hamer's gift which enabled the Company to pay regular quarterly pensions to five or six poor weavers. Two entries in the Court minutes for 1618–19 read: 'Gabriel Grette is ordered to have the first pensioner's place for Mr. Hamer's gift that falleth', and 'Richard Ferries is appointed to have the next pensioner's place that happeneth out of the gift of Mr. Ralph Hamer.'[5] These pensions continued to be paid for many years; as one pensioner died another was elected, and there was never any shortage of applicants! Thus, in October 1648 the Court of Assistants 'ordered that John Street, a freeman of this Company, being poor, shall immediately receive the pension of Mr. Ralph Hamer now void, viz., 10s. on the quarter of the year'.[6] By this time another benefactor, Mrs Mary Paradine, was also providing pensions, so that Robert Elliott was able 'to receive Mrs. Mary Paradine's pension of 5s. p. ann. in place of Widow Preene, deceased'; and a month later (November 1648) two poor freemen were granted pensions—one to be paid from Mrs Paradine's fund and the other 'to be the Company's pensioner in the room of Hump. Hall late deceased'.[7] When Andrew Fordam, a Paradine pensioner, died in January 1649, his pension was 'continued unto his widow'. Moreover, by the early 1660s the Company was making very substantial pension payments from its own funds (see Table 12.1). And in the following year the Company paid no less than £42. 5s. to its pensioners.[8] Originally it was Mrs Paradine's intention that her pensions should number twenty-four, but after the deaths of five Paradine pensioners in 1664 the Company decided that in future 'there shall be 20 . . . to the end that every one may have the more'.[9]

Table 12.1 *Pension payments*

Date	Paid to	£	s.	d.
1662–3	Mrs. Mary Paradine's pensioners	6	0	0
	Mr. Hamer's pensioners	11	0	0
	Mr. Hammond's pensioners	2	16	0
	the Company's pensioners	28	16	0

The increase of periodical pensions did not mean that occasional appeals for help went unheeded. The Court minute book for 1651, for example, shows that £4. 10s. was 'Laid out for the poor' by the Renter Warden, and 'More to 2 poor women, 3s. 6d.' On another occasion the Company gave 5s. 'to goodman Turner that have 8 children naked for want of clothes'.[10] Appeals from sick or disabled members were never ignored, as we see in the case of John Ball who was ill in hospital in 1654, 'and his wife being distracted', a gift of five shillings was sent for his relief.[11] Or there was Mr Taverner, very poor and desperately ill, who was provided with 'a pair of sheets, 2 shifts [nightshirts] and a straw bed . . . and such other necessaries as they [the Officers] shall think fit for [him], who lies in a very deplored condition, and ye charge thereof to be out of ye Poor's box: [and] to give a woman 1s. a week to look to and tend him'. The sequel is recorded on 11 July 1667, when the Court resolved that 'The bedding, etc., bought for Mr. Taverner's use (he being dead) shall be given to Widow Davis who hath taken pains with him.'[12] In June 1668 5s. was given to Thomas Hicks, 'a poor blind man, a freeman of this Company', and a similar sum to Thomas Doding 'to relieve his present necessities'.[13] Anna Wilkinson, being blind, was recommended for the next available pension. John Tomkin received a gift of 8s. 6d. from the Company, he having sustained 'great loss by the ship that was fired [burned] at London Bridge'.[14] Occasionally, men who had held high office in the Company were brought low by disease or business misfortunes. For example, in June 1676, 'Upon request of Francis Wharton, late an Assistant, now in great want, it [was] Ordered he be paid a pension of £3 p. ann. by 15s. a quarter.'[15] Gabrielle Hoare, a Liveryman who had, in his time, served the office of Steward, but 'through great Losses' had fallen to 'a low and mean condition', asked to be discharged from the Livery. The Court regretfully agreed and gave him £4. In a similar case in March 1684 the Court granted £2 to a 'very poor' Liveryman and a month later awarded him a yearly pension of 20s.[16] When Richard Hill, one of the Assistants, was reported (January 1677) as 'reduced to a very low mean Estate, through great disappointments and losses by trade', the Court deputed four of its members to call immediately upon him and his wife, to talk over the situation with them, and if the misfortune appeared to be genuine, to make a gift not exceeding £12. A few months later the Company gave Richard Hill a chaldron of coal.[17] The Company's occasional gifts were sometimes relatively large, sometimes quite small; which suggests that each case was carefully considered on its merits. Thus, in 1687 'a poor Member', a 'very poor woman' and a 'poor ancient man', each received 2s. 6d.; but only 6d. was given to 'a poor man'; and in 1689–90 one 'poor Member' received £3; another 10s., while a third was awarded only 1s.[18]

Imprisonment for debt, which was very common in the seventeenth and eighteenth centuries, could be a terrible fate for anyone who had no friends able and willing to 'help him out', for, as we have seen in Chapter 2, the debtors' prisons or 'compters' were dreadful dens of dirt, disease, degradation and vice, even by the standards of those times. Dekker, who had first-hand experience of London's prisons, voiced a heartfelt plea for 'the distressed in Ludgate, the miserable souls in the Holes of the two Counters, the afflicted in the Marshall-sea, the Cryers-out for Bread in the King's Bench, and White Lyon'. In May 1654, the Weavers' records run: 'This Court taking notice of the condition of Reynold Collins, late servant of the Company, he being now in prison, do order that [the Renter Bailiff] shall disburse 5s. to the said Mr. Collins towards his relief.'[19] When somebody told the Court in the autumn of 1662 that Edward Hager, a freeman, had been a long time in prison (doubtless for debt) and 'might now come forth if he had but Money to pay his fees, and he had 5s. in his hand for that use already', the Court instructed the Renter Warden to 'make up that 5s. to 40s. and he is desired to see the same laid for his (Hager's) enlargement accordingly'. Shortly afterwards the Court, having heard that George Bridge, a Liveryman, was 'ruined' and lying in the King's Bench prison, decided to pay from the Company's funds a reasonable fee to the prison keeper so that Bridge might be 'removed into the Rules',[20] where he would be able to work at his trade; and then the balance of £5 (his original Livery fine) was to be returned to him and he was to be discharged from the Livery.[21] In November 1668 the Company gave five shillings to secure the release of 'John Nicholls, one of our Livery now prisoner in the Marshalsea, in part of his [livery] fine of £5 intended to be returned to him'.[22] On another occasion the Court granted up to £3 to procure the release of one Jennings, 'an ancient member' of the Company, who 'now lyeth in Wood Street Compter for a small debt'.[23] Another member, William Burnham, was rescued from Newgate in January 1673, by a grant of £1 from the Company.[24] Two years later, 'upon Petition of John Crouch, a poor Member, having been in Prison and now sick' the Court voted 5s., and a similar sum to another poor member, Daniel Wilcox, whose condition was 'very sad'. In 1677, two members—one a Liveryman—who were in prison for debt, regained their liberty with the Company's help.[25]

Poor widows were always treated with kindness and compassion, their poverty being relieved usually by gifts in money or kind, by pensions and, after the erection of the twelve almshouses in 1670, by election to places among the almswomen. When a male pensioner died, his pension might, at the Company's discretion, be settled upon his widow.[26] The grant of pensions to widows seems to have been quite usual at least as early as the beginning of the seventeenth century. Thus, Widow Thorpe was promised 'the next pension which shall happen in the Company' after 6 October 1612, and Widow Mott, 'late wife of John Mott, deceased', was given a similar promise in 1618.[27] When Mrs Hester Jackson, the widow of a freeman who 'had borne all offices in the Company', was left almost destitute after her husband's death, the Court rose to the occasion by giving her 30s. immediately out of the poor's box and promising 10s. a quarter until a regular pensioner's place fell vacant, when she should have it.[28] Ann Rash, widow of an active and respected member of the Company, appeared and told the Court in June 1664 that her late husband 'by reason of great losses and crosses in the World did leave her in a very sad and deplorable condition with 10 children (8 being now alive)', but no money with which to 'drive a small trade towards their maintenance'. Whereupon 'in tender consideration' the Court voted £3.[29] Another sad case of a woman who had known better days was that of Mrs Daniell, the widow of Richard Daniell, 'an ancient master of the Company' who was Renter Bailiff in 1651 and Upper Bailiff in 1655, 'now (1669) reduced to low condition'. She was given a pension of 15s. a quarter.[30] The Renter Bailiffs' accounts contain many records of small occasional gifts such as:

21 October 1668
  Given Widow Shepheard of Hackney   2s. 6d.
23 December 1668
  Given Widow Troughton a Poor Petitioner   2s. 6d.
4 October 1675
  Given Widow Cuckoo a poor woman   5s. 0d.[31]

There were, of course, other useful ways of helping widows, such as putting their children into apprenticeships or employment,[32] or finding employment for the widows themselves. In the spring of 1662, Widow Elizabeth Major reminded the Court of Assistants that her late husband had 'been at the charge of buying racks and spits and all other things needful and convenient for the use of this Company, and she having a great charge of Children', applied to be appointed cook to the Company 'in the room or stead of her late husband'. To this the Court agreed on condition 'that she do from time to time give content unto the Stewards of the Company . . . she providing such assistants' as shall also give satisfaction.[33]

A unique case, at least so far as the Weavers' records go, comes to light from the first decade after the Restoration. In August 1660 John Ash, Citizen and Weaver of London, executed a deed of gift (confirmed in his will) whereby he gave £500 to the Weavers' Company

. . . in Trust to pay £30 by half-yearly payments . . . during his life, and after his Death to his wife Elizabeth during her life, and after both their deaths to James Ash their son during his life. And after his decease then in Trust to Dispose of the principal sum, and all Interest, to and for the Use and Benefit of the said Corporation and the poor People thereof according to the discretion of the Bailiffs, Wardens and Assistants of the said Company.[34]

The Company's Bailiffs and Wardens were named as trustees and executors of the will, and when John Ash died at the beginning of 1661, it was decided to purchase of William Lambert a house in Bread Street for £200, by way of partial investment of the trust fund. This house was entirely destroyed in the Great Fire and (as we have noted in Chapter 9) the empty site was sold to Thomas Bostock, a scrivener, in the spring of 1668 for £142. Meantime the balance of John Ash's gift was put towards the purchase price (£620) of a farm at Shenfield in Essex. The dates of the deaths of Elizabeth Ash and her son, James Ash, are not recorded, but on 14 September 1668 the Court minute book tells us that

> Whereas heretofore Mr. John Ash deceased late a member of this Company, did in his life time give and bestow upon this Company £500 for certain uses. . . . Now at this Court John Ash eldest Grandson of the said Mr. Ash together with his Uncle . . . appearing and producing Certificates of the death of James Ash, son of ye said John (deceased) . . . and declaring that they were lately arrived from Holland in expectation of receiving somewhat by the death of his Grandmother, but being therein disappointed and having been at very great charge in their voyage, lying 7 weeks at Sea, and praying ye charity of this Company towards their return, this Court in rememberance of the said deceased Mr. Ash and in pity and compassion to his Grandchildren, especially to him and Uncle now present, do agree and order for supplying their present necessities and enabling them to return home that [the Renter Bailiff] do presently pay . . . six pounds as of the free gift of this Court. And the same was accordingly now paid in Court to ye hands of the said Grandson.[35]

Two other benefactions by well-to-do members which date from this period are Mr William Cade's legacy of £50 in trust to enable the Company to 'pay to three poor men such as they think fit, 20 shillings a piece every year quarterly',[36] and Rowland and John Morton's conveyance to the Company in consideration of a cash payment of £50, of 'all their freehold messuages called Hatchett's and Gillett's', and of some six acres of farmland at Billericay in the parish of Great Burstead in Essex, upon trust to pay £13 a year to Richard Morton for life, to be distributed by him among the Company's poor, and after his death the whole income to be used by the Company for the benefit of poor members. The deeds were sealed on 28 July 1664, and in gratitude the Court of Assistants ordered that 'the Effigies of Mr.

Rowland Morton be drawn and put in the hall for a good benefactor to the poor of this Company'. The Weavers owned the two Essex farms for over two centuries, and their management gave many a good excuse for the Officers to get away from the smell and smoke of the 'great wen' into the fresh air of the pleasant Essex countryside.[37]

In the early summer of 1669, when the new Weavers' Hall was nearing completion, the Company received from William Watson, one of its members, a most generous offer, which was communicated to the Court of Assistants by the Upper Bailiff at their midsummer meeting.

> Our Mr. [Master or Upper Bailiff] now intimating the willingness of one, Mr. Watson, a Member of this Company, to give and bestow £200 towards some Almshouses to be built for some poor Members of this Company do thankfully accept and imbrace and do order that our Mr. and Mr. Warden James do return to Mr. Watson ye hearty thanks of this Court for this his charitable intention. And this Company do agree that 12 rooms be built upon a piece of ground at Shoreditch which Our Mr. and Warden James are in treaty for and near conclusion with ye Parish; and ye Company to pay what ye said £200 shall fall short in that affair.[38]

The piece of land, 'near the highway leading from the Parish Church of St. Leonard [Shoreditch] . . . unto Hogsdon', was leased from the parish trustees for a term of 200 years at a yearly rental of 6s.[39] Drawings were prepared and building began at once. During July and August 1669 the master carpenter received £45, and the master bricklayer £50, for materials and labour 'upon acct. for ye Compa. Almshouses', and a number of similar payments were made to various master craftsmen early in the following year, including £12. 10s. in April 1670 to a carpenter 'for setting up Rails abt. ye Almshouses'. The water supply was by a hand-pump from a well until 1707, when a supply of New River water was laid on. Digging the well cost 24s. and lining it with bricks 13s. 6d.[40] The principal master craftsmen were Jonah Lewis and Thomas Seagood, both of whom were employed on the rebuilding of the Hall. Jonah Lewis's son was also employed on the almshouses.[41]

Quite a number of groups of almshouses, such as William Watson's, and those given by Sir Robert Geffreye (1715) which still adorn the Kingsland Road a little to the north of Shoreditch Church, were built in the seventeenth and eighteenth centuries. The eastern fringe of London's liberties was ideal for this purpose,[42] for land was cheap, the situation open and rural, yet the pensioners were not too remote from their friends nor from the Companies' Halls in the City where they had to present themselves to collect their pensions. The Weavers' almshouses, their twelve rooms clean and bright with new whitewash, were ready for occupation by August 1670. A plaque on the façade told the passer-by that 'This Building was erected by the Company of Weavers, London, towards the charge whereof Mr. William Watson, a Member of the same Company, was a good benefactor, 1670'. The first person to be admitted, early in August, was Sarah Scruby, widow, of Cripplegate. Three weeks later, when two more from Cripplegate and four from Shoreditch were admitted, there seems to have been a modest celebration, for the Renter Bailiff 'Spent when the Alms People were admitted, 8s. 2d.'[43] Early in October 1670 an eighth almswoman, Alice Clay, recommended by the Churchwardens and overseers of the Poor of the Parish of St Giles, Cripplegate, was admitted to one of the 'houses'. But men, it seems, were not excluded at this time, for the almshouses were built 'for some poor Members' of the Company, not for widows only. Having observed the courteous rule 'Ladies first', the Company admitted, in 1671, 'John Jenkins, Citizen and Weaver, an ancient Inhabitant in Cripplegate parish', and Philip Mould, another 'ancient member' who was recommended by none other than the benefactor, Mr Watson.[44]

The admission of parishioners from St Giles, Cripplegate, to the new almshouses made the overseers of the parish of St Leonard, Shoreditch, apprehensive lest the almsfolk from Cripplegate could be deemed to have gained a legal settlement in Shoreditch whereby they might, at some future date, become chargeable not to Cripplegate but to Shoreditch for the provision of necessaries, medical care and nursing during sickness and senility, and perhaps burial expenses also. Thus, when Rachel Goodhead of the parish of St Giles without Cripplegate, a weaver's widow, was admitted to the Weavers' Almshouses, the Churchwardens of St Giles's gave a written undertaking to indemnify both the Weavers' Company and the Churchwardens of St Leonard, Shoreditch, against all such expenses in the future.

Normally, relations between the two parishes and the Company were businesslike and amicable. There was, however, a slight skirmish in the summer of 1671, when the Shoreditch Churchwardens asked the Company to modify the line of a wall so as to 'better the passage' of the inhabitants of Hoxton. To this the Company agreed in principle, but when the Shoreditch vestry tried to avoid paying for the work involved, the Company threatened 'not to receive any of the Poor' of Shoreditch into their almshouses in future. And their annoyance increased in May 1672, when the Company was indicted for encroaching upon common land by 'setting up rails and posts in ye King's waste before their Almshouses at Hogsdon', and was forced to withdraw its fence. Happily, a month later the tension relaxed and a satisfactory settlement was reached regarding the wall.[45]

The Company next turned its attention to the immediate surroundings of the almshouses; a gardener was employed and, in December 1671, £7 were spent on plants, trees and labour.[46] The worthy Mr Watson, however, being elderly himself, was less concerned about the outdoor amenities than with the indoor comforts of the almspeople. In the winter of 1672 we find him

> proposing to lay the poor of the Compa. Almshouses in yearly 3 Chaldrons of Coals and offering [to the Company] fifty pounds towards ye same, towards payment of which he delivered 11 pairs of broad Garters, 12 pairs of 8*d*., 10 pieces of 10*d*., and 15 pieces of 6*d*. ribbons, amounting according at his rate to £20. 19*s*. which offer the Compa. kindly accepted as also ye said Garters and Ribbons at ye rate aforesaid.

When these goods were sold by the Company they realised only £15 which was 'in the judgement and opinion of the Court as much as the same are worth having been long made and the colours greatly prejudiced and out of fashion'. On 19 February 1672 Mr Watson paid to the Company £30 in cash, which, with the proceeds of the sale of the garters and ribbons, would enable four sacks of coal to be given every year to each of the old people in the Almshouses.[47] Sad to relate, this was probably the last of his benefactions, for on 27 February 1673 a Court minute records that 'Mr. Will. Watson, a Member of this Company, dying ye 25th instant, was this day buried from the Hall.'[48] We cannot doubt that a numerous company of Citizens and Weavers gathered to pay their last respects to such a 'good Benefactor' and that the Company's pall was used.

The City companies' palls, or hearse cloths, were often magnificent examples of embroiderer's work,

> Most prized for art, and laboured o'er with gold,

consisting usually of a centre rectangle of cloth of gold measuring about 6 feet by 2 feet, to the sides and ends of which were attached embroidered and fringed velvet flaps, some 10 or 12 inches in depth. The Saddlers' pall was of crimson velvet with a centre of yellow silk; the Pewterers had 'an hers cloth of gold' with the Company's arms embroidered thereon and four figures of St Michael the Archangel with twelve 'flowers of gold'.[49] The richly embroidered pall of the Merchant Taylors' Company is illustrated in Unwin's *Gilds and Companies of London* (opposite page 226); and he mentions somewhat similar palls used by the Ironmongers, Fishmongers and Vintners. As for the Weavers' Company, an item in the inventory of 1575 mentions a 'hearse cloth with certain arms in yellow cotton'; probably on blue velvet, since yellow and blue are the Company's colours. But later records point decisively to a much richer and more elaborate cloth, which may have been made early in the seventeenth century.

We know that it bore the Company's arms and at least six figures (of which some or all may have been saints) almost certainly embroidered in gold wire. Also there may have been symbols suggesting weaving, such as shuttles and sheep, intermingled with some conventional floral decoration. In 1650 the Weavers were able to pawn this hearse cloth for £20—quite a large sum—and as we have seen in Chapter 5, seven years later 125 silver spoons were sold for £47 to meet the cost of repairing it.[50] Occasionally the pall was hired, presumably by members of the Company or their widows, for fees which ranged from £1 to £3. For example, in September 1671 the Company 'Recd. of Widow Shepheard for the use of the hearse cloth, £2'.[51] Towards the end of 1718 the Company, apparently short of money, decided to sell the pall 'for the best price obtainable'; but there were no offers[52] and the pall was reprieved for fifteen years. The end came in 1733 when the Court of Assistants 'Resolved that six of the figures of the Company's pall be burnt [? melted down] and the produce of them reported to the next full Court and that the four Officers in place see this Resolution executed'; and a month later 'Ordered that the four in place do buy a Blue Cloth to cover the Table in the Court Room, and that the Arms upon the Pall be placed upon the said cloth.'[53]

To return to the seventeenth century. Another benefactor who, like Rowland Morton, had his portrait hung in Weavers' Hall, was Richard Mulford. He first appears in the autumn of 1674 when three Assistants and the Clerk were deputed to discuss with him his proposal to give £150 towards 'the building of 6 rooms for Almspeople of the Company on a piece of ground near the Halfway House, Islington'. But when it seemed likely that the scheme would involve the Company in too much expense, the matter was dropped.[54] Shortly afterwards, perhaps as an alternative to the original plan, Mr Mulford lent £200 to the Company, receiving interest at 6 per cent per annum until his death in 1683, when the Company repaid £100 to his widow, retaining the other £100 upon trust to provide, from the income, two coats every year for two poor men and two gowns for two poor women, being freemen and freemen's widows living in the parish of St Botolph, Bishopsgate. The gifts were made each Good Friday[55] 'on the certificate and request of the churchwardens' who had little difficulty in finding four 'suitable objects' among the closely packed population of weavers in their parish.[56] Any money over and above the tailor's bill was shared among the chosen four.[57]

Several similar gifts were received during the seventeenth century. In 1675, John Satchwell left to the Company a legacy of £60, the interest to be used to provide new shoes and stockings for eight freemen or widows living in the parish of St Giles without Cripplegate. James Kymier provided £50 in 1679 on condition that the Company would 'lay out yearly for ever £2. 8s. 0d. in seacoles and distribute

them among the Alms People at Shoreditch and lay out 12s. for meat
and drink for them on St. Andrew's day for ever'.[58] Richard Gervies
advanced £100 to the Company in 1692 on condition that £4 per
annum should be paid to him during his lifetime, and after his death
the same sum to be used annually—£2 to bind an apprentice from the
parish of St Leonard, Shoreditch, and £2 to be given to poor weavers'
widows in the parish of St Leonard, Shoreditch and St Giles, Cripplegate.[59] If no suitable 'poor man's son' could be found in any year,
then the churchwardens divided the £4 between twenty-four poor
widows, twelve from Shoreditch, six from Cripplegate Within and six
from Cripplegate Without. Towards the end of the century another
donor, John Drigue, gave £50 to the Company, 'the interest thereof
[about £2 per annum] to be employed for the clothing of one poor
Weaver and the Widow of one Weaver of Bishopsgate to be nominated by the Company on 24th August, those once nominated to have
it during life unless the circumstances be altered'.[60] About the same
time, John Hall created a somewhat complicated charity by bequeathing to the Company a house in Nicholas Lane, the rent from
which was to be applied as shown in Table 12.2.[61]

Table 12.2 *Charitable uses of rent income from John Hall's gift*

Application of rent	£	s.	d.
To St. Bartholomew's Hospital at Christmas	2	0	0
To the Preacher of the Wednesday Lecture in the Church of St. Clement, East Cheap, to be paid on the Thursday next before Easter	1	10	0
To the Churchwardens of that Parish, same day, to buy 2 Turkeys for the Parishioners to be eaten that day at the Feast called the Reconciling Feast or Love Feast		10	0
To the Heirs of John Hall at Christmas	3	0	0
To 6 poor Freemen of the Weavers' Company each St. James's Day	1	16	0
To the 4 Officers of the Company 2s. each		8	0
To the Clerk of the Weavers' Company for writing the names of the 6 poor		2	0
	9	6	0

Provided that the Heirs and Assigns shall out of the £3 yearly
pay 20s. to some Pious and Learned student in Divinity for his
better Encouragement and Subsistence.

The premises, 'then known by the sign of the Swan', were on the east
side of Nicholas Lane in the parish of St Martin Orgar, and eventually
became No. 20. The house was a tall, narrow, brick building consisting

of a shop at ground-floor level, and over the shop two rooms, one above the other, one having 'a wooden balcony fronting the street'. Higher still there was a garret. Beneath the shop was a cellar, and under the street in front of the house, a vault.[62]

About the turn of the century Samuel Saunders provided that from the interest on a capital sum of £200 the Company was to spend yearly, on the first Monday in October, '£8 in the clothing of 3 poor Freemen [aged] 50 years at least, and 3 poor Freemen's Widows [aged] 50 years at least, as the Court shall appoint'; each to have 'a Coat or Gown of Cloth of a Brown Colour of the Value of 18s.: and a pair of Shoes and Stockings of 6s. price, and 2s. and eightpence in money'; the recipients were to be two persons within Norton Folgate ('if none be found, then in Shoreditch'), two persons in Shoreditch and two in Bishopsgate. Usually one man and one woman from each of the three districts received 'Saunders' Gift' during the eighteenth century (see Table 12.3).[63]

Table 12.3 *Accounts of 'Saunders' Gift', 1748*

Each man	£	s.	d.	Each woman	£	s.	d.
Coat, 3 yds. cloth @ 4/–		12	0	Gown, 3⅓ yds. @ 4/–		13	4
Making		2	6	Making		2	0
Buttons		1	0	Shoes		2	6
Shoes		4	6	Stockings		2	0
Stockings		2	0	Paid in money		6	10
Paid in money		4	8				
	1	6	8		1	6	8

One of the Company's most loyal members and 'good benefactors' in the seventeenth century was Alexander Hosea (b. c. 1620; d. 1686) who was a useful, co-operative Liveryman during the 1660s and was for many years a member of the Court of Assistants. He did his duty as Steward in 1662. In 1667 he gave advice on engine-looms and was chosen to serve on a special committee 'touching the rebuilding of the Hall', generously subscribing £20 to the Hall rebuilding fund. These services brought him the offices of Upper Warden in 1669, Renter Bailiff in 1671, and Upper Bailiff in 1675.[64] He gave £7 to the barge building fund in 1672 and presented seven trumpeters' cloaks and three coats for the drummers. During his year as Renter Bailiff he was appointed with his friend John Shewell, six other Assistants, six of the Livery, and four of the Yeomanry, to be 'Appraisers of such forraign Work as shall be imported & taken by ye officers of ye Customs'.[65] He signed as one of the Company's Auditors in 1676–7 and again in 1680–1.

Hosea was a native of the small Gloucestershire town of Wickwar, near Wotton-under-Edge, where the chief industry, apart from farming, was the manufacture of woollen cloth.[66] As a lad he was apprenticed to weaving, probably in his native place; but ambition moved him to try his fortune in London, where, under Cromwell and Charles II, this enterprising 'foreigner' from the West Country became a successful all-round 'man of mixed enterprise'—manufacturer, merchant, moneylender, ship and property owner, with a network of interests at home and abroad. As a master silk and lace weaver he had apprentices, and men and women in his employ: as a merchant he exported silk goods (ribbons and lace chiefly) to the West Indies and New England, and imported sugar, rum, wine and other valuable commodities. Evidently he was in a flourishing trade at the right time, for as 'the West Indians grew rich . . . the merchants who dealt with them grew richer still'.[67] A number of entries in his executors' accounts indicate that his shipping interests were far from negligible and probably contributed substantially to the growth of his fortune.[68] Five ships are named: *Constant, Friendship, Morea, John and Sara* and *Speedwell* (see Table 12.4).

Table 12.4 *Entries from Hosea's executors' accounts*

Date	Item	£	s.	d
Aug. 31 1686	Received of Capt. Wm. Barnham for 1/8th part of ye Ship *Constant* valued by 2 of Trinity House & Some others at £379.3.6.	47	7	10
Feb. 2 1687	Of Mr. Gregory Page for 1/8th pt. of £17 divided for 4 guns upon ye Ship *Morea*	2	2	6
Nov. 16 1688	Of Mr Jno. Huntington . . . for 1/8th part of ye Ship *Speedwell* (being sunke at Hull) as p. appraisement	6	0	0
Apr. 27 1689	For 1/8th pt. of ye Ship *John & Sara* & Cargo sold to ye African Company for £1,100, and share of trading profits £23.4.5. (less legal and other expenses) Net	151	14	5

As his fortune grew, Hosea made a number of substantial loans at interest, some of them to his young relatives to help set them up in business either at home or abroad. For example, to John Hosea of Jamaica (son of Alexander Hosea's cousin, Robert Hosea, carrier, deceased) the testator left a legacy of £300, from which the executors deducted John Hosea's debt of £226; and to Thomas Collins and his son he gave £100 and £200 respectively, 'which said sums Thomas Collins the Father hath already in his hands and is to pay mee interest for it'. After Hosea's death his executors set about collecting the many sums due, but it was slow work.[69] Fifteen years after Hosea's death his executors, still trying to collect outstanding debts, compiled a list (see Table 12.5).

Table 12.5 *Money owed to Hosea's estate, July 1701**

Debtor	£	s.	d.	
Voyage to Canary, Robt. Sanderson	32	4	7	
Tho. King,	11	12	0	dead
Symon Smith,	20	10	7	denys it
Ben. Mountfort, New England	10	19	6	
Nath. Byefield, New England	9	18	10	
Richd. Gyles in Kent	4	10	0	

* Incomplete list.

From time to time, Hosea seems to have done a little pawnbroking, for his executors found among his belongings, 'a silver spoone formerly pawned by Peter Collidge and 5 plaine gold rings and a silver seal, pawned by Mrs. Jane Baker'. These unredeemed pledges were sold to Mr Sweetapple, the jeweller, for £2. 11s. 10d.[70]

Lastly we come to Hosea's investments in real estate: a tavern, six freehold houses, five tenements, and 33 leasehold houses in London; a farm and farmhouse in Kent, and some mills at Kingston-on-Thames.[71] Not long before he died he had leased a private residence at Hackney (then a quiet village on the rural fringes of London), and in his will he gave to his cousin, Anne Lazanby, £200 'besides what I owe her', and 'the household goods in my new dwelling house if I dye before she marries, and I doe forgive her all she owes mee for dyett in consideration of the Interest I owe her'.[72] Hosea's business premises —workshops, warehouse and counting house—were probably in Basinghall Street and Mumford's Court, Milk Street, where he leased no fewer than seven houses from the Mercers' Company.[73]

The spring of 1686 found Hosea a very sick man, and early in May he left London to stay with his cousin, Thomas Collins, at Nind (probably Nind Farm) in his native Gloucestershire[74] where, three weeks later, he died, despite the efforts of two doctors (father and son) and the local apothecary, supported by the compassionate nursing of two servants—'Sara Prout and Mary Taylor yt helped him at his death'. Nor must we overlook Obadiah Williams who received ten shillings 'for fetching and applying Leeches to him'.[75]

Hosea's will, dated 19 March 1684, requested that he should be buried 'by or near my loving Wife in the parish church of St. Law-rence Jury [Jewry], London', and directed that not more than £400 should be spent upon his funeral. As executors he appointed his cousin (and business partner) Joseph Collins, and his 'loving friends' John Shewell, Citizen and Weaver of London (who was Upper Bailiff in 1679–80) and 'Thomas Powell of Key Court in the parish of St. Mary Aldermary, Master of Arts'. He appointed also two 'overseers' of his will: John Mumford, Citizen and Grocer of London, and William James, Citizen and Weaver, who preceded Hosea as Upper Bailiff in 1674–5.

Hosea's body was brought back to London[76] where it lay at Weavers' Hall as befitted such a highly respected past Upper Bailiff and benefactor. The Hall was heavily draped with black baize, and on 1 July 1686 eight bearers, wearing mourning hatbands, black scarves and 'broad black ribbons', bore the coffin, which was doubtless covered with the Weavers' funeral pall, to the church of St Lawrence Jewry where it was interred in 'the Little Vault'.[77] The executors' accounts show the customary funeral expenditure upon mourning dress for the executors, overseers, close relatives and their wives, and upon burial rings, escutcheons, gloves, hatbands, scarves, rosemary etc.[78] The total was £387. 12s. 8d.

For the executors the funeral was little more than a prelude to their main task of realising Hosea's assets, paying his debts and distribut-ing the legacies in accordance with his will: a long and complicated business which, as it turned out, dragged on for eighty years. The early stages of this marathon, which were simple enough, included a careful search to make sure that the will of 1684 was, in fact, Hosea's last will. Relevant entries in the executors' cash book (f.1) are shown in Table 12.6.

Having failed to find a will more recent than that of March 1684, with its codicil dated 13 September of the same year, the executors turned to the settlement of the Testator's debts and legacies (Table 12.7.)

To his many relatives Alexander Hosea left some fifty pecuniary legacies, ranging from £5 to £300, and amounting in all to £3,685; but his gifts to non-relatives were only five in number: £50 to Thomas Pitts, Citizen and Weaver of London; an annuity of £10 'to the lame son of Thomas Pitts'; £10 and £40 respectively to two former men-servants, and £70 'to Elizabeth Tallent my now servant'. To St Bartholomew's, St Thomas's and Bethlehem Hospitals, Hosea left legacies of £200 each, and to the Mayor, Aldermen and Borough of Wickwar £600 'for and towards the maintenance of a public School there' for children whose parents 'are poore, that they may be taught to write and read'.[79] Before all these legacies could be paid in full the executors needed to raise over £5,000; not an easy task because the properties were, on the whole, in a poor state of repair.[80] The houses

Table 12.6 *Entries from Hosea's executors' cash book*

1686	Item	£	s.	d.
May 24	To cash, resting as p. his cash booke at his death	213	2	9
	For 8 pieces of 20s. gould in his drawers at Hackney	9	8	0
	Of Eliz. his maide being left of yt. money Mr. Hosea had about him when he died more than wt. she laid out in ye Country & her charges to London		6	6
	In a paper 4s. 2d. being recd. formerly of Mr. Thomas Smith for pewter		4	2
June 7	For a coatch to Hackney & back with Mr. Shewell, Mr. James & Capt. Hosea to See for another will		6	0
	For opening ye Locks & Mending of ym		2	0

Table 12.7 *The settlement of Hosea's debts and legacies*

Date	Item	£	s.	d.
1686				
July 12	To Mr. Daniell Collins for his charges & horse going into Glostershire at Mr. Hosea's death	2	0	0
	To Mr. Thomas Collins for Mr. Hosea's being at his house, his horse & other charges	12	18	0
	To Mr. Gyles Biddle for his service to Mr. Hosea & in his last Sickness & coming up to London &c.	5	7	6
July 21	To Mr. Thomas Ward & Mr. William Meakins for apraising ye goods at Hackney & at London	3	0	0
Oct. 12	To Mr. Thomas Hilliard ye Brewer for beer & ale delivered at Hackney from ye 1 Jan. to 22 September '86	8	8	0
Oct. 12	To Mr. Wm. Harney for ¾ rent for ye house at Hackney	10	9	6
Nov. 13	To Mr. Vernam ye furrier for 4 years ¾ keeping Mr. Hoseas goune		19	0
1687				
May 21	To Capt. Jas. Bayley for 5 gall. & 3 pints Canary at 5s. 6d. sould to ye Testator in his life time	1	9	6

in Knuckles Alley, Long Acre, were sold in 1687, for £600, and in the same year the sum of £325 was realised by the sale of some of the Kentish farmland. It was not until four years later, however, that the executors were able to sell the houses at Broken Cross, Westminster, together with the mills and land at Kingston, to the same purchaser, for a total of £1,875.[81] After this a number of legacies could be discharged, including those to St Bartholomew's and Bethlehem hospitals. Meanwhile 'the household goods & wares . . . appraised in ye Inventory of Joseph Collins' realised £164. 10s. 6d., and '2 Servants of ye Testator formerly sold in Jamaica for £20' brought in £16. 10s. net, after deduction of commission and expenses.[82]

Hosea's will provided that the 'overplus', or residue, of his estate should go 'to such poore Tradesmen and women as they [his executors] shall think fit, no one to have less than £5': a distribution which took seventy years to complete; from May 1695 when the first payment of £10 from the overplus was made 'to Mr. Hercules Beaufoy, Weaver,[83] ye Testators intimate acquaintance, being aged and poor and low', until January 1766 when the successors of the original executors finally closed the account. Legacies amounting in all to more than £1,000 were distributed to eighty men and sixty women, nearly a quarter of whom were employed in the making of silk textiles, lace and garments in and around London. The chief occupational sub-groups are shown in Table 12.8.

Table 12.8 *Chief occupational sub-groups to benefit under Hosea's will*

| | No. of | |
Occupation	Men	Women
Weavers	8	2
Bonelace makers (all employees of Alexander Hosea)	—	4
Buttonmakers	—	2
Wire-drawers and silver spinners	6	1
Silk spinners or throwsters	—	3
Stocking-frame weavers	2	—
Mantua makers	—	3
Milliners	—	4
Tailors	3	—
Shopkeepers	—	8

Poor and needy workers in other occupations were also helped, like 'Sara Bowne, tobacco cutter & stripper, being very poor & blind', who received £10, and Robert Langden of Poplar, a ship's carpenter, aged about sixty-four years, 'haveing been a careful labouring man in his business, & being poor & following his Trade', to whom the executors granted £10. 15s.[84] Legacies were given, too, to seven tradesmen and women of Hackney and Homerton, where Hosea resided: a shoemaker, barber, farrier, chimney sweep, milliner, chandler, and washer each received between £5 and £7. Very little was distributed outside London and Hackney. Two women—a windster and a mantua maker—living in Colchester received legacies, and so did two clothiers of Nind and a serge weaver of Wotton-under-Edge, all three of whom were men.[85]

Hosea's bequest to the Weavers' Company 'towards the relief of the poor of that Company' took the form of houses in Holborn, joining with the Swan tavern, on the north side of Holborn opposite Holborn Bars, on the west corner of Baker's Court or Alley and partly over the entry to the court.[86] The executors' accounts to Michaelmas 1693 show rent arrears amounting to £50. 16s.,[87] and any rosy hopes raised by this benevolent bequest were short-lived for the state of the premises was so bad that only immediate heavy expenditure could prevent rapid dilapidation. Moreover, certain tenants were such bad payers that the Company had to threaten, from time to time, 'to seize for the rent'. The Weavers' account book for the period immediately after October 1694, when the Company entered into possession, contains the following illuminating entry:[88]

> The report of this Charity being spread among the poor of the Company they became so pressing . . . that for the space of eight years the Company were constrained to augment their Charities twenty pounds per ann. upon this account though they did not receive one penny . . . till [15 January 1694], so that from the time this Charity was left to the time possession was delivered to the Company, the Compa. have paid to their poor Members towards their relief . . . £160.

The rent roll at Michaelmas, 1695, stood as shown in Table 12.9. In the following year the Company, dealing with the most urgent repairs, paid £129 for brickwork, carpentry, plumbing, glazing and painting; and among sundry smaller items, it is recorded, with unconscious humour, that they paid 'for cleaning the common sewer and trained bands £1. 1s. 8d.' Table 12.10 shows the disbursements down to July 1696. The total receipts during the same period were only £235. 1s. 8d.; leaving the Company £288. 19s. 2d. out of pocket.[89] On the other hand, seventy-two poor members had received between them, each year, a total of £67. 12s.

Although the Holborn property was in a rotten, ruinous state, it was, apparently, not ripe for development. When, eventually, Hosea's Charity was put in order, some forty guineas were distributed

Table 12.9 *Hosea's bequest: rent roll, 1695*

Tenants	Gross income from rents p. ann.
	£
Mr. Stanion, baker, in Baker's Court	34
Mr. Isbell	28
Mr. Fisher	6
Mr. Skelton	6
Mr. Trueman	8
Roger Fowler, a room and cellar £3	
Susan Reeves, a chamber £2	8
James Eades, a chamber & garrett £3	
	90
plus An empty house formerly let at	7

Table 12.10 *Payments by the Company under Hosea's will*

	£	s.	d.
Advanced by the Company to the poor, 8 years at £20 p. ann.	160	0	0
Payments, e.g. pensions, repairs, taxes etc:			
1694–5 £51 3s. 6d.			
1695–6 £312 17s. 4d.			
	364	0	10
	524	0	10

annually among the Company's poor; but only by dint of careful management by the Company's officers over many years. At the turn of the century the Company paid £474 'towards rebuilding of a house in Holborn'.[90] Early in 1704, Stanion the baker, who was in arrears with his rent, had 'withdrawn himself', and in May, when he gave up his tenancy, the Company made a compassionate grant of £3 to his wife 'towards her relief'. The bakehouse and shop were then let to another tenant at a slightly reduced rent.[91] Six years later a small committee of inspection recommended repairs to the baker's oven, the paving of the passage, the fixing of a watercock near the bakehouse, and the whitewashing of some empty premises so as to improve the prospects of letting.[92] And so things went on for over twenty years until, in 1733-4, the Company began seriously to consider letting the property as a whole 'for a long Term or upon a Building Lease'. This was done early in 1735 when William Westbrook leased the estate for sixty-one years at forty guineas a year.[93] Unfortunately, he allowed the property 'to run to Ruin' and 'great Arrears of Rent' to accumulate, and finally died insolvent in 1751. The Upper and Renter Bailiffs tried to sort out the mess, but litigation dragged on, and not until June 1757 did the Weavers' Company regain possession of the estate.[94] Eventually a new tenant, John Frostick, a carpenter, agreed to pay £40 per annum (the Company paying land tax, £3; and the fire insurance premium of £6. 6s. 6d.) for a lease of forty-one years from Christmas 1757, the lessee to spend £200 on repairs within the first eighteen months.[95] It was this tenant who complained in 1760 that 'the Watch House & Stocks erected partly on the King's Highway and partly on this Company's ground' were a public nuisance and 'greatly detrimental' to the Company's property;[96] but the outcome is not recorded. Ten years later Frostick, like his predecessor, went bankrupt, and one John Noldret took over the remainder of his lease.[97] When this lease expired in 1799 the Company was fortunate enough to let the property to a Mr Solomon Lange for thirty-one years at a much increased rent of £100 per annum, the tenant covenanting to spend £500 on repairs, which were honestly carried out.[98]

The summer of 1727 brought the Weavers the largest windfall they had ever had. Nicholas Garrett of Wandsworth, a wealthy man of Huguenot descent and at one time a silk weaver, who owned several properties in the City of London, in Cambridge, and at Hummerton in Worcestershire, died on 19 June 1726 at the age of sixty-seven, and by a codicil added to his will only six months before, he bequeathed £1,000 East India stock to the London Weavers' Company for the building and endowment of six almshouses for poor members.[99] This was indeed a generous gift, for the market price of East India stock then stood around 173-4, so that the cash value of the legacy was well over £1,700; enough to pay for a site and buildings and leave a balance for pensions and maintenance. In March 1728 the Company's officers spent 2s. at Batson's Coffee House, 2s. 1½d. at the Royal Oak and 11s. 10d. at the Three Tuns in Bishopsgate when they went to look for a suitable site; and in April and May they went as far afield as Bow and Pimlico. Finally, in October, they 'agreed for Mr. Tilliard's ground in Porter's fields, to build ye 6 Almshouses directed by Mr. Garrett's Will' at a price of £100, and marked the occasion by spending 25s. on a little celebration at the Three Tuns.[100]

Unlike the Hoxton almshouses which provided only one room for each pensioner, the new ones were designed to 'consist of two Rooms one over the other'. It was decided to build in red brick, with a tiled roof, and in March 1729 a tender of £420 was accepted by the Company; £250 to be paid when the roof tiles were fixed, and the balance on completion of the work. By early October the work was finished, the builders received their second payment (£170) and a bill of extra charges amounting to £32. 12s. 3d. was under consideration by the Court.[101]

At a Full Court in mid-October Mr Malton, one of the Assistants, announced that he intended to resign from the Court and become a candidate for one of the new almshouses. His colleagues were astonished but not hostile, and he was duly elected to Nicholas Garrett's almshouse No. 1. The same Court, having decided that the houses should be for men only, proceeded to elect five poor men to occupy houses Nos. 2 to 6. New River water was laid on; posts were set up in the street five feet from the wall, and a footway outside the wall was made of 'small pebbles or raggs'. Another footway was made 'within the wall from the gate to the Houses and . . . to each of the Bogg Houses with square Wraggs and two foot wide'. Lastly, trees were planted, 'within the wall'.[102] Towards the end of the year, when the Committee inspected the buildings and grounds, the Renter Bailiff recorded: 'Spent at a Review of Mr. Garrett's A.H. with the 4 in Place, &c., 10s. 9d.' A similar visit three months later cost only 3s. 6d. for 'A Pot of Coffee, A Bottle of Wine & Bread & Butter'.[103]

Sometimes it seems that one charitable gift prompts another, which reinforces or supplements the first. This certainly happened in 1731 when Thomas Carpenter, Citizen and Haberdasher of London, bequeathed £300 to the Weavers' Company 'in trust to lay out the interest and profits thereof yearly in the purchasing of coals and candles to be equally distributed between the six Pensioners' living in the Nicholas Garrett almshouses. The legacy, invested in Bank Stock, yielded £11 a year, enough to provide a chaldron of coals and three-and-a-half dozen candles to each almsman; a welcome addition, we may be sure, to their meagre pensions of about £8 a year, or 3s. weekly. It is significant that in 1756 the almsmen asked, and the Company readily agreed, that all the money available from Carpenter's Charity should be spent on coals, for at their time of life warmth was more important than candlelight.[104]

James Limborough, Citizen and Weaver of London, another generous eighteenth-century benefactor and a pious Christian, seems to have had a special concern for the education of children, and for the weavers' spiritual welfare, for by the terms of his will, dated 25 July 1774, he bequeathed £1,800 to be divided between six charity schools, and a capital sum of £3,500, invested in 3 per cent Consolidated Bank Annuities, 'for the support and maintenance' in the neighbourhood of Spitalfields of an annual course of lectures or sermons. Since 1783 these have been known as 'The Limborough Lectures'.

At the time of his death (at the end of 1774 or early 1775) James Limborough was a much respected member of the Weavers' Court of Assistants and, to judge from the terms of his will, quite well off. He was then living at Clapton near Hackney, a rural village overlooking the green and pleasant valley of the River Lea. Here he had acquired a 'new built house' amply and comfortably furnished, where he kept his pictures, plate, jewels, carriage and horses, and employed a small staff of servants. He was a friend of Richard Lea who later became Upper Bailiff (1791–2) and master and father-in-law of Samuel Wilson, a future Lord Mayor.[105] Lea witnessed Limborough's will and, in March 1775, was able to swear to the authenticity of two codicils which were in the testator's handwriting, being 'well acquainted with James Limborough . . . for several years before and to the time of his death and . . . with his manner and character of handwriting'. Limborough left more than twenty legacies to his relatives and servants, his executors, and the four clergymen of the parish of St John at Hackney, amounting in all to £8,140. He left £300 to the London Hospital, £100 to the parish charity school in Hackney, and £300 to each of the parish charity schools of Christ Church, Spitalfields, St Matthew, Bethnal Green, St Botolph, Aldgate and St Botolph, Bishopsgate. He also bequeathed £500 to the Boys' Free School in the Liberty of Norton Folgate, adding at this point the following interesting and unusual proviso:

> and it is my desire that none of the Boys belonging thereto may by virtue or means of this bequest be provided with cloaths, caps or bands or any kind of uniform dress or colour, but that they may continue distinguished in this respect from the general plan of parish Charity Schools for encouragement of the Industrious sort of Poor People who may be glad of an Opportunity of Educating their Children in a decent private manner.

The income from the trust fund did not become available for the Limborough lectures until after the death of James Limborough's wife, Mary, who had a life interest in the fund and who survived her husband for about eight years. After her death the Weavers' Court of Assistants met, in January 1783, 'to accept the Trust concerning £3,500 three p.cts.' Four trustees were appointed (the Upper Bailiff and three Assistants) and arrangements were made to hold the first course of lectures.[106] The will had named the three churches in or near the Spitalfields district in any one of which the lectures might be held, viz., Christ Church, Spitalfields;[107] or St Botolph, Aldgate; or St Botolph, Bishopsgate; and had provided for 'an Evening Lecture to be performed and preached . . . every Sunday for Eight Months in the Year' beginning on the first Sunday in September and ending on the last Sunday in April, 'the same to be performed with the usual Evening Service . . . to begin at or near six of the clock and to end about eight'. The testator wished to benefit 'the Inhabitants in and about the Neighbourhood of Spitalfields where there are a great many Manufacturers of both sexes, several of whom of various conditions may be glad of the Assistance hereby offered to them to fill up the latter part of the Lord's Day in a Religious and pious manner'. [108] Having obtained from the Rector and Churchwardens of Christ Church, Spitalfields, permission to use 'that Church and Pulpit', the Court held a special meeting, on 18 February 1783, attended by the Upper and Renter Bailiffs and eighteen of the Livery, to consider applications from four reverend gentlemen 'of Character and Abilities'. In an election by ballot, nineteen votes were cast, ten of them for the Rev. Henry Foster, who thus became the first Limborough Lecturer, and gave the inaugural Lecture on the first Sunday evening in September 1783.

Each Limborough Lecturer held office for three years at a salary of £50 per annum, and the will empowered the Bailiffs, Wardens and Assistants of the Weavers' Company to expend £7 on 'providing a Dinner for them annually', and to use the residue of the income in paying gratuities to the parish clerk and other officers of the church in which the lectures were given, and upon such necessary expenses as candles. Table 12.11 shows the first disbursements made under the terms of the Limborough lectureship.

The pattern is much the same year after year, but occasionally an unusual item appears. For example, in 1787 '2 Patroles' received 14s., and in 1789 £3. 7s. 4d. was paid to 'Boys for attendance at Doors &c.' In 1792 Mary Pettit received 9s. 7d. 'for Repairs of the Lanthorns', and in 1798 10s. 6d. was paid to an unnamed man 'pr. order of Mr. Lea, Gallery Keeper'. A few small surpluses must have accumulated by this time, sufficient to enable the trustees to grant £25 'for the repair of Christ Church, Spitalfields, out of the Limborough Lecture fund'.[109] A similar grant was made in 1822 towards the installation of gas-lighting in the church.[110] In 1921 and again in 1968 the Charity Commissioners varied the terms of the Trust to bring it into line with modern requirements. An annual sermon is delivered by the Company's Chaplain and Limborough Lecturer. In recent years the Lecture has been given at the Queen's Chapel of the Savoy and has been followed by a reception to the members of the Livery and their guests at the Savoy Hotel.

Table 12.11. *Disbursements made under the terms of the*
Limborough lectureship

1784	Item	£	s.	d.
Mar. 13th	By Cash pd. The Revd. Henry Foster half a years Salary due at Xmas 1783	25	0	0
June 3rd	By -Do- due 26th April 1784	25	0	0
	By Abram. Dupree, Parish Clerk of Christ Church, Spitalfields	5	5	0
	By -Do- John Rondeau, Sexton of -Do-	2	2	0
	By -Do- James Lenham, Beadle of -Do-	1	1	0
	By -Do- James Rogers, Bell Ringer	1	1	0
	By -Do-　　　? 　　　Organist	1	1	0
	By -Do- Susan Bruges, Elizth. Bowster Elizth. Wiltshire, Mary Goddard, Mary Cossar, Nathl. Spurging ⎫ 6 Pew ⎬ Openers ⎭	4	10	0
May 24th	By -Do- Messrs. Cowper & Chapman, Tallow Chandlers Bill	28	19	10
	By -Do- Mr. Briggs, [Weavers'] Company's Clerk	3	3	0
June 3rd	By -Do- Robert LeMare, Beadle of Weavers' Compy.	2	2	0
	By -Do- for the Court of Assistants Dinner	7	0	0
	By -Do- for 6 Rect. stamps		1	6
		106	6	4

NOTES

1 Unwin, *Gilds*, pp. 47, 53
2 MS. 4647, f.413.
3 MS. 4655/3, f.49b.
4 MS. 4655/4, February 1667.
5 MS. 4655/1, ff.81, 87.
6 MS. 4655A, 3 October 1648.
7 MS. 4655A, 3 October and 27 November 1648.
8 MS. 4646, ff.96–7; MS. 4655/2, ff.26, 83.
9 MS. 4655/3, f.164.
10 MS. 4655A/2, 7 and 15 April 1651; MS. 4655/2, f.131.
11 MS. 4655/2, f.107.
12 MS. 4655/4, ff.37b, 63; March–July 1667.
13 MS. 4655/5, ff.63b, 66b.
14 MS. 4655/9, f.43b; MS. 4655/12, f.125.
15 MS. 4655/88, f.89b.

16 MS. 4655/9, ff.6, 17, 26.
17 MS. 4655/8, ff.112b–113b, 128.
18 MSS. 4649B/1 and 2.
19 MS. 4655/2, f.105.
20 A limited district surrounding or adjacent to the prison, in which the prisoners were allowed to move about or ply their trade.
21 MS. 4655/3, f.63. This, of course, created a vacancy on the Livery, which, when filled, enabled the Company to collect a new fine.
22 MS. 4648/1, 18 November, 4 and 7 December 1668. This John Nicholls had contributed 5s. to the Hall building fund through the French Congregation; see MS. 4648/1, August 1668.
23 MS. 4655A/3. cf. E. Hatton, *A New View of London* (1708), p. 783.
24 MS. 4655/7, f.15b.
25 MS. 4655/8, ff.36, 40b, 133, 133b.
26 MS. 4655/8, ff.72b, 74.
27 MS. 4655/1, ff.20, 80, 96.
28 MS. 4655/3, f.73b. The ages of widows applying for pensions are not usually recorded, but in 1684 the ages of three applicants are given as 67, 71 and 84 (MS. 4655/9, ff.20b, 43b).
29 MS. 4655/3, f.129b.
30 MS. 4655/5, f.52.
31 MS. 4648/1, 1666–82.
32 See, e.g., MS. 4648/1, 19 June 1682.
33 MS. 4655/3, ff.27, 28b.
34 *The Clerk's Report on the Charities*, 1742, f.1; MS. 4646, f.254b.
35 MS. 4655/5, 14 September 1668.
36 MS. 4646, f.255
37 MS. 4646, ff.252; MS. 4655/3, ff.119, 122b–123, 142b.
38 MS. 4655/5, f.64b, 21 June 1669; MS. 4655/6, f.3b; MS. 4646, f. 103.
39 MS. 4646, f.252b. The inventory of 1688 (MS. 4646, ff.295–6) includes 'a lease of the ground at Hogsdon (Hoxton) whereon the Almshouses are built'. cf. MS. 4649A, 2 August 1680 and 31 July 1682; and MS. 4655/22, 7 December 1858.
40 MS. 4648/1, April–August 1670; MS. 4648/3, 20 October 1707; *Reports of the Royal Commission on the Livery Companies of London*, vol. 39 (1884), Part V, pp. 341–64. A new pump was bought in 1690 for £2. 10s. (MS. 4649B/2, 9 August 1690).
41 MS. 4655/6, ff.18, 23, 40.
42 Rose, *The East End of London* (1951), pp. 48–9.
43 MS. 4655/6, f.45b; MS. 4648/1, 22 August 1670; Hatton, op. cit., p. 764.
44 MS. 4655/6, ff.61, 75b, 78b.
45 MS. 4655A/3, *passim*.
46 MS. 4649A.
47 MS. 4655A/3, 15 January and 19 February 1672; MS. 4648/1, 19 January 1672.
48 MS. 4655/7, f.20.
49 C. Welch, *History of the Company of Pewterers* (1902) I, pp. 88–90.
50 MS. 4646, ff.88, 92. See Victoria and Albert Museum/Board of Education, *An Exhibition of Works of Art belonging to the Livery Companies of the City of London* (1927), Plates LXXI–LXXVIII, for examples of Companies' palls.
51 MS. 4646, ff.112, 116; MS. 4648/1, 4 September 1671.
52 MS. 4655/11, f.264b.

53 MS. 4655/13, ff.99, 102. The Pewterers may have done much the same; see Victoria and Albert Museum/Board of Education, op. cit., Plate LXXIX.

54 MS. 4655/8, ff.9b, 35.

55 MS. 4655/9, f.62b. On 24 October 1687 the Renter Bailiff 'Paid to a Painter for changing the picture frame and writing Richd. Mulford a good Benefactor, 8s.'

56 MS. 4655/10, f.43b.

57 In 1829 the Charity Commissioners, after inquiry, held that a charity did exist and that the Company should be spending £6 per annum upon its objects (MS. 4655/20, ff.82–3, 143b).

58 MS. 4646, ff.254b–255.

59 MS. 4655/10, f.10b.

60 MS. 4655/11, f.45a.

61 MS. 4648/6; MS. 4655/10, f.1. The Indenture is dated 11 April 1691.

62 *Clerk's Report on the Charities*, 1742; cf. *Mr. Hare's Report*, 1865. See also a *Scheme for the Regulation and Management of the Charity of John Hall . . . approved by Order of the High Court of Justice (Chancery Division), 1895.*

63 MS. 4655/11, ff.1b, 2b, 27, 45a; MS. 4655/14, f.29; *The Clerk's Report on the Charities*, 1742, f.9.

64 MS. 4655/3, ff.69, 71; MS. 4655/4, f.66; MS. 4655/5, f.9; MS. 4655/6, 8 August 1670; MS. 4655/8, f.56b; MS. 4650; MS. 4646, ff.109, 296; MS. 4648/2.

65 MS. 4655A/3, 8 July 1672.

66 Leland visited the district between 1535 and 1543 and referred to Wickwar as a 'pratye clothing tounlet'. Quoted by J. Tann, *Gloucestershire Woollen Mills* (1967), p. 29. For a detailed study of the numbers employed in agriculture and industrial occupations in Gloucestershire early in the seventeenth century see A. J. and R. H. Tawney, 'An Occupational Census of the Seventeenth Century', *Economic History Review*, October 1934.

67 J. H. Parry, *The Age of Reconnaissance* (1963), p. 265.

68 MS. 4653, ff.4–11, 9, 14–15, 24, 37, 45–7, 51, 56; N. Carlisle, *The Endowed Grammar Schools in England and Wales* (1818), I, p. 463. Local legend has it that Hosea was sent to the bakehouse with a special dish of 'white pot', but on the way he dropped it, 'which so terrified him that he durst not return to his master' but ran away to London.

69 Hosea's Will; MS. 4653, ff.7, 9, 15, 53.

70 MS. 4653, ff.13–14.

71 MS. 4653, ff.12, 16. This property was on the banks of the Hogsmill river, a small stream rising at Ewell and flowing into the Thames at Kingston, which 'abounded in gunpowder mills' driven by water wheels (*V.C.H., Surrey*, II, pp. 312, 327). Hosea's tenant, Mrs Rosamine Rose, may have been in business as a silk throwster; but there is no evidence on this point. In December 1687 the executors allowed her a year's rent 'for ye repairing of ye mills'.

72 P. C. C. Wills, XI, 1686, 90 (Somerset House).

73 MS. 4653, f.3.

74 Hosea's Will; A. H. Smith, *The Place-Names of Gloucestershire*, Part III, pp. 39, 47. In the seventeenth century there was an old fulling mill at Nind and around it a cluster of larger buildings grew up during the eighteenth and nineteenth centuries; but 'by

1897 Nind Mills, the sole cloth mill left in Kingswood had failed'
(J. Tann, op. cit., pp. 52, 92–3, 121).

75 MS. 4653, f.4.

76 The executors paid £24. 7s. to Wm. Russell 'for sending a Hearse
& his man into Glostershire & charges & to bring up the Testators
corpse to London, & being at his house &c.' (MS. 4653, f.10).

77 MS. 6975, Parish Register of St Lawrence Jewry, 1538–1715.

78 MS. 4653, ff.2, 13. Compare Pepys's funeral expenses given in H. B.
Wheatley (ed.), *The Diary of Samuel Pepys* (1928), pp. lv-lviii.
Evelyn mentions Pepys's death (*Diary*, 26 May 1703) and a suit of
mourning presented to him: 'Mr. Jackson [John Jackson, Pepys's
nephew and heir] sent me compleat mourning, desiring me to be
one to hold up the pall at his *magnificent obsequies*. . . . ' Mourning
garments were presented to 40 persons in all, and 123 burial rings
were distributed to Pepys's relatives, godchildren, friends, and
servants, and to representatives of the Royal Society, Oxford and
Cambridge Universities, the Admiralty, the Navy Office, etc.

79 Hosea's Will. The £600 was paid in two equal instalments in 1692
and 1693 (MS. 4653, ff.45, 49–56). The school's governing body
consisted of five trustees who had power 'upon every misdemeanour
to turn out any schoolmaster and place another in his room'. Two
masters were appointed; a Latin, or grammar, master, and a
writing master; their salaries and expenses to be paid from the
income from the Swan tavern, Holborn, with which Hosea had
endowed the school towards the end of his life. The writing master
usually had, on an average, 25 boys and girls on his roll, but the
Latin master never had more than 4 pupils; sometimes none at all.
In 1734 certain inhabitants of Wickwar petitioned the Court of
Chancery, unsuccessfully, to abolish the Latin school and to appoint
'a master to teach boys to read, write and cast accounts, and a
mistress to teach girls to read, knit and sew', for this would be
'most conducive to the good of the poor sort of inhabitants, for
whose benefit the said charity was intended'. The Charity Commissioners visited the school in 1834 and found but few persons in
Wickwar 'who attach importance to a classical education', therefore
'the grammar-school has seldom more than 3 or 5 boys, sometimes
only one, sometimes none'. But the writing school under the parish
clerk who taught reading, writing and common arithmetic, had an
average of 25 *boys*. (Where were the girls?) There was also a rather
unsatisfactory Sunday school, 'but the boys of the free-school are
not required to attend'. The Latin master, the Rev. David Rees,
received £28 per annum, free living accommodation over the school-
room, and a good garden: 'appointed in 1827 . . . he has had no
scholar for three years past; very few since his appointment, and
none whose parents are poor'. It is no surprise to learn that he had
left the town 'on urgent business' a day or two before the Commissioners arrived (*Report of the Charity Commissioners*, XVII
(1827), pp. 388–90; XXIX, Part I (1835), pp. 271–2). In 1795 Lord
Chief Justice Kenyon remarked that a great many grammar schools
were in a 'lamentable condition . . . empty walls without scholars,
and everything neglected but the receipt of salaries and emolu-
ments, in some instances . . . not a single scholar . . .' (quoted in
Curtis and Boultwood, *An Introductory History of English Education since 1800* (1964), pp. 80, 87–8. cf. N. Carlisle, *Endowed*

Grammar Schools of England and Wales (1818)). Hosea's school is now regulated under a scheme made by the Board of Education in January 1935.

80 For example, in July 1698 one of the executors visited 'Ringlestone', the farm in Kent, 'about repairing ye house, barn & stable, being so bad yt ye Tenant will not live in it'. Early in August a quantity of 10, 11 and 14 ft. deals and some sacks of nails were shipped by hoy from Wapping; some thatching was done, also, and the well was repaired (MS. 4653, ff.56–8).

81 MS. 4653, ff.14, 42–4, 46, 53.

82 MS. 4653, ff.18, 33.

83 Renter Bailiff of the Weavers' Company, 1679–80; Upper Bailiff 1683–4 (MS. 4646, ff.113, 117).

84 MS. 4653, ff.53, 58.

85 MS. 4653, ff.60–4.

86 Hosea's Will; *Reports of Charity Commissioners*, VIII (1823), p. 390. This property was almost on the City boundary slightly east of the corner of Gray's Inn Lane and facing the picturesque Staple Inn, which still survives. See E. Williams, *Early Holborn and the Legal Quarter of London* (1927), II, pp. 1232–3; H. Phillips, *Mid-Georgian London* (1964), p. 193.

87 MS. 4653, ff.79–81.

88 MS. 4655/10, ff.8b, 13b, 17b, 20, 22b.

89 MS. 4653A; *The Clerk's Report on the Charities*, 1742, f.6.

90 MS. 4646, ff.135–6.

91 MS. 4655/11, ff.18, 20.

92 MS. 4655/11, ff.64, 173.

93 MS. 4655/13, ff.142, 152, 167.

94 MS. 4655/16, *passim*.

95 MS. 4655/16, f.183b; MS. 4648/7, 2 December 1757.

96 MS. 4655/16, ff.237, 241.

97 MS. 4655/17, f.144.

98 MS. 4655/19, ff.21, 33b, 50b, 132b. The fire insurance cover (premium 15s. 6d. per £100) was increased from £800 to £950 in 1799.

99 A. Boyer, *The Political State of Gt. Britain*, vol. 31 (1726), p. 648. J. T. Squire, *Mount Nod; a Burial Ground of the Huguenots*, gives a summary of Nicholas Garrett's will. He is buried at Mount Nod, of which S. P. Myers writes: 'Near the top of East Hill (Wandsworth) the road comes to life with, oddly enough, a cemetery, the old Huguenot Cemetery with its story on a stone. 'Here rest many Huguenots who, on the revocation of the Edict of Nantes in 1685, left their native land for conscience' sake, and found in Wandsworth freedom to worship God after their own manner. They established important industries, and added to the credit and prosperity of the town of their adoption. . . . The Huguenots . . . brought to Wandsworth the secret processes of felting which made the hat-making of the town famous. They established factories for dyeing and silk and calico printing' (*London South of the River* (1949), p. 123).

100 MS. 4648/4, ff.148–50, 154, 179, 213; MS. 4655/12, f.194. The site chosen was in Elder Street, Porters Fields, in the Liberty of Norton Folgate, and just within the boundary of the parish of St Leonard, Shoreditch. Chassereaux's map of this parish in 1745 shows the position.

101 MS. 4655/12, ff.241, 244–6, 250b. William Tayler and William
    Goswell were the master carpenters (*Survey of London*, vol. 27, pp.
    91–2).
102 MS. 4655/12, ff.250b, 251.
103 MS. 4648/4, ff.226, 254.
104 MS. 4655/13, ff.38, 75; MS. 4655/16, ff.133b, 141; MS. 4646, f.256b.
    In the 1740s the coal usually cost between 31s. and 35s. a chaldron,
    the candles 8s. a dozen. The almsmen's pensions were slightly
    increased in 1771 to £9. 6s. 8d. or 3s. 7d. weekly (MS. 4648/8, June
    1771).
105 See Chap. 16.
106 MS. 4655/17, ff.431–2, 434–5, 442; MS. 4648/10, 17 January 1783.
107 One of the 'new' churches, built by Nicholas Hawksmoor between
    1723 and 1729.
108 James Limborough's Will, ff.2–3.
109 MS. 5234/1; MS. 4655/18, f.334.
110 MS. 4655/19, f.488.

Chapter 13

A New Charter and By-laws

When King William III died on Sunday, 8 March 1702, a 'queer, unnatural interlude in English History' came to an end. 'There was a sigh of relief throughout the capital, and then, with scarcely the pause which decorum enjoined, a very general jubilation for Her Majesty Queen Anne'.[1] Loyal addresses from all parts of the kingdom, near and far, welcomed and acclaimed the new monarch. Her 'sunshine day' having dawned, she lost no time in meeting and addressing first her Privy Council, and soon after (on 11 March), both Houses of Parliament. She was right regally attired and, making excellent use of her pleasant melodious voice, she 'charmed them both, for never woman spoke more audibly or with better grace'. The matter as well as the manner of her speeches created a most favourable impression, in tune with the popular mood at the time. In the City of London the merchants and bankers, 'that fourth Estate of the Realm', relieved and re-united by the agreement to amalgamate the two rival East India Companies, felt buoyant and ready for new ventures.[2] The climax came, of course, with the Queen's coronation on St George's Day, 1702, when 'all things [were] performed with great Splendour and Magnificence, the day concluding with bonfires, illuminations, ringing of bells, and other demonstrations of a general satisfaction and joy'.[3]

For the Weavers' Company, however, the opening of the new century and the new reign was much less auspicious. To begin with, the financial state of the Company was causing so much anxiety that the four Auditors were asked to investigate and report. Their findings, presented in September 1702, were that (i) the Company's funds had been much diminished in recent years by the great expense of dinners provided at the various Court meetings; (ii) the Company, already in debt, must shortly face further necessary expenses likely to arise from parliamentary proceedings, repairs to the Hall, and sundry other workmen's bills; and (iii) 'if the same disbursements should be longer continued it will be very difficult to prevent the damage and disgrace that may reasonably be expected to fall on the Company'. The Auditors made three recommendations which the Company accepted: (*a*) for one year the expenses for dinners on Full Court days and pension pay-days should be limited to £1. 10*s*. on each occasion; (*b*) that at every Private Court 12*d*. should be allowed in lieu of dinner to every person who, having been summoned, arrived before 11 a.m. and stayed to the end of the business; the Clerk to have 12*d*. and the Beadle, 6*d*.; (*c*) the amount spent on the Livery on the election days of the Lord Mayor, Sheriffs, Parliament men and others, should not exceed £2 on each occasion.[4]

Shortly afterwards the Auditors reported that the action taken 'touching the Intrenching of Expenses of Court Dinners . . . might, if continued, bring the Company out of debt'. But the process was gradual; at the end of 1704 money was still 'wanting for payment of debts and other necessary occasions'.[5]

An even more serious problem was worrying the Officers and Assistants at this time, for in addition to the inevitable strains and tensions between masters and journeymen, there appeared within the Company sinister symptoms of a widening cleavage which threatened to sap its efficiency as a controlling body. The root of the trouble was, once again, fear of the increasing numbers and competition of foreign and alien interlopers, and it was alleged that the Court of Assistants made no use of the Company's powers to check this and other abuses. In March 1703 'divers Liverymen and others' asked the Court not to admit foreign masters who could not prove that they had served a seven-years' apprenticeship at least. To this the Court agreed (3 May 1703), adding a proviso that 'persons might be admitted journeymen they proving their service according to the customs of the Country where they were brought up'. Four months later, however, the new order was rescinded, greatly to the chagrin of certain Liverymen, who straightway began a door-to-door canvass, telling weavers that the Court was abusing its position, and asking for money to finance legal proceedings against the Company,[6] based upon the Letters Patent granted by Charles I in 1638, which they erroneously referred to as a 'charter'.

This takes us back to the 1630s, another period of acute dissension within the Company, when a simmering cauldron of discontent, comprising many ingredients, at last boiled over in 1636. Led by William Counley, nineteen of the Commonalty made formal charges against the Officers and Assistants; viz. that they did not hold monthly and quarterly Courts openly 'at and in Common Hall' but they did 'assemble themselves weekly in a parlour privately, permitting none to be present but their Clerk and Beadle who are sworn to be secret'; and at these meetings, fees and fines were exacted much in excess of

the lawful amounts. For example, a number of poor members had
been summoned to the Livery in order to extract from them the £5
livery fine; but 'since the taking of the said sums of money' the poor
men 'have lived in great want and necessity' and their families also.
Thus it was that in the five years 1631-6, the Livery had been increased from thirty to eighty persons. Another serious charge was that
although the Yeomanry and Commonalty had reported to the Court
many intruders into the trade, nevertheless the intruders had been
'licensed and admitted to weave' although many of them 'could
neither begin nor finish any piece of work'.[7] Furthermore, the Court
had ignored the fraudulent certification of illegal 'apprentices', who
thus could become freemen of the City. Indeed, the Company's
Beadle, Thomas Pell, was personally involved in this form of fraud,
for on information laid before the Lord Mayor's Court in 1638, Pell
was convicted, fined £5 and ordered to be 'utterly dis-franchised'.
When some of Pell's friends appealed for clemency the Weavers'
Commonalty, who hated Pell and all his works, were furious and
requested the Lord Mayor and Aldermen to rule that Pell 'may still
stand dis-franchised by reason of many other abuses which he have
committed against the Company and Tradesmen of the same . . .'.
Nor was this all, for while they were on the subject of apprentices, the
Commonalty attacked the Bailiffs' and Wardens' right to keep two
additional apprentices and two extra looms; a privilege said to be
worth £20 a year to each of them for life.[8] The deepest thrust of all,
however, was the scepticism voiced by the Commonalty and certain
of the Liverymen regarding the Officers' financial competence and
integrity. The critics thought that between £100 and £200 from the
Company's income should have been 'added yearly to the increasing
of the Hall stock' (i.e. capital) so that land could be bought, almshouses built, or loans granted 'to young men to set up their Trade
as other Worshipful Companies do . . . yet it is still reported the
Company to be very poor having neither lands nor stock of money'.
The Officers were actually accused of dividing the money among
themselves or else spending it recklessly 'without due consideration
of the poor sort of the Company'.[9]

Against this background the Letters Patent of 1638 first made their
appearance. The whole document exudes the greatest confidence in
the Weavers' Company and indeed confers upon it powers and duties
so extensive that it would have been quite impossible to exercise and
perform many of them. If the Company solicited the Letters Patent
by petition, it is almost certain that the royal response went much
beyond their request. The preamble speaks of tissues, silk and stuffs
deceitfully and slightly made by intermixing refuse and waste silk,
thread, cotton and other base materials, and of reductions in the
dimensions of fabrics to the discredit of the trade and the impoverish-

ment of the honest and expert craftsmen therein. Moreover, these abuses had lately much increased by reason of 'the excessive multitude of Aliens that daily have resort in this Kingdom', taking upon themselves the said Trade and 'living without regulation, government or order therein'. (The Mercers also complained of similar abuses.) For all stuffs made of foreign or part-foreign materials, such as silk, the Company of Weavers of London was granted power to make laws and ordinances enforceable by 'reasonable' fines upon all persons, whether freemen, foreigners, denizens or strangers, throughout the whole of England and Wales. The London Weavers, moreover, were authorised to appoint Deputy Bailiffs, Deputy Wardens and Assistants in any other cities, towns, or places where foreign or part-foreign materials were woven: all such stuffs were to be viewed and sealed at designated centres.[10] Thus stuffs manufactured in London, Westminster or Southwark or within five miles thereof, were to be viewed and sealed at Weavers' Hall by the Weavers' Company acting in co-operation with the Mercers' Company; the two Companies being empowered to make levies on members in order to pay specially employed searchers.

There is no evidence that any of these extremely wide powers were ever exercised by the Weavers, who probably realised that the whole grandiose scheme would have been unworkable because of the bitter local opposition it would have evoked (e.g. in ancient cities such as Coventry or Norwich!), and the lack of adequate administrative machinery. Therefore the Weavers, to use their own words, 'always acted by other Charters and Ordinances',[11] but the existence of Charles I's Letters Patent enabled the disgruntled members or 'complaynors', as they were called, to cite, over sixty years later, certain clauses which provided that all persons admitted to the Company, except the Weavers of Canterbury, must be natural-born subjects who had served a legal seven-years' apprenticeship to weaving. This, said the 'complaynors', had been flagrantly flouted. Moreover, the Officers and Assistants had elected new Wardens without the consent or vote of the Livery, contrary to the words of the 'charter' of 1638; and although that document expressly provided that one Bailiff, one Warden and ten of the Assistants must be broad weavers, while the other Bailiff and Warden with ten Assistants must be narrow weavers,[12] the present Officers and Assistants 'have procured themselves to be composed all or greatest part of narrow weavers, and freemen of the Company *not being Weavers*'. The Officers and Assistants were accused of conniving at the admission of 'aliens and others not duly qualified to use the Trade of Weaving', and neglecting to prosecute such intruders. Several of the Livery, wishing to ventilate these complaints, had 'oftentimes desired' a Common Hall, 'that the Charter might be read that they might know their rights and privileges therein specified [but] the same had been denied to them'.[13]

All this was bad enough, but worse followed when proceedings in the Court of Chancery were actually begun in March 1705 by fourteen Liverymen and six of the Commonalty. The Officers and Assistants then appealed for negotiations, and before the case came up for trial the contestants agreed provisionally to form a negotiating committee of three representatives from each side. In the interests of peace within the trade it was thought advisable to seek ratification of this arrangement at a Common Hall to which all master weavers, whether Liverymen or not, were bidden. A tense and potentially ugly situation developed, however, when a turbulent crowd of journeymen, who had been told by the malcontents that they had every right to be present at the meeting, rushed the doors, thrust the Beadles aside—'though the Beadles were set to guard them and keep them out'—and poured in like a torrent. The Hall was packed to suffocation, and the hubbub became so appalling that 'one could scarce stir or be heard to speak'. The Upper Bailiff and certain other Officers 'admonished them [the journeymen] to depart as having no business here', but they were enjoying themselves too much and would not go. At last, 'after proclamation for silence was several times made', the Clerk read, on behalf of the Court, a prepared statement which described the so-called charter of 1638 as 'inconsistent . . . to the welfare and interest of the Trade and Company . . . and . . . our forefathers thought the same to be destructive both to the Trade and Company, otherwise they would have pursued the directions thereof'. The statement stressed the importance of the matter under discussion and asked that 'the same may be thoroughly debated . . . calmly and sedately without any heat and with as much decency and order as possible'; but, despite this plea, 'several debates arose which lasted a considerable time in great heat and confusion'. The sense of the meeting, so far as it could be gathered, seemed to favour the nomination of a committee 'out of the Livery' to treat with a committee chosen from the Court of Assistants; 'but the Hall being in such confusion no Question could be agreed on to be put, whereupon our Master left the Chair and dismissed the Common Hall'.

Ten days later, a Special Court, consisting of the Bailiffs, Wardens, Assistants and Livery, tried to reach a settlement, only to stumble upon a new bone of contention; should the Liverymen's representatives on the proposed committee be chosen from the *whole* Livery, or from among the disgruntled Liverymen, 'the complaynors'? Those Liverymen who were opposed to the latter argued that they had 'as much right to give their vote for anything concerning the good of the Company and Trade as the complaynors had'. Whereupon, tempers flared again and after a long, confused debate, amid much 'shouting and noise in a riotous manner by the Complaynors . . . our Master dismissed the Court'. The next move was quite unexpected, and not without its humorous side. On 20 August 1705, 'being the feast on the Inauguration of the new Bailiffs and Wardens', five of the chief 'complaynors' came with their wives to the dinner 'and tendered 2s. a piece for the same pursuant to the Ordinance, but that usage having been discontinued time out of mind, and the Liverymen and their wives having been treated on the Election day in lieu thereof, the Court refused to accept of their 2s. a piece; however, the said persons stayed and dined'. Ten uninvited and, probably, unwelcome guests! Were they, one wonders, given the cold shoulder?[14]

By this time the Officers and Assistants had become alarmed and anxious: alarmed at the threat of heavy legal costs which lengthy proceedings in the Court of Chancery might bring upon the scarcely solvent Company; and anxious to preserve the Company's good name and reputation as a decorous, responsible body. In the end the Court decided that, despite the expense, a new charter would offer the most satisfactory and permanent solution of the problem. Therefore the Clerk was instructed to prepare a draft and try to borrow the necessary funds. Luckily, about this time (February 1706) a Mr John Drew wished to buy from the Company an annuity of £20, for which he agreed to pay £220.[15]

But the way was still not clear. Certain of the 'Complaynors', unwilling to admit defeat, drew up their own draft charter and delivered it to the Upper Bailiff towards the end of March. Obviously this document could not be ignored or swept aside; it had to receive, and be seen to receive, proper consideration, and for this purpose the Court appointed an *ad hoc* committee of six members. When this committee had reported, the Court convened a Common Hall (30 May 1706) which had the unenviable task of discussing two rival drafts. 'Whereupon and after a long debate of the matter the Question was put, whether the Company's draft should be proceeded on to be made a Charter or not? It was carried in the affirmative by a great majority. Nevertheless, some present seeming to be dissatisfied, the Master told them they should have a poll if they desired it, but they all declined the same.' The 'complaynors', however, had certainly not 'laid aside their animosities', for their next move was a petition to the Lord Privy Seal against the proposed new charter. This necessitated yet another Common Hall at which, after a long but (this time) orderly debate, a poll revealed a majority of 30 to 1 in favour of the new draft charter. But now it was the Lord Keeper who delayed matters by requiring from every Liveryman his written consent or dissent. In the end sixty-five 'subscribed consent . . . and 17 not consent to the New Charter'; a result which was reinforced by a statement that 'many others of the Livery' had also 'testified their consent'.[16] Faced with this overwhelming majority the 'complaynors' at long last fell silent.

As one looks back upon the whole protracted, noisy and bitter contest, the absence of any reference to the Charter granted by James II at the beginning of his brief reign seems very odd. This document had to be rushed through because the death of Charles II (1685) in the middle of his high-handed *Quo Warranto* proceedings[17] had left the Weavers' Company to face the approach of Election Day bereft, strictly speaking, of the legal power to elect any Officers at all! Obviously, urgent action was called for. The Charter of 1685, drawn on traditional lines, did not repeat the ambitious impracticalities of Charles I's Letters Patent. It provided that the Company's members should be those who had served a seven-years' apprenticeship, and 'all other persons being expert and skilful in the said Art and Mistery as have been admitted or shall hereafter . . . be lawfully admitted freemen or members'. The Company, governed by two Bailiffs, two Wardens and twenty-six Assistants, was given jurisdiction in the Cities of London and Westminster and the Borough of Southwark and within twenty miles thereof. Within this extended area the Company had the right of search 'at seasonable and convenient times' in houses, work-houses, warehouses, cellars, etc.[18] Why, then, was this relatively recent Charter never cited? The answer lies in the statute 2 William and Mary, c. 8; 'An Act for reversing the judgement in *Quo Warranto* against the City of London . . .', which declared void all charters and letters patent granted by Charles II and James II as a consequence of the *Quo Warranto* proceedings.

As soon as Queen Anne's assent to the new charter was quite certain, the Court of Assistants, with a tremendous feeling of relief and release, held a thanksgiving celebration. Trumpeters, watermen, standard bearers and porters were hired and a shilling was paid 'to Mr. Christmas for a bonefire'. In the morning and evening they had 'rolls, cheese, butter and drink' which cost £1. 4s. 8d. But the midday meal was best: eight large sirloins of beef were eaten, and there was bread, wine and tobacco aplenty. These items, plus 'dressing [the dinner] and servants' and paying the reckoning on 'the night we came from my Lord Keeper', cost the Company £16. 7s.[19]

These sums, however, were small compared with the many legal fees and bribes inseparable from the tricky business of soliciting a royal charter and steering it through the many intricate channels. This cost more than £330;[20] a large sum which the Company could ill afford at that time. In the financial year 1706-7, £192. 4s. 6d. was spent on the new charter, which turned a credit balance of £125. 12s. 10d. brought forward from 1705-6 into a debit balance of £34. 6s. 10d. Moreover, the Company borrowed at this time nearly £241, and it already owed the Renter Bailiff about £100 secured by a bond.[21]

Between 1706 and 1709 a special effort was made to collect more quarterage, with the results set out in Table 13.1. For the following two years, 1713–15, the average was little more than £120 per annum.

Table 13.1 *Quarterage collected, 1706–12*

Date	£	s.	d.	Date	£	s.	d.
1706–7	151	6	3	1709–10	130	8	6
1707–8	173	6	3	1710–11	144	16	3
1708–9	188	7	9	1711–12	135	9	3

The new Charter, dated 17 November 1707, engrossed on four skins of vellum with a portrait of the Queen at the beginning and her great seal appended at the end, was received by the Weavers with a fanfare of trumpets (which cost them ten shillings) on 25 November, when the Officers 'expended this day ye Charter coming down £1. 11. 3.'.[22] A Common Hall was convened for 9 December 1707 at which the new Charter was formally presented and read by the Clerk,[23] its preamble and main provisions being:

1   The Charter of Henry II, confirmed by successive kings and queens and by Act of Parliament in the reign of Henry VI, is confirmed.

2   Of late years the number of foreigners and others engaged in weaving have greatly increased and many such people have settled in various out-parishes adjacent to London and Southwark, thereby avoiding the jurisdiction of the Company of Weavers.

3   In order to remedy this undesirable trend and to enable the Queen's natural-born subjects in the weaving trade to be better provided with employment, the Charter seeks to strengthen the Ancient Gild or Company of Weavers.

4   The territorial extent of the Company's jurisdiction is defined as the Cities of London and Westminster and the Borough of Southwark and 'ten miles distant thereof and round the same'.

5   Within these limits no persons are permitted to engage in weaving unless they are members and free of the Company or 'duly qualified according to the Laws for exercising the same'.

6   There shall be two Bailiffs and two Wardens, and not less than sixteen and not more than twenty-four Assistants. Between these limits the actual number is to be fixed by 'the Bailiffs, Wardens and Assistants or the major part of them for the time being'.[24]

7   The Bailiffs and Wardens are to hold office for one year

(unless re-elected). The Assistants and Clerk to hold for life unless removed by the Court of Assistants for misdemeanour in office.

8 The Bailiffs and Wardens must take the oaths prescribed by Act of Parliament (instead of the Oaths of Allegiance and Supremacy) and the oaths for the due execution of their respective offices. The Assistants and Clerk must take appropriate oaths administered by the Bailiffs and Wardens or any two of them.

9 'A Court' for managing the Company's affairs must consist of the Bailiffs and Wardens or any two of them, with at least nine of the Assistants.

10 Every year on the Feast Day of St James the Apostle (25 July) the Company must hold a General Court or Common Hall consisting of Bailiffs, Wardens, Assistants and Livery, or the major part of them, to elect two Bailiffs and two Wardens for the year next ensuing. The nomination of these four officers to be 'as anciently made and performed'.

11 Any nominee refusing or neglecting to serve will be liable to a fine not exceeding £20, assessed by the Court of Assistants.

12 The Court of Assistants may choose and elect from the Livery as many additional Assistants as they deem necessary, provided that the total number does not exceed 24 at any time.

13 When a new Clerk is required he is to be chosen by the Court of Assistants 'or the greater part of them for the time being'.

14 Power is given to the Court of Assistants 'to call and make choice of such fit persons being Freemen . . . to be of the Livery . . . when and as often as they shall think fit'.

15 The Auditors, Beadles, 'and other Officers, Ministers and Servants for the use and service of the Company' to be chosen by the Court of Assistants.

16 For the 'well ordering, Rule and Government' of the Company and Trade, the Court of Assistants, with four Liverymen appointed by 'the major part of the Livery duly assembled', are empowered to make by-laws and ordinances, which, however, are not valid unless ratified and confirmed by the Court of Assistants and Livery in a Common Hall.

17 Offenders against the by-laws and ordinances may be fined by the Court of Assistants, which may mitigate or cancel such fines, or sue at law by action of debt, or otherwise.

18 No merchants, mercers or other persons are allowed to keep any loom or warping frame in a house or other place unless they have 'served to the Trade of Weaving'.

19 The Company's right of search within the trade is confirmed.

20 Members of the Company may take natural-born subjects or others as apprentices, provided that they are presented to the Court and bound at Weavers' Hall for a term of seven years at least.

21 Apprentices 'out of their time' may be made free of the Company by the Bailiffs and Wardens, or any two of them.

22 The Court may, at its discretion, admit to the freedom any other 'fit and expert persons in the Trade of Weaving', if over the age of twenty-one and 'duly qualified by Law for the exercise of the said Trade'.

23 The ancient custom of receiving from each Freeman a silver spoon of 1½ oz. weight, or its value in money, for the charitable and public uses of the Company is confirmed.

24 The Charter confers the usual rights to purchase, hold and dispose of land; to sue and be sued in all Courts; and to have a common seal.

25 Justices of the Peace, mayors and other civic officers are enjoined to help the Company, when so requested, to carry out its lawful functions.

The ten-miles radius (reduced from the twenty miles laid down in James II's Charter) meant a circle around London reaching from Enfield in the north to Croydon in the south; and from Hammersmith and Putney in the west to Barking and Woolwich in the east, and including hamlets such as Walthamstow, Hackney, Hampstead, Kilburn, Paddington, Fulham and a score of others 'in the fields'.

It now remained to draft new by-laws in accordance with the Charter, which required, as we have seen, four Liverymen, chosen *ad hoc* by their fellows in a Common Hall, to act with the Court of Assistants. This election was made without difficulty early in February 1708, and the draft was prepared, discussed, amended and finally approved by a Common Hall on 26 April 1708.[25]

The provisions of these by-laws and ordinances fall into two main categories: (*a*) those which implement in detail the provisions of the Charter for the organisation of the Company and the discharge of its lawful functions; and (*b*) those which state in writing long-standing usages and rules (some of considerable antiquity) touching such matters as the limitation of the numbers of apprentices, the almost complete exclusion of women, the terms upon which 'foreigners' and 'alien strangers' were eligible for membership, and so forth. One of the most important clauses runs: 'for the Improvement of the Manufacture of Weaving and for giving all due Incouragement to all Ingenious persons as well Foreigners as others as are skilful therein . . . any alien stranger or foreigner who have served as an Apprentice according to the Custom of the Country from whence he came shall be eligible for membership', and foreign journeymen shall be eligible to become Masters provided they can prove that they are 'duly qualified'. Apprentices 'out of their time' who wish to use the weaving trade must apply for their freedom, proving at least seven years' apprenticeship and that they 'are become Artists in the said Trade, Art or Mistery'. There is a clause requiring the Bailiffs and Wardens to wear their gowns at all Courts 'the better to be had in Reverence and esteem by all such as shall appear before them', and another which prescribes a penalty of twenty shillings for divulging the Company's secrets to persons other than the members of the Court of Assistants. The fines for declining to take office, to act as Steward or to join the Livery are also stated.[26]

The prevailing financial famine did not deter the Weavers from giving tangible proof of their loyalty and gratitude to the Queen by acquiring a large portrait of her, in June 1709, at a cost of £12. Indeed, they went further, for six weeks later (and long after his death in 1702) they paid £14. 10s. 'for King Wms. Picture'.[27] Thus seven portraits of British sovereigns were now proudly displayed in Weavers' Hall: Queen Elizabeth I, James I, Charles I, Charles II, James II, William III and Queen Anne.[28]

For well over twenty years no charter or by-law troubles arose. In the autumn of 1733, however, the Company failed in a lawsuit against a recalcitrant weaver because its Officers were unable to produce the original minute which authorised the making of the by-laws upon which the Company's case relied. The shock of this decision evoked a quick response. On the last day of November 1733 a Full Court 'took into Consideration their present By-laws and the want of the original Minutes of their making the same . . . and . . . Resolved to proceed in making New By-laws . . .' by setting up, as prescribed by the Charter, a special committee comprising the Assistants and four Liverymen. But, by comparison with the drafting committee of 1708, this committee was extremely dilatory and did not finish its work until October 1735,[29] when 'a Subscription was proposed and agreed to amongst the Gentlemen of the Court of 3 Guineas each towards the Expenses of forwarding the Company's By-laws, [and] It was Resolved . . . that it be repaid by the Company and if not sooner out of the monies payable . . . from their Irish Estate.'[30] The completed document and a petition to the Lord Chancellor and the Lord Chief Justices of the King's Bench and Common Pleas praying for their confirmation were approved by the Weavers on 20 November 1735—nearly two years after the original decision to proceed.[31] Then followed further long and inexplicable delays until, in October 1737, the Court somewhat impatiently requested that the four Officers in place 'do forthwith take the most speedy and effectual method to get the present By-laws as they now stand presented to the Lord Chancellor and the Lord Chief Justices for approbation'.[32] But still the way was not clear, for the judges objected that the draft was defective in form and appeared to assign to the Company a jurisdiction not warranted by the Charter. We can readily imagine the effect of this bombshell in a Common Hall at which the four Officers, fourteen Assistants and no fewer than seventy-six Liverymen were present. Fortunately, Lord Chief Justice Willis volunteered to settle the draft within a few days; an offer which was most gratefully accepted and quickly implemented. So, on 13 February 1738, the new by-laws were passed by the Weavers' Court, 'ingrossed in a Book upon Vellom', and formally approved by a Common Hall held a week later.[33]

Under the new regulations, as under the old, the tussles with illegal interlopers, weavers of inferior goods, employers of 'unlawful boys, girls, journeymen, and the like', continued throughout the eighteenth century; a century marked by an increasing tendency to challenge the Company's rights and to flout its authority. Indeed, so many infringements accumulated on all sides that, in order to keep costs down, the Company was frequently compelled to select, from a long list, a small number of alleged offenders against whom proceedings were to be taken, choosing, for the sake of the Company's prestige, only cases in which the prospects of success were good. Thus, when four men 'who are not Members and exercise the Weaving Trade' were ordered by the Court of Assistants to be 'forthwith arrested at the charge of the Company', the Court stipulated 'that special care be taken for sufficient evidence to prove the facts'.[34] In 1744, the Company's Committee of Law Suits, having taken Counsel's opinion, made an onslaught upon a number of non-members who were exercising 'the trade, art or mystery of weaving' or 'who do Intermeddle therewith', in breach of the Company's 'ancient franchises'. The Court of Assistants decided to take immediate legal action against two recalcitrant persons and to summon twenty-five others to appear at the next Court 'to shew their right to Exercise the Trade and that they may be admitted to the Freedom'. Of the twenty-five, four took their freedom forthwith, nine promised to do so, two were made free in June 1745, and the remaining ten ignored the summons, apparently with impunity.[35]

Throughout the second half of the eighteenth century evasion and infringement of the Company's regulations persisted on a considerable, and probably increasing, scale. Apprentices were still bound before justices of the peace and not at Weavers' Hall; 'learners', never indentured as apprentices, were still being taught weaving for trifling fees; many a qualified weaver obstinately refused to take his freedom, and there were numbers of unqualified ones who, with equal tenacity, refused to leave the trade. And all the time the Company was hampered by the heavy costs of legal actions. In 1766, for example, four prosecutions cost the Company £129. But it did not give up the struggle entirely. In the spring of 1781 thirty non-members were summoned, and in 1784 the Clerk was ordered to write to no fewer than fifty unadmitted weavers, nine of whom were on the list of 1781. When the response proved disappointing, the Court of Assistants decided to prosecute fourteen of those summoned, which meant that between 1784 and 1787 the Company sacrificed more than £440 in what we now know was a losing battle.[36]

NOTES

1 Winston S. Churchill, *Marlborough; His Life and Times* (1933–4), II, p. 498.
2 G. M. Trevelyan, *England under Queen Anne: Blenheim* (1930), p. 164.
3 Abel Boyer, *History of the Reign of Queen Anne . . . Year the First* (1703), pp. 2–9, 22–7.
4 MS. 4655/11, ff.11–11b.
5 MS. 4655/11, ff.16, 20, 21b.
6 MS. 4655/11, ff.13b, 14, 16b, 21.
7 MS. 4647, The Ordinance and Record Book, ff.388–40, 417–18. Doubtless this refers to the highly skilled work of setting up the warp threads in the loom ready to begin a new piece, and the removal of the finished piece from the loom.
8 MS. 4647, f.452.
9 MS. 4647, ff.413, 451–2.
10 The London Pewterers' Company had the right to search for false wares throughout the whole kingdom; but the country pewterers revolted against such supervision by the London pewterers, who became increasingly unwilling to assert their authority outside London and the suburbs. The pewterers of the City of Bristol were known to flout the ordinances and authority of the London Pewterers (C. Welch, *History of the Pewterers' Company*, I, p. iii; II, pp. viii–ix, 103, 184).
11 The Letters Patent of 1638 were supplemented by an Indenture of the same date whereby the Weavers covenant 'to pay or cause to be paid' to the King certain duties on wrought and dyed silks (MS. 4637). At the end of 1638 the Privy Council, the King being present, had these duties under consideration (MS. 4655/1, ff.110–11). No doubt the whole scheme fell into abeyance during the Civil War.
12 MS. 4636, The Letters Patent, 4 July 1638. Broad weaving is defined in this document as 'above one quarter of a yard broad'. See also MS. 4647, The Ordinance and Record Book, ff.480–8.
13 MS. 4655/11, f.22, December 1704.
14 MS. 4655/11, ff.23b, 25, 26b.
15 The Company received this sum on 18 February 1706.
16 MS. 4655/11, ff.30, 33, 35, 35b.
17 Herbert, *History of the Twelve Great Livery Companies*, I, pp. 212–19.
18 MS. 4639; Repertories, 91, ff.67, 92, March and June 1686. The

Weavers' Company had to apply to the City 'to be again ranked among the Livery Companies of this Citie'. A list of the names of sixty-one Liverymen (almost all English names) who were formally approved by the Court of Aldermen is given in Repertories 91, f.92.

19 MS. 4648/3, 5 May 1707.
20 MS. 4646, ff.142–3.
21 MS. 4655/11, f.36b.
22 MS. 4648/3, 25 November, 12 December 1707.
23 MS. 4655/11, f.38.
24 In addition to the four officers—Ralph Titford, Henry Soames, Gilbert Mace and William Edmunds—nominated in the Charter to hold office from 17 November 1707 to Election Day (25 July) 1708, the sixteen members of the Court of Assistants are named.
25 MS. 4655/11, f.41.
26 In 1709–10 the Clerk was given ten guineas for his work on the new by-laws and £8 for 'providing a Book for and engrossing and entering the Charter and By-laws therein' (MS. 4655/11, ff.47b, 64b). This book still exists.
27 MS. 4648/3, 20 June and 1 August 1709.
28 MS. 4646, ff.284b, 286b. The Company still has five of these portraits; see Chap. 19 below.
29 MS. 4655/13, ff.128, 162, 170, 186.
30 Sixty guineas were subscribed in 1735 and repaid in 1738.
31 MS. 4655/13, ff.189, 193.
32 MS. 4655/14, ff.3, 7.
33 MS. 4655/14, ff.7, 23, 32, 38, 42, 56, 61–2.
34 MS. 4655/11, ff.167, 177, 183; MS. 4655/12, ff.83b, 179b; MS. 4655/13, ff.22, 32.
35 MS. 4655/15, ff.85b, 192, 224.
36 MS. 4655/16, f.208b; MS. 4655/17, ff.309, 330, 467, 474b, 476b; MS. 4655/18, f.31b; MS. 4648/8, *passim*; MS. 4648/10, *passim*. William Scowfield, summoned in June 1753, pleaded poverty, 'ill-health by shortness of breath', a large family, 'and his wife ready to lye in'. He was excused for three months (MS. 4655/16, f.76b).

Chapter 14

Daniel Defoe and the Calico Madams

It was fortunate that the Weavers had composed their internal differences, closed their ranks and settled down to work under the new charter and by-laws before the great calico controversy reached its crisis between 1719 and 1721. English silk weavers had been menaced by competition from Indian textiles since 1621 when the powerful monopolistic East India Company first began seriously to consider marketing Bengal silks in England. Although their advisers disliked the project at that time, it was never completely abandoned. Indeed, the main part of the East India Company's business in the second half of the seventeenth century was the importation of piece-goods and silk stuffs into the English and European markets.[1] Indian wrought silks and painted and dyed calicoes became extremely fashionable, taking the place of English silks, half-silks, slight silks, worsted stuffs, says and perpetuanos, 'not only for the clothing of both sexes, but for curtains for rooms, beds, etc.',[2] especially after the import prohibition laid upon French silks and linens by Parliament in 1678. The English weavers derived only a partial benefit from this, for the consumers turned largely to Indian fabrics for linings as well as outer garments to replace the French wares, and, said a pamphleteer, 'on a sudden, we saw all our women, rich and poor, cloath'd in Callico, printed and painted; the gayer and the more tawdry the better.' The demand sprang up in all classes: from ladies of high rank and fashion, who often appeared on special occasions 'like an embassy of Indian Queens'; from 'the greatest gallants' and 'the meanest cookmaids', so that many a man had difficulty in distinguishing his wife from his chambermaid[3] for they all looked 'more like the Merry Andrews of Batholomew Fair' than the womenfolk of a trading people. Moreover, there were changes of fashion within 'the fashion'. Around 1680 all sorts of novel chintzes were much in demand; by 1687 striped chintzes were more in demand than flowered ones; in the 1690s Bengal muslins were asked for 'with

292

great flowers, birds, beasts, and any other odd fancies of the country'.[4]

Against these serious encroachments upon their trade and livelihoods the London weavers struggled incessantly; the Company mainly by petitioning Parliament, the small masters and journeymen by continual angry grumbling and occasional riots.[5] It was a long, hard fight not only against powerful commercial interests grouped within and around the East India Company, but against the intangible, almost invincible 'universal Female Fancy'. Despite some set-backs the Weavers persevered and, by the turn of the century, had achieved a measure of success. Although the London Weavers' petition against the wearing of East India fabrics was rejected by Parliament in 1680, an additional duty of 10 per cent on imported Indian calicoes, wrought silks and various mixtures was imposed in 1685. Moreover, this duty was doubled in 1690 and renewed by successive Acts of Parliament until it was made permanent in 1711. But the profit margins on Indian fabrics were so wide and the amount of smuggling so great that even these tariffs were ineffective as protective measures. The recorded imports of Indian calicoes and Bengal wrought silks in the four years 1698–1701 are shown in Table 14.1.[6]

Table 14.1 *Recorded imports of Indian calicoes and Bengal wrought silks, 1698–1701*

Date	Calicoes (*pieces*)	Bengal wrought silks (*pieces*)
1698	247,214	57,269
1699	853,034	24,445
1700	951,109	116,455
1701	826,101	115,504

During the 1690s the weavers' plight became even more desperate, for besides the competition from abroad they appeared to be suffering from serious overcrowding of their industry at home. Some of the journeymen went tramping; some went to sea; all were at breaking point.[7] According to Macaulay, numerous copies of a ballad, probably Jacobite in origin, exhorting the weavers to rise against the Government were discovered in 1693. But the most powerful stimulants to violent action were economic, 'bread-and-butter' arguments, not other people's political ambitions. In January 1697, when Parliament was discussing a Bill designed to prohibit imports of Indian wrought silks, between 4,000 and 5,000 weavers and their wives marched to the House, crowded into the lobby and threatened to invade the Chamber itself. The same evening a mob attacked East India House, broke open the outer door, pulled down rails, smashed windows and knocked down an officer of the Poultry Compter, who lost his hat and halberd; but when the Lord Mayor and Sheriffs arrived with a guard and arrested three men (who were later sent to Newgate) the rest of the rioters dispersed. The Commons, extremely angry, declared that those who had incited the rioters had committed a high crime and misdemeanour against the constitution and freedom of Parliament.[8] The next day (22 January) small groups of weavers entered some shops in the City and tore up calicoes and imported silks.

Two months later (22 March 1697) the weavers rose once more and attacked a house in Spitalfields belonging to a Mr Bohmer, a Member of Parliament and Deputy Governor of the East India Company. The trained bands (with perhaps some regulars) arrived post-haste and fired upon the mob, killing two and wounding several others; whereupon the rioters dispersed—but not for long. After a brief lull of two days large numbers of weavers assembled in a field near Hackney and threatened to go and destroy the house of Sir Josiah Child, the merchant-economist and 'uncrowned king' of the East India Company who lived at Wanstead. The military acted promptly enough to prevent serious damage, and when a press-gang made hay by seizing several of the younger men, the remainder made off. They remained, however, in a state of seething revolt,[9] and rioted again in April when they 'very near seized the treasure of the East India House'.

The Weavers' Company always deprecated such disturbances and tried hard to discourage or prevent them, while at the same time it continued to press by peaceful, constitutional means for that complete prohibition of the wearing and use of Indian fabrics which alone promised adequate protection to its members and their employees. At last, in February 1700, a Bill 'for the more effectual employment of the poor and encouraging the Manufactures of England' was passed by both houses of Parliament and was hailed with great jubilation in all weaving districts. The new Act provided that calicoes, 'painted, dyed, printed or stained', as well as all manufactured pure or mixed silk fabrics imported from India, China or Persia 'shall not be worn or otherwise used within this Kingdom'.[10] But after the first flush of rejoicing, the Weavers realised that the Act provided no penalties for the *wearing* of prohibited goods, and it did not cover calicoes printed or painted in England.

What, in practice, were the effects of this piece of legislation? Although the evidence is somewhat conflicting, the truth seems to be that the weavers benefited from an encouraging recovery in their industry for several years until the competition of calicoes printed in England began to take effect. The infant English calico-printing industry (founded probably in 1676) flourished and grew rapidly after 1700 under the stimulus provided by the exclusion of similar goods printed in India. The Commissioners for Trade and Plantations reported in 1702 and again in 1707 that 'the allowing calicoes unstained to be brought in had occasioned such an increase of the printing and staining calicoes here that it is more prejudical' to the English weavers than before 1700.[11] Soon the weavers realised that what they had hailed as a victory was likely to prove little better than a defeat. Womenfolk hesitated, for a time, to appear in 'prohibited' clothing, but they soon became bold again and returned to their forbidden fashions, so that before long more chintzes and coloured calicoes than ever were being worn and used 'as well in the country as in the city'. The calico printers themselves admitted in 1711 that about a million yards of calico were being printed annually, of which approximately three-quarters were coarse calicoes from India 'printed for Frocks, Aprons, Quilts, etc.' and sold at 2d., 3d. or 4d. a yard.[12] In response to the weavers' complaints Parliament levied excise duties on printed calicoes and linens in 1712, and increased them two years later. Although this checked the expansion of the competing industry for the time being, the marked popularity of printed fabrics continued to threaten the woollen and silk weavers.

The Weavers' Company realised only too well that a time of crisis was fast approaching when they would have to fight a great battle to save their industry from a swift and permanent decline. They were facing a two-pronged attack, for in addition to the calicoes and linens printed in England they were up against the widespread activities of the 'Clandestine Traders' who not only smuggled English wool to the Continent, and French wines and brandy into England, but illegally imported Indian wrought silks and printed fabrics of all sorts through Holland and France. There was also the lucrative practice of defrauding the revenue by re-landing prohibited goods after they had been entered for re-export and the Customs had allowed drawback; though it seems that few such goods found their way into the London market.[13] Seamen ashore, seamen's wives and other 'strowlers' often helped to dispose of smuggled goods, and it was known that great quantities were illegally sold by wandering hawkers and pedlars.[14] From 1713 to the beginning of 1718 the Weavers' Company was continually at grips with this smuggling menace. A special standing committee of nine was set up and the Company informed the Lords Commissioners of the Treasury that it was more than ready to recommend persons of skill and knowledge to assist the customs officers to discover, seize and identify illegal goods.[15]

As time passed the situation became steadily more explosive. A trade recession, which had been threatening since 1717, was aggravated by the outbreak of war with Spain in 1719.[16] Some of the journeymen weavers were already engaging in the 'sport' of calico chasing, from which it was but a short step to large-scale tumults and riots.[17] The Weavers' Company quickly saw the danger and issued 'The Advice of the Master Weavers to the Journeymen of their Trade, approved by the Court of Assistants and ordered to be printed and published July 1, 1719', expressing great concern 'for the many poor journeymen and their families reduced to great distress for want of employment', but deploring 'the Violence which many have run into of late, upon Account of the Wear of Printed Callicoes', and pointing out that the redress of grievances which must come from Parliament, might be seriously set back by disorderly behaviour. The journeymen were enjoined not to insult or molest anybody on any account whatsoever.[18] But this appeal was ignored. 'This week', reported the *Weekly Journal* on 4 July 1719, 'the Gibbet on Stonebridge was hung from top to bottom with fragments of Callicoe, Stuffs torn or rather stolen from Women by Journey Men Weavers.' And not only men; women and boys, and even girls were among the assailants. On one occasion 'a young woman in Whitechapel being rudely assaulted by a parcel of weavers who tearing her Callicoe Gown from off her back' so terrified her that she fainted, and although she 'was bled by a surgeon' her life was 'despaired of'.[19] Another incident, much less serious in its consequences, occurred when 'a woman in a callicoe Gown' was confronted by a journeyman weaver 'who swore he would strip her of her Gown, unless she would do it herself'. To which her spirited rejoinder was that she would give him half-a-crown 'if he had the Boldness to do it; upon which he tore it off'. Before long he found himself in a magistrate's court, where his ingenious defence was 'that she had hired him to divest her of the Gown, and [he] insisted upon being paid what she promised'. It seems that the magistrate (unlike Queen Victoria) *was* amused; the weaver was 'dismissed' and the lady 'was ordered to go about her Business', whatever that may have been.[20] Throughout the summer the newspapers reported case after case of assault and insult. *Aqua fortis* was thrown on women's clothes. When three ladies in a coach drove up to look at a weavers' ringleader in the pillory, they were stripped of their calicoes 'as clean . . . as a butcher does a partridge of its feathers'. Other women were 'frightened into fits' or miscarriages. Some of the weavers impudently entered people's houses 'at the very doors of magistrates' to search for calicoes, and any they found they carried off in triumph on the tops of poles, to the accompaniment of shouts of 'King George for ever' to show that they were not seditious.[21] So intense did popular feeling become that the writers and sellers of broadsheets released a cascade of doggerel verses, of which the following 'Weaver's Complaint' is a prime example:

The Weaver's Complaint against the Callico Madams[22]
To the tune of 'For an Apple of Gold'

In the Ages of Old,
We Traded for Gold,
Our Merchants were Thriving
    and Wealthy:
We had Silks for our Store,
Warm Wool for our Poor,
And Drugs for the Sick and
    Unhealthy:
And Drugs for the Sick and
    Unhealthy.

But now we bring Home
The Froth and the Scum
To Dress up the Trapes like a
    Gay-Dame;
And Ev'ry She Clown
Gets a Pye-spotted Gown,
And sets up for a Callicoe
    Madam.
O! tawdery Callico Madam . . .

Here they Stamp 'em and
    Print 'em,
And Spot 'em and Paint 'em,
And the Callico Printers
    Brocade 'em;
They cost little Pay,
And are tawdery gay,
Only fit for a Draggle-tail
    Madam,
O! this tawdery Callico Madam.

Ev'ry Jilt of the Town
Gets a Callico Gown;
Our Own Manufack's out of
    Fashion:
No Country of Wool
Was ever so dull,
'Tis a test of the Brains of the
    Nation:
O! the test of the Brains of the
    Nation,

To neglect their own Works,
Employ Pagans and Turks,
And let foreign Trump'ry
    o'er spread em:
Shut up their own Door,
And starve their own Poor,
For a tawdery Callico Madam.
O! this Tatterdemalion Madam.

Were there ever such Fools!
Who despising the Rules,
For the common Improvement
    of Nations:
Tye up the Poor's Hands,
And search foreign Lands,
For their Magpie ridiculous
    Fashions.
For their Magpie ridiculous
    Fashions.

They're so Callico wise,
Their own Growth they despise,
And without an inquiry, 'Who
    Made'em?'
Cloath the Rich and the Poor,
The Chaste and the Whore,
And the Beggar's a Callico
    Madam.
O! this Draggle-tail Callico
    Madam.

Nay, who would lament it,
Or strive to prevent it,
If the Prince of Iniquity had
    'em:
Or if, for a Bride,
They were heartily ty'd
To some Pocky Damn'd
    Callico Madam.
To some Pocky Damn'd
    Callico Madam.

On the other hand, many a voice was raised on behalf of the women 'against the Riotous Weavers'. It was intolerable, declared one spirited champion of women's rights, 'for a Gang of Audacious Rogues to come and fall upon us in the Streets, and tear the Clothes off our Backs, insult and abuse us, and tell us we shall not wear what they do not weave; is this to be allowed in a Nation of Liberty? . . . have all the People the use of Liberty but us?'[23]

In September 1719 the Company prepared a petition 'touching calicoes', which was referred to the Commissioners for Trade and Plantations, who invited the petitioners to send a deputation to explain and clarify their views. The Officers, well aware that the Company might be entering upon a stern and costly struggle, called a Full Court early in November 1719 'to concert methods' of raising 'money to defray the charges of the Company's Petition . . . against Calicoes and to prosecute the same in Parliament'. This was followed on 13 November 1719, by a Common Hall at which the Four in Place, nine Assistants and some forty of the Livery were present. It appeared that the Committee set up six years before to help to suppress the smuggling and wearing of 'prohibited and uncustomed' silks had collected from weavers and mercers over £450, of which £336 had been spent. Taking into account £60 earned by way of interest, there remained in hand £174. This sum, augmented by £100 from current funds, was now to be used in the fight against 'the Clandestine Importation and Consumption of prohibited East India wrought silks and the . . . Wearing and Use of Calicoes and Linen both foreign and home-printed'. The original committee of nine was strengthened by seven new members.[24]

About the same time the Officers and Assistants took another bold and imaginative step by engaging Daniel Defoe—who was nearly sixty years of age but still vigorous and seemingly tireless—to present the weavers' case and keep it constantly before Members of Parliament, other influential people and the public at large in a periodical entitled the *Manufacturer*. They could not have made a better choice, for Defoe, the first and foremost English journalist, was then at the very peak of his power. He had published *Robinson Crusoe* in April 1719 and *The Further Adventures of Robinson Crusoe* only four months later. That astonishing trio, *Captain Singleton*, *Moll Flanders* and *Colonel Jack*, were to follow in 1721-2. And, as Professor Sutherland has said, Defoe 'was never more of an artist than when he was building up a simple, direct case for adopting one line of action rather than another . . . given a case to put, he was a master at putting it clearly and convincingly'.[25] Moreover, his long-standing and sympathetic interest in the English textile industry was well known. As early as 1708 he had noticed, with regret, that the ladies had promoted 'the chintz from . . . their floors to their backs' and calico had so completely crept into all parts of the house that curtains, cushions, chairs and beds 'were nothing but Callicoes or Indian stuffs', instead of the English worsteds and silks formerly used.[26] Nearly twelve years later he was still deploring the fact that the streets were 'crowded with calico madams' and the houses 'stuff'd with calico furniture'.[27]

The *Manufacturer: or The British Trade fully Stated, wherein the Case of the Weavers, and the Wearing of Callicoes, are considered*[28] made its début under a cloud, for the journeymen weavers' riotous behaviour and their rough handling of women in the streets, shops and places of entertainment had aroused widespread disapprobation and censure. It is, therefore, not surprising that in the first issue of the *Manufacturer* (Friday, 30 October 1719) Defoe opens with an oblique apology for 'the late Tumults'. 'The Weavers', he wrote,

> have done mobbing; and now they hope to be heard calmly,
> as they intend to speak coolly. If they have been to blame,
> they are not going to justify themselves here. . . . Their
> Design in this Paper is to have their Grievances laid open,
> and their Story fairly told, in a Manner less offensive than they
> have been able to tell it in the Street; that they may complain
> without Rabbling and Noise, and be answer'd with milder
> Arguments than those of a Prison and a Pillory. . . . They
> know their Cause to be good, and think 'tis pity it should
> suffer by their having a little more Passion than Patience. They
> acknowledge their Warmth may have been their Mistake; but
> they recommend it to their Enemies to take a small Dose of
> starving Patience and tell how it works with them. They
> assure the World that two Drams of it is a Vomit for a Dog.

The wearing of calicoes was like a contagion 'that if not stopped . . . will, like the Plague in a Capital City, spread itself o'er the whole Nation [so] . . . that the whole manufacture of Great Britain will be destroyed by this Callico Plague as People are swept away by a General Infection, unless some timely Relief may be had'. Henceforth the 'Violence of Persuasion' would be tried, for ' 'tis as well to the Weavers if they can bring the Women to be ashamed to wear Callicoes, as if they were afraid to wear 'em'. The *Manufacturer* appealed to all mothers still wearing calico to 'consider how many Families of Mothers and Children they help to starve by gratifying their Callico-Fancy . . . and employing Pagans and Indians, Mahometans and Chineses, instead of Christians and Britains'.

In the second issue of the *Manufacturer* Defoe pictured the weavers in and around Spitalfields as 'poor, rash, but exasperated People who . . . broke out into some violences', because of 'their miseries and the Hardship of their Circumstances; Want of Work, and, by

Consequence, Want of Bread: a sad Prospect of a ruin'd Manufacture, and no Hope of recovering it'.[29] Worse still, he explained, the future of every textile manufacturer in the whole kingdom was at stake, for the 'wearing of callicoes stops the Clothiers of Gloucestershire, Worcestershire, Oxfordshire, Wiltshire and other Clothing Counties'. He was, moreover, careful to stress the interdependence of all classes, 'from the meanest spinner in the Nation to the Prince upon the Throne', for 'if, for a few years only, Providence should order things so that the Sheep should yield no fleece, we should see how sensibly the Landlords would feel the loss of their Tenants, . . . and when the Weavers' looms ceased to go, or the Spinners' wheels to turn round, the Farmers' teams would learn to stand still, and the Gentlemen's coaches soon have no wheels'; for ' 'tis by the spinning-wheels going round in the Village, that the coach-wheels go round in the Park'. Surely people must feel concern, even alarm, at this grave threat to Britain's principal manufacture, except perhaps the few who were engaged in bringing in 'these Things' and 'cooking them up to the gay Imaginations of our Ladies'. And as a gentleman in a coffee-house said, the weavers would never succeed so long as 'all the Women were against them to a man'. Therefore let every manu-facturer and merchant, every woolcomber and spinner, every dealer in wool or silk in any form, *begin at home* by trying to convince his wife and daughters that by wearing calico they were destroying British manufactures and starving the poor.

Having written four numbers of the *Manufacturer*[30] in a fortnight, even Daniel Defoe was reduced (in nos. 5 and 6) to repetition, irrelevancy, and a rather garrulous attack upon the governors of the East India Company who were accused of trying to curry favour with the Government by offering large loans on easy terms. But, says Defoe, 'let 'em not flatter themselves with the Magnipotence of their Cash; for . . . the Manufacturers, however poor and declining, shall out-bid them', because once Parliament has rescued trade and manufacture from the calico plague, prosperity will return and far more funds will become available than the Government has need of. In no. 7 Defoe is obviously trailing his coat hoping that somebody—anybody—will enliven the proceedings by joining issue with the *Manufacturer*. His wish was swiftly granted, for early in November 1719 there had appeared in the lists the *British Merchant, or a Review of the Trade of Great Britain, so far as it is Falsely Stated by The Manufacturer*, 'proving that the Author ought to have rank'd the Heads of his first Papers under the word Clamour and not Argument'.[31] This exactly suited Defoe and gave him a second wind. Week after week the wordy warfare raged. The *British Merchant* attributed the decline in the English silk manufacture, not to the competition of printed calicoes, but to the imported foreign wrought silks; and ascribed any general decline of prosperity and employment to idleness, extravagance and the consequent high costs of manufacture, 'for 'tis a certain Maxim that Cheapness of Labour, and consequently the Cheapness of Goods, is the only Means to increase their Consumption either at home or abroad; and without this all Laws will be of no great Effect.' Then followed in successive issues (to use the *British Merchant*'s own words) 'a Repeated Confutation of all that the *Manufacturer* has asserted against Printed Callicoes as the Principal Cause of the Decay of the Woollen Manufacture', and arguments to sustain the proposition 'that printed calicoes are more beneficial to the nation than the silks they interfere with'.[32]

Defoe began his work as 'author' of the *Manufacturer* anonymously, but very soon the *British Merchant* challenged him to say openly whether he had 'been formerly concern'd in a Paper call'd the *Mercator* . . .'. This Defoe admitted, adding that 'some of the Gentlemen who opposed my Management of *The Mercator* then, do me the honour not to be asham'd of my managing *The Manufacturer* now'.[33]

Towards the end of 1719 massive support for the Calico Bill was forthcoming from all parts of the country. It seemed indeed that the time was ripe and the weavers willing. On 24 November the House of Commons received and referred to a Committee of the Whole House a petition from 'the Weavers, Walkers, and others', freemen of the Company of Clothiers of Worcester complaining of the 'Deplorable and Declining Condition' of the clothing trade and the woollen manufactures throughout the kingdom by reason of the export of wool and the wearing of stained and printed calicoes and linens. This was the beginning of an avalanche. Day after day for nearly three months similar petitions poured into Parliament from the London weavers, dyers and silk throwsters, and from weavers, woolcombers, websters, spinners, fullers, clothiers and mercers, in upwards of a hundred cities, towns and villages in twenty-seven counties spread throughout the length and breadth of the land, from Durham and Westmorland to Hampshire and Dorset; and from Devon, Somerset and South Wales to Norfolk, Suffolk and Essex.[34] The Petition of the London Weavers' Company to the Commissioners for Trade and Plantations was transferred in due course to the House of Commons, and when the Company's deputation appeared before the Committee of the Whole House on 21 January 1720,[35] their case was supported and strengthened by a timely report and recommendations submitted by the Commissioners for Trade and Plantations after a thorough sifting of the evidence submitted by all the interests mainly concerned, such as the weavers of London, Norwich and Canterbury, the Turkey and Italian merchants, the Scottish linen merchants, drapers and factors, the calico printers and the East India Company.

The London Weavers' evidence was given by Thomas Eades, Colonel Lekeux and his son, Peter Lekeux, Josiah Tidmarsh, John Dent and several other prominent members of the Company. Eades (Renter Bailiff of the Weavers' Company in 1719–20 and Upper Bailiff in 1720–1) was a Quaker and a manufacturer of 'callimancoes and camblitts partly for the foreign trade', who normally employed between 180 and 230 looms, but after some two years of declining trade he had but 100 looms in use, of which only one-third were fully employed. He estimated that about 1,500 of his employees (men, women and children) were without work in the autumn of 1719, and he had on his hands £7,000 worth of unsold silk and woollen goods. The numbers of weavers in London had not increased since 1714–15, but their employment had 'lessened every year for 3 or 4 years past and weavers' wages had fallen 25 per cent'.[36] As additional evidence the London Weavers' Company submitted to the Commissioners seven pages of samples of the fabrics chiefly affected by the competition of printed calicoes—some light worsteds, many half silks and a few slight silks—with details of widths and prices, to prove that consumers had, in fact, a great range and variety of home-produced stuffs to choose from, and at prices lower than those charged for printed calicoes and linens, for example: woollen stuffs from 4d. to 4s. per yard, silk and worsted stuffs from 9d. to 5s. per yard, silk and thread stuffs from 10d. to 5s. 6d. per yard, and silk stuffs from 1s. 6d. to 28s. per yard.

When it was suggested that they had taken excessive numbers of apprentices, the London Weavers replied that in 1660, in obedience to an Order in Council, they 'did indeed admit many foreign weavers into their Fellowship, but for ten years past they have bound no more than 3,213 apprentices'. The Canterbury weavers had bound only eighty-five apprentices in seven years (1713–20) 'and at Norwich their Trade is, and has been, under such Discouragement that not above one-eighth part of the weavers have any apprentices', and most of these had but one apprentice each.[37] Defoe saw nothing surprising in this, for, said he, when textile manufactures were declining, parents hesitated to apprentice their children to such crafts because 'it seems to be only bringing them up to Misery and Beggary, and putting them Apprentice to learn the Art and Mystery of Starving'.[38] The Commissioners estimated that when trade was good some 16,000 looms were employed 'in and about London, which kept at work and maintained 160,000 persons in combing, spinning etc.', and at Norwich another 130,000 people were similarly employed by the textile manufacture. But large-scale smuggling of foreign wrought silks and Indian calicoes, and the fashion of wearing printed calicoes and linens had forced British weavers to 'lessen the number of their looms and discharge many of their people'. On the other side of the account only about 800 people, including labourers, women and children, were employed in printing and staining calicoes and linens in England.

The tide of affairs now seemed to be flowing in favour of the weavers. Both the Commissioners for Trade and Plantations, and the Committee of the Whole House recommended that the use of all printed, painted, stained and dyed calicoes and linens in apparel, household furniture, or otherwise in Great Britain should be prohibited; except linens grown and manufactured in Great Britain and Ireland. The Committee also took the view that the prevalent smuggling of English wool into foreign countries was 'a great Occasion of the Decay of the Woollen Manufacturers of this Kingdom'.[39] Defoe proclaimed (prematurely) that the weavers' enemies had been 'smitten . . . under the Fifth Rib'. An anti-calico Bill was brought in and passed by the Commons, but failed to pass the Lords; which meant for the weavers 'hope deferred' until the next session of Parliament.[40] Great and bitter was the disappointment, especially among the journeymen and small master weavers. In and around Spitalfields men and women could think and talk of nothing else. Rumours were soon abroad that this or that person had tried to obstruct the Bill; that A.B. or C.D. had said that the journeymen weavers were a lazy lot and would not work if they had it to do; or that a certain firm had stocks of printed calicoes hidden in a house. The result was a highly explosive situation, which the Weavers' Company tried to damp down by exerting its influence among members and by the issue of a public notice early in May 1720.[41]

> Weavers Hall,
>   At a Court of Assistants of the said Company,
>   held the 6th Day of May, 1720.

> Whereas the Application that has been made to the Parliament and to the Government in behalf of the Manufacturers of this Kingdom, against the Mischiefs arising to them from the Wearing and Use of Calicoes, has been so successful, that although for Reasons of State, they have not obtained an immediate Redress according to their Hopes, and as the Necessity of the Poor requir'd: yet since it hath been publickly declared, not only in their Lordships' Address to his Majesty, but in his Majesty's most gracious Answer thereto, that their Complaints are just, and that their Grievances ought to be redressed; there appear much greater hopes than ever that the Manufacturers will receive effectual Relief the very next Sessions of Parliament. . . . We farther earnestly recommend

it to you, That in Compassion to the Poor, you would exert your utmost Ability to keep them in Work as much as possible, to prevent the Distresses and Miseries they must otherwise be reduced to. And above all, we recommend to you to use your Authority with Your Servants, and your Interest among your Workmen, to prevail with them to bear patiently the Delay of their Deliverance, and at least to behave themselves peaceably and dutifully that they may not render themselves unworthy of his Majesty's Concern for them, or put themselves out of his Royal Favour and Protection; and especially that they may give no Advantage to their Enemies to represent them as People unworthy of the Good that is intended for them.

Persuasion, however, proved powerless; the soothing tones of the calm voice of reason and all the counsels of prudence and patience went unheeded. According to Maitland's *History of London*, the weavers were so inflamed that:

> . . . some thousands of them, with their Wives and Children, repaired in a tumultuous manner from Spitalfields to Westminster; where, crowding the passages to the House of Lords, they demanded justice of their Lordships as they passed. But detachments of the Horse-Guards being sent to prevent their doing mischief the Mutineers returned home, without doing other damage than tearing a few Calico Gowns off the backs of divers Women they met; and being arrived at their respective habitations, peace was preserved in that neighbourhood by the Trained Bands of the Tower-Hamlets for a few days. But the hot fit returning, they threatened to demolish the house of a French weaver and rifle that of the East India Company; but detachments of the Horse and Foot-Guards being timely sent into the City, and the Trained-Bands drawn out, their pernicious designs were happily prevented; and divers of the Rioters being apprehended and committed to Prison, the rest immediately dispersed.[42]

The 'French weaver' referred to may have been James Dalbiac of Brick Lane in 'Bednal Green Hamlet'. An angry mob carrying staves and stones smashed his windows and threatened to pull down his house and tear him limb from limb. Another weaver, Peter Nettle, of Steward Street in the Old Artillery Ground, also had his windows smashed by the mob.

The year 1720 saw the inflation of the South Sea Bubble and a hundred others; when all sorts of people rushed 'to buy shares in the most glorious money-for-jam' speculative frenzy ever known. The

London Journal reported that there was 'nothing but running about from coffee-house to coffee-house and subscribing without knowing what the proposals were'. The poet Prior, who, like John Gay, had plunged heavily, wrote: 'I am lost in the South Sea; the roaring of the waves and the madness of the people are justly put together. It is all madder than St. Anthony's dream.'[43] Amid all this glitter of riches, real and imagined, the weavers' troubles received scarcely a thought, except from Daniel Defoe and the Weavers' Company. 'The manufacturers', said Defoe, 'are as willing to give place to Superior Business as any other People, but not quite so able. Poverty and Distress, Decay of Trade, Loss of Employment, and Cries of Families are clamant and vexatious things, not soon quieted or easily borne.' But, he asked, is the South Sea Bubble superior business? Surely not; for the 'late Fractures and Fall' of the bubble companies 'have given a Terrible Blow to the whole Nation'; confidence and credit have been destroyed and honest trade and manufactures brought to a standstill, so that many poor people 'are greatly distress'd by the Disaster of it'. Priority in Parliament's time-table ought to be given not to 'Bubble Business' but to manufacturers' business—the Calico Bill—for 'Projects and Stocks are but accidents, were born of yesterday and die tomorrow; but Manufactures are the Life of the Nation.'[44]

Meantime the Company was preparing yet another petition to Parliament, stressing the plight of the many hundreds of poor weavers and their families, and pointing out that in anticipation of some relief from Parliament the master weavers were giving employment to their journeymen and, consequently, were accumulating in their hands great stocks of finished goods; but they could not continue to do this 'unless encouraged by a Bill' passed in their favour.[45]

When Parliament reassembled, the long agitation on the weavers' behalf—petitions and pamphlets without number, the powerful pen of Daniel Defoe in the eighty-six issues of the *Manufacturer*, the weighty facts and calculations produced in the *Weaver*,[46] and a general public concern that the poor should be employed in spinning and weaving rather than rioting—at last blossomed and bore fruit. The so-called 'Calico Bill' became an Act[47] which forbade the use or wear in Great Britain, after Christmas Day 1722, of all printed, painted, stained and dyed calicoes (but not linens) in any garment, or apparel, or on any bed, chair, cushion, under-cushion or other household purpose. The scope of the Act included 'all stuffs made of cotton or mixed therewith, which shall be printed or painted with any colour or colours, or chequered or striped, or stitched or flowered in foreign parts with any colour or colours or with coloured flowers made there' with the exception of muslins, neckcloths, fustians and calicoes dyed all blue. The wearers, users, buyers and sellers of the prohibited fabrics were liable to fines ranging from £5 to £20, the money so forfeited to be shared between the informers or prosecutors and the poor of the parish in which the offence was committed. The justice and compassion of Parliament, said Defoe, 'gives Life to our Trade' by opening the way to 'a general Re-cloathing of so many thousand Women at once with our own Growth and Workmanship'. Was it not, indeed, more reasonable 'that our own People should be cloathed by the Labour of our own People, than by the Labour and to the Profit of Pagans and Mahometans'? Defoe, of course, realised the importance of proper enforcement of the law:

> Not a Callicoe should ever pass the Streets after this Act excludes them, without just Measures taken to call them to Account; it will then be no Mobbing decently to desire the Callicoe Lady to walk before a Justice of the Peace, with her Tawdry Geer, and give such an account of herself as the Law directs. No poor Weaver will be liable to be Transported and, as we may call it, sold into Slavery, for pulling a Callicoe Madam by the Elbow, but the Crime will be then of the Callicoe side, and it is our Fault if we let any of them escape unpresented. . . . From this day we may date the resurrection from the dead, as well of our foreign declining commerce as of our manufactures.[48]

This was, indeed, the nub of the matter. The weavers' victory did not bring a permanent peace because, in practice, enforcement of the new law on any adequate scale was impossible. Calico fever, a particular manifestation of what Defoe called the ladies' 'passion for fashion', was sometimes assuaged, but never completely cured. Women continued to wear, and weavers continued to tear, the forbidden fabrics. Only a few weeks after the new Act came into force Defoe, out of patience at last, sharply rebuked the journeymen weavers for 'outrages' against women thought to be wearing prohibited calicoes. If, he said, the weavers proceeded legally their many friends would be ready 'to help and assist them, and to appear for them as they have formerly done; but this [violent] way Nobody can appear for them . . . or say anything in their behalf'.[49] Five years later, Defoe himself, the weavers' champion, was ready to admit defeat at the hands of the army of Amazons who steadily refused to 'dress by law or clothe by Act of Parliament . . . they claim English liberty as well as the men, and as they expect to do what they please, and say what they please, so they will wear what they please, and dress how they please'.[50] Thus, despite the Act of 1721, and the prohibition of the importation of wrought silks, plus export bounties given, in 1722, on English silk, the restocking revival of trade soon

passed and the London weavers felt once again the cold grip of a
creeping depression. In July 1728, a crowd of journeymen weavers
presented a humble petition to the Weavers' Company, stressing the
severe recession of trade and mounting unemployment 'these three
years last past' which had caused 'the utmost Poverty and Want'
and asking, fearfully, 'what will it be when the Winter comes on?'
They attributed 'this excessive Badness of Trade . . . chiefly and
principally' to the increasing use and wearing of printed and stained
fabrics and all sorts of prohibited wrought silks. The petitioners
asked the Company to press the Government for some limitation
of the use and wear of competing goods, otherwise they feared that,
driven by hunger among themselves and their wives and children,
some of their fellows might again resort to 'Riots, Tumults, and
Assaults, which are generally the Product of Misery and Despair:
which Publick Disorders pick-pockets and common Rogues never
fail to foment and cultivate, that they may thereby the better pilfer
and steal; and when they have so done, to father those Villanies on
the poor Weavers, as they did in the Time of the Tearing of the
Callicoes'. With the same object in mind, a full Court of the Weavers'
Company promptly printed and published the journeymen's petition
prefaced by their own observations upon it, viz., that the Court
'were all to a Man' of the opinion that the petition was just and
reasonable, and they would do all in their power to procure some
relief, by laying the 'Petition and Reasons' before one or other of the
first Officers of State.[51]

That the wearing of forbidden fabrics still continued in the 1730s
is proved by the words of warning offered to the ladies by the
Gentlemen's Magazine in 1735:

> The silkworms form the wardrobe's gaudy pride;
> How rich the vests which Indian looms provide;
> Yet let me here the British nymphs advise
> To hide these foreign spoils from native eyes;
> Lest rival artists murmuring for employ,
> With savage rage the envied work destroy.[52]

Prosecutions against the wearers of printed calico were also brought,
from time to time, *pour encourager les autres*, and in 1741, after
several accused persons had pleaded ignorance of the law of 1721,
the Lord Mayor recommended the Weavers to publish in several
newspapers the relevant sections of the Act as a warning to the
unwary.[53] This was done at intervals during 1741–3 by notices in the
Daily Advertiser and the *London Evening Post*.[54] But the struggle
still went on. In June 1745, the Weavers' Company appointed a
special committee of nine 'to put the Act of Parliament . . . in force
against the sellers and wearers of printed calico', with powers to

act on information received and to press prosecutions at the Company's expense.[55] Three weeks later, the Court had before them a petition presented by a deputation of journeymen silk weavers on 'behalf of themselves and great Numbers of their poor Brethren Weavers in and about London' calling attention to the 'great difficulties and Distresses for want of sufficient Employment' that they had suffered 'for a considerable time past', because of 'the great Increase of late Years in the Using and Wear of printed Callicoes, Chints and prohibited East India Silks, contrary to the Acts of Parliament'. They asked for immediate action, for they were 'Reduced to the Utmost Poverty and Distress and in danger of Starving'. The Court assured the men that the Company was resolved to prosecute all offenders against whom sufficient evidence could be found. At the same time

> it was Earnestly recommended by the Court to the Petitioners that they would take especial Care themselves and also recommend it to the rest of the journeymen Weavers to behave themselves quietly and not Commit any Violence which might break the Peace. But that such Information as they should be able to make against any Offenders Complain'd of by their Petition they should give to the Company's Clerk . . . and then the Petitioners withdrew.[56]

Shortly afterwards the Company issued a public notice:

> Weavers Hall,
> London,
> July 11th 1745.

> The Legislature . . . having thought fit by divers Acts of Parliament to prohibit the Use, Sale and Wear of all East India Silks, Chints and printed Callicoes whatsoever; the Weavers Company, London, have resolved, at the request of the poor Manufacturers effectually to put the Laws in execution against all Offenders, and hereby give Notice . . . that the Penalty upon any Persons having a Gown, Apparel or Furniture, of East-India Silk or Chints, besides the loss of the said goods, is £200. . . . Every person's house, on information, is liable to be search'd and such goods to be seized as prohibited Goods. The Penalty on wearing a printed Callico Gown is to the Informer £5 for every offence, which is every day the same is worn, if information be given within 6 days. The Penalty on . . . having Furniture of printed Callico is £20, one half to the Informer. The like Penalty for . . . selling printed Callicoes or exposing the same for sale (unless for Exportation) . . . and printed Cottons, tho' manufactured in this Kingdom, are

under the same Penalty, unless the Warp be entirely of Linen Yarn.[57]

And about a fortnight later a supplementary notice appeared in the press:

> Weavers Hall,
> London,
> July 25th 1745.
>
> Whereas several Persons have within six months last past bought Gowns of printed Callico, thro' Inadvertency of the Penalties incurr'd by wearing them; the Weavers Company, London, give Notice, that if such Persons will apply to the Draper or Drapers who sold them, and he or they shall refuse to return the Money the Gown cost, on applying to the said Company's Clerk at any Time within twenty Days before the six Months expire, he will, at the Company's Expense, on due Proof of such Sale, oblige the Seller or Sellers to return the Money for the same.[58]

We know that proceedings were begun against a number of sellers of printed calicoes, but it is impossible to estimate the degree of success achieved in this direction. Drapers usually had either the means to defend themselves or the wit to evade the law; but poor, ignorant and illiterate persons were especially vulnerable. The Weavers' Court minutes record the case of Mary Andrews, convicted at Guildhall and fined £5 for wearing a printed calico gown, 'but she being really very poor' and 'an object of charity', appealed to the Weavers not to press for payment of the fine; whereupon the Court of Assistants remitted £4 5s. taking only 15s. towards the legal charges.[59] About the same time the following public apology appeared in the London press:

> Whereas I, Abraham Burton, Porter and free of the Weavers' Company, did on Friday last insult a Lady in the publick Streets for wearing a painted gown, and as I was then in liquor and entirely ignorant of the Penalty I have incurred . . . and now being sensible of, and sincerely sorry for the Crime I have committed, do . . . ask Pardon for the same of the Lady and all others concern'd, and hope, out of Compassion to my Wife and numerous Family now unprovided for, they will not prosecute me according to my deserts, promising for the future to behave myself peaceably and quietly. . . .

The maximum penalty was transportation for seven years, so we must hope that the lady decided to forgive the repentant porter.

In 1746 the Weavers had to drop half-a-dozen cases against sellers of prohibited goods because four eminent lawyers advised that, in their opinion, the Company, being a corporation, could not itself act in a lawsuit as a common informer.[60] But it could act on the information given by individuals, and this it continued to do, in selected cases, for over thirty years. Between 1766 and 1769, for example, the Company paid a number of rewards to certain common informers who seem to have followed a lucrative, if unsavoury, trade. Entries in the Renter Bailiffs' accounts are self-explanatory (see Table 14.2).[61]

Table 14.2 *Company payments to informers*

Date	Item	£	s.	d.
23 October 1766	Paid John Peck reward for convicting Esther Seymour for wearing Callico	20	0	0
8 October 1767	Cash paid John Peck for his services against the Wearers of Chintz	15	15	0
16 November 1767	To John Peck for his services in convicting wearers of Chintz	10	10	0
	and Wm. Ward for ditto . . .	15	15	0
21 December 1768	The Clerk's bill on account of the Information and Convictions of the Wearers of Chintz or Printed Callicoes	31	4	0

Similar rewards were paid, from time to time, for 'services in promoting seizures of foreign and Indian wrought silks'. A pair of wily Welshmen seem to have been especially active in this sector. Thus in March 1768 the Court of Assistants, 'ordered that Ten guineas be paid to David Davis for . . . giving information for Foreign Silks, in consequence of which several Seizures were made'. Three months later, Thomas Jones, a journeyman tailor by trade, received a reward of five guineas 'for his service in procuring a seizure of a Foreign Coat and Waistcoat . . . by Mr. Lycet, a Customhouse Officer'.[62] In the following year, Peck and Ward, still very active, received from the Weavers' Company twenty and thirty guineas respectively for giving information and 'procuring Several Persons to be Convicted of Wearing Printed, Painted, Stained or Dyed Callicoes contrary to Law'.[63] After 1769 such rewards were paid much less frequently, for the Company seems to have reached the conclusion that it was unprofitable to continue an active repressive policy, since the results achieved hardly justified the expenses incurred. There is, however, in the Renter Bailiffs' Voucher and Receipt Book, under the date 7 February 1780, a receipt for '£5, being a gratuity for my Trouble in Convicting Persons of Wearing Chintz, &c. . . . (signed) Edward Wheston.'[64] And as late as 1785 it was reported in the press that

'Last week a gentlewoman of Mile-end had a new linen gown entirely destroyed by pouring spirits on it, by some wicked fellows, supposed to be Spitalfields silk-weavers. This practice is grown so common at the eastern end of the town that most of the females are fearful of leaving home in cottons or linens, especially in the evenings.'

NOTES

1 Bal Krishna, *Commercial Relations between India and England, 1601–1757* (1924), pp. 98, 139.
2 Ibid., p. 140.
3 P. J. Thomas, *Mercantilism and the East India Trade* (1926), pp. 26–9, 38.
4 Ibid., pp. 45–6.
5 The distress and desperation among the journeymen weavers was so great in 1683 that it was suggested that a troop of cavalry should be quartered in Whitechapel (Cal. S.P. Dom., 1683 (2), p. 330; quoted in M. Beloff, *Public Order and Popular Disturbances* (1938), p. 83).
6 Krishna, op. cit., pp. 257–9.
7 Pamphlet, *England's Danger by Indian Manufactures* (1699).
8 Beloff, op. cit., pp. 84–6; Thomas, op. cit., p. 108.
9 N. Luttrell, *A Brief Historical Relation of State Affairs*, IV, pp. 167, 172, 197, 198–200, 510.
10 It was hoped that such goods would be re-exported to Europe, and this was the Act which introduced the bonded-warehouse system.
11 For an excellent section on early English calico-printing see Thomas, op. cit., pp. 121–8, 174.
12 Wadsworth & Mann, *The Cotton Trade and Industrial Lancashire, 1600–1780* (1931), p. 133.
13 *The Case of the Fair Traders: Being a clear View and State of the Clandestine Trade, as now carry'd on in Gt. Britain* (a pamphlet, c. 1719).
14 *A Letter to a Member of the Honourable House of Commons* (c. 1720); *The Case of the Shop-Keepers in Great Britain, humbly recommended to the ensuing Parliament* (c. 1720); *Jnl of Commissioners for Trade and Plantations* (1719), p. 118.
15 MS. 4655/11, ff.177b, 179, 182.
16 Natalie Rothstein, 'The Calico Campaign of 1719–21', in *East London Papers*, July 1964, p. 5.
17 In mid-June 1719, four men said to be weavers were imprisoned for rioting, and two others for 'feloniously tearing' a woman's gown (*V.C.H.*, *Middx.* (1911), p. 134).
18 *Weekly Journal*, 4 July 1719, p. 1395.
19 *The Original Weekly Journal*, 2 January 1720, quoted in Rothstein, op. cit., p. 8n.; G. B. Hertz, 'The English Silk Industry in the 18th Century', in *English Historical Review*, XXIV (1909), p. 725. cf. *The Case of the Retailers of Printed Callicoes* (1720) and *The Case of the Linen-Drapers* (c. 1720).

20 *Weekly Journal*, 4 July 1719, p. 1394.
21 Thomas, op. cit., pp. 141, 145.
22 Printed for W. Boreham in Paternoster Row, 1719.
23 *Mist's Journal*, 15 August and 12 September 1719.
24 MS. 4655/11, ff.279–83.
25 James Sutherland, *Defoe* (1937), p. 183.
26 *Weekly Review*, 31 January 1708.
27 The *Manufacturer*, 15 December 1719.
28 Published every Wednesday and Friday for three-and-a-half
   months, but after 12 February 1720 on Wednesdays only: printed
   for W. Boreham at the Angel in Paternoster Row; price $1\frac{1}{2}d$.
29 The *Manufacturer*, no. 2, 4 November 1719.
30 Each number was a single foolscap sheet closely printed on both
   sides. Copies of these and many other similar documents were
   bound and kept by the Weavers' Company. In 1893 the City
   Librarian asked that this book, 'recently exhibited at Merchant
   Taylors' Hall', should be given to the Guildhall Library, but the
   Company declined to part with it (MS. 4655/28, August and October
   1893). It has now (1969) been deposited there. See A.1.3, no. 64.
31 The *British Merchant*, no. 1, Tuesday 10 November 1719. This
   counterblast to the *Manufacturer* was a weekly sheet (price $1\frac{1}{2}d$.)
   financed by the drapers and edited by 'Mr Asgill', probably John
   Asgill (1659–1738), writer, barrister, and speculator; member of
   Irish House of Commons from which he was expelled *c*. 1703;
   subsequently member for Bramber in the English House of Commons.
32 See, e.g., the *Manufacturer*, no. 10, December 1719 and no. 22,
   January 1720; the *British Merchant*, nos 1, 3, 5 and 10.
33 The *Manufacturer*, no. 10, 2 December 1719. The *Mercator, or Commerce Retrieved* was published twice weekly from 26 May 1713 to
   20 July 1714, to advocate the Government's free-trade policy. In
   his *Appeal to Honour and Justice* (1715) Defoe denies that he was its
   author or that he had any payment or profit from it; but he con-
   tradicts himself in the *Manufacturer* as to his authorship, though
   he still maintains that he was not paid for his work. Professor
   Sutherland points out that Defoe was paid £500 during the first
   seven months of 1714 out of Secret Service Funds (Sutherland,
   op. cit., p. 201). cf. J. T. Boulton (ed.), *Daniel Defoe* (1965), pp.
   189, 280; J. R. Moore, *A Checklist of the Writings of Defoe* (1960);
   and *Daniel Defoe, Citizen of the Modern World* (1958), pp. 100–2.
34 *Votes of the House of Commons*, 24 November 1719–6 February
   1720.
35 Ibid., January 1720, pp. 66, 78; MS. 4655/11, ff.279–280b.
36 MS. 4655/11, ff.269, 281, 299; City of London Records: Companies,
   8.3, *Journal of the Commissioners for Trade and Plantations, 1719*,
   p. 128; N. Rothstein, 'The Calico Campaign of 1719–21', in *East
   London Papers*, July 1964, pp. 10 and 15; the *Manufacturer*, no.
   26, January 1720. Callimancoes were striped, glazed worsteds
   woven in satin in bright colours, and sold at $11d$. to $13d$. a yard.
   Flowered callimancoes had a floral design made by the weft
   crossing the stripes, and were a little more expensive. These
   materials were used for men's gowns and waistcoats, children's
   coats and furnishings.
37 *Journal of the Commissioners for Trade and Plantations, 1718–22,*

pp. 118, 133–5. A copy of the petition of the Norwich City Council and the Norwich worsted weavers is printed in the *Manufacturer*, no. 10, 2 December 1719.

38 The *Manufacturer*, no. 19, 1 January 1720.

39 *Votes of the House of Commons*, February 1720, f.112.

40 MS. 4655/11, ff.289b, 290b; *Manufacturer*, no. 31, 17 February 1720, no. 34, 9 March 1720, and no. 43, 11 May 1720.

41 MS. 4655/11, ff.292b–293; *Manufacturer*, no. 42, 4 May 1720.

42 Maitland, *London*, I, p. 530; MS. 4655/11, f.294 refers to 'the late Riots and Insults', 19 May 1720.

43 E. T. Powell, *The Evolution of the Money Market* (1916), p. 153n., gives a list of twenty-six 'bubbles' and the fantastic peak prices reached by their shares. P. F. Gaye, *John Gay: His place in the 18th Century* (1938), pp. 204–5; E. H. Lecky, *History of England in the 18th Century*, I, pp. 371 et. seq. Pope was among the fortunate few who came through 'with half of what they imagined they had'. P. Quennell, *Alexander Pope* (1968), p. 167.

44 *Manufacturer*, no. 65, 13 October 1720, no. 75, 22 December 1720, and no. 79, 19 January 1721.

45 MS. 4655/11, ff.308, 312.

46 *Manufacturer*, nos. 1–86, which ran from 30 October 1719 to 9 March 1721. The *Weaver* came out eight times from 23 November 1719 to 11 January 1720. The *British Merchant*, opponent of the *Manufacturer*, appeared only twelve times, from 10 November 1719 to 11 February 1720.

47 7 Geo. I, c. 7.

48 *Manufacturer*, nos. 82–5. The Weavers' Company promptly printed and circulated an abstract of the Act of 1721.

49 W. Lee, *Daniel Defoe: His Life and Recently Discovered Writings* (1869), III, pp. 90–4.

50 Defoe, *A Plan of the English Commerce* (1726), p. 253.

51 MS. 4655/12, ff.186, 191, 209–10.

52 A stanza taken from the *Chronologist*; quoted in Krishna, op. cit., p. 264.

53 MS. 4655/15, f.115. Whether printed fustians made of linen and cotton were exempt from the Act of 1721 was doubtful. The Manchester men sought confirmation of their right to manufacture such fabrics, and in 1736 the so-called Manchester Act expressly permitted the use of printed fabrics made of linen yarn and cotton wool, provided that the warp was entirely of linen yarn.

54 MS. 4648/6, 6 October 1742; MS. 4655/15, f.162b.

55 MS. 4655/15, f.225b.

56 MS. 4655/15, f.226b.

57 The law was complicated and required expert technical knowledge for its just enforcement; also it was open to abuses, such as false or malicious information laid by dishonest persons or out of private spite.

58 But any garment of 'printed linen, cotton, lawn or other sort of cloth, *not being calico*', could legally be worn.

59 MS. 4655/15, ff.234b, 235b, 261b.

60 MS. 4655/15, ff.272, 284b.

61 MS. 4648/8.

62 MS. 4655/17, ff.77b, 83, 102b.

63 MS. 4655/17, f.103; MS. 4655/17, ff.413–14, 4 June 1782. Even the

embassies of foreign governments might become involved in clandestine activities, as when the Customs Officers seized several thousand pounds' worth of foreign laces, silks, and other prohibited goods in the apartment of a secretary at the Bavarian Embassy.
64 MS. 4649, f.49.

Chapter 15

Special Treatment for Spitalfields

From the early part of the eighteenth century down to 1773 the London silk industry was plagued by 'grievous discontents' and not a few civil disturbances which became ever more serious as the years passed. It was, as we know, a fashion trade, subject to sharp fluctuations of fortune, peaks of temporary prosperity being followed by depressions which quickly plunged the poorer weavers, their families and auxiliary workers into the depths of privation. 'As soon as the market stops, they [the master weavers] stop. If they cannot sell their work they immediately knock off looms and the journeymen as immediately starve.' Certain masters might have to discharge from fifty to a hundred men and, perhaps, put a similar number on short-time. Some, indeed, mindful of the distress which threatened their employees, were prepared to manufacture goods for stock; but to do so in the fashion sections of the trade was to run the risk of heavy losses—even bankruptcy—because a capricious fluke of fashion might suddenly render a master weaver's stock wellnigh valueless. Furthermore, there were, from time to time, dearths of raw materials —most of which had to be imported from Turkey and the Levant, Italy, India and China—arising from natural causes or the outbreak of foreign wars.

Although the English silk manufacturers were protected by high import duties from 1713 to 1765, they still had to face strong competition from attractive foreign fabrics, many of which were smuggled in. The French manufacturers were the most formidable competitors, and, we are told, 'their smuggled goods caused despair in Spitalfields'. The fondness of English buyers for French alamodes and lustrings, for example, became almost a craze, and ladies of fashion thought it a triumph if they secured new and rare French silks but lately brought in by smugglers. 'Women asked for Pompadour caps, Orleans handkerchiefs, and Conti mantlets at the bidding of cosmopolitan dressmakers, who . . . insisted on recommending French gowns and styles.' Smuggled silk was, indeed, prized so highly that some English makers actually tried to pass off their goods as having been lately smuggled from France.[1] And when 'prodigious quantities' of Chinese and Indian silks were also smuggled via Ireland, the Isle of Man, and the Plantations, it is small wonder that the English silk manufacturers became alarmed and despondent, with

> The poor in our streets complaining too;
> They fain would work, but have no work to do.

In the eighteenth century, too, the widening gulf between the master manufacturers and the 'working hands' added internal stresses and struggles between masters and journeymen to the difficulties which beset the industry. Journeymen in many of the crafts were turning away, slowly but surely, from the craft gilds, in which they had little status and less influence, and seeking to form societies of their own. The journeymen feltmakers, for example, seem to have had a trade club able to call and organise strikes as early as 1696–9;[2] although, in the end, they were made to confess, with deep contrition, that they had

> conspired and combined together to enhance the prices for making of hats, for which several of us now stand indicted, and being now . . . fully convinced of the unlawfulness of such conspiracies, do hereby . . . promise . . . the Masters, Wardens and Commonalty of the Company of Feltmakers, London, [never to] . . . do any act . . . that may in any wise tend to the promoting or encouraging of such conspiracies or combinations.

The journeymen wheelwrights formed a club in 1714 and during the following twenty years they struck three times for higher wages and shorter hours. In 1718 we hear of the master coachbuilders' complaint of a journeymen's combination and in 1721 the master tailors asked Parliament to put a stop to a recent combination among their journeymen (numbering some seven thousand in London and Westminster) to raise wages and reduce working hours. This journeymen's organisation was based upon several taverns where they met and collected 'several considerable sums of money to defend any prosecutions against them'. This, said the master tailors, is a

> very ill example to journeymen in all other trades; as is sufficiently seen in the journeymen Curriers, Smiths, Farriers, Sail-makers, Coach-makers, and artificers of divers other arts and misteries, who have actually entered into confederacies of the like nature; and the Journeymen Carpenters, Bricklayers and Joiners have taken steps for that purpose, and only wait to see the event of others.[3]

Towards the middle of the century the master masons became alarmed because the free journeymen masons had 'entered into unlawful Combination busying themselves more to prevent others from Working than to procure or Deserve Employment for themselves', and complained of 'an intractable Spirit in the lower Class of Freeman which made them Negligent in their Callings, Exhorbitant in their Demands and Disrespectful to their Superiors'.[4] Among the London silk weavers, too, the same forces were at work and similar trends can be discerned, exacerbated from time to time by fortuitous set-backs to the industry. Excessive drinking and failure to work at a steady pace were among the weavers' chief failings, not in London only, but throughout the country.[5] Many a weaver who could subsist on the earnings of three days' work was sorely tempted to be idle—and perhaps drunk—during the rest of the week. Monday (sometimes called Saint Monday) was usually a no-work day, and on Saturday the weaver took finished work to his employer's warehouse and received payment for it. Even on the four days, Tuesday to Friday, work could be interrupted from time to time by tippling and talking. In 1751 'A Citizen of London' ventured to offer some well-meant advice intended to discourage resort to taverns and clubs.

Men who spend their time in Clubs, contract bad Habits;
and too much drink makes a Man unfit for Business. Late
hours prevent early rising; and coming late to Work is the
cause of less work being done . . . if by Intemperance and bad
conduct of the Husband, a family is in a perishing Condition,
the Cause must not be attributed to Want of Trade. . . . A Man
who smoakes his Pipe at Home saves by doing so, and his
Wife gets some of his Beer; he goes to bed soon, and rises
early; he finishes his work well, is healthy and strong, and
thereby able to work better. . . . [Eventually] by Contentment
and Frugality he may rise from as mean Cottages as his first
Masters inhabited, to dwell in Houses like Palaces (Spittle
Square) which they now live in; or from Garrets with smoaky
Chimneys . . . to Country-houses in fine Air (Sydenham), which
they now occupy.[6]

The Weavers' records show that in the autumn of 1750, acting mainly through William Reynolds, an energetic Assistant, the Company was trying 'to keep the journeymen weavers in a quiet and peaceable Disposition' and taking precautions to prevent disturbances which threatened to arise from the adverse effects upon trade and employment of the 'excessive dearness' of raw silk and silk yarn. Again, in 1757, when a serious shortage of fine organzine thrown silk was feared, the Company made an urgent appeal to the

Government, and a Bill authorising imports from Italy was quickly rushed through.[7]

Early in the following decade, the Weavers' Company decided to try a policy of admitting qualified persons to the freedom at half fees in approved cases, hoping thereby to strengthen the Company, and at the same time to check the tendency of weavers 'in low circumstances' to form a combination or to resort, in hard times, to 'bargaining by riot'. In September 1761 the Court of Assistants decided that for the ensuing year any qualified persons 'desirous to be made free, but by reason of their low circumstances not able to bear the expense' might be admitted on payment of one-half of the usual fees. Non-members of all ages and various lengths of experience as weavers responded. Edmond Butler of Bethnal Green, for example, had been

> bred to the Weaving Business by his mother, Frances Butler, in Monmouth Street, Spitalfields, weaver, who was an Undertaker and had divers Looms standing in her House where the journeymen worked by whom he was instructed in the silk weaving, and has since exercised the Trade for 20 years. He now has a large family and is in low circumstances.

Among several Scotsmen who took advantage of the new dispensation were Robert Berenger, John Maxwell and John White, all of whom had been apprenticed in Edinburgh—Berenger more than twenty years before.[8] A number of weavers of French origin were also admitted at this time on payment of half fees. Peter Dusse of Bethnal Green had been bred to weaving in Picardy, 'as by Certificate dated 16th April 1758 appears, and has exercised the weaving business in England ever since his arrival, being upwards of six years'. John Ferry, 'who was bred to weaving in Normandy', and John Descarrieres, a foreman weaver, were similarly admitted. And, as a last example, we may notice the case of Lewis Gasquel, a French Protestant refugee weaver from the city of Nîmes,

> who left his country to avoid the Persecution in May 1752 and from thence went to Lausanne in Switzerland, and from thence to Holland, thence to Ireland where he took the Oaths and made the Declaration appointed by the Statute of King William for encouraging French Protestants to settle in Ireland, Prays to be admitted on payment of half fees, having a Wife and 3 children and being in low circumstances, was made free accordingly.[9]

The number of freemen admitted annually during the years immediately preceding the introduction of half fees was between forty and fifty. In the year 1761-2 the total number of freemen admitted rose steeply to 123, of whom 48 paid full fees and 75 half

318

fees. A second attempt was made in 1764–5 to attract new members in this way, but only half-a-dozen weavers availed themselves of the opportunity: a disappointing response.[10] Probably the poorer weavers were looking elsewhere for a solution to their problems and saw no point in joining the Weavers' Company. Many were leaving the industry because it was so overcrowded. Charlotte Clarke, Colley Cibber's daughter, writing her autobiography in the early 1750s, remarked that the companies of strolling players were being 'horribly invaded by barbers, 'prentices, taylors, and journeymen weavers'.[11] At the same time, there is evidence of a steady counter-flow of 'country' weavers into London and its suburbs.[12] The Weavers' records reveal a rising tide of complaints against the 'great encroach-ments' of interlopers, such as 'haberdashers and others' (including 'divers Jews') who exercised 'the said trade tho' not bred to the same' nor admitted to the freedom of the Weavers' Company. The Com-pany, while theoretically sympathetic to such complaints, pursued a selective policy, taking care not to embark upon a costly campaign of prosecutions at law against all and sundry. So, when James Buxton, a broad weaver, complained of the competition of unlawful workers, the Court of Assistants pointed out that he himself was not free of the company and was, therefore, 'a Transgressor by refusing to take up his Freedom, which he persisted to refuse . . . until the Company would exert themselves to put the Laws in force against Interlopers'. Such effrontery was a challenge not to be ignored, and the Court 'Resolved *nem. con.* that the said James Buxton be forth-with sued for Exercising the Trade within this Company's Guild, not being admitted to the Freedom.'[13] At another Court, in October 1763,

> divers Persons, Masters & Journeymen in the Worsted Lace weaving attended, complaining of Great Injury done to their Trade by Edward Thornhill and Henry Soley of Long Acre carrying on the said Trade in a very irregular and Illegal manner, and not being admitted to the Freedom of this Company. But it appearing that most of the Persons now complaining were themselves unlawful workers not being admitted to the Freedom. . . . It was Objected to the Regularity of Receiving this Complaint till the Parties Complaining had taken up the Freedom of this Company, if they were Intitled to the same. And that when they had done so, this Court would be ready to hear their Complaint if properly presented by a Memorial in Writing.

Whereupon 'the said Persons withdrew', doubtless much deflated.[14]

The Company did take legal action in a limited number of cases. For example, after several ineffective summonses, it decided to prosecute John Hallett, a non-member who was accused of carrying

on 'a considerable Trade within this Company's Guild'. This threat
soon brought about his 'submission', together with his partner, John
Wills, and they were both made free by redemption (not by servitude), towards the end of December 1763, on payment of the costs
of the suit and the usual fees.[15] Such cases suggest strongly that the
London silk industry was on the verge of domination by partnerships
of capitalist–entrepreneurs, of whom some, at least, had never been
apprenticed to the trade.

Meanwhile, many of the journeymen weavers, utterly discontented
with their rates of pay and total earnings, became dangerously
hostile to their employers in a general atmosphere of smouldering
resentment which some small incident might spark off into a violent
explosion. We know that in 1762 the journeymen had a list of
increased piece-work prices 'inserted in a Book, which they have
caused to be printed and delivered to each Master'.[16] When the
masters rejected 'the Book' some 2,000 weavers destroyed looms and
materials and began a strike which might have developed into
serious rioting had not the Guards been called out.[17] But the cauldron
continued to boil. On 28 March 1764 Mr John Dell, a Liveryman of
the Weavers' Company, reported to the Court of Assistants that
great numbers of journeymen were assembled in Weavers' Hall 'and
in the street about the Hall Gate', to pray that 'an application
might be made to Parliament to hinder the Exorbitant Increase and
Wear of Foreign Wrought Silks'. A small deputation of six or eight
of the journeymen having been admitted to the Court Room, the
Court professed itself well disposed to consider and pursue

> every reasonable measure . . . to promote their Trade and
> Manufacture, in which they were most essentially concerned,
> on behalf of themselves as well as the Journeymen. . . .
> But . . . the Journeymen by their Disorderly and Riotous
> Behaviour in many late instances of Cutting and Destroying
> Looms and Works, and other Outrageous Conduct, in Breach
> of the Peace, had rendered themselves very offensive, and to
> be looked upon as a very disorderly and turbulent set of People.

Any relief would obviously depend upon the restoration among
them of 'peaceable and orderly behaviour and obedience to the
Laws . . . as Good Subjects'. The journeymen's deputies 'promised
to Engage as much as they could a quiet behaviour in future',
and said that the journeymen were willing to collect £100 towards
the expenses of an application to Parliament.[18]

Then the journeymen went away and waited, and the months
passed, but no relief came. They waited nearly a year before, their
patience exhausted, they turned out and marched upon the houses
of Parliament 'with drums beating and banners flying', to present a

petition praying for a total prohibition of the importation of foreign-wrought silks. The lace-makers joined in, bearing flags to which they had attached floating pieces of French lace. They accosted several Members of Parliament who were not only shocked by the weavers' 'wretched situation' but alarmed at the sight of such a multitude and by a report that weavers from other towns were preparing to march to London. Arms from the Honourable Artillery Company's armoury were hastily sent to the Tower of London, lest they should fall into the weavers' hands; but the demonstrators contented themselves with smashing a few windows.[19] The Weavers' Company pressed Parliament, in March 1765, to lay additional duties upon all silks and velvets imported from the Continent whether plain wrought or brocaded, flowered, figured or clouded; and when this application failed another was prepared and presented a year later.[20]

The early summer of 1765 brought little or no improvement in the weavers' situation, so in sheer desperation they resolved to go direct to the King himself. Horace Walpole, painting, as he claimed, a portrait of the times, tells us that on 14 May between 3,000 and 4,000 of these poor men went very 'quietly and unarmed to Richmond, to petition the King for redress'. The Queen, walking in the paddock, was alarmed by their numbers; but they gave no offence, and marched off, peaceably enough, to Wimbledon, whither the King had gone to a review. When he promised to do all in his power to relieve them, 'they returned pleased and orderly'. But the next day, the Bill for imposing high duties on Italian silks having been rejected by the Lords, a great crowd of weavers went to the House of Lords, where they behaved 'in the most riotous manner, abusing the Peers, and applauding the Commons, who had passed their Bill'. The Chancellor's coach was stopped, but he boldly faced the mob who were 'abashed at his firmness' and let him pass.

> When the Duke of Bedford appeared, they hissed and pelted him; and one of the mob taking up a large stone . . . dashed it into the chariot: the Duke broke the force of the blow by holding up his arm, but it cut his hand and bruised him on the temple; so narrowly he escaped with his life. They then followed him to his own house, where with great good temper he admitted two of the ringleaders to a parley, and they went away seemingly appeased. The next day [16 May] the House of Lords issued out orders for preservation of the peace; but the weavers continued to parade the streets and the park, though without committing any violence.

Later that day, however, the Duke of Bedford was warned that his house would be attacked that night,[21] on which he sent away his jewels and papers, and demanded a party of horse, . . . and as was foreseen, the rioters in prodigious numbers assaulted the house in the evening and began to pull down the wall of the Court; but the great gates being thrown open, the party of horse appeared, and sallying out, while the riot act was read, rode round Bloomsbury square slashing and trampling on the mob, and dispersing them; yet not till two or three of the guards had been wounded. In the meantime a party of the rioters had passed to the back of the house, and were forcing their way through the garden, when fortunately fifty more horse arriving in the very critical instant, the house was saved, and perhaps the lives of all that were in it. . . . The disappointed populace vented their rage on the house of Carr, a fashionable mercer, who dealt in French silks, and demolished the windows. All Saturday they remained peaceable; and . . . no further mischief ensued.

Horace Walpole's story continues:

On Sunday evening I went to compliment the Duke and Duchess . . . on their escape. I found the square crowded, but chiefly by persons led by curiosity. As my chariot had no coronets, I was received with huzzas; but when the horses turned to enter the court, dirt & stones were thrown at it. When the gates were thrown open I was surprised at the martial appearance. The horse-guards were drawn up in the court, and many officers and gentlemen were walking about as on the platform of a regular citadel.[22]

Despite the disorders, Parliament was not completely deaf to the weavers' cries; and in 1765 it passed legislation prohibiting imports of fully manufactured foreign silk goods, continuing high duties on other silks and reinforcing the existing prohibition on silk ribbons, laces and girdles by imposing heavier penalties for smuggling.[23]

But, once again, no substantial improvement came about. Indeed by 1767 there seemed to be no end to periodical riots and incipient rebellion. Some masters who had insisted on reducing journeymen's piece rates, had had partly finished work cut out of the looms. When a group of masters and journeymen appeared before the Weavers' Court of Assistants in November 1767, the masters asked the Court 'to consider of some method to settle the Prices in such a manner as to prevent in future the mischief which had been done by cutting works out of the Lomb', and the journeymen told the Court that the prices of their work had been so much reduced that they wished the Court 'would interfere in settling the prices between the Masters and Men'. The prices the journeymen wanted were those in the Book of

Prices agreed upon in 1762. The Court's considered opinion was that these were not unreasonable and that their reduction by certain masters had been

> the chief causes of the late disturbances in the Trade. And further it appearing . . . that the said Masters have lately agreed and given it under their hands that they will comply with the prices contained in the said Book, this Court did earnestly recommend it to the Masters strictly to observe the Agreement, and to the Journeymen an orderly and peaceable Behaviour.

This recommendation, which was given in writing to the journeymen's representatives and printed in the newspapers, was so ineffective that early in 1768—one of several successive years of high food prices and increasing unrest—the Weavers' Company felt obliged to set up a special committee of seven members 'to consider of, and do what they might think necessary, in order to put a stop to the disturbances among the journeymen'.[24] But this committee's task was hopeless because the desperate weavers had already begun to fight among themselves. The old hostility between the single-loom and the engine-loom weavers flared up and some of the more militant characters were arrested with arms in their hands. On 30 November 1767, according to the *Gentleman's Magazine*,

> A body of weavers, armed with rusty swords, pistols and other offensive weapons, assembled at a house on Saffron-hill with an intent to destroy the work of an eminent weaver near that place, but were happily dispersed without much mischief. Some of them were apprehended, and being examined before the justices at Hicks's-hall, it appeared that two classes of weavers were mutually combined to distress each other, namely the *engine* and *narrow* weavers. . . . The men who were taken up were engine weavers, and they urged . . . that they only assembled in order to protect themselves from a party of the others who were expected to rise. As they had done no mischief, they were all dismissed with a severe reprimand for not having applied to the civil magistrate for protection.[25]

Worse still, in April 1768 a mob of weavers, 'armed with cutlasses, pistols, etc. and in disguise, went at midnight to the houses of several journeymen weavers in Spitalfields and 'cut to pieces 16 looms, with their contents, which belonged to Messrs. Everard and Phipps', master weavers of fancy goods, and on a 'subsequent nocturnal excursion these miscreants narrowly escaped from a party of soldiers who had nearly surrounded them unperceived'.[26] Four months later a number of Spitalfields weavers 'arose in a body', broke into Nathaniel Farr's house in Pratt's Alley, cut the silk in two looms and shot dead Edward Fitch, a lad of seventeen. Rewards were offered, but the murderers were never brought to justice.[27] Indeed, the extremists, quite undeterred by the prospect of transportation or hanging, audaciously formed a club called 'The Cutters' and tried to levy a tax upon anyone who owned or possessed a loom. They met at the Dolphin tavern in Cock Lane, whence they issued their impudent and illegal demands in such terms as: 'Mr. Hill, you are desired to send the full donation of all your looms to the Dolphin in Cock Lane. This from the conquering and bold Defiance to be levied four shillings per loom.' When Mr Hill wisely reported this demand to the Bow Street magistrates in October 1769, prompt action was taken. Having learned that 'the Cutters' were actually in session, a magistrate, several members of the newly created police force and a party of soldiers raided the Dolphin, where, sure enough, they found the club assembled, its members fully armed 'receiving the contributions of terrified manufacturers'. The troops and police were instantly fired upon. A soldier fell dead, and the Cutters tried to escape over the housetops; but two were killed and four arrested. Afterwards a detachment of the Guards was quartered in the district; a precaution which put an end to the Cutters' audacious activities.[28] Altogether, five Cutters were executed before the end of 1769.[29]

Meanwhile, a negotiating committee of masters and men who genuinely desired to reach a just and peaceful settlement had succeeded in producing a revised Book of Prices, of which a rare copy is preserved in the Goldsmiths' Library in the University of London.

> *A list of the Prices in those Branches of the Weaving Manufactory, called The Black Branch and The Fancy Branch, together with the Persians, Sarsnets, Drugget-Modes, Fringed and Italian handkerchiefs, Cyprus and Draught Gauzes, and plain and laced Nets. Printed in the Year 1769, at the Expense of those Manufacturers who were Subscribers for carrying on the Work.*
> Black Branch. A list of the Prices agreed to be Paid for Making the different Kinds of Work . . . as settled and signed by the several Manufacturers whose names are hereunder Written, (that is to say) by the Masters . . . on behalf of themselves and the rest of the Masters and by the Journeymen, whose names are hereto subscribed on behalf of themselves, and the rest of the Journeymen.

Then follow seven pages of prices, agreed and approved by the negotiating masters and journeymen:

MASTERS	JOURNEYMEN
Ouvry and Prichard	Thomas Baker
Jacob Jamet	James Saunders
Daniel and Charles Mesman	William Durant
Andrew Benjamin Guivaud	Jacob Buckey
Solomon Hesse	Thomas Haddon
Legrew and Son	John Murphy
Peter Serret and Son	
James and Charles Dalbiac	
John Fremont and Son	

Then, in turn, follow the prices fixed for the Fancy Branch, running to eleven pages and subscribed to by the same six journeymen, but by a different list of masters, except for Jacob Jamet whose name appears again.

Daniel West	Samuel Lawrence
Jacob Jamet	J. B. Hebert and Co.
Thompson and Meadows	John Lemaitre
Phipps and Everard	John Hoskins
John Roy	

Lastly, there is a list of prices 'agreed to be paid for the making of Drugget Modes, Fringed and Italian Handkerchiefs, the Cyprus and Draught Gauzes, and Plain and Laced Nets' (six pages), signed at the end by the same six journeymen and by Andrew Benjamin Guivaud, Bowland and Co., and John Hoskins, Masters. This list places a partial prohibition on the employment of women and girls, except upon certain limited classes of work such as 'any sort of Handkerchiefs of above the usual or settled price of 4s. 6d. per dozen for the making thereof'. The prices in all three lists were to take effect from 1 January 1769.[30]

It is significant that the journeymen's negotiators thought it expedient to insert at the end of the Book a justification of their action in sitting down with the masters to negotiate these prices. Their statement is most illuminating:

> We doubt not [they said] but envy and ill-will may induce
> many to raise objections to different articles in the aforegoing
> pages; notwithstanding the pains which have been taken, both
> by masters and men, to settle every article on the most just
> and equitable terms. . . . We know there are some of that
> unhappy cast, that they are never contented long with any
> thing, as it would be labour lost to try to please such, so we

hope their number are but small. Upon the whole we are enabled to say, (which with the utmost gratitude we would acknowledge) we have found much more merit amongst our masters, than we at first expected. . . . With respect to the objections that some may make to the persons who undertook this difficult task, as wanting such and such requisite qualifications . . . let it be remembered what a critical situation our affairs were then in, and how difficult . . . to find any persons . . . that had the public peace so much at heart, as to inspire them with resolution sufficient to enter on so arduous an employ. However, we have, we think, taken the most effectual method to preserve ourselves from censure, by carefully avoiding to do any thing of ourselves; but on the settlement of every article in debate, have taken pains to procure a sufficient number of the most able and approved workmen the different branches in debate afforded . . . we have at all times not only admitted, but even requested the attendance of all who had any connections with the business. . . . Again, let it be remembered, that at our first setting out, we did not propose to make advancements, only to establish what we had, which, by the assistance of many worthy masters, it is presumed we have.

The Book of Prices ends with a dozen delightful patterns of figured silks, which still retain their pleasant colours after two centuries, and, more surprisingly, a poem:

> When base oppression wav'd its iron rod,
> And under foot an helpless people trod,
> Distressed families felt the direful smart,
> Keen anguish pierc'd the honest labourer's heart,
> Provisions high, and wages vastly low,
> Starving at home, not knowing where to go;
> In this dilemma, think what could they do,
> What method take, what course must they pursue?
> Made by oppression mad, their minds distracted,
> Shut up from all relief, such parts were acted;
> By some who void of sense, were void of fear,
> Oh! may such dreadful scenes no more appear.
> What grateful sentiments must fill our hearts
> When we reflect on those who took our parts;
> Who, touch'd by tender feelings of compassion,
> Were mov'd by justice only, not by passion;
> May bounteous providence their labours bless,
> Who help'd to crown our labours with success,
> And may no treacherous, base, designing men
> E'er make encroachments on our rights again;

> May upright masters still augment their treasure,
> And journeymen pursue their work with pleasure,
> May arts and manufactories still increase,
> And Spitalfields be blest with prosperous peace.

Unfortunately this earnest and honest attempt to bring peace to Spitalfields achieved only temporary success. The winter of 1770–1 brought serious unrest, culminating tragically on 16 April 1771 when a mob stoned to death Daniel Clark, who had given evidence against certain offenders in previous riots.[31] Once again the poorer weavers were face to face with unemployment and hunger, and numbers of them, in desperation, were shipping to America as indentured servants.[32] Two days before Christmas 1772 the Weavers' Company, 'taking into consideration the great Distress of many poor people in the Weaving Manufacture arising from the General Stagnation of Trade', gave £100 to start 'a Subscription for the relief of such poor objects as are out of Employment and shall appear deserving'.[33] All this meant, as the silk weaver Samuel Sholl tells us, that the less scrupulous masters were in a strong position to reduce piece rates below the 'Book prices';[34] while the journeymen demanded, most urgently, 'that some means may be devised to compel the Masters to abide by the prices of their work, as settled between them and the Journeymen'.

So it came about that, after long hesitation and delay, and years of unrest, turbulence and rioting, it was decided to use compulsion. Many prominent persons, such as the Lord Mayor and Sir John Fielding, the famous blind Bow Street Magistrate, showed a great deal of sympathy for the journeymen weavers, as, indeed, did Parliament by passing the first and most important of the Spitalfields Acts (13 Geo. III, c. 68) in 1773. On 1 May 1772 Sir John Fielding wrote to William Eden, Under-Secretary of State, requesting him to inform Lord Suffolk, the Secretary of State for the Northern Department, that the London magistrates chiefly concerned had met at Bow Street on the previous day and that 'the Committee of the journeymen weavers and several of the masters attended there, when the Bill . . . was read and approved by the magistrates, masters and men'. Then, accompanied by three colleagues—Pell, Sherwood and Wilmot, all justices in the Spitalfields–Bethnal Green district—Fielding personally delivered the Bill to Lord North 'and had some conversation on the subject'. Fielding's opinion was that 'the masters will have more reason to rejoice than the men (if the Bill was passed), as it frees them from their outrages', and will probably 'turn the journeymen weavers' road from the Palace to the Quarter Sessions'. All went according to plan, the Bill became an Act, and on 9 July 1773 Sir John Fielding was able to report to the Secretary of

State that at the Quarter Sessions held on 8 July the weavers' wages had been fixed under the new Act 'to the entire satisfaction of those masters and journeymen weavers who appeared there in behalf of their respective bodies', adding his fervent hope 'that this step will prove a radical cure for all tumultuous assemblies from that quarter'.[35]

This important statute (13 Geo. III, c. 68), which came into force on 1 July 1773, empowered the Lord Mayor, Recorder and Aldermen of the City of London and the justices of the peace for the City and Liberty of Westminster, the Liberty of the Tower of London, and all places in the County of Middlesex, 'to settle, regulate order and declare the wages and prices of work of the journeymen weavers' employed and working 'in the Silk Manufacture within their respective jurisdictions'. Normally, a negotiating committee of masters and journeymen in a certain section of the industry—such as 'the several branches of the Silk-Velvet and Silk-Shag Manufactory'—submitted to the appropriate justices a list of prices,

the said List having been agreed to and signed by both Masters and Journeymen after the most mature Deliberation in the most open, publick, and conspicuous Manner, and by previous Advertisements in Two daily Newspapers . . . (on three separate days) that all Partys interested therein might attend and have notice of the same.[36]

If the justices approved, they made an order which had to be printed three times in any two daily newspapers published in London and Westminster. On the relatively few occasions on which the masters and journeymen failed to agree, the magistrates found themselves in some difficulty, for they were not competent to deal with the technicalities arising from the manufacture of the great variety of fabrics then made in the London silk industry; but they usually sought a solution, by 'inquiring into the price of provisions and what the weaver could earn, and decided accordingly'.[37]

The magistrates were fixing legal rates of pay—not legal minima—and once they had made their order, no master weaver could legally pay *more or less* than the rates so fixed. The penalty, on conviction, was a fine of £50 to be paid, after deduction of the expenses of the prosecution,

into the hands of the Master of the Weavers' Company . . . to be distributed by him, in conjunction with the Wardens of the Company, to any distressed journeymen weavers or their families, who shall have been last employed in . . . the aforesaid jurisdictions, at their discretion.

The journeymen weavers were forbidden to 'ask, receive or take' more or less wages or prices for their work or to 'enter into any combination to raise' such wages or prices, or to 'decoy, solicit or intimidate other journeymen, so that they quit their masters'. Nor must they assemble in groups exceeding ten persons in order to present petitions or make other representations, except to the proper magistrates designated in the Act. The penalty on conviction was a fine of 40s., to be paid (like the masters' penalties) to the Weavers' Company. In default of payment an offender was liable to imprisonment with hard labour not exceeding three months.

The Act also provided (a) that no master weaver residing within the defined districts might employ any journeyman weaver out of, or beyond, those limits 'with intent to elude or evade' the law, and (b) no silk weavers so residing might have more than two apprentices at any time. The penalty fixed was £20 for every offence on conviction, to be paid, like the other penalties, to the Weavers' Company. All the evidence suggests, however, that these provisions were easily and often evaded or infringed with impunity, and the convictions were negligible in number and effect.[38]

The records of the Weavers' Company contain remarkably few references to this special Spitalfields legislation, and there is nothing to suggest that the Company's charitable funds benefited very much from the well-meant provisions of the Act of 1773. The first Court minute on the subject is dated 20 December 1775 and refers to 'Mr. John Timmings [who] attended and informed the Court of the Circumstances of his Conviction . . . for paying less wages than is settled by the Book of Prices.' The Court directed that the money received by the Company 'upon the conviction of Mr. Timmings' be not distributed pending the result of an appeal which he intended to make.[39] If any similar sums were received by the Company under the penal provisions of the Act, they must have been distributed directly to sundry poor weavers, for no entries appear to have been passed through the Company's accounts. When a journeyman weaver had laid an information successfully, he usually asked for 'all or part of the fine'.[40]

There can be little doubt that many 'failures' to pay and receive legal prices went unpunished, despite the formation of a journeymen weavers' society with the object of exposing and, in the last resort, prosecuting employers who evaded the list prices. At the Ribbon Weavers' inquiry in 1818 documents were produced showing the existence of such a body 'to protect the Act' as the weavers put it; an aim which was quite legal. In a letter dated 13 October 1817 addressed to 'Brother Tradesmen', the anonymous committee claimed that within 'the last nine months, upwards of 50 persons . . . have obtained the lawful price of their work . . . by means of the trade society', and urged the journeymen to attend all 'trade meetings'. In the same minutes of evidence we find the 'Rules to be observed by a few Friends called the *Good Intent*', which seems to have been an association of the silk weavers of Bethnal Green to support, so far as the funds would allow, any member 'turned out of work for demanding his price (in a becoming manner)'; and any member who helped another to get work was to have 10s. When any matter was in dispute, the society selected one or two members to go and look into it: a practice which might save time and tempers in the long run. In December 1813 there were eighty-three members and £5. 8s. 11½d. 'in the box'.[41] Doubtless some journeymen surreptitiously and illegally accepted lower prices, especially in very slack periods, for fear that they might lose their employment entirely if they complained. Moreover, new fabrics or variations of old ones, introduced between the periodical revisions of the Book of Prices, might have, in practice, no legal prices for two or three years, or even longer.

Whatever may have been its defects and limitations, the Act of 1773 replaced a decade of discord and violence, crime and punishment, by a half-century of comparative calm, orderly negotiations and, on the whole, fair rates of pay; a transformation greatly envied by weavers in other parts of the country, such as Coventry and Macclesfield.[42] The Weavers' Company was second to none in its desire for industrial peace. Although it could not be a party to wage negotiations, it was always ready to use its influence on the side of moderation and just dealing; it advertised, at the Company's expense, meetings of the trade (e.g. on the request of a substantial number of journeymen), and willingly granted the use of Weavers' Hall for meetings of masters and men.[43] Perhaps the period of most severe strain occurred between the outbreak of the French Revolution in 1789 and the years immediately following the final defeat and downfall of Napoleon in 1815. The economic and political repercussions of these shattering events upon life in England have often been described. Advanced Radicals in this country—especially the 'English Jacobins'—nurtured wild hopes that the new French Republic's promise of 'fraternity and assistance' to all peoples would take the form of a military invasion of England which would bring liberty to the toiling masses and turn George the Third into 'George the Last'. We know that the London Corresponding Society's Spitalfields and Moorfields 'divisions' in 1792–3, although low in funds, had a large membership, including many silk weavers.[44] If John Thelwall is to be believed, the journeymen weavers were having a bad time in the last decade of the eighteenth century.

Even in my short remembrance [he said in September 1795]

bare-foot, ragged children . . . in that part of the town were very rare. I remember the time . . . when a man who was a tolerable workman . . . had generally, beside the apartment in which he carried on his vocation, a small summer house and a narrow slip of garden, at the outskirts of the town where he spent his Monday, either in flying his pigeons or raising his tulips. But those gardens are now fallen into decay . . . and you will find the poor weavers and their families crowded together in vile, filthy, and unwholesome chambers, destitute of most common comforts, and even of the common necessaries of life.[45]

The Weavers' Officers and Assistants, mindful of the serious civil disturbances of the 1760s, decided to make clear their loyalty to King and Constitution in a public declaration, dated Weavers' Hall, 18 December 1792:

We the Bailiffs, Wardens and Court of Assistants of the Worshipful Company of Weavers (the most antient Corporation in London) being sensible of the Blessings we enjoy as Britons, anxious to unite with all faithful Subjects in expressing our Loyalty to his Majesty and our zealous attachment to our most excellent Constitution consisting of King, Lords and Commons, as established at the Revolution, Resolve unanimously, and we do hereby express our determination to pay due Obedience to the Laws of our Country, and that we will use every lawful means in our power to preserve the Peace and good order of Society.[46]

This document was left for a fortnight in the Clerk's office to be signed by 'such Liverymen and Freemen as may approve thereof', and was presented 'to the Secretary of the Treasury to be conveyed to Mr. Pitt'. It was published in various newspapers and 2,000 copies were printed and distributed in and around Spitalfields.

The fact that no tumults occurred among the London silk weavers at this time, despite the rising prices of food and other common commodities, the distress among the poor in Spitalfields, and the activities of certain extremists,[47] may be attributed, at least in part, to the existence of recognised negotiating facilities under the Act, supplemented in 1792 by an Act covering weavers of silk mixed with other materials in the Spitalfields district. It is significant that no fewer than six reviews and revisions of the Book of Prices were made in the eleven years from 1795 to 1806.[48] The Weavers' Company, too, tried to help. In 1793, for example, it spent £4. 5s. 'For advertising [a] Meeting of the Trade on the Petition of Journeymen weavers'; and sent a donation of £100 to the 'Treasurer of a Committee for relieving poor Weavers'.[49]

A copy of what seems to be the last Book of Prices to be issued before the repeal of the Spitalfields Acts in 1824 has been found (1967) in the strong room at Weavers' House, Wanstead. Compiled by James Buckridge, senior, and reprinted by E. Justins of 34 Brick Lane, Spitalfields in 1821, it was once the property of William Cecil, a Liveryman of the Weavers' Company.[50] It lists all piece-work rates (usually at so much per yard) settled in the 'several branches of the silk and silk-mixed manufactures', under the Acts, in and after 1795.[51] The lists of prices cover ninety-one printed pages; twenty-seven types of fabrics are mentioned, numbers of them being made in five or six varieties and many different widths; and more than 2,150 separate prices are specified. On the last page, under 'General Provisions', we read 'All bad jobs that require extra assistance, and take above one hour, for every extra hour the same are employed to pay 1s.'

This last sentence serves as a reminder that, quite apart from slackness of trade, there were other circumstances which could cause delays or interruptions of the flow of work, so reducing the weavers' earnings. As the Spitalfields manufacturer, William Hale, said, in 1818, 'Silk is a very delicate article to manufacture; a man has got a certain quantity (of warp) in the loom that will occupy him perhaps five or six weeks to weave it; after he has done a part of it, he has sometimes to wait a few days before the remainder of the silk (weft) comes from the dyers; this is a loss of time, and it falls on the journeyman weaver.' Sometimes the yarns came to hand wrongly dyed as to colour, or spoiled in the dyeing process.

> I can [Hale said] produce many instances of journeymen, steady men who work for me, who have frequently earned two guineas a week for weeks together, yet (taking) the aggregate amount of their earnings (in the plain silk trade) through the year, . . . and though I make use of every means to keep them employed . . . the average . . . does not exceed 13s. per week, for every weaver who works for me.[52]

On figured silks high pay could be earned, but the time needed to set up the looms—called 'building their harness'—was very much longer. Therefore, the weaver gained greatly if, once his loom was set up, he could have a long run of work on the same figured pattern; but, conversely, his average earnings were much reduced if runs of work were of short duration.

During the post-war decade, 1815–25, the forces in favour of unrestricted enterprise and free trade rapidly gained momentum. The mere mention of the names of the economists David Ricardo, J. R. M'Culloch, Horne Tooke, and the politicians Henry Brougham, William Huskisson, F. J. Robinson (Viscount Goderich) and Thomas

Wallace, all of whom had complete faith in the 'liberal principles of political economy', is enough to recall the history of the last phase of Mercantilism in England. The pressure and events leading up to the repeal of the Spitalfields Acts in 1824, the removal of import prohibitions on foreign silk fabrics in 1826 and the subsequent gradual reduction of the import duties are all part of that history.[53] At the same time the introduction of power looms seriously threatened and ultimately destroyed the livelihoods of the hand-loom weavers. Echoes of the agonies of these unfortunate weavers come to us through the voluminous reports of a number of Royal Commissions and Select Committees of the Lords and Commons, of which one of the most revealing is that of the Select Committee on the Petition of the Ribbon Weavers in 1818.

Several leading London silk manufacturers, prominent members of the Weavers' Company, gave evidence before this Committee, but they did not speak as with one voice. Some held that the Spitalfields Acts had been beneficial to the London silk industry, on the whole; but others, especially those doing business on a big scale, were in favour of early repeal. Among the former was William Hale,[54] who had been in the industry since 1791, in the broad plain branch, having been in partnership with his father-in-law until the latter retired. For many years before 1818 he had employed 'some hundreds' of weavers to make goods for the home market, but not for export. His considered opinion was that the Acts had been very beneficial to the district, because the journeymen had received agreed 'fair' prices for their work, the district had been quiet, and the poor rates had been kept down. He admitted that some work had been taken away into districts outside the operation of the Acts; and he was careful to point out that the increase in the quantities of silk goods made between c. 1810 and 1818 was general throughout the country and not peculiar to Spitalfields.[55] One must remember, however, that some branches had begun to move away from London *before* 1773, influenced, it may well be, wholly or partly by the violent and re-current labour disturbances; and it is not improbable that this movement would have continued but for the passing of the Act of 1773. It is significant, too, that masters and journeymen outside London wished to have the Acts extended to them. For example William Pears of Coventry, who employed some sixty engine looms on narrow ribbons and at least 300 single hand looms on wider ribbons, was strongly in favour of a general extension of the Spital-fields system. So was William Goostry of Leek and Jacob Field, a journeyman weaver who had worked under the same system in Dublin.[56] John Ames of Ames and Wilkinson, silk manufacturers, St Paul's Churchyard, said that his firm manufactured broad silks in London and ribbons in and around Coventry where they employed 'several hundred persons'. He favoured the extension of the Acts to other parts of the country.[57] In the end, no fewer than eighty-eight well-established manufacturers or firms signed a statement in support of the Acts and their extension to the country at large.[58]

Prominent in the opposite camp was Stephen Wilson of Lea Wilson and Company, silk manufacturers, who employed, perhaps, some 400 to 500 weavers; he could not say definitely, 'it is really mere guess'. He disliked, chiefly, the rigidity of wages under the Acts, which, he alleged, had already driven the manufacture of crêpe, gauze, bandanna handkerchiefs and bombazine out of Spitalfields 'into the country'. The competition of places like Coventry, Kidderminster, Macclesfield and Manchester, where wages were much lower, was severely felt in Spitalfields.[59] Stephen Wilson's evidence is especially interesting because it reveals some of the practical difficulties of working under the Acts, and some of the loopholes. He cited the negotiations of 1807, when the joint committee of masters and men had under revision a 'book' of twenty-two folios. One folio alone might contain between thirty and forty items, on any one of which there might be as much as four to five hours of haggling. When agreement could not be reached the list was referred to the magistrates for arbitration on the outstanding differences, which usually arose, said Wilson, on the most technically difficult and controversial items. In one such instance the magistrates had fixed a price of 14s. 6d. 'a square'; but because (by some oversight) the price for that particular type of work had not been thrice advertised, 'it was not considered as law', said the witness, who added with obvious relish, 'I have made some thousands of them since [paying] at 8s. a square, instead of 14s. 6d.; . . . [and] I have had young women of 22–23 years of age that have made me ten in a week.'[60] Thomas Gibson, another London master weaver, had a warehouse in the City, employed 70 to 100 looms on plain and figured broad silks, and was evidently a capitalist–entrepreneur; he had never been apprenticed to weaving, nor had he worked as an operative weaver. Like Stephen Wilson, he was against the Acts and for much the same reasons, but he did concede that, while all masters and men should be free to agree to diverge from 'official' prices if they wished, there should be in reserve, so to speak, official prices which would come into operation in cases of deadlock.[61]

At the end of a long, patient inquiry, the Select Committee reported that the 'great privations and distress, arising out of inadequate wages, . . . reducing thousands of [silk and ribbon weavers] . . . to seek parochial aid . . . in the parishes of Coventry and in the County of Warwick, . . . do not exist in London, Westminster, and Middlesex', where the Spitalfields Act is in force. Therefore the Committee, with the concurrence of many masters and weavers, recommended the

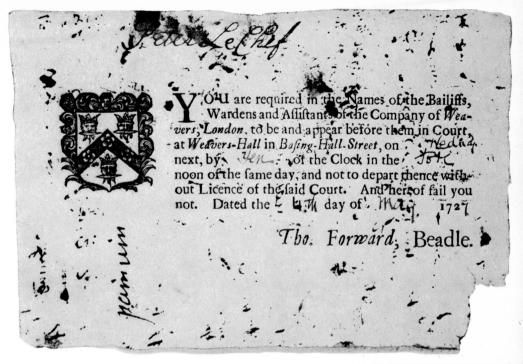

YOU are required in the Names of the Bailiffs, Wardens and Assistants of the Company of Weavers, London, to be and appear before them in Court, at Weavers-Hall in Basing-Hall-Street, on _____ Wedn 4 next, by _____ of the Clock in the _____ noon of the same day, and not to depart thence without Licence of the said Court. And hereof fail you not. Dated the 4th day of May 1727

Tho. Forward, Beadle.

1 Summons to appear before the Weavers' Court of Assistants, May 1727.

(1)

THE

C A S E

OF THE

COMMONALITY

OF THE

CORPORATION

OF

VVeavers of London

truly Stated.

Humbly presented to the Consideration of the Honorable House of Commons.

ALL Legall Jurisdictions over a number of people or society of men must either be primitive or derivative, now primitive jurisdiction is undoubtedly in the whole body and not in one or more members, all men being by nature equall to other, and all jurisdictive power over them being founded by a compact and agreement with them, is invested in one or more persons, who represent the whole, and by the consent of the whole are impowred to govern by such Rules of equality towards all, as that both governours and governed may know certainly what the one may command, and what the other must obey;

B   without

2 Page one of a pamphlet entitled *The Case of the Commonality of the Corporation of Weavers of London truly Stated*, c. 1659.

I _Anthony Halder_ — — a Member of the Company of WEAVERS _London_, do hereby promiſe and engage to pay unto the preſent Bailiffs and Wardens of the ſaid Company, their Succeſſors or Aſſigns, the ſum of
_0 — 5 — 0_ _Five Shillings_ — as my voluntary Gift, for and towards the Re-building of the Common-hall of the ſaid Company. Witneſs my hand the 27th — day of _September_ — 1669·

anthony holder

I _James Maud_ — a Member of the Company of WEAVERS _London_, do hereby promiſe and engage to pay unto the preſent Bailiffs and VVardens of the ſaid Company, their Succeſſors or Aſſigns, the ſum of
Paid
_0 — 10 — 0_ _Ten Shillings_ — as my voluntary Gift, for and towards the Re-building of the Common-hall of the ſaid Company. VVitneſs my hand the 27th — day of _September_ 1669

I _Thomas Alsop_ — a Member of the Company of VVEAVERS _London_, do hereby promiſe and engage to pay unto the preſent Bailiffs and VVardens of the ſaid Company, their Succeſſors or Aſſigns, the ſum of
_0 — 10 — 0_ _Ten Shillings_ — as my voluntary Gift, for and towards the Re-building of the Common-hall of the ſaid Company. VVitneſs my hand the 27th — day of _September_ — 1669

ye mrk of Tho. ☩ Alſop.

3 Members' promises to subscribe to the Weavers' Hall rebuilding fund, 1669.

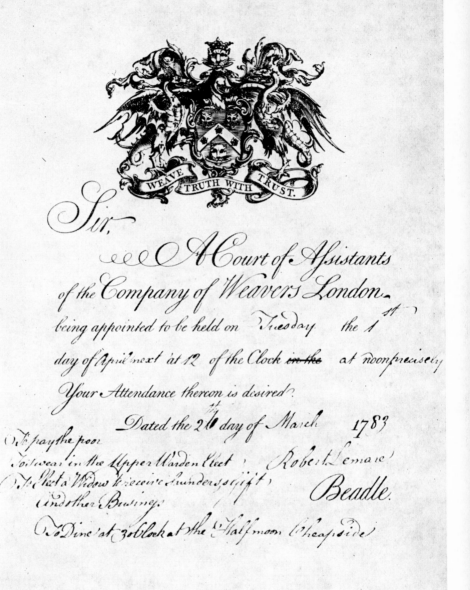

Sir,

A Court of Assistants of the Company of Weavers London being appointed to be held on Tuesday the 1st day of April next at 12 of the Clock in the at noon precisely Your Attendance thereon is desired.

Dated the 20th day of March 1783

To pay the poor
To swear in the Upper Warden Elect
To Elect a Widow to receive Saunders's gift, and other Business
To Dine at 3 oClock at the Halfmoon Cheapside

Robert Lemare

Beadle.

4 Summons to an Assistant to attend a meeting of the Court, March 1783.

22

Per Dozen.—s. d.

From 32 to 36 inches for the second, and every
   other shuttle used in border only - - 0 6
But if used in the body, to be paid double the
   price on each.

Aug. 1795. From 36 to 45 inches for the second and every
   other shuttle - - - - 1 0
From 45 to 54 inches, for the second and every
   other shuttle - - - - 2 0
Borders not to exceed 3 inches each.

Aug. 1795. If an extra course of treadles is brought on any
   silk handkerchief, 36 inches or under, to turn
   the border or stripe, when the whole of the
   harness does not exceed 8 lambs - - 1 0
But if the harness exceed 8 lambs, for turning
   border or stripe - - - - 2 0
N. B. From 36 to 45 inches - - - 2 0
     From 45 to 54 inches - - - 3 0

Aug. 1795,
and
April, 1805.
If an extra harness to make tabby or bias border,
   four lambs or under, on any of the aforesaid
   grounds, 36 inches and under, for the borders
   allowed 75 reeds each - - - 1 0
And should it exceed 75 reeds, for every 25 reeds
   extra, or under - - - - 0 3
From 36 to 45 inches, the borders allowed 110
   reeds each - - - - 2 0
And for every 25 reeds extra - - - 0 6
From 45 to 54 inches, the borders allowed 150
   reeds each - - - - 3 0
And for every 25 reeds extra, or under - 0 9
From 54 to 59 inches, 150 reeds each other border 4 6
From 59 to 63 inches, 200 reeds each other border 6 0
And for every 25 reeds extra - - 1 0
The borders not to exceed 2 threads in a lish, or
   4 lishes to the reed.
If these borders are made the one to face up, and

April, 1805,
and
April, 1806.
   the other down, 32 inches and under, to be paid
   extra for that addition more than when made
   in the regular way, for 32 inches and under - 1 0
From 32 to 36 inches - - - - 1 6
From 36 to 40 inches - - - - 2 0
From 40 to 45 inches - - - - 2 6
From 45 to 50 inches - - - - 3 0
From 50 to 54 inches - - - - 3 6
And should they be made wider, for every 4
   inches extra to advance - - - 0 6

April, 1805. If an extra harness from 4 to 6 lambs, to make
   satinet bias or tabby borders, to be paid as
   follows, 32 inches and under - - - 1 6

23

Per Dozen.—s. d.

From 32 inches to 36 inches, the borders allowed
   75 reeds each - - - - 2 0
And should it exceed 75 reeds, for every 25
   reeds, or under, extra - - 0 3
From 36 to 40 inches - - - 2 6
From 40 to 45 ditto, to be allowed 110 reeds for
   each border - - - - 3 3
Should it exceed 110 reeds, then to be paid for
   every 25 reeds, or under - - 0 6
From 45 to 50 inches - - - 4 0
From 50 to 54 inches, to be allowed 150 reeds
   for each border - - - 5 0
And should it exceed 150 reeds, for every 25
   reeds extra - - - - 0 9

   N. B. Should this 6 lamb satinet, or bias   *April, 1805.*
   border, be made the one to face up, the
   other down, then to be paid sixpence
   more for each breadth, than that addition
   provided for the 4 lamb.

If the master requires an extra role or bobbins to
   be used in stripes or borders, to be paid extra 1 0
Satin bars made by shoot, where there is no up-   *April, 1805.*
   right satin, 1000 shoots or under in the square.
36 inches or under - - - 6 0
From 36 to 40 inches - - - 8 6
From 40 to 45 inches - - - 11 0
From 45 to 50 inches - - - 13 6
From 50 to 54 inches - - - 16 0
For every 200 shoots extra - - 1 0
This work 36 inches and under, to be allowed
   one shuttle besides the ground shuttle; if above
   36 inches, 2 shuttles besides the ground shuttle.
If satin bars across be brought on handkerchiefs   *April, 1805.*
   made with 8 lambs or treadles to the ground,
   and 4 lambs or treadles for the upright bias, not
   to be deemed real satin bordered handkerchiefs. But should there be more than 12
   lambs or treadles, then to be paid as real satin-
   bordered handkerchiefs.
If a tissue be brought on any handkerchiefs   *April, 1805.*
   where there is no flush out of the ground, made
   in a harness all short eyes, of the under-men-
   tioned breadths, to advance the price of the
   ground as follows:
              36 inches or under.
For 8 lambs or treadles, or under - 1 6
From 8 to 12 ditto - - - 2 6
From 12 to 16 ditto - - - 1 6

5   Specimen pages from a list of prices paid for silk weaving in
Spitalfields between 1795 and 1821.

6 Weavers' Hall carved
staircase and doors.

7 Weavers' Hall (interior).
Rebuilt after the Great
Fire by Edward Jerman in
1688–9.

8 (*left*) The Leading Staff: rosewood
with silver gilt mounts, the arms of
England and the Weavers' Company are
chased on the ends. Sixteenth century.
(*right*) The Mace: silver, George V. 1934,
presented by William B. Ingle to
commemorate his year of office as Upper
Bailiff, 1933–4.

9 (*opposite*) The Upper Bailiff's badge, presented by Frederic Ouvry, Upper Bailiff, 1878–80.

10 (*above*) The Upper Bailiff's chair, bought in 1707.

11   Silver loving cup, 1662.

12   The poor's box, 1666.

13 Portrait of Queen Anne, bought by
the Weavers' Company in 1709. Probably
a copy of the portrait painted by Sir
Godfrey Kneller for the Inner Temple in
1703.

14 Alderman Samuel Wilson, Lord
Mayor of London 1838–9. An engraving
by William Walter from a picture by
Thomas A. Woolnoth.

15   Francis Dearman (1831–1904), silk
weaver, Globe Road, Spitalfields.

16   Samuel Higgins, silk weaver, in his loom-shop at Gauber Street,
Spitalfields. A drawing by D. MacPherson for the *Daily Graphic*, 7th
April 1899.

17   A typical silk weaver's house in Spitalfields, built *c.* 1825. A
drawing by D. MacPherson for the *Daily Graphic*, 7th April 1899.

20   The Weavers' Almshouses built at Wanstead in 1859 by Joseph
Jennings, architect and surveyor to the company.

18   (*left above*) The William Watson Almshouses in Shoreditch
(Hoxton), built 1669–70; rebuilt 1824. From a drawing by Thomas
Hosmer Shepherd.

19   (*left below*) The Nicholas Garrett Almshouses in Porter's Fields,
built 1729. From a drawing by Thomas Hosmer Shepherd.

21 The Weavers' visit to Belgium in June 1930: a tribute to the
Unknown Warrior.

extension of the Act to cover Coventry and Warwickshire, either permanently or 'at least [as] a trial for . . . a few years, by way of experiment'. But this was never done, for such action would have been against the set of the tide of Liberalism, which was flowing strongly in the opposite direction. The enemies of the Spitalfields Acts were bent on complete repeal and no tinkering.

In 1820 the merchants of London petitioned the Commons, stressing the importance of buying in the cheapest market and selling in the dearest, a principle 'which regulates every merchant in his individual dealings [and] is strictly applicable as the best rule for the trade of the whole nation'. The petitioners were opposed to 'every restrictive regulation of trade not essential to the revenue—against all duties merely protective from foreign competition—and against the excess of such duties as are partly for the purpose of revenue and partly for protection'.[62] A House of Lords Committee on foreign trade (silk and wine) reported in 1821 against the Spitalfields Acts as being restrictive of the free employment of capital wherever it seemed most profitable.[63] William Hale fought a stubborn rearguard action by publishing his pamphlet, *An Appeal to the Public in defence of the Spitalfields Acts* (1822), and by giving evidence in 1823 before the Lords' Committee 'on the Bill to repeal four Acts relating to the wages of persons employed in the manufacture of silk'.[64] But here, as in the ribbon weavers' inquiry five years before, his evidence was countered by that of men like Stephen Wilson who 'thought the Acts a relic of barbarism, an interference with capital and political economy', and a forcing-ground of combination among journeymen.[65] Such views found an eloquent echo in Ure's *Philosophy of Manufactures*: 'If it were possible', he wrote, '. . . to make a calculation of the quantity of labour that is wasted' by artificial bolstering of various old industries, '. . . the mind of men would turn in disgust from the protective system, so tenaciously clung to by the Spitalfields weavers, and so absurdly lauded by their parliamentary patrons.'[66]

The final phase of the struggle began in May 1823 when the master manufacturers of London and Westminster presented to Parliament a petition for the repeal of the Acts. With one accord the journeymen weavers presented counter-petitions praying for the preservation of the Acts, 'which we humbly conceive to be our greatest Blessing'. They collected 11,000 signatures in three days, and on the day of the third reading of the repeal Bill, Palace Yard was crammed with anxious silk weavers. Although this Bill passed the Commons it was so extensively amended in the Lords that the Government dropped it. But not for long. An amended Bill was introduced in May 1824, passed through all its stages with little discussion and no serious amendments, and received the Royal Assent in the following month.

No angry demonstrations, no rioting ensued; the journeymen weavers remained quiet, stunned by the news.

Although this was a victory for the big silk manufacturers, their triumph was short-lived, and it was not long before they themselves were put under pressure by the free traders. Indeed, more medicine had already been prepared, for it was in 1824 that William Huskisson, President of the Board of Trade, and F. J. Robinson, Chancellor of the Exchequer, 'fashioned the first free trade budget of the century, with important consequences to the silk industry'.

> Since 1765 fully manufactured silks had been prohibited, and on other silks high duties were imposed. An *ad valorem* duty of 30 per cent. was now proposed instead of the former prohibition on such manufactured silks as shoes and gloves; on plain manufactured silks a duty of 15s. a lb.; on figured silk 20s. a lb.; and on other silks 30 per cent. *ad valorem*. On raw silks similar reductions were made. The duty on raw silk from the East Indies was reduced from 4s. to 3d. per lb.; on raw silk from China and Italy, from 5s. to 6d., while the duty on organzine was brought down from 14s. 10d. to 7s. 6d.[67]

In order to give the silk manufacturers time to sell existing stocks and to prepare for foreign competition, the new duties were not put into force until 5 July 1826.[68]

While the silk manufacturers naturally welcomed the marked cheapening of their raw materials, they did not relish the prospects of open competition from foreign makers, especially the French, in addition to the substantial surreptitious competition of the persistent imports of smuggled goods, which had, indeed, become so normal that it was possible to insure such merchandise 'with as much facility against loss by seizure, as for protection against the elements'.[69] According to a Custom House statement, 50 per cent of the goods shipped from France to Britain between 1827 and 1843 were smuggled.[70] Small wonder that the master manufacturers in the London silk industry became alarmed at the Government's new free-trade policy; especially as they had reason to fear further reductions of import duties at no distant date; for 'the statesmanship that began with Pitt's careful perusal of Adam Smith was reaching fruition in the policy of Huskisson and Robinson'.[71] Mercantilism was finished; Liberalism had arrived.

NOTES

1 G. B. Hertz, 'The English Silk Industry in the 18th Century', *English Historical Review*, XXIV (1909), p. 720.

2 Unwin, *Gilds*, p. 350; Bland, Brown, and Tawney, *English Economic History: Select Documents* (1921), pp. 619–22.
3 The master tailors' petition was successful in securing an Act of Parliament (1721) which declared illegal all combinations of journeymen tailors within London, Westminster, and the Bills of Mortality, and fixed their rates of wages and hours of labour (Bland, Brown and Tawney, op. cit., p. 624).
4 Quoted by Kellett, 'The Breakdown of Gild and Corporation Control . . . in London', *Economic History Review* (1958).
5 A. Plummer and R. E. Early, *The Blanket Makers, 1669–1969* (1969), pp. 75–80.
6 A Citizen of London, *Serious Advice to the Silk Manufacturers; in a Letter to the Master and Wardens of the Weavers* (1751).
7 MS. 4655/16, ff.4, 168, 171.
8 MS. 4655/16, ff.272, 284.
9 MS. 4655/16, ff.272, 276b, 288b, 301b.
10 MS. 4655/16, ff.342b. Other similar attempts to attract new members in 1784 and 1788 were equally unsuccessful (MS. 4655/17, f.475; MS. 4655/18, f.87b).
11 *A Narrative of the Life of Mrs. Charlotte Clarke, written by herself* (2nd edn, 1755), p. 188.
12 George, *London*, pp. 179–80.
13 MS. 4655/16, ff.287, 303b, 318.
14 MS. 4655/16, f.325b.
15 MS. 4655/16, ff.319b, 321, 326, 330. Several similar prosecutions were undertaken by the Company at this time.
16 MS. 4655/17, ff.66–8; Hammond, *The Skilled Labourer* (1919), p. 205.
17 Paul Mantoux, *The Industrial Revolution in the 18th Century* (rev. edn, 1948), pp. 82–3.
18 MS. 4655/16, f.336.
19 D. Macpherson, *Annals of Commerce* (1805), III, pp. 415–16; F. B. Palliser, *History of Lace* (3rd edn, 1875), pp. 321–2; G. A. Raikes, *History of the Honourable Artillery Company* (1878–9), II, p. 12.
20 MS. 4655/17, ff.1b, 19, 21.
21 Bedford House was a great mansion built from a design by Inigo Jones. It stood on the north side of Bloomsbury Square and had low walls in front and a garden at the back, 'with a fossé to the fields'. It has now disappeared. From Bedford House a man could walk, at this period, past the duck ponds and hawthorn hedges of Tottenham Court Road through open country to the village of Hampstead on the northern hills.
22 Horace Walpole, *Memoirs of the Reign of King George III* (1845), II, pp. 154–8.
23 Macpherson, op. cit., p. 418; A. Brady, *William Huskisson and Liberal Reform* (1928), pp. 96, 98.
24 MS. 4655/17, ff.66–8, 73. According to Raikes, *History of the Honourable Artillery Company* (1878–9), II, pp. 17–18, a crowd of weavers actually rescued three men who had been arrested and accused of rioting, while they were being examined by the magistrates at Whitechapel.
25 *Gentleman's Magazine*, vol. 37, p. 606.
26 J. P. Malcolm, *Anecdotes of the Manners and Customs of London in the 18th Century* (2nd edn, 1810), II, pp. 69–70.
27 G. F. Rudé, *The Crowd in History* (1964), p. 74.

28 Malcolm, op. cit., pp. 101–2.
29 Hammond, op. cit., p. 208; Rudé, op. cit., p. 76. It will be remembered that this was the Wilkes-and-Liberty period; a time of civil commotion and mob riots in support of Alderman John Wilkes, the popular hero, who was 'agin the Government' and the House of Commons over the *North Briton* case. Wilkes was fined £500 and imprisoned; he was four times elected an M.P. but rejected by the Commons. The majority of the livery companies were pro-Wilkes and addressed two bluntly worded and far-from-humble petitions to the King, in the second of which they accused Parliament and the King's ministers of blatantly unconstitutional conduct; they told George III that the Commons were 'corruptly subservient' to his ministers, and demanded their dismissal and the dissolution of Parliament. The Goldsmiths, Grocers and Weavers, however, disapproved of such strong language. On 28 February 1770 the Weavers' Court of Assistants resolved 'unanimously that this Court entirely Disapproves of the said (draft) as disrespectful to his Majesty's Person and Dignity and injurious to the supreme authority of Parliament, and subversive of the happy Constitution of this Kingdom'. They ordered the resolution to be printed in the *Public Advertizer*. It must be remembered that the time for the renewal of the prohibition upon the importation of foreign wrought silks and velvets was fast approaching, and the Weavers were anxious not to offend the Government. The prohibition was, in fact, renewed in 1771, much to the Weavers' satisfaction (MS. 4655/17, ff.126–126b, 154; R. R. Sharpe, *London and the Kingdom* (1895), III, pp. 80–94). Both before and during the war with the American Colonies, the Weavers remained aloof, adhering to their resolution of February 1770 (MS. 4655/17, f.236, 4 April 1775).
30 The unit of measure is either the yard of 37 inches, or the ell of 46 inches.
31 Hertz, op. cit., p. 726.
32 George, *London*, pp. 145–6.
33 MS. 4655/17, f.186b; MS. 4648/9, 4 January and 31 March 1773.
34 Samuel Sholl, *Short Historical Account of the Silk Manufacture in England* (1811).
35 R. Leslie-Melville, *Life and Work of Sir John Fielding* (1934), pp. 181–3; H.O. Papers 86 (26).
36 City of London Records, Companies 7, 26.
37 Hand-loom Weavers, II, p. 360.
38 J. H. Clapham in *Economic Journal*, December 1916, pp. 462–3.
39 MS. 4655/17, f.249b.
40 *R.C. on Municipal Corporations, 2nd Report* (1837): section on London Companies, p. 213.
41 *Ribbon Weavers*, pp. 54–5, 57; cf. also evidence of Stephen Wilson (Upper Bailiff 1811–12 and 1829–30) and Ambrose Moore (Upper Bailiff 1826–7, 1847–9), pp. 60, 164–5, 194.
42 Ibid., pp. 61, 71, 89–90.
43 See, e.g., MS. 4655/18, f.282; MS. 4648/11, 25 June 1793.
44 E. P. Thompson, *The Making of the English Working Class* (1965), p. 121.
45 Lecture reported in *Tribune*, XXIV, quoted by Thompson, op. cit., p. 143. John Thelwall (1764–1824) was the son of a silk weaver. He was a natural orator, a gifted lecturer, and became a leading English

Jacobin, glorying in the basic principles of the French Revolution, 'notwithstanding all its excesses', and a prominent member of the famous London Corresponding Society.

46 MS. 4655/18, ff.233–5.

47 Raikes, *Hist. of the Honourable Artillery Company* (1878–9), II, p. 198.

48 W. Hale, *Letter to S. Whitbread on the Distresses of the Poor in Spitalfields* (1806); *Ribbon Weavers*, p. 188.

49 MS. 4648/11, 25 June and 9 November 1793.

50 This is probably the William Cecil mentioned in the Court minutes in 1810: 'Charles Plummer, son of George Plummer, of Wheeler Street, Spitalfields, Sawyer, apprenticed for 7 years to Wm. Cecil of St John Street, Bethnal Green, C. & W. of London. No consideration' (MS. 4655/19, f.249b).

51 After 1811 women weavers were included under the Spitalfields Acts.

52 *Ribbon Weavers*, Evidence, pp. 46, 141. Hale revised his original average of 20s. to 24s. after referring to his cash book.

53 See A. Brady, *William Huskisson and Liberal Reform* (1928), especially Chaps IV and V.

54 Upper Bailiff of the Weavers' Company, 1823–4; he resided at Homerton and died in 1841.

55 *Ribbon Weavers*, Evidence, pp. 39–47.

56 Ibid., pp. 122, 131–3, 136. In 1813 the cotton weavers envied the Spitalfields silk weavers who 'have law to secure their prices . . . but cotton weavers, when their work is done, know not what they shall receive' (*Commons Journals*, vol. 68, 25 February 1813).

57 Ibid., p. 185.

58 Ibid., pp. 197–8. Fourteen Spitalfields manufacturers, each of whom employed from 20 to 130 looms, are named on pp. 181 and 185.

59 Ibid., pp. 51–3, 57.

60 Ibid., p. 58.

61 Ibid., pp. 141–3.

62 Brady, op. cit., p. 84.

63 Lords Committee on Foreign Trade, Second Report (1821), VII, 421, p. 6.

64 Lords Committee on a Bill to repeal the Acts relating to Wages in the Silk Manufacture (1823), Evidence, *passim*.

65 J. H. Clapham in *Economic Journal*, December 1916, p. 464.

66 A. Ure, *Philosophy of Manufactures* (1861 edn), pp. 455–6.

67 Brady, op. cit., p. 99.

68 G. R. Porter, *The Progress of the Nation* (1836), p. 255.

69 Lardner, *Silk*, pp. 84–5, 320 (Note N).

70 Brady, op. cit., pp. 105–6.

71 Ibid., p. 101.

Chapter 16

An Early-Victorian
Lord Mayor

Early in the month of May 1813, a young silk weaver named Samuel
Wilson was made free of the Weavers' Company by servitude, and
on the same day he paid to the Company his Livery and Steward
fines (£25) and was admitted a freeman of the City of London.
Twenty years later he was elected a Sheriff of London and Middlesex,
and in 1838, in the second year of the young Queen's reign, he became
Lord Mayor of London—the only Lord Mayor from the Weavers'
Company ever to be elected.[1]

Samuel Wilson was born in 1792, the son of John Wilson, a weaver
of Wood Street, London (who hailed originally from Stenson in
Derbyshire), and Elizabeth, daughter and heiress of James Wyght, a
London merchant. On 4 February 1806 Samuel was apprenticed for
seven years to Richard Lea of Old Jewry, a prominent, prosperous
citizen and weaver, who was elected to the Court of Assistants of the
Weavers' Company in 1786, served as Renter Bailiff in 1790–1 and
became Upper Bailiff in 1791–2. Richard Lea served also as a City
Alderman from 1803 to 1808.[2] As soon as he was 'out of his time',
Samuel Wilson, following the traditional romantic pattern, married
his master's daughter, Jemima Lea, in 1813, when she was 'sweet and
twenty'. Two years later she bore him a son, whom they named
Cornelius Lea, and who, in due time, grew up to be a worthy successor to his father.[3]

Young Samuel Wilson began his business career in favourable
circumstances. He was well connected and, in all probability, not
short of funds. Stephen Wilson (Upper Bailiff of the Weavers'
Company in 1829–30) was a member of the well-established firm of
Lea, Wilson and Company, silk manufacturers,[4] and as a junior
partner in the same house, Samuel Wilson would certainly meet men
who were both capable in business and influential in the City. There
can be little doubt that he was conscientious in his attention to
business, and respected, even popular, among his colleagues and

customers. He was, moreover, an active and generous member of the Weavers' Court of Assistants, to which he was elected in 1828 at the early age of thirty-six, and held office as Upper Bailiff no fewer than four times—1832-3, 1846-7, 1862-3 and 1863-4. He became a City Alderman in 1831 and served upon the aldermanic bench—first for Castle Baynard ward (1831-53) and then for Bridge Without (1853-71)—for forty years.[5]

Samuel Wilson's election as one of the Sheriffs of London and Middlesex[6] for the year 1833-4, brought in its train an Indian summer of pageantry for the Weavers' Company. Although the year was 1833, not 1733, and the Company's barge which used to make such a brave show in the seventeenth and eighteenth centuries had long since been broken up, the Court of Assistants felt that certain 'marks of respect should be paid to Samuel Wilson upon entering upon that high office'. So they set up a committee which, in due course, reported and recommended:[7]

(1) That it is customary for the Court of the Company to which each Sheriff belongs to attend him when he is sworn in at Guildhall and on the following day when sworn at Westminster.

(2) That a barge should be provided in which to proceed to Westminster, and carriages to the place of embarkation.

(3) That the other Sheriff's Company (the Spectacle Makers) should share the cost of the barge with the Weavers' Company.

(4) That six flags or banners are necessary for the barge and for procession through the streets, viz.,

    The Royal Standard
    ,,   City Arms
    ,,   Weavers' Arms
    ,,   Spectacle Makers' Arms
    ,,   Arms of Alderman Wilson
    ,,   Arms of Alderman Harmer (the other Sheriff-elect).

(5) That Livery gowns be hired for the Members of the Court of Assistants for the occasion.

(6) That the Weavers' Court dine together on 9th November instead of having the usual quarterly dinner in October.

(7) That a sum not exceeding £100 be voted for the above-mentioned purposes.

The Spectacle Makers readily agreed to co-operate, 'a proper supply of Scarfs and Cockades' was ordered, and Mr Sheriff Harmer and the Master and Wardens of the Spectacle Makers' Company were invited to the Weavers' quarterly Court Dinner in January 1834.[8] Meantime the ceremonial arrangements for swearing in the Sheriffs on Saturday 28 September 1833 were publicly announced:[9]

> The Courts of Assistants of the Weavers' Company and the Spectacle Makers will meet at Weavers' Hall . . . at ten o'clock in the morning precisely to Breakfast. . . . The procession will leave the Hall ¼ before eleven—
> > Peace Officers to clear the way
> > The Beadle of the Spectacle Makers Company
> > The Clerk in his Carriage
> > The Members of the Court in their Carriages
> > The Master and the Warden in the last Carriage
> > The Beadle of the Weavers' Company on foot
> > The Clerk in his Carriage
> > The Court of Assistants in theirs
> > The Upper Bailiff & Wardens in theirs
> > The Under Sheriff Sandell's Carriage
> > The Under Sheriff Stokes
> > The Sheriff-elect Harmer
> > The Sheriff-elect Wilson
> > Two Police Officers.

Having arrived at the Guildhall, the two Companies ranged themselves to the left and right, leaving a passage between them for the Sheriffs, who passed into the Court of Aldermen to be sworn. Afterwards the members of the two Companies could return home in their carriages or accompany the Corporation to church to hear a sermon, returning to the Common Hall at 1 p.m. to elect the new Lord Mayor.

On 30 September the Sheriffs were presented to the Barons of the Court of Exchequer at Westminster to receive the King's approbation of their appointment. The Courts of the two Companies met at Weavers' Hall and went in procession as before, but led this time by the Barge Master (Captain Searle), the Watermen bearing the Sheriffs' Banners, and a band of music. The Colours, except the streamer of the Weavers' Company, and 'the Music' went aboard the barge with the Officers and members of the two Companies. The Lord Mayor's barge headed the river procession until it neared Westminster Bridge, when the Company's barge passed to the landing stairs first, so as to be ready to receive the Lord Mayor and his party when they landed. At the end of the return journey the Sheriffs passed 'to the [London] Tavern first to be ready to receive their Guests'.[10]

Afterwards came the bills. By far the largest item was for the banners and flags: £68. 10s. 6d.; the hire of the barge cost £28. 11s.; and the carriages, £32. 1s. 2d.; the bills for scarves and cockades totalled £8. 14s. 9d.; the Beadle had a new hat which cost £1. 6s., and re-gilding his staff cost nearly as much (£1.5s.). At the final reckoning the Spectacle Makers paid £33. 17s. 10d. and the Weavers, £120. 7s. 11d. At a Court meeting of the Weavers' Company on 3 November 1834 certain members, shocked by the expense, moved 'that it is expedient for the Court to declare that on any future occasion of a member of this Compy. being called to fill the office of Lord Mayor or Sheriff of this City, this Court will not contribute to the pageantry on such occasions further than the loan of its Hall and Banners'. This was lost by only one vote (four against five).[11]

During the ensuing decade the Company was faced with no fewer than three important ceremonial occasions. The first was the visit of the young Queen Victoria to the City on Lord Mayor's Day, 1837, the year of her accession to the throne; a royal occasion which was heralded by a letter from the Town Clerk:

12 October 1837

Gentlemen,

I am instructed by the Committee of the Court of Aldermen to suggest to the Livery Companies of the City of London the expediency and propriety of their availing themselves of the opportunity of the Queen's proposed Visit to the City on Lord Mayor's Day, the 9th November next, to adopt some mode of exhibiting their loyalty and affection . . . for Her Majesty on that occasion, by their taking up their ancient and accustomed standings, in their Livery Gowns, in the public streets of the City through which Her Majesty may pass to the Guildhall, and by the display of their flags and banners, . . . or in such other manner as the Companies might deem more advisable. It is expected that Her Majesty will leave St. James's Palace about two of the clock of that day, so as to arrive at the Guildhall at or before Four of the clock in the Afternoon. . . .[12]

The Weavers' Company decided to have their stand erected in St Paul's Churchyard, but they lent the Company's banners of the Royal Standard and the arms of the City of London to the Parish of St. Lawrence Jewry for the day.

The second important ceremonial occasion was the election of Alderman Samuel Wilson as Lord Mayor for the year 1838–9. With the expenses incurred in 1834 fresh in their minds, the Weavers' Assistants prudently referred the question of attending on the new Lord Mayor to their Income and Expenditure Committee. Three weeks later this committee reported as follows:[13]

(1) It was customary for sixteen of the Liverymen of the Company to which the Lord Mayor-elect belonged to attend him at the Guildhall at his swearing-in ceremony, and on the following day—Lord Mayor's Day—when he

was sworn before the Barons of the Exchequer at Westminster.

(2) The hire of carriages for those days (8 and 9 November) was recommended, but not the hire of a barge on the 9th because the 'great expense' of £28 upon the 'long and uncomfortable journey by water' did not seem to be justifiable.

(3) The Bandmaster and fifteen of the band of the 1st Battn. of the Rifle Brigade (then stationed in the Tower of London) could be engaged to play for the procession on Lord Mayor's Day and the Company's dinner afterwards at the Albion tavern for one guinea each bandsman and two guineas for the bandmaster.

(4) The banners and flags bought when Alderman Wilson became Sheriff could be used again, but new cockades would be needed for the coachmen, Banner Bearers and others.

(5) The estimate of expenses which 'should be incurred . . . consistently with respect due to the important Office of Lord Mayor' was:

	£	s.	d.
Repairing Long Streamer Banner		7	6
Altering Royal Standard Banner to meet circumstances of present reign by taking out Hanoverian Escutcheon and making good the arms	3	13	6
72 yards of ribbon to make 23 Cockades of Lord Mayor's Colour at 7d. and a scarf for Beadle	2	2	0
Making up ditto		6	0
Band of 1st Batt. Rifle Brigade	17	17	0
Coaches £15, Coachmen £3	18	0	0
Hire of Livery Gowns: 12 @ 5/- p. day, 2 days	6	0	0
Banner Bearers and 2 assistants for Streamer: 7 @ 5/- p. day, 2 days	3	10	0
Refreshments for attendants; Breakfast for Court, &c on 9th November, say	5	0	0
	56	16	0

These recommendations and the estimate were accepted without modification, and on 8 November the Bailiffs, Wardens and Assistants, sixteen in all, went from Weavers' Hall to the Mansion House to attend the Lord Mayor-elect to the Guildhall and back to the Mansion House. The next day, the sixteen again assembled at Weavers' Hall and went in procession to Guildhall as follows:

The Beadle
The Band
The Royal Standard
The Weavers' Arms   The Arms of the City
The Arms of the Lord Mayor
The Long Streamer
The Junior City Marshal
The Clerk of the Company
The Court and Livery (15 members)
The Upper Bailiff

From the Guildhall they attended the Lord Mayor-elect to the waterside, and after he had embarked, the Weavers' procession went by land to Westminster whence they returned in time to meet the new Lord Mayor at his landing place.

On yet another ceremonial occasion—Queen Victoria's visit to the City in 1844 to open the new Royal Exchange, which replaced Edward Jerman's building, burnt down in 1839—the Weavers' Company had 'standing' space in the Poultry, to which the Livery went in procession with banners and flags, from Weavers' Hall, after taking breakfast as guests of the Upper Bailiff. The Court minutes record that on this occasion 'the Upper Beadle had intimated his inability to attend 'because . . . his duty at Fishmongers' Hall had clashed with his duty as Beadle of the Weavers' Company, and that as the same thing might occur again he begged that it might be understood by the Court that he was ready, if required, to resign his Office'. The Court resolved that the Beadle be told from the Chair that should he again fail to obey the orders of the Court or Officers he would be discharged, 'but that no further notice will on this occasion be taken of the recent occurrence'.[14]

At this time Samuel Wilson was living at Village Place (later called The Cedars) in the quiet Kentish village of Beckenham. The house, built about the year 1717, stood in extensive wooded grounds through which flowed a stream known as the Beck. The property had been bought by Alderman Richard Lea, father-in-law of Samuel Wilson, to whom the house and grounds passed on Richard Lea's death in December 1828,[15] at the age of eighty-two. During 1838–9 there must have been quite a stir in the village every time the Lord Mayor set out to attend a civic function.[16]

The record of Wilson's activities during his mayoralty reveals the nature of his special civic interests and political leanings. Quite early in his year of office he won considerable public approval by his determined attempt, in his capacity as chief magistrate, to improve and humanise the administration of the poor law at parish level. A leading article in *The Times* of 21 December 1838 accused the poor-law authorities of gross neglect of their duties and commended the 'persevering exertions of the Lord Mayor and others for the relief of the wretched objects whose famished looks and naked limbs shock the sight and feelings in almost every street'. Wilson was prepared to censure any parish officer who refused relief without reasonable cause or neglected to investigate properly and take appropriate action. 'I do not consider it to be my duty', he said on one occasion, 'to write letters to overseers to request that they will be so good as to do their duty.' Therefore, he did not hesitate to inflict upon one, Stockham, overseer of Allhallows-on-the-Wall, a fine of £5 (followed by a threat of distraint for non-payment) for refusing to relieve Mary Dodds, a poor, illegitimate girl, on the pretext that she did not belong to that parish. The Lord Mayor quickly proved the contrary by having her mother found and brought into Court, and, said he, 'If the overseer [still] refuses to relieve her, tell him he must take all the consequences, and that I shall . . . have him indicted.'[17] But he would never condone unreasonable insubordination on the part of able-bodied paupers, and when six such men refused to do the work required of them by the poor-law officers, Wilson sentenced them to fourteen days on the treadmill in the House of Correction.[18] On the other hand, he could be lenient, as when he refused to gaol a very old woman who had taken relief from two parishes simultaneously.[19]

The opening years of Queen Victoria's reign were filled with widespread unrest and deep-seated discontent among the working class. Unemployment, low wages, long hours of work, wretched housing, and bitter disappointment at the 'great betrayal' of 1832, when the parliamentary vote was not given to the working man by the Reform Act of that year, were some of the ingredients in an explosive political atmosphere in 1838–9. The popular hostility and agitation against the new Poor Law rose to its climax and merged almost imperceptibly into Chartism, the newly born, first working-class political reform movement on a national scale in British history. Radical political unions revived; democratic societies and working men's associations became active in London and the large provincial towns; the 'People's Charter' providing (*inter alia*) for universal manhood suffrage was drafted and published in 1838, and the first Chartist Convention which opened at the British Hotel, Cockspur Street by Charing Cross, on 4 February 1839, drew a quarter of its forty-nine members from London.[20] The Chartists' delegates sat and talked—sometimes rather wildly—in London until 13 May 1839, when they moved to Birmingham where, by that time, a much more revolutionary atmosphere had spread abroad and where serious rioting and incendiarism actually broke out early in July. On 8 July the Convention returned to London, but the magistrates of the City and the County of Middlesex were not called upon to deal with any similar disturbances.[21] When some 500 Chartists marched in procession from Smithfield to St Paul's Cathedral on 11 August there was no disorder and they 'conducted themselves peaceably during divine service'. According to Mark Hovell, the Chartists had failed to draw together a substantial following among the Londoners. 'A meeting addressed by Pitkeithly and Smart at Rotherhithe on March 28 (1839) drew only fifty or sixty persons. . . . The notion that the populace of London would play in a Chartist Revolution the part of the Paris folk in the French Revolution, if it were ever entertained, was hopelessly impossible.'[22]

Although Samuel Wilson would never countenance violence or sedition, there is good reason to suppose that he believed in freedom of speech and peaceful assembly, and wished to see a further extension of the franchise. On 30 May 1839 the Court of Common Council, with Lord Mayor Wilson in the chair, had a brisk debate on a resolution supporting an extension of the liberties and franchises of the people; recognition of 'equal civil rights without distinction of sect or party'; improvement of the condition of the working classes, and promotion of the cause of universal education, 'which by purifying and reforming our institutions wherever abuses exist, may secure to the Throne the only safe and permanent basis for a constitutional Monarchy, [namely] the sincere affection and support of a free and contented people'. Although this resolution was defeated by 121 votes against 75, there was clearly a substantial minority—nearly two-fifths of those voting—in the Common Council in favour of further parliamentary reform and a national system of education for all.[23]

The year 1838–9 saw, also, an intensification of the City's struggle to retain its own police force by securing exemption from the proposed Metropolis Police Act, and it was Lord Mayor Wilson who led a deputation of City Aldermen and Common Councillors to Buckingham Palace on 21 March 1839 to present an address and petition to the Queen. Although, on this occasion, the City Fathers received a somewhat curt answer, they won their fight in the end, for only the Thames river police, not the City police, were merged in the Metropolitan Police by the Act of 1839.[24]

A more cordial, relaxed atmosphere prevailed on 26 September 1839, when the Lord Mayor was received in private audience by the Queen, and conveyed to her the City's thanks for the portrait of herself which she had recently presented. He reported to his colleagues that he had been most graciously received and the Queen had said that it would always give her pleasure to promote the interests of the citizens of London.[25]

Meanwhile, from 22 to 27 July 1839 the Lord Mayor had made a six-day ceremonial progress by water 'on the business of the conservancy of the Thames' (another of his special interests), which included a visit to Windsor Castle, a public dinner at the White Hart in Windsor, and a landing on Magna Carta Island, where he was greeted on the landing stage by 120 charity-school boys and girls in medieval costume.

One of Samuel Wilson's far-sighted aims was the broadening of the scope of the City Corporation's hospitality and social functions. In May 1839 *The Times* reporter, commenting upon a Mansion House banquet given by the Lord Mayor to a distinguished company of learned, scientific and other professional men, concluded: 'The Mansion House entertainments . . . are no longer churlishly confined to members of the corporation. The present Lord Mayor, upon reaching the mayoralty, acted upon the principle of including eminent members of all professions and occupations not connected with the City of London.'[26]

On another occasion the Lord Mayor struck a distinctly personal note by giving a ceremonial banquet for all connections of the Wilson Family over the age of nine; a function attended by no fewer than 111 members of his family, who gave him two silver-gilt loving cups and covers, inscribed as follows:

> Presented to the Right Honourable Samuel Wilson, Lord
> Mayor of London, to commemorate an entertainment given by
> his Lordship and the Lady Mayoress in the Egyptian Hall in
> the Mansion House on the 5th day of April, 1839, to his
> Lordship's Family . . . and in remembrance alike of the
> Spendour and Hospitality of the scene, and of the great
> kindness shewn by the Lord Mayor and the Lady Mayoress
> to their guests.

Towards the close of Samuel Wilson's year of office the Common Council debated a draft Motion of Thanks to the outgoing Lord Mayor, which expressed warm appreciation of his interest in the conservancy of the Thames and improvements in its navigation, his staunch resistance to all attempts to encroach upon or reduce the City's 'long cherished and ancient right to self-government and internal jurisdiction', and his liberal attitude to poor relief under the exceedingly controversial Poor Law Amendment Act, 1834, especially the urgent immediate necessities of the poor 'whose only crime was their utter destitution'. Similar approval was expressed for 'his respect and attachment to the rights and liberties of the people in permitting them to assemble publicly to discuss and petition for redress of their supposed grievances', and for his energy in checking proceedings of an 'illegal character'. This last significant paragraph, however, evoked objections and was eventually replaced by a shorter, rather colourless expression of thanks.[27]

Both during and after Samuel Wilson's mayoralty his friends and fellow citizens spoke often of his unfailing urbanity and courtesy; his bestowal of credit and praise where they were due; his vigour, firmness and impartiality; his humanity and his 'anxious regard to the interests of all classes in the exercise of his magisterial duties'.[28] So strong, indeed, was this appreciation of his services to the community that, in addition to a function in his honour at the London coffee-house early in December 1839, an entertainment was held at the Albion tavern on 18 June 1840, at which he was presented with a 'splendid piece of plate' in the form of a triple-branched candelabrum, by Green and Ward of Cockspur Street, which had a central pedestal composed of three female figures representing the City of London, Justice and Humanity, and among other decorative features, the arms of the City, and of Alderman Wilson.[29]

For many years after his mayoralty Alderman Wilson continued to interest himself in the Company's affairs and the proper maintenance of its status and dignity. During his second term as Upper Bailiff (1846–7) the Company entertained to dinner the Prime Minister, Lord John Russell, and the Lord Mayor (13 January 1847).[30] The Court minute book records:

> 1st June 1847 . . . the Upper Bailiff reported that considering that the Silver cups belonging to the Company used at the dinners of the Court and Livery were incomplete [i.e. without Covers] he had provided Covers which he begged the Court to accept in commemoration of Lord John Russell . . . having honoured the Court with his Company at dinner on the 13th Day of January 1847. *Resolved* That the thanks of the Court be presented to Mr Alderman Wilson, Upper Bailiff, for his gift of Covers to the Loving Cups . . . and for his continued attention to the interest of the Company . . . [and that] a suitable inscription . . . be placed on the Cups to perpetuate the liberality of the Upper Bailiff.

When he vacated the chair at the end of his year of office, he was again warmly thanked for his assiduous and dignified performance of his duties and his unflagging interest in the Company's prosperity.[31]

If Samuel Wilson was shrewd and successful in business, he was also generous. Early in 1845, as the Weavers' records show, he was seriously considering the creation of a trust fund 'for certain beneficial objects'.[32] Five years later he gave £2,000 to the Weavers' Company upon trust to devote the income, after his death and that

of his wife, to the upkeep and repair of his family vault in the churchyard of Beckenham Parish Church, and from the surplus to pay 10*s*.
each to ten poor parishioners, not receiving parish relief, in each of
the parishes of St Mary, Islington and St George, Beckenham, and
the Ward of Castle Baynard in the City of London, 'and to ten like
poor Weavers the sum of 10*s*. each'. Any proceeds remaining were
to be used to provide a dinner each year in the month of June for the
Officers and Assistants of the Weavers' Company, who must invite
the male heir (if any) of Alderman Wilson, the Lord Mayor of
London, and a number of other distinguished guests.[33] During his
long life the donor kept a watchful eye upon the trust funds, increasing, from time to time, the income or the capital by judicious
sales and reinvestments. In June 1864, for example, he informed the
Court that the original £2,000 had grown to £2,600, and he proposed
to give a further £400 to make up the fund to £3,000.[34]

The Company's Almshouse Endowment Fund was another worthy
cause for which Samuel Wilson worked untiringly during the early
'sixties, after it had been decided to move the almsfolk to new and
better buildings at Wanstead. As chairman of the Almshouses Committee he served on numerous deputations to bankers, brewers, silk
brokers, merchants, and well-known philanthropists. Approaches
were also made to the Members of Parliament for the City, Finsbury,
the Tower Hamlets and Middlesex. During 1861 Alderman Wilson
and his committee succeeded in collecting about £100 a week,[35]
and in May 1864 the fund passed £4,500; a result which enabled the
Company to install pensioners in six additional almshouses for men.
At this period, too, Wilson was again elected Upper Bailiff (1863–4)
and re-elected in the following year,[36] doubtless in recognition of his
devoted work for the Company.

About three years later, when the City Corporation undertook
some restoration work in the Guildhall, the Weavers' Company was
asked to contribute an illuminated window to fill the space 'over the
stone steps leading to the Council Chamber'. The ever-generous
Samuel Wilson at once offered to bear the cost, so enabling the
Company to accept the invitation without anxiety on the score of
expense. When the work was finished early in 1868, the Upper Bailiff
received the following letter:[37]

> 3 Sussex Square, Brighton.
> Feby. 1868
>
> My Dear Sir,
> I have pleasure to inform you the Weavers Window is now
> finished, and placed in the best position in Guildhall over the
> Steps in the centre leading to the Courts of Aldermen &
> Common Council.
> The right hand compartment represents Henry Fitz Elwyne,

the first Mayor of London, who retained the Office for Twenty five years, he left all his lands to the Drapers Company.

In the left hand compartment is Sir Richard Whityngton, 'thrice Lord Mayor of London', in his robes of office, in one corner is the famous Cat so generally mixed up with the name of Whittington!—he was a member of the Mercers Company.

In the right hand lower compartment is represented the Sword, the Mace, the City Purse and the Arms of the Weavers Company.

In the left hand compartment the Sceptre of the City, the Collar of S.S., the Jewel and the City Seal with the City Arms.

The inscription is as follows:—

'Presented by the Weavers Company, the most ancient of all the City Guilds'.

The window is much admired as a Work of Art, and gives great satisfaction—it is considered equal in merit to any Window in the Guildhall.

I am, My dear Sir,
Yours very truly,
Samuel Wilson.

The busiest men, it is often remarked, always seem able to find time for yet more work, and this was true of Samuel Wilson, for in addition to his business activities and his services to the City of London and the Weavers' Company, he gave zealous service as a magistrate for the counties of Middlesex, Essex, Kent, Sussex and Surrey.[38] Nor must one forget his long period of service as a part-time volunteer soldier in the Royal London Militia. From 1851 he is frequently referred to as 'Colonel Wilson', for he had become second in command of the regiment in that year, with the rank of Lieutenant-Colonel. Four years later he was promoted to Colonel and became commanding officer of the Royal London Militia (with headquarters in Finsbury), a command which he held for the next sixteen years, performing his duties with characteristic keenness and judgment. Every summer, for three or four weeks, he took charge of the annual full-time training, presiding over an officers' mess of some twenty-five to thirty members, and having at the same time 600 other ranks under his command. When the Militia was embodied during the Crimean War (1854–6) he travelled to Aldershot every week to inspect the regiment and, it is said, 'took great pride in the large number of men' who transferred to the regular army from his Corps. In 1870, after an illness, and probably on medical advice, for he was then seventy-eight years of age, he resigned his command and was succeeded by Colonel Sir William Rose.[39]

351

The Wilsons, staunch members of the Church of England, were closely identified with the old parish church of St George, Beckenham, in which is the family vault. Here, in April 1865, after over half a century of married life, Samuel Wilson's wife, Jemima, was buried; and here he too found a last resting place after his death in 1881, in his ninetieth year. In the south transept of the church, below a large 'Wilson window', are memorials to Samuel and Jemima Wilson.[40]

NOTES

1 MS. 5234, f.57, 4 May 1813; MS. 4661/104; Beaven, *Aldermen*, I, p. 353.
2 MS. 4661/87 and 96; *Cobbett's Political Register*, III, p. 721.
3 Cornelius Lea Wilson became a freeman of the City on 24 June 1851; he was thrice Upper Bailiff of the Weavers' Company (1857–8, 1873 (3 months), and 1884–5); Prime Warden of the Goldsmiths' Company in 1869; and a magistrate for Westminster, Middlesex and Kent. He married Mary Ann, daughter and heiress of Isaac Wilcox of Pembury, Kent, in 1842, and died on 19 December 1911 at the age of ninety-six. See *The Times*, 22 December 1911, p. 9; R. Borrowman, *Beckenham, Past and Present* (1910), opp. p. 228; Walford's *County Families*; Weavers' Company Court minute books, *passim*.
4 *Ribbon Weavers*, p. 51.
5 MS. 4661/107; Beaven, *Aldermen*, II, p. 144.
6 On Midsummer Day, 24 June, every year, freemen of the city companies meet at Common Hall in the Guildhall to elect two Sheriffs and certain other City Officers for the ensuing year. A Sheriff becomes eligible to be elected Lord Mayor at some future date.
7 MS. 4655/20, ff.157–63.
8 MS. 4655/20, ff.169, 185b. James Harmer, Master of the Spectacle Makers' Company 1831–2 and 1843–4. The son of a Spitalfields weaver, he was the first Spectacle Maker to become a City Alderman. Said to have been rejected at the poll for Lord Mayor in 1840 because he owned the radical *Weekly Dispatch*. Died 12 June 1853 (Beaven, *Aldermen*, II, pp. xxvi, 204).
10 We read that Mr Samuel Wilson presented to the Company the banner of his armorial bearings as a token of his appreciation of the honour his Company had done him.
11 MS. 4655/20, f.193b.
12 MS. 4655/20, ff.247–9.
13 MS. 4655/20, ff.263–9.
14 MS. 4655/20, ff.392–4.
15 R. Borrowman, *Beckenham Past and Present* (1910), pp. 56, 265.
16 Ibid., p. 59.
17 *The Times*, 1 and 3 January 1839.
18 *The Times*, 2 January 1839.
19 *The Times*, 7 January 1839.

20 M. Hovell, *The Chartist Movement* (1918), pp. 121–2.
21 *The Times*, 14 May, 6 and 9 July, 12 August 1839; Hovell, op. cit., Chaps 7 and 9.
22 Ibid., p. 144.
23 C.C.C. Proceedings, 1839, pp. 144–5.
24 C.C.C. Proceedings, 1839, pp. 77, 80; C. Welch, *Modern History of the City of London* (1896), pp. 181–2; *The Times*, 22 March 1839.
25 C.C.C. Proceedings, 1839, p. 231.
26 *The Times*, 23 May 1839.
27 C.C.C. Proceedings, 1839, pp. 315–16.
28 MS. 4655/20, f.283.
29 *The Times*, 5 December 1839 and 20 June 1840.
30 MS. 4655/20, ff.459, 466; *The Times*, 15 January 1847.
31 MS. 4655/20, f.471b.
32 MS. 4655/20, f.409.
33 MS. 4655/20, ff.531–3.
34 MS. 4655/21, 1 October 1850; MS. 4655/23, 7 June 1864; Letter Book, 1863–75, f.268.
35 Weavers' Almshouses Committee Minute Book, 1861.
36 MS. 4655/23, 3 May and 25 July 1864.
37 MS. 4655/24, 1 October 1867 and 3 March 1868. This window was destroyed when London was bombed from the air during the Second World War.
38 Borrowman, op. cit., p. 58. An appointment which did not absorb much of his time was that of King's (or Queen's) Harbinger, an ancient office, the duties of which were to provide for the accommodation of the band whenever the Court moved in procession, on royal visits, progresses, and similar occasions. See Dodd's *Dignities* (1842), pp. 133–4.
39 Muster and Pay Rolls of the Royal London Militia, P.R.O., W.O. 13/1390–4. In 1857–8 Alderman Wilson's address in the list of Assistants of the Weavers' Company was changed from 40 Ludgate Street to 'Head Quarters, Finsbury', which suggests that he was spending a good deal of time on Royal London Militia duties (MS. 4661/109).
40 Borrowman, op. cit., pp. 72–3, 108, 120, 264, 266. Jemima Wilson died 31 March 1865 and Samuel Wilson on 7 July 1881 (*The Times*, 9 July 1881, p. 12; *City Press*, 13 July 1881, p. 5).

Chapter 17

Change of Pattern I

The lifetime of Alderman Samuel Wilson spans the period in which
the hand-loom silk weavers 'were being crushed out with infinite
misery'[1] and the London silk industry was slowly fading away, while,
at the same time, the London Weavers' Company, after a chequered
career through more than seven centuries, entered upon the last stage
of transformation from an old-style craft gild to its modern form as a
City livery company. The salient features of these changes must now
be described.

Looking back upon the history of the gilds and companies we can
discern, at least as early as the 1730s, symptoms of the creeping
decline which eventually paralysed their traditional functions. It is
true that in 1712 the City Corporation affirmed that it was still
determined to punish in the City's courts any un-free persons who
used 'any manual occupation or handicraft' within its jurisdiction:[2]
a declaration which may have delayed for a time—but only for a
time—the progress of decline. By the middle of the eighteenth century the Weavers, while holding in theory to their rights, privileges
and ordinances (and taking sporadic action, from time to time, as
though to prove it), were apparently well aware that conformity to
their regulations on any substantial scale could be neither induced
nor enforced. Indeed, certain offences, such as the operation of
excessive numbers of looms, were completely ignored, presumably
because the more prosperous and influential masters did not want
such 'irregularities' to be brought into the open. Restrictions on the
number of apprentices taken by master weavers had become a dead
letter long before the fact was pointed out by the Royal Commission
on Municipal Corporations in 1837.[3] The final abandonment of the
search of the trade in 1736 is certainly a highly significant milestone
on the Company's long road from medieval craft gild to modern
livery company. The long-established gild practice of admitting to
the freedom by patrimony; the old and obstinate 'Custom of London';

and the increasing number of apprentices formally bound at Weavers' Hall but immediately turned over to masters in quite different trades, added immeasurably to the atmosphere of confusion in which traditional regulation and control broke down, largely because of the mounting difficulties of giving legal definition to offences, let alone inflicting deterrent punishment upon the offenders.[4]

The maintenance, however, of a numerous, cohesive body pursuing a policy of resistance to the competitive encroachments of 'illegal' interlopers was still regarded by the Weavers' Company as feasible and desirable. Hence the attempts to increase the Company's membership by concessions or other changes, such as admission to the freedom at reduced fees in approved cases; the abolition of the distinction between freemen and admissioners; and attempts to press 'users' of the trade into membership. Recorded membership (Officers, Livery and Commonalty), which had decreased gradually from a peak of 6,330 in 1692 to 5,240 in 1720, rose again to 6,258 in 1730, and in 1736, when the Company dropped the distinction between freemen and admissioners (whether foreigners or strangers), it touched the highest figure ever recorded—6,426. The summer of that year saw the last search of the trade by the Company's Officers; and no sooner were the searches abolished than the recorded membership slumped steeply—to 4,923 in 1740: a loss of 1,500 in only four years. Moreover despite the Company's efforts, prompted by the journeymen's complaints,[5] to track down and bring to book persons 'exercising the Trade of Weaving without having any Right thereto', the recorded membership ten years later was only 2,613, which means an average yearly loss of 230 members over the decade 1741–1750.

The general attitude in the trade was expressed in 1748 by Ephraim Flamar, who told the Court of Assistants that although he had been 'duly brought up to the Weaving Trade which he had exercised many years . . . he did not consider it would be of any use to be admitted to the Freedom of the Company and therefore would not be at any expense to be admitted'. Apparently he was not frightened by the Company's threat to sue him. James Voisin, 'living in Coleman Alley, Bunhill Row, Gold and Silver Orice Weaver', could have taken his freedom by patrimony, for his father had been a member of the Weavers' Company, but he protested that 'he had not money to pay the charges nor ever should have, and peremptorily refused to be admitted'. Faced with many similar cases, the Court ordered the Beadles, in October 1748, to make a list of 'all persons who exercise the Trade and are not admitted'.[6] But nothing could arrest the decrease in membership, which continued without a break, though much less steeply, throughout the second half of the eighteenth century, until at the turn of the century the total fell below 1,000

(983 in 1800). In 1810 it went down to 818, but recovered slightly, to 905, by 1820. Nor could anybody possibly deny the definite separation of 'the direction of industrial operations' from 'their execution in detail' which had emerged in the seventeenth century and become quite widespread by the middle of the eighteenth century,[7] by which time the main line of cleavage in the London silk industry was not between members and non-members of the Weavers' Company, but between the journeymen weavers and their employers: between the men who actually did the work and those who gave it out to them and marketed the finished fabrics. In the industrial disputes drama in which tension between employers and journeymen often reached breaking-point in the third quarter of the eighteenth century, and also throughout the fifty years of comparative peace following the first Spitalfields Act of 1773, the Weavers' Company, as we have seen, was cast for only a minor part. But the Company was slow to accept this great change in its position and powers.[8] As late as the 1840s people in the trade were still being summoned to take up membership or to show by what right they exercised 'the Art and Mystery of Weaving, without being admitted to the Freedom of the said Company'. During the year 1817, for example, the Court of Assistants called for a list of names of non-members—especially those who had ignored the Company's summons—and appeared to be contemplating some coercive measures on an unusually large scale. The Company's Summons Book (1787–1856) shows that in 1821 over 100 summonses to take up freedom were issued, and during the 1830s and 1840s more summonses were sent out at fairly regular intervals, though in smaller numbers. In May 1830, when Mr Davies of Foster Lane, a silk trimmings manufacturer, was duly summoned to take up his freedom, he answered 'that he shall not do so and the Company might do as it pleased'.[9] The Royal Commission on Municipal Corporations, reporting in the mid-1830s, said that 'Parties carrying on the trade of Weavers in London are summoned to take up their Freedom in the Company, the Court having the power by the Charter to compel them so to do.' People within the City's jurisdiction usually submitted, 'but in several cases it has been necessary to proceed by actions at law, in all of which the Company has been successful, and judgments obtained against the parties refusing'.[10] If those summoned did not respond, the summons was repeated a second and a third time. One of these third summonses, issued in 1843, was couched in the following peremptory terms: '. . . as the Court [of Assistants] possesses the most conclusive evidence that you are carrying on the business of Weaving in violation of the rights and privileges of the Company it is their determination to enforce the same. . . .'[11] It would seem that no summonses to the freedom were issued after 1847.

The spread of free-trade ideas during the earlier half of the nineteenth century had implications for local trade and industry, as well as for international trade. Many master manufacturers wanted to be protected, but a large and increasing number of others favoured the removal of all restrictions on freedom of enterprise. This major difference on commercial and industrial policy which split the members of the Weavers' Company at the turn of the century lay at the root of the conflict of evidence given, as we have noted, by a number of prominent London silk manufacturers before various government committees of inquiry. Divided internally in this way, the Company was inevitably much weakened for the task of enforcing any of its now obsolescent 'rights'.[12] The Royal Commission on Municipal Corporations remarked that the advantages, if any, resulting to the members of the Weavers' and a score of other companies,

> must be confined . . . to the opportunities afforded to the more substantial classes, of occasionally being brought into contact with each other. . . . Advantages to the community at large, there are none; and the disadvantages to those who are compelled to come into the Companies, on account of their exclusive privileges, is measured by the extent of the fine paid upon admission. . . . No qualification whatever is required [of a Liveryman-elect], provided the party pays his fine, and [the smaller companies] . . . look to the Livery merely as a source of revenue . . .[13]

But more than two-thirds of the Weavers' Court of Assistants either were or had been connected with the weaving trade.[14]

After the 'shackles were removed' by Parliament's adoption of Huskisson's free-trade policy, the English silk industry enjoyed (especially after 1829) a period of rapid growth. G. R. Porter, the Board of Trade's chief statistician, with all the latest official statistics at his fingertips, recorded, enthusiastically, that:

> the silk manufacture in all its branches has spread itself into various districts, and is conducted upon a scale, and according to principles which admit of so great a degree of economy, as not only to place the products of our silk looms within the reach of the humbler classes of the community in this country, but to enable us successfully to compete in other markets with goods produced in foreign countries.

Having recovered from the set-back caused by the grave commercial crisis of 1825, British exports of manufactured silk goods began to show a marked increase in 1830, when they reached an aggregate value of £521,000. By 1833 the total was over £737,000, and in 1835 the figure exceeded £972,000, the principal overseas markets being found in Canada, U.S.A., and the West Indies.[15] John Dillon, a warehouseman, told the Select Committee of 1832 that not only were sales of English silks increasing, but their quality had much improved since 1826; indeed, he said, 'in plain gros de Naples the English have now almost, if not altogether, superseded the French'. Another witness spoke of an immense increase in the manufacture of certain silks at Manchester, and it is clear that the expansion was mainly in the north-west and Midlands where wage-rates and other costs were appreciably lower than in London, and where power-driven machinery was gradually being introduced and improved. The Factory Inspectors' reports for 1834–5 show that the numbers of 'silk factories' and their male and female employees were far greater in the counties of Chester, Lancaster, and Derby than in Essex. Even Somerset had more silk factories than Essex (twenty-three against eight), and employed 1,890 people on silk manufacture compared with 1,527 in Essex.[16] A report (1828) on the state of the British wool trade remarks that 'though there is not a full manufacture of cloth at present . . . we have a manufacture of silk lately established' near Ilminster.[17] Within a few years, power looms were weaving silk at Shepton Mallet and Ottery St Mary, where it was estimated that 'a woman can, with a power-loom, do twice as much as a man can in a hand-loom'. In 1830–1 Porter had, with unwonted pessimism, doubted 'whether the use of power-looms, however they may be modified, is susceptible of much extension in any save the commonest branches of the silk manufacture'.[18] Yet in 1832 the go-ahead partnership of Courtauld, Taylors and Courtauld built a power-loom factory at Halstead, Essex,[19] and at the close of 1835 there were 1,714 power looms weaving silk fabrics in England. Assistant Commissioner J. C. Symons, writing in 1838–9, was convinced that 'whenever mechanical invention has sufficiently softened the action of the power-loom, its inroads will be as great on silks as on cottons', while his colleague, Commissioner W. E. Hickson, reported that among the silk weavers he had 'met universally with a deep-rooted conviction that the power-loom would never interfere with them' because of the many technical difficulties. Yet, as he goes on to show, after eighteen years of persistent experimentation 'these difficulties have been triumphally conquered'. In a Manchester silk factory he had seen sixty-four power looms weaving plain silks, attended by a woman or a girl to each loom; and in another factory he found Jacquard looms making figured silks with one man attending to two looms. He was convinced that very shortly this man might be replaced by a girl, and that ribbons and bandannas would soon go over to power weaving. Only velvet weaving might, perhaps, escape the competition of the power looms, though even this might eventually be taken over.[20]

In London, where the situation contrasts sharply with that in the north-west, Midlands, and west of England, one sees a marked failure to move with the times, followed by all the symptoms and consequences of decline concentrated within a relatively small, close-built urban area. The boundaries of 'Spitalfields' in the middle of the nineteenth century ran from St Leonard's Church, Shoreditch, along the Hackney Road to the Regent's Canal, along the line of the canal to the Mile End Road; then westwards through Whitechapel to St Botolph's Church, Aldgate; thence along the length of Houndsditch to St Botolph's Church without Bishopsgate, and finally, turning northwards along Norton Folgate, to the starting point at Shoreditch Church. Within this irregularly shaped area, known universally as 'Spitalfields', although it included parts of Bethnal Green, Shoreditch, Whitechapel and Mile End, large numbers of silk weavers were concentrated.[21] It was, therefore, a community district extremely vulnerable to any and every kind of set-back in the silk trade.

Even supposing that the Weavers' Company had succeeded in retaining and enforcing its rights as a craft gild in the London silk industry, it would have had little enough to control by the middle of the nineteenth century. Ample evidence comes down to us from the journeymen hand-loom weavers and their masters; from qualified medical men and experienced social investigators, all of whom paint the same sombre picture of 'a crying national tragedy', a doomed and dying industry. Richard Cray, a Bethnal Green silk weaver who had been driven to Radicalism and Chartism by excessive labour and hard times, tells of a master silk manufacturer—Mr Newberry of London Wall—who had 'about 200 looms at work in 1824', but 'now in 1838 he has about 12, the rest of his work he has made in Exeter by the power Looms where he has a few boys at work at 3 shillings and 2 shillings per week'.[22] William Brunskill, who manufactured broad silks in Spitalfields and ribbons in Coventry, had become a considerable importer and dealer in foreign silk goods 'since the ports have been opened'. Giving evidence before the Select Committee on the state of the silk trade since the legislation of 1824, he said that foreign imports had beaten many Spitalfields fancy fabrics out of the market, which caused more manufacturers and weavers to turn to plain fabrics, and greatly intensified competition for employment in the plain section. The formidable competition of the Manchester silk manufacturers was also mentioned, and the lamentable fact that many of the smaller Spitalfields manufacturers had gone out of business, ruined.[23] Barrett Wadden, another witness, had been a silk manufacturer for nearly ten years in Spitalfields and for fourteen years before that in Dublin. Before the repeal of the prohibition on foreign silk goods he had employed 300 weavers: by 1832 he employed, on an average over the whole year, only 60–70, because he now found it 'a very unprofitable trade'. 'I have had', he said, 'some opportunities of seeing the weavers at their own houses . . . many of them have their bed gone to the pawnbrokers . . . in very many instances, the midnight lamp has no longer oil in it . . .' even 'the shuttles are gone to pawn . . . nothing in their room but a loom and a pallet on the floor; no table, no chair'. He thought that the majority of the weavers were mainly employed—when they were employed at all—on 'plain low-priced goods made from inferior silks'.[24] It is significant that, at this time, one London Board of Guardians, accustomed though they were to extreme poverty and privation, resolved to apprentice no more children to the silk weavers.[25] In this period, too (1829–32) 'Mr. Hanbury, the Secretary of the Spitalfields Soup Society' was appealing for funds 'for the relief of the distressed Manufacturers and others in that district'.[26] James Phillips Kay, M.D., an Assistant Poor Law Commissioner (who later became Sir James Kay-Shuttleworth), stated in Appendix B to the *Annual Report of the Poor Law Commissioners for England and Wales*, 1837, that the Spitalfields weavers had but a meagre diet, scanty clothing and 'a very low amount of household convenience'. Trade depression had halved the industry's output, one-third of the 14,000 looms being totally unemployed, while many of the remainder were only partially in use. This was disastrous where whole families relied upon the earnings of two, or perhaps three, looms. Some weavers took to portering at the docks or Billingsgate market 'during seasons of distress', but 'a considerable number . . . are reported to be too feeble for great bodily exertion. . . . The children at such periods are also hired at a market (held at Bethnal Green every Monday) by shopkeepers in all the adjoining parishes, as nurses of children, errand boys and girls, etc., and earn 2s. 2d. or 4s. 2d. per week.'[27] According to Richard Cray, the silk weavers' piece-work rates in 1839 had fallen to between 50 and 60 per cent of the 1824 level, i.e. 'before the introduction of French silks and the repeal of the Spital-fields Act'.[28]

Ample confirmation came, shortly afterwards, from the famous Reports on the condition of the hand-loom weavers throughout the country. The report on Spitalfields (1840) was written by Dr James Mitchell, an Assistant Commissioner, but we know that W. E. Hickson, one of the four Commissioners, also made a thorough investigation in the district. He it was who took a statement from William Bresson of Daniel Street, Spitalfields, a velvet weaver and loom-broker, and a great-grandson of Raymond Bresson, a French Protestant refugee who settled in London in the seventeenth century.[29] William Bresson, born in 1786, had been in the silk industry all his life. As a loom-broker he let out looms to other weavers, charging from $3\frac{1}{2}d.$ to $4d.$ a week. The value of each loom was about £1, and, said he, 'I should do very well, as I have about 200 looms out, if I could get my money; but the fact is I lose half of it. I am obliged, of course, to take security, but the neighbourhood is so poor that security and all are often good for nothing. When, however, the trade prospers, I prosper. . . .' Evidence was taken from a number of journeymen weavers. Thomas Heath, for example, had been a sailor for twelve years, but in 1816 he said, 'I took to weaving [and] worked at plain satin for 12 months, until I got acquainted with the loom, and then I took to figured work, and have been at it ever since. . . .' Doubtless he had a natural flair for the craft, for he was thought to be one of the best silk weavers in Spitalfields in 1839. Another self-taught weaver was John Druce, who said that, although his father had made woollen cloth, 'I was never taught weaving by anybody, and in 1802, being then 16 . . . I tried silk weaving and succeeded' in various branches, but 'many men never get beyond the plainest work. . . . Whenever the trade is brisk men come to it from other employments and begin at the simplest work. . . . The weavers bring up their families to be weavers from a desire to get something from their [children's] labour as soon as possible.' A note in Lardner's *Treatise on the Silk Manufacture* (1831) cites the case of a family consisting of husband, wife, and ten children, all of whom, excepting the two youngest, were organised like a small factory.

> The father, assisted by one of his sons, was occupied with a machine . . . punching card slips from figures which another son, a fine intelligent lad about thirteen years of age, was 'reading on'. Two other lads, somewhat older, were in another apartment, casting, drawing, punching, and attaching to cords the leaden plummets or lingos, which form part of the harness for a Jacquard loom. The mother was engaged in warping silk with a machine. . . . One of the daughters was similarly employed at another machine, and three other girls were in three separate looms weaving figured silks. . . . An air of order and cheerfulness prevailed throughout this busy establishment . . . and, with the exception of the plummet-drawers, all were clean and neatly clad. The particular occupation wherein each was engaged was explained readily, and with a degree of genuine politeness, which proved that amid the harassing cares attendant upon daily toils of no ordinary degree, these parents had not been unmindful of their duty, as regards the cultivation of their children's minds and hearts.[30]

James Hoyles, who came of an old-established weaving family, had begun at an early age, as was usual, by winding quills; then from eleven to eighteen he worked at fancy trimming, but left it because of slack trade. At eighteen he took up silk weaving and, under his father's instruction, became proficient in twelve months. He estimated net weekly earnings as follows:

Best Velvets	17s.	Ladies' Velvets	14s.
Second Velvets	12s.	Slight Velvets	10s.
		Best plain silks	9s. 6d. to 10s. 6d.
Young unmarried women		8s.	
Married women		4s.	

Charles Cole and a committee of weavers handed in the names of twenty plain weavers, who used, with their families, a total of 37 looms, and averaged net weekly earnings of 8s. 6d. per loom.[31] Table 17.1 shows weavers' earnings on the cheaper fabrics, allowing a deduction for their expenses of approximately 3s. a week, *averaged*, over the year's work and taking slack with busy times.

Table 17.1 *Weavers' earnings*

Material	s. d. per week
Plain lutes	8 1 (to 6s. 9d.)
Plain garment silk	7 5
Light satins	5 11
Plain sarsenet	4 1

Thomas Heath, one of the most skilful weavers in Spitalfields, produced 40 samples of his own work—'exceedingly beautiful' figured silks. His detailed records of his earnings for upwards of eight years showed a weekly average of 15s. gross (or 11s. to 11s. 6d. net after deduction of his expenses) to which he added his wife's earnings of about 3s. a week. 'I have been as fortunate as most of the trade', he told the Commissioners; 'I have never been discharged altogether; I have always been attached to some warehouse, but then I have had a great deal of play [unemployment], as others have had. I have not been able to buy a coat for these five years.'[32]

The engine-loom weavers, who made narrow goods such as ribbons, hatbands, edge-bindings and laces, were also suffering from 'the loss of their Book of Prices', the introduction of power looms in the North, and a disastrous reduction of their earnings. For example,

Charles Leagoe was engaged in making double ribands. Before 1824, he got £1. 8s. 4d. a week; in 1826 the work was done for 18s., and in 1831, for 15s., and that work is now [1839] paid only 13s. 4d., and, deducting 1s. for extra rent and 9d. for candles, the net earnings of the weaver is about 11s. 7d. a week. In this branch the weaver must wind his own quills, as a child cannot be trusted. Of this work there is now but little, and the weavers engaged in it suffer from 'play'. The trade is gradually becoming extinct.

For the past seven years this man had been employed chiefly on galloons,[33] and he estimated his net earnings from his loom at 5s. 9d. a week, adding that 'even at those wages there is often little to do'. To supplement these meagre earnings he went out 'attempting to sell tin-ware', while his wife took his place in the loom, and he earned a little more by working 'at the Borough market from 4 to 12 on the Saturday afternoon'. Thus he managed to scrape together a total income of 11s. 6d. a week for himself and his family. He could see no prospect of relief apart from 'getting out of the trade to something else', and he would certainly not let his children enter it. He shrank from accepting parish relief, and had never had such help except when he and his whole family were 'laid up by the typhus fever'. Leagoe's evidence was fully corroborated by other witnesses.[34]

Even the highly skilled and somewhat more highly paid velvet weavers had little real security. At times when velvets were in vogue, they prospered; but 'should a change come in public taste (which a few months may bring about), and velvet dresses, mantillas, velvet bonnets, shawls, collars and waistcoats go out of fashion, some thousands of the best paid class of weavers would suddenly be reduced below the common level'.[35] Nevertheless, their plight was, on the whole, less desperate than that of the plain and narrow weavers, and 'the contrast between the two classes of operatives was most observable when on Saturdays, the general pay-day, they were to be seen waiting about the doors of the various manufacturers' offices to receive their weekly "draw" of wages'.[36]

Hickson's opinion (always worth having) was that although

the silk weavers in the manufacturing districts [of the North] work for lower wages than the weavers of Spitalfields and Bethnal Green, they are on the whole in better circumstances than the latter. In the suburbs of Manchester house room is much cheaper than in Spitalfields; a weaver being able to obtain a small house, with four rooms, for the rent of one room in London. Provisions also are somewhat cheaper . . . but the most important advantage is cheap fuel. Next to bread, perhaps, in this cold and damp climate, the most important necessary of life is fuel; [and] . . . I doubt whether anything can prevent the rapid decline of all the principal London manufactures, by their removal to the northern counties,

unless means can be devised to cheapen here [London] the
supply of fuel.

During the hard winter of 1838 the Manchester weavers were paying
9*d*. a cwt. for coal, while the Spitalfields weavers had to pay 2*s*. 2*d*.,
with the thermometer at zero and three-quarters of the looms idle.
'Often, Sir, and often,' said a Spitalfields weaver's wife, 'were we
obliged, when half starving, to go without a pennyworth of bread,
and buy a pennyworth of coals, or take the children over to a
neighbour's to borrow a warm at their fire, or put them early to bed
shivering and crying with cold.'[37]

Hickson also gave some figures, obtained from Morrison and
Company of Fore Street (one of the largest silk merchant houses in
the City of London), indicating the trend of trade away from London
and towards the North between 1826 and 1838 (see Table 17.2).[38]

Table 17.2 *Broad silks: rateable proportion (%) of purchases
in different markets*

Market	5 years ending 31.7.1826 £ s. d.			5 years ending 31.7.1831 £ s. d.			5 years ending 31.7.1838 £ s. d.		
Spitalfields	66	10	6	53	6	0	43	5	9
Manchester & Macclesfield	33	9	6	44	2	8	51	19	3
France	—			2	11	4	4	15	0
	100	0	0	100	0	0	100	0	0

As to hours of labour, John Druce's working day was from 8 a.m.
to 8 p.m. Taking two hours for meals, he spent ten hours in his loom:
'quite enough too', he said. William Garland worked twelve hours
in the loom, when he had work to do. Thomas Heath reckoned to
work a thirteen-hour day (7 a.m.–9 p.m.), taking only one hour for
meals. Weavers who worked in their own homes could stop work
when they chose; some who fell behind with their work tried to catch
up by working into the night: 'You will sometimes hear the looms
going at 2 or 3 in the morning,' Thomas Heath said, 'and, besides
that, in some of the back streets and courts and alleys, where the
poorest class of weavers dwell, you will see the lights and hear the
looms on Sunday evenings. . . . Some rush the work and exhaust
themselves by relatively short bursts of intensive labour; others
work more deliberately and sensibly.'[39] An important reason for
last-minute rushes was the fact that completion of the piece meant
payment of its price (less any advances already received).

Evidence on the parlous physical condition of a great many of the silk weavers comes from all sides. They are described as diminutive, weak, subject to tuberculosis, and usually among the earliest victims of epidemics such as cholera. 'Fever is never for a single day in any season of any year, entirely absent from a considerable portion of the Spitalfields and Bethnal Green districts.'[40] The parish of Christ Church, Spitalfields, had long been grossly overcrowded, and Bethnal Green rapidly became so in the first three decades of the nineteenth century. Originally a hamlet in the Manor of Stepney, Bethnal Green was created a separate parish by Act of Parliament in 1740, when it had 1,800 houses and 15,000 inhabitants.

> In the boom that followed the Napoleonic Wars, a whole district of Bethnal Green was built over with small houses expressly designed for one class of worker, the hand-loom weavers. They spread east from the old centre of the trade . . . adjoining Spital Square, and in the ten years 1816 to 1826 . . . new streets of two-storey houses were built for them, with living rooms below and a workshop above. These houses can at once be recognised by the 'long windows' of the upper storey . . . access from the living to the working floor was often by a ladder through a trap-door. . . .[41]

Between the census of 1801 and that of 1831 Bethnal Green's population grew from 22,310 to 62,018—an increase of nearly 40,000 which degraded the old rural village into a festering slum. The census of weavers taken in Spitalfields in July 1838 revealed a total of 4,299 families of weavers in the whole district, of whom 3,512 were in Bethnal Green. Moreover, 1,063 of the Bethnal Green weavers' families had only one loom, and another 1,251 families had only two looms. The number of looms in Bethnal Green returned as 'unemployed' was 776, while another 189 were 'said to have been parted with'. Table 17.3 gives a statistical summary of the situation in

Table 17.3 *Families with looms*

Neighbourhood	1	2	3	4	5	6 or more	Total
Bethnal Green	1,063	1,251	702	351	113	32	3,512
Christ Church, Spitalfields	184	139	42	13	3	2	383
Mile End New Town	149	135	42	22	8	5	361
Shoreditch	22	13	3	3	—	2	43
Totals	1,418	1,538	789	389	124	41	4,299

Bethnal Green compared with the Christ Church, Mile End New Town and Shoreditch neighbourhoods.

Families having more than three looms often let out one or more, receiving from the renter a small weekly sum for 'loom-standing'. Of the unemployed looms, 202 belonged to 143 families 'not having any employment'; 97 of them relying upon only one loom.[42]

Table 17.4 *Census of silk weavers in the Spitalfields district, July 1838*

	(A) *Number of looms worked by*						
Neighbourhood					*Apprentice*		
	Men	*Women*	*Boys*	*Girls*	*Boys*	*Girls*	*Total*
Christ Church, Spitalfields	415	227	15	11	1	—	669
Bethnal Green							
(*a*) The Green	929	648	84	57	10	1	1,729
(*b*) Church	1,535	1,095	147	114	34	7	2,932
(*c*) Town	1,486	985	136	84	8	4	2,703
(*d*) Hackney Road	282	169	20	9	3	—	483
Mile End New Town	396	254	34	19	1	—	704
Shoreditch	55	17	4	1	5	—	82
Totals	5,098	3,395	440	295	62	12	9,302

	(B) *Types of silk fabrics made in Spitalfields* (*all neighbourhoods*)						
Fabrics				*Made by*			
	Men	*Women*	*Boys*	*Girls*	*Apprentice*		*Total*
					Boys	*Girls*	
Plain	2,820	2,790	336	242	52	12	6,252
Velvets	1,871	526	76	46	8	—	2,527
Jacquard velvets	15	1	8	—	—	—	24
Jacquard or figured	392	78	20	7	2	—	499
Totals	5,098	3,395	440	295	62	12	9,302

In February 1832 6,000 people were on parish relief in Bethnal Green and another 1,100 on indoor relief in the workhouse which had only 370 beds.[43] All were easy victims in a cholera epidemic like that of 1831–2. The Hand-loom Weavers Commissioners tell much the same story as the Poor Law Commissioners, in statements asserting that 'The chances of life of the labouring classes of Spitalfields (including the weavers) are amongst the lowest that I have met with', and that it is bad air, bad lodging and bad food 'which cause children to grow up an enfeebled and diminutive race of men'. William Bresson would not have been described as 'poor' at that time and place; but this is what the Commissioner (W. E. Hickson) said of his house and its surroundings:

> William Bresson . . . lives in a small house containing but three very small rooms, and a fourth barely large enough to contain six looms, by which it is completely choked up. For this house, which could be built . . . for £80, the two families occupying it pay the disproportionate rent of £16, and £2. 5s. additional for the small strip of flower garden in front. There is no cesspool nor sewer to carry off the soil from the privy; and close to the house runs a stagnant ditch filled with abominable black filth, for which there is no drain, and the stench from which is often insupportable. The neighbourhood is, of course, seldom free from fever; and I was informed that a whole family were lying dead, through fever, in a street in the vicinity at the time of my visit.[44]

Despite such reports there was no improvement. Dr Hector Gavin, in his *Sanitary Ramblings* in Bethnal Green nearly ten years later, found the dwellings of the poor still surrounded by heaps of refuse and garbage, which with 'the filthy cess-pools and privies . . . everywhere pollute . . . this dirty parish'. He visited one house in which eight persons lived and slept in one ground-floor room, 10 ft by 6 ft by 9 ft high; and it is not surprising that the children had 'low fever'. Another family occupied the other ground-floor room, and above was a workroom, shared by the two families. Close behind no. 1 Paradise Row the doctor found 'Paradise Dairy', where sixteen cows and twenty pigs were kept. Here animal dung and vegetable refuse 'were piled up a considerable height above a hollow adapted to receive them', while 'the soakage from the neighbouring privies found its way into this receptacle for manure and filth. . . . The occupiers of this dairy nevertheless asserted the place to be perfectly clean and wholesome.' And so on. Shoreditch, too, is described as unhealthy, while Spitalfields (where unemployed silk weavers and 'many thousands of labouring men herd together'), Mile End (Old and New Towns) and Whitechapel were found to be 'still more unhealthy'.[45] Wide publicity was given to the condition of the Spitalfields weavers in the middle of the century by Henry Mayhew (now well-remembered for his studies of *London Labour and the London*

Poor) in a series of frank, detailed, humane articles, written in his capacity as 'Metropolitan Commissioner' of the *Morning Chronicle* newspaper. He found many of the weavers on the brink of destitution, although they worked twelve to fourteen hours a day when they had work to do: the father and mother working on by lamplight while their children lay sleeping amid the dust and clatter of the workroom. Sitting at midnight with one starving weaver, he saw 'patience in his misery that gave it more an air of heroism than desperation'. Mayhew's careful investigations revealed a people struggling bravely against enormous odds. Nor did they, in large numbers, seek a fleeting solace in excessive drinking. In 1850 only 1 weaver in 99 was an habitual drunkard, compared with 1 in 22 among musicians, and 1 in 68 among medical men.[46]

In striking contrast to the journeymen and their families, the master weavers or manufacturers were living in good style in and about Spital Square, Devonshire Square, Great St Helen's, White Lion Street, or in more suburban neighbourhoods such as Bishop Bonner's Fields or Old Ford.[47] For the most part, they left the details of the work and wages to managers and foremen, who farmed out the work—what there was—to petty master weavers who 'made their own terms with the hands they employed in their crowded cottage workshops'. The result was, inevitably, the further beating down of wages and 'an immense amount of sweated labour' among men, women and children alike; the journeyman being 'obliged to take the work out to make at what price he could get or starve'.[48]

The death blow to the already weakened Spitalfields silk industry was struck in 1860 by the commercial treaty with France, 'a product of the most secret diplomacy', negotiated by Cobden and his opposite number on the French side, Chevalier. This treaty abolished the English silk duties which, before 1860, were 'turbans 3*s*. each; dresses 30*s*. each; plain silk ribbons 6*d*. a lb.; with many specific rates; and on all silks not otherwise specified, 15 per cent *ad valorem*'.[49] The details of the new treaty attracted little opposition in Parliament for it was in harmony with the general policy to which the victorious free-traders had been committed for forty years. Gladstone secured a majority of 122 in the Commons against the retention of the existing duties on imported silk manufactures; and a modest motion that the duties be retained until 1 October 1861 was negatived by a majority of 128.[50] *The Times* printed the full text of the treaty on 11 February 1860, with the comment: 'Protection, expelled from palaces, has been lurking in comfortable corners, among people . . . standing out each for his own little craft. A crowd of small manufactures and petty produce, from silk to eggs, are [henceforth] to be admitted duty free.' Spitalfields and Coventry petitioned and protested in vain. 'Let the silk trade perish and go to countries to which it properly belongs' is the contemptuous comment attributed to Cobden. Within a very few weeks, British ports were flooded with duty-free French and Swiss silks—a flood which submerged, for all time, many a family of silk weavers in Spitalfields and Essex. Some emigrated; some joined the wretched ranks of the casual labourers in the docks; but still there remained large numbers 'unable to find any means of support'.[51] Many firms gave up the ghost and sold their stocks for what they would fetch, thus glutting the market and depressing yet further prices and wages; 'the aspect of Spitalfields and Bethnal Green began immediately to change for the worse. . . . The offices and warehouses were given up. Some manufacturers could not meet their liabilities, and were ruined'; others took offices in the City and dealt in goods made in the provinces and abroad; a few 'built factories in the provinces and transplanted to them the most skilful of the hand-loom silk weavers who still remained . . .'[52] Many a young manufacturer 'whose father had made his fortune in the better times of protection, who probably thought there was no necessity for renewed exertion on his part, found himself unequal to, and consequently beaten in, the match with his more thoroughly grounded continental confrère.'[53]

The misfortunes of Spitalfields soon spread into Essex, a county in which a number of towns, notably Colchester, Coggeshall, Saffron Walden, Chelmsford, Braintree, Bocking and Halstead, had gradually developed into 'outposts or dependencies' of the London master silk weavers during the seventeenth and eighteenth centuries. In these towns and in the Essex villages on the eastern outskirts of London— East Ham and Stratford-by-Bow, for example—a host of home-working weavers depended largely on work put out to them by the Spitalfields masters. As early as 1645 a silk weaver named Paul Fox, 'a man of honest life and conversation', is recorded as having dwelt in Plaistow many years, weaving fine lace and 'ribbaning' with the help of his son and two journeymen. A directory of 1793 gives the names of two silk weavers—James Rogers of Epping and Michael Boyle of Colchester—and it is clear that at the turn of the century a number of City and Spitalfields firms, whose partners were members of the London Weavers' Company, had regular links with Essex. 'Norwich' crape was being woven (c. 1815) at Saffron Walden, where a small factory, owned by Grout, Bayliss & Co., of London and Bocking, employed 'many hands, principally young females'. Jones and Foyster made ribbons and broad silks at Halstead and Samuel Courtauld began to manufacture crape about 1825. J. & W. Robinson of Milk Street, City, employed velvet weavers in and around Coggeshall and so did Bailey, Fox & Co., a firm founded in Spitalfields by Charles Bailey and Edward Fox in 1829, who manufactured figured velvets and silks for waistcoats, black and coloured velvets for coat collars, and tailors' facings and linings. Two other partnerships, Carter Vavasseur and Rix of Trump Street, Cheapside and John Vanner and Sons (now of Sudbury) were manufacturing silk fabrics in Braintree until the early 1860s. And in the same town, Daniel Walters and Son had 150 jacquard looms making furniture silks, damasks, rich brocatelles, etc.[54] In 1832, Peter Bedford, the Quaker philanthropist, was living in Castle Street, Saffron Walden, and carrying on business as a silk manufacturer in London and Essex, although, it seems, he had never been apprenticed to the craft.[55]

From 1773—perhaps earlier—to 1824, it was customary for master silk weavers and manufacturers to pay two-thirds of the Spitalfields 'book prices' for work done in Essex, and when the London weavers 'lost their Book' the Essex weavers, too, were involved in the subsequent difficulties about rates of pay. At Coggeshall, for example, wages fell soon after 1824 and the weavers anxiously complained of many unsettled disputes with their employers. Average net earnings were about 7s. 6d. a week for men, and 3s. 6d. to 4s. for women. By 1839 the average net earnings of hand-loom silk weavers at Braintree had fallen below those of the bricklayers' labourers, 'who had 9s. a week and three pints of porter a day', and the agricultural labourers, who suffered no deductions and might glean, cut firewood, and grow some potatoes and cabbages. The weavers pointed out that the trade was overcrowded because entry was easy, and alleged that the London manufacturers deliberately kept large numbers of weavers on their books by giving out small amounts of work to as many weavers as possible, so assuring themselves of a large reserve of labour which could be called upon suddenly in busy periods.[56] After the French treaty of 1860 a number of the firms already mentioned either closed down or severely curtailed their manufacturing activities, until, by the end of the century, only Warner and Sons, Bailey, Fox & Company, and Samuel Courtauld and Company continued to manufacture in Essex, while John Vanner and Sons carried on business over the county border at Sudbury in Suffolk. Courtaulds were fortunately saved from a set-back in the sixties by the prevailing crape-wearing fashion, and in 1870 'the Franco-Prussian War inflated the French demand for the company's crape, sales of which in that year were unprecedented'.[57] Large numbers of unemployed silk workers migrated to Braintree, Bocking and Halstead in the hope of being employed by Courtaulds.

Meanwhile, the 'unhappy decadence' of the silk industry continued in Spitalfields. An official report on the English silk industry in 1884, made in connection with the investigations of the Royal Commission on Technical Instruction, revealed that in the sixty years between 1824–5 and 1884 the annual consumption of silk yarn in 'London, including Spitalfields', had fallen from $1\frac{1}{2}$ million lb.

to 80,000 lb.; the number of 'operatives employed' had decreased from 60,000 to less than 4,000; the surviving hand looms numbered only 1,200, while only 40 power looms had been set up, all in one factory making umbrella silks. Some firms had only their winding and warping done in London, the weaving being done in the country. The types of goods still being made included plain and figured silks for furniture; chenille and trimmings; high-quality scarves and ties; umbrella and parasol silks. There was keen competition from foreign manufacturers, especially those of Roubaix, Lyons, Crefeld and Milan. The weavers' wages ranged from 15s. to 50s. a week. Many of the younger men had left the trade, apprentices were no longer coming in, and a large number of weavers' houses 'suitable to the trade' had been pulled down.[58]

Such demolitions, however, were sometimes opposed by the weavers. For example, as late as December 1900, George Dorée, a velvet weaver and warp spreader living and working at Albion Road, Bethnal Green, sought the help of the Weavers' Company in resisting the demolition of certain houses 'specially adapted for weaving' which the Borough Council was proposing in order to use the cleared site for an electric station and a dust destructor. Dorée, a descendant of Huguenot craftsmen and an alert, intelligent man, was looked upon in Spitalfields 'as the representative and champion of the . . . silk weavers', and was much respected by the manufacturers. He worked for Bailey, Fox & Company, and had been a prize-winner in one of the Weavers' silk-weaving competitions. He occupied a typical silk weaver's dwelling which had four rooms on the ground floor, two of the rooms being situated on either side of a central passage running from front to back. Through the open back-door an interested visitor could see a small back-yard, gay with flowers in spring and summer, and 'furnished with a large, neat aviary'. On the upper floor, reached through a trap-door, was a large work-shop 'flooded with light', and in one of the looms sat Mrs Dorée 'weaving a rich black silk of an extraordinary solid texture'.[59] The Weavers' Company held, quite rightly, that such houses and work-shops were worth preserving, and that their skilled artist-craftsmen should not lightly be driven out. So the Company wrote to the Local Government Board asking that 'due regard' should be had 'to the special needs of the hand loom weaving industry'. When this appeal proved successful the 'poor weavers . . . so often hardly pressed', were not slow to convey their gratitude to George Dorée and to the Company.[60] Dorée it was who wove the purple and crimson velvet for King Edward VII's coronation robes, and he continued to weave exquisite silk fabrics of the highest quality until his death in 1916.

In the early dawn of the twentieth century appeared Charles

Booth's monumental detailed study of the *Life and Labour of the People in London*, which gave dreadful definition to the incidence of poverty in slum areas, such as the East End districts of Bethnal Green, Whitechapel, and Hoxton where over 44 per cent of a congested population of 240,000 were poor, very poor, or destitute, and where:

> . . . the pale weaver, through his window seen,
>   In Spitalfields, looked thrice dispirited.

The categories of the poor ranged from the lowest 'loafers and occasional labourers' through the 'casual labourers' to 'those whose earnings are small because of irregularity of employment, and those whose work, though regular, is ill paid'.[61] The percentages of poverty in the East End, worked out by Charles Booth and his colleagues, were among the highest in the whole Metropolis. The remnants of the silk industry were, they said, 'being held together partly by the superior character of the work and the special efforts of the manufacturers, and partly by a semi-philanthropic endeavour to develop amongst the wealthy a fashion for Spitalfields silks. . . . The bulk of the operatives are getting on in years, and there are few learners to take their place.'[62] The House of Liberty had tried to help by arranging, in May 1888, an exhibition of English silk on their premises in Regent Street, making a special feature of Spitalfields silk brocades in the hope of bringing about 'the renaissance of this beautiful and once important national industry'. The purity of material, its durability, and the beauty and delicacy of design and colouring were stressed, and brocades with such attractive names as 'Chrysanthemum', 'Iris', 'Cornflower' and 'Ox-eye Daisy', in a variety of colours, were strongly recommended as 'particularly suitable for dinner, evening, and reception dresses, and court trains', as well as for tea-gowns. Early in the nineties Liberty's had a selection of Spitalfields and other English silks permanently on exhibition at 218–20 Regent Street.[63]

By 1900 furniture damasks and umbrella silks were being made, to an increasing extent, on steam-power looms in factories out of London. The diminishing remnant of the silk weavers worked in hand looms in their homes or in small hand-loom workshops, the heavy and highly skilled work being done mainly by men, while on plain, light work more than half the weavers were women or girls.[64]

Among the few stubborn survivors was Samuel Higgins, the 'particularly interesting weaver' living and working in Gauber Street on the eastern fringes of the Spitalfields district, who was interviewed by the *Daily Graphic*'s representative in 1899. The weaving-room, approached by the steepest of stairs and entered through a trap-door, contained three looms—two jacquards for the weaving of figured silk, and a more primitive latch loom commonly called a 'Jack-in-the-Box'.

> One of the jacquards was worked by the weaver himself, who was engaged on weaving the richest of red silk, shot with black, for gentlemen's ties. The other jacquard loom was occupied by his elder daughter, who was manufacturing silk shot with satin, while the 'Jack-in-the-Box' was deftly worked by his younger daughter for the production of silk lining for gentlemen's coats. At either end of the room were quilling wheels for winding the silk for the shuttles. . . . The room was a model of cleanliness and in apple-pie order.

Born in 1828, Samuel Higgins had been apprenticed to silk weaving at an early age, and in course of time he had become an expert weaver of brocade, silk velvet, shot, figured and watered silk. In 1884 he was entrusted by Messrs Evan Howell & Co., of St Paul's Churchyard, with the weaving of watered silk for a dress for Queen Victoria, and nine years later the freedom of the Weavers' Company was conferred upon him for his meritorious services in reviving the almost forgotten art of producing 'the old-fashioned English moiré antique'.[65] 'He is an Englishman,' said the reporter, 'but his wife is a direct descendant of the Huguenots. . . . Although 71 years of age, he is as active as a young man, and his sight is perfect. Teetotallers will no doubt attribute this to the fact that he is a total abstainer and a non-smoker.' This weaver's house had been built about 1825. The living-rooms were on the ground floor and the whole of the upper storey was taken up by the weaving-room, which was amply lighted by a window extending along the whole length of the back of the house, and two windows at the front so large as to leave very little brickwork to obstruct the light. But by the end of the nineteenth century many of the weavers' houses were being used as ordinary workmen's dwellings, while others had been pulled down. Certainly, no new ones would be built, for the industry was fast vanishing from its old home in Spitalfields, never to return.[66]

Almost by chance, in the mid-1960s the author met Mr Joseph Deane who had worked, like his father before him, in the London silk industry as an upholsterers' trimmings weaver. He was born in Hoxton in 1873, and although over ninety years of age at the time of the interview he was still active in mind and body (he had only recently given up cycling!) and his memory was remarkably clear. He recalled that he left school at twelve years of age and began to work incredibly long hours as a barber's lather-boy, but about a year later he was apprenticed to an uncle who made upholsterers' trimmings on narrow single hand looms mainly for wealthy customers of firms such as Maples and Shoolbreads. His working day was from 8 a.m. to 8 p.m., which meant $10\frac{1}{4}$ hours in the loom and a total of $1\frac{3}{4}$ hours allowed for meals. On Saturdays work stopped at 2 p.m. The goods made, such as braids for curtain-edgings, ranged from 2 inches to 4 inches in width, and the pay went from $1\frac{1}{2}d$. a yard for 'little fringes' up to maxima of $3d$. and $4d$. a yard for wider and more intricate weaving. 'The old weaving in Spitalfields was slavery,' he said, 'but ours wasn't.' On the contrary, the work was light, interesting and well-paid; his earnings averaging £2 a week all the year round, which compared very favourably with many other crafts at that time. However, during the First World War Mr Deane had to work in a munitions factory, and having, perforce, made a break, he never afterwards returned to weaving.

Among the little community of retired weavers now spending the evening of their lives in the comfort and peace of Weavers House at Wanstead, two have been chosen as representatives, so to speak, of their fellows and neighbours. There is Mr George Darlison, who was born in 1880 into an old silk-weaving family, his father, grandfather, and great-grandfather having been hand-loom silk weavers before him. From the age of thirteen he was employed in the industry, and worked for well-known firms such as Bailey, Fox & Co., and Vavasseur, Carter & Coleman, for whom he wove velvets. He has a carefully preserved photograph of himself weaving silk scarves in a jacquard hand loom. Younger than Mr Darlison by some five years is Miss Rose Dearman, who left school in 1899 at the age of fourteen to become a silk weaveress. She was taught by her father, Francis Dearman (1831–1904), who owned four looms and occupied a weaver's house in Globe Road, where he worked, when trade was brisk, from 6.30 a.m. to 8 p.m., taking a break for breakfast and 'sometimes a rest in the afternoon'. This suggests from eleven to twelve hours a day actually at work in his loom. The weaving shop was on an upper floor of his house and was entered through a trap-door. (This particular house was pulled down in 1905.) After dark they wove by the light of hanging oil lamps with green shades. Miss Dearman remembers that they worked mainly for J. H. Buckingham & Co., of Ropemaker Street, on 27-inch and 36-inch men's and women's figured silk scarves and mufflers. The firm's foreman paid occasional visits to the Dearmans and a long-standing friendly relationship seems to have existed between Mr Dearman and his employers. During the early years of the twentieth century, as more and more work went to the power looms, the length of the 'play' or waiting periods between orders greatly increased. Miss Dearman continued to weave for some ten years after her father's death in 1904, but in the end she was forced to give up silk weaving and go over to the millinery trade.

Sooner or later many others of the silk weavers' rearguard must have been forced out in much the same way; but they were a tough and tenacious remnant. There were, in 1914, 46 workshops still occupied by some 114 hand-loom weavers, men and women, mostly on the eastern edge of Bethnal Green, with between 50 and 60 ancillary workers—winders, warpers, shuttle-makers, card-cutters and draughtsmen. Over twenty years later (July 1935) the minutes of the Weavers' Company carry a reference to 'the colony of weavers still living in and about Bethnal Green', comprising some ten or eleven elderly folks in the last of the looms.[67]

NOTES

1 J. H. Clapham, *Economic History of Modern Britain* (1926), I, pp. 551–2.
2 J. R. Kellett, 'The Breakdown of Gild and Corporation Control . . . in London', *Economic History Review* (1958).
3 Second Report, section on London Companies, p. 210.
4 See, e.g., MS. 4655/4, ff.60, 67, 75 (1738). The Clothworkers abandoned their right of search in the 1740s.
5 MS. 4655/18, f.250, 1 October 1793, refers to a petition from sundry orris weavers against persons exercising their craft without having served a proper apprenticeship.
6 MS. 4655/15, ff.32b, 35b–45b, 300b, 304–5, 308.
7 J. K. Ingram, Address on 'Work and the Workman' (1880); quoted in Webb, *History of Trade Unionism* (1907 edn), p. 25. cf. MS. 4655/19, f.454.
8 See, e.g., the Court minutes from 1798 to 1814 (MS. 4655/19, *passim*).
9 MS. 4655/19, ff.384b, 393, 394b–395b, 405b, 410b; MS. 4655/20, f.103; cf. also f.112.
10 Second Report (1837), pp. 210–11. The average annual number of freemen admitted was: 1801–10, 25; 1821–30, 20; and the trend was downwards.
11 MS. 4655/20, various minutes from f.346 to f.414. The Company's fees, etc. were:
An apprentice bound to a master weaver
£1. 11*s*., plus duty £2. 2*s*.=£3. 13*s*.
,,   ,,   ,,   ,, a journeyman
£1. 0*s*. 6*d*.,   ,,   ,,   £2. 2*s*.=£3. 2*s*. 6*d*.
A parish binding (no duty payable), 15*s*.
A turnover,   8*s*.
Admission to the Freedom: by servitude,   £2. 6*s*.
                          by patrimony,   £2. 4*s*.
                          by redemption, £9. 2*s*.
Admission to the Livery, £10. 12*s*., plus compounding for quarterage, £1. 1*s*.
12 MS. 4655/19, ff.96b, 101b. See MS. 4655/20, f.64, 1 July 1828, for a reference to 'the existing differences of opinion in the silk trade'.
13 Second Report (1837), section on London Companies, pp. 18, 20.
14 Ibid., p. 211.
15 G. R. Porter, *Progress of the Nation* (1836), pp. 259–60.

16 Brady, op. cit., pp. 103–4; Porter, op. cit., p. 261. A silk factory
   usually carried out various processes other than weaving, such as
   throwing and winding.
17 *Report of the Select Committee of the Lords on the . . . British Wool
   Trade* (1828), p. 116.
18 Lardner, *Silk*, p. 275.
19 C. H. Ward-Jackson, *History of Courtaulds* (1941), pp. 35–6.
20 *Hand-loom Weavers*, vol. 24, pp. 21, 591, 615. Also in this Report
   (pp. 23–4n.) are the revealing statements of 9 (parish)
   apprentices found in prison, about the apprenticeship system and
   its defects, lack of schooling, etc. An official return published in
   1862 shows that there were 10,635 power looms in use in silk
   factories in England in 1861, the majority driven by steam
   (*Accounts and Papers* (1862), LV: *Return of Silk Factories in 1861*).
21 C. Knight, *London* (1842), II, pp. 386–7.
22 B.M. Add. MS. 34,245B, ff.3–16. See also below, Appendix 2.
   Richard Cray was one of the earliest members of the London
   Working Men's Association (founded in 1836), and was chosen by
   that body, with two other members, James Watson and Charles
   Cole, to investigate the state of the Spitalfields silk weavers
   (B.M. Add. MS. 37,773, f.7). Watson was a well-known Radical
   bookseller and publisher; Cole was secretary of the (unofficial)
   journeymen weavers' committee which collected and presented
   evidence to the Hand-loom Weavers' Commission.
23 W. E. Hickson said that the Spitalfields weavers were threatened
   less by foreigners than by their own countrymen in the North,
   'and this competition is so formidable that, had the book prices
   been maintained, in all probability the trade would long before
   this (1838–9) have left London altogether' (*Hand-loom Weavers*,
   vol. 24, p. 15).
24 *Select Committee on the Silk Trade* (1832), Evidence, vol. 99, pp. 18,
   319, 338, 648, 652–5.
25 M. Sturt, *The Education of the People* (1967), p. 46.
26 MS. 4655/20, ff.76, 133b.
27 Parliamentary Papers, 1837, vol. 31, Appendix B.
28 B.M. Add. MS. 34,245B, ff.17–18; printed below in Appendix 2,
   B and C.
29 See Appendix 3 below.
30 Lardner, *Silk*, p. 328, Note GG.
31 *Hand-loom Weavers*, vol. 23, pp. 228–38, 259.
32 Ibid., p. 233.
33 Galloon is a narrow close-woven braid, of silk, gold, silver or cotton
   used for binding. Furniture fringes, braids, gimps, galloons, etc.,
   were known collectively as passementerie.
34 *Hand-loom Weavers*, vol. 23, pp. 276–8.
35 *Hand-loom Weavers*, vol. 24, p. 6.
36 Sir Frank Warner, *The Silk Industry of the United Kingdom* (1921),
   p. 73
37 There was at this time a tax of 1s. 1d. a ton on all coals consumed
   in London and Westminster and within twenty miles thereof; all
   other coal was untaxed. This tax, introduced in 1667 to help the
   city after the Great Fire, was not finally abolished until 1890
   (1 & 2 William IV, c. 76; *Hand-loom Weavers*, vol. 24, p. 17).
38 Adapted from *Hand-loom Weavers*, vol. 24, p. 15.

39 *Hand-loom Weavers*, vol. 23, pp. 237–8.
40 Ibid., pp. 239–41.
41 M. Rose, *The East End of London* (1951), pp. 159–60.
42 *Hand-loom Weavers*, vol. 23, p. 228. On distress, discontent and rioting in Bethnal Green in 1827–9 see Cobbett's *Political Register*, 7 July 1827, and Welch, *Mod. Hist. of the City of London* (1896), p. 163.
43 N. Longmate, *King Cholera* (1966), p. 92; cf. C. Creighton, *A History of Epidemics in Britain* (1965 edn), II; and Parliamentary Papers relating to Cholera and the Report of the Board of Health, 1831–2 (155), XXVI, 475.
44 *Hand-loom Weavers*, vol. 24, Appendix, p. 79; cf. *Poor Law Commissioners' Report on Sanitary Condition of the Labouring Population* (1842).
45 Hector Gavin, M.D., *Sanitary Ramblings: Sketches and Illustrations of Bethnal Green* (1848), pp. 4–5, 10–12; *The Times*, 4 February 1847.
46 Rose, op. cit., pp. 171–2, 185n., 208–9.
47 Warner, op. cit., Chap. VI; an excellent chapter on 'a typical silk master' in the decade 1850–60.
48 B.M. Add. MS. 34,245B.
49 J. H. Clapham, *Economic History of Modern Britain* (1932), II, pp. 1–2, 244. No other manufacture had more than 10 per cent tariff protection in the 1850s; many none at all. See also Clapham, *The Economic Development of France and Germany, 1815–1914* (4th edn, 1936), pp. 260–2.
50 Warner, op. cit., p. 81; C. F. Bastable, *The Commerce of Nations* (9th edn, 1923), p. 57.
51 MS. 4655/23. A. Ure, *Philosophy of Manufactures* (3rd edn, 1861), p. 644; Appendix by P. L. Simmonds.
52 Warner, op. cit., p. 90. For a full study of the treaty of 1860 see A. L. Dunham, *The Anglo-French Treaty of Commerce of 1860 and the Progress of the Industrial Revolution in France* (1930).
53 *Report on the English Silk Industry* (1884), vol. 31, p. lxxiv.
54 *V.C.H.*, *Essex* (1907), II, pp. 462–8; Warner, op. cit., p. 297; *Second Report of the R.C. on Technical Instruction* (1884), III, p. liii. On the employment of Suffolk weavers by Spitalfields manufacturers see *V.C.H.*, *Suffolk*, II, pp. 273–4.
55 *V.C.H.*, *Essex*, II, p. 465. For his biography see W. Tallack, *Peter Bedford* (1865).
56 *Hand-loom Weavers*, vol. 23, pp. 285–7.
57 Ward-Jackson, op. cit., pp. 55–7.
58 C. Booth, *Life and Labour of the People in London*, 1st Ser. IV, pp. 254–5; *Report on the English Silk Industry* (1884), vol. 31; Report by Thomas Wardle. Some weavers' houses were demolished when the railway was taken through to Liverpool Street. Sir Thomas Wardle (1831–1909) was born in Macclesfield and later worked in his father's business at Leek-brook, Staffs. In 1882 he established the silk and cotton printing business of Wardle & Co. at Hencroft, Leek. Recognised as an authority on silk, he founded the Silk Association of Great Britain and Ireland, and was its president until 1909. He was knighted in 1897 and became an Honorary Freeman of the Weavers' Company on 3 February 1903. See Warner, op. cit., Chap. XLIII and a portrait on p. 142.

59 Warner, op. cit., pp. 99–100; there is a picture of George Dorée at work in his loom opp. p. 74.

60 MS. 4655/29, 4 June 1901, 3 June 1902, 9 June 1903.

61 Booth, op. cit., 1st Ser. II: *Poverty* (1902), pp. 20, 25.

62 Ibid., 1st Ser. IV, pp. 245, 254–5; 2nd Ser. II, p. 314.

63 *The Queen*, 28 May 1892; Messrs Liberty's Dress Fabric Catalogue. I am grateful to Miss Elizabeth Aslin of the Bethnal Green Museum for bringing this to my notice.

64 Booth, op. cit., 1st. Ser. IV, pp. 247–52.

65 MS. 4655/27, ff.375–6.

66 *Daily Graphic*, 7 April 1899.

67 MS. 4655/33, 25 July 1935; Warner, op. cit., pp. 98–9, 103–5; A. K. Sabin, *The Silkweavers of Spitalfields and Bethnal Green* (1931), p. 19.

Chapter 18

Change of Pattern II

At the opening of the nineteenth century the Company's Officers were greatly concerned about the state of Weavers' Hall. Evidently the cheap job done by Mr Benson in 1798 had been no more than superficial, which was only to be expected since the cost was but £35. Scarcely had he completed his work than it became necessary to call in three surveyors, who found that the north-east wall of the Court Room was in a dangerous state and still sinking, despite a certain amount of shoring up. 'Many other defects and unsound parts, particularly in the south wall', were discovered. Indeed, the Clerk's apartments were so bad that the Company permitted him and his family to move out in April 1800, allowing him £60 (?per annum) towards the rent of alternative accommodation. Meantime, the anxiety having spread to the Livery, a full meeting of Liverymen was convened to consider the best course of action. Finally it was decided that the Hall and the two houses facing Basinghall Street should be advertised to be let by auction, unless previously let by private contract. The Company wished to get £300 a year in rent for the Hall and two houses; the lessee to spend at least £500 upon repairs. No extensions were to be built upon the garden, and 'no trade usually deemed a nuisance' to be carried on upon the premises. But when the lease was put up for auction at Garraway's Coffee House on 3 April 1800 not a single bid was forthcoming.[1]

An alternative scheme for a partial letting of the premises was then substituted, with the result that the lower part of Weavers' Hall, the Clerk's office and apartments, and the two houses were let on lease for fourteen, twenty-one or thirty years to Mr Jacob Osborne, a Hamburg and Russia merchant,[2] at a rental of £110 plus all taxes and costs of repairs, provided that the Company undertook to rebuild the south wall. This work, together with repairs to the Court Room and rooms adjoining, and the construction of a water closet, was put in hand by the Company in the summer of 1800.[3] By this arrangement the Company retained the use of the main Hall and the Court Room (with the kitchen and cellar) for meetings and social functions. In August 1800 the Court resolved 'that Mr Osborne [the new tenant] may alter the front of the houses at the Hall Gate in any way he thinks fit reserving a sufficient Space to place the Company's Arms over the outer Gate at his expence'.[4]

The Company's finances at this time were in a somewhat muddled state, and there is evidence not only of overspending, but of general slackness and apathy among the members, except when some big issue, such as the fate of Weavers' Hall, temporarily stirred them. Indeed, it was sometimes impossible to form a quorum, and not always easy to fill the office of Upper Bailiff. By the spring of 1818 the falling away was such that the idea of reviving non-attendance fines was seriously considered.[5] However, no positive action was taken and attendances at meetings dwindled still further. At the General Court or Common Hall held on St James's Day, 1825, only the four Officers, one Assistant and three Liverymen were present, and similar very poor attendances are recorded in 1826 and 1828. Meantime, a special committee was set up to consider the best means of securing an income equal to the necessary and proper expenditure of the Company. One change which resulted from the work of this committee was the introduction in 1811–12 of lump-sum payments in lieu of annual quarterages. New freemen were to pay 10s. 6d. in lieu of all quarterages, and new Liverymen, one guinea. It was also resolved 'that this Court do recommend to the Livery at large the propriety of redeeming the quarterage payable by them of two shillings per annum, as a means of increasing the Funds of the Company . . . and that . . . the sum of 21s. be accepted from each Person in lieu of all quarterage.' Shortly afterwards this resolution was amended (4 February 1812) to read: 'Every Freeman admitted as a Master shall pay 21s., and every Journeyman 10s. 6d. in lieu of quarterage, and 10s. 6d. more if admitted, afterwards, to the Livery. Applicants for the Freedom and Livery at the same time, to pay 21s. in lieu of quarterage.'[6]

Additional income was produced, after 1810, by letting the ground floor under the Hall to a firm of factors for office and storage purposes; and when, in 1820, 'the basement storey formerly used as the Kitchen of the Hall' was let to the same tenants, the kitchen utensils were sold. The holding of major social functions in Weavers' Hall was discontinued. In 1822, the Association of the Silk Trade wanted to call a meeting at Weavers' Hall of 'such silk manufacturers as employ not less than 20 looms', but the Company was obliged to say that although they would gladly allow the Association the use of Weavers' Hall for small committees, it was probably unsafe for large meetings.[7]

Since Weavers' Hall was no longer safe for large gatherings and its kitchen was closed, it now became customary to hold the Livery dinners biennially and outside the City, at the Trafalgar Tavern, Greenwich, or the West India Dock Tavern at Blackwall. For example in April 1827, the Court resolved 'That a Dinner be provided on St James's Day next for such of the Livery as have paid the Steward's Fine of £15 and arrears of Quarterage, [and] that £30 be contributed from the Company's general funds towards the expenses.'[8] The trail to Greenwich had been blazed by the Assistants at least as early as January 1814, when the dinner bill at Greenwich for the 'Court & many Visitors' came to £23. In the following August £25. 10s. was spent for the same purpose in the same place.[9] By 1842 the Company's finances had recovered sufficiently to allow annual Livery dinners to be resumed. Attendances at Court Meetings and Common Halls were also showing a modest improvement, following a sharp comment, minuted and sent out to every Assistant in October 1837, on the great difficulties in conducting the Company's affairs which arose from the

> systematic non-attendance of some, and by the frequent neglect of attendance on the part of other Members of the Court, and this inconvenience has never been greater, nor the neglect . . . more striking, than the impossibility that has arisen therefrom both on the 21st August [1837] and again on this day, of swearing in the Officers chosen on St James's Day last, and which has also prevented the transaction of other important business.[10]

Study of the relevant records from 1816 to 1885 reveals certain changes in the Company's membership. To begin with the apprentices: in the first decade of the nineteenth century apprentices were bound at Weavers' Hall at the rate of some 25 per annum. This influx, however, was not maintained as we see from Table 18.1, in which the figures reflect the general decline of the London silk industry.

Table 18.1 *Apprentices bound under the auspices of the Weavers' Company*

Decade	Total
1816–25	152
1836–45	58
1856–65	6
1876–85	10

During the decade 1816–25 nearly all the apprentices came from the adjacent districts of Spitalfields, Bethnal Green, Mile End New Town, Whitechapel, Shoreditch and Hoxton. Only eight among the total of 152 were country lads; five of them from the Home Counties and three from Hampshire, Yorkshire and Denbigh respectively. Classification according to the occupation or status of the parents is shown in Table 18.2.

Table 18.2 *Occupations of parents of apprentices bound, 1816–25*

Parents	No.
Silk manufacturers, mercers, brokers, etc.	15
Weavers	40
Other craftsmen	31
Miscellaneous trades	17
Widows	27
Labourers	3
'Gentlemen'	4
Miscellaneous or occupations not stated	15
Total	152

This shows that the sons of weavers, other craftsmen, and widows numbered ninety-eight, or nearly two-thirds of the total. For the majority of these and the other apprenticeships either no premiums were paid or only a small sum (e.g. £4) which was usually paid from a charitable fund such as the Dixon Charity administered by the Drapers' Company. But a few remarkably large premiums were paid in certain cases: for example, the son of a deceased sea captain was apprenticed to a London ribbon and silk manufacturer for a premium of £100; a City hatmaker paid £500 when his son was apprenticed to a silk broker; and the parents of two apprentices to chemists and druggists paid £299 and £300 respectively.

During the decade 1836–45 the apprentices were still coming from much the same districts, but in greatly reduced numbers (see Table 18.3).

Sons of weavers, other craftsmen and widows number thirty-one, which is slightly more than one-half of the total and a smaller proportion than in 1816–25. Thirty-three were taken without premiums, and for thirteen others premiums of only £4 each were paid from Dixon's Charity. The highest premium recorded in this decade is £99 paid by a Kentish surgeon to a silk and velvet manufacturer. By 1850 the last vestiges of the old traditional craft-

Table 18.3 *Occupations of parents of apprentices bound, 1836–45*

Parents	No.
Silk manufacturers, mercers, brokers, etc.	6
Weavers	17
Other craftsmen	12
Miscellaneous traders	11
Widows	2
Labourers	2
'Gentlemen'	3
Miscellaneous or occupations not stated	5
Total	58

apprenticeship system were fast disappearing. Between 1856 and 1865 only six apprentice bindings are recorded. Of these, two lads were apprenticed without premiums; a third had his premium of £4 paid by Dixon's Charity, and a fourth was apprenticed to a Liveryman of the Weavers' Company who received a premium of £15 from the same source. This lad is the only one of the six whose apprenticeship seems to have had anything to do with silk; one entry is incomplete and therefore doubtful; the remaining four clearly did not go into any branch of the silk trade. Between 1876 and 1885 four apprentices were bound to firms of silk manufacturers, fringemakers, and umbrella and parasol manufacturers; two to account book manufacturers; one to an ironmonger, another to a commercial traveller. Each was apprenticed to his father. No premiums were paid in this decade, and not one weaver's son was bound. Only two apprenticeships are recorded in 1886 and 1887: one to a silk manufacturer and the other to an umbrella and parasol manufacturer. Thereafter, for twelve years, no apprentices were bound at Weavers' Hall.

Significant changes can be traced also in the records of admissions to the Freedom of the Company. For example, during the decade 1816–25, 202 freemen were admitted, of whom 80 qualified by servitude (apprenticeship), 37 by patrimony, and no fewer than 85 by redemption. The redemptioners were, for the most part, in business in the silk industry as manufacturers, merchants, mercers, brokers and warehousemen, but a few manufacturers and merchants from other trades, such as timber and floorcloth, were admitted by this method. A somewhat similar pattern is revealed by analysis of the admissions, 92 in all, in the decade 1836–45, except that the total number is much less, and the admissions to the Freedom by patrimony are proportionately higher (see Table 18.4).

Table 18.4 *Admissions to the freedom of the Company, 1836–45 and 1876–85*

| Occupation | Admitted to Freedom by | | |
	Servitude	Patrimony	Redemption
1836–45			
Silk manufacturers, merchants, brokers, etc.	3	3	31
Other manufacturers, merchants, brokers, etc.	2	5	4
Weavers	16	2	—
Other craftsmen	4	7	—
Miscellaneous traders	6	3	—
Labourers and porters	—	3	—
'Gentlemen'	—	3	—
Total	31	26	35
1876–85			
Silk manufacturers, merchants, brokers, etc.	—	—	—
Other manufacturers, merchants, brokers, etc.	—	1	1
Professional men (accountants, lawyers, etc.)	2	3	4
Weavers	—	1	—
Other craftsmen	1	2	—
Miscellaneous traders	2	3	1
'Gentlemen'	1	2	1
Total	6	12	7

Here we see that operative weavers had almost disappeared from the Company's records.

About the middle of the century the state-of-the-Hall question again raised its head. A special Survey Committee set up in 1847 reported that 'The premises are very old and some repair is required; the Hall itself is very dirty and the Rooms over, being in the occupation of Tenants on lease, the inconvenience of dirt is increased by the occasional falling of Vermin.' The Committee also drew attention to the unprotected state of the property after office hours and on Sundays. We are not told what, if anything, was done about the vermin and other nuisances, and although the Officers were asking, in 1848, whether the time had come to pull down 'the entire buildings in Basinghall Street', and erect a new building on the site,[11] nothing of importance was done until 1855, when a general financial review revealed that the annual loss on the Hall and the adjoining houses (although fully let at the time at a total rental of £135) was nearly £28, by reason of rates, taxes and repairs, and the rent payable to the Merchant Taylors' Company for part of the site on which the Weavers' garden had been laid out many years before. The Income and Expenditure Committee pointed out that, as the various leases would fall in at Lady Day 1856, 'a large increase of the Company's income may be derived from improving this property, but no time should be lost in deciding what will be the most advisable course'. In April 1855 this committee reported that:

1   there is no probability that the Merchant Taylors' Company will either sell or let the piece of Ground on which the back part of the Company's Hall is now built at such price as it would be advisable to give;
2   the present buildings were not capable of being repaired or improved so as to indemnify the Company for the outlay.
3   On the other hand, the committee felt sure that 'every member of the Company and the Court would regret that the oldest Gild . . . of London should lose the respectability which attaches to having their own Hall.

The Committee therefore favoured a plan to pull down the Old Hall and houses and rebuild on the same site at an estimated cost of £6,000; but in October 1855 the Court decided, much against the obvious preference of its Income and Expenditure Committee, to relinquish the Hall and offer to let the ground on a seventy-years' building lease, 'without any reservation as to the adaptation of the building for the use of the Company', from Lady Day 1856; the lessee to spend at least £5,000 and to have the option to purchase, within the first twelve months, the ground rent at 33 years' purchase.[12]

Once this momentous decision was taken, no time was lost. The Court of Assistants held its last meeting in Weavers' Hall on Tuesday, 18 March 1856. The Upper Bailiff, Mr John Guillemard, and the other Officers were present with nine of the Assistants. It must have been a sad occasion, but if any nostalgic sentiments were expressed they were not recorded in the minutes, which remain strictly practical in tone. Negotiations regarding accommodation and service having been satisfactorily concluded with the London Tavern, the next meeting of the Court was held there on 1 April 1856.[13]

The famous London Tavern stood on the west side of Bishopsgate Street almost at the junction with Cornhill. It was an imposing building, erected in 1767–8 from designs by Richard Jupp on the site of the old White Lion Tavern which was burnt down in 1765. In the days of Dr Johnson and James Boswell the tavern was excellently managed by a celebrated landlord named Bleaden, formerly a waiter at White's, and its famous dinners and wines made it a gourmet's paradise. In its basement live turtles swam in tanks of sea water, and from its bill of fare the epicure could choose 'exquisite beefsteaks', game in season, and a variety of special omelettes. He could also test the resources of its cellar, amply stocked with a wealth of choice wines. Some 350 people could dine in comfort in its largest room. East India Company dinners were held there, and so were Masonic, political and philanthropic meetings, such as that convened by the Garibaldi Committee of the City of London Tradesmen's Club in August 1860 to raise money to aid Garibaldi's attempt to free the Italian people from foreign conquerors. After more than a century of success the London Tavern closed in 1876 when its site and buildings were sold for £80,000. Had Boswell been alive to hear the news, he might have derived a crumb of comfort from the fact that the purchaser was the Royal Bank of Scotland.[14]

When the Weavers' Company moved from Weavers' Hall arrangements had to be made for the safe-keeping of its more valuable items of movable property. It was decided that 'the pictures, plate, breakfast service and other articles bearing the insignia of the Company, together with the Upper Bailiff's Chair and Desk be removed to the London Tavern for the use of the Court, and that other articles, such as the chairs and tables in the Court Room and Hall be disposed of'.[15] At this juncture the damaged state of many of the Company's old record books was discovered. The Court minute books, the Renter Bailiffs' account books and other documents were kept at one time in an oak chest, about 4 feet 6 inches long and fitted with three iron locks, in the basement strong-room at Weavers' Hall. But there came a time when, for some unknown reason, the books had been removed from the chest and placed on top of a cupboard near the ceiling, through which water from a leaking gutter percolated, unnoticed, for quite a long time. Not until the old Hall was about to be pulled down did the serious discoloration and rotting away of pages, covers and bindings come to light. The damaged documents were then restored to the old chest and deposited in the cellar at the London Tavern where they remained for about twelve years.[16]

From the Basinghall Street site the Company expected to obtain a yearly rent of at least £300; but on 4 March 1856, the day fixed for receiving offers, only one bid was received—£50! Fortunately, before the end of the month a far better offer came in from Mr Charles J. Corbett, an architect in practice at No. 17 Gracechurch Street, who was willing to take a building lease of the premises for eighty-two years at £305 per annum; the lessee to spend at least £5,000 on rebuilding, and to have certain old materials including the stained glass windows. This offer was accepted,[17] and shortly afterwards a quantity of 'Building Materials, Fixtures and Fittings-up of Weavers' Hall and Two Houses adjoining' was offered for sale by auction on the premises on Wednesday, 16 April 1856. The catalogue included:

Oak and fir timbers in roofs

10 tons of Lead in flats, gutters and pipes, Wainscoting and Carved oak panels and mouldings

Marble chimney pieces

Gas fittings, stoves, Coppers and Cisterns

A Brussels carpet 8 yds. × 5¼ yds.

A deal Table on turned legs, 15½ ft. by 3 ft. with green cloth cover

A deal Table on turned legs, 26 ft. by 3 ft.

33 Mahogany chairs

4 elbow chairs

A pair of oak folding doors, with carved panels . . . and the storey of stairs, with turned balusters

The carved oak lions' [i.e. leopards'] heads and griffins [i.e. wivern] on stairs

The mahogany glazed shop front of No. 21 (Basinghall Street) with outside shutters

The glazed shop front of No. 23, with outside shutters, sash door and shutters, facia and entablature, panelled & glazed enclosure of Counting House, wainscoting . . . cloth door and fittings.

The new premises took slightly less than a year to build, and early in April 1857 the Weavers' Court expressed the opinion that the new buildings on the site of their old Hall were very pleasing. The Clerk of the Company and his professional partner agreed to rent most of the first floor, and by April 1861 'the Chambers built on the site of the Hall (were) all occupied by good tenants'.[18]

Meantime, the Company was holding its meetings at the London Tavern, which it continued to do until early in 1868, when the possibility of securing better accommodation at the new Terminus Hotel at Cannon Street Station presented itself. A special committee having reported favourably, the move was made in May 1868, though the Company's pictures were not transferred until later in the year.[19] This new arrangement continued until November 1873, when the Company decided to move back to the London Tavern, taking its pictures and the two carved coats of arms of the Weavers' Company. Unfortunately, within a little over two years the sale and closure of the London Tavern forced the Company to move yet again. This time the Albion Tavern in Aldersgate Street was selected, but it could not take the five pictures, four of which were very large indeed. The Court therefore resolved to offer the royal portraits of Queen Elizabeth I, Charles II, James II, William III and Queen Anne[20] to the Corporation of the City of London to be hung in their library and museum at the Guildhall, subject to the Company's right to resume possession on giving six months' notice. The City Corporation accepted this offer and in August 1876 the City Librarian was able to report that the five pictures had been hung in the Guildhall Library, and the large coat of arms in the museum.[21]

Not until the nineteenth century was fairly well advanced did the Weavers' Company succeed in settling its finances upon a firm basis. In earlier centuries, as we have seen, the Company led a somewhat precarious financial life scraping through recurrent crises by various short-term expedients, but lacking a long-term economic policy. During the nineteenth century, however, all this was changed. The Company's resources were carefully husbanded and, riding on the tide of Victorian industrial and commercial expansion in the second half of the century, the Weavers' capital assets and annual income were steadily increased. The variety of forms of sound investments available were, of course, much greater in this period than ever before. In 1816, for instance, the Court weighed the merits of ground rents as a form of investment, and early in 1820 certain changes in the Company's investments, designed to improve future income, were made.[22] This prudent policy was pursued for many years. In 1837, for example, the Company substantially reduced its 'funded property' (mainly by selling Consols) and re-invested the proceeds (over £4,000) in the freehold ground rents of certain properties in the City, which were acquired at thirty-and-a-quarter years' purchase.[23] The Company's expenditure, however, both general and on charities' account, tended so persistently to outstrip income that early in 1835 the Court of Assistants set up an Income and Expenditure Committee composed of the Bailiffs, Wardens and three of the Assistants, to supervise and manage all the Company's income and estates, including authorising normal repairs and other items of everyday expenditure. Abnormal repairs and other 'extraordinary' expenditure still needed the authority of the Court of Assistants as a whole, after consideration of a report from the Income and Expenditure Committee.[24] Between 1836 and 1843, the Company's accounts showed that its property and funds had increased from less than £6,000 to more than £7,000; but these figures represented valuations at cost, not at current values. In 1845 the Auditors recommended that the funded property (e.g. stocks and shares) should in future be valued at the prices prevailing 'on the day of making up the Company's Accounts, and that an expert valuation of the real property should be made once in seven years'. The accounts for 1844–5 reflect the revised values (see Table 18.5).

Table 18.5 *The Company's property
after the 1845 revaluation*

Item	£
Funded Property	3,100
Freehold Ground Rents	4,786
Real Property	9,358
Furniture, etc. at Hall	455
Cash at Bankers	473
Total	18,172

This total compares with £7,164 calculated in 1843 by the old method of valuation.[25]

The general accounts covering the middle of the century remind us that this was the great railway era. Thus in 1848 the Company sold a large part of its holdings of stocks such as Consols and re-invested the proceeds in the debentures of the South Eastern and the Caledonian railways, from which they hoped to obtain a yield of $5\frac{1}{3}$ per cent.[26] These debentures, which the Company bought at a discount, were repaid at par during the 1850s.[27] Further investment in railways followed; this time in the South Wales Railway and the Monmouth Railway and Canal Company. In the year 1856–7 the Company's income from these two investments was £110, while its holding of 3 per cent Consols (valued at £205) produced only £6. 3*s*. The major sources of income at this time were the Shenfield farm and the properties in Basinghall Street and Nicholas Lane, which together brought in an aggregate rental of approximately £400, and the City (Moorgate Street) ground rents yielding nearly £156 per annum.[28] When the redemption of the South Wales and Monmouth Railway debentures, in 1860, made £2,500 available in cash, the Company used some of this money to convert their old Hoxton almshouses into shops, and re-invested the remainder in Indian railway stocks,[29] which were held for many years.

The Great Exhibition housed in a 'crystal palace' in Hyde Park in 1851, aroused enormous public interest and resulted (*inter alia*) in a determined attempt to improve and extend English technical and art education. But the Weavers' records, strangely enough, are silent on the subject, although we know that certain individual silk and orris weavers submitted examples of their work.[30] Nor do we find the Weavers' Company in the forefront of the subsequent educational movement, launched with the blessing and staunch support of the Prince Consort, and so ably led by Lyon Playfair.[31] But a limited interest on the Company's part in certain aspects of technical and art education is suggested by a subscription voted annually from 1843 onwards to the Spitalfields School of Design,[32] which was situated at no. 37 Crispin Street, a house thought to have been occupied at one time by James Limborough.[33] This school, founded with government aid in 1842, sprang from a suggestion in a report to the Handloom Weavers' Commission in 1840, and was chiefly concerned with the production of designs for woven silk fabrics. In 1849 it was adversely criticised by several witnesses before a Parliamentary Committee of Inquiry on the grounds that the instruction given was not related closely enough to actual silk manufacture, little progress had been made in the art of designing for silk weaving, and many designs produced could not be executed. In face of these strictures it is encouraging to discover that a fine piece of brocaded silk, called 'Queen's Pattern', was designed by the school's students and woven by them on their own loom set up at the Great Exhibition of 1851.[34]

Early in 1864 the Weavers' Company received from Miss (later Baroness) Burdett-Coutts a donation of £25 for its Almshouses Endowment Fund and a suggestion that a school of design should be established for the children of Spitalfields weavers. The Clerk, in his letter of thanks, informed the kind donor that 'such a School . . . was already in operation' and that her letter had been 'handed to John Vanner, Esq., a Member of the Court then present, who was Chairman of the Committee of the School in question'. In the following year the School moved to Folgate Street, and in 1868 it is described in a work on London as 'the Government School of Design where are awarded prizes for designs for fabrics, drawing and painting from nature, crayon-drawing, etc.' Later the School seems to have been merged in the Bishopsgate Ward School in Primrose Street, but it did not disappear without trace, for in the Victoria and Albert Museum 'impressive examples of silk woven at the School' are still preserved.[35]

The Company's records reveal little activity in the matter of technical education until December 1871, when one of the Assistants, Mr Thomas James Nelson,[36] moved for a special committee 'to consider and report in what way, if any, this Company can promote technical instruction in the branch of trade with which it is connected, and also in what way, if any, it can encourage and reward the skill of the handicraftsmen employed in the production of woven silk fabrics'. A committee of Officers and eight Assistants was set up, and reported early in 1873 that 'the majority . . . were of opinion that there was no practical way for carrying out Mr. Thomas Nelson's idea, considering the peculiarities of the Weaving Trade'. Shortly afterwards Baroness Burdett-Coutts wrote urging the Company to consider the foundation of prizes for skilled workmen in the trade. But even this influential lady could evoke no positive response; nor could the organisers of the International Exhibition of Trade who wished to make a special feature of the manufacture of silks and velvets, and asked (unsuccessfully) for a subscription of ten guineas towards the prize fund. Later in the year a number of circulars and other papers received from the Secretary of the Commissioners for the International Exhibition at South Kensington, requesting the Company's 'adhesion to movements relating to technical education in the various City Guilds', were merely acknowledged and 'laid before the Court'. No further action seems to have followed.[37]

Some three years later a meeting of representatives of the City livery companies, held at the Mansion House, resolved 'that it is desirable that the attention of the Livery Companies be directed to the promotion of education not only in the Metropolis but throughout the country, and especially to technical education, with the view of educating young artisans and others in the scientific and artistic branches of their trades'.[38] This historic meeting eventually resulted in the incorporation (in 1880) of the City and Guilds of London Institute for the Advancement of Technical Education, which for many years thereafter took the lead and set the pace in the development of English technical education. The Committee of the Associated Livery Companies formed a working party to draw up a detailed scheme of technical education. The Weavers' Company sent a representative to the first meeting on 7 June 1877, and maintained its interest in the proceedings of this committee throughout the following year.[39]

Then followed a few years of lethargy, from which the Company was aroused early in 1888 by its Upper Bailiff, Mr William Robert Fox, who put forward a plan to stimulate the trade by 'offering prizes for the best workmanship of the handloom weavers of this country', the first prize in each class of work to be the Freedom of the Company, conferred gratuitously as an award of merit. This proposal, which chimes in with the renaissance movement in the industry, was agreed to, and a scheme, limited to the employees of firms employing fifty or more weavers—subsequently amended to thirty because 'the number of workmen engaged by manufacturing firms has been so reduced in later years'—in London or within a ten-mile radius, was drafted. Three classes of work were selected as covering the hand weaving carried on in and near London at that time; viz. (I) plain silks; (II) figured silks (including furniture silks); (III) velvets. The first competition held in the summer of 1888 attracted twenty-four competitors from nine firms of silk manufacturers; the numbers in each of the three classes are shown in Table 18.6.

Some of the firms manufactured more than one type of fabric, usually plain and figured silks; but one firm, Bailey, Fox & Co., made plain and figured silks and velvets. The firms' names are not without

Table 18.6 *Number of competitors for the*
Company's weaving prizes, 1888

Class		No. of competitors	No. of firms
I	Plain silks	11	6
II	Figured and furniture silks	11	6
III	Velvets	2	2

interest, for they represent the small fighting rearguard of a once numerous army (see Table 18.7).[40]

Table 18.7 *The competing firms*

Class		Name of firm	No. of competitors
I	Plain silks	F. & R. Gillett	1
		Vavasseur, Carter & Coleman	3
		Slater Bros. & Co.	1
		Bailey, Fox & Co.	2
		Duthoit, England & Co.	2
		J. H. Buckingham & Co.	2
II	Figured and furniture silks	Vavasseur, Carter & Coleman	2
		Slater Bros. & Co.	2
		A. N. Thomas	1
		Duthoit, England & Co.	2
		J. H. Buckingham & Co.	2
		Warner & Ramm	2
III	Velvets	Bailey, Fox & Co.	1
		J. & W. Robinson & Co.	1

The judge chosen by the Company, Mr H. C. Soper of Noble Street in the City, described the workmanship in each class as 'excellent', and awarded prizes as shown in Table 18.8.

Second prizes went to Mrs Pratt of J. H. Buckingham & Co., William Morgan of Slater Bros. & Co., and Thomas McNeill of Vavasseur, Carter & Coleman, in Classes I, II, and III respectively.

The seven successful competitors were invited to attend a Court meeting on 2 October 1888, at which, after an address by the Upper Bailiff, the four winners of first prizes were admitted to the Freedom of the Company, and silver badges for excellence in weaving were presented to all seven.[41]

This competition evidently stimulated and heightened interest in technical education among members of the Weavers' Company, and

Table 18.8 *The prizewinners*

	Class	Weaver	Employer
I	Plain silks	Joseph Turner	Vavasseur, Carter & Coleman
II	Figured and furniture silks	George John Clarke	Warner & Ramm
III	Velvets	John Dormer ⎱ Equal John Yetton ⎰	Bailey, Fox & Co. J. & W. Robinson & Co.

in the autumn of 1888 a donation of fifty guineas was sent to Sir Philip Magnus, Director of the City and Guilds of London Institute, with a letter suggesting

> that it would be a very great advantage to the London Hand Loom Silk weaving industry if a school were started at which young people of both sexes might be thoroughly instructed in the art of plain, figured and velvet weaving, as for a great many years past the old system of apprenticing young people to the trade has been given up and the trade already suffered from a want of good hand loom weavers.

The letter referred to the recent competition, expressed regret that that Company had insufficient funds to set up a 'school of instruction so much required in the East End of London', and went on to suggest that young women might be encouraged to take up plain silk weaving while the young men were trained for figured silk and velvet weaving. The letter of thanks from the City and Guilds Institute drew attention to the fact that under its system of technical education, classes were already established for the silk industry, but its available resources would not permit of the establishment of a School of Silk Weaving.[42]

The second silk-weaving competition was held in the following year (1889) when twenty-six weavers (eighteen men and eight women) entered from seven firms, including on this occasion, J. Vanner and Sons. The number of classes was increased from three to five by the addition of 'Fancy Harness', 'Figured silk with one or two shuttles' and 'Figured silk with two or more shuttles', to the existing 'Plain silk' and 'Velvet' classes. First prizes were awarded to four men and a woman—Emma Macaree, who worked for J. H. Buckingham & Co., taking a 'first' for fancy harness weaving—and in due course these five weavers received the freedom of the Company.[43]

The competitions continued throughout the 1890s but with

diminishing entries in the second half of the decade. From a peak of thirty-six entries in 1891, the numbers fell to less than a dozen in 1900, after which the competition was discontinued. To the end the standard of craftsmanship remained high, the entrants being very keen to excel. In 1893, for example, the excellence of the furniture brocades was specially commended by the judge, Mr Soper, who, in the same year, was admitted to the Freedom and Livery of the Weavers' Company in recognition of his outstanding services.[44] A sixth class called 'Moiré antique' was added in 1894, a year in which there were 29 competitors and 6 first prize winners, all working in Bethnal Green. The following year saw the entries fall to 15; but 6 first prizes were won, 4 by men and 2 by women; 4 were from Bethnal Green, 1 from Old Ford, and 1 from Bow. In all, the Freedom of the Company was awarded to 65 highly skilled hand-loom silk weavers between 1888 and 1900 as a result of these annual competitions.

The newly created London County Council exchanged letters with the Weavers' Company in 1892 regarding the provision of technical education in London, and the Authority was told of the Company's annual silk-weaving competition. But when the Council invited the Company, in April 1893, to help with the expenses of founding a Technical Education Board[45] to expand and co-ordinate technical education in London, the Company replied that it felt unable to do more in this field than continue the annual competition.[46] Little more was done by the Company in the sphere of technical education—indeed, the subject was seldom mentioned in the minutes —until 1910, when the Weavers gave support to a Textile Industries Committee set up to promote the interests of the various sections of the textile industry in Britain.[47] In 1918 the Textile Industries Committee, having sent a questionnaire to 95 textile firms in London, ascertained that some 36 firms could find employment for about 300 trained weavers if they were available. Sir Robert Blair, the Education Officer to the London County Council, was asked whether the Council would be prepared to set up a 'small practical school of weaving' to train young persons of both sexes, and possibly some disabled soldiers and sailors, as working weavers, not amateurs; but upon close investigation of the probable future demand for trained weavers in the London area it did not appear either to the L.C.C. Higher Education Committee or to a committee of the Weavers' Company that such a step could be justified.[48]

During the following decade the Company continued to show interest in art and design applied to textiles and appointed a representative to the committee of the London Section of the Textile Institute. Donations were sent to the Textile Institute,[49] the Textile and Architectural Decoration Committees of the Royal Society of

Arts, and the British Institute of Industrial Art. Furthermore, in 1928–9, the Company decided to provide

(a) a scholarship of £100 for one year to be awarded to a candidate of graduate or equivalent status for silk research at Leeds University;

(b) a similar scholarship for wool research at Torriden, Leeds;

(c) a Royal Society of Arts studentship in textiles of £50 per annum; and

(d) prizes to the value of £25 per annum to be awarded by the City and Guilds of London Institute.[50]

Another earnest of the Company's concern for the furtherance of textile education and technology was given in 1923 when the Honorary Freedom of the Company (with admission to the Livery) was conferred upon Professor A. F. Barker, Professor of Textile Industries in Leeds University, and Professor A. J. Turner, Professor of Technology in Manchester University,[51] 'in recognition of their valuable services to the Textile Trade'.[52]

At least one salient feature of the old pattern changed very little in its essentials, namely, the traditional care and relief of poor weavers. Before the advent of the Welfare State this was a most necessary and humane function. During the distressful period of the Revolutionary and Napoleonic Wars, the Company made known its 'earnest desire that further and more effectual assistance may be dispensed for meliorating the situation of those who by age or infirmity are rendered incapable of work', and strongly recommended such persons, 'who are much Distressed and very Numerous . . . to the notice of the public at large, and the members of this Company in particular, who may be inclined to relieve them either by donation or Will'.[53] In this spirit the Company sent £100, in 1793, to the treasurer of 'a committee for relieving poor Weavers', and distributed Solomon Hesse's legacy of £30 in the years 1797–1801 in grants ranging from 5s. to £10.[54] During the same period the Company granted £10 to James Walker 'on condition that he goes to America in the course of 3 months, to be paid to the owners of the ship as part of the expense of his passage, but on no other terms whatever'. In and after 1805 the dividends from a gift of £400 Deferred 3 per cent Annuities were paid quarterly to the widows in the Hoxton Almshouses, and the income on Thomas Cook's legacy of £2,100 3 per cent Consols was applied to the same purpose after January 1812. William Taylor, a Liveryman, left a legacy of £90 in the same year to be distributed among poor members of the Company, and various other substantial donations to the General Benevolent Fund were received from time to time.[55] Furthermore, from its own funds the Company subscribed twenty guineas in 1812 to the Spitalfields Soup Society.[56]

The long war against Napoleon was causing high food prices and much distress among the poor, including many 'decayed silk weavers of deserving characters in great want of support in their declining age', for 'very few even amongst the industrious and most frugal of the working hands ever have it in their power to make a provision for their support under the infirmities of old age owing to the great fluctuations of the weaving trade'. The Weavers' Company decided to appeal to silk merchants, master manufacturers, silk dyers and others engaged in the London silk industry to raise a fund 'for relieving the necessities and promoting the comfort of the aged, infirm and truly deserving silk weavers in the decline of life by erecting and endowing a few more almshouses'. The fund was opened in October 1819 with a handsome donation of £500 from Richard Lea (Upper Bailiff, 1791–2), followed by £200 from Daniel Agace. Later, another large donation came in from Mr Beckwith, of Cateation Street, a silk manufacturer, who gave £100 to the Fund on behalf of himself and his partner, Mr Varnish, 'stating that sum to be part of a penalty recovered . . . on a prosecution against a vendor of smuggled thrown silk, and also stating that the remaining part [of the penalty, viz. £60. 14s. 7d.] was to be divided between the London Dispensary and the Spitalfields and Bethnal Green National Schools'.[57] Shortly afterwards the General Association of the Silk Trade subscribed £100 for the Company's poor, in recognition of the use of Weavers' Hall kindly allowed to the Association for their committee meetings.[58]

After the passing of the Charitable Trusts Acts, 1853 (16 & 17 Vict., c. 173) it became imperative that the Company should review its charitable funds to make certain that the administration and accounts were in accordance with the new Act, since henceforth accounts had to be submitted annually to the Charity Commissioners. This task fell upon the hard-working Income and Expenditure Committee, and it was found that some of the money was being transferred to the General Charitable Fund, while some had been allowed to accumulate. For example, the payments to the heir of John Hall had been discontinued; no coats and gowns had been given under Richard Mulford's charity for many years; and nothing under John Drigue's charity since 1833. The major charities' income, however, was being spent, in every sense, regularly. The Holborn property, bequeathed by Alexander Hosea, was producing about £182 per annum, which was used to pay pensions. The proceeds of the sale of the men's almshouses had been properly invested pro tem. in trustee securities. The 'General Benevolent Fund' was invested in 3 per cent Consols, which in 1855 were producing a yearly income of some £59. Of this nearly £49 was distributed to pensioners, leaving £10 to be carried forward each year. After consultation with the Charity Commissioners the difficulties were resolved and the Company's charities accounts and administration were settled upon a more businesslike basis.[59]

During the 1870s the Company received two generous legacies; one in 1871 under the will of Lady Jane Morrison, and the other in 1877 under the will of Mr William Frederick Graham. Lady Morrison bequeathed £2,000 to the Weavers' Company, directing that the income should be used in perpetuity to provide pensions for one widow and one widower living in the Wanstead Almshouses. The legacy, when invested in trustee stock, was expected to yield an income of some £70 per annum, or sufficient to provide two pensions of about 13s. a week.[60] The prospect of such an income brought applications from eleven widows ('almost without exception the widows of weavers by trade') and four widowers when the Morrison pensions were first awarded in March 1872. The applicants' ages ranged from fifty-eight to eighty. Having interviewed all the applicants and chosen two to receive the Morrison pensions of £35 per annum, in lieu of their present pensions, the Officers recommended that the pension money so released, slightly supplemented, should be distributed among the remaining almspeople so as to increase the men's pensions from £18 to £20 and the women's to £16. 10s. The Officers hoped that these increases

> will be highly acceptable to the pensioners generally (most of whom are very necessitous and have no means of support beyond their present pensions) not only because of the extra comfort they will be able to obtain in their declining years, but as tending to lessen the possible feeling of disappointment at two of their number only, by the terms of the gift, being so largely benefitted.[61]

The records of these interviews are human documents which cannot fail to arouse our sympathy and a certain modest satisfaction that, through its various funds, the Company has been enabled to provide protection and peace for many aged, lonely and sometimes ailing folk, as they pass through life's eventide. This work, on an improving scale, the Company is still doing.

The William Frederick Graham bequest, in 1877, of £1,000 'free from duty and unfettered by conditions' was the generous gift of a past Upper Bailiff (1864–5), whose family had already contributed substantially to the Almshouses rebuilding fund twenty years before.[62]

Despite sundry welcome windfalls, however, the Company tended to overspend on charitable objects throughout the nineteenth century, for the Court of Assistants was constantly concerned that they were unable to comply with all the appeals from 'decayed and deserving members of the Company'.[63] A 'Statement of Charitable Income and Expenditure' for the year 1877–8 shows that the Company's property (land, houses and stocks) earmarked for benevolent purposes was then valued at £22,830, and produced an annual income of approximately £850. Against this the Company's actual expenditure on charitable objects was £915; leaving a deficit of £65. This was by no means exceptional; indeed the annual deficits were often much larger. During the eighteen years from 1885 to 1903 there was one small surplus and seventeen deficits ranging from £5 to £405, and averaging £110 per annum. But after 1902–3 the charities account was brought into better balance by the gradual increase of income.[64]

Yet another source of anxiety had arisen early in the nineteenth century when the Company's almshouses in Old Street Road, Hoxton (built in 1670), were found to be in such a bad state structurally that, obviously, 'something would have to be done' very soon. Therefore the Officers must have been more than thankful when, at the beginning of 1824, a senior member, Mr Charles James Coverley, of Providence Row, Moorfields, who had been Upper Bailiff in 1810–11 and again in 1821–2, 'offered to take down the Almshouses at Shoreditch and rebuild the same at his sole charge'.[65] By the end of the same year the work was done and it only remained to add the finishing touches which took the form of 'the putting up the Arms of the Company' and a large stone tablet paying permanent public tribute to Mr Coverley's generosity:

Erected A.D. 1670
for the Widows of twelve poor Freemen
Rebuilt A.D. 1824
at the sole charge of Charles James Coverley, Esq.,
a benevolent Member of the Court of Assistants

In addition, the Court caused its resolution of thanks to be 'transcribed on Vellum . . . handsomely emblazoned, framed and glazed and presented' to the generous donor.[66] When Charles James Coverley died in 1835 it was found that he had extended his earlier gift by bequeathing property sufficient to give £4 a year to each of the twelve almswomen.[67]

By 1845 the other almshouses, built in 1729 in Elder Street, Porters Fields, in the Liberty of Norton Folgate, were in such a 'generally decayed state' that the Company was forced to consider a proposal to rebuild them on a site on the fringe of London. Indeed, a special committee had looked at land in Old Ford, Hackney Wick, and Cambridge Heath (near Victoria Park), but no decision had been reached. A new factor came into the committee's calculations when the Commissioners of Woods, Forests, Works and Buildings notified the Weavers' Company that the Elder Street property would be required for the construction of a new street, to be called Commercial

Street, passing through Spitalfields to Shoreditch. Receiving this news with well-concealed joy, the Weavers doubtless anticipated that prompt action would follow, and all repairs and redecorations to the almshouses were stopped. But the negotiations between the Company and the Commissioners were, in fact, extremely protracted, and the six almshouses were still standing, 'dilapidated and dirty', as late as 1851. Eventually, in the late summer of 1851 a purchase price of £2,400 was agreed and the Company moved the six almsmen into temporary accommodation in three houses in Bonners Fields.[68]

The idea of combining the Company's almshouses—if possible on a somewhat increased scale as to accommodation and numbers of almspeople—on a single site well away from the centre of London gained appreciable support during the 1850s. A small committee, set up in 1854 to keep the matter under review, had Alderman Samuel Wilson as chairman and he continued to take an active interest in the building and financing of the almshouses for many years thereafter.[69] Early in 1857 the committee reported that an attractive site had been inspected near Wanstead. The soil was 'gravelly' and there was a railway station within easy reach. The price, including fees and stamps, might be about £250 per acre. Negotiations were authorised and by October 1857 the Company completed the purchase[70] of three acres of 'copyhold enfranchised' land, with a frontage of 300 feet and a depth of 440 feet, for £750. Before the end of the year plans were prepared for a building providing two rooms for each of twelve women and twelve men, and residential accommodation for a superintendent. The estimated cost was £5,000.[71]

The funds available or promised were set out in March 1856 as shown in Table 18.9.

The plans drawn up by Joseph Jennings (for many years the Company's faithful surveyor) provided, in a two-storey building, twelve 'dwellings' for men, with a common kitchen and a reading room, and twelve for women, also with a common kitchen and reading room. There was also an office and residential accommodation for the Superintendent. In the central portion, on the upper storey, was a large Court Room 'which might be used as a Chapel if desired'; and was so used from time to time.[72] The entrances to the dwellings, said the surveyor, 'are placed at the back or garden side as being the warmest aspect, and the upper Dwellings are approached by a covered balcony as preferable to passages and desirable as a walk for the infirm, at the same time forming a covered way to the Dwellings below'.

The Court lost no time in inviting tenders and launching, simultaneously, a public appeal for funds. Early in June the lowest tender, that from Pritchard and Son of Warwick Lane, quoting £5,350, was accepted, and Mr John Coleman was appointed clerk of the works[73]

'at two pounds and seven shillings per week'. On 3 August 1858 the
Court of Assistants met at the Eagle Hotel, Snaresbrook, whence
(having concluded normal business) they proceeded to the Wanstead
site, where the Upper Bailiff, Cornelius Lea Wilson, son of Alderman
Wilson, laid the foundation stone in the presence of the Court and a
number of distinguished guests. Under the stone they deposited a
copy of the Charter of King Henry II, a statement setting forth the
history of the men's and women's almshouses down to 1858, and a list
of the donations to the Almshouses Fund so far received. The buildings were ready for occupation by the beginning of July 1859.

Table 18.9 *Funds for new almshouses, 1856*

Item	£	s.	d.
Money received from Commissioners for Porters			
Fields (men's) almshouses	2,424	4	10
Money invested from time to time	1,774	0	6
Invested in Consols at 96 (say)	4,000	0	0
Floating balance in Company's hands	571	6	11
Donations received or promised:[74]			
Mr. Graham 500			
Mr. Durant 500			
Mr. Stone 500			
Mr. Dalton 100			
Mr. Vanner 100			
Mr. Holt 25			
—			
	1,725	0	0
	6,296	6	11
Deduct purchase of land	750	0	0
	5,546	6	11

Mr West, one of the almsmen, was placed 'in temporary authority'—
a sort of senior (old) soldier! On the women's side a Mrs Ransom was
put in charge and was allowed to have her daughter to help her, the
Company paying the girl £15 per annum.[75] By July 1860 the Almshouse Committee had become convinced that West was 'not a
fit person to be allowed to continue Superintendent', because of
'numerous and well-founded complaints . . . that he is scarcely ever
on the premises, and absent without leaving the keys or anyone in
charge'. Furthermore, 'habits of insobriety are alleged by some of the
almspeople'. A month later Samuel Hotine, the Company's Beadle,
was appointed, at his request, Superintendent of the Almshouses, and

was given a list of duties, which included responsibility for the general care and cleanliness of the buildings as well as for the cleanliness and orderly conduct of the inmates. For this he received free quarters, coals, candles, and an allowance of £15 in cash.[76] The unreliable Mr West retained his almshouse but was sternly warned that 'any repetition of his habits of intemperance or any other misconduct' would mean prompt expulsion.

Occasional misbehaviour was certainly not unknown among the almsfolk, 'confirmed Drunkenness' being the most common cause from the seventeenth to the nineteenth centuries. The Court usually admonished and warned the offender once or twice, but if he or she persisted in disregarding the rules, expulsion was the ultimate penalty. A rather serious case came to a head in 1794 when two of the almswomen at Hoxton were given a month's notice to vacate their rooms because they had continued 'to suffer men and other improper persons to reside in their respective Almshouses contrary to the repeated orders of this Court'. On another occasion one of the married almsmen was accused by his neighbours of getting very drunk, using 'disgusting and blasphemous language (such as some of the witnesses were unwilling to repeat)', and ill-treating his wife, whom he finally turned out of doors, thus making her chargeable to the parish and bringing disgrace upon the Weavers' Company. After an investigation he was dismissed from his almshouse. Lastly, we may notice the case of the old almswoman who was dismissed 'for confirmed uncleanliness in her house and person'. The fact that she died less than six months later suggests that the real root of her trouble may have been progressive ill-health. On the whole, the serious cases resulting in expulsion were remarkably few and far between,[77] but they continued to crop up, despite the Rules and Regulations drafted and displayed for the almspeople's guidance in 1866. In 1885 the Company drew up new regulations which were ordered to be 'printed, framed and exhibited outside each pair of Almshouses'.[78]

As to the Almshouses Fund, many encouraging donations (including one of twenty-five guineas from H.R.H. the Prince of Wales) were received by the middle of 1865, largely as a result of 'the untiring zeal and interest shown and the time devoted by Col. and Alderman Wilson'. Table 18.10 shows the position at the beginning of May 1864.

By June 1865 the Fund stood at £4,700, together with a gift of securities valued at £500 from Mr John Remington Mills to found an additional pension.[79] To this must be added 'the annual income and accumulations' of half-a-dozen 'obsolete charities' dating from the seventeenth and early eighteenth centuries—a sum of about £300—which the Charity Commissioners agreed could be applied towards the support of the almspeople in the new Wanstead Almshouses. In 1865–7 there were also Mr Samuel Ridley's pension fund (£100) and

Table 18.10 *The Almshouses Fund, 1864*

Item	£	s.	d.
Donations from the Bailiffs, Wardens and Members of the Weavers' Company	2,502	10	8
Donations from Persons connected with the Silk Trade and others	2,066	4	4
	4,568	15	0

Miss Mary Copp's legacy of £300 which enabled the almspeople's pensions to be augmented.[80]

Meantime the Company had had to decide what to do with the old almshouse buildings in Hoxton. If they were let as they stood a total yearly rental of about £45 could be expected; but the tenants would certainly be 'of a very inferior type'. The Almshouses Committee felt that

> moral, social and sanitary considerations would prevent the Company so dealing with the property, as it . . . would only be underlet to poor families probably in single rooms, and the yard and other accommodations (bad enough when inhabited by Almswomen only) would be disgraceful and unwholesome, and a public body like the Weavers' Company would be justly blameable to sanction it.

An alternative scheme, favoured by the Committee, was the conversion of the premises into three or six shops by building on at the ground floor level. This might cost £500, but the aggregate annual income would probably be some £120–£140.

Eventually, three shops 'of very economical construction', were made, and let quite readily to a toyseller and stationer, a bird fancier, and a fruiterer and confectioner. All went harmoniously enough until 1862 when the Company, having learned that the shops were open for business on Sundays, informed the tenants of its strong disapproval of 'the flagrant desecration of the Sabbath'. The shopkeepers, on the other hand, were more than reluctant to lose their profitable Sunday trade, but by way of compromise they undertook 'to conduct their business with as little show and parade as possible on Sundays'.[81] The tenants of the three shops were, in fact, prospering; the premises were 'in a fair state of repair although dirty'; and from the Company's point of view the conversion proved a good investment, for the total rents from the three shops which amounted to nearly £164 per annum in 1870–1, had risen to £290 by 1884.[82] About this time the shops were numbered 335, 337 and 339 Old Street, and in 1886 we learn that no. 339 had been divided into two parts: one part remained a confectioner's, but the 'other shop with the premises at the rear extending behind the confectioner's shop and including the upper rooms' was sub-let to a cabinetmaker, upholsterer and bedding manufacturer, who made beds of flocks and shoddy in one of the upper rooms, while the ticking was stitched in the others. These changes at once raised the question of additional fire risk in the minds of the Company's visiting committee.[83] At the turn of the century the bedding manufacturer was still there and no fire had occurred; but the other tenants had gone and their places had been taken by a firm of retail clothiers, and by the British Tea Table Company which conducted a tea-rooms and eating house.[84]

Shortly before Christmas 1901, the Receiver of the Metropolitan Police informed the Weavers' Company of his wish to purchase and demolish their Old Street property to make part of a site for a new Police Court and Station, and after negotiation a price of £8,400 was agreed. In 1908 a scheme for the future administration by the Company of these funds, which then stood in the books at £8,764. 11s. 6d., was agreed by the Charity Commissioners.

During the half-century after 1880 the Company sold not only its old almshouses but several other properties which it had owned since the seventeenth century. The first to be sold were the buildings at Holborn Bars and Bakers Alley (sometimes called Bakers Court) which Alexander Hosea bequeathed to the Weavers' Company in 1686, directing that the income be used to relieve the Company's poor. Doubtless the Officers and Assistants were delighted to be rid of this property for it had been a perpetual source of trouble, anxiety and expense ever since the Company took it over from Hosea's executors in 1694. The very old rickety buildings constructed mainly of wood quickly became dilapidated unless kept under constant repair. Although the Company usually let the premises on repairing leases, many of the tenants were impecunious, some insolvent, and all apt to neglect their duties in this respect. Indeed, some neglected to pay the rent. A surveyor's report presented early in 1846 stated that the house facing Holborn was in 'fair condition', but the 'state of the houses in Bakers Court is altogether most filthy [and] the whole state of repair and drainage' very bad. In 1848 the Company seriously considered pulling down the Bakers Alley premises when the leases expired, clearing the site and letting it on a building lease; but nothing was done, and five years later these houses were still 'occupied by the lowest class and [were] much out of repair'.[85] Apparently the demolition took place in 1857, but the building lease proved difficult to dispose of, for there were many empty houses in the vicinity at that time. Several projects were considered. A proposal to erect model lodging houses came to nothing; a scheme to build 'a first-class cigar divan with billiard rooms, baths and racquet court' was rejected by the Company, and so was an offer of £200 per annum from a prospective tenant who wished to erect a music hall on the site, so designed as to have a 'handsome entrance' in Holborn. He was willing to agree not to allow dancing, not to use the premises 'for billiard rooms nor in any way in a disorderly manner'. But, despite the high rent offered, the Court twice rejected the idea of a music hall (by 9 votes against 7). Eventually a more acceptable lessee was found who agreed to pay a yearly rent of £150 for a term of 42 years.[86] By the spring of 1864 this lessee had built a range of spacious, well-lighted workshops on the Bakers Alley site and had succeeded in letting them at good rentals for various business uses, including a coffee roasting plant and warehouse 'equipped with steam power'. The Renter Bailiff reported, with evident satisfaction, 'that as the lease is a short one, the Company's reversion to the property may be considered very valuable'. A cloud obscured the sun, however, when the tenant, having become involved in litigation, was committed to a debtors' prison until he could pay the attorneys' costs.[87] Evidently other tenants were found, for in the spring of 1872 the Court of Assistants was informed that the Holborn premises were now all let, the shops and warehouses in rear being occupied by a school stationer apparently in a good way of business.[88] Six years later it was reported that the premises continued in a very satisfactory state and were let to 'tenants exclusively in the stationery, printing and lithographic trades'. Meantime, Parliament had passed the Metropolitan Street Improvement Act, 1877, which enabled the Metropolitan Board of Works 'to make certain New Streets and Street Improvements within the Metropolis', including the widening of Gray's Inn Road on its east side; and this resulted in the compulsory purchase, in 1880, of the Holborn property which had been held by the Company under the terms of Alexander Hosea's will for nearly two centuries. The purchase price was £7,177.[89]

No other substantial sales of the Company's property holdings took place until 1910–12 when the Irish rent charge was finally redeemed, the Weavers receiving through the Vintners' Company a capital sum of £162; a payment which brought to an end a chapter in the Company's history which had opened, as we know, exactly three centuries before, when James I tried to 'plant' English and Scottish settlers in Ulster.[90]

The next old property to be disposed of was the house known at one time 'by the sign of the Swan and . . . situated in St. Nicholas Lane on the East side thereof', but bearing the number 20 in 1915 when the Weavers sold it. Readers will remember that it was given to the Company by John Hall in 1691, subject to a number of annual rent charges, including '11s. a piece . . . to be paid to the 4 Officers in

Place and 2s. to the Clerk'.[91] For many years this house, like the Holborn property, was unprofitable and troublesome to manage. For instance, in the middle of the eighteenth century the place was empty for several years and fell into serious disrepair.[92] Again, in 1792, the tenant having died, his lease was assigned; but shortly afterwards the assignee also died, leaving such large arrears of rent that the Company had to threaten to distrain; whereupon the new tenant paid £30 and promised to clear the balance by instalments. The lease was again assigned, in 1808, to Sarah Maslin, a dealer in oysters, who, we are told, bore 'a good character in the neighbourhood'.[93] During the 1850s no. 20, which was the last house before the corner of King William Street, was joined as one property with a newly built corner shop.[94] By 1867 another lessee had converted the upper floors into offices, but the cost of the work involved was heavy and this tenant, too, fell seriously into arrears with his rent. The new accommodation was, it seems, not well planned, so that the offices proved difficult to let. In 1869 the ground floor—let as a luncheon bar—and the offices were occupied; but in 1871–2 the premises were 'untenanted and shut up' and six months' rent remained unpaid.[95] Soon afterwards no. 20 and the corner premises were let together, and in the 1880s Messrs Spiers and Pond ran a restaurant there. Some twenty years later a similar business was still being carried on in these premises, for in 1902 the Weavers' records speak of 'the Windmill P.H. and Restaurant'.[96] Finally, in 1915, no. 20 Nicholas Lane was sold to the Skinners' Company, the owners of the adjoining property, and after consultations with the Charity Commissioners, the proceeds (£6,000) were invested in trustee securities.[97] Some four years later, after the end of the First World War, the Company sold to the Royal Mail Steam Packet Company the freehold of nos. 14 and 16 Moorgate for £25,250,[98] thus realising certain ground rents purchased at the beginning of the reign of Queen Victoria when the Company decided to introduce rather more variety into its investment holdings.

We have seen in an earlier chapter how Rowland and John Morton, by a deed dated 28 July 1664, created 'Morton's Charity' which provided that in due course all the rents of the freehold properties known as Hatchett's and Gillett's in the parish of Great Burstead, Essex, should be administered by the Weavers' Company for the benefit of its poor.[99] This property consisted of an old farmhouse built of timber, lath and plaster, which stood in a street running parallel to the main street of the little country town of Billericay. There was also a barn, a stable, cattle sheds and some six acres of land. Like all property of its time and type, it was costly to maintain for it had a high dilapidation rate, and tenants who took it on repairing leases were likely to find that they had over-reached themselves. In the autumn of 1754, for example, John Cowden of Rotherhithe, carpenter, leased the farm and undertook to build a new brick house there. But when, a year later, he had shown no intention of even beginning the work, the Company evicted him and had him arrested and imprisoned for breach of covenant. After six months in the King's Bench prison, Cowden tried to negotiate with the Company, but was sternly told that he had 'lost all claim to favour' by reason of his dishonesty and the great expenses he had caused the Company to incur.[100] The next tenant, Richard Falkner, was a much better type, and spent £120 on repairs and improvements in four years. Unfortunately, he died in 1761, and John Hirst of Billericay, landlord of the Red Lion inn, took over the remainder of his lease. The rent was unchanged at £14 per annum 'neat . . . clear of all taxes, outgoings or deductions'. This tenant, too, was honest and a man of substance.[101] From a report of a visit by the Weavers' Company in 1845 one learns that the lessee at that date was one George Burgess, 'a very respectable and thriving' saddler and harnessmaker, who was paying a rent of £15 a year to the Company. The six acres of land were described as two paddocks of meadowland and about four acres of arable. The old farmhouse which had been divided into five tenements, was found to be 'in a state of great and dangerous dilapidation', the roof threatening to fall in; but it might 'last a great many years if properly repaired'. By sub-letting, the enterprising saddler was able to raise some £28 a year, and it is clear that after the negotiation of a new fourteen-years' lease (at £41 per annum) he spent freely in putting the property into a good state of repair.[102] But tenants come, and tenants go; and by the end of the century the buildings had become so utterly ramshackle and insanitary that the rural district council was pressing for their demolition. To this the Weavers' Company agreed, for it was unwilling to incur public censure for owning insanitary property. Moreover, within a few years, the value as building land would certainly far exceed its agricultural value. By the middle of 1903 all the old buildings were pulled down and the site cleared of rubbish, but the whole property was not finally disposed of for building purposes until 1919–21.[103]

It will be remembered that in 1666, under pressure from sundry discontented members, the Company had bought, as an investment, a farm at Shenfield in Essex. Despite its distance from London, this rural property, known as Brook Farm, had proved, on the whole, a better investment and less troublesome to the Company's Officers, than the town properties in Holborn and Nicholas Lane. Some tenants, needless to say, were bad farmers and worse payers; but others, like the Perrys, father and son, who occupied and worked the farm during most of the first half of the nineteenth century, were excellent 'improving tenants', who kept the land clean, thoroughly drained and amply manured; the farm buildings well repaired, and the fences and gates in good order.[104] A surveyor's report, dated 7 March 1854, shows that there were about thirty acres of arable and grass with a little more than one acre of 'garden waste', and that 'in consequence of the Railroad the grass land is not so valuable as it used to be'. The surveyor put the 'farming value' at £58. 10s. per annum and thought it unlikely that the sitting tenant would renew his lease.[105] The next tenant was a bad one who fell so far behind with his rent that the Company distrained, only to find that 'the crops had been removed and there was nothing on the premises'. After an interval, a dairy farmer leased the farm and soon made a number of improvements.[106]

The surveyor's reference to the 'railroad' takes us back to the early days of the railways and to the negotiations, in 1836, between the Eastern Counties Railway and the Weavers' Company for some of the Shenfield farm land for railway building. Eventually, the railway agreed to pay £300 for 2 acres, 2 roods, 31 perches; this sum to include 'compensation for severance and compulsory sale'. The railway also undertook to construct an 'occupation bridge' and suitable fences.[107]

Following a report in 1876 that the old farmhouse was in a bad condition, the roof, especially, being 'much decayed', and the bedroom floors 'in a wretched state', the Officers began to think of selling the farm; but in the end no action was taken.[108] At the turn of the century (1890–1909) the land was in good heart and bringing in about £70 per annum in rent. The venerable buildings, however, needed recurrent repairs. In 1909, the Company's surveyor in a report in which he pointed out that 'no less than 19 pairs of semi-detached houses (with frontages 25 ft. and average depth 150 ft.) and a block of six shops' had recently been built 'immediately facing the farm . . . and with one exception they are all occupied', went on to suggest that the Company might undertake in the near future a similar building development on about nine acres of Brook Farm, and with this in view he recommended the planting of a line of trees to screen the railway.[109] The trees were planted, but the Company seemed very reluctant to sell the farm piecemeal, except occasional strips for railway building.[110] At last, in 1934 Brook Farm was sold as a whole for £17,800, and when they relinquished their ownership the Weavers presented to Shenfield church a silver almsdish to commemorate the Company's association with the parish over an unbroken period of 268 years.[111]

Apart from a brief description of the octocentenary celebrations in 1930, this chapter must end as it began—with a reference to the evergreen question of Weavers' Hall. In 1912 the leasehold interest in the office buildings on the Weavers' Hall site at no. 22 Basinghall Street was offered at auction and was bought by the Weavers'

Company for £5,800.[112] For ten years afterwards the Company continued to look upon the site and buildings as an investment; but towards the end of 1922 the Court of Assistants set up a sub-committee, consisting of Mr C. J. Fox, Mr Charles Wigan and Dr H. B. Nelson, with the Surveyor, Mr J. W. S. Burmester, and the Clerk, Mr L. E. Tanner, as advisers, 'to consider the question of the future utilisation of the Hall, and report to the Estates Committee'. The sub-committee found that the block of buildings, which were some sixty-five years old, consisted of four floors and a basement and were divided into twenty-two suites of offices, together with the house-keeper's accommodation on the top floor. The gross annual rent received was about £2,200. Two main questions were discussed by the sub-committee:

(1) Whether it would be practicable for the Company to pull down the existing building (after the expiry of all the tenancies in 1928) and build on the site a Hall for the Company; or

(2) Whether the existing building might be so adapted as to provide a Court and Luncheon Room on one of the floors.

The Surveyor having reported that the capital cost of pulling down and rebuilding as proposed in (1) would be between £60,000 and £70,000, the sub-committee formed the opinion that expenditure on this scale, plus the concomitant loss of income from rents, 'was an impossible proposition to entertain at the present time'. Project (2) would probably cost £5,000 for conversion of the premises, and entail an annual loss of rent of approximately £624. In return the Company would be getting a Court Room to seat 34 persons, a Luncheon Room to seat 28, with a 'service room for kitchen purposes', a General Waiting Room, cloak-room and lavatory. A Luncheon Room of the size proposed was, in the sub-committee's view, inadequate: a room large enough for at least forty people was the minimum acceptable size. Taking the long view, the sub-committee concluded that, although at that time the Company could not afford to demolish and rebuild on the site,

the provision of a Hall would add to the prestige and standing of the Company, and . . . the Court might consider whether a definite sum should be set aside each year with this end in view. . . . The Sub-Committee are much impressed with the desirability of securing premises where the Company's pictures, plate, and other possessions can be housed, and can be seen by members of the Company.

Then followed a tentative suggestion that a Weavers' Hall sinking fund might be created by setting aside a sum of £500 each year.[113]

For several years following this report a good deal of thought and discussion went on about the idea of building a new Weavers' Hall, and the all-important question of ways and means; but gradually interest waned and the iron was no longer hot.

The summer and autumn of 1929 saw the Court of Assistants busily making plans to celebrate the 800th anniversary, not of the founding of the Weavers' Gild—an event lost in the mists of the Middle Ages—but of the earliest known record of the existence of the London Weavers' gild and its recognition by the Crown. This is the entry in the Pipe Roll of the Exchequer in the year 1130, during the reign of Henry I, recording the payment of £16 by Robert, son of Levestan, to the Crown on behalf of the Weavers.[114] The celebrations began in the middle of May with a special Court dinner at which H.R.H. the Prince of Wales was the guest of honour. The Court Circular for 13 May 1930 announced that 'H.R.H., attended by Brig.-General G. F. Trotter, was present at the Octocentenary Dinner of the Worshipful Company of Weavers, which was held at the Grocers' Hall this evening'. The small gathering included the Belgian Ambassador, the Earl of Crawford and Balcarres, and the Deputy Master of the Grocers' Company, as guests; the four Officers of the Weavers' Company (Mr G. R. Y. Radcliffe, Upper Bailiff, Mr W. R. Fox, Renter Bailiff, Major the Hon. George H. Chubb, Upper Warden, Dr J. C. Ingle, Renter Warden), fourteen Assistants, three Liverymen (Lord Illingworth, Sir Henry Birchenough and Mr E. R. W. Radcliffe), the Chaplain (the Rev. A. A. Slack) and the Clerk to the Company (Mr L. E. Tanner).[115] Among the Assistants present was Mr James Harold Early, who had been Upper Bailiff in the previous year (1928–9) and who, shortly after, gave to his sister-in-law a vivid, eyewitness account of the Prince and the proceedings.

Letter from Mr. J. H. Early to Miss K. W. Elliott, C.B.E.

Newland, Witney.
16th May 1930

My dear Kay,

I see from your letter to Alice that you want to know what I thought about the Prince.

Well, we had a thoroughly good time of course. Before the show we had all received, as you may imagine, pretty strict and precise orders as to what we were to do and how we were to do it; the suggestions having been submitted to the Prince and approved by him. However, once he blew into the room there was very little stiff adherence to programme. Instead of standing solemnly with the Officers of the Company so that we might be presented to him in turn, he at once sailed round the room, the Upper Bailiff panting after him and H.R.H. shaking

hands with everyone he met with the utmost heartiness. I had
wondered beforehand whether it would be a case of just
standing in front of him and bowing, but he grabbed hold and
gave one quite a good grip. He was looking slightly tanned,
and in good hard condition. He has a rather harsh voice, but
the use he makes of it simply charms everybody. If he once
came across your second cousin, or met your great-aunt in
Timbuctoo, he remembers it and takes care to mention it and
tells you to be sure to tell your great-aunt next time you see
her that he remembers their pleasant meeting.

At Dinner we were quite a small company sitting round an
oval table. The chief guest kept up an animated conversation
all the time. He had the Belgian Ambassador on his right and
seemed to be speaking to him alternately in English and
French. We had speeches at the close, but they were very
short, his amongst them. Afterwards he circulated round the
big drawing-room talking to anyone who approached him.
Finally, at 10.30 or so, his equerry wanted to drag him away,
but he had the greatest difficulty, and the Prince went all
round the room saying good-night to everyone separately, and
from time to time stopping and involving himself in a fresh
conversation. Altogether he produced a very good impression,
and it was possible even for a hard-bitten democrat to feel it
was a most interesting evening. . . .

J.H.E.[116]

As to the Prince's speech, Dr L. E. Tanner, C.V.O., who, as we have
noted, was present as Clerk to the Weavers' Company, recalls that
the Dinner was 'a very informal affair' and when speech-time came
the Prince showed some reluctance to make the formal speech which
had been written for him, and 'eventually made a little impromptu
speech in reply to the toast of his health'. Among the gifts made to
the Company to mark its Octocentenary was a silver-gilt sheep given
by Lord Illingworth of Denton, and a silver rose-water dish, presented
by the Court of Assistants and first used by the Prince of Wales at the
dinner on 13 May.

Another memorable feature of the celebrations was a visit made by
three of the Company's Officers and seven members of the Court and
Livery, attended by the Chaplain,[117] Clerk and Beadle, to Belgium in
June 1930. Although, at first, a visit to France, the country in which
so many of the London silk weavers had their origins, was contem-
plated, support was not unanimous. But there was never any doubt
on either side of the Channel about the visit to Belgium. The Foreign
Office in London, the British Embassy in Brussels, and the chief
municipal officers of Brussels and other leading Belgian cities received

the proposal warmly. Considerable interest was shown by Ghent and Courtrai, both long-famous for their linen manufactures, which in times past were largely marketed, together with great quantities of fine Flemish cloth, through Bruges, with its sixty-eight flourishing trade gilds; a commerce which reached its highest peak of prosperity during the fourteenth century. As the Burgomaster of Bruges[118] said in his address of welcome to the Weavers' party on 16 June,

> it is thanks to the cloth trade that the bonds of friendship, which have existed for centuries past, between England and Flanders, and particularly between England and Bruges, have been tied. And not only bonds of friendship, but also political and economic connections, which have been producing almost at every moment great advantages to both our peoples.

The numerous preliminary arrangements having been meticulously made by the Clerk, the Weavers' party set out for Belgium on 12 June 1930 and 'after a smooth crossing from Dover to Ostend, reached Brussels in a violent thunderstorm at 7 o'clock'. The next day a cordial welcome to the party by the Burgomaster of Ghent was followed by a luncheon given by the Ghent Branch of the Anglo-Belgian Union, of which General Maton, a former Belgian Military Attaché in London, was the head; and

> after luncheon the Court and their hosts embarked on the Municipal launch for a tour of the docks, etc. In spite of the fact that some of the party got lost, and that at the furthest point the launch, owing to a mechanical breakdown, refused for half-an-hour or more to go either forward or backward, an enjoyable afternoon was spent and . . . the Palace Hotel, Brussels, was reached in time for dinner.[119]

On 14 June the party was entertained in Brussels by Burgomaster Adolphe Max and the Town Council;[120] and on 16 and 17 June similar hospitality was enjoyed at Bruges and Courtrai. On the last day of the visit, 18 June, a few of the party made time to visit the Antwerp Exhibition where they particularly wished to see the British Section. Also on that day, which by some felicitous chance happened to be the anniversary of the Battle of Waterloo, the Weavers gave a dinner in token of their appreciation of the great kindness and generous hospitality of their Belgian hosts. Among the principal guests were the Counsellor of the British Embassy in Brussels, Mr Nevile Bland, C.M.G. (who was Chargé d'Affaires during the Ambassador's absence on leave), and a number of eminent Belgians, including General Maton and three high officials of the Belgian Ministry of Foreign Affairs.

Dr Lawrence Tanner, looking back over the space of nearly forty years, has no doubt that the Belgian visit:

> was a great success and . . . much of the sucess was due to the fact that the Upper Bailiff (Geoffrey Radcliffe) was in terrific form, and ready to talk and make speeches in fluent French—and with an accent all his own—at any hour of the day or night! The most notable event was the 'City Dinner' (with all the usual ritual, Loving Cup,[121] etc.) which we gave in Brussels on the last night, with the famous Burgomaster Max as our chief guest.

A month later, on 16 July 1930, the Weavers concluded their celebrations, pleasantly and appropriately, with a Livery Dinner for the Lord Mayor (Sir William Waterlow) and the Sheriffs of London. On this special occasion doubtless a deeper note than usual crept into the voices of members and guests alike as, pausing briefly at the 800th milestone, they drank the time-honoured toast:

The Upper Bailiff
and
The Worshipful Company of Weavers
Root and Branch, and may it flourish for ever.

NOTES

1 MS. 4655/19, ff.2, 20, 22, 26–29b, 42–46b.
2 P.O. Directory, 1805–7.
3 The Company sold £400 4 per cent Bank Annuities at this time, probably to finance this work. It was agreed that the lessee should provide insurance cover of £2,500.
4 MS. 4655/19, ff.49b–52, 54, 58, 66. The sale catalogue of 1865 shows that shop fronts were put in at some date between 1800 and 1856.
5 MS. 4655/19, ff.395b, 402, 430–2.
6 MS. 4655/19, ff.161, 279b, 283, 368b–369, 402, 435b. In 1815–16 quarterages collected totalled £43, of which 25 guineas were paid for redemption of quarterages; but many dues remained unpaid.
7 MS. 4655/19, ff.439, 443b, 479, 481b; MS. 4655/20, f.18. Repairs to Weavers' Hall cost £223 between 1822 and 1825.
8 MS. 4655/20, ff.41, 82, 121b, 154b, 239, 323b, 359.
9 MS. 5234/1. The West India Dock Tavern at Blackwall was noted for its banquets of whitebait and various other fish followed by duck, cutlets, bacon and meat pies, with choice wines, all served, as Dickens remarked, 'at the highest prices known to civilisation'.
10 MS. 4655/20, ff.243b, 244b, 415b, 513b.
11 MS. 4655/20, ff.463b, 482b, 502b.
12 MS. 4655/21, *passim*. On the lease of ground from the Merchant Taylors see MS. 4655/20, ff.93, 101b, 251.

13 Estimated expenses at the London Tavern: Room for Court meetings, twelve meetings at 10*s.* 6*d.*, £6. 6*s.*; breakfast for ten persons at 1*s.* 6*d.* a head on twelve days, £9.

14 D. B. Wyndham Lewis, *The Hooded Hawk* (1946), p. 266; B. Lillywhite, *London Coffee Houses* (1963), p. 710.

15 MS. 4655/21, 15 January, 5 February 1856.

16 W. C. Waller (ed.), *Extracts from the Court Books of the Weavers' Company of London* (1931), Huguenot Society publications, pp. xi–xii. About the year 1868 the chest and books were moved to the porter's lobby at the Cannon Street Hotel, and in 1873 to the Weavers' Almshouses at Wanstead (MS. 4655/25, 13 January 1874; see also J. Corbet Anderson's report, 1883).

17 MS. 4655/21, 1 April, 6 May 1856. The new lease was sealed on 4 August 1857.

18 MS. 4655/22, 7 April 1857; MS. 4655/23, April 1861. The old Hall had three storeys, including the ground floor; the new building had an extra storey.

19 MS. 4655/24, 14 January, 3 March 1868; Letter Book 1863–79, ff.183–4. A year later the Court decided to spend £60 to have all the pictures overhauled, repaired, and reframed if necessary.

20 For many years it was wrongly supposed that this was a portrait of Queen Mary, the wife of William III; but see MS. 4648/3, 20 June 1709 and MS. 4655/19, f.540b.

21 MS. 4655/25, November 1873; March 1874; April and August 1876. Four of these portraits now hang in the Library of Westminster Abbey; see Chap. 19 below.

22 MS. 4655/19, ff.375, 439, 532, 537b.

23 MS. 4655/20, f.256.

24 MS. 4655/20, ff.195, 201.

25 MS. 4655/20, ff.412, 431b.

26 MS. 4655/20, ff.485b, 500b.

27 The Caledonian Railway Debentures, repaid in 1852–3, gave the Company a capital profit of £105 (MS. 4655/21, *passim*).

28 MS. 4655/22, 5 May 1857.

29 Madras Railway and Great Indian Peninsular Railway (MS. 4655/23, *passim*).

30 e.g. William Elam submitted specimens of figured silk and orris weaving; these are now in the possession of the Weavers' Company.

31 M. Argles, *South Kensington to Robbins* (1964), Chap. 2.

32 MS. 4655/20, f.350.

33 F. Warner, op. cit., p. 96.

34 A. K. Sabin, *The Silkweavers of Spitalfields and Bethnal Green* (1931), pp. 15, 20; Cat. no. 152, Plate X. Also at the 1851 Exhibition a selection of patterns of silks made at various dates between *c.* 1650 and 1850 were displayed. Many of these are kept at the excellent Bethnal Green Museum, which is a branch of the Victoria and Albert.

35 *Survey of London*, XXVII, p. 139; MS. 4655/23, 19 January 1864. John Vanner was Upper Bailiff in 1861–2 and 1868–9. J. Timbs, *Curiosities of London* (1868 edn), p. 745; J. F. Flanagan, *Spitalfields Silks of the 18th and 19th Centuries* (1954), Plates 45 and 49.

36 Sir Thomas Nelson (1827–85), City Solicitor, son of Thomas Nelson of Mark House, Walthamstow, and the City of London, merchant. He was admitted a solicitor in 1848 and appointed City Solicitor

in 1862. During the 1870s he was involved, on behalf of the City
Corporation, in the protracted litigation which ended in the preservation of Epping Forest for the enjoyment of the public for ever
(see G. Shaw Lefevre, *English Commons and Forests* (1894), Chap.
VIII). He was Upper Bailiff of the Weavers' Company 1873–4, and
was anxious that a history of the Company should be written. He
was knighted in 1880.

37 MS. 4655/25, *passim*. On Baroness Burdett-Coutts's charitable
works among the Spitalfields weavers and others see C. B. Patter-
son, *Angela Burdett-Coutts and the Victorians* (1953), Chap. 8.

38 Livery Companies Committee, *Report on Technical Education* (1878).

39 MS. 4655/25, March–July 1877 and June 1878; MS. 4661A/14,
Letter Book, 1863–79, circular letter, 5 June 1878.

40 MS. 4655/27, ff.80, 86, 97, 107.

41 MS. 4655/27, ff.123–4, 130.

42 MS. 4655/27, ff.132, 140–3, 166, 175, 182, 207; MS. 4661A/14,
Letter Book, October 1888, ff.146–7; City & Guilds, *Programme of
Classes*, 1888–9.

43 MSS. 4655/27, ff.183–7, 192–3. In Class III (figured silk with one
or two shuttles) an 'honourable mention' certificate was gained by
Francis Dearman, whose daughter worked with him as a weaveress,
and is (in 1969) living in Weavers' House, Wanstead, as an
almswoman of the Company.

44 MS. 4655/27, f.295; MS. 4655/28, December 1893; MS. 4661A/14,
Letter Book 1891–3, f.15, gives a list of fifteen firms in the London
silk industry in 1891.

45 This Board was set up in 1893, under the Technical Education
Acts of 1889 and 1891, with Sidney Webb as its first chairman, and
Dr William Garnett as secretary.

46 MS. 4655/27, ff.348–9, 386; MS. 4661A/14, Letter Book 1891–3,
f.630.

47 MS. 4655/30, 5 April 1910. Manufacturers, distributors and the
Board of Trade also gave support.

48 MS. 4655/31, 3 December 1918 and 5 April 1921. Estimated earnings of male weavers were put at £3 per week, and of female
weavers at 30*s*. to 40*s*. (MS. 4661A/14, Letter Book 1916–19, ff.378,
419–21, 428). In 1906 a School of Weaving established by Miss
Grasett was inspected by a sub-committee of the Weavers' Company, which reported that 'her work was without commercial
value', but recommended a donation of ten guineas as a token of
the Company's interest (MS. 4655/29, 20 August 1906).

49 C. C. Hawkins, *Technical Education and the City Livery Companies*
(1923), p. 14.

50 MS. 4655/31 and 32, *passim*.

51 Upper Bailiff, 1962–3.

52 MS. 4655/32, 5 June 1923.

53 MS. 4655/18, f.340b; MS. 4655/19, f.243.

54 MS. 4655/19, f.74; MS. 4648/11, 9 October 1793.

55 MS. 4655/18, f.323b; MS. 4655/19, ff.155, 282, 307; MS. 4655/20,
ff.13, 17b, 37.

56 MS. 5234/1, 4 March 1812. In 1830, under the will of Thomas Platt,
formerly an Assistant, the Company received invested funds producing £10 a year, to be paid to the occupants of its almshouses
(MS. 4655/20, f.99).

57 MS. 4655/19, ff.412, 435, 484b, 507–9.
58 MS. 4655/19, f.531b.
59 MS. 4655/21, 6 March 1855; MS. 4655/22, 3 June and 2 December 1856. cf. MS. 4655/28, 21 August 1893.
60 MS. 4655/24, 1 August 1871; MS. 4655/25, 6 February 1872.
61 MS. 4655/25, 5 March 1872, and cf. 1 October 1878.
62 MS. 4655/21, 6 May, 3 June 1856; MS. 4655/25, March 1877; 7 May 1878. Robert Graham was Upper Bailiff in 1856–7.
63 MS. 4655/19, ff.157, 229, 356.
64 In December 1921 the Auditors warned the Company that it was, once again, overspending on its Charities (MS. 4655/31, 6 December 1921).
65 MS. 4655/19, ff.515, 517–18b; MS. 4661/96; and see the Livery list for 1799–1800. Charles James Coverley came of a family long established as weavers and members of the Weavers' Company. For example, in 1751 Robert Coverley of Tenter Alley, Little Moorfields, weaver, son of Robert Coverley, Citizen and Weaver of London (deceased) and Jane Coverley, widow, was made free by servitude; and a year earlier Robert's younger brother, Charles, was apprenticed for 7 years to his mother. Charles Coverley was made free in due course, and later elected to the Livery (in 1762). In 1753 another son, entered in the books as Roger de Coverley, who had been apprenticed to his father in 1745, was made free by servitude on the testimony of Jane Coverley, widow. Ten years later (1763) he is listed among the Liverymen (MS. 4655/15, f.340b; MS. 4655/16, ff.12, 76, 195b). 'Coverleys Fields' were in Mile End New Town, originally a hamlet in the Manor of Stepney.
66 MS. 4655/19, f.535.
67 MS. 4655/20, ff.205b, 319b.
68 MS. 4655/20, ff.174–5, 450, 456, 528b; MS. 4655/21, *passim*.
69 MS. 4655/21, 1 November 1853, 17 January 1854.
70 Largely through the good offices of Mr Robert Graham, who was Upper Bailiff in 1856–7.
71 MS. 4655/22, *passim*.
72 e.g. MS. 4655/23, 3 July 1860; MS. 4655/24, 4 August 1868.
73 He was recommended by Mr John Vanner, a member of the Almshouses Committee, Upper Bailiff 1861–2 and 1868–9, who was present at the laying of the foundation stone (see MS. 4655/22, 3 August 1858). The cost of entertainment at the Eagle Hotel was £28. 9s. 5d., and £9. 12s. was paid for a silver trowel.
74 MS. 4655/21, 1 June 1852, 6 May 1856; MS. 4655/22, 3 June, 1 July 1856, 6 October 1857.
75 Mr John Vanner supplied Bibles to those almspeople who wanted them and arranged for one of the City Missionaries to attend to their spiritual welfare (thus by chance forestalling the Vicar of Wanstead, who, a little later, offered his services). Mr Vanner also provided some chairs (MS. 4655/22, 6 December 1859).
76 MS. 4655/23, 3 July and 7 August 1860.
77 See, e.g., MS. 4655/18, f.262b; MS. 4655/19, ff.120–1; MS. 4655/20, ff.519b, 524b; MS. 4655/24, 6 July 1869.
78 MS. 4655/24, 2 October 1866; MS. 4655/26, ff.304, 327; MS. 4655/27, ff.74–5.
79 MS. 4655/23, *passim. City of London Livery Companies Commission, Report* (1865), pp. 341–2, 345–7. John Remington Mills was Upper Bailiff in 1831–2 and 1845–6.

80 MS. 4655/24, 17 January 1865; 2 July 1867.
81 MS. 4655/22, and 23, *passim.*
82 MS. 4655/24, 3 May 1870; MS. 4655/26, f.278.
83 MS. 4655/27, ff.4–5.
84 MS. 4655/28, April 1899.
85 MS. 4655/20, ff.26, 433, 438b, 483; MS. 4655/21, 4 April 1853; MS. 4655/22, October 1856–May 1857.
86 MS. 4655/22, 19 January and 5 April 1859; MS. 4655/23, 17 December 1861 and 3–4 February 1863.
87 MS. 4655/23, 5 April 1864; MS. 4655/24, 4 July 1865.
88 MS. 4655/25, 2 April 1872 and April 1878.
89 On the re-investment of these trust funds see MS. 4655/27, f.174, and MS. 4655/30, February 1909–June 1910.
90 MS. 4655/30, 1 February 1910, 3 October 1911, 19 August 1912; Letter Book, 1905–8, f.19b.
91 The payments to the Officers and Clerk appear to have been discontinued in 1731 (*Report on the Charities,* 1742, f.15).
92 MS. 4655/12, f.140; MS. 4648/4, ff.207, 231, 262; MS. 4655/16, ff.85, 89, 97b.
93 MS. 4655/18, ff.218–19; MS. 4655/19, f.210.
94 MS. 4655/21, 6 February 1855.
95 MS. 4655/24, *passim*; MS. 4655/25, 2 April 1872.
96 MS. 4655/29, 3 April and 1 May 1902.
97 MS. 4655/30, 17 August 1914, 30 March 1915.
98 MS. 4655/31, 18 August 1919.
99 MS. 4655/3, f.142b.
100 MS. 4655/16, ff.110, 119b, 130b, 140, 172. The Clerk's bill 'for the Ejectment at Billericay' amounted to £29. 9s.
101 MS. 4655/16, ff.161b, 183b, 242b, 257b, 263; MS. 4648/7 (1761).
102 MS. 4655/20, ff.420b, 424, 479b.
103 MS. 4655/28, June, August 1899, February 1900; MS. 4655/29, 9 June 1903; MS. 4655/31, 2 December 1919, 1 February 1921; MS. 4661A/14, Letter Books, 1879–85, ff.117, 372; 1908–10, ff.274, 279, 382.
104 MS. 4655/19, ff.487b, 523–4b, 537; MS. 4655/20, f.427.
105 MS. 4655/21, 7 March 1854.
106 MS. 4655/22, 7 October, 4 November 1856, 6 April 1858.
107 MS. 4655/20, ff.217, 258b.
108 MS. 4655/25, 4 April 1876, 7 August, 2 October 1877.
109 MS. 4655/30, 7 December 1909, 11 June 1912; MS. 4661A/14, Letter Book, 1908–10, ff.541–2.
110 In 1930 a strip of land (3 acres 8 perches) was sold to the L.N.E.R. for railway widening at a price of £2,500 (MS. 4655/32, 1 April 1930).
111 MS. 4655/33, 25 July 1934, 5 February 1935.
112 MS. 4655/30, 2 April 1912.
113 *Report* of the Sub-Committee on Weavers' Hall (1922).
114 MS. 4655/32, 1 and 7 October 1929, 13 May 1930.
115 *The Times,* 14 May 1930. The signatures of the Prince, the other guests and members of the Weavers' Company who were present are in MS. 4655/32, 13 May 1930.
116 I am indebted to Mr Richard E. Early for telling me of this letter (now in his possession) written by his father, and for allowing me to quote from it. Mr J. H. Early was three times Upper Bailiff—

in 1928–9, 1940–1 and 1951–2. In 1922 he stood as Liberal candidate in the North Oxfordshire Parliamentary Election, and came second in a three-cornered contest.

117 The Very Rev. the Dean of Gloucester acted as Chaplain to the Company during the visit to Belgium, because the Limborough Lectureship was temporarily vacant (MS. 4655/32, 1 April 1930).

118 M. Victor Van Hoestenberghe.

119 MS. 4655/32, 12–13 June 1930. The members of the party were: G. R. Y. Radcliffe, Esq., Upper Bailiff, Major the Hon. G. H. Chubb, Upper Warden, J. C. Ingle, Esq., LL.D., Renter Warden, the Right Hon. Lord Askwith, K.C.B., K.G., the Right Hon. Lord Illingworth, P.C., W. B. Ingle, Esq., J. H. Early, Esq., J. W. S. Burmester, Esq., K. C. Fox, Esq., Professor A. D. Barker, M.Sc., the Very Rev. Canon Courtenay Gale, Chaplain, L. E. Tanner, Esq., Clerk, and Mr W. E. Willis, Beadle.

120 In February 1911 the Weavers' Company had given a luncheon in London to the Burgomaster of Brussels (MS. 4661A/14, Letter Book, 1910–13, ff.76–7).

121 The Ceremony of the Loving Cup. Immediately after dinner and Grace, the Bailiffs and Wardens drink to their Guests a hearty welcome; the Loving Cup is passed round the table, and each guest, after he has drunk, applies his napkin to the mouth of the Cup before he passes it to his neighbour. The person who pledges with the Cup stands up and bows to his neighbour, who, also standing, removes the cover with his right hand and holds it while the other drinks. On passing the Cup, the one who has pledged should immediately turn his back on his neighbour until he in turn has passed the Cup on. This ceremonial is said to originate in the precaution of keeping employed the right or 'dagger' hand of the person removing the cover, while the person standing behind the one who is pledging guards his back against a possible treacherous attack.

Chapter 19

Mid-Twentieth Century

The octocentenary celebrations might have been chosen as an eminently suitable point at which to bring to a close this history of the Weavers' Company since 1600. But the Company itself goes on, and since 1930 a number of events have occurred and certain important decisions have been taken which ought to be recorded, however briefly.

In 1931 Dr Frances Consitt, who had been working for several years on a history of the Company based upon its early records covering the Middle Ages and the Tudor period, completed her task. Arrangements were made for publication by Oxford University Press and the book appeared in 1933 under the title *The London Weavers' Company from the Twelfth Century to the close of the Sixteenth Century*.[1]

At about the same time the Court of Assistants, together with certain prominent members of the Livery, met to consider the desirability of bringing up to date the Company's By-laws, which had not been revised since 1737 (under circumstances described in Chapter 13 above). New By-laws and Ordinances were drafted by Sir John Miles, a member of the Court and a former Upper Bailiff, and these were duly confirmed in Common Hall on 26 July 1937, just two hundred years and four months after the old By-laws and Ordinances had been 'approved, allowed and confirmed' in the reign of George II.[2]

The outbreak of the Second World War in September 1939, with its imminent threat of aerial attacks, raised many problems for all the City Livery Companies, not the least of which was the protection of their priceless historic possessions—their halls, ancient documents, antique pictures, furniture, and plate. At first, from September 1939 to May 1941, the Weavers were fortunate, but on the night of 10–11 May 1941 Weavers' Hall was seriously damaged by incendiary bombs which fell on the adjoining buildings, no. 21 Basinghall Street, and the premises at the rear. The Company's Surveyor reported that the rooms in the 'back part of Weavers' Hall from the rear ground floor and first floor upwards . . . were burnt out with all the contents'. Some relics of the old Hall were completely destroyed, including the seventeenth-century carved over-mantel and panelling, and the seventeenth-century carvings on the staircase, but the old carved doors at the head of the staircase, which were made in 1669 after the Great Fire, survived.[3] The five royal portraits—Queen Elizabeth I, Charles II, James II, William III and Queen Anne—which, before the war, were hung in the Guildhall Library, had been taken to a 'place of greater safety' shortly after the beginning of the war, otherwise they, too, might have been destroyed in the 'blitz'.[4] It was even more fortunate that the Company's ancient charters and records were neither damaged nor destroyed. However, the Court of Assistants prudently decided to run no further risks and the documents were soon afterwards taken out of London, part to New College, Oxford, and part to Glebe House, Knebworth, the house of Dr G. R. Y. Radcliffe.[5] During the last phase of the war the Almshouses at Wanstead were damaged by a rocket bomb, which made it necessary for a number of the almsfolk to seek temporary shelter with relatives or friends.[6] Fortunately there were no casualties.

Those who remembered the octocentenary visit to Belgium, and how the Court had been entertained at Brussels by the famous Burgomaster Max, must have been moved by the exchange of messages between the Company and the City of Brussels at the time of his death, early in 1940.[7] Shortly afterwards the Nazi hordes swept across the Low Countries and normal communications were cut for over four years. Memories of 1930 stirred once more when, early in October 1944, the Court of Assistants resolved to send a letter to the Burgomaster of Brussels 'conveying their pleasure at the liberation of his ancient City and the Country of Belgium', and enclosing a donation of 5,000 francs 'for the alleviation of distress'. The gift was accepted with courteous appreciation and used to help the children of Brussels.[8]

Shortly after the restoration of peace the Honorary Freedom of the Company was conferred upon H.R.H. Princess Alice, Countess of Athlone, in recognition of her services to the British Empire. The Princess thus became the first Honorary Freewoman of the Weavers' Company.[9]

In 1953, Mr Norman Cleverton Tremellen, C.C., a Liveryman of the Company, was elected to the office of Sheriff, an honour which had not fallen to a Weaver since Samuel Wilson was elected Sheriff in 1833. Four years later, another Weaver, Mr Deputy Samuel Richard Walker, C.B.E., was elected Sheriff, much to the satisfaction of his fellow members.[10]

The Company benefited very considerably under the will of the late

Sir Cecil Bigwood, D.L., J.P. (1863–1947). Sir Cecil was a distinguished lawyer who served London as a magistrate for over half a century. Elected to the Livery of the Weavers' Company in 1891, he was for many years an active and devoted member. He became Upper Bailiff in 1911, and was re-elected in the following year. Under his will the Company became entitled, on the death of his sister in 1957, to substantial residential properties comprising mainly houses and flats at Lewisham, Beckenham, and Catford. The Lewisham Estate, which was leasehold, was sold to the freeholders, the Mercers' Company, in 1960, and most of the houses at Park Langley, Beckenham, were sold to the tenants. The Catford Estate, comprising about 140 houses, flats or maisonettes, with a rent-roll of about £21,000, has been retained, and the Court has adopted a policy of extending the estate by the purchase, when possible, of adjoining houses or houses situated between the blocks of property already owned. A long-term policy of major repairs, improvements, and modernisation is being systematically carried through.

During the past thirty to forty years the Company has maintained and strengthened its links with the weaving industry by electing into the Livery, or on to the Court, many who were or are actively concerned with weaving in any of its branches. In this connection the names of Viscount Rochdale and Mr J. P. Early (both of whom succeeded their fathers as members of the Court), Sir Charles Allom, Sir Frank Warner, Sir Ernest Goodale, the Earl Peel, Mr J. Sugden Smith and Mr D. R. B. Mynors come to mind. In recent decades the Company has been fortunate indeed in having as Upper Bailiffs—besides those already mentioned—a number of members, distinguished and active in other spheres, who have devoted much of their time and talents to building up the status and usefulness of the Weavers' Company. In particular several families, notably the Chubbs, Foxes, Ingles and Radcliffes, have provided Upper Bailiffs who have given outstanding service to the Company. As a result the Company has developed from what was little more than a dining club in the twenties and thirties to an active and forward-looking body devoting many thousands of pounds a year to the furtherance of technical knowledge in the British Textile Industry or to appropriate charities, such as its own almshouses.

Since the end of the Second World War the Company has not only maintained but increased its keen interest in higher technical education for the textile industry and tried to move with the times. The Court were fortunate in having the expert guidance of two former Upper Bailiffs (Sir Ernest Goodale, C.B.E., M.C., and Dr A. J. Turner, C.B.E.). At their suggestion a Scholarships (Studentships) Committee was formed in 1945 and the former research scholarships were replaced by two Senior Research Studentships in Textile Technology and Design tenable by approved students recommended by Leeds University (Textile Department), Bradford Technical College, the Shirley Institute, the Linen Research Institute, Belfast, the Wool Industries Research Association, and Manchester College of Technology. These awards, which are for one year in the first instance but can be renewed for a further one or two years in appropriate cases, were increased to £500 per annum in 1961 and are (in 1970) limited to Leeds, Bradford and Manchester Universities; they impose no age limits and are open to British subjects by birth or naturalisation who intend to make a career in the design, production or distribution of textiles, or in textile education or research. In 1966 the Company took a further step forward in this field by instituting an American Scholarship for one year's postgraduate study. This is now worth £1,900, and provides for nine months at North Carolina State University, followed by three months in the American textile industry. In addition to these grants the Weavers' Company awards bursaries through the Royal College of Art for short courses of training in colleges and/or textile mills in the United Kingdom, or at textile centres abroad. Grants are made periodically through the Royal Society of Arts to enable practising designers and teachers in the textile industry to travel abroad to study methods in other countries. In short, the whole scheme is reasonably flexible and adaptable.[11]

In 1933 the Court transferred investments from the General Estate to a Trust Fund which came to be known as the General Charitable Trust Fund. The income (supplemented in recent years by substantial annual payments under covenant from the Company) is applied first in the provision of studentship grants, and secondly for donations for other charitable purposes; any residuary income being available to supplement the Weavers' Almshouses Charities income if required.

Mr E. E. Willis, the Beadle and Superintendent of the Almshouses, upon whom the Company had conferred the Honorary Freedom in 1945, retired in 1953, after thirty years' service.[12] He was succeeded by Mr John Jackson who was made an Honorary Freeman of the Company in 1968.

In 1960 Mr Lawrence E. Tanner, C.V.O., who had been Clerk to the Company for over forty years, expressed a wish to retire as he was nearing the age of seventy and felt that 'the time had come when the Clerkship should be in younger hands'. The Court of Assistants, with understandable reluctance and regret, accepted Mr Tanner's decision and in due course appointed one of its Liverymen, Mr Romilly S. Ouvry, to succeed him with effect from 1 August 1960. In October 1960 the Company expressed its appreciation of Mr Tanner's long period of devoted service by electing him to the Court of Assistants. Two years later, Mr Tanner was elected to serve as Upper Bailiff for

1963–4; and it was during his year of office that the writing of the Weavers' history from 1600 to the present time was put in hand.

At the Octocentenary Dinner on 16 July 1930 the Upper Bailiff expressed the hope that 'when the 900th birthday came round, they would meet in a Hall of their own',[13] and for many years thereafter hope persisted that a new Weavers' Hall would one day rise upon the old site in Basinghall Street. In 1947–8 the cost of such a scheme was roughly estimated to be £75,000, while the probable annual revenue from rents was put at £7,000. But nothing was done beyond urgent war-damage repairs and, in 1952, the renovation of the front of the building. The rear portion, which was damaged during the war, remained derelict.[14] Towards the end of 1957 all hope of building a new Weavers' Hall in Basinghall Street faded away when the Court resolved that the old site should be developed solely as an office building and that the Company 'should look elsewhere for the possible site of a new Hall'. The prospect of finding a place in the City's Barbican development area was under consideration for a time, but nothing came of this.[15] Finally, in 1961, the Court decided to sell the freehold of the Basinghall Street property, and, 'in view of soaring costs', to give up all idea of buying a site and erecting a new Hall, or acquiring and adapting an existing building within, or adjacent to, the City. These decisions were made with the greatest reluctance. Various propositions had been examined from time to time, but in every instance the costs of acquisition and adaptation, and the estimated net expenses of future maintenance were deemed to be beyond the Company's resources.[16] This meant that permanent 'homes', other than Weavers' Hall, had to be found for the Company's records, pictures and plate. Already, in 1948, the Court had agreed with the City Corporation to deposit the Weavers' records 'on loan' at the Guildhall Library,[17] where they have been expertly indexed and stored by professional librarians. Four of the five royal portraits presented a more difficult problem because of their great size. Ultimately, in 1962, arrangements were made for these portraits, suitably restored and framed, to be hung in the Library at Westminster Abbey;[18] while not far away the fifth and much smaller portrait, that of Queen Elizabeth I, now adorns the Clerk's office. Arrangements have recently been made for the safe-keeping of the Company's plate in the strong-room of the Company's Bankers, Messrs Glyn Mills & Co., whence it is taken out for use and display on special occasions.

In 1956 the Company sold a portion of the land at the rear of the almshouses, and the School of Our Lady of Lourdes was built thereon. In 1964, following a recommendation by the Almshouses Committee, the Court decided to enlarge the accommodation at Weavers' House[19] to house a greater number of old people, to apply to the

Charity Commissioners for a Scheme to widen the scope of the Charity (which, hitherto, had been limited to former members of the weaving industry), and to modernise and rearrange some thirty-one of the charitable funds into two main groups. The Charity Commissioners issued a Scheme in 1968 whereby nineteen of the charities were grouped in the Weavers' Almshouse Charities and twelve in the Weavers' Pension Charities. The Scheme also enlarged the scope of the Charity to admit inmates at the Company's discretion in the following categories:

(1) Poor Freemen, their wives or widows, and poor Freewomen;
(2) Sons over sixty years of age of poor Freemen, and daughters in reduced circumstances;
(3) Poor persons connected with the textile industry, either in the wholesale, retail or distributive branches;
(4) Poor Freemen and other poor of the City of London;
(5) Poor persons generally, at the discretion of the Trustees.[20]

The Scheme also authorised the Company, as Trustees of the Charity, to come into line with modern practice by charging residents contributions towards the cost of upkeep, recoverable largely by way of Supplementary Pensions from the Ministry of Social Security. The proposals also contemplate a substantial loan from the Local Authority (the London Borough of Redbridge), the balance of the cost of the rebuilding being found by the Company from its General Estate under Deeds of Covenant and additional loans made or guaranteed by the Company. It is anticipated that subsidies under the Housing Subsidies Act, 1967, over the next sixty years will provide for the repayment of the loans and create a fund for major repairs and ultimate rebuilding.

NOTES

1 MS. 4655/32, 13 June 1927, 3 February 1931; MS. 4655/33, 6 October 1931, 7 February 1933.
2 MS. 4655/33, 1 October 1933; 9 June, 13 October, 1 December 1936; 6 April 1937.
3 Court minutes, 27 May 1941.
4 MS. 4655/33, 11 October 1939.
5 Court minutes, 25 July 1941.
6 Ibid., 6 February 1945.
7 MS. 4655/33, 6 February 1940.
8 Court minutes, 3 October, 5 December 1944; 6 February 1945.
9 Court minutes, 4 February 1947.
10 Court minutes, 6 October 1953; 25 July, 8 October 1957.
11 See, e.g., minutes of a meeting of the Studentships Committee, 28 November 1967.

12 Court minutes, 4 December 1945; 3 February 1953.
13 *City Press*, 18 July 1930, p. 2.
14 Court minutes, 1 June 1948; 25 July, 7 October 1952.
15 Ibid., 8 October 1957; 3 June, 1958.
16 Ibid., 2 June, 3 October 1961.
17 Court minutes, 3 February, 6 April, 1948.
18 Ibid., 2 October 1962. Mr L. E. Tanner, besides being Clerk to the
    Company, had been for many years Keeper of the Muniments and
    Librarian at Westminster Abbey.
19 This name for the Company's Almshouses was adopted for postal
    purposes in April 1952.
20 Court minutes, 5 October 1965.

A. 'AN INVENTORY *of the Plate, Linen, Pewter, Implements of Household &c. in Weavers' Hall, London, belonging to that Company* TAKEN AND MADE IN OCTOBER 1677' (MS. 4646, Old Ledger Book, f.203)

	WT.				WT.		
PLATE	*Oz.*	*d.*	*gr.*	PLATE	*Oz.*	*d.*	*gr.*
One Basin contains	56	10	–	One Cup	8	4	–
One Ewer	37	–	–	One Cup	6	7	–
One Standing Bowl	38	17	–	One Cup	6	4	–
One Standing Bowl	39	5	–	One Cup	6	–	–
One Cover for those				One Cup	5	17	–
Bowls	13	–	–	One Cup	4	–	–
Another Cover for				One Cup	3	15	–
those Bowls	12	8	–	One Cup	3	14	–
One Salt	40	3	–	One Trencher Salt	4	14	2
One Salt	24	3	–	One Trencher Salt	2	8	–
One Salt	24	–	–	One Trencher Salt	2	7	–
One Salt	17	11	–	One Trencher Salt	2	7	–
One Tankard	22	–	–	One Trencher Salt	2	6	12
One Tankard	20	15	–	One Trencher Salt	2	6	12
One Bowl	18	9	–	One Trencher Salt	2	–	8
One Bowl	9	–	–	One Silver Gilt			
One Trencher Plate	14	11	–	Spoon	3	–	–
One Sugar Dish	5	5	–	Twenty-eight			
One Cup	10	12	–	Silver Spoons			
One Cup	9	–	–				

LINEN
(not recorded)

PEWTER

12	15 lb. Dishes		53	7 lb. Dishes
11	11 lb. Dishes		23	5 lb. Dishes

17	4 lb. Dishes	24	Pie Plates
(?)	Dozen and (blank)	18	Pewter Flagons
	Trencher Plates*	2	Monteiths†
1	Pewter Cistern	1	Chamber-pot &c.
12	Pastry Plates	2	Sweetmeat Frames

The Company's Common Seal with a small chain to it
One other Seal for sealing of Admissions
The Company's Barge Cloth
The Hearse Cloth‡
The Company's Leading Staff
The Company's Mace
One broad cloth Carpet
One Turkey work Carpet
Cushions
Seven Cloaks for Trumpeters ⎫
Three Coats for Drummers ⎭ §
Four old Coats for Footmen
The two Beadles' Gowns
Eight pieces of Tapestry Hangings in the Hall
One Watch and Case in the Parlour
The King's Arms in a frame
The Company's Arms in a frame
Queen Elizabeth's Picture
The Picture of King James
The Picture of King Charles I
The Picture of King Charles II
The Picture of James, Duke of York
Five Pictures of Benefactors
A Testament to swear freemen
The Poor's Box
A Bell & Hammer for the Court Table
One Musket, Bandoliers and two Swords
One Pike
Three Spanish Tables

BANNERS
One long and large Streamer ⎫
One King's Arms ⎪
One City Banner ⎪
One Ensign of the Company ⎬ for the Barge
One Company's Banner ⎪
Two large Pendants ⎪
Thirty small Pendants etc. Escutcheons ⎭
One Fife Banner

* Given as 22 dozen in the Inventory of 1684.
† A large bowl for cooling punch glasses.
‡ Embroidered.
§ Given by Mr Alexander Hosea.

CHARTERS

The Charter of Henry II
A Confirmation p. Hen. VI
A Confirmation of Edwd. IV
A Confirmation of Hen. VIII
A Confirmation of Phil. & Mary
A Confirmation of Qu. Eliz.
A Confirmation of K. James
Another for Mitigation of Fee farm rent
A Confirmation of K. Charles I

The Allowance of the Company's Arms under seal in two parts
The Ordinances confirmed by the Judges
The Same transcribed in a Book
An indenture wherein the Company conditions with Mrs Paradine to pay
   £6 p. ann. to the Poor of the Company
This Ledger Book of Accompts
A Statute Book
The Books of proceedings in Court
The Books of Admissions etc. Presentmts.
The Counterpt. of an Indenture Between the Feofees in Trust for the
   Compa. 12 January 1648
Eighteen pieces of Evidence touching the Company's Hall
A Deed of Gift to the Company of £500 by Mr John Ash with his Will
The Deeds of a House & land in Great Bursted, als. Billericay, Essex
The Deeds of a House & land at Shenfield in Essex
A Lease for the New River Water
The Charter of King James II
Mr Kinear's Gift
Lease of the Bargehouse
Eighteen white linen Waistcoats for the Watermen with Tin Eschutcheons
Two blue satin Coats for the Barge Mr and Steerman (with tin eschutcheons)
Three large Tables in the Hall
Nine Wainscot forms in the Hall
Nine Spanish Tables
Two Wainscot forms in the Parlour
Six joint Stools
One fire grate Shovel & Tongs
One little table with a draw
Six spits
One Boiling Pot
Two Iron Grates in the Garretts
One Iron bound Trunk
Two Chests in the Garret
One Chest wherein the Silver Plate lies
One Copper
A Map of the City
Eighteen Leather Chairs
Three leaden Cisterns

One small Chest
One velvet Chair
The Compa. Barge
Seven Pictures*
One Ladder
One Carved gilt Cupid
One large folio Bible†

B. *An annotated list of the thirty items of the Company's plate,*
alms box, officers' badges, etc., in chronological order

(September 1969)

During the Civil War the Weavers' Company, like many other corporations, sold its plate to raise funds. After 1657—and particularly after the Restoration in 1660—we can trace in the accounts the process of replacement by purchases and gifts. From time to time batches of the silver spoons customarily presented by newly fledged freemen were sold, the proceeds being used to buy cups, bowls, salts, etc. Thus in 1660–1 sixty-two spoons were sold for £23. 14s. 2d., which enabled the Company to buy a large silver bowl and a slightly heavier silver salt—in all 86¾ oz. Two years later the Company bought two silver salts and 'a great standing bowl, with two covers, one for that and the other for one as big'. These so-called standing bowls are the silver chalices or loving cups listed below. Among the plate presented to the Company was a silver bowl, weighing some 20 oz., which was a legacy left by Thomas Hall in 1657; a silver tankard bequeathed by Abraham Vanhack in 1662; a silver salt given in December 1663 by Mr William James, an active Liveryman who became Upper Bailiff in 1674–5; and a silver cup and trencher plate given by Samuel and Abraham, the two sons of Mr Arnold Beake (Upper Bailiff, 1660–1), when they both became freemen on the same day in 1667. Ten years later, as the Inventory taken in 1677 shows, the Weavers' stock of plate stood at thirty-one items (not including twenty-nine spoons), weighing in all some 475 oz.

The Company's
inventory no.

23   BEADLE'S BATON OR LEADING STAFF
Rosewood with silver-gilt mounts. The arms of England and of the Weavers' Company are chased on the ends. Sixteenth century. Listed in the Inventory of 1677.

7   TWO LARGE SILVER CHALICES OR LOVING CUPS
made in 1662 by 'R.F. and W.H.',
engraved with the arms of the Weavers' Company:
no other decoration.

*   Hanging in the Court Room, according to the inventory of 1685.
†   Embossed in brass; the gift of Mr John Drigue.

Appendix 1

*The Company's
inventory no.*

These appear in the Inventory of 1677 as
'One Standing Bowl,   38 oz. 17 d.
One Standing Bowl,   39 oz. 5 d.
One Cover for these Bowls,   13 oz.
Another Cover for these Bowls, 12 oz. 8 d.'
The two seventeenth-century covers were subsequently
lost or stolen and were replaced in 1847 by two early-
Victorian silver covers engraved with the Company's
arms and the words: 'The Covers to the Loving Cups
of the Worshipful Company of Weavers were presented
by Samuel Wilson, Esqr. Alderman of London and
Upper Bailiff of the Company for the Second Time, in
Commemoration of the Right Honourable Lord John
Russell, the First Lord of Her Majesty's Treasury,
having honored the Court with his company at dinner,
on the evening of Wednesday the 3rd of February
1847.'*

20   THE ALMS OR POOR'S BOX
Rosewood, cylindrical, with steel hasp and lock, and
two silver shields, one engraved with the arms of the
City of London and the other with the arms of the
Weavers' Company.
Carved on wooden top:
'Benjamin Ducane
George Heginbotham   } Bailiffs,   1666
Richard Bealy
Mathew Porter   } Wardens, 1666'
Made in December 1666 to replace the poor's box
destroyed in the Great Fire: cost, £2 for the box and
10s. for the two silver escutcheons.
Listed as 'The Poor's Box' in the Inventory of 1677.
Silver bands hall marked George IV, 1820, evidently
added to strengthen the rosewood sides.

13   A PAIR OF SILVER PORRINGERS
William III, 1696. Plain bodies, two handles, engraved
with arms of the Weavers' Company; weighing, together,
15 oz. Purchased c. 1920.

10   THE 'ROCHDALE' SILVER TANKARD WITH HINGED COVER
AND THUMBPIECE
William III, 1697. Weight, 24 oz.
Plain body engraved with contemporary coat of arms.
Inscription beneath the base:
'A Gift from George, Baron Rochdale of Rochdale,

* This date is wrong; the correct date is 13 January 1847. See *The Times,* 15 January 1847, p. 4.

429

*The Company's
inventory no.*

Upper Bailiff 1926–7, 1939–40, woollen weaver, to the
Worshipful Company of Weavers.'

4

THE 'HOLLINGWORTH' SILVER CUP, WITH HANDLES
Queen Anne, 1710. Weight, 17 oz. Made by H. Green.
Engraved with arms and crest of the Weavers' Com-
pany, also with crest of a previous owner—a serpent
curled around a tree trunk above two Maltese crosses.
Presented by Howard Hollingworth, Esq., Citizen and
Weaver, 31 March 1914.

24

SILVER INKSTAND
Base 11 in. × 6½ in., gadroon bordered, centre vase
decorated with four leopard head medallions; also a
separate pair of Georgian silver vases *c.* 1777, on
square bases with decorations and engravings similar
to centre vase, fitted with glass inkwells. Engraved with
arms of Weavers' Company and inscribed:
'George Hilditch, Upper Bailiff, 1894–5, 1889–90,
Upper Warden, 1883–4.'

16

A PAIR OF SILVER COFFEE POTS
(*a*) George IV, 1825.   Weight, 40 oz.
(*b*) William IV, 1836.   Weight, 43 oz.
Probably re-made from certain seventeenth-century
pieces melted down. (The Inventory of 1677 shows
two silver tankards weighing together 42 oz. 15 d.)
(*a*) is engraved with the Company's arms and inscribed:
'This plate presented to the Worshipful Company of
Weavers in the forms and by the persons hereon
recorded was made Anno Domini 1826.
Thomas James, Esquire   Upper Bailiff
Ambrose Moore, Esquire   Renter Bailiff.'
(*b*) is engraved with the Company's arms and inscribed:
'The Worshipful Company of Weavers.
John Josiah Buttress, Esqre. Upper Bailiff
Lea Wilson, Esqre.   Renter Bailiff.'

19

SILVER SALVER WITH FOUR FEET
Victoria, 1840. Weight 80 oz.
Chased with conventional floral design.
Engraved in centre the Weavers' arms and the words,
'William Robert Fox, 1867–1935, Silk Weaver.'
On back:
'Presented by Kenneth Charles Fox, Upper Bailiff,
1942–43' and the letter 'F'.

14

METAL GILT STANDING SALT AND COVER
Probably Victorian electro-plate. 16 in. high, gilt

The Company's
inventory no.

metal salt cellar and cover with lining; body heavily
chased and decorated with masks, flowers, fruit, etc.,
three pod feet.

18   THE 'ASKWITH' SILVER CASKET
Edward VII, 1901. Weight 103 oz.
$9\frac{1}{2}$ in. $\times$ 6 in. $\times$ $4\frac{3}{4}$ in., lined in blue velvet and
engraved with the arms of the City of London and the
Weavers' Company. Inscriptions:
(i) On top: 'Presented to Sir George R. Askwith, K.C.B.,
K.C. on his admission to the Freedom of the Worshipful
Company of Weavers. 23 October 1911.'
(ii) On end: 'This casket presented to Lord Askwith on
his admission to the Honorary Freedom of the Company
in 1911 in recognition of his Great Public Services in
settling Lockouts and Strikes by Arbitration.'

12   SILVER CIGAR BOX
Edward VII, 1909. Weight, 59 oz.
14 in. $\times$ $6\frac{1}{2}$ in., hand-wrought, cedar lined casket on
six cast feet, engraved with arms of the Weavers'
Company and inscribed:
'Presented by the Court of Assistants to Commemorate
the year of Office of the Right Hon. the Earl of Athlone,
G.C.B., G.C.V.O., C.M.G., D.S.O. as Upper Bailiff in
1919–20.'

5   THE 'CHUBB' SILVER CUP AND COVER
George V, 1910. Weight, 55 oz. Height, $14\frac{3}{4}$ in.,
with two handles and scroll band with festoon and
acanthus leaf decoration on body.
Cover fluted, with acanthus leaves. Presented to the
Company by Sir George Hayter Chubb, Bt., J.P.
(later Lord Hayter), Upper Bailiff, 1910–11.

6   THE 'INGLE' SILVER CUP AND COVER
George V, 1928. Weight, 46 oz.
Cup with two handles, plain body, hand-raised bead
and rope mount top and bottom, engraved with arms
of the Weavers' Company. Cover with ivory knob.
Presented by J. C. and W. B. Ingle in memory of
John B. Ingle, Esq., Upper Bailiff, 1885–6.

15   SILVER AND ENAMEL ROSEWATER DISH
George V, 1929. Weight, 13 oz.
Hand-raised with four raised embossed shields and hob-
nail mounted border, raised carved centre with
enamelled arms of the Weavers' Company surrounded
by rope mount. Given by members of the Court of

Assistants to commemorate the Company's Octocentenary in 1930, and first used by H.R.H. Edward,
Prince of Wales, K.G., when he dined with the Court
on 13 May 1930.

2 SILVER GILT MODEL OF A RAM
George V, 1929.   Weight, 575 oz.
On silver gilt base 17½ in. × 17½ in. × 1⅞ in., with two
enamelled coats of arms on ebonised base. Presented
to the Weavers' Company by the Rt. Hon. Lord
Illingworth of Denton, P.C. on the occasion of the
Company's Octocentenary in 1930.

3 THE 'HAYTER' SILVER GILT CUP
George V, 1931.   Weight, 15 oz.
Hand-raised shaped body, knob decorated with four
leopards' heads holding shuttles in mouths; plain stem,
chased stepped foot with arms of the Weavers' Company
and Lord Hayter. Inscriptions:
(i) On lip of cup: 'Given by the 1st Lord Hayter,
Upper Bailiff 1931–2.'
(ii) On base: 'The Upper Bailiff's Cup.'
Made by Omar Ramsden.

1 SILVER MACE
George V, 1934.   Weight approx. 59 oz.
Presented to the Company by William B. Ingle, Esq.
to commemorate his year of office as Upper Bailiff,
1933–4.

9 THE 'CHUBB' SILVER MAZER BOWL
George VI, 1937.   Weight, 50 oz.
Heavy hand-raised leaf and *fleur-de-lys* mount, centre
knob with arms of Weavers' Company. Presented by the
2nd Lord Hayter to mark his second term of office as
Upper Bailiff, 1936–7.
Made by Omar Ramsden.

11 A PAIR OF SILVER CANDELABRA
George VI, 1937.   Weight of the pair, 65 oz.
Height 15 in.
Three-light, plain branches, half-fluted holders
supported by two shields each bearing a leopard's head
and shuttle, plain round base, engraved with arms of
the Weavers' Company, and inscribed:
'Presented to the Worshipful Company of Weavers by
Sir Henry Birchenough, Bt., G.C.M.G., Upper Bailiff,
1934–5.'

*The Company's
inventory no.*

8   THE 'INGLE' SILVER BOWL
George VI, 1942. Weight, 54 oz.
A 12 in. silver bowl, plain body with arms of Weavers'
Company chased in bottom, and sunray fluting.
Inscription:
'Presented to the Company in Memory of the late
John Curzon Ingle, LL.D., sometime Solicitor to the
Company, by Mary, his wife, 1942.'
Made by C. J. Shiner.

17   THE 'BURMESTER' SILVER LOVING CUP AND COVER
Elizabeth II, 1962. Weight, 35 oz.
Cup engraved with arms of the Weavers' Company,
silver and ivory handles, slender stem. Cover with
ivory knob.
Presented by J. W. S. Burmester, sometime Surveyor
to the Company.
Made by Brian Marshall.

17A   THE 'SAVAGE' LOVING CUP AND COVER
Elizabeth II, 1962. Matches no. 17, the 'Burmester'
Loving Cup and Cover, but has no inscription.
Presented to the Weavers' Company by W. H. Savage,
Esq., Citizen and Weaver.
Made by Brian Marshall.

25   SILVER CIGARETTE BOX
Elizabeth II.
Presented to the Weavers' Company by the Hon.
G. C. H. Chubb in 1962 following his year of office as
Upper Bailiff, 1961–2.

21   THE GHENT BELL
A metal bell mounted on a wooden frame or plinth,
approx. 10 in. high.
Various inscriptions include:
'Myn naam is Roeland' and the dates 1314, 1651, and
1948.
? A model of a famous cathedral or city bell.
Presented to the Weavers' Company by the City
Corporation of Ghent, in London, on 5 October 1950.

26   THE UPPER BAILIFF'S BADGE
Presented to the Company by Frederic Ouvry, Upper
Bailiff, 1878–9 and 1879–80.

27   THE UPPER BAILIFF'S CHAIN
Presented to the Company in June 1965 by Col.
C. R. Wigan, M.C., T.D., Upper Bailiff, 1947–8 and
1955–6.

The Company's
inventory no.

28   THE RENTER BAILIFF'S BADGE
Central medallion presented by Nathaniel R. H.
Humphreys, Esq., in 1881, and the mounting to the
central medallion presented by J. W. B. Ingle, Esq.,
Upper Bailiff, 1960–1.

29   RENTER WARDEN'S BADGE
And UPPER WARDEN'S BADGE, both presented by the
Livery to mark the Company's Octocentenary in 1930.

30   THE CLERK'S BADGE

A. 'THE CONDITION OF THE SILK WEAVING TRADE'
(*written by 'A Weaver' in 1838 and sent to the Secretary of the*
Chartist Convention in 1839 (British Museum Add. MS.
34,245B., ff.3–16))

Of all trades the Weaving is one of the most useful and one of the most
Ingenous of our manufacturs, therefore the persons Employd in that
Branch of Trade ought to be sufficiently paid for their Labour, for two
reasons, the first because it is a unhealthy and sedentry employment,
secondly because every man that lives by his Labour ought to earn a
sufficiently weekley sum if he is a careful man to enable him to put bye
something so that he may not become a burden on his fellow man by
seeking Charity and thereby making himself a Slave by accepting Charity
in any form. Instead of that of all Trades the Weaver is the worst paid
for his Labour being obliged when he has work to Labour from 14 to 16
hours per day for the Miserable pittance of 7 or 9 shillings per Week, a
sum not sufficient to keep him in Existance and thus he his obliged to drag
on his miserable life pale and Emaciated Brought on by Excessive Labour
and want of food, many a Night after working 18 hours in the day have I
gone to bed with Excessive pain in my Chest that I could not Sleep the
remaining 6 hours of the twenty four, and althow I have left Weaving two
years I still have at times pains in my Chest and Back, through Working so
many hours, Because I never would Except of the various Charities. A
Weaver is not like many other artizans he must have room for his Loom
and Expences attacht to it which [in] many other trades the master finds,
then if a Weaver is such a useful Mechanic why should he be left to starve
in a Land of plenty, seeking Charity wherever he can find it and therby
Loosing his Independence as a man. What is the Cause that has [?brought]
the Weaving trade to this Miserable Condition, the Silk Trade being a
fancy trade was protected up to 1824 by an act of Parliament Prohibiting
foreign Silks into this Country and by another act Compelling Manufacturers to pay a certain price for Weaving agreed on between Master
and man, this act was in force for London onley. My opinion is it ought

to have been all over the Country, thus the 16,000 Weavers in London was Protected against the unprincipled Master who takes every advantage to undersell the fair Master by every petty way he can, but in 1825 the parliament not the peoples, for the Mass had nothing to dew with Parliament then and very little now, in that year the Parliament Brought in a Bill to repeal those laws and make what they calld free trade by Asisting the French weaver to the Starvation of the English Weaver. Now I am an advocate for free trade but not a partial one, when the trade was thrown open for Silks it ought in Common Justice to be thrown open in Corn &c., for how is it possible saddled has we are by heavy taxes and no voice in making those taxes we could compete with the foreigner who have not so many taxes and in whose Country the raw Silk can be got so much Cheaper, besides the man who is benefited by this Cheap Labour is the Man of Fixed Income, the non producer. Then came the power Looms. I am an advocate for Machinery but under the present system it is a Curse because it enriches the few at the Misery of the Many and Prevents other Manufact[urers] who have not large Capital from Employing hands but at a low rate to compete with the power Loom and the power Loom to Compete with the Foreign Market. Then comes the Great Slaughter Houses to compleate their Misery those Houses will send out their Agents to the little Manufacturers and buy up a great quantity of goods, perhaps all they have in their Warehouse at a Reduced price for the sake of ready Money almost at the price the silk and Labour cost him. Then he will to make up his loss Reduce his workman a halfpenny per yard. The Large Master, when he finds that out, Reduces his hands to sell with him and so the thing goes on. But if they was Compelld to pay a [Certain] price they could not then undersell each other to the misery of the men. In 1824 there was in London in Spitalfields and Bethnal Green about 600 Ribbon or Engine Looms a Going, now in 1838 there is about 100, the rest all gone to the Power Looms. A Mr. Newberry of London Wall had about 200 Looms at work in 1824, now in 1838 he has about 12, the rest of his work he has made in Exeter by the power Looms where he has a few boys at work at 3 shillings and 2 shillings per Week. Such has [been] the effect of power Looms upon hand Labour, which makes Mr. Newberry a rich man at the [?expense] of the many he Employed, and thus the Weavers Wages in town has bean Reduced from 60 to 70 per cent and the Masters in town who had not Capital like Mr. Newberry to buy Machinery Reduced there hands to compete with him and the Weaver has been obliged to take the work out to make at what price he could git or starve.

The only thing in my opinion that will benefit the Condition of the Weaver is a fair Representation in the Commons house of Parliament by Uneversial Sufferage &c., for I do not think out of 12,000 Weavers in London there are 20 got their Franchise. So that we might have cheaper Taxation, a Repele of the Corn Laws to compeate with the Foreigner, a Tax of 10 per cent on the power Looms or a Property Tax and a Bord of Trade [i.e. a trade board] to regulate the Prices of Weaving every 6 months which Board of Trade should be established in London, for if all the Masters paid alike for their Labour they would not undersell each other has they now dew to the Injury of the fair Master and the Misery of the Men. Some persons think that Emigration will benefit their condition but that is all Nonsence, for a Weaver that is bean brought up to the Loom all his Life Cannot and does not know how to Cultivate the Land, his frame is so wasted by over Labour and low Diet, many Handreds not knowing the taste of Meat once a week, that he has not strength for such work. The great evil is the Weaver works two many hours he produces two much, no Man ought to work more than 10 hours per day then he would have some time to instruct his mind and that of his family, there is many whole families in Bethnal Green and Spitalfield &c., that has not common Understanding for the want of Education. It is no wonder that some of them do not make the best use of their money what little they do git when they are so devoid of knowledge, wile others that is possest of knowledge cannot and will not make appearance among fellow men Because they are in that Degradid Condition they will not and are ashamed to mix in Society having not sufficient Clothing to appear [?among other] men, their Spirits are broken and many that are weak fly to Intoxicating Liquors to Stimulate them and drown their thoughts and Misery and all this is keep up to enable the great fund holder Capitalist and non producer to live in Luxury and Riches to the Misery of the Millions that produce it.

B. 'PRICES PAID FOR [NARROW SILK] WEAVING *in Bethnal Green and Spitalfields before the Introduction of French Silks and the Repeal of the Spitalfields Act*' (British Museum Add. MS. 34,245B., f.17)

Name of work	Prices paid in 1824: per length	Prices paid in 1839: per length	The quantity of work a man can make in a week	The number of hours he must work per day	Expenses that he has to pay out of his Earnings for Light & Wear & Tear of Machinery
	s. d.	*s. d.*			
Galloon in a 20-shuttle loom	15 0	7 6	a little more than a length	14–16	
4 Doubles; 20-shuttle loom	21 8	10 0	1 length	14–16	From 1*s.* 3*d.* to 1*s.* 6*d.* per week
6 doubles; 16-shuttle loom	24 0	11 8	1 length	14–16	

Some Masters is paying 10 per cent less than this.

The great depression in this Trade is chiefly owing to the Power Looms.

Price of Bread: 4 lb. loaf
1824   1839
7 pence   9 pence

A Weaver's house which in 1814 fetched 5s. per week, is now letting for 4s. 6d. and 4s.

C. 'PRICES PAID FOR BROAD SILK WEAVING *in 1824 & 1839*'
(British Museum Add. MS. 34,245B., f.18)

Name of work	1824 per yard	1839 per yard	How many yards a day, working from 14 to 16 hours per day	Expenses of a Weaver for Quilling, Candle, Wear & Tear of Machinery for one loom:
	s. d.	*s. d.*		
3 Singles	– 9	– 4½ and – 5	(omitted)	
4 Singles	– 10	– 6	3½ to 4	
3 Doubles	– 11	– 9	3	1s. 6d. per week
4 Doubles	1 2	2 3 & 2 6	2½ to 3	
Ladies' Velvets	4 0		¾ to 1	
Collar Velvets	5 0	3 3	¾	

The Slaughter Houses such as Morrison's, Leaf & Co., &c., are a great Curse to the Trade, they buy of the Little Masters for ready money and they cut down to sell to them. As for the Tyranny of the Masters I must refer you to C. Cole* or my friend Saml. Sully, 72 Seabright St, Beth. Green and he will give you every information on that Business.

---

* Charles Cole of Church Street, Bethnal Green, was one of the original members of the London Working Men's Association (Add. MS. 37,773, f.7) in July 1836, and was secretary of the journeymen weavers' committee which gave evidence to the Asst. Commissioners on Hand-loom Weavers in 1838–9. Probably the 'Weaver' who wrote the above was Richard Cray (of Twivile Street, Bethnal Green). He also was a member of the Working Men's Association (1836), and was chosen by the Association, with Charles Cole and James Watson, to investigate the state of the weavers in Spitalfields.

D. 'POLITICAL OPINIONS OF THE WEAVERS'
(same writer, 'A Weaver')
(British Museum Add. MS. 34,245B., ff.15–20)

The Weavers at the time they was well paid for their Labour was a Loyal set of men and made Politics very little of their study and there [are still a] few now that clings to the Higher orders with the view of Encouraging their Trade but the great Majority of them Laugh at this Idea for they know that the Tory Party with the W(h)igs first ruiened the Trade in 1824 by Opening the Foreign Markets for the Introduction of the French Silks. The great Majority of the Weavers now is from Loyal Subjects [? converted] to Radicals nay I may say Democrats, their extreme misery has done some good, it has taught them to think, Particular the Young Branch of the Trade for they are more Enlightened and many of the Old ones has Different opinions now to what they had when they was in Prosperity. They have not been used to Politics being more used to fancy such as Birds, Dogs and Skittle Playing but that is fast dying away, a great many are fanciers in Flowers, In my opinion their wants some good Missionaries among them to teach them Politics, a great number of them have signed the National Petition and subscribed towards the Rent out of a Meeting that I got up one Evening consisting of about 50 persons, they subscribed 10s. 0d. which considering the wretched condition they are in is not so bad, but such a man as Vincent their would dew good to keep up a good Agitation, the few good Men their of any Talent cannot afford time to git up and attend Meetings being so bad paid for their Labour.

'ON SOCIETYS' *(same author and source)*

There is very few Societys among the Weavers Excepting Benefit and Burial Clubs, there is a Trade Union consisting of four or five lodges but I believe they are but thinley attended owing to the apathy of a few and the want of funds of the many not being able to pay the Subscription of $1\frac{1}{2}(d.)$ per week for Unfortunately the Lodges is held at Public Houses and if a Man goes there he is Compeld of Course to support the House by having the Accomodation of the Room and this he cannot dew and pay his Subscription too, out of his miserable wages Except those that are making the best work. There is a Mechanics Institution in Hackney Road, the amount of the Subscription is one Pound per annum, or 5s. quarterly, and this is much too high for the Weavers, consequientley it is I believe support mostley by Clerks &c., who are done business soon in the Evenings, and at this Institution I hear that Political affairs is not allowed to be Discussed. There is no Book Societys that I am aware of in Existence. Myself and a few more Establish(ed) one and wee carryed it on for two years by great Exertion and got several Books but at last it *fell*, owing I believe to men not likeing to come out to meet their fellow men for the want of sufficient means and Clothing and for the want of a private Place to meet instead of a Public House. A great many of the Weavers are bad

Scholars particular many of the Old ones many of them cannot Read or Write, but the younger Branch of Society I think are better men both in Education and Political Knowledge and I am certain that knowledge is fast progressing among them, particular Political, for I am always among them and when ever I speak or address them on Politics they pay great attention and seam to have a wish to learn if their was a Public Place or Building where they could meet without drayning their little funds to pay for it, it whould be the means of doing a great deal of good for there is many that will not come out from the time they begin their work in the Loom till they finish it, they are so depress and their work generally last five or six weeks and during that time they seldom stir outside the door for the reason above stated, viz., the want of Sufficient Clothing particularly those that have seen Better Days (ff.15–16).

The condition of the hand-loom weavers
(*1840 Report*: *Appendix, Report of Commissioner W. E. Hickson*)

William Bresson, 2, Daniel-street, Orange-street, Spitalfields;
Examined by Mr Hickson, July 14 1838.

I am a velvet-weaver and loom-broker; have been all my life in the weaving trade; and am now 52 years of age. I am the great grandson of Raymond Bresson, one of the French protestants who took refuge in England after the revocation of the edict of Nantes, and established the silk trade in Spitalfields. I have now by me his bill of naturalization, which he was obliged to take out when he came to this country: it is dated 1710, and is decorated with the portrait of Queen Anne. From that time to the present our family have remained in the same place; we have never visited the land of our forefathers, but the French language is not quite extinct among us; I speak it imperfectly, but some have a much better knowledge of it than myself. By intermarriages, however, the distinctive character of the French weaver is now lost; but the number of French names in Spitalfields shows how large a portion of them are of French extraction. In consequence of their distress when they first came over, from the persecution they had endured, many of them were in part supported for a length of time at the expense of Government. The fund set apart for the purpose was called 'La Munificence Royal'. There are some who still receive pensions from this fund, but the pensions will expire with their lives, and no new cases are relieved.

What is the nature of your trade as a loom-broker?—I purchase looms, and let them out to weavers who cannot afford to buy one, or to those who want an extra loom, and who might afford to buy one, but who would not think it worth while, for the sake of an additional job which might not last, to purchase a new loom when one hired would answer the purpose. I charge from $3\frac{1}{2}d$. to $4d$. per week, and the value of the loom is about 20s. I should do very well, as I have about 200 looms out, if I could get my money; but the fact is, I lose half of it. I am obliged, of course, to take security, but the neighbourhood is so poor that security and all are often good for nothing. When, however, the trade prospers, I prosper; when it is depressed, I suffer. My cash-book is, therefore, a pretty good thermometer of the state of trade for the last 17 years; for trading always upon about the same capital, and being quite certain to let my looms when there is work to be had, the money I receive each year will show whether the trade generally was in a good or bad state.

Here the witness put in the following extract from his cash-book, showing his receipts each year during the last 17 years:—

	£	s.	d.		£	s.	d.
1822	60	4	7½	1831	41	8	3
1823	52	4	7½	1832	35	15	9
1824	75	14	11	1833	49	14	4
1825	101	9	9	1834	44	4	−½
1826	42	8	5	1835	52	14	–
1827	78	9	11	1836	50	3	2½
1828	67	9	4	1837	26	6	1
1829	28	10	1	1838	9	18	6 (6 months only)
1830	29	3	1				

This statement proves that the trade has always been liable to great fluctuations.

The weaver would do pretty well if he could depend upon full employment throughout the year, one year with another, and especially upon the best fabrics; but the trade has always been uncertain and precarious. Every five or six years there comes a period of stagnation, which often lasts for two years before trade is brisk again. The last winter was one of the worst we have known. The weather was unusually severe; and the trade almost destroyed, owing to the panic which affected the American houses. The holders of silk could not sell at any price, and the manufacturers therefore completely stopped. I and my family were always able to get work, but thousands could not; and, owing to the inclemency of the season, they suffered much. At the present moment there are still many looms idle, though the greater part are employed.

Do you ever remember a similar period of stagnation in former times?—About 30 years ago, I remember the weavers in a similar state. This was when, through the Berlin decrees, we were unable to procure raw silk from Italy. Silk was then sold at 5s. per ounce; and the cost of the manufactured article was so great, in consequence, that only the richer classes could afford it, and the demand was greatly limited. This lasted till one of our silk-throwsters tried what could be done with the India silk, and, finding that it could be made to answer very well, we became independent of the supply from Italy.

What sum of money is a silk-weaver able to earn weekly at the loom?—It is difficult to speak with any accuracy upon this point. To determine the earnings of a weaver, it is necessary to ascertain what is his skill, and whether he is quick or slow at his work. Fancy fabrics and fine velvets require a great amount of skill; and there are some weavers (though not many), working upon these, who can make £100 per annum, with one loom; but then there are a multitude of others, working upon plain goods, who do not make above £25 in a year; and there are some poor creatures who do not make above £20. This arises, not altogether from differences of price paid for different kinds of work, but from some being quicker work-men than others, and also more steady, perhaps at their work. I have a son, 18 years of age, who is remarkably quick; he will earn 25*s.* per week on plain satins, paid for at the rate of from 5*d.* to 7*d.* per yard, when it will commonly take two men, employed at two different looms, to earn this sum at the same kind of work. Again, I have known a man earn 30*s.* in a week upon satins at 8*d.* per yard, but this was a remarkable case.

Are there many families in Spitalfields unable to earn more than £20 in the year at weaving?—When we speak of families, we must remember that in a family, when the trade is in a good state, there is invariably more than one loom employed. One man at a loom earns, perhaps, but 10*s.* in a week, but when able to enploy the labour of his wife, children, or apprentices, perhaps three looms, and often four, are kept going, so that I cannot say. I know many families who, when in full work, earn, or might earn, *20s.* per week. My son-in-law, for instance, lives with me in the house, and earns about 18*s.* This would be a poor sum for his family to live upon; but then his wife, my daughter, is very quick at the loom, and earns as much, or rather more, than he does himself. They have at present but one child. One of my neighbours, who has finer work than myself, and a large family, keeps six looms employed among them, and can earn with their assistance, £5 per week; but, being a man of dissipated habits, he does not save money.

Are the earnings of weavers now less than they were formerly: during the war, for instance?—Certainly: though I must say I never expected the war prices to be kept up; and, as every thing else has fallen, the difference practically is not so great as some of my friends will have it. There never was a time in my recollection when some in the weaving trade would not earn very large sums, and others again next to nothing. The decline in wages has chiefly been in the article of fancy-figured fabrics; and this was occasioned by the invention of the Jacquard machine in France. Before the Jacquard machine was introduced in Spitalfields there were weavers among us able to earn (under peculiar circumstances) a guinea a day. The work, however, was not so steady as that of fine velvets; and a great deal of time was lost in waiting for fresh patterns, &c. Now, in fine velvets—that is to say, the velvets called Geneva velvets, Dutch velvets, and Dutch bastard velvets—there has been no decline of wages; the price paid per yard is about 6*s.*, and I have known some weavers quick at their work make six yards per week. The reason fine velvets have kept up is, that the work requires a degree of skill which not one weaver in a hundred attains. A common weaver, in cutting the thread next the cane wire, would cut right through the cane, and spoil the whole piece. Ladies velvets, upon which I work, are not so well paid, and have fallen in price since the war; but they do not require so great a degree of care. Plain goods have fallen, most especially the article of gros-de-Naples, which used to be the staple commodity, or what familiarly we used to call the bread-and-cheese of Spitalfields. The price paid for weaving a yard of gros-de-Naples has fallen from 8*d*. to 5*d*. I account for this partly by the circumstances that gros-de-Naples has been to a certain extent superseded by other fabrics, what we term *struck-up-satin*, for instance. We now scarcely know what to call the staple of Spitalfields, there are so many varieties of fabrics. If the majority were employed upon gros-de-Naples, they would be very ill paid; but I do not think the majority are employed upon this fabric. It must be borne in mind that our earnings are not so great as they would at first appear, owing to various little expenses connected with the loom, and the loss of time arising from attending shop. It is necessary to make continued applications to the warehouse for shoot,* &c., while the work is going on; and, when it is done, measuring and examining the work, where a great number of hands are employed, causes great delay. I attend shop for the whole of the five looms employed in my family, and lose in this way, going backwards and forwards, at least two whole days in every week.

Did you never contemplate bringing up your son and daughter to some other branch of industry?—Yes, on account of the fluctuations to which the trade has always been liable. This led me to take great pains with their education; and thinking a little musical talent might be turned to account, I had my son taught to play the violin when a child, and my daughter the piano. As they grew up, however, I never could discover any means of bettering their condition by getting them into other trades. In fact, although we are not so well off as we could wish, there are few trades in which a woman is able to earn as much as my daughter gets by working at the loom; though I must say it is a sort of slavery for a woman which I have never liked to see. And as to my son, I do not think from what he sees of the condition of the journeymen shoemakers and tailors, that he would be disposed to change with them if he could. Carpenters get better paid; but then their trade appears to me more precarious than that of hand-loom weaving.

Do the weavers ever combine to raise their wages by means of a trades' union?—There is no trades' union among us at present, but there was formerly. At present the only unions that exist are the shop-meetings, and these are rather encouraged by the masters than otherwise, as they do not interfere with wages. They arise in this way:—the weavers, being poor, are obliged to apply for part of their money on account, before they bring the whole piece home. Sometimes it will happen that a weaver, having been paid for nearly the whole of his piece, sells it and runs away. To prevent being defrauded in this manner, the master now requires the joint security of the whole shop; and the men, therefore, subscribe 6*d*. or 1*s*. each, occasionally, to raise a fund for the purpose. In return, the shop-meetings usually require that the master shall not employ a man upon whose integrity they cannot depend; and make also various other regulations. A manufacturer is, however, generally content to trust his property, without security, in the hands of a weaver who does not draw on account, but waits for his money till his work is finished. I have no occasion to draw on account, and am not, therefore, required to subscribe to the fund.

In my father's time combinations existed to raise wages, and were then very formidable. Men were employed called *cutters*, who went about openly

* i.e., weft yarns.

in large parties destroying, by cutting, the property of the master in the loom. When meeting at a public-house, they would station a sentinel at the door, armed with sword and pistol. These men were very determined and desperate in what they undertook. Many of them had been sailors; and the sentinel did not hesitate, in one instance, to shoot a soldier belonging to a serjeant's guard sent to apprehend the party. This ended in several of the cutters being taken up and executed and in the Spitalfields Act being passed, which it was hoped would put an end to the differences which had existed between masters and men. When the Spitalfields Act was repealed, an attempt was made to revive the old system of cutting, in order to compel the masters to give the book-prices. I know one man who had work in the loom destroyed to the value of £30. A great deal of property was destroyed, but the cutters went about it so secretly that they were never detected. The alarm was so great, that I purposely kept myself *idle* a month or six weeks, lest I should not be able to protect the work, and lest I should be supposed to be implicated in any injury it might suffer while in my hands.

This system was suddenly abandoned, and the *sealing* system adopted. A party went round, inserted a piece of paper in the warp of every loom, and sealed it. When a loom was sealed in this manner, it was understood to be at the peril of the weaver if he broke the seal to resume his work. The trade was put under a spell by this means, and whole families were reduced to starvation. At last the masters made a feint of giving way. They agreed to give the book-prices, with the understanding, at which many of us connived, that they should be reduced to their former level in a week or so. We celebrated this as a great victory, which most of us knew in our hearts to be a great delusion. The book-prices only lasted five weeks. Since then there was an attempt made to form a secret society, and I was asked to belong to it, but refused. I believe now there is no combination or trades' union among us. The shop-meetings used to send deputies to a conference (which was a kind of trades' parliament), but have ceased to do so. The secretary was paid 35*s*. per week, and ran away with about £20 of their money; and the number of persons unemployed have always defeated every attempt to get wages raised by such means. It was impossible to prevent wages falling, when so many persons were coming into the silk trade, whose labour had been superseded at cotton and linen weaving by the power-loom. There are many Irish weavers in Spitalfields, and although the wages of the weaver are higher in their own country, as I have understood, through their trades' unions, yet they come and work among us at a lower rate than they are willing to do at home, and thus injure both themselves and us.

What is the state of education among the weavers of Spitalfields?—We have never wanted for men of superior intellectual qualifications, who have had the advantages of education, when it was thought desirable to go up to Ministers, or give evidence before a Committee of the House of Commons; but, as a body, I cannot say that the Spitalfields weavers are an educated class. Perhaps the majority are not able to read and write; certainly this is the case with a very large portion of them. One of the best things the Government could do for us would be to establish schools in the district; there are now very few. Good evening schools I think very desirable. In the day-time the children are generally employed at home in winding quills, or in picking the work in the loom; but they might attend evening schools, if such were provided. I think, also, assistance might be given in establishing reading-rooms and mechanics' institutions among us, and the effect would be very beneficial. Books and newspapers are now almost inaccessible to a weaver; the new law, which accompanied the reduction of the stamp-duty in newspapers, put down the un-stamped papers which were read in Spitalfields, without substituting stamped papers sufficiently cheap in their place; I think, therefore, there is now less reading than formerly. To buy a sixpenny paper, five or six persons usually subscribe together, and the news is stale before the last subscriber gets it. I belong to a mutual instruction society, connected with the chapel in Spicer-street, and we have a reading-room; but I know of no other instance of the kind. The weavers, as a body, do not appreciate the advantages of education for their children.

Is the moral state of the hand-loom weavers in your neighbourhood equal, or inferior, in your opinion to that of other classes?—I do not think the moral state of the hand-loom weavers is lower than that of many other classes of journeymen, although it is not what could be wished. I would rather take the personal security of a weaver for the hire of a loom, than of a journeyman tailor or shoemaker; indeed, I have so often lost my money through trusting tailors and shoemakers, that I have come to the resolution never to take their security again. I cannot depend upon a journeyman tailor or shoemaker remaining long in the same place; and although he sometimes puts on a very smart appearance, yet, if you visit his home, it is astonishing how seldom you find him possessed of the most necessary articles of furniture, so that a broker would find nothing in his room to seize for rent. The weaving trade is, on the whole, more favourable to morality than many other trades, because the children are brought up at home under the eye of the parent. They have not, therefore, the same opportunities of intercourse with idle and dissolute companions, which printers have, for example, and all who work together in a common workshop; but the number of spirit-shops in Spitalfields shows that we have nothing to boast of in this respect. There are three large spirit-houses close together, at the corner of Church-street, which I have known supported out of the wages of weavers for the last 20 years. Beer-shops are not so great an evil; I know some very respectably conducted; and it seems to me much better to encourage the sale of beer than that of gin. Distress among the weavers is always felt first among those given to intemperance and the most improvident. The steady, sober workman, upon whom the master can most rely, and with whom his property is the most secure, is always the last person out of work, even in bad times.

Have the weavers any means of rational amusement or pleasurable relaxation?—They used to be very much given to gardening, and were great tulip-fanciers; but one of our greatest grievances is that most of the open spaces formerly let out in gardens are now built over, and there are no public walks or places for out-door exercises, as at the west-end of the town, where those who have private parks of their own have the benefit of the public parks. This is one reason why the weavers are generally such a short, stunted race; there are few athletic men among them. During the war there was a brigade raised among the weavers, most of whom were not above five feet two inches. A few open spaces, however, are still left. My house is in one, containing about three acres, all let out in strips of gardens, each only 90 feet by 20. They are at the present moment filled with flowers cultivated to great perfection. Spitalfields was once very famous for tulip-beds. A tradesman, named Bartlet, a butcher, had a bed of tulips valued at £2,000; and not long since I knew an operative weaver who was able by the proceeds of his tulip-bed to set up a beer shop, which could not have cost him less than £40.

What is the sanatory state of the district?—We have suffered greatly from fever during the last winter, and this arises in a great measure from dirt and filth of some of the close neighbourhoods, inhabited chiefly by Irish weavers, and from the want of a proper drainage in other parts. There ought to be regulations for causing every house to be frequently lime-washed, and every court and alley to be cleansed of its accumulations of rotten vegetables and dirt; the sewers, also, ought to be better attended to. I know a gentleman who built 120 houses without either cess-pools or sewers; some time after they were added, but still there are hundreds without cess-pools or sewers. After a heavy rain, some of the streets are for a length of time impassable. It is impossible for a neighbourhood to be free from fever where so much noxious effluvia is generated as in Spitalfields.

What remedies appear to you desirable to be adopted for the relief of the Spitalfields weavers?—I cannot help thinking a repeal of the Corn Law would be one of the most efficient, though I am aware this is not the opinion of many among us; they think wages would be reduced in proportion to the price of bread; but I cannot see that, for it appears to me that it would improve trade; and if it improve trade, wages would have a tendency to rise. It would also be a great blessing to a Spitalfields weaver if something could be done to supply him with coals at a cheap rate in the winter. During the severe frost of last winter the suffering was very great. Coals were only to be obtained at 20*d.* per bushel, and there were hundreds of families obliged to make one bushel last for the firing of a whole week. Had it not been for some charitable societies, by whom coals were distributed, many poor creatures must have perished, and perhaps many did, though the public might not be aware that the want of fuel accelerated their death. As to the Spitalfields Act, I do not expect to see it made again the law; but perhaps some law could be framed by which masters and men might be enabled to make regulations for their mutual benefit.

(signed)   William Bresson.

N.B.—William Bresson, the above witness, lives in a small house containing but three very small rooms, and a fourth barely large enough to contain six looms, by which it is completely choked up. For this house, which could be built from ground for £80, the two families occupying it pay the disproportionate rent of £16, and £2. 5*s.* additional for the small strip of flower-garden in front. There is no cess-pool nor sewer to carry off the soil from the privy; and close to the house runs a stagnant ditch filled with abominable black filth, for which there is no drain, and the stench from which is often insupportable. The neighbourhood is, of course, seldom free from fever; and I was informed that a whole family were lying dead, through fever, in a street in the vicinity at the time of my visit.

Appendix 4

Charities administered by the Weavers' Company (1969)

*Approximate
value of fund*
.£60,000

General Charitable Trust Fund

Weavers' Almshouse Charities, comprising the following:
1 The Charity known as the Weavers' Almshouses
   otherwise known as Weavers' House, Wanstead
2 The Charity known as the Almshouses Building and
   Subscription Fund
3 The Charity of Obadiah Agace
4 The Charity of Henry Baker
5 The Charity of William Ballance
6 The Charity of Benjamin Carpenter
7 The Charity of Thomas Cook
8 The Charity of Mary Wotton Copp
9 The Charity of John Drigue
10 The Charity of Nicholas Garrett
11 The Charity of Robert Graham
12 The Charity of James Bracebridge Hilditch
13 The Charity of James Kymier
14 The Charity of Samuel Mills
15 The Charity of Richard Mulford
16 The Charity of Thomas Platt
17 The Charity of William Satchwell
18 The Charity of Samuel Saunders
19 The Charity known as Vanner's Gift   (Items 2–19)   £20,000
Note: The Almshouses Rebuilding Fund (increasing at the
   rate of £7,000 per annum under a Covenant by the
   Company) stood at over £37,000 on 31 December 1969

Weavers' Pension Charities, comprising the following
20 The Charity of Charles Albert Bannister
21 The Charity of Emily Dowling

449

22 The Charity known as the General Benevolent Fund
23 The Charity of Thomas Lampard Green
24 The Charity of John Hall
25 The Charity of Alexander Hosea
26 The Charity called Lady Morrison's Gift
27 The Charity of Rowland and John Morton
28 The Charity of William Prater
29 The Charity of Samuel Ridley
30 The Charity of Kathleen Warde Tanner
31 The Charity known as Samuel Wilson's Pensions
    Charity   (Items 20–31) £18,000
    Freehold Property 3 Johnsons Court, E.C.1

Fox Memorial Trust   £300

The Charity of James Limborough   £1,500

Colonel Wilson's Trust Fund   £1,000

Richard Gervies's Gift   £60

*A list of Upper Bailiffs of the Weavers' Company
from 1600 to 1970*

*Year of
office
beginning
in*

1600	Peter Reynolds
1601	Roland Colston
1602	Ambrose Smyth
1603	Elize Parrye
1604	William Wiliecott
1605	Thomas Smyth
1606	Blaze Gratewoode
1607	John Cooke
1608	John Dutton
1609	Richard Woodhouse
1610	John Rowdon
1611	George Andrewes
1612	John Rowth
1613	Hercules Taylor
1614	John Cane
1615	Robert Watkinson
1616	John Rowdon
1617	George Brice
1618	John Rainshall
1619	Charles Alman
1620	William Stevens
1621	John Rowdon, jnr.
1622	Batholomew Sowthey
1623	Robert Cryst

*Year of
office
beginning
in*

1624	Robert Hembrye
1625	John Wilson
1626	Uncertain: probably Abraham Rowe
1627	John Hawkins (Alderman 1626)
1628	Abraham Baker
1629	John Lamott (Alderman 1648)
1630	Gabriel Stone
1631	Nicholas Elliott
1632	Ezechiell Reeve
1633	Francis Foster
1634	John March
1635	Nicholas Fawcett
1636	Robert Hanch*
1637	Robert Hanch re-elected
1638	Alexander Colston
1639	Peter Barker
1640	Samuel Rivers
1641	Walter Stavers
1642	Rowland Morton
1643	Robert Arden

* Sometimes spelt Haunch(e), elected to the Livery 22 October 1616.

Year of
office
beginning
in

1644 Richard Worsamand
1645 John Sherman
1646 Gratian Allen
1647 George Davis
1648 To 19 Feb. 1649
     Thomas Jackson
1649 To 31 Mar. 1650
     William Jackson*
1650 To 7 Apr. 1651
     John Hewett
1651 Thomas Mabberley
1652 Thomas Mabberley
     re-elected
1653 William Cade
1654 Richard Richardson
1655 Richard Daniell
1656 William Bolnest
1657 Thomas Westwood
1658 Robert Fleming
1659 Edmond Bearstow
1660 Arnold Beake
1661 Richard Hill
1662 John Adams
1663 John Adams
     re-elected
1664 Daniel Fairvacks
1665 William Marriott
1666 Benjamin Ducane
1667 Benjamin Ducane
     re-elected
1668 Paul Dobie
1669 Abraham Broadway
1670 Jonathan Reeve
1671 George Heginbothom
1672 Richard Bailey
1673 Mathew Porter
1674 William James
1675 Alexander Hosea
1676 John Upcher
1677 John Slater
1678 James Pitman
1679 John Shewell
1680 John Burton

Year of
office
beginning
in

1681 William Shaw
1682 John du Bois
1683 Hercules Beaufoy
1684 Josiah Ricraft
1685 Joshua Sabin
1686 Joshua Sabin
     re-elected
1687 John Merry
1688 Henry Soames
1689 John Drigue
1690 Thomas Coles
1691 Richard Awbrey
1692 William Johnson
1693 William Harding
1694 Nathan Sully
1695 John Satchwell
1696 Richard Lavington
1697 John Adams
1698 Thomas Parry
1699 Joseph Webster
1700 William Norris
1701 Richard Carrington
1702 Thomas Wilkes
1703 Thomas Smythe
1704 Thomas Reynolds
1705 Ralph Titford
1706 Henry Soames
1707 (1) William Edmunds
         elected, 25 July 1707
     (2) Ralph Titford *appointed*
         U.B. under the New
         Charter (Queen Anne)
         on 17 November 1707:
         William Edmunds then,
         under the Charter,
         became Renter Warden.
         He was re-elected
         Upper Bailiff in 1709
1708 Richard Blowing
1709 William Edmunds
1710 Edward Richier
1711 Thomas Deacon
1712 William Hornblower

* Apparently forced upon the Company: the accounts for this year were 'cooked' (MS. 4646, f.86b).

Appendix 5

Year of
office
beginning
in

1713	Benjamin Graves
1714	Gilbert Mace
1715	Humphrey Burroughs
1716	Jonathan Forward
1717	Samuel Malton
1718	John Tredwell
1719	John Dent
1720	Thomas Eades
1721	Thomas Pearce
1722	Thomas Fitzhugh
1723	Cornelius Dutch
1724	William Daintry
1725	Humphrey Hill
1726	William Dawson
1727	Gabriel Bestman
1728	John Johnson
1729	Thomas Excelbee
1730	Benjamin Burroughs
1731	Joseph Willet
1732	Gamaliel Maud
1733	Edward Whitehouse
1734	Joseph Harris
1735	Peter Lekeux
1736	William Terret
1737	Benjamin Champion
1738	William Phillips
1739	Sir William Baker
	(Alderman,
	Bassishaw Ward, 1739–70)
1740	Henry Thompson
1741	Thomas Bray
1742	Captain John Baker
1743	John Willett
1744	Joseph Humble
1745	William Reynolds
1746	James Godin
1747	Daniel Booth
1748	John Cooper
1749	John Turner
1750	William Marsh
1751	Henry Baker
1752	Samuel Nicholson
1753	James Johnson
1754	Samuel Jordan
1755	John Gibson

Year of
office
beginning
in

1756	Abraham Deheulle
1757	Daniel Cabanell
1758	James Gibson
1759	Abraham Jeudwine
1760	Peter Ogier
1761	Walter Locke
1762	Peter Campart
1763	Thomas Abraham Ogier
1764	Peter Lekeux
1765	John Hinde
1766	William Dolman
1767	Zachariah Agace
1768	Joshua Pickersgill
1769	James Walker
1770	John Kirkman
	(Alderman 1768–80)
1771	Joshua Warne
1772	John Garsed
1773	Peter Arnaud
1774	James Turner
1775	Charles Triquet
1776	Alexander Champion
1777	Daniel West
1778	Obadiah Agace
1779	Jacob Agace
1780	Benjamin Mills
1781	Daingerfield Taylor
1782	Charles Brown
1783	Peter Alavoine
1784	William Poole
1785	John Howard
1786	William Bartlett
1787	James Cranch
1788	James Brooke
1789	John Dangerfield
1790	Thomas Towle
1791	Richard Lea
1792	James Maze
1793	James Walker
1794	Aubrey Joseph Lum
1795	Richard Packer
1796	Henry Stokes
1797	Thomas Platt
1798	William Sharpe
1799	Abraham Thorn

Year of office beginning in		Year of office beginning in	
1800	James Grugeon	1842	Thomas James
1801	John Wesley	1843	Samuel Ridley
1802	William Wilson	1844	Ambrose Moore
1803	James Hammond	1845	John Remington Mills
1804	Samuel Mills	1846	Samuel Wilson
1805	John Jourdan		(Alderman)
1806	Joshua Jones	1847	Ambrose Moore
1807	John Hammond	1848	Ambrose Moore
1808	Abraham Favenc		re-elected
1809	Joseph Tayler	1849	William Lynes
1810	Charles James Coverley	1850	Thomas Winkworth
1811	Stephen Wilson	1851	George Taurke Kemp
1812	Thomas Jackson	1852	John Bradbury
1813	William Lane	1853	Edward Wilson
1814	Robert Lum	1854	Robert Gamman
1815	Peter Alavoine	1855	John Guillemard
1816	John Perrell	1856	Robert Graham
1817	Thomas Towle	1857	Cornelius Lea Wilson
1818	Oliver Hatch	1858	Stephen Lewis
1819	Samuel Mills	1859	Benjamin Risden Thomson
1820	Joseph Wilson	1860	William Ballance
1821	Charles James Coverley	1861	John Vanner
1822	William Smart	1862	Colonel Samuel Wilson
1823	William Hale		(Alderman)
1824	David Nevill	1863	Colonel Samuel Wilson
1825	Thomas James		re-elected
1826	Ambrose Moore	1864	William Frederick Graham
1827	John Ham	1865	Patrick Comrie Leckie
1828	Joseph Wilson	1866	Samuel William Ridley
1829	Stephen Wilson	1867	Henry Henderson
1830	George Stokes	1868	John Vanner
1831	John Remington Mills	1869	William Nevill
1832	Samuel Wilson	1870	Herbert Sturmy
	(Alderman 1831–71)*	1871	Nathaniel James Powell
1833	Joseph Grout	1872	Edward Fox
1834	John Smart		Died in office April 1873.
1835	William Stone		Cornelius Lea Wilson elected
1836	John Josiah Buttress		to serve from 13 May to
1837	Lea Wilson		25 July 1873
1838	Folliot Scott Stokes	1873	Thomas James Nelson
1839	Joseph Carter	1874	Charles W. C. Hutton
1840	John Ballance	1875	William Whitley
1841	Charles Pritchett Bousfield	1876	John Alexander Radcliffe

* Sheriff 1833–4; Lord Mayor 1838–9.

1877 James Howell
  Died before he could take
  office. John Alexander
  Radcliffe was asked to
  continue in office during
  1877–8
1878 Frederic Ouvry
1879 Frederic Ouvry
  re-elected
1880 Thomas Owthwaite Hutton
1881 Nathaniel Robert Henry
  Humphrys
1882 James Engelbert Vanner
1883 Henry Ellis
1884 Cornelius Lea Wilson
1885 John Brouncker Ingle
1886 William Tullet Howard
1887 William Robert Fox
1888 William Robert Fox
  re-elected
1889 George Hilditch
1890 Francis Reynolds Yonge
  Radcliffe
1891 James Bigwood, M.P.
1892 James Bigwood, M.P.
  re-elected
1893 Henry Ellis
1894 George Hilditch
1895 Thomas Owthwaithe Hutton
1896 John Brouncker Ingle
1897 John Brouncker Ingle
  re-elected
1898 William Robert Fox
1899 Francis Reynolds Yonge
  Radcliffe
1900 James Bigwood, M.P.
1901 James Engelbert Vanner
1902 Henry Ellis
1903 George Hilditch
1904 John Brouncker Ingle
1905 William Tullet Howard
1906 William Robert Fox
1907 Francis Reynolds Yonge
  Radcliffe, K.C.
1908 James Bigwood

1909 Samuel Forde Ridley
1910 Sir George Hayter
  Chubb, Bart.
1911 James E. C. Bigwood, J.P.
1912 James E. C. Bigwood, J.P.
  re-elected
1913 Frank Warner
1914 Charles James Fox
1915 William Brouncker Ingle
1916 Horace Bertram Nelson
1917 William Newburn, J.P.
1918 James Vanner Early
1919 The Rt. Hon. The Earl of
  Athlone, K.G.
1920 Charles Wigan, J.P.
1921 Sir John Charles Miles
1922 Charles Archibald Chubb
1923 Percy William Nelson
1924 Sir Charles Carrick Allom
1925 The Rt. Hon. Lord Askwith,
  K.C.B.
1926 The Rt. Hon. Lord Rochdale
1927 Sir Walter P. Nevill, J.P.
1928 James Harold Early
1929 Geoffrey Reynolds Yonge
  Radcliffe
1930 Samuel Forde Ridley, J.P.
1931 The Rt. Hon. Lord Hayter
1932 The Rt. Hon. The Earl of
  Athlone, K.G.
1933 William Brouncker Ingle
1934 Sir Henry Birchenough,
  Bart., G.C.M.G.
1935 Sir John Charles Miles
1936 The Hon. C. Archibald
  Chubb, C.C.
1937 Sir Charles Carrick
  Allom, F.S.A.
1938 The Rt. Hon. Lord
  Askwith, K.C.B.
1939 The Rt. Hon. Lord
  Rochdale, C.B.
1940 James Harold Early
1941 Geoffrey Reynolds Yonge
  Radcliffe, D.C.L.

Year of
office
beginning
in

1942 Kenneth Charles Fox,
F.C.A.
1943 Ernest Davies, C.B.E.
1944 The Rt. Hon. Lord Gorell,
C.B.E., M.C.
1945 The Rt. Hon. Lord Gorell,
C.B.E., M.C.
re-elected
1946 Major H. A. R. Graham
1947 Colonel C. R. Wigan, M.C.,
T.D.
1948 John Sugden Smith
1949 The Rt. Hon. Lord Rochdale,
O.B.E., T.D., D.L.
1950 The Rt. Hon. Lord Hayter,
C.C.
1951 James Harold Early
1952 Geoffrey Reynolds Yonge
Radcliffe, D.C.L.
1953 The Rt. Hon. Lord Gorell,
C.B.E., M.C.
1954 Major H. A. R. Graham
1955 Colonel C. R. Wigan,
M.C., T.D.

Year of
office
beginning
in

1956 Brigadier The Rt. Hon.
Lord Rochdale, O.B.E.,
T.D., D.L.
1957 Sir Ernest W. Goodale,
C.B.E., M.C.
1958 The Rt. Hon. Earl Peel
1959 Dr N. Langdon-Down
1960 J. W. B. Ingle
1961 The Hon. G. C. H. Chubb
1962 Dr Arthur James Turner,
C.B.E.
1963 Lawrence E. Tanner, C.V.O.,
F.S.A.
1964 John Patrick Early
1965 John Patrick Early
re-elected
1966 Richard Glanville Fox
1967 Guy Lushington Yonge
Radcliffe
1968 David Rickards Baskerville
Mynors
1969 Hugh Henry Valentine Ellis,
F.C.A.
1970 Norman D. Ouvry

Glossary

*Silk fabrics and other materials**

Alamode	A thin, light and glossy silk
Armozine	A strong corded silk used for women's gowns and men's waistcoats
Birdseye	A spotted fabric of muslin or silk
Bombazine	A slight, twilled fabric of silk and worsted, much used for mourning dresses
Boratto	A light material of silk and wool, resembling bombazine
Brocade	A silk fabric with a pattern of raised figures in colours
Camlet	A light fabric made of mixed yarns, e.g. silk and camel hair
Chintz	A calico with a pattern painted or printed in colours
Crape	A thin silk gauze, with a crimped or wrinkled surface; usually black and worn as a sign of mourning
Damask	A rich figured silk stuff, with reversed pattern on the back
Damassin or Damasquitte	A sort of brocade
Ducape	A heavy corded silk
Ferrandine	A coloured fabric made of silk and wool
Ferret	A narrow silk ribband or tape (also a cotton tape)
Florentine	A twilled silk, striped, figured or plain
Fustian	A fabric with linen warp and cotton weft
Galloon	Narrow ribbon or braid of spun silk, cotton thread, or gold and silver tissue
Gartering, garters	Garters not only secured the stocking but served for display. Woven of silk and gold and silver thread into a braid, often in a chequered or 'diced' pattern. Elegant

* Principal authority: C. W. and P. Cunnington, *Handbook of English Costume in the 17th Century* (1955); *Handbook of English Costume in the 18th Century* (1957).

457

	specimens were fringed or trimmed with spangles
Gauze	A very thin silk fabric
Grogram	A coarse fabric of mixed silk, wool and mohair, often stiffened with gum
Lace, laced	The words 'lace' and 'laced' had various meanings. Thus stays were laced when the sides were drawn together with strings or strong tapes. A coat was laced when it was trimmed with braid or metallic lace; so, too, with a man's 'laced' hat. A woman's gown might be trimmed with needlework lace, or the wearer might have lace at her throat and wrists. Laced shoes were shoes trimmed or decorated with braid, not shoes with shoe-strings
Lawn	A very fine linen
Lawn, Cobweb	A very fine linen used for ruffs, cuffs, veils, kerchiefs, etc.
Lutestring or Lustring or Lustrine	A glossy silk fabric
Mantua or Manteau	An open robe worn with a petticoat on social occasions in the first half of the eighteenth century. Frequently of rich material, elaborately embroidered. 'A long trailing mantua sweeps the ground.' (John Gay, *Trivia* (1716))
Norwich crape	A worsted and silk fabric; not real crape
Paduasoy	A strong corded silk fabric
Philoselle	A wrought silk
Poplin	A woven fabric having a silk warp, a worsted weft and a corded surface
Ribbon	In the seventeenth century many thousands of yards of ribbon were worn by upper-class people, both men and women, for 'points' to close openings in garments and for decoration, such as ribbon loops, bows, wrist-ties, shoulder-knots, and sashes. Numerous gaily coloured ribbon loops were worn by men of fashion to form a fringe round the waist and the bottoms of the breeches. One pair of breeches, now preserved in the Victoria and Albert Museum, is trimmed with at least 250 yards of ribbon arranged in bunches
Rug	A coarse frieze or napped cloth
Sarsenet	A fine soft silk material, much used for linings
Satin	A silk fabric with a glazed or shiny surface
Satinesco	Probably a cheap sort of satin
Shagreen	A silk material used for linings
Shalloon	A light woollen stuff used chiefly for coat linings and women's dresses

Stockings	Early in the seventeenth century knitted stockings of wool, wool-mixtures, and silk were rapidly displacing cloth stockings among men and women of the upper and middle classes. Framework knitters using the newly-invented stocking frame or 'engine' were increasing in numbers and dexterity
Tabaret	An upholstery fabric of alternate satin and watered-silk stripes
Tabby	A watered silk
Tabin or Tabinet	A watered silk and wool fabric
Taffeta	A fine smooth glossy silk of plain texture
Tiffany	A very thin gauze-like silk fabric
Tissue	A woven fabric of gold, silver and silk thread

Source Materials

I. *Manuscripts and printed documents belonging
to the Weavers' Company**

A. CHARTERS, LETTERS PATENT, ORDINANCES, AND GRANTS,
DATING FROM 1604 TO 1738

*Guildhall Library
  Reference No.:*
MS.

4632	Inspeximus Charter of King James I, dated Westminster, 23 May 1604, granted to the Weavers of London, confirmed the Inspeximus Charter of Queen Elizabeth of 1559.
	(Vellum; first Great Seal with casts of obverse and reverse. Finely illuminated initial showing the sovereign enthroned, and heraldic borders.)
4635	Inspeximus Charter of King Charles I, dated Westminster, 20 November 1626, granted to the Weavers of London, confirmed the Inspeximus Charter of James I of 1604.
	(Vellum, two skins; appended fragment of second Great Seal of Charles I with casts of obverse and reverse. Illuminated initial (the sovereign enthroned) and illuminated heraldic borders on skin 1.)
4636	Letters Patent of King Charles I, dated Can[on]bury, 4 July 1638, confirming the Charter of Henry II . . . and granting to the Weavers' Company rights [*inter alia*] of searching and sealing silks and stuffs . . .
	(Vellum, five skins, two of them illuminated, including the royal arms and the arms of the Weavers' Company with supporters; appended Great Seal of Charles I with casts of obverse and reverse.)

* The records of the Weavers' Company from 1155 to 1600 are listed in Frances Consitt, *The London Weavers' Company from the Twelfth Century to the Sixteenth Century* (1933), Appendix I, pp. 172–80.

4637 — Indenture, dated 4 July 1638, between King Charles I and the Weavers' Company whereby in consideration of the Letters Patent of 1638 certain dues or taxes on wrought silk tissues were to be paid to the King. (Vellum, three skins; appended fragment of third Great Seal of Charles I with casts of obverse and reverse.)

4638 — Certified copy of the Letters Patent of 1638, made 4 December 1639, with short subject index, in a contemporary hand.

4639 — Charter of King James II, dated 24 October 1685, giving the Weavers' Company jurisdiction over all persons practising the art of weaving within the cities of London and Westminster, the borough of Southwark, and all other places within twenty miles distance.
(Vellum, four skins; has a clear, well-preserved portrait of James II.)
Note: This Charter, which re-incorporates the Weavers' Company after the surrender of their powers to King Charles II during his *quo warranto* proceedings, was ignored in subsequent negotiations and controversies because a subsequent Act of Parliament declared void all such charters granted by James II.

4640 — Charter of Queen Anne, dated Westminster, 17 November 1707, confirming previous charters, making further provision for the regulation of the Weavers' Company and limiting their jurisdiction to London, Westminster, Southwark, and places within ten miles distance.
(Vellum, four skins; has a clear engraved portrait of the Queen by J. Nutting; appended is the third Great Seal of Queen Anne with casts of obverse and reverse.)

4641 — Laws and Ordinances dated 30 November 1708, for the better government of the Company, confirmed by the Livery in a General Court or Common Hall assembled on 26 April 1708.
(Vellum, four skins; with signatures and signet seals of William, Lord Cowper, Lord Chancellor; Sir John Holt, Chief Justice of the Queen's Bench, and Sir Thomas Trevor, Chief of the Court of Common Pleas.)

4642 — By-laws and Ordinances, dated 15 and 20 March 1738, prepared by the Court of Assistants and confirmed in a General Court or Common Hall in accordance with the Charter of Queen Anne.
Signed by the Bailiffs, Wardens, twelve Assistants and four of the Livery; ratified by the Lord Chancellor, the Chief Justice of the King's Bench, and the Chief Justice of the Court of Common Pleas.

Guildhall Library
  Reference No.:

4644   Grant, dated 10 August 1616, of Supporters to the Company's Arms.

B. COMPANY RECORDS

4646   Old Ledger Book, 1496–1732, contains annual summaries of the Renter Bailiffs' and Renter Wardens' receipts and payments, as well as memoranda and inventories.

4647   Ordinance and Record Book, 1577–1641, containing copies of the Company's Ordinances, Petitions stating Weavers' grievances, etc.

4648A/1–2   Renter Bailiffs' Annual Accounts for financial years 1675–6 to 1722–3 (incomplete; seven accounts are missing, viz., 1678–9, 1692–3, 1695–6, 1717–18, and 1719–22) and Renter Warden's Account of Quarterages received and payments made in 1735–6.

4648B   Limborough Lectures Trust Account Book, 1783–1813.

4648C   Weavers' Company Property Ledger, 1817–27.

4648D   Weavers' Company Trust Property Ledger, 1817–27.

4648/1–11)   Renter Bailiffs' Account Books, 1666–1797 (incomplete), 11 vols.

4649B/1–2)   Renter Bailiffs' Account Books, 1687–8 and 1689–90.

4649   Renter Bailiffs' Acquittance or Receipt Book, 1767–1783. On the first page is an 'Account of new pewter bought for the Company, of Thomas Swanson, 1786 July 25, in exchange for the Company's old pewter'.

4649A   Renter Bailiffs' Acquittance Book, 1670–82.

4650   Book of Subscriptions towards rebuilding the Common Hall, 1667–9. Contains also accounts with the bricklayers, mason, carpenter, and other craftsmen.

4651 ⎫
4651/2 ⎬   Clerk's Account Books (rough), 1757–73 and 1773–84.

4652   Clerk's Sundry Account Book (rough), 1784–93.

4653   Cash Book of the Executors of Mr Alexander Hosea (deceased May 1686), 1686–1766, with particulars of several houses in Holborn, a list of tenants, etc., and a detailed account of the funeral expenses of Alexander Hosea.

4653A   Alexander Hosea's Charity Account Book, 1694–6.

4654   Pensioners' Books, 1724–1911 (incomplete), 4 vols.

4655A   Court Minute Book (rough), 1648–51.

4655A/2–3   Court Minute Books, 1651–2 and 1671–2.

4655 (1–33)   Court Minute Books, 1610–1940 (incomplete), 33 vols. Note: MS. 4655/1 contains, at the back, memoranda and copies of documents variously dated from 1617 to 1642.

Guildhall Library
  Reference No.:

4655B	Summons Book, 1787–1856.
4655C	Court of Assistants' Agenda Book, 1885–1911.
4655D	Clerks' rough Note Book, 1889–93.
4656 (1–7)	Freedom Admission Books, 1600–1769 (incomplete), 7 vols.
4657B	Apprentice Binding Book, 1655–9.
4657 (1–2)	Apprentice Binding Books, 1694–1865, 2 vols.
4657A (1–5)	Modern Indices of Apprentice Bindings, Turnings-over, and Admissions to Freedom, extracted from the Court Minute Books, 1661–1765 (incomplete), 5 vols.
4658	Book of Forms of subscription towards the rebuilding of the Common Hall, 1669–70. The forms show the amounts given or promised, and are signed by the donors.
4659	Tithe Rate Assessment for the parishes of St Lawrence Jewry and St Mary Magdalen, Milk Street, 1718.
4660	Calendar of Apprentices, 1665–1706. An alphabetical list of names of apprentices.
4661 (1–109)	Quarterage Books, 1681–1872 (incomplete), 109 vols, containing lists of names of Officers, Assistants and Livery, and alphabetical lists of the Commonalty. Certain volumes contain details of sums collected on searches of the craft.
4661A/14	Clerk's Out-letter Books, 1863–1919, 14 vols.
4782A	An inventory of the Company's Plate, Linen, Pictures and Effects, taken 2 February 1829.
5234 (1–2) 5236	Renter Bailiffs' Account Books, 1802–18, 3 vols.
5235	Pensions Distribution Books and Estate Accounts, 1800–17.
5237 (1–2)	Court Minute Books (rough), 1798–1816.
5238	Partial transcript (mid-seventeenth century) of the Company's Ordinances (ratified in 1577).
10,596A	Weavers' Almshouses Committee Minute Book, 1861.
	A List of Surnames of Foreign Origin, compiled from the records of the Weavers' Company, *c.* 1883, containing over 2,000 names.
	A Report on certain old Books belonging to the Weavers' Company, by J. Corbet Anderson, 1883.
	Report of Committee on the Company's Charities (1742).
A.1.3. No. 64	A Collection of Papers for and against a Bill to prohibit the Wear and Use of Dyed, Printed, and Painted Calicoes, in the years 1720 and 1721.
	The table of contents contains the following entries in manuscript: 'The Manufacturer, being a Paper that was Printed at the Charge and by the direction (for the

most part) of the Company of Weavers London. 86 in
all by Dan: De: Foe.'

'The British Merchant being a paper printed at the
Charge & ye direction of the Drapers; 12 in all by Mr
Asgill.'

'The Weavers; being a paper that was Printed at the
Charge, and by the Direction of some Warehouse Men &
Others; 8 in all by Overall &c.'

In addition, there are 38 pamphlets, petitions, open
letters, etc., dating from 1719–21, presenting various
views on the calico controversy.

Freedom Admission Book, 1804–1920.

A List of Prices in the Several Branches of the Silk and
Silk-Mixed Manufactures; as settled from time to time
by the Lord Mayor, Aldermen, and Recorder of the
City of London, and the Justices of the Peace for the
County of Middlesex, and the Liberty of His Majesty's
Tower of London, in their respective Quarter Sessions,
in pursuance of Two several Acts of Parliament, made
and passed in the 13th and 32nd years of the Reign of
George III. Commencing in the year 1795. Compiled by
James Buckridge, Sen. London: Re-printed by E.
Justins, 34 Brick Lane, Spitalfields (1821).

(87 printed pages of prices; approximately 2,000 separate items are listed; dates in margins show when prices
for that section were last fixed; the index (pp. 93–5)
indicates the range of fabrics made in Spitalfields
between 1795 and 1821.)

Weavers' Company, *Affectionate Advice to Apprentices*
(n.d.)

*Mr Hare's Report to the Charity Commissioners . . . on
the Charities of the Weavers' Company* (1864).

*A Scheme for the Regulation and Management of the
Charity of John Hall . . .* (1895).

Weavers' Company, *Particulars of Charities* (1896).

II. *Other manuscripts*

Guildhall Library MS. 6497/7, Parish Register of St Giles without Cripple-
gate, 1663–7
Guildhall Library MS. 6975, Parish Register of St Lawrence Jewry,
1538–1715
Records of the City of London:
   Repertories 3, 33, 34, 41, 57, 73, 91, 127
   Remembrancia, VII
   Journals of the Court of Common Council
   P.A.R. Book 5

Companies 7–26; 8–3

Minutes of the Proceedings of the Court of Common Council, 1839

British Museum Additional Manuscripts 34,245B (3–20)

Public Record Office:

Home Office Papers 86 (26)

Muster and Pay Rolls of the Royal London Militia, 1851–70; W.O. 13/1390–4

Registry of the Prerogative Court of Canterbury (Somerset House):

Copy of the Will of Alexander Hosea (1686)

Copy of the Will of James Limborough (1774)

III. *Parliamentary papers and reports*

Journal of the Commissioners for Trade and Plantations, 1718–22

Votes of the House of Commons, 1719–20, 1739

Select Committee on the Ribbon Weavers' Petitions, 1818

Lords Committee on Foreign Trade, Second Report, 1821

Lords Committee on a Bill to repeal the Acts relating to Wages in the Silk Manufacture, 1823

Select Committee of the Lords on the . . . British Wool Trade, 1828

Parliamentary Papers relating to Cholera and the Report of the Board of Health, 1831–2

Select Committee on the Silk Trade, 1832

Royal Commission on Municipal Corporations, Second Report, 1837

Royal Commission on the Condition of the Hand-loom Weavers, Reports, 1839–41

Poor Law Commissioners' Report on the Sanitary Condition of the Labouring Population, 1842

Accounts and Papers, 1862, LV: Return of Silk Factories in 1861

City of London Livery Companies Commission, Report, 1865

Royal Commission on the Livery Companies of London, Report, 1884

Report on the English Silk Industry, 1884

Royal Commission on Technical Instruction, Second Report, 1884

IV. *Other printed material*

A. PAMPHLETS, TRACTS, ETC.

W. Lithgow, *The Present Surveigh of London . . . with the several Fortifications thereof* (1643)

A Breviate of the Weavers' Business before the Honourable Committee of the House of Commons in Star Chamber (1648)

A Letter of H. E. Thomas, Lord Fairfax to the Lord Mayor of London (9 December 1648)

The Case of the Commonalty of the Corporation of Weavers of London truly stated (c. 1649)

The Humble Representation of the Weavers' Company . . . (1650)

John Tatham, *London's Tryumph* (1658)

Englands' Danger by Indian Manufactures (1699)

The Just Complaints of the Poor Weavers (1719)

The Case of the Weavers humbly offer'd to the Parliament of Great Britain (c. 1719)

The Case of the Fair Traders: Being a clear View and State of the Clandestine Trade, as now carry'd on in Great Britain (c. 1719)

The Weavers' Complaint against the Callico Madams (1719)

A Letter to a Member of the Honourable House of Commons (c. 1720)

The Case of the Shop-Keepers in Gt. Britain, humbly recommended to the ensuing Parliament (1720)

The Case of the Retailers of Printed Callicoes (1720)

The Case of the Linen-Drapers (c. 1720)

The Humble Petition of many Journeymen Weavers (1728)

'A Citizen of London', *Serious Advice to the Silk Manufacturers; in a Letter to the Master and Wardens of the Weavers* (1751)

A List of the Prices in those Branches of the Weaving Manufactory, called The Black Branch and The Fancy Branch . . . (1769) [In the Goldsmiths' Library, University of London]

W. Hale, *A Letter to S. Whitbread on the Distresses of the Poor in Spitalfields* (1806)

B. PERIODICALS

The *Loyal Protestant & True Domestick Intelligence* (July 1681)

The *Weekly Review*, 1708.

The *Weekly Journal*, 1719

Mist's Journal, 1719

The *Manufacturer: or the British Trade fully stated . . .*, 1719–21

The *British Merchant, or a Review of the Trade of Great Britain . . .*, 1719–20

The *Weaver*, 1719–20

Gentleman's Magazine, November 1767

The Times, 1839–40, July 1881

City Press, July 1881

Daily Graphic, 7 April 1899